BESTSELLING BOOK SERIES

Florida For Dummies
3rd Edition

D0846422

Greater Miami

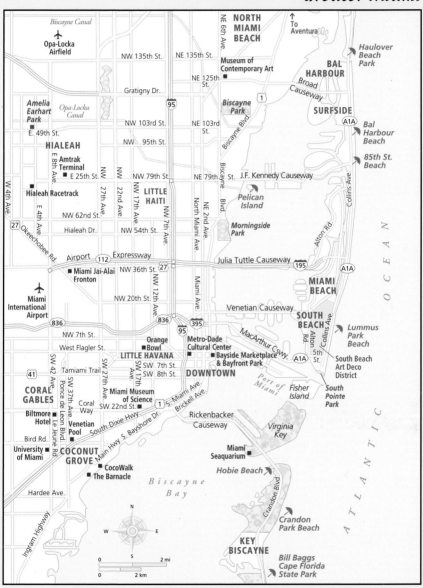

Biscayne Canal

Opa-Locka Airfield

North Miami Beach

↑ To Aventura

Haulover Beach Park

NW 135th St. / NE 135th St.

Museum of Contemporary Art

BAL HARBOUR

Broad Causeway

NE 125th St.

Gratigny Dr.

95

Biscayne Park

1

SURFSIDE

A1A

Bal Harbour Beach

Amelia Earhart Park

Opa-Locka Canal

NW 103rd St. / NE 103rd St.

E. 49th St.

NW 95th St.

85th St. Beach

HIALEAH

Amtrak Terminal

E 25th St.

NW 79th St. / NE 79th St.

J.F. Kennedy Causeway

Collins Ave.

Hialeah Racetrack

LITTLE HAITI

Pelican Island

NW 62nd St.

Hialeah Dr.

NW 54th St.

Morningside Park

Alton Rd.

27 Okeechobee Rd.

Airport 112 Expressway

Julia Tuttle Causeway

195

A1A

Miami Jai-Alai Fronton

NW 36th St. 27

MIAMI BEACH

Miami International Airport

NW 20th St.

Venetian Causeway

SOUTH BEACH

Lummus Park Beach

836 / 836

95 395

MacArthur Cswy.

Alton Rd. / Collins Ave.

NW 7th St.

Orange Bowl

Metro-Dade Cultural Center

5th St.

South Beach Art Deco District

West Flagler St.

LITTLE HAVANA

SW 7th St.

SW 8th St.

Bayside Marketplace & Bayfront Park

A1A

41

Tamiami Trail

DOWNTOWN

Port of Miami

Fisher Island

South Pointe Park

CORAL GABLES

Coral Way

Miami Museum of Science

SW 22nd St.

1 S. Miami Ave.

Brickell Ave.

Biltmore Hotel

Venetian Pool

Rickenbacker Causeway

Bird Rd.

University of Miami

COCONUT GROVE

Virginia Key

Miami Seaquarium

CocoWalk

The Barnacle

Hobie Beach

Hardee Ave.

Biscayne Bay

Crandon Blvd

Ingram Highway

Crandon Park Beach

ATLANTIC OCEAN

N / W E / S

0   2 mi
0   2 km

KEY BISCAYNE

Bill Baggs Cape Florida State Park

Sarasota and Bradenton

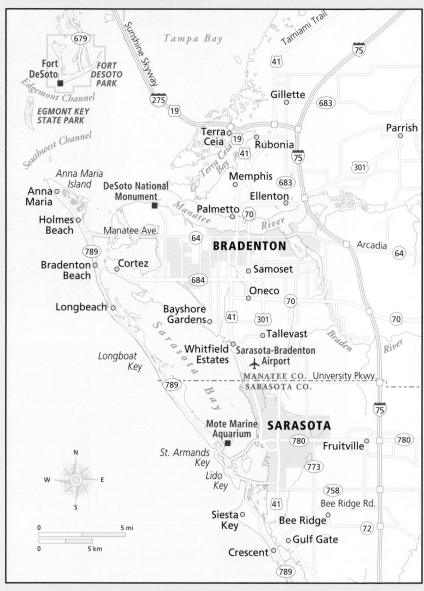

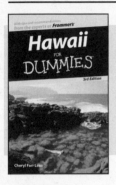
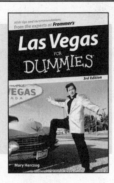

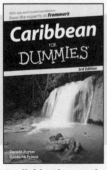
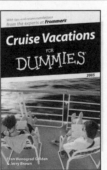

Florida

FOR

DUMMIES®

3RD EDITION

Florida
FOR
DUMMIES®
3RD EDITION

by Lesley Abravanel

WILEY

Wiley Publishing, Inc.

Florida For Dummies,® 3rd Edition

Published by
Wiley Publishing, Inc.
111 River St.
Hoboken, NJ 07030-5774
www.wiley.com

For general information on our other products and services, please contact our Customer Care Department within the U.S. at 800-762-2974, outside the U.S. at 317-572-3993, or fax 317-572-4002.

For technical support, please visit www.wiley.com/techsupport.

Wiley also publishes its books in a variety of electronic formats. Some content that appears in print may not be available in electronic books.

Library of Congress Control Number: 2005923791

ISBN-13: 9-7807-6457-7451

ISBN-10: 0-7645-7745-X

Manufactured in the United States of America

10 9 8 7 6 5 4 3 2 1

3B/QU/QX/QV/IN

WILEY

About the Author

Lesley Abravanel is a freelance journalist and a graduate of the University of Miami School of Communication. When she isn't combing South Florida for the latest hotels, restaurants, and attractions, she's on the lookout for vacationing celebrities, about whom she writes in her weekly nightlife and gossip column, "Velvet Underground," for both the *Miami Herald* and its weekly entertainment newspaper, *Street*. She is a contributor to *Star Magazine* and the Miami correspondent for *Black Book Magazine* and is the author of *Frommer's South Florida*.

Author's Acknowledgments

Thanks to my parents, Arnold and Francine — without them, I am nothing; to Aunt Trish, who knows more about schlepping through Florida than anyone else I know; to Mrs. Ritchie, for teaching me to aspire to greatness; to the publicists out there who understand the importance of getting back to me; and to all those who appreciate the humor and irony of my involvement in this very book.

Publisher's Acknowledgments

We're proud of this book; please send us your comments through our Dummies online registration form located at www.dummies.com/register/.

Some of the people who helped bring this book to market include the following:

Editorial

Editors: Jennifer Connolly

Project Editor: Naomi Kraus

Development Editor:
Jennifer Moore

Copy Editor: Jennifer Connolly

Cartographer: Roberta Stockwell

Editorial Manager: Michelle Hacker

Editorial Supervisor:
Carmen Krikorian

Editorial Assistant: Melissa Bennett

Senior Photo Editor: Richard Fox

Cover Photos: *Front cover:*
© Richard Cummins/Corbis,
South Beach; *Back cover:*
© Tom Salyer/Panoramic Images,
Miami Beach.

Cartoons: Rich Tennant
(www.the5thwave.com)

Composition Services

Project Coordinator: Kristie Rees

Layout and Graphics: Carl Byers,
Lauren Goddard, Joyce Haughey,
Lynsey Osborn,
Melanee Prendergast,
Heather Ryan

Proofreaders: David Faust,
Leeann Harney, Jessica Kramer,
Carl William Pierce,
TECHBOOKS Production
Services

Indexer: TECHBOOKS Production
Services

Publishing and Editorial for Consumer Dummies

Diane Graves Steele, Vice President and Publisher, Consumer Dummies

Joyce Pepple, Acquisitions Director, Consumer Dummies

Kristin A. Cocks, Product Development Director, Consumer Dummies

Michael Spring, Vice President and Publisher, Travel

Kelly Regan, Editorial Director, Travel

Publishing for Technology Dummies

Andy Cummings, Vice President and Publisher, Dummies Technology/
General User

Composition Services

Gerry Fahey, Vice President of Production Services

Debbie Stailey, Director of Composition Services

Contents at a Glance

Maps at a Glance

Table of Contents

Part II: Planning Your Trip to Florida 33

Chapter 3: Managing Your Money 35

Chapter 4: Getting to Florida 45

Introduction

*E*ven those of you who, like me, reside in the Sunshine State feel as if you're on a permanent vacation, and it's not just because of the sun, the palm trees, and the ocean. Whether your passion involves water sports, beach bathing, theme-park hopping, shopping, art and historical sighting, or wining and dining, Florida offers a wealth of opportunities for you to experience at your leisure.

Florida has come a long way since 1513, when Ponce de Leon landed and alligators ate his men, and the natives sent their *bon voyage* wishes via Flaming Arrow Express. From diving with dolphins to daring rides on roller coasters that zoom from 0 to 60 mph in less than three seconds, you'll find experiences here like nowhere else on Planet Earth. If you're interested in the past, you can immerse yourself in St. Augustine, the oldest city in the U.S. — but the Sunshine State also has plenty of attractions that can bring you tantalizingly close to the future. Florida's theme parks, especially those clustered around Orlando, are constantly trying to out-duel each other with high-tech animatronics, virtual experiences, and all-too-real thrill rides where you strap yourself in and pray your bladder doesn't become a stranger with a mind of its own. Miami's sizzling South Beach offers some of the hottest nightlife on American soil. Daytona Beach is world-renowned — or infamous, depending on your point of view — for Bike Week and spring break. And, Destin and Fort Walton Beach have miles of sand on which to tan your body.

Florida's a big place, and your number-one priority should be navigating your way through all the fun and sun without exhausting yourself — after all, you are on vacation. All you need to ensure a great trip to Florida is some patience, some advance planning, and some suntan lotion — now how hard is that?

About This Book

With a little help from us, you won't have to

- ✔ Do it anyone else's way.
- ✔ Pay full price.
- ✔ Read the fine print.

There's no need for any of that. You chose this book because you know the *For Dummies* name and have probably already made your first decision — you're thinking hard about a trip to Ponce de Leon's favorite flatland, Florida. You probably also know how much you want (or can afford) to spend, the pace you want to keep, and how much planning

Dummies Post-it® Flags

As you're reading this book, you'll find information that you'll want to reference as you plan or enjoy your trip — whether it be a new hotel, a must-see attraction, or a must-try walking tour. Mark these pages with the handy Post-it® Flags included in this book to help make your trip planning easier!

you can stomach. Most of *y'all* (forgive our Southern slang) also don't want to tend to every little detail. Yet you don't trust just anyone to do it for you. That's why you're reading this book.

My job is to boil down what, honestly, is a very long spit of real estate — 542 miles from Key West to Jacksonville, then left and westward 364 miles to Pensacola. (That doesn't count most of the Gulf Coast!) At current count, Florida has 16 million residents and five times that many tourists per year — all crowded into about 22 percent of the land. The rest of the state is pasture, swamp, and public land that most folks never see. Because your time and money are valuable, I focus on the cities and regions in Florida that deserve your attention. This book doesn't cover Florida comprehensively (that would require volumes). It highlights the best Florida has to offer. I don't worry you with the secondary stuff that, although perfectly fine, isn't up to snuff for most vacations.

How can anyone sort through that kind of mess, you ask? It takes experience. After stomping through the state for over a decade, I know where to find the best deals (of the non-rip-off variety). In this book, I guide you through Florida in a clear, easy-to-understand way, enabling you to find the best hotels, restaurants, and attractions without having to read this book like a novel — cover to cover. Although you can read every page if you choose, you can also flip to only those sections that interest you. I also promise not to overwhelm you with choices. I simply deliver the best, most essential ingredients for a great vacation.

Conventions Used in This Book

To make this book an easier reference guide for you (and because Florida does its best to make you max them out), we use the following abbreviations for commonly accepted credit cards:

> **AE:** American Express
>
> **CB:** Carte Blanche
>
> **DC:** Diners Club
>
> **DISC:** Discover
>
> **JCB:** Japan Credit Bank

MC: MasterCard

V: Visa

I also include some general pricing information to guide you as you decide where to unpack your bags or dine on the local cuisine. I've used a system of dollar signs to show a range of costs for one night in a hotel (the price refers to a double-occupancy room) or a meal at a restaurant. (The room rates do not include taxes of up to 12 percent. The cost of each meal is the main course only; so allow for the 6–7 percent sales tax, as well as appetizers, drinks, or other extras you desire.) Check out the following table to decipher the dollar signs:

Dollar Signs	Hotel	Restaurant
$	$99 or less	$14 or less
$$	$100–$199	$15–$24
$$$	$200–$249	$25–$39
$$$$	$250 or more	$40 or more

I've listed exact prices for every establishment, attraction, and activity, but keep in mind that prices are subject to change.

In addition, I've divided the hotel listings into two categories — my personal favorites and those that don't quite make my preferred list but still get my hearty seal of approval. Don't be shy about considering these "runners up" hotels if you're unable to get a room at one of my favorites or if your preferences differ from mine — the amenities that the runners up offer and the services that each provides make all these accommodations good choices to consider as you determine where to rest your head at night.

For those hotels, restaurants, and attractions that are plotted on a map, a page reference is provided in the listing information. If a hotel, restaurant, or attraction is outside the city limits or in an out-of-the-way area, it may not be mapped.

Foolish Assumptions

As I wrote this book, I made some assumptions about you and what your needs may be:

- ✔ You may be an inexperienced traveler trying to determine whether to take a trip to Florida or looking for guidance to decide when and how to make this trip.

- ✔ You may be an experienced traveler, but you don't have much time to devote to trip planning or to spend in Florida when you get here. You want expert advice on how to maximize your time and enjoy a hassle-free trip.

✔ You're not looking for a book that provides all the information available on Florida or one that lists every hotel, restaurant, or attraction in the state. Instead, you want a book that focuses on places that give you the best or most unique experiences in the Sunshine State.

If you fit any of these criteria, *Florida For Dummies,* 3rd Edition, gives you the information you're looking for!

How This Book Is Organized

Florida For Dummies is divided into seven parts. The chapters in each part lay out the specific details of that part's topic. Each chapter and part is written so you don't have to read what came before or after, though I sometimes refer you to other areas for more information. Here's a brief look at the parts.

Part 1: Introducing Florida

Think of this part as the hors d'oeuvre. In this part, I tempt you with the best experiences, hotels, eateries, and attractions in Florida. I throw in a weather forecast, look at special events, and then help you plan a budget. I also provide special tips for families, seniors, travelers with disabilities, and gay and lesbian travelers.

Part 11: Planning Your Trip to Florida

Should you use a travel agent? How about buying a package tour? Where can you find the best airfare? In this part, I answer those questions and also talk about the advantages — and disadvantages — of booking your trip on the Internet as well as list some good online resources. In addition, I get into money matters, discussing whether you're better off using credit cards, ATMs, traveler's checks, or cash. Before moving on, I tie up some last-minute details and talk about travel insurance, car rental, and packing tips.

Part 111: South Florida

This part of the book deals with Miami, the Keys, the Everglades, Fort Lauderdale, Palm Beach, and their 'burbs. I introduce the neighborhoods and then explore some of the *modus transporto* (local buses, trolleys, taxis, shuttles, and other vehicles to get you from hither to yon). I also give you some advice on where to stay, where to eat, and which attractions to see. Finally, I profile the best shopping areas, present the best clubs, and offer some suggested itineraries.

Part 1V: The Gulf Coast

Florida's left coast has pockets of development, particularly around the Tampa Bay area, but the Gulf Coast is not nearly as cramped as the Atlantic side. In this part, I introduce you to Tampa, St. Petersburg, and

the Gulf beaches and then venture south to Sarasota, Fort Myers, and
Naples. I include the region's best accommodations, restaurants, attractions, shops, and clubs, as well as sightseeing itineraries.

Part V: Visiting Central Florida: Mickey Mania

So much is shoehorned into Orlando and the Walt Disney World area that
this section of Florida deserves its own part — three meaty chapters.
First off, I show you how to get there, profile the neighborhoods, and
present the best accommodations and eateries in town. Then I devote a
chapter to the major theme parks operated by Disney, Universal, and
SeaWorld. Last but not least, I present some of the smaller, cheaper, and
more relaxing attractions, explore shopping and partying venues and
then take side trips to the Kennedy Space Center and Cypress Gardens.

Part VI: The Great North

Except for a few development clusters — most notably along the upper
Atlantic Coast — North Florida is pretty wide-open. Most of the places
here are oriented more toward backpackers, paddlers, and cow tippers
than typical tourists. In Northeast Florida, I offer you a front-row seat in
the oldest city in the United States, St. Augustine, and explore Daytona
Beach, Amelia Island, Fernandina Beach, and Jacksonville.

Part VII: The Part of Tens

Every *For Dummies* book has The Part of Tens. The appearance of this
part is as certain as annual rate increases at Florida's theme parks. Here,
I give you parting advice on the state's best beaches and foods.

You can also find an appendix, your "Quick Concierge," which contains
lots of handy-dandy information you may need when traveling in Florida,
like phone numbers and addresses for emergency personnel or area hospitals and pharmacies, protocol for sending mail, and more. Check out
this appendix when searching for answers to lots of little questions that
may come up as you travel.

Icons Used in This Book

Several icons (those little pictures in the margins) are scattered throughout this guide. Consider them your road map for finding specific information you may need.

The Best of the Best icon highlights the best Florida has to offer in all
categories — hotels, restaurants, attractions, activities, shopping, and
nightlife.

Find out useful advice on things to do and ways to schedule your time
when you see the Tip icon.

Watch for the Heads Up icon to identify annoying or potentially danger-ous situations, such as tourist traps, unsafe neighborhoods, budget breakers, and other things to beware of.

I use the Kid Friendly icon to identify particularly family-friendly hotels, restaurants, and other places, although most of Orlando is receptive to small fry.

Keep an eye out for the Bargain Alert icon as you seek out money-saving tips and/or other great deals.

The Natural Wonder icon highlights particularly noteworthy beaches, parks, preserves, and other natural attractions in Florida, a state known for its natural beauty.

Where to Go from Here

Okay. You know what to expect from this book and how to use it to plan a sun-filled, fun-filled vacation to Florida. So, start reading. There's much to do before you arrive, from arranging a place to stay each night to exploring the best beaches, attractions, and nightlife that Florida has to offer. Like the Boy Scouts, the successful Florida traveler needs to be prepared; follow the advice in this book, and you will be. And, last but not least, have fun — this state was designed to bring sunshine into its visitors' lives, so you may as well enjoy it.

Part I
Introducing Florida

The 5th Wave   By Rich Tennant

"I appreciate that our room is so near the ocean I can hear the waves crashing, but I had to get up to go to the bathroom 6 times last night."

In this part . . .

Deciding on a vacation destination shouldn't cause angst, but making a few decisions now — before the landing gear lowers — can help you get the most out of your vacation. My goal in this part is to help you cut through the first wave of options that you encounter when deciding on a Florida destination.

But before I do, you get to do a little dreaming about the premier experiences Florida offers, and the grand excursions you can embark upon when you get there.

Chapter 1

Discovering the Best of Florida

In This Chapter
- ▶ Dining in the top restaurants
- ▶ Landing in the most intimate spots
- ▶ Playing like an all-star
- ▶ Partying with the best of them

*W*hether you prefer diving with dolphins, working on your suntan, or gorging on great food, Florida's wealth of activities, dining opportunities, and entertainment can impress even the most jaded traveler. Millions of visitors flock here each year, drawn by the promise of warm winters, a bounty of beaches, and fabulous attractions — both man-made and natural. But before I dive into the details, I review some of Florida's best places to stay, eat, and have fun. In these first pages, I tell you about some of the things that convince snowbirds, families, honeymooners, and outdoor enthusiasts to come here every year and, in the process, I show you a few things that can fill your to-do list.

Of course, selecting the *best* from such a large, visitor-friendly state is no easy job, and the choices I list here are simply some of the highlights. You can discover hundreds of other hotels, restaurants, activities, and attractions in the following chapters. And, dare I say, you'll probably find a few of your own after you arrive in the Sunshine State. Throughout the book, the "Best of the Best" icon is attached to the places and activities mentioned in this chapter.

I'm going to keep an ace in the hole and save my favorite Florida beaches for Chapter 22, but for now, here are the all-stars.

The Best Fine-Dining Experiences

- ✔ **Chef Allen's** (North Miami Beach; ☎ 305-935-2900). This outstanding Floribbean (a term used to describe the best of Caribbean and Floridian cuisines' offerings) restaurant boasts a show kitchen and a menu that features goat-cheese-encrusted lamb chops and mesquite-grilled soft-shell crabs. See Chapter 9.

- ✔ **Norman's** (Coral Gables; ☎ 305-446-6767). A perennial award winner thanks to such treats as venison *au poivre* and pork tenderloin with Haitian grits, Norman's is consistently one of So Flo's best. See Chapter 9.

- ✔ **Louie's Backyard** (Key West; ☎ 305-294-1061).This stellar, scenic waterfront spot serves up grilled yellowfin tuna and spice-rubbed venison while you watch a spectacular sunset. See Chapter 11.

- ✔ **Cap's Place Island Restaurant** (Lighthouse Point; ☎ 954-941-0418). This barge-turned-restaurant on a private island near Fort Lauderdale offers the total South Florida experience, serving excellent, reasonably priced seafood. And there's a bonus: The boat ride to the restaurant is free. See Chapter 13.

- ✔ **Euphemia Haye** (Longboat Key; ☎ 941-383-3633). This cozy culinary standout offers unique continental cuisine and a romantic atmosphere. See Chapter 16.

- ✔ **Emeril's** (Universal Orlando; ☎ 407-224-2424). TV Chef Emeril Lagasse's original eatery at Universal's CityWalk beckons with creative Creole dishes, an open-to-view "wine loft" with 12,000 bottles, and a delightful atmosphere. See Chapter 17.

- ✔ **Beech Street Grill** (Jacksonville; ☎ 904-277-3662). Housed in a historic two-story home, this perennial award winner serves tasty, upscale cuisine. See Chapter 21.

- ✔ **Marker 32** (Jacksonville; ☎ 904-223-1534). This Jacksonville foodie hot spot features a million-dollar view of the Intracoastal as well as a killer chipotle-rubbed beef tenderloin. See Chapter 21.

The Best Places for Fresh Seafood

- ✔ **Joe's Stone Crab** (Miami's South Beach; ☎ 305-673-0365). This South Beach institution wins the Great Crab War by serving the most succulent stone crab in town (some say it's a monopoly), providing an amusing see-scape of Miami's movers, shakers, and most curious — and crab-crazy — tourists. See Chapter 9.

- ✔ **Atlantic's Edge** (Islamorada; ☎ 305-664-4651). This Keys standout makes a mean Thai-spiced snapper, or you can bring your own catch, and the staff will prepare it for you. See Chapter 11.

✔ **Testa's** (Palm Beach; ☎ 561-832-0992). The Palm Beach mainstay continues its 75-year family tradition with seared tuna, almond-crusted prawns, and an amazing seafood marinara. See Chapter 13.

✔ **Ted Peters' Famous Smoked Fish** (St. Petersburg; ☎ 727-381-7931). Life doesn't get much better than sipping a cold beer while diving into red-oak-smoked mullet, mackerel, and more at this open-air St. Petersburg institution. See Chapter 15.

✔ **Blasé Café** (Sarasota; ☎ 941-349-9822). Don't be fooled by the name of this awesome local favorite. There's nothing blasé about Chef Todd's fresh fish du jour. See Chapter 16.

The Best Romantic Hideaways

✔ **Little Palm Island** (Little Torch Key; ☎ 800-343-8567). This sublime resort, tucked away on a 5-acre isle near Little Torch Key, is only accessible by boat. Kids under 16 are prohibited, and the rooms don't have phones, TVs, or alarm clocks. See Chapter 11.

✔ **Cheeca Lodge** (Islamorada; ☎ 800-327-2888) Cheeca, appropriately pronounced *chic*-aahh, is a world-class resort with a laid-back style that positively encourages the sharing of private moments. See Chapter 11.

✔ **Marquesa Hotel** (Key West; ☎ 800-669-4631). The Marquesa Hotel's 40 rooms have the charm of a romantic bed-and-breakfast, to go along with four-poster beds, marble baths, and private porches. See Chapter 11.

✔ **Renaissance Vinoy Resort** (St. Petersburg; ☎ 800-468-3571). This swank St. Pete stay has a pampering spa and an ambience straight out of an F. Scott Fitzgerald novel. See Chapter 15.

✔ **Don CeSar Beach Resort & Spa** (St. Pete Beach; ☎ 800-637-7200). This sprawling pink structure is the epitome of a Gatsby-style mansion with a seafront setting. See Chapter 15.

✔ **Peabody Orlando** (Orlando; ☎ 800-732-2639). The Peabody exudes a sophistication that ranges from its famous marching mallards to candlelit dinners at its restaurant. See Chapter 17.

✔ **Casa Monica Hotel** (St. Augustine; ☎ 800-648-1888). Built in 1888, the Casa Monica Hotel has the charm and Spanish architecture common to the oldest city in the United States. See Chapter 21.

The Best Family Attractions

✔ **Miami MetroZoo** (Miami; ☎ 305-251-0400). The city's only zoo enthralls visitors of all ages thanks to a petting zoo and 700 critters, including white tigers, black rhinos, and Komodo dragons. See Chapter 10.

✔ **Dolphin Research Center** (Marathon; ☎ 305-289-1121). The Dolphin Research Center boasts the best of Florida's swim-with-the-dolphin programs. See Chapter 11.

✔ **Lion Country Safari** (Loxahatchee; ☎ 561-793-1084). This little piece of Africa near West Palm Beach lets you drive through and walk grounds that not only harbor lions but also elephants, rhinos, and wildebeests. See Chapter 13.

✔ **Busch Gardens** (Tampa; ☎ 866-353-8622). Tampa's biggest attraction offers close-up views of African animals as well as guided tours, shows, flume and raft rides, and five roller coasters. See Chapter 14.

✔ **Disney's Magic Kingdom** (Orlando; ☎ 407-824-4321). This theme park of all theme parks is an American classic. See Chapter 18.

✔ **Disney–MGM Studios** (Orlando; ☎ 407-824-4321). A large piece of Hollywood comes to life in central Florida at the Disney–MGM Studios. See Chapter 18.

✔ **Universal Studios Florida** (Orlando; ☎ 800-711-0080). Less kitschy than MGM, you can find lots of action and adventure at Universal Studios. See Chapter 18.

✔ **Islands of Adventure** (Orlando; ☎ 800-711-0080). Thrill rides and cartoon faves make this Universal theme park one of Orlando's must-do's. See Chapter 18.

✔ **Kennedy Space Center** (Cape Canaveral; ☎ 321-449-4444). Blast off with tons of fun centering on the past, present, and future of space travel. See Chapter 19.

✔ **Daytona USA** (Daytona Beach; ☎ 386-947-6800). A state-of-the-art, interactive vehicular attraction that's even popular with non-race fans, Daytona USA is one of the few places in the world where speeding is a way of life. See Chapter 20.

The Best Chills and Thrills

✔ **The roller coasters at Busch Gardens** (Tampa; 866-353-8622). This African-themed adventureland offers five whopping coasters. The newest is **Gwazi,** a wooden coaster whose 50 mph thrills include weightlessness. **Kumba** and **Montu** are 10 mph faster. **The Python** offers a double corkscrew and a 70-foot plunge, while **The Scorpion** has a 60-foot dive and a 360-degree loop. See Chapter 14.

✔ **Summit Plummet** at Disney's Blizzard Beach starts slow but finishes with a 120-foot, wedgie-inducing freefall. You know that this one must be good because there are viewing stands to watch the suckers — er, riders — make the journey. See Chapter 18.

✔ **The Amazing Adventures of Spider-Man** at Islands of Adventure is a 3-D simulator that dips and twists through comic-book action. Watch out for the simulated, but very realistic feeling, 400-foot drop. See Chapter 18.

✔ The **Incredible Hulk Coaster** at Islands of Adventure launches you from 0 to 40 mph in two seconds and then does seven rollovers and two deep drops — you'll feel weightless, and possibly nauseated. See Chapter 18.

✔ **Dueling Dragons,** also at Islands of Adventure, catapults frail bodies on dueling coasters through five inversions at 55 to 60 mph, and — get this — you come within 12 inches of the other coaster on three occasions. See Chapter 18.

✔ **Rock 'n Roller Coaster** at Disney–MGM Studios rips from 0 to 60 mph in 2.8 seconds and goes right into an inversion, as the 120 speakers in your stretch limo blast Aerosmith. And as if that isn't enough, all this takes place in semidarkness. See Chapter 18.

✔ **The Twilight Zone Tower of Terror,** also at Disney–MGM, is a free-fall experience that leaves your stomach hanging at several levels — Rod Serling would have loved it. See Chapter 18.

The Best Places to Get Tipsy

✔ **Nikki Beach Club** (South Beach; ☎ 305-538-1111). This outdoor oasis is a cross between the Playboy Mansion and an episode of *Survivor,* with tiki huts, teepees, and, of course, bars, not to mention a colorful array of scantily clad barflies. See Chapter 10.

✔ **Alabama Jack's** (Islamorada; ☎ 305-248-8741). Don't drive too fast or you'll miss this converted gas station on the water that's home to delicious smoked fish and a colorful mix of Harley dudes, old–school, Hee Haw–esque line dancers, and passers-by en route to or from the Florida Keys. See Chapter 11.

✔ **Woody's Saloon and Restaurant** (Islamorada; ☎ 305-664-4335). This raunchy roadhouse bar features nightly headliners Big Dick and the Extenders. The leader of the band is a frequently profound and almost as frequently profane Native American who loves to pick on his audience. See Chapter 11.

✔ **Captain Tony's** (Key West; ☎ 305-294-1838). Some believe that this joint was the original Sloppy Joe's frequented by Ernest Hemingway. Undergarments left hanging from the ceiling pretty much set the tone of this dive. See Chapter 11.

✔ **Stan's Idle Hour Seafood Restaurant** (Goodland; ☎ 941-394-3041). This off-the-beaten-path bar-cum-restaurant has gained fame as the home of some odd events, including the Goodland Mullet Festival, the Buzzard Lope Queens, and Polish Octoberfest. See Chapter 16.

The Best Places to Party Until Dawn

- ✔ **South Beach** (Miami). South Beach, a.k.a. Glitter Beach, is just the two southernmost miles of Miami Beach but feels much larger in stature as an Art Deco District with clubs and bars featuring everything from rock to rhumba. See Chapter 10.

- ✔ **Duval Street** (Key West). The Bourbon Street of South Florida, Duval Street is yet another great place to cruise the bars; also take in the Sunset Celebration at nearby Mallory Square. See Chapter 11.

- ✔ **Las Olas Boulevard** (Fort Lauderdale).What used to be a dirt road leading to the Atlantic is now a tony street of cafes, galleries, boutiques, and bars. See Chapter 13.

- ✔ **Clematis Street** (West Palm Beach). This downtown West Palm Beach street offers lively action in pubs and clubs. See Chapter 13.

- ✔ **Ybor City.** This Cuban enclave near Tampa really gets lively with salsa-fied fun after the sun goes down. See Chapter 14.

- ✔ **Orlando.** The crème de la crème of prefab clubs and bars, most with a specific theme à la Planet Hollywood, Orlando is central Florida's mecca of entertainment. The city has two very themey entertainment districts. Disney's **Pleasure Island** and Universal's **CityWalk** let you party well into the wee hours. See Chapter 19.

The Best Places to Cast Your Reel

- ✔ **The Keys.** The Florida Keys are heaven for game fishermen (blue and white marlin, bonefish, tarpon, and permit) as well as anglers looking to put something on the dinner table. See Chapter 11.

- ✔ **Fort Lauderdale.** Fort Lauderdale offers good launching points for anglers looking for redfish, trout, snook, Spanish and king mackerel, sailfish, snapper, and grouper. See Chapter 13.

- ✔ **Treasure Island.** A good place to cast a line for grouper, amberjack, sea bass, and snapper. See Chapter 15.

- ✔ **Boca Grande.** The fishing off Boca Grande is wonderful, and things really heat up in July when The World's Richest Tarpon Tournament is staged. See Chapter 16.

Chapter 2

Deciding Where and When to Go

*F*lorida is a year-round destination — it has only a few rain dates — but some places are best sampled in the so-called off season. Unless you're into togetherness, two of our most popular destinations are best avoided during certain times of the year. **Walt Disney World** and Orlando's other major theme parks amount to instant insanity any time kids are out of school, such as summer and holidays. The more popular **Florida beaches** (Miami, Daytona, and St. Petersburg/Clearwater) also do a feverish business in summer as well as during the annual snowbird season (winter) and spring break.

I give you ammunition so you can decide when to go, but it's quite likely that personal factors will end up cementing your decision. Some of you, for example, plan a vacation to avoid wicked weather back home. Others take advantage of seasonal savings that are too good to pass up. And many of you have to travel when the school calendar allows. The good news is that there's a season for everyone.

Where you go depends on your interests and budget. Do you want to soak in the sun? Avoid another human life-form for a while? Hook a tuna? Explore the oldest city in the United States? Lose lunch on our best thrill rides? This guide offers all these possibilities and more.

Diving Into Florida's Regions

If you want to come to Florida but don't know much about it, you're in good company. Even Florida natives are lucky if they get to know everything about their own backyards.

Florida

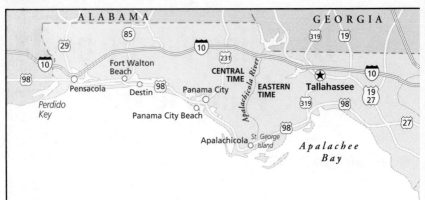

Gulf of Mexico

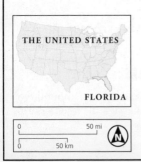

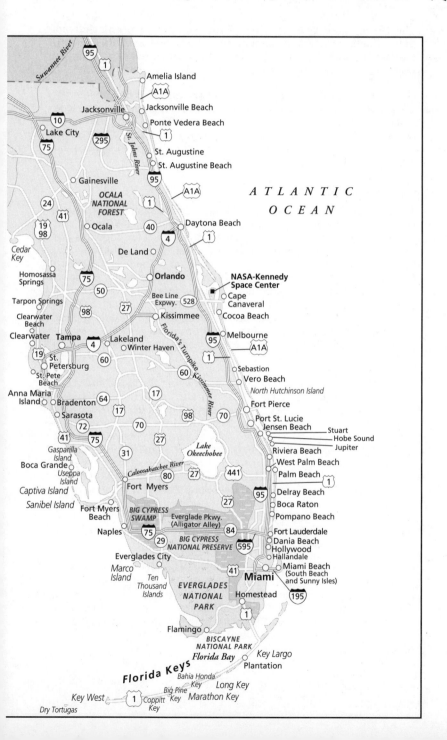

This is a big state. Don't even try to tackle it all at once. Biting off more than a fraction of the state in one visit is futile. So I separate the state into manageable chunks that you can study before deciding what you want to cover this year (and perhaps, in the many years to come).

For starters, here are thumbnail sketches of the cities and regions to get you thinking about a wish list. Do you want nightlife? Are the kids making the decisions for you? Do you like the beach? Hate the forest? Don't be bashful. It doesn't cost a thing to dream, and you'll have time later to whittle your list down to size. I give you all the tools necessary to make the decision that's right for you.

South Florida

The unofficial capital of the South Florida region, Miami is both pictur-esque and sophisticated, with a pulsating nightlife. **South Beach** is where La Dolce Vita fuses with La Vida Loca, known for hot clubs and cool people watching along a beach that's been described as America's Riviera. **Villa Vizcaya** and **Coral Castle** are two of the region's finest (and most ambitious) architectural marvels, while kitschier attractions such as the **Miami MetroZoo** and **Miami Seaquarium** have been tickling tourists for decades. The sports scene includes pro football, baseball, basketball, and hockey franchises. But Miami is a moderately expensive destination, and it has many of the other problems associated with a metropolis, including crime, congestion, and pollution. (See Chapters 9 and 10 for details about Miami.)

Things thin and chill out a bit in the Keys, where the mood and the magic are a little off-center, but that's just the Conch Republic's way of life. Only a single road stretches over the 110 miles from the mainland to **Key West.** This single highway can make the drive seem like an endless journey when accidents close one or both lanes. The Keys are best for those of you who want to kick back and forget about following a sched-ule or a dress code. Water sports rule through most of the Keys, espe-cially at such gems as **Bahia Honda State Recreation Area** on Big Pine Key and **John Pennekamp Coral Reef State Park** in Key Largo. Key West was a favorite stomping ground (and watering hole) for several of the most notable literary and artistic figures of the 20th century. Its attrac-tions include the **Audubon House** and the **Ernest Hemingway Home and Museum** (see Chapter 11).

South Florida is also the gateway to Florida's greatest natural treasure, **the Everglades** (see Chapter 12). And **Palm Beach** is the winter home of some of America's rich and famous. To match the size of his ego, Donald Trump bought Mar a Lago, Palm Beach's largest and most resplendent home. Even if you're not on *Forbes'* list of the richest people in the world, it's fun to window shop along **Worth Avenue,** known as the Rodeo Drive of the South (see Chapter 13).

Fort Lauderdale has several of Florida's best **golf courses,** and the burgeoning yet **historic downtown riverfront** area, with shops, dining, and
assorted amusements, is one of the region's most popular new tourist
draws.

The Gulf Coast

With some exceptions, this coast hasn't experienced the explosive growth
that the Atlantic side has. The water is part of the reason. The Atlantic
is alive with crashing waves, which is as good as the surf gets in Florida.
Across the way, the Gulf of Mexico is calm and tepid, like a soothing tub.

Tampa's Latin influence adds a welcome touch to the region's food, culture, and architecture. The city has a moderately good arts calendar, a
dandy nightclub scene in the Cuban enclave of Ybor City, and in **Busch
Gardens,** a theme park that rivals Orlando's offerings. St. Petersburg's
signature attractions include its **Gulf Beaches,** the **Salvador Dalí Museum,**
and the **Florida International Museum.**

The two cities have a top-rated sports calendar that includes big-league
baseball, football, and hockey teams. But tourism is an afterthought on
Tampa's side of the bay, and St. Petersburg is nearly as overbuilt as Miami.
(See Chapters 14 and 15 for more on Tampa and St. Petersburg.)

Sarasota's **Asolo Theatre** and the **Ringling Museum of Art** give the
cultural community plenty of reason to crow. Gulf-view towns, such
as Naples, Marco Island, and Fort Myers, are quieter than most of
Florida's other beachfront cities. This stretch of the coast has more than
10,000 islands including **Sanibel, Captiva, Gasparilla,** and **Boca Grande.**

 On the downside, this area is spread far and wide. There are few day-
filling activities, and you have to drive a while to get to your next stop.
(See Chapter 16 for information on Sarasota, Naples, and Fort Myers.)

Central Florida

If Orlando were a rock group, it would be called "Mickey and the
Wannabes." In Central Florida, Walt Disney World is the lead vocalist,
Universal Orlando and **SeaWorld** play the guitar and keyboards, and
dozens of smaller attractions are behind the drums. This area truly is
fantasyland, but the crowds, cost, and confusion can turn your trip into
a frightful experience.

As late as 1970, Orlando was a small town dotted with cow patties, orange
blossoms, and palmetto stands. A year later, Disney changed that forever.
Uncle Walt's legacy spawned four theme parks (**Magic Kingdom, Epcot,
Disney–MGM Studios,** and **Animal Kingdom**) and nearly a dozen minor
attractions, plus a supporting cast of resorts, restaurants, and stores —

enough to be its own city. Orlando is also home to the ever-expanding world of Universal Orlando (**Universal Studios Florida, Islands of Adventure,** and more) as well as **SeaWorld** and its younger sister, **Discovery Cove.** (Check out Chapter 18 for information on all the Disney, Universal, and SeaWorld attractions.)

If ever there were a destination that virtually had it all, Orlando is it, which is why many people love it. It's a reasonably convenient place to park yourself — much of the hoopla is in two areas, Lake Buena Vista and International Drive, and most of its neighborhoods have just about everything you need for an amusing vacation.

On the flip side, traffic and crowds can be brutal, and the theme parks are expensive. (Most visits cost a family of four $180 — just for admission.)

The Great North

Daytona Beach's calling cards are bikinis, bikers, and bullet cars. The city bills itself as "the world's most famous beach." The title is disputable, but Daytona is a wide stretch of white sand, bathed in frothy Atlantic waters. Aside from the beach, Daytona's most popular tourist attractions are the **Daytona International Speedway** and **Daytona USA,** a high-tech, interactive, jump-and-shout exhibit in front of the speedway (see Chapter 20). But if you're not into sun, sand, and speed, Daytona may feel like you woke up in *Wayne's World* with a Southern twang. And if you arrive in March and aren't a member of the spring-break squad, you're likely to feel out of place on the beach.

The oldest city in the United States, **St. Augustine** (founded in 1565), is located a little farther north of Daytona on the Atlantic coast. If the idea of forts and other musty mysteries appeals to you, here's a chance to go back to the days of the earliest colonization. **Castillo de San Marcos** is a precious link to the past as are several storefronts that stake a claim to being the oldest something or other (jail, school, and so on). Although the city has its share of tourist trappings (a pseudo **Fountain of Youth,** for example), it also has some nifty places to visit, such as the **St. Augustine Alligator Farm and Zoological Park** and the **Bridge of Lions** (see Chapter 21).

Continuing north, **Jacksonville** is a Navy town that has traded paper mills for sprawl and interstate clutter. The **Jacksonville Zoo** and the natural beaches, such as the one at **Little Talbot Island State Park,** are pluses, but most tourists find themselves having to scatter to find things to do in the Jacksonville area. One of northeast Florida's nicer resorts, **Amelia Island Plantation,** is 30 miles north. This resort blends environmental consciousness with top-flight golf, tennis, and beach activities. At the other end of the island, **Fort Clinch State Park,** near **Fernandina Beach,** offers living-history presentations that are a joy to see (see Chapter 21).

Revealing the Secret of the Seasons

Seasons? You bet Florida has them.

Of course, some of them are far less pronounced than in places like Europe, Canada, and New York. Sometimes it's hard to even tell if Florida has an autumn or spring. Summer's heat and humidity often last six months or more. During hurricane season, which lasts from June through November, intense storms can send even the most diehard Floridians running for shelter (see the "Heeding Weather Warnings" section, later in this chapter). As a tradeoff, winters are generally mild and pleasant. Florida skies are unusually sunny, except for the first day of winter cold fronts, a short spring rainy season, and the daily thunderstorms that come and go quickly in summer. Temperatures in Florida are more moderate along the coasts, particularly on the Atlantic side, which has a decent sea breeze; the center of the state tends to be a bit colder in winter and hot as blazes in summer.

Most people enjoy their vacations more when crowds are thin and the weather is mild — spring and fall in Florida. Except in Orlando, rooms and (in some cases) other expenses are cheaper during these seasons.

 If you have youngsters, think about pulling them out of school for a few days during the off season to avoid crowds and lines at theme parks and other attractions. Ask their teachers for schoolwork to take with you. You can also suggest that your kids write a report on some educational element of the vacation. If you're a senior who can travel when you please, think about avoiding the peak of the winter snowbird season as well as the summer and holiday family times.

Here's our seasonal score sheet.

Discovering springtime in Florida

Spring is a popular vacation time for most travelers, and Florida is no different. Here are some of the best reasons to go to Florida in the springtime:

- ✔ The weather is mild.
- ✔ Spring is when Florida really blooms. Think flower power.
- ✔ Accommodations that give discounts give them now.

However, keep in mind the following springtime pitfalls:

- ✔ Without a winter, a long spring is rare. Temps can get warm and sticky in April (heat + humidity = Hades).
- ✔ The pollen drives hay-fever sufferers crazy.
- ✔ Spring break cometh. Avoid it unless you're a breaker.

Heating up the scene in summer

Florida bustles during the summer season, in spite of the sizzling temperatures. Here are some points to consider:

- Wow — picturesque 6 a.m. sunrises and 9 p.m. sunsets.

- August means back-to-school sales at malls and outlets.

- Air-conditioning is alive and well. Savvy travelers spend the middle of the day indoors, whether it's in a cool attraction or their accommodations.

But, again, keep in mind the following:

- The heat and humidity are oppressive.

- Summer thunderstorms cool things off a little, but they pass quickly, allowing the sun to turn concrete and asphalt walks into frying pans. Summer is also the heart of hurricane season (see the "Heeding Weather Warnings" section, later in this chapter).

- Discounts? Ha! Why cut prices with these crowds?

Falling into the tropics

Fall is a beautiful time of year to visit Florida. Here are some of the state's autumn bonuses:

- Ah, fall foliage. Florida has the same fiery reds, brilliant oranges, and screaming yellows as New England. The difference is that ours last about 17 minutes.

- Accommodations that give discounts do so in the fall, too.

- Lines and crowds begin to shrink.

Some things to look out for, however:

- It's cooler, but temps aren't as mild as those in spring until Thanksgiving or later.

- The hurricane season lasts through November, and storm activity can run high in September and October (see the "Heeding Weather Warnings" section, later in this chapter).

Heading south for the winter

Winter brings visions of softly falling snowflakes (and slick roads and salt trucks) to most travelers, but that's not the case in Florida. You should consider the following pluses when planning a winter vacation in Florida:

✔ There isn't a true winter, just a few days at or near freezing, followed by mild, sunny weather. So leave those winter blues back home.

✔ Lines are short in many tourist areas during most of the winter season.

Winter does have its downside, however. Consider the following:

✔ The mid-December to early January holidays are nearly as crowded as the dead of summer.

✔ Forget about a white Christmas. It's common for temperatures to be in the 90s during Hanukkah, Christmas, and Kwanzaa.

✔ After mid-December arrives, prices rise.

Wising Up about the Weather

You can check out Table 2-1 for the average 24-hour temperatures for selected Florida cities. Beyond these averages and the seasonal information I provide in this chapter, there's no way to get a true-blue, long-term forecast. But you can find short-term forecasts (presuming you trust meteorologists) at the following venues:

✔ **The Weather Channel:** The 24-hour cable channel features Florida on a regular basis, and it offers ongoing coverage when big weather news happens. You can also get information on the Internet at www. weather.com.

✔ **The Weather Center:** This Tampa-based service is a good source for statewide weather information. The Weather Center (www.weather center.com) features data on tides, rainfall, temperatures, and severe weather warnings as well as a link to the National Weather Service (NWS). Speaking of the NWS, you can jump to its site at www.nws.noaa.gov for more information.

Table 2-1	Average 24-Hour Temperatures for Sample Cities (°F/°C)										
Miami											
Jan	Feb	Mar	Apr	May	June	July	Aug	Sept	Oct	Nov	Dec
69/21	70/21	71/22	74/23	78/26	81/27	82/28	84/29	81/27	78/26	73/23	70/21
Tampa											
Jan	Feb	Mar	Apr	May	June	July	Aug	Sept	Oct	Nov	Dec
60/16	61/16	66/19	72/22	77/25	81/27	82/28	82/28	81/27	75/24	67/19	62/17

(continued)

Table 2-1 *(continued)*

Orlando

Jan	Feb	Mar	Apr	May	June	July	Aug	Sept	Oct	Nov	Dec
60/16	63/17	66/19	71/22	78/26	82/28	82/28	82/28	81/27	75/24	67/19	61/16

Jacksonville

Jan	Feb	Mar	Apr	May	June	July	Aug	Sept	Oct	Nov	Dec
57/19	58/14	64/18	69/21	77/25	80/27	81/27	82/28	79/26	73/23	65/18	61/16

Heeding Weather Warnings

There's no need for paranoia, but knowing a little about Florida's climatic temper tantrums can reduce the odds of one or all of them ruining your vacation.

Making hurricane waves

Should you worry about hurricanes? No, but it helps to be aware of them. The hurricane season runs from June 1 through November 30. In an average year, 12 or so tropical storms are born somewhere in the Gulf and Atlantic waters, half or more develop into hurricanes, and, again on average, 1 or 2 may touch part of Florida, especially coastal areas. The hurricane season was particularly brutal in 2004 with four hurricanes — Charley, Frances, Ivan, and Jeanne — hitting Florida in a period of six weeks.

If you're unlucky enough to be here when a hurricane is threatening, modern tracking gives you plenty of warning. In severe cases, your hotels may be evacuated and you may end up in a shelter. At that point, there's really nothing more you can do but wait out the storm in safety. If the thought of a hurricane really bothers you, consider steering clear of Florida in the most active months, which are usually July to mid-October, the same months that Florida is hottest and most crowded.

If one week before your much-anticipated vacation Hurricane Harry plows right through your destination, how can you tell if Miami's Fontainebleau Hilton Resort is still standing? You could ask a reservationist or someone at the local chamber of commerce. But if you're a Doubting Danielle, you may want to turn to a third party. The state **Division of Emergency Management** in Tallahassee (☎ **850-413-9900**) is the agency in charge of putting Florida back together again. You should get a fair, impartial report on damage to specific areas. You can also find information on the agency's Web site at www.dca.state.fl.us/fdem.

Tumbling tornadoes

Tornadoes are fairly uncommon, but they and waterspouts are a fringe benefit of summer thunderstorms. You're more likely to run into one at Universal Studios' "Twister" attraction, but don't take any chances. When tornado warnings are issued, go indoors and stay clear of windows. April, May, and June are considered peak periods — though some nasty ones have dropped into the Florida Panhandle (a region not covered in this book so I can cover more popular areas more thoroughly) in February and March.

Don't take lightning lightly. Here are a few quick facts:

- ✔ Lightning is 50,000°F, five times hotter than the sun.

- ✔ Lightning can reach out from the sky and zap you from 10 miles away.

- ✔ Lightning travels fast — a radar gun clocked its speed at 186,000 miles per second.

But you have to be pretty unlucky to be standing in the wrong place (under an oak tree, wading in water, or trying to hit a golf ball while wearing metal cleats and holding a metal club) at the wrong time (again, usually during a thunderstorm). Lightning will more than likely entertain you: The pyrotechnics really light up the sky. But keep your distance. The fireworks are better and safer at Walt Disney World.

Much of central Florida is considered the Lightning Capital of the United States. Tampa and St. Petersburg are among the most common targets, with 88 days of lightning activity and some 50 strikes per square mile a year. An average house in this part of the universe gets hit every 20 or 30 years. If you were as big as a house and never moved, well, then that gives you an idea of the likelihood of a run-in with lightning.

Forgoing some sun

Floridians are as proud of that big orange thing in the sky as Bubba is of his prize pickup truck. We even nicknamed ourselves the Sunshine State. The sun certainly is a friend of Florida tourism, but it isn't always a friend of Florida tourists, especially the ones who arrive unprepared for its sucker punches. One of these blows from the sun, sunburn, is a bad hombre, but its evil twin, sun poisoning, can ruin your vacation. Most burns can be eased with over-the-counter creams or aloe. But sun poisoning — sunburn to the fourth or fifth power — is far more dangerous. It can result in fever, chills, headaches, dizziness, nausea, and in the worst cases, sunstroke.

Protecting yourself from sunburn and sunstroke is simple. Lather your skin with a sunblock that has an SPF (sun protection factor) rating of 30 or higher. (*Do not* use tanning oil. That's like slathering yourself with bacon grease before jumping into a low-burning skillet.) You may think the ultimate souvenir is a Florida tan, but tans aren't all they're cracked up to be. Ask any native the state's skin cancer rates. If nothing worse happens, your Florida tan will start to peel by the time you get back on the block.

If you skip this prevention advice and go straight to the I'm-on-fire-and-I-feel-a-bit-woozy phase, helping hands are on standby at **Poison Control** (☎ 800-282-3171).

Remember to bring a wide-brimmed hat and don't forget a native's favorite fashion statement — sunglasses.

Raining down

Rain doesn't hurt anyone, but it can dampen a beach vacation and outdoor activities. Much of the Atlantic coast in Miami-Dade, Broward, and Palm Beach counties gets 60 or more inches of rain a year, 7 more inches than the state average. The Keys get about 40 inches. Summers bring brief but daily rains to much of the state. You can often wait out a rainstorm if some shelter is nearby; don't automatically pack up for the day unless it looks like there's no end in sight.

Checking Out Florida's Calendar of Events

Florida packs the schedule with dozens of exciting festivals and special events throughout the year. In the following sections, I list some highlights.

Keep in mind that although many of Florida's events are fun-filled, some are especially rowdy and crowded. Here are a few of the more notorious:

- ✔ **Gasparilla Pirate Fest (Tampa):** On the last Saturday in January, hundreds of boats and hundreds of thousands of revelers fill the bay and downtown Tampa for Gasparilla, a festival capped by a pirate invasion. A barge masquerading as a ship, mostly filled with city bigwigs, invades and captures Tampa on behalf of the mythical pirate, Jose Gaspar. Most of the bigwigs have 80-proof blood when this happens (even though it's 10 a.m.). In all, there are two weeks of events, including foot races, street parties, and parades. It's a smaller version of Mardi Gras, but one that should be experienced in limited doses, if at all. If you want a dose, call ☎ 813-251-4500 or go to www.gasparillapiratefest.com.

- ✔ **Bike Week (Daytona Beach): The Sturgis of the South,** Daytona Beach's Bike Week events, which take place sometime between February and mid-March, are to be avoided at all costs unless you like motorcycles and bikers in all sizes, shapes, and states of consciousness. Daytona doesn't exaggerate when it says more than 500,000 two-wheel enthusiasts show up for the events, which include parades, races, shows, entertainment, and a fair share of falling down on the beach. If you're a glutton for noise and crowds, call ☎ 800-854-1234 (U.S. only) or 386-255-0981 or go to www.bikeweek.com.

- ✔ **Spring Break:** Arrggghhhh!!! Spring break, spanning March and April, brings an annual invasion of partying college kids to beach hot spots including Panama City, Daytona, Key West, and Miami. Orlando gets its share of mayhem, too.

✔ **Fantasy Fest (Key West):** Fantasy Fest, in which Mardi Gras goes
south the last week in October, sees Key West overtaken by wildly
costumed (and some wildly undercostumed) revelers who have no
shame and no parental guidance. This weeklong, hedonistic, X-rated
Halloween party is not for children. If you're going, make reservations
early because hotels tend to book up very quickly for this event.
Call ☎ 305-296-1817 or go to www.fantasyfest.net.

✔ **Biketoberfest (Daytona Beach):** If Bike Week tickles your fancy, the
Daytona Beach Biketoberfest blowout probably will, too. Races,
touring rides, parades, costumed bikers, and other activities —
such as biker tipping — fill the final weeks of October. Give them a
loud shout at ☎ 800-854-1234 (U.S. only) or 386-255-0415 or check
them out online at www.biketoberfest.org.

✔ **Guavaween (Tampa):** At the risk of sounding like we're picking on
Daytona and Tampa, the **Guavaween** festival held in Tampa's Ybor
City is a Latin-style Halloween celebration that has become seedier
over the years. Still, you may be curious enough to call ☎ 813-248-
3712 or 813-621-7121 or refer to their Web site (www.guavaween.net)
to get more information.

January

Held on Miami's South Beach, **Art Deco Weekend** (☎ 305-672-2014; www.
mdpl.org), features bands, vittles, antiques vendors, artists, tours, and
lots of traffic in a celebration of the whimsical architecture that's made
this restored area one of America's most unique neighborhoods. Second
week of January.

Football fanatics flock to Miami's **FedEx Orange Bowl Classic** (☎ 305-
371-4600; www.orangebowl.org), held at Pro Player Stadium, featuring
two of the year's best college football teams. January 1.

The four-day **Zora Neale Hurston Festival** (☎ 407-647-3307; www.
zoranealehurstonfestival.com), is held just north of Orlando in
Eatonville, the first incorporated African-American town in America,
and it highlights the life and work of author Zora Neale Hurston. Last
week in January.

February

Dusty midways, hopeless games, and greasy food join hands with live-
stock exhibits, arts and crafts, and big-name country entertainers at the
Florida State Fair (☎ 813-621-7821; www.floridastatefair.com), a
fair held on the east side of Tampa. Second and third week of February.

Megayachts, dinghies, and everything in between are featured at
the **Miami International Boat Show** (☎ 305-531-8410; www.discover
boating.com/boatshows/miami), which draws hundreds of thousands
of boat enthusiasts to the Miami Beach Convention Center. Mid-February.

Twenty of Major League Baseball's teams use Florida for their **spring training** camps. Pitchers and catchers land in mid-February; exhibition games are played from early March to the beginning of April. You can get information through your hometown Ticketmaster, or you can look online at www.springtrainingmagazine.com. February to early April.

March–April

If you need proof that Miami's predominantly Hispanic community knows how to throw a party, head for the **Carnaval Miami/Calle Ocho** (☎ 305-644-8888; www.carnavalmiami.com). The largest of its kind in the country, the nine-day ethnic celebration comes to a pounding finale with the 23-block Calle Ocho street festival. Early March.

Cypress Gardens comes alive with hundreds of annual blossoms at **Spring Flower Festival,** featuring more than two dozen real-life figures decked out in flowers and over 35,000 plants (☎ 800-282-2123; www.cypress gardens.com). March 14 through May 15.

More than 100 acts from around the world participate in the eclectic **Orlando International Fringe Festival** (☎ 407-648-0077; www. orlandofringe.org), held at various locations in downtown Orlando. Entertainers perform drama, comedy, political satire, experimental theater, and a seven-minute version of Hamlet, all on outdoor stages. Ticket prices vary, but most performances are under $10. Ten days in April and/or May.

May

Accurately billed as Florida's largest music, art, and waterfront festival, **SunFest** (☎ 561-659-5980; www.sunfest.org), in West Palm Beach features 40 bands, which perform on three stages. There's also an art show, fireworks, and more. End of April and beginning of May.

The **Fernandina Beach Shrimp Festival** (☎ 800-226-3542 (U.S. only) or 904-277-0717; www.shrimpfestival.com), in the northeast corner of the state, is held in Florida's oldest port, the birthplace of Florida's shrimp industry and features live music, entertainment, and slews of fisher-folk dressed up as pirates. The first weekend in May.

At **McDonald's Air and Sea Show** (☎ 954-467-3555; www.national salute.com), it's a tough call as far as what's more crowded — Fort Lauderdale's air, sea, or ground, which combine to attract more than 2 million onlookers craning their necks for a view of big-name air wolves such as the Blue Angels and the Thunderbirds. Early May.

Key Largo hosts the largest fishing tournament in the Keys, the **Coconuts Dolphin Tournament** (☎ 305-453-9794; www.coconutsrestaurant.com), enticing anglers with a $26,000 prize fund, including $7,000 for the winner. Mid-May.

June

Gay Disney (www.gayday.com or www.gaydays.com), draws tens of thousands of gay and lesbian travelers to Central Florida. This event grew out of Gay Day, an unofficial event at Disney World dating to the early 1990s, when it drew 50,000 people. Universal and SeaWorld also roll out the red carpet for gays and lesbians over this weekend. First weekend in June.

Not to be outdone by Carnaval Miami/Calle Ocho, the **Coconut Grove Goombay Festival** (☎ 800-283-2707 or 305-372-9966; www.goombay festival.com), is billed as the largest black-heritage festival in the United States. Last weekend in June.

July

Held at the Looe Key National Marine Sanctuary on Big Pine Key, the **Underwater Music Festival** (☎ 800-872-3722 or 305-872-3580), gives divers a chance to listen to an underwater symphony. Call the festival for dates.

Held on Boca Grande, the **World's Richest Tarpon Tournament** (☎ 941-964-0568; www.worldsrichesttarpon.com), offers approximately $250,000 in prize money for anglers working the tarpon-rich waters off Southwest Florida. Mid-week in the second week of July.

August

The west-coast city of Venice, the self-described "Shark's Tooth Capital of the World," hosts the **Shark's Tooth and Seafood Festival** (☎ 941-488-2236; www.veniceflorida.com/shark.htm), which lets kids scramble for mako molars while grown-ups gorge on fruits of the sea, browse through arts and crafts, and enjoy ice sculptures. First weekend in August.

September

St. Augustine Birthday Festival (☎ 904-825-1010; www.staugustine info.com), celebrates the 1565 birth of the nation's oldest city. The annual event includes a re-enactment of the landing of the city's founder, Pedro Menendez, followed by a Catholic mass and then a day filled with entertainment and food. Second week in September.

On the **Night of Joy** (☎ 407-824-4321; www.disneyworld.com), the Magic Kingdom is home to a contemporary Christian music festival featuring top artists. This is a very popular event; if it's on your dance card, get tickets ($30 per night or $50 for the pair) early. Contact Disney for dates.

October

The month-long **Destin Fishing Rodeo** (☎ 850-837-6734; www.destin fishingrodeo.org), is held in an area that's billed as the "World's Luckiest Fishing Village." That may be a stretch, but it is a hot spot for anglers. The entire month of October.

Come to the **Epcot International Food and Wine Festival** (☎ 407-824-4321; www.disneyworld.com) if you'd like to sip and savor the food and beverages of several cultures. In addition, more than 60 wineries from across the United States participate. Events include wine tastings, seminars, food, dinners, and celebrity-chef cooking. October to mid-November.

The world's largest boat show, the **Fort Lauderdale International Boat Show** (☎ 954-764-7642; www.showmanagement.com), has boats of every size, shape, and status symbol displayed at the scenic Bahia Mar marina and four other locations in the area. Traffic-phobes beware. Call or check Web site for dates.

During **Halloween Horror Nights** (☎ 800-837-2273 or 407-363-8000; www.universalorlando.com), Universal Orlando transforms into a haunted attraction with live bands, a psychopath's maze, special shows, and hundreds of ghouls and goblins roaming the streets. The studio closes at dusk and then reopens in a new, macabre form at 7 p.m. Special admission is charged for this event, where liquor flows freely. Nineteen fright-filled evenings in late October.

November

For its annual **Chrysanthemum Festival** (☎ 800-282-2123; www.cypressgardens.com), Cypress Gardens gets decked out with, get this, 3 *million* blooms that use a cascading waterfall for a centerpiece. Mid-November.

Bibliophiles, literati, and some of the world's most prestigious and prolific authors descend upon downtown Miami for the **Miami Bookfair International** (☎ 305-237-3258). The weekend street fair is the most well-attended of the entire event, in which regular folk mix with wordsmiths such as Tom Wolfe and Jane Smiley, while indulging in snacks, antiquarian books, and literary gossip. All lectures are free, but they fill up quickly, so get there early. One week in mid-November.

The **Walt Disney World Festival of the Masters** (☎ 407-824-4321; www.disneyworld.com), one of the largest art shows in the South, takes place at Downtown Disney Marketplace. The exhibition features top artists, photographers, and craftspeople, all winners of juried shows throughout the country. Admission is free. Second weekend in November.

December

In a stirring welcome to the holiday season, re-enactors in period costumes lead a torch-lit procession through St. Augustine's historic district during **British Night Watch and Grand Illumination** (☎ 904-829-1711; www.staugustine.com). Daytime events include living-history displays. First weekend in December.

People who complain that the holiday season just isn't as festive in Fort Lauderdale as it is in colder parts of the world probably have missed the spectacular **Winterfest Boat Parade** (☎ **954-767-0686**), held along the Intracoastal Waterways. Forget decking the halls. At this parade, the decks are decked out in magnificent holiday regalia as they gracefully — and boastfully — glide up and down the water. If you're not on a boat, the best views are from waterfront restaurants or anywhere you can squeeze in along the water. Mid-December.

During the **Disney Christmas** festivities (☎ **407-824-4321;** www.disney world.com), Main Street in the Magic Kingdom is lavishly decked out with lights and holly, and carolers greet visitors. Thousands of colored lights illuminate an 80-foot tree. Epcot, Disney–MGM Studios, and Animal Kingdom also offer special embellishments and entertainment throughout the holiday season, as do all Disney resorts. Contact Disney for dates.

Amelia Island, located between Jacksonville and Fernandina Beach, puts on a month-long **Victorian Seaside Christmas** celebration that includes tours of bed-and-breakfasts, teddy bear teas, and sleigh rides on the beach (☎ **800-226-3542** [U.S. only] or 904-277-0717; www.amelianow.com). The entire month of December.

Part II
Planning Your Trip to Florida

The 5th Wave   By Rich Tennant

"Maybe we shouldn't have gotten a time-share so close to the Everglades."

In this part . . .

Okay, it's time to slide into some serious planning. I open this part of the book by talking about money matters, such as whether to use traveler's checks or credit cards, and by providing you with information that guides you through planning a budget for your trip. Then I discuss getting to and around Florida and suggest ways for zeroing in on a room that's right for you. Finally, I consider the pros and cons of travel and medical insurance, and offer up some specialized resources for travelers with unique travel needs or interests.

So, if you're ready, sing a little traveling music with me!

Chapter 3

Managing Your Money

· ·

In This Chapter

▶ Managing your dollars and cents
▶ Avoiding surprise expenses
▶ Cutting costs and gleaning other frugal tidbits
▶ Sorting out your money options
▶ Preventing and recovering from theft

· ·

Developing a realistic budget is an important key to enjoying your vacation. The last thing you want to experience when you get to Florida is sticker shock — and the state has been known to exact a pound of flesh from even the most cost-conscious travelers. From hotel rooms to restaurant tabs to admission fees, you can ring up a high tally if you don't do your homework in advance. The good news is that I can help you make sure that you don't bust your bankroll.

Planning Your Budget

 Budgeting a Florida vacation is easy. The hard part is sticking to the budget. Sometimes tourist attractions, souvenir stands, beaches, and 80-proof fun make people so giddy that they get separated from both their common sense and their finances. They end up in shock — especially when credit card bills begin arriving in the mail. But if you avoid too much impulse bingeing — er, buying — and draft an honest budget, you're home free.

 Make sure to include everything in your vacation budget. Add in the cost of getting to the airport; airport parking (if you drive yourself); airline tickets (you can find tips for getting the best airfare in Chapter 4; transportation from your destination airport to your hotel, or the rental-car charge if you're driving yourself; the room rate; meals; admissions to attractions (multiplied by the number of days you'll visit them); sightseeing tours; souvenirs; and entertainment expenses. Then tack on another 15 percent to 20 percent as a safety net.

Later in this chapter, I offer you a few ways to beat the high cost of Florida travel. (Also, check out the destination chapters for more money-saving travel tips.) But first, here are some things to expect in the way of prices when you get to Florida.

Transportation

If you're going to stay put in some of Florida's big cities, you can get by without a rental car. You can get around Orlando (see Chapter 19), and to a lesser degree, Fort Lauderdale (see Chapter 13), St. Petersburg (see Chapter 15), and Daytona Beach (see Chapter 20) by hotel or private shuttles and tour services, especially if you pick a room that's near the places you want to visit. You can also get by without a car in Miami Beach, St. Augustine, and Key West because most of their hot spots are concentrated in reasonably small areas.

That said, you'll be at the mercy of the aforementioned services, you may waste a good deal of time getting around using public and private transportation, and in some cities (Miami for one), relying on taxis will cost you a bundle. If you don't want the hassle or you're visiting a smaller destination, rentals are advisable, if not a necessity. Their rates start at about $35 a day or $110 a week. Don't forget to add in any hotel and attraction parking fees, noted in the destination chapters, as well as the 20 percent state taxes assessed on rental cars in Florida.

Lodging

Florida is a big state that wears several different faces, so don't pay attention to hotel price information that mentions a statewide average — it really doesn't exist here. A $50-a-night room in Crystal River (see Chapter 15) may be a little above average, while a similarly priced room in Miami will put you in a neighborhood where you definitely don't want to be. Due to these differences in rates, I give you a range in the destination chapters that goes from low to high like this: $99 or less, inexpensive; $100 to $199, moderate; $200 to $249, expensive; and $250 and higher, very expensive. If you insist on an average (don't hold me to it) room rate, you should expect to spend

- ✔ $30 to $60 in towns that are off the beaten path.

- ✔ $70 to $100 in the mid-Atlantic coastal region, north of Palm Beach and south of Cocoa Beach/Titusville, and on the Gulf Coast, north of the St. Petersburg/Tampa area and south of Sarasota (excluding Naples).

- ✔ $100 to $150 for the mainstream hotels in Miami and Orlando; the beaches of Daytona, Fort Lauderdale, and Naples; and the corporate zones in Tampa and Fort Lauderdale.

- ✔ $150 to $250 for the expensive (but not top-notch) accommodations around Key West, Miami, Orlando, and Palm Beach; the state's golf and spa resorts; and the upper-end corporate and business zones in Fort Lauderdale, Jacksonville, Miami, Orlando, Tampa, and so on.

- ✔ $250 and into the ionosphere at the high-end resorts and corporate retreats found in Miami, Naples/Marco Island, Orlando, Palm Beach, and the Jacksonville area.

Dining

In most Florida cities, you can buy three squares for about $35 per person, per day (excluding tax, tip, and the 80-proof fun I mentioned a little earlier). You won't eat at gourmet restaurants for that amount, but you won't be condemned to Uncle Mel's No-Frills Grille, either. Allowing for $35 per person per day gets you into B to C+ eateries. Major tourist cities, such as Miami and Orlando, as well as business destinations, such as Jacksonville and Tampa, are a pinch pricier for the same class of cuisine. And if you doom yourself to the theme parks, expect to pay 20 percent more for the same or lesser quality food.

I promise to give you four price levels in the dining areas of the destination chapters — $14 and under, $15 to $24, $25 to $39, and $40 and up — although I cater more to people on moderate budgets.

Sightseeing

When it comes to a day's entertainment, the amount you spend depends on what city you visit and what attractions and activities interest you the most. Orlando will unquestionably cost you more than any other Florida city. SeaWorld's sister park, **Discovery Cove** (see Chapter 18) has raised the bar on Florida attraction prices. Tickets are $229 from January 1to March 21 and September 1 to December 31; and $249 from March 22 to August 31 for a daylong adventure that includes a 30-minute swim with the dolphins, seven days' admission to SeaWorld, lunch, and a few other wet-and-wild goodies. (It's $129–$179 depending on season, if you can skip the dolphin swim.)

Orlando's theme parks are part of the next tier. Single-day passes cost $55 for adults and $44 for kids 3 to 9 years old at **Disney's** four parks. **Universal's** two theme parks cost $55 for adults and $45 for kids 3 to 9, and the **SeaWorld** admission is $54 for adults and $45 for kids 3 to 9. Those prices do not include 6 percent sales tax. If you're going to be a regular, buy one of the multiday, multipark passes outlined in Chapter 18. **Busch Gardens** in Tampa (see Chapter 14) also falls in this tier.

The fees for Florida's other attractions range downward from those that you would pay at theme parks to free or next to nothing for an endless string of museums. Table 3-1 has a cross section.

Table 3-1   A Sampling of Florida's Entertainment Options

Attraction	Cost
Cypress Gardens (see Chapter 19)	$34.95 adults, $19.95 kids 6 to 17
Daytona USA and Daytona International Speedway Tour (see Chapter 20)	$20 adults, $14 kids 6 to 12
Florida Aquarium (see Chapter 14)	$16 adults, $8 kids 6 to 12
Kennedy Space Center (see Chapter 19)	$35 adults, $25 kids 3 to 11
Key West Conch Tour Train (see Chapter 11)	$20 adults, $10 kids 4 to 12
Parrot Jungle Island (see Chapter 10)	$24 adults, $20 kids 3 to 10
Salvador Dalí Museum (see Chapter 15)	$13 adults, $6 kids 10 and over

Shopping

You won't find many bargains here. You also won't find much that's patently Florida, except citrus, overpriced seashells, stuffed Mickeys, and T-shirts from tourist-courting bars. Our best advice: Avoid the shops in the vacation zones. If you must buy, scout local newspapers for ads aimed at the townies and shop where they do. Also, be wary of the so-called factory outlets that promise deep discounts. Most of them don't deliver. (Know suggested retail prices before you walk in the door.) Being an international city, Miami features the most diverse shopping in the state.

Florida has many of the same retailers found in other U.S. states: **Macy's, Bloomingdale's, Nordstrom, Neiman Marcus, Sears, Saks, Burdines,** and **Dillard's.** Their sales will probably appeal to travelers coming from another country, but Americans can find the same prices at home. Ditto for the discount chains, such as **Kmart, Target, Wal-Mart,** computer sellers, such as **CompUSA,** and electronics marts, including **Circuit City** and **Radio Shack.**

Nightlife

Here's a good guideline when it comes to Florida nightlife: If a destination has a beach, it has a bar that hops from midmorning into the wee hours. Miami, specifically **South Beach,** arguably has the hottest nightclub scene, thanks to its Latin culture, 5 a.m. liquor licenses, and an infusion of celebrities who don't come out before midnight. Disney's **Pleasure Island** and Universal's **CityWalk** have given Orlando reason to shine after dark. (Table 3-2 lists examples of expenses you're likely to encounter during an Orlando stay.) To a smaller degree, that's also the case in **Ybor City** near Tampa, where the music also has Latin spice.

Most bars are free. Cover charges in clubs generally run from nothing to $20, depending on the city; Miami and Orlando clubs usually have the highest covers in the state. The most expensive clubs are located in the hot spots mentioned, where drinks tend to be pricey ($7 and up), so try to hit during happy-hour bargains. Clubbing — assuming that you can find a club in some of the quieter spots — usually costs much less in the smaller cities. (Table 3-3 lists sample expenses you may encounter in Miami.)

Table 3-2	What Things Cost in Orlando	
Item	U.S. $	U.K. £ (At press time, $1.93=£1)
One-way taxi ride from airport to Walt Disney World	50	26
Roundtrip shuttle from airport to Walt Disney World (adult fare)	30	16
Double room at Disney's Grand Floridian Resort & Spa	329–2,195	170–1,136
Double room at Portofino Bay Hotel	259–2,200	134–1,139
Double room at Disney's Coronado Springs Resort	133–219	69–1130
Double room at Disney's All-Star Movies Resort	77–124	40–64
All-you-can-eat buffet dinner at Akershus in Epcot, not including tip or wine	19.50	10
Dinner entrees at Pebbles	10–21	5.20–11
Bottle of beer (restaurant)	2.50	1.30
Coca-Cola (restaurant)	1.25	0.65
Roll of Kodak film, 36 exposures, purchased at Walt Disney World	9.45	4.90
Adult 1-day, 1-park admission to Walt Disney World	55	28
Child 1-day, 1-park admission to Walt Disney World	44	23
Adult 1-day, 1-park admission to Universal or SeaWorld	55	28
Child 1-day, 1-park admission to Universal or SeaWorld	45	23

Table 3-3	What Things Cost in Miami	
Item	*U.S. $*	*U.K. £ (At press time, $1.93=£1)*
One-way shuttle Miami International Airport to South Beach (per person)	15	7.75
Double room at the Delano	345–675	179–349
Double room at the Abbey Hotel	99–255	51–116
Dinner entrees at Van Dyke Café	9–17	4.65–8.80
Dinner entrees at Chef Allen's	25–40	13–21
Coca-Cola (inside attraction)	1.75	1.19
Roll of Kodak film, 36 exposures, at Walgreens	6.99	3.60
Adult admission to Miami MetroZoo	12	6.20
Child admission to Miami MetroZoo	7	3.60
Adult admission to Miami Seaquarium	25	13
Child admission to Miami Seaquarium	20	10

Keeping a Lid on Hidden Expenses

Be on the lookout for these not-so-nice surprises:

✔ **Sales tax:** Florida adds a 6 percent sales tax to most items, except groceries and medical services. Additionally, some communities have a local-option sales tax and a bed tax on hotel rooms that can push the total tax to 12 percent or more on a room. So ask when booking.

✔ **Rental-car charges:** Sales tax, surcharges, and various other required add-ons could add 20 percent to 25 percent to the rates that rental-car companies quote you. Ask about add-ons when you book.

✔ **Phoning home:** If ever there were a travel commandment that should not be broken, this is it: Thou shalt not make a telephone call from thy hotel room without first asking how much it will cost. Although some hotels don't charge for local calls, most do. And the charge for a long-distance call can be marked up by as much as 200 percent. Some hotels charge you even if you use your calling card or dial a toll-free number. Save yourself a coronary and ask before you dial, or better yet, use pay phones — almost all hotels have them in their lobbies.

✔ **Minibar charges:** Sure those peanuts are convenient, but are they worth the price of your kids' college tuition? Even looking isn't free; many of the minibars at better hotels have a built-in sensor system that charges you 15 seconds after you lift an item.

✔ **Tipping:** Don't forget to budget for tips! Gratuities generally run 15 percent for restaurant service and cab rides. (In the case of restaurants, double-check the bill before you tip. Some restaurants automatically add a gratuity to the check.) Housekeepers at your hotel may be worth $1 to $2 a day *if* you feel they should be rewarded for cleaning your messy mess or honoring your "do not disturb" until late in the day. Baggage handlers usually get $1 per bag.

✔ **Park food:** As I mentioned earlier, if you spend time at the major theme parks and some smaller attractions, such as the Kennedy Space Center or Parrot Jungle, you may be stuck paying high prices for low- to middling-quality food.

Cutting Costs — but Not the Fun

Considering the warnings I've already dished out, by now you must be wondering whether you can afford this place. Of course you can. It's simply a matter of choosing a vacation that fits your budget. Florida isn't as pricey as some folks think. Sure, the prices at five-star crash pads will steal your breath, but the millions of tourists who arrive every year have created considerable competition, and that can result in bargains.

After you've settled on your accommodations and airfare, you can keep the other expenses in check by regulating what attractions you see, where you eat, and how much time you spend doing the free stuff or things that are included in your room rate. (A day at the motel pool is cheaper than taking a family of four deep-sea fishing in Destin or visiting one of the costly theme parks.) You can find plenty of ways to cut costs, including the following:

✔ **Go in the off season.** During nonpeak times — October and November, April and May, and the two weeks before Christmas — you'll find that the airlines and hotels slash their prices by as much as 40 percent. These are the best times of year to travel, if you're trying to save money (and avoid crowds).

✔ **Buy a package tour.** For many destinations, one call to a travel agent or packager can net you airfare, hotel reservations, a car, and some attractions tickets, all for much less than if you tried to put the trip together yourself. Even if you don't want to go with a complete package — say, if you want to buy your airfare with frequent-flier miles or you just don't like what a full package offers — you can book room/car deals or other special packages directly through some hotels. (See Chapter 4 for more information in package tours.)

✔ **Always ask about discounts.** Membership in AAA, frequent-flier plans, trade unions, AARP, the military, your company, or other groups may qualify you for discounted rates on plane tickets, hotel rooms, car rentals, and even meals. Many attractions also offer discounts to members of certain organizations. Ask about everything — you could end up pleasantly surprised.

✔ **Reserve a room with a refrigerator and coffeemaker.** You don't have to slave over a hot stove to cut a few costs; several motels have minifridges and coffeemakers. Buying supplies for breakfast will save you money — and probably calories. Also remember that room service is among the costliest ways to eat, and the food quality often rivals cardboard.

✔ **Skip the room with a view.** Rooms with great views are the most expensive accommodations in any hotel. Because you probably won't be hanging out in your room all day anyway, why pay the price? (See Chapter 6 for more about room rates and views.)

✔ **Ask if your kids can stay in your room with you.** A room with two double beds usually doesn't cost any more than one with a queen-size bed, and many hotels won't charge the additional-person rate for children. Even if you have to pay $10 or $15 for a rollaway bed, you'll save a ton by not taking two rooms.

✔ **Don't rent a gas guzzler.** Renting a smaller car is cheaper, and you save on gas to boot. Unless you're traveling with kids and need lots of space, don't go beyond the economy size. For more on car rentals, see Chapter 5.

✔ **Pick up those free, coupon-packed visitor magazines.** Detailed maps, feature stories, dining and shopping directories, and discount coupons give these pocket-size giveaways a good wallop. Look for them in your hometown Sunday newspaper or, after you land, in the lobbies of hotels or restaurants.

✔ **Skip souvenirs.** Make your photographs and memories the best mementos of your trip. If you're worried about money, do without the T-shirts, seashells, key chains, salt-and-pepper shakers, mouse ears, and other trinkets. Set a spending limit and stick to it!

Handling Money

You're the best judge of how much cash you feel comfortable carrying or what alternative form of currency is your favorite. That's not going to change much on your vacation. True, you'll probably be moving around more and incurring more expenses than you generally do (unless you happen to eat out every meal when you're at home), and you may let your mind slip into vacation gear and not be as vigilant about your safety as when you're in work mode. But, those factors aside, the only type of payment that won't be quite as available to you away from home is your personal checkbook.

Using ATMs and carrying cash

The easiest and best way to get cash away from home is from an ATM
(automated teller machine). Florida has an ample supply of 24-hour
ATMs. You can find the machines at most malls, banks, and convenience
stores, such as 7-Eleven and Circle K. Frequently, one or more ATMs are
located inside theme parks and larger tourist attractions as well as in
shopping or downtown districts.

Check the back of your ATM card to see which network your bank
belongs to and look for ATMs that display your network's sign. You're
probably connected to one of the two most popular networks: The
Cirrus (☎ 800-424-7787) and **PLUS** (☎ 800-843-7587). You can call
their toll-free numbers to obtain convenient locations in Florida.

Be sure you know your personal identification number (PIN) before you
leave home and be sure to find out your daily withdrawal limit before you
depart. Also keep in mind that many banks impose a fee every time your
card is used at a different bank's ATM. On top of this, the bank from which
you withdraw cash may charge its own fee. To compare banks' ATM fees
within the U.S., use www.bankrate.com. For international withdrawal
fees, ask your bank.

Charging ahead with credit cards

Credit cards are a safe way to carry money: They also provide a convenient record of all your expenses. Most major credit cards are accepted
throughout Florida, though some places only accept American Express,
MasterCard, and Visa. You can get cash advances from your credit cards
at any banks (although you start paying hefty interest on the advance
from the moment you receive the cash, and you don't receive frequent-
flier miles on an airline credit card). At most banks, you don't even need
to go to a teller; you can get a cash advance at the ATM if you know your
personal identification number (PIN). If you've forgotten your PIN or didn't
even know you had one, call the phone number on the back of your credit
card and ask the bank to send it to you. It usually takes between five and
seven business days, though some banks will give you the number over
the phone if you tell them your mother's maiden name or pass some
other security clearance.

Toting traveler's checks

These days, traveler's checks are less necessary because most cities
have 24-hour ATMs that allow you to withdraw small amounts of cash as
needed. However, keep in mind that you will likely be charged an ATM
withdrawal fee if the bank is not your own, so if you're withdrawing money
every day, you may be better off with traveler's checks — provided that
you don't mind showing identification every time you want to cash one.

You can get traveler's checks at almost any bank. **American Express**
offers denominations of $20, $50, $100, $500, and (for cardholders only)
$1,000. You'll pay a service charge ranging from 1 percent to 4 percent.

You can also get American Express traveler's checks over the phone by calling ☎ **800-221-7282**; Amex gold and platinum cardholders who use this number are exempt from the 1 percent fee.

Visa offers traveler's checks at Citibank locations nationwide as well as at several other banks. The service charge ranges between 1.5 percent and 2 percent; checks come in denominations of $20, $50, $100, $500, and $1,000. Call ☎ **800-732-1322** for information. AAA members can obtain Visa checks for a $9.95 service fee at most AAA offices or by calling ☎ **866-339-3378**. **MasterCard** also offers traveler's checks. Call ☎ **800-223-9920** for a location near you.

If you choose to carry traveler's checks, be sure to keep a record of their serial numbers separate from your checks in the event that they are stolen or lost. You get a refund faster if you know the numbers.

Dealing with a lost or stolen wallet

Be sure to contact all your credit card companies the minute you discover your wallet has been lost or stolen and file a report at the nearest police precinct. Your credit card company or insurer may require a police report number or record of the loss. Most credit card companies have an emergency toll-free number to call if your card is lost or stolen; they may be able to wire you a cash advance immediately or deliver an emergency credit card in a day or two. Call the following emergency numbers in the United States:

- ✔ **American Express** ☎ **800-221-7282** (for cardholders and traveler's check holders)

- ✔ **MasterCard** ☎ **800-307-7309** or 636-722-7111

- ✔ **Visa** ☎ **800-847-2911** or 410-581-9994

For other credit cards, call the toll-free number directory at ☎ **800-555-1212**.

If you need emergency cash over the weekend when all banks and American Express offices are closed, you can have money wired to you via **Western Union** (☎ **800-325-6000**; www.westernunion.com).

Identity theft and fraud are potential complications of losing your wallet, especially if you've lost your driver's license along with your cash and credit cards. Notify the major credit-reporting bureaus immediately; placing a fraud alert on your records may protect you against liability for criminal activity. The three major U.S. credit-reporting agencies are **Equifax** (☎ **800-766-0008**; www.equifax.com), **Experian** (☎ **888-397-3742**; www.experian.com), and **TransUnion** (☎ **800-680-7289**; www.transunion.com). Finally, if you've lost all forms of photo ID call your airline and explain the situation; airline personnel may allow you to board the plane if you have a copy of your passport or birth certificate and a copy of the police report you've filed.

Chapter 4

Getting to Florida

*G*etting there *isn't* half the fun for most travelers, especially those of us enduring longer airport lines, stewing over flight delays, or getting bumped involuntarily by airlines that overbook their flights. But the trip doesn't have to be an expensive hassle. In this chapter, I cut through the baloney and make sure you have an easier time than those who didn't map out their campaign in advance.

Flying to Florida

All the major U.S. domestic carriers, many of the international ones, and some charter services offer regular flights into Florida's top four destinations. (In order, they are Miami, Orlando, Tampa, and Fort Lauderdale–Hollywood International airports.) Combined, this four-pack handles up to 100 million passengers in a banner tourism year. (See the Appendix in the back of the book for a list of toll-free numbers and Web sites for the major airlines.) And if the mainstream airports don't serve your preferred drop zone, the state has 13 more international and regional airports with moderate to limited jet service, meaning you may have to deal with an extra connection, but you shouldn't have trouble landing near most any Florida destination.

Getting the best deal on your airfare

Competition among the major U.S. airlines is unlike that of any other industry. Every airline offers virtually the same product (basically, a coach seat is a coach seat is a . . .), yet prices can vary by hundreds of dollars.

Business travelers and others who need the flexibility to buy their tickets at the last minute and change their itineraries at a moment's notice — and who want to get home before the weekend — pay the premium rate, known as the *full fare*. But if you can book your ticket far in advance, stay over Saturday night, and are willing to travel midweek (Tues, Wed, or Thurs), you can qualify for the least expensive price — usually a fraction of the full fare. On most flights, even the shortest hops within the United States, the full fare is close to $1,000 or more, but a 7- or 14-day advance purchase ticket may cost less than half of that amount. Obviously, planning ahead pays.

The airlines also periodically hold sales, in which they lower the prices on their most popular routes. These fares have advance purchase requirements and date-of-travel restrictions, but you can't beat the prices. As you plan your vacation, keep your eyes open for these sales, which tend to take place in seasons of low travel volume — November, December, and January (excluding holidays). You almost never see a sale around the peak summer vacation months of July and August, or around Thanksgiving or Christmas, when many people fly, regardless of the fare they have to pay.

Consolidators, also known as bucket shops, are great sources for international tickets, although they usually can't beat the Internet on fares within North America. Start by looking in Sunday newspaper travel sections; U.S. travelers should focus on the *New York Times, Los Angeles Times,* and *Miami Herald.*

Bucket shop tickets are usually nonrefundable or rigged with stiff cancellation penalties, often as high as 50 percent to 75 percent of the ticket price, and some put you on charter airlines with questionable safety records.

Several reliable consolidators are worldwide and available on the Net. **STA Travel** (☎ 800-781-4040; www.statravel.com), the world's leader in student travel, offers good fares for travelers of all ages. **FlyCheap** (☎ 800-FLY-CHEAP; www.1800flycheap.com) is owned by package-holiday megalith MyTravel and so has especially good access to fares for sunny destinations. **Air Tickets Direct** (☎ 800-778-3447; www.air ticketsdirect.com) is based in Montreal and leverages the currently weak Canadian dollar for low fares; it'll also book trips to places that U.S. travel agents won't touch, such as Cuba.

Here are some tips for discovering the best values on airfare to Florida:

> ✔ **Ask the airlines for their lowest fares.** Be certain about your travel dates before you call because many of the best deals are nonrefundable. Also, call more than once — often, you'll get different rates on different days, as cheap seats get sold out, or added, as airlines try to fill up the planes. The best time to call: just after midnight, when airlines tend to release additional cheap seats into their "inventory." If you do get a rate that's lower than previous quotes, get a confirmation number (the airlines will usually hold a reservation for 24 hours before making you book a ticket). After shopping around, go with the best rate, and cancel the others.

Check fares both by phone and on the Internet. Airlines often offer cheaper fares on their Web sites than through their telephone reservation lines.

✔ **Be flexible.** The more flexible you are about your travel schedule and length of stay, the more money you're likely to save. Flying during off times (at night, for instance) saves you money.

✔ **Consider using a travel agent to find out about all your available options.** Sometimes a good agent knows about fares that you won't find on your own. Also, Internet providers offer travel sections that may include pricing comparisons.

✔ **Travel on "no-frills" airlines.** Several so-called no-frills airlines — with low fares but no meals or other amenities — serve Florida. The biggest is **Southwest Airlines** (☎ 800-435-9792; www.southwest.com), which flies to Jacksonville, West Palm Beach, Fort Lauderdale, Orlando, and Tampa. **Spirit Air** (☎ 800-772-7117; www.spiritair.com) is another option. **JetBlue Airways** (☎ 800-538-2583; www.jetblue.com) is a low-cost carrier that operates mostly on the eastern seaboard but also flies from the West Coast.

✔ Consider joining a travel club, such as **Moment's Notice** (☎ 718-234-6295) or **Sears Discount Travel Club** (☎ 800-433-9383 for information or 800-255-1487 to join). They supply unsold tickets to members at discounted prices. (You pay an annual fee to receive the club's hotline number.) Of course, your choices are limited to what's available, so you have to be flexible. Keep in mind, however, that you may not have to join these clubs to get such deals because many airlines now unload unsold seats directly through their Web sites.

Booking your flight online

The "big three" online travel agencies, **Expedia** (www.expedia.com), **Travelocity** (www.travelocity.com), and **Orbitz** (www.orbitz.com) sell most of the air tickets bought on the Internet. (Canadian travelers should try www.expedia.ca and www.travelocity.ca; U.K. residents can go for expedia.co.uk and opodo.co.uk.) Each has different business deals with the airlines and may offer different fares on the same flights, so shopping around is wise. Expedia and Travelocity will also send you an **e-mail notification** when a cheap fare becomes available to your favorite destination. Of the smaller travel agency Web sites, **SideStep** (www.sidestep.com) receives good reviews from users. It's a browser add-on that purports to "search 140 sites at once," but in reality only beats competitors' fares as often as other sites do.

If you're willing to give up some control over your flight details, use an *opaque fare service* like **Priceline** (www.priceline.com) or **Hotwire** (www.hotwire.com). Both offer rock-bottom prices in exchange for travel on a "mystery airline" at a mysterious time of day, often with a mysterious change of planes en route. The mystery airlines are all major, well-known carriers — and the possibility of being sent from Chicago to Tampa via Los Angeles is remote. But your chances of getting a 6 a.m. or 11 p.m. flight are pretty high. Hotwire tells you flight prices before you buy; Priceline usually has better deals than Hotwire, but you have to play their "name our price" game. *Note:* In 2004 Priceline added nonopaque service to its roster. You now have the option to pick exact flights, times, and airlines from a list of offers — or opt to bid on opaque fares as before.

Great last-minute deals are also available directly from the airlines themselves through a free e-mail service called *E-savers*. Each week, the airline sends you a list of discounted flights, usually leaving the upcoming Friday or Saturday and returning the following Monday or Tuesday. You can sign up for all the major airlines at one time by logging on to **Smarter Living** (www.smarterliving.com), or you can go to each individual airline's Web site. Airline sites also offer schedules, flight booking, and information on late-breaking bargains.

Driving to Florida

Can't stand to fly? Can't afford the extra expense? You're not alone. Each year, many people get behind the wheel and drive themselves to their sunny Florida destination.

Driving to Florida is a less expensive and potentially more scenic option than flying, but the distance may be so great that it eats up too much of your vacation. Here's how far several cities are from Orlando. (If you're going to Miami, add about 200 miles to each figure; if you're only going to northern Florida, subtract about 200.)

- ✔ **Atlanta:** 436 miles
- ✔ **Boston:** 1,312 miles
- ✔ **Chicago:** 1,120 miles
- ✔ **Cleveland:** 1,009 miles
- ✔ **Dallas:** 1,170 miles
- ✔ **Detroit:** 1,114 miles
- ✔ **New York:** 1,088 miles
- ✔ **Toronto:** 1,282 miles

Need directions? No problem. Use the following routes and after you're in Florida, pick up the highway that leads to your destination:

- ✔ **From Atlanta,** take I-75 South.
- ✔ **From Boston and New York,** take I-95 South.

- ✔ **From Chicago,** take I-65 South to Nashville and then I-24 South to I-75 South.

- ✔ **From Cleveland,** take I-77 South to Columbia, South Carolina, and then I-26 East to I-95 South.

- ✔ **From Dallas,** take I-20 East to I-49 South, to I-10 East, to I-75 South.

- ✔ **From Detroit,** take I-75 South.

- ✔ **From Toronto,** take Canadian Route 401 South to Queen Elizabeth Way South, to I-90 (New York State Thruway) East, to I-87 (New York State Thruway) South, to I-95 over the George Washington Bridge, and continue south on I-95.

AAA (☎ **800-222-4357;** www.aaa.com) and some other automobile clubs offer free maps and driving directions to their members.

Getting to Florida by Rail

Don't want to fly but can't stand the thought of driving all the way to Florida? Hop a train! **Amtrak** trains (☎ **800-872-7245;** www.amtrak.com) pull into several stations across Florida.

Amtrak's **Auto Train** allows you to bring your car to Florida without having to drive it all the way. The service begins in Lorton, Virginia — about a four-hour drive from New York; two hours from Philadelphia — and ends at Sanford, Florida, about 23 miles northeast of Orlando. The Auto Train departs Lorton and Sanford daily at 4:00 p.m., arriving at the other end of the line the next day at about 8:30 a.m. Fares for the Auto Train vary according to season and schedule, but fares for two passengers and a car begin at $368.

As with airline fares, you can sometimes receive discounts if you book train rides far in advance. However, discounts usually aren't offered around the very busy holiday periods. Amtrak features money-saving packages, which include accommodations, car rentals, tours, and so on. For package information, call ☎ **800-321-8684.**

Choosing a Package Tour

For popular destinations, such as Florida, packages can be a smart way to go because they often offer discounts that you could never get if you booked all the elements of your vacation separately. Package prices are low because they're sold in bulk to tour operators, who resell them to the public. It's kind of like buying your vacation at Sam's Club or one of those other membership discount clubs. Except here, the tour operator buys the 1,000-count box of garbage bags and resells them ten at a time, at a cost that undercuts what you'd pay at your neighborhood supermarket.

Package tours can vary as much as those garbage bags, too. Some offer a better class of hotels than others; others provide the same hotels for lower prices. Some book flights on scheduled airlines; others sell charters. In some packages, your choice of accommodations and travel days may be limited. Some let you choose between escorted vacations and independent vacations; others allow you to add on just a few excursions or escorted day-trips (also at discounted prices) without booking an entirely escorted tour.

To find package tours, check out the travel section of your local Sunday newspaper or the ads in the back of national travel magazines such as *Travel & Leisure, National Geographic Traveler,* and *Condé Nast Traveler.* **Liberty Travel** (call ☎ **888-271-1584** to find the store nearest you; www.libertytravel.com) is one of the biggest packagers in the Northeast and usually boasts a full-page ad in Sunday papers.

Some of the most popular Florida packages revolve around Orlando and its theme parks. The major parks themselves offer numerous packages:

✔ **Walt Disney World** (see Chapters 17–19) offers a dizzying array of packages, some of which include airfare, a room in a Disney or related property, theme-park passes, a rental car, meals, a Disney cruise, and/or a stay at Disney's beach resorts in Vero Beach, Florida, or Hilton Head, South Carolina. You can get more information about Disney packages by calling ☎ **800-828-0228** or 407-828-8101, heading online to www.disneyworld.com, or writing to Walt Disney World, Box 10000, Lake Buena Vista, FL 32830-1000. Ask for a *Walt Disney World Vacations* brochure or video.

✔ **Universal Orlando** packages, although not on the same scale as Disney, have improved greatly, with the addition of the Islands of Adventure theme park (see Chapter 18); the CityWalk food-and-club district (Chapter 19); and the Portofino Bay, Hard Rock, and Royal Pacific resorts (Chapter 17). The menu includes rooms, VIP access to the parks, and discounts to other non-Disney attractions. Universal also offers packages that include travel, transportation, and cruises. Contact Universal Studios Vacations at ☎ **888-322-5537** or 407-224-7000, or go online to www.universalorlando.com.

✔ **SeaWorld** offers two- and three-night packages that include rooms at a few Orlando hotels including the Renaissance Orlando Resort at SeaWorld (see Chapter 17), car rental, tickets to SeaWorld (see Chapter 18), and in some cases, other theme parks. Get information at ☎ **800-423-8368,** or online at www.seaworld.com.

The competition is stiff not only in Orlando but also in other major Florida tourist destinations, including Miami, Fort Lauderdale, Daytona Beach, and Tampa/St. Petersburg. Check the packagers I list in this section to see what options they offer in your chosen destination.

Airline packages

Another good source of package deals is the airlines themselves. **Delta Vacations** (☎ 800-872-7786; www.deltavacations.com), the big fish in the pond, offers selections that can include round-trip airfare, lodging (including tax and baggage tips), a rental car with unlimited mileage or round-trip transfers from the airport, admission to some theme parks, accommodations, and so on. Prices for Delta Vacations usually vary depending on the package, property, departure city, and season.

Continental Airlines Vacations, (☎ 800-301-3800; www.coolvacations.com), offers several packages that include airfare, car rental, and hotel stays at numerous central Florida hotels and **WDW** resorts. You can apply the airline's frequent-flier miles to some packages and you can make reservations with or without air service.

For other airline-package possibilities, see the phone numbers and Web sites for various airlines listed in the Appendix in the back of this book.

Other package resources

Besides airline and theme-park packages, you can also find packages elsewhere. One option is **American Express Travel** (☎ 800-732-1991; http://travel.americanexpress.com/travel/travel). It lets American Express card holders book reservations around the state while throwing in perks like discounts on merchandise, dinner shows, and sometimes tours.

Other package specialists include the following:

- ✔ **Touraine Travel** (☎ 800-967-5583; www.tourainetravel.com) offers a wide variety of tour packages to **Disney** and Disney properties, **Universal Orlando, SeaWorld,** and other parts of Florida.

- ✔ If you're a linkster, you have several packagers from which to choose. **Golf Getaways** (☎ 800-800-4028; www.golfgetaways.com) and **Golfpac Vacations** (☎ 800-327-0878; www.golfpacinc.com) offer a slate of play-and-stay packages — from basic to extraordinarily comprehensive ones.

Chapter 5

Getting around Florida

- -

In This Chapter

▶ Traveling around Florida by car
▶ Booking commuter flights
▶ Chugging along on the choo-choo
▶ Riding the magic bus

- -

*F*lorida feeds on tourists — conservatively, about 50 million a year. So, the tourism czars make sure that you and your fellow 49,999,999 travelers can go from Point A to Point B as quickly as possible.

You may end up flying to Florida and rarely venturing more than 25 miles from the airport. Or you may do a little in-state traveling. In this chapter, I provide information on the four most popular ways to get around Florida, in case you want to hit the road while you're here.

By Car

You won't need a car if you stick to single-destination vacations, including Disney/Orlando, Fort Lauderdale, Miami Beach, Key West, Daytona Beach, and St. Petersburg/Clearwater. However, bringing or renting a set of wheels is the best and easiest way to see the sights, especially if you plan to visit more than one city.

 The fact that traveling around Florida is easy and convenient, doesn't mean that it's quick. The large distances between cities — 542 miles from Key West to Jacksonville, for example — can make for a lengthy drive, and the traffic on the state's major highways will only make the trip longer. See the "Florida Driving Times and Distances" map in this chapter to get an idea of how much time you'll spend on the road.

Minding the road rules

Here are a few tidbits about driving in Florida:

Florida Driving Times and Distances

Boldface numbers *indicate distances in miles*
Lightface numbers *indicate driving times*

✔ **Rush hour:** In Florida, rush hour generally runs from 7 to 9 a.m.
and 4 to 6 p.m. on weekdays. Traffic during these times can be
brutal in cities such as Miami, Orlando, and Tampa, more so if
you use the interstates and other major highways. (Orlando has
rush hour on the weekends, too, thanks to the theme parks.)
Most toll roads, however, tend to be less congested, so it does
pay to pay up.

✔ **The more the merrier:** Several counties (most notably Miami-Dade)
operate special High Occupancy Vehicle (HOV) lanes on major
roads and highways. In order to use these lanes (usually faster than
the regular traffic lanes), you need to have a minimum number of
passengers in the car (usually three or higher). Don't get in an HOV
lane if your car isn't carrying the requisite number of passengers —
you could be fined several hundred dollars.

✔ **Red means go:** Florida law allows drivers to make a right turn on red, after coming to a full stop and making sure the coast is clear (unless signs say otherwise).

✔ **Speed demons beware:** Posted speed limits are enforced pretty vigorously. The speed limits on Florida's interstates and major highways usually are 55 to 70 mph. The limit is 55 mph on many other roads, but it dips as low as 10 to 20 mph in school zones. Fines for speeding begin at more than $150. In particular, mind the reduced speed limits in school zones, where fines are doubled.

✔ **Buckle up:** Driving without using a seat belt is illegal, and the local police actively ticket violators.

✔ **Safety issues:** Ask someone at your hotel's front desk, your rental-car agency, the local chamber of commerce, or the police department about which routes in the area are safe for travel and which should be avoided. Be particularly wary of high-crime areas and ultrarural roads. Also, be extra careful at night, especially regarding where you park. Try to stay in well-lit, public areas.

✔ **Permits:** A handicap permit is required for parking in places designated for the disabled. Handicap permits from other states are honored, but a disabled license plate alone won't do the job.

✔ **Emergencies:** You can reach the Florida Highway Patrol on a cellphone by dialing *FHP. From a regular phone, dial 911.

Renting some wheels

Car-rental rates depend on the size of the car, the length of time you keep it, where and when you pick it up and drop it off, special discounts, and other factors. Asking the following questions can help save hundreds of dollars when renting a car:

✔ **Is the weekend rate lower than the weekday rate?** Ask if the rate for Friday-morning pickup is the same as on Thursday night. If you're keeping the car five or more days, a weekly rate should be cheaper than the daily rate.

✔ **Will I be charged a drop-off fee if I return the car to a location that's different from where I rented it?** Some companies assess a drop-off charge, while others, notably National, do not. Ask if the rate is cheaper if you pick up the car at the airport or in town.

✔ **May I have the price I saw advertised in the newspaper?** Be sure to ask for that rate; otherwise, you may be charged the standard (higher) rate. Don't forget to mention membership in AAA, AARP, frequent-flier programs, and trade unions, which usually entitle you to discounts ranging from 5 to 30 percent. Ask your travel agent to check these special rates. Also remember that most car rentals add at least 500 miles on your frequent-flier account.

If you want information about the major rental-car companies serving Florida, see the Appendix in the back of this guide.

Ringing up the cost of renting a car

On top of the standard rental prices, other optional charges apply to most car rentals. The *Collision Damage Waiver (CDW),* which covers what you would be required to pay for damage to the car in a collision, is charged on rentals in most states. However, many credit card companies cover this expense. Check with your credit card company before you go so that you can avoid paying this hefty fee (as much as $15 a day).

Rental companies also offer additional liability insurance (if you harm others in an accident), personal-accident insurance (if you harm yourself or your passengers), and personal-effects insurance (if your luggage is stolen from your car). If you have insurance on your car at home, you're probably covered for most of these unexpected events. If your own insurance doesn't cover you for rentals, or if you don't have auto insurance, consider buying additional coverage (rental companies are liable for certain base amounts). But weigh the likelihood of getting into an accident or losing your luggage against the cost of this extra coverage, which can run as much as $20 a day.

Some companies also offer refueling packages — you pay for an entire tank of gas upfront. The price is usually fairly competitive with local gas prices, but you don't get credit for any gas remaining in the tank when you return the car. If you reject this option, you pay only for the gas you use, but you have to return the rental with a full tank or face charges of $3 to $4 a gallon for any shortfall. If a stop at a gas station on the way to the airport will make you miss your plane, by all means take advantage of the fuel-purchase option. Otherwise, skip it.

Also expect some hefty taxes — as much as 20 percent — to your base rental rate. If you rent your car in an airport, you may be charged an additional fee on top of the taxes. To estimate the true rental price, ask for a rundown of all the applicable taxes and fees assessed on your car.

Most rental companies have a minimum age requirement for renters, usually 25, and some have a maximum age limit. When they do rent to the under-25 crowd, rental companies charge an extra $10 to $20 *per day* in young-renter fees. Most companies will also refuse to rent you a car if you have a poor driving record or you don't have a credit card.

Booking a rental on the Internet

Using the Internet can make comparison shopping and reserving a rental car much easier. All the major booking Web sites — including **Travelocity** (www.travelocity.com), **Expedia** (www.expedia.com), and **Yahoo! Travel** (www.travel.yahoo.com) — offer search engines that find discounted rental rates. Enter the size of the car you want, pickup and return dates, and the city where you'll rent it, and the server returns a price. You can also make reservations through these sites.

By Plane

The commuter branches of several major airlines provide extensive service to many Florida cities. Fares for short hops are usually reasonable. The three most popular airlines for intrastate travel are:

- ✔ **Continental:** ☎ **800-525-0280;** www.continental.com

- ✔ **Delta:** ☎ **800-221-1212;** www.delta.com

- ✔ **US Airways:** ☎ **800-428-4322;** www.usair.com

Cape Air (☎ **800-352-0714;** www.flycapeair.com), a small commuter airline, flies from Key West to Fort Myers, Naples, and Fort Lauderdale, which means you can avoid backtracking to Miami from Key West if you're touring.

All major carriers offer service to Florida's busiest airports: Miami International (☎ **305-876-7000;** www.miami-airport.com) and Orlando International (☎ **407-825-2001;** www.orlandoairports.net). Tampa International (☎ **813-870-8700;** www.tampaairport.com) and Fort Lauderdale-Hollywood International (☎ **954-359-6100;** www.broward.org/fll.htm) are nearly as popular.

Most big-name domestic airlines serve the following international airports. If you fly into these airports from outside Florida, you may have to make an extra connection, and fares are often higher than flying into a bigger airport such as Miami or Orlando. This group includes:

- ✔ Palm Beach (☎ **561-471-7412;** www.pbia.org)

- ✔ Southwest Florida, Fort Myers (☎ **941-768-4700;** www.swfia.com)

- ✔ Jacksonville (☎ **904-741-2000;** www.jaxairports.org)

- ✔ Sarasota Bradenton (☎ **941-359-2770;** www.srq-airport.com)

Many large domestic carriers, their express services, and commuter airlines serve this next tier in the airport food chain:

- ✔ Pensacola Regional (☎ **850-436-5000;** www.flypensacola.com)

- ✔ Orlando Sanford International (☎ **407-585-4000;** www.orlandosanfordairport.com)

- ✔ St. Petersburg–Clearwater International (☎ **727-535-7600;** www.stpete-clwairport.com)

- ✔ Daytona Beach International (☎ **386-248-8030;** www.flydaytonafirst.com)

- ✔ Melbourne International (☎ **321-723-6227;** www.mlbair.com)

✔ Key West International (☎ **305-296-5439;** www.keywest
internationalairport.com)

✔ Panama City–Bay County International (☎ **850-763-6751;** www.
pcairport.com)

 In most cases, you'll choose the airport closest to your vacation base.
For example, if your destination is the Pinellas County Gulf beaches
(see Chapter 15), you can save yourself a one-hour drive from the
major airport in the area, Tampa International, if you instead fly into
St. Petersburg–Clearwater International. Likewise, if Key West is your
goal, you'll save at least three hours in driving time by landing there
instead of Miami International. However, far fewer carriers serve the
smaller airports, and airfares often are more expensive.

See the Appendix in the back of this book for the toll-free phone numbers
and Web sites of the most popular airlines that serve Florida.

By Train

Train travel from one Florida destination to another isn't very feasible
due to sporadic scheduling and frequent stops and starts. Getting from
Daytona Beach to Fort Lauderdale, for example, takes 8½ hours by train,
but by car the same trip takes less than 4 hours. However, if trains are
in your travel plans, **Amtrak** (☎ **800-872-7245;** www.amtrak.com) runs
trains to 50 cities in Florida, including Daytona, Fort Lauderdale, Key West,
Miami, Orlando, Tampa, and St. Petersburg.

By Bus

 I list public transportation services in the destination chapters.
Greyhound (☎ **800-231-2222;** www.greyhound.com) is an option for
intercity travel, but it has the same problems — slow and sporadic
service — as train travel. It also doesn't give you the flexibility that a
rental car does.

Chapter 6

Booking Your Accommodations

In This Chapter

▶ Considering your options

▶ Getting the best for less

*H*otel, motel, Holiday Inn! Florida is a haven of hotels ranging from kitschy mom-and-pop spots, reliable chains, swanky destination resorts, theme stays, B&Bs, and boutique hotels. It all depends on what you're in the mood for and how much you are willing to spend.

In this chapter, I focus on the essentials about accommodations, including what you get for your money (and how to get more). I also offer some tips throughout for finding particularly personable digs.

Getting to Know Your Options

Although Florida sports a wide variety of accommodations, for the most part, this guide concentrates on Florida's four main lodging types. I use a handy little dollar sign code for the amount of dough you have to hand over when you decide to stay in these places. The explanation for the code is in the "Key to Hotel Dollar Signs" table, later in this chapter.

✔ **Resorts** usually offer just about everything you can get with a room. Features vary from property to property, but amenities are often in the $$$$ category. The resorts are usually right on the beach, in the best neighborhoods, or in the heart of the action. If you're so inclined, resorts can be one-stop destinations that offer package deals and good rates during the off-season. But keep in mind that you won't feel like part of the family, and they usually cost top dollar.

✔ **Hotels** sometimes have accommodations similar to resorts, but they're generally smaller and offer fewer activities and facilities. Hotels usually offer daily housekeeping service, one or more swimming pools, one or more lounges and restaurants, room service, and an activities desk. Hotels can be more intimate than a resort and offer slightly cheaper rates, but they have fewer amenities and services. The locations may not be as good, and hotels can have thin walls.

✔ **Motels,** whether chains or mom-and-pop operations, generally have basic rooms and amenities, the kind found in the $ and, in a few cases, $$ categories. The rooms tend to be smaller, a good restaurant (or perhaps any restaurant) likely won't be on the premises, and their locations are often farther from the action. But the price is right, and most of us don't go on vacation to spend much time in the room.

✔ **Bed-and-breakfasts** are plentiful in Florida and a good way to experience a home-style visit. The locations, usually situated outside of the tourist mainstream, may be a perk for you, particularly if you're the kind of traveler who likes the feeling of staying in someone's home. Bed-and-breakfasts vary widely in size and services. On one end of the scale, some have tight quarters and shared baths, while others have private sitting areas, lavish amenities, and private whirlpool tubs. At either end, don't expect a great deal of service beyond breakfast, bed and towel service, and, sometimes, evening dessert or a glass of wine. Bed-and-breakfasts are hardly ever on the beach, so if your heart's set on that ocean view, you should consider another style of accommodation.

The Florida Bed & Breakfast Inns Association, P.O. Box 6187, Palm Harbor, FL 34684 (☎ **800-524-1880;** www.florida-inns.com), publishes a nifty guide, *Inns of Florida,* which offers descriptions of a number of inns and bed-and-breakfasts in the state. The association inspects all the listed properties.

In addition to the four main lodging categories, I also touch on a few **condominiums** and **vacation rentals.** These accommodations are good if you have a large family, like the spaciousness of a house or an apartment, or plan to stay in an area for a few weeks or longer. But they tend to be pricey, and there usually isn't on-site management, so service is slow or nonexistent.

The hotels, motels, and resorts listed in the destination areas of this book (see Chapters 9 through 21) are grouped by price, from budget motels to very expensive rooms and apartments. The rates I quote in those chapters are per night, based on double occupancy. To give you a better idea of what you can expect to get for your money, here's a menu of the amenities that may be offered in each price category:

Table 6-1		Key to Hotel Dollar Signs
Dollar Sign(s)	*Price Range*	*What to Expect*
$	Less than $100	Accommodations at this level generally have pretty basic trimmings and limited space. They also tend to lean toward the no-frills side (although almost all come with swimming pools and air-conditioning). Accommodations at the higher end of this category may have hair dryers and coffeemakers, cable TV, and kids' play areas, and they sometimes offer free continental breakfasts. If they're multistory, they usually have an elevator.
$$	$100–$199	Within this category, you'll probably have a choice of king-size or double beds, a full range of amenities (coffeemakers, hair dryers, two TVs in two-room models, multiline phones, maybe modem lines, VCRs, free daily newspapers, and so on), designer shampoos, and room service. Rooms are slightly larger, and the pools may be joined by a whirlpool and fitness center. The continental breakfast probably has fresh fruit, granola, and muffins, rather than day-old doughnuts and those pint-size boxes of dry cereal. The hotel may even have a palatable on-site restaurant.
$$$	$200–$249	Hotels at this level tack on guest-services desks where you can arrange sightseeing trips, attractions tickets, and restaurant reservations. They probably have large, resort-style pools with multiple whirlpool tubs (some of the higher-end rooms have their own), fitness centers, and, occasionally, small spas. Rooms have multiple phones, beds, and TVs. They also often have minibars and separate tubs and showers.
$$$$	$250 and up	With these accommodations, nothing is outside the realm of possibility, including a world-class fitness center. In addition to the nicer amenities in the earlier price categories, many of the hotels here have concierge levels, loaded rooms, 24-hour room service, gorgeous pool bars, and live entertainment in their lounges. Some have full-service spas, gourmet restaurants, and tight security.

Getting the Best Room at the Best Rate

Some folks call a hotel, ask for a rate, and pay it — no questions asked. This practice is like going to a car lot and paying the sticker price. If this description hits a little too close to home, just read on. In this chapter, I show you how to find the best hotel rates and get the best room that your money can buy.

Finding the best rate

The **rack rate** is the maximum rate a hotel charges for a room. It's the rate you get if you walk in off the street and ask for a room for the night. You sometimes see these rates printed on the fire/emergency exit diagrams posted on the back of your door.

Hotels are happy to charge you the rack rate, but you can almost always do better. Perhaps the best way to avoid paying the rack rate is surprisingly simple: Just ask for a cheaper or discounted rate. You may be pleasantly surprised.

In all but the smallest accommodations, the rate you pay for a room depends on many factors — chief among them being how you make your reservation. A travel agent may be able to negotiate a better price with certain hotels than you can get by yourself. (That's because the hotel often gives the agent a discount in exchange for steering his or her business toward that hotel.)

Seasons also affect room rates, especially as occupancy rises and falls. Most Florida destinations are in peak season during summer and holidays (when kids are out of school and their families travel) and during winter (mainly between Jan and Mar when snowbirds come south). If a hotel is nearly full, it's less likely to offer you a discount. Likewise, if the hotel is nearly empty, an employee may negotiate a room rate with you, especially if the hotel is locally owned. Some resorts offer midweek specials, and downtown hotels often offer cheaper weekend rates.

Orlando, for the most part, doesn't have a normal pattern of high and low seasons. Blame two things for this: Disney's year-round tourist appeal, and a convention schedule that never takes much of a breather. Many Orlando hotels do, however, offer lower rates from early January through March (it's not a mecca for snowbirds), from just after Labor Day to just before Thanksgiving, and for the first two weeks of December. If you plan to hit a destination during its busy season, your best shot at getting a discount is to reserve early — months in advance, if possible.

 Please note that room prices are subject to change without notice, so even the rack rates quoted in this book may be different from the actual rate you receive when you make your reservation.

Finding the best hotel rate requires a bit of detective work. For example, reserving a room through the hotel's toll-free number may result in a lower rate than calling the hotel directly. On the other hand, the central reservations number may not know about discount rates at specific locations. For example, local franchises may offer a special group rate for a wedding or family reunion, but they may neglect to tell the central booking line. Your best bet is to call both the local number and the toll-free number and see which one gives you a better deal.

Ask about discounts if you're a student, senior, military or government employee, police officer, firefighter, or member of AAA or AARP. Also, if you own stock in a hotel company, you may be eligible for some kind of a price break or other perk. When you settle on your destination, make sure to contact the local visitor information center (see the Appendix in the back of this book) by phone or via the Web to see if it has any discounts available. Most have plenty of them.

When budgeting for your room, don't forget to allow for the combined sales and bed taxes that are charged in the state's various counties. In some parts of Florida, they add as much as 12 or 13 percent to your bill.

Getting the view — or not

Views are one of the most heavily advertised amenities offered by hotels located in Florida's coastal cities. Sure, it would be nice to see the sun appear or disappear over the ocean from your room, but is a room with a view worth the money? You may pay an extra $50, $100, or more per night for a view of sea oats, sand dunes, and frothy waves. If money's no object or if that restful view is the top priority of your vacation, then damn the torpedoes. Full speed ahead. But if you won't be hanging out in your room very much, you can find better ways to blow your inheritance.

Want to know exactly what you get when the hotel offers you a view? Here's the scorecard:

- ✔ **Oceanfront:** This usually means your room is smack-dab on the beach, which is synonymous with being 8 feet under water during a hurricane tide. It also means you're going to pay for that location. But it doesn't necessarily mean you actually get a view of the ocean, so ask. Some of Florida's less-than-reputable innkeepers advertise themselves as oceanfront because a room in a building faces the tides, even if your room doesn't. You also may not be able to walk straight out your door to the beach — many of these places are high-rises where it's highly recommended that you go down before you go out. Don't forget to ask about elevator service. Going downstairs is a piece of cake; going up is a gravity-defying experience. Be sure to find out exactly what you're getting.

- ✔ **Oceanview:** These rooms are usually guaranteed to be at the top of the price chart. Your shoulders will be squared to the beach, but you may not be oceanfront. You may actually be several hundred feet back, overlooking air-conditioning units on some shorter buildings. Again, remember to ask. Remember, too, when staying in a high-rise, that if surf sounds are what's important, make sure you're on one of the first few floors. You won't be able to hear the waves above the fourth or fifth floors. Their sounds usually yield to the roar of airline engines or the complaints of high-flying gulls.

✔ **Partial oceanview:** This is where semantics come into play. If you look east, at sunset on an odd-numbered Thursday . . . well, you get the idea. You may be able to see the surf from half the windows in your L-shaped condo, or maybe you can see it if you press your nose into the glass and stare cross-eyed to the left. It may be a great deal or a great rip-off. Our best advice: Take it if it's offered, but don't pay a penny extra.

✔ **Other views:** Depending on where you land in Florida, you may encounter a room with views of a marsh, garden, wildlife habitat, or any of Florida's other natural treasures, including waste-treatment plants. But don't buy in if the brochure promises a mountain view — there are none.

Surfing the Web for hotel deals

Shopping online for hotels is generally done one of two ways: by booking through the hotel's own Web site or through an independent booking agency (or a fare-service agency like Priceline). These Internet hotel agencies have multiplied in mind-boggling numbers of late, competing for the business of millions of consumers surfing for accommodations around the world. This competitiveness can be a boon to consumers who have the patience and time to shop and compare the online sites for good deals — but shop they must, because prices can vary considerably from site to site. And keep in mind that hotels at the top of a site's listing may be there for no other reason than that they paid money to get the placement.

Of the "big three" sites, **Expedia** offers a long list of special deals and "virtual tours" or photos of available rooms so you can see what you're paying for (a feature that helps counter the claims that the best rooms are often held back from bargain booking Web sites). **Travelocity** posts unvarnished customer reviews and ranks its properties according to the AAA rating system. Also reliable are **Hotels.com** and **Quikbook.com**. An excellent free program, **Travelaxe** (www.travelaxe.net), can help you search multiple hotel sites at once, even ones you may never have heard of — and conveniently lists the total price of the room, including the taxes and service charges. Another booking site, **Travelweb** (www.travelweb), is partly owned by the hotels it represents (including the Hilton, Hyatt, and Starwood chains) and is therefore plugged directly into the hotels' reservations systems — unlike independent online agencies, which have to fax or e-mail reservation requests to the hotel, a good portion of which get misplaced in the shuffle. More than once, travelers have arrived at the hotel, only to be told that they have no reservation. To be fair, many of the major sites are undergoing improvements in service and ease of use, and Expedia will soon be able to plug directly into the reservations systems of many hotel chains — none of which can be bad news for consumers. In the meantime, it's a good idea to **get a confirmation number** and **make a printout** of any online booking transaction.

In the opaque Web site category, **Priceline** and **Hotwire** are even better for hotels than for airfares; with both, you're allowed to pick the neighborhood and quality level of your hotel before offering up your money. Priceline's hotel product even covers Europe and Asia, though it's much better at getting five-star lodging for three-star prices than at finding anything at the bottom of the scale. On the downside, many hotels stick Priceline guests in their least desirable rooms. Be sure to go to the BiddingforTravel Web site (www.biddingfortravel.com) before bidding on a hotel room on Priceline; it features a fairly up-to-date list of hotels that Priceline uses in major cities. For both Priceline and Hotwire, you pay upfront, and the fee is nonrefundable. *Note:* Some hotels do not provide loyalty program credits or points or other frequent-stay amenities when you book a room through opaque online services.

Florida Hotel Network (www.floridahotels.com) offers a centralized reservations service for accommodations in a variety of price ranges for major cities in Florida. If you want to book rooms for large groups, you can do it here.

Most of the visitor information centers listed in the Appendix in the back of this book have links to some of the hotels in their areas. Also, many of the accommodations listings in Chapters 9 through 21 include Web addresses. And you can also link to specific hotels at **Visit Florida** (www.flausa.com) and **Absolutely Florida** (www.funandsun.com), although getting to your desired choice on these sites will probably require some patience.

Reserving the best room

After you make your reservation, asking one or two more pointed questions can go a long way toward making sure you get the best room in the house. Always ask for a corner room. They're usually larger, quieter, and have more windows and light than standard rooms, and they don't always cost more. Also ask if the hotel is renovating; if it is, request a room away from the renovation work. Inquire, too, about the location of the restaurants, bars, and discos in the hotel — all sources of annoying noise.

If you book your room through a travel agent, ask the agent to note your room preferences on your reservation. When you check in at your hotel, your preferences will pop up when the reception desk pulls your reservation. Special requests can't be guaranteed, but ask in advance anyway. If you aren't happy with your room when you arrive, talk to the front desk. If they have another room, they should be happy to accommodate you, within reason.

Chapter 7

Catering to Special Travel Needs or Interests

- -

In This Chapter

▶ Traveling with a family
▶ Visiting Florida, senior-style
▶ Realizing a world without barriers
▶ Gaining another barrier-free view

- -

*I*t's time to dispense a little advice for travelers with special needs. The last thing you want or need is a vacation that's too old, young, restrictive, or full of obstacles for you or your lifestyle. There are so many things to see and do in Florida that anybody should be able to find something suitable. Many cities also provide specialized services for those with special needs; so if you need help, just ask.

Traveling with the Brood: Advice for Families

 Most of Florida's major attractions were designed with kids in mind, nearly all restaurants have special menus for young diners, and many hotels let youngsters stay in their parents' room at no extra charge or for a small one. Many of Florida's beach resorts offer activities for kids, and in some cases, full daily programs to occupy their time. A number of hotels also offer baby-sitting services so moms and dads can have a night on their own. And Disney and Orlando cater to youngsters, day or night.

You can find good family-oriented vacation advice on the Internet from sites like the **Family Travel Forum** (www.familytravelforum.com), a comprehensive site that offers customized trip planning; **Family Travel Network** (www.familytravelnetwork.com), an award-winning site that offers travel features, deals, and tips; and **Family Travel Files** (www.thefamilytravelfiles.com), which offers an online magazine and a directory of off-the-beaten-path tours and tour operators for families.

Here are some general rules and reminders for your family to consider when planning a trip to Florida:

- **After you arrive, keep an eye out for discount coupons on meals and attractions.** Some are two-for-one specials, while others offer a percentage taken off the regular price. You can find these coupons in giveaway newspapers and magazines in the lobbies of hotels and restaurants. Also, check the Friday entertainment sections in many local newspapers.

- **Remember — kids under 12, and in many cases under 18, stay free in their parents' room in most hotels.** If you're not sure of a property's policy, ask when making a reservation. Look for places that have pools and other recreational facilities and then spend a no-extra-expense day or two away from costly tourist attractions.

- **Consider setting up rules on such things as bedtimes and souvenirs.** It can soften the disappointment after you arrive.

- **Talk with your kids about what to do if they become separated from you.** It's easy to get lost inside the larger tourist attractions and areas. In their guide maps, many attractions outline what to do if you and your child get separated. If your kids are 7 or under, attach a nametag to the inside of their shirt or jacket. (If young children are crying and scared, they may have trouble giving park staffers their name.) For older kids, choose a place to reunite if they get separated.

- **Keep in mind that your home may be toddler-proof, but hotel rooms aren't.** Bring blank plugs to cover outlets and whatever else is necessary to prevent an accident from happening in your room. Also, pack sunscreen and hats for the entire family, including infants and toddlers. If you forget to bring sunscreen, buy some at a convenience store or drugstore. Get a waterproof one that has an SPF rating of 25 or higher. Young children should be slathered with sunscreen, even if they're in a stroller. Adults and children should also drink plenty of water to avoid dehydration during Florida's hot months, especially May through September.

- **Bring some lightweight snacks and bottled water in an easy-to-carry backpack.** They may save you headaches and money (concessions at attractions sometimes charge double or more what the free world charges).

- **Don't try to do too much.** By overextending yourselves, all you'll gain are hot, tired, and cranky kids. Take frequent breaks when touring the major attractions and, if possible, go back to your hotel room and spend a little down time before hitting the sights again.

> ✔ **Plan playtime for parents.** It's your vacation, too! If your hotel offers
> a baby-sitting service, book a sitter for the night and go out for a
> romantic dinner or another adult-oriented activity.

Making Age Work for You: Tips for Seniors

With the possible exception of kid-crazy Orlando, Florida is as popular among seniors (especially during the fall and winter months) as it
is with the families that come during holidays and summers. Many
Florida hotels, restaurants, and attractions roll out the red carpet for
older travelers.

Members of **AARP** (formerly known as the American Association of
Retired Persons), 601 E St. NW, Washington, DC 20049 (☎ **888-687-2277**
or 202-434-2277; www.aarp.org), get discounts on hotels, airfares, and
car rentals. AARP offers members a wide range of benefits, including
AARP: The Magazine and a monthly newsletter. Anyone over 50 can join.

The **U.S. National Park Service** offers a **Golden Age Passport** that gives
seniors 62 years or older lifetime entrance to all properties administered
by the National Park Service — national parks, monuments, historic
sites, recreation areas, and national wildlife refuges — for a one-time
processing fee of $10, which must be paid in person at any NPS facility
that charges an entrance fee. Besides free entry, a Golden Age Passport
also offers a 50 percent discount on federal-use fees charged for such
facilities as camping, swimming, parking, boat launching, and tours.
For more information, go online to www.nps.gov/fees_passes.htm
or call ☎ **888-467-2757**.

Elderhostel (☎ **877-426-8056;** www.elderhostel.org) arranges study
programs for those aged 55 and over (and a spouse or companion of
any age) in the United States, including Florida, as well as in more than
80 countries around the world. Most courses last five to seven days in
the United States, and many include airfare, accommodations in university dormitories or modest inns, meals, and tuition.

Recommended publications offering travel resources and discounts
for seniors include: the quarterly magazine *Travel 50 & Beyond* (www.
travel50andbeyond.com); *Travel Unlimited: Uncommon Adventures
for the Mature Traveler* (Avalon); *101 Tips for Mature Travelers,*
available from Grand Circle Travel (☎ **800-221-2610** or 617-350-7500;
www.gct.com); *The 50+ Traveler's Guidebook* (St. Martin's Press);
and *Unbelievably Good Deals and Great Adventures That You
Absolutely Can't Get Unless You're Over 50* (McGraw-Hill), by Joann
Rattner Heilman.

Accessing Florida: Advice for Travelers with Disabilities

Most disabilities shouldn't stop anyone from visiting Florida's popular tourist areas. There are more options and resources out there than ever before, and the major destinations do a lot to lift barriers, including on many of their rides.

You can get a free copy of the *Planning Guide for Travelers with Disabilities* from Visit Florida, P.O. Box 1100, Tallahassee, FL 32302-1100 (☎ 888-735-2872; www.flausa.com). Additionally, all the major theme parks in Orlando offer guidebooks and other services that are specially geared to disabled guests. Ask for these publications at the parks' guest services desks when you arrive.

The U.S. National Park Service offers a **Golden Access Passport** that gives free lifetime entrance to all properties administered by the National Park Service — national parks, monuments, historic sites, recreation areas, and national wildlife refuges — for persons who are visually impaired or permanently disabled, regardless of age. You may pick up a Golden Access Passport at any NPS entrance fee area by showing proof of medically determined disability and eligibility for receiving benefits under federal law. Besides free entry, the Golden Access Passport also offers a 50 percent discount on federal-use fees charged for such facilities as camping, swimming, parking, boat launching, and tours. For more information, go online to www.nps.gov/fees_passes.htm or call ☎ 888-467-2757.

Many travel agencies offer customized tours and itineraries for travelers with disabilities. **Flying Wheels Travel** (☎ 507-451-5005; www.flyingwheelstravel.com) offers escorted tours and cruises that emphasize sports and private tours in minivans with lifts. **Access-Able Travel Source** (☎ 303-232-2979; www.access-able.com) offers extensive access information and advice for traveling around the world with disabilities. **Accessible Journeys** (☎ 800-846-4537 or 610-521-0339; wheelchair travelers and their families and friends.

Avis Rent a Car has an "Avis Access" program that offers such services as a dedicated 24-hour toll-free number (☎ 888-879-4273) for customer with special travel needs; special car features such as swivel seats, spinner knobs, and hand controls; and accessible bus service.

Organizations that offer assistance to disabled travelers include the **MossRehab** (www.mossresourcenet.org), which provides a library of accessible-travel resources online; **SATH (Society for Accessible Travel and Hospitality)** (☎ 212-447-7284; www.sath.org; annual membership fees: $45 adults, $30 seniors and students), which offers a wealth of travel resources for all types of disabilities and informed recommendations on destinations, access guides, travel agents, tour operators, vehicle rentals, and companion services; and the **American Foundation for the Blind (AFB)** (☎ 800-232-5463; www.afb.org), a referral resource for the blind or visually impaired that includes that includes information on traveling with Seeing Eye dogs.

For more information specifically targeted to travelers with disabilities, the community Web site **iCan** (www.icanonline.net/channels/travel/index.cfm) has destination guides and several regular columns on accessible travel. Also check out the quarterly magazine *Emerging Horizons* ($14.95 per year, $19.95 outside the U.S.; www.emerginghorizons.com); **Twin Peaks Press** (☎ 360-694-2462), offering travel-related books for travelers with special needs; and *Open World Magazine,* published by SATH (subscription: $13 per year, $21 outside the U.S.).

Following the Rainbow: Advice for Gay and Lesbian Travelers

Although Florida has a few pockets of intolerance, most of the larger destinations have active gay and lesbian communities. Many of those cities and several of the smaller coastal ones are especially receptive to gay and lesbian guests. Miami's South Beach and Key West are extraordinarily popular with gay and lesbian travelers, and Orlando's Gay Days Celebration in June (corresponding with Gay Disney, which takes place the first Saturday in June; see "Checking Out Florida's Calendar of Events" in Chapter 2) attracts thousands.

Speaking of Gay Days, you can get information about those events as well as events that occur throughout the year from Gay, Lesbian & Bisexual Community Center of Central Florida, 934 N. Mills Ave., Orlando, FL 32803 (☎ 407-228-8272; www.glbcc.org). Welcome packets usually include the latest issue of *Triangle,* dedicated to gay and lesbian issues, and a calendar of events pertaining to Florida's gay and lesbian community. The welcome packet includes information and ads for the area's clubs.

For state-specific information on the Web, try **The Gay Guide to Florida** at http://gay-guide.com, which this has a wealth of information, especially nightlife listings.

The International Gay and Lesbian Travel Association (IGLTA) (☎ 800-448-8550 or 954-776-2626; www.iglta.org) is the trade association for the gay and lesbian travel industry and offers an online directory of gay- and lesbian-friendly travel businesses; go to their Web site and click on "Members."

The following travel guides are available at most travel bookstores and gay and lesbian bookstores, or you can order them from **Giovanni's Room** bookstore, 1145 Pine St., Philadelphia, PA 19107 (☎ **215-923-2960;** www. giovannisroom.com): *Out and About* (☎ **800-929-2268** or 415-644-8044; www.outandabout.com), which offers guidebooks and a newsletter ($20/yr; 10 issues) packed with solid information on the global gay and lesbian scene; *Spartacus International Gay Guide* (Bruno Gmünder Verlag; www.spartacusworld.com/gayguide/) and *Odysseus,* both good, annual English-language guidebooks focused on gay men; the *Damron* guides (www.damron.com), with separate, annual books for gay men and lesbians; and *Gay Travel A to Z: The World of Gay & Lesbian Travel Options at Your Fingertips* by Marianne Ferrari (Ferrari International; Box 35575, Phoenix, AZ 85069), a very good gay and lesbian guidebook series.

Chapter 8

Taking Care of the Remaining Details

● ●

● ●

*T*he launch pad is just ahead. All you need to do is take care of a few last-minute details: Stuff your bags with everything that's clean, water the geraniums, pay the rent, and finish 50 other 11th-hour chores. Then you're on your way to Ponce de Leon's land of dreams!

Feel free to skip this chapter if you're not worried about insurance matters, airline security, and advance reservations for restaurants and events. Otherwise, join us!

Playing It Safe with Travel and Medical Insurance

Three kinds of travel insurance are available: trip-cancellation insurance, medical insurance, and lost luggage insurance. The cost of travel insurance varies widely, depending on the cost and length of your trip, your age and health, and the type of trip you're taking, but expect to pay between 5 and 8 percent of the vacation itself. Here is my advice on all three:

✔ **Trip-cancellation insurance** helps you get your money back if you have to back out of a trip, if you have to go home early, or if your travel supplier goes bankrupt. Allowed reasons for cancellation can range from sickness to natural disasters to the State Department declaring your destination unsafe for travel. (Insurers usually won't cover vague fears, though, as many travelers discovered who tried to cancel their trips in October 2001 because they were wary of flying.)

A good resource is **"Travel Guard Alerts,"** a list of companies considered high-risk by Travel Guard International (www.travel insured.com). Protect yourself further by paying for the insurance with a credit card — by law, consumers can get their money back on goods and services not received if they report the loss within 60 days after the charge is listed on their credit card statement.

Note: Many tour operators can arrange insurance policies through a partnering provider, a convenient and often cost-effective way for the traveler to obtain insurance. Make sure the tour company is a reputable one, however: Some experts suggest you avoid buying insurance from the tour or cruise company you're traveling with, saying it's better to buy from a "third party" insurer than to put all your money in one place.

✔ For domestic travel, buying **medical insurance** for your trip doesn't make sense for most travelers. Most existing health policies cover you if you get sick away from home — but check before you go, particularly if you're insured by an HMO.

✔ **Lost luggage insurance** is not necessary for most travelers. On domestic flights, checked baggage is covered up to $2,500 per ticketed passenger. If you plan to check items more valuable than the standard liability, see if your valuables are covered by your homeowner's policy, get baggage insurance as part of your comprehensive travel-insurance package or buy Travel Guard's "BagTrak" product. Don't buy insurance at the airport, as it's usually overpriced. Be sure to take any valuables or irreplaceable items with you in your carry-on luggage, as many valuables (including books, money, and electronics) aren't covered by airline policies.

If your luggage is lost, immediately file a lost-luggage claim at the airport, detailing the luggage contents. For most airlines, you must report delayed, damaged, or lost baggage within four hours of arrival. The airlines are required to deliver luggage, once found, directly to your house or destination free of charge.

For more information, contact one of the following recommended insurers: **Access America** (☎ 866-807-3982; www.accessamerica.com); **Travel Guard International** (☎ 800-826-4919; www.travelguard.com); **Travel Insured International** (☎ 800-243-3174; www.travelinsured. com); and **Travelex Insurance Services** (☎ 888-457-4602; www.travelex-insurance.com).

Staying Healthy When You Travel

Getting sick will ruin your vacation, so I *strongly* advise against it (of course, last time I checked, the bugs weren't listening to me any more than they probably listen to you).

For domestic trips, most reliable health-care plans provide coverage if you get sick away from home. For information on purchasing additional medical insurance for your trip, see the previous section.

Talk to your doctor before leaving on a trip if you have a serious and/ or chronic illness. For conditions such as epilepsy, diabetes, or heart problems, wear a **MedicAlert identification tag** (☎ 888-633-4298; www.medicalert.org), which immediately alerts doctors to your condition and gives them access to your records through Medic Alert's 24-hour hotline.

Keeping Up with Airline Security Measures

With the federalization of airport security, security procedures at U.S. airports are more stable and consistent than ever. Generally, you'll be fine if you arrive at the airport **one hour** before a domestic flight and **two hours** before an international flight; if you show up late, tell an airline employee and she'll probably whisk you to the front of the line.

Bring a **current, government-issued photo ID** such as a driver's license or passport. Keep your ID at the ready to show at check-in, the security checkpoint, and sometimes even the gate. (Children under 18 do not need government-issued photo IDs for domestic flights, but they do for international flights to most countries.)

In 2003, the TSA phased out **gate check-in** at all U.S. airports. And **e-tickets** have made paper tickets nearly obsolete. Passengers with e-tickets can beat the ticket-counter lines by using airport **electronic kiosks** or even **online check-in** from your home computer. Online check-in involves logging on to your airlines' Web site, accessing your reservation, and printing out your boarding pass — and the airline may even offer you bonus miles to do so! If you're using a kiosk at the airport, bring the credit card you used to book the ticket or your frequent-flier card. Print out your boarding pass from the kiosk and simply proceed to the security checkpoint with your pass and a photo ID. If you're checking bags or looking to snag an exit-row seat, you will be able to do so using most airline kiosks. Even the smaller airlines are employing the kiosk system, but always call your airline to make sure these alternatives are available. **Curbside check-in** is also a good way to avoid lines, although a few airlines still ban curbside check-in; call before you go.

Security checkpoint lines are getting shorter, but some doozies remain. If you have trouble standing for long periods of time, tell an airline employee; the airline will provide a wheelchair. Speed up security by **not wearing metal objects** such as big belt buckles. If you've got metallic body parts, a note from your doctor can prevent a long chat with the security screeners. Keep in mind that only **ticketed passengers** are allowed past security, except for folks escorting disabled passengers or children.

Federalization has stabilized **what you can carry on** and **what you can't.** The general rule is that sharp things are out, nail clippers are okay, and food and beverages must be passed through the X-ray machine — but that security screeners can't make you drink from your coffee cup. Bring food in your carryon, rather than checking it, as explosive-detection machines used on checked luggage have been known to mistake food (especially chocolate, for some reason) for bombs. Travelers in the U.S. are allowed one carry-on bag, plus a "personal item" such as a purse, briefcase, or laptop bag. Carry-on hoarders can stuff all sorts of things into a laptop bag; as long as it has a laptop in it, it's still considered a personal item. The Transportation Security Administration (TSA) has issued a list of restricted items; check its Web site (`www.tsa.gov/public/index.jsp`) for details.

Airport screeners may decide that your checked luggage needs to be searched by hand. You can now purchase luggage locks that allow screeners to open and relock a checked bag if hand-searching is necessary. Look for Travel Sentry certified locks at luggage or travel shops and Brookstone stores (you can buy them online at `www.brookstone.com`). These locks, approved by the TSA, can be opened by luggage inspectors with a special code or key. For more information on the locks, visit `www.travelsentry.org`. If you use something other than TSA-approved locks, your lock will be cut off your suitcase if a TSA agent needs to hand-search your luggage.

Beating the Crowd: Reservations and Tickets

You'll want to spend your time in Florida on the beach or at attractions, not waiting hours for a restaurant table or a theater ticket. Although, in most cases, an advance reservation (for dining and other activities) is not mandatory, having one helps your day run smoothly.

Reserving a table

Getting a restaurant reservation in Florida is comparatively easy. In most cases, you can make same-day reservations or even walk into the restaurant when you feel your first hunger pangs. There are, of course, plenty of exceptions, such as **Emeril's** in CityWalk in Orlando (see Chapter 17) or many of the restaurants on Miami's **South Beach** (see Chapter 9). Even at places that are less in demand, I recommend that you make reservations as far in advance as you can (including before you leave home) for any restaurant accepting them. You can find all the information you need to make a reservation in the dining listings in the destination chapters. After you arrive, your hotel's concierge or front desk can help with reservations, too.

If you're a smoker, don't plan on lighting up over dinner. Smoking is prohibited in Florida's public work places, including restaurants and bars that serve food. Stand-alone bars that serve virtually no food are exempt, as are designated smoking rooms in hotels and motels.

Reserving a ticket and getting event information

Ticketmaster is the key player for reservations to most of Florida's major events, including concerts, shows, and pro sports events. If you know of an event that happens while you're in town, check first with your hometown Ticketmaster outlets to see if they sell tickets for the event. (If you live as close as Atlanta or New Orleans, they probably do.) Otherwise, go to the Ticketmaster Web site at www.ticketmaster.com, or call the outlet in the city you'll be visiting. The Ticketmaster numbers for a few of Florida's larger cities are:

- ✔ Fort Lauderdale: ☎ **954-523-3309**
- ✔ North Florida: ☎ **904-353-3309**
- ✔ Miami: ☎ **305-358-5885**
- ✔ Orlando: ☎ **407-839-3900**
- ✔ St. Petersburg: ☎ **727-898-2100**
- ✔ Tampa: ☎ **813-287-8844**

Most of the ticket outlets are open from 9 a.m. to 9 p.m., Monday through Friday, and 9 a.m. to 7 p.m., Saturday and Sunday.

You can pick up information on what's playing in your part of Florida from a few solid sources. Most of Florida's midsize and larger daily newspapers publish an entertainment section on Friday that includes events, restaurants, and more. Many of them have free online publications.

The **International Association of Convention and Visitor Bureaus** has a Web site at www.officialtravelinfo.com — another good place to find out what's happening during your stay. Use the site's links page to find your destination, and then choose the services or activities you want to see. The same goes for **Visit Florida** (☎ **888-735-2872;** Internet: www.flausa.com) and **Absolutely Florida** (☎ **305-865-9420;** Internet: www.funandsun.com), which include information on sightseeing, cultural events, accommodations, and more.

The visitor centers listed in the destination chapters are also good sources of event, restaurant, and sightseeing information.

Reserving a green

Golfers can get information on many of Florida's courses and make reservations through **Golfpac** (☎ **800-327-0878** or 407-260-2288; www.golfpacinc.com). Or you can contact **Tee Times USA** by calling ☎ **888-465-3356** or visiting the Web at www.teetimesusa.com.

Part III
South Florida

By Rich Tennant

"I can replace your bridge, Mr. Dolan, but in this part of Miami, the Historic District mandates that I do it in the Art Deco style."

In this part . . .

*Y*ou may already be zeroing in on South Florida as your top-draft pick. Arguably, it has as much diversity as any other landing zone in Florida. Party people find it hard to resist the glam-ified energy of Miami's South Beach (see Chapters 9 and 10) or the eclectic, laid-back lifestyle of Key West (see Chapter 11). And if you prefer to relax when vacationing, you aren't left out, thanks to such natural treasures as John Pennekamp Coral Reef State Park in Key Largo (Chapter 11), Bahia Honda State Park on Big Pine Key (Chapter 11), and the Everglades (Chapter 12).

The following five chapters offer all you need to know about the best places to eat, sleep, and be merry in the frequently frenetic, though sometimes soothing, south.

Chapter 9

Settling into Miami

*I*f you think Miami is all palm trees and little substance, you're wrong. Miami is one of the few cities that actually benefits from multiple-personality disorder. Biscayne Bay ripples in the sunset as the last speedboats come home for the night. Little Havana provides a glimpse of pre-Castro Cuba juxtaposed by the Mc-pleasures of modern life. And the alluring sands of South Beach glitter with glitz, glam, and all the makings of a juicy gossip column. This is as chic as *La Florida* gets, where La Dolce Vita fuses with La Vida Loca, creating a tropical cocktail that's guaranteed to both shake and stir. With the exception of theme parks and Mouse-ka-things, you can find just about everything worth finding in Florida in Miami.

First-time visitors are most surprised by the city's cultural and natural resources. Sapphire-blue water, gleaming quartz beaches, and tropical gardens are complemented by such standouts as **Villa Vizcaya, Biscayne National Park,** and **Bill Baggs Cape Florida State Recreation Area.** And yes, if you need an attraction fix, some of Florida's most enduring — among them, the **Miami Seaquarium** and **Metrozoo** — are here to prove that animal life does exist beyond the maniacal drivers on I-95.

I'll chauffeur you to those as well as to other attractions in Chapter 10, but for now I get you here, through the check-in line, and parked at a dinner table.

Getting There

Most folks come by air because flying is convenient and in most cases reasonably economical. Trains can be tedious, and even rail buffs find them time-consuming if they only have a week off. Ditto for drivers — they're staring at about 450 miles between the state line and Miami.

By plane

Touch down at **Miami International Airport (MIA),** which handles 34 million passengers annually. The tenth busiest airport in the world, it's served by more than 100 domestic and foreign airlines, offering direct links to 200 cities on five continents. The airport's 121 gates may seem overwhelming, but the layout isn't quite as complicated as it appears. For further information, call ☎ **305-876-7000,** or visit the airport's Web site (www.miami-airport.com).

After picking up your luggage — the route to baggage claim is clearly marked — you can take advantage of a number of services:

- ✔ **Car-rental desks** for Avis, Budget, Dollar, Hertz, National, Value, and Royal are on the first level near the baggage-claim exit. (See the Appendix for rental-car agency information.)

- ✔ **Customs** has two inspection areas. Passengers arriving at Concourses D, E, and F exit at Concourse E, Level 1. Those arriving at Concourses A and B exit at Concourse B, Level 3.

- ✔ **Foreign currency exchange booths** are at six locations on Level 2 and on Level 3 in the Greeter's Lobby Concourse B. A booth at Concourse E operates 24 hours a day. If you're coming from another country, convert to U.S. dollars at a bank back home. The exchange rate may not be better, but you'll save on fees.

- ✔ The **24-hour information center** is on Level 2, at Concourse E across from the hotel. There are four other centers, including two at baggage claim on Level 1, Concourses D and G (open 11 a.m.–7 p.m.). You can also get information by calling ☎ **305-876-7000.**

- ✔ A **full-service bank** is located on Level 4 of Concourse B. **ATMs** are also located at the Passenger Service Centers between Concourses B and C and between Concourses G and H on Level 2 of the Terminal. The bank is open from 9 a.m. to 6 p.m. on weekdays and from 10 a.m. to 4 p.m. on Saturdays.

Interstate 95, toll roads, and interior highways link Miami International Airport, 6 miles from downtown Miami and about 10 miles from the beaches, to the tourist areas. As I mentioned earlier, all the major car-rental agencies are located at the airport, or they run shuttles to their nearby offices. If you reserved your rental car before you left home, head for the rental agency's desk after you've collected your baggage.

Cabs cost from $1.50 to $3 to start the meter and $2 for each mile. So a one-way fare for up to five people from the airport to the beaches would range from $24 and up. Cab rides from the airport are blissfully short: To South Beach, it's only about 15 minutes; downtown is less; Coral Gables and the South, about 20 minutes, which is the same for the North Miami area. Taxis line up outside the airport's arrival terminals. **SuperShuttle** is one of the city's busiest van services. Its rates from the airport to South

Beach are $13 per person one-way. That's not a bargain for larger families. Be prepared to make several stops because you're likely to share a ride with several strangers. For more information, call ☎ **305-871-2000,** or visit the shuttle's Web site (www.supershuttle.com).

I don't recommend using public buses. They're unreliable and brutally slow, taking an hour or more to travel the 10 miles to South Beach.

If you are headed to the northern section of Miami you may be better off flying in and out of **Fort Lauderdale Hollywood International Airport** (☎ **954-359-6100;** www.co.broward.fl.us/fll.htm). Oftentimes, flights routed through this airport are cheaper than those flying into and out of MIA. Located in the middle of Broward County, it's actually closer to North Miami Beach and Aventura than Miami's own airport. See Chapter 13 for more on this airport.

By car

If you're coming by car, there are only two routes worth considering:

- ✔ Connect with Interstate 75 in north Florida and the Florida Turnpike (a toll road) at Wildwood.
- ✔ Ride Interstate 95 down the East Coast.

I-95 is the major north–south artery here. From it, you can reach the beaches, downtown, and points south. But it's the highway system's answer to bronchitis — highly congested — and poorly marked, so it's easy to get lost. (See Chapter 4 for northerly routes into the city.)

By train

Amtrak (☎ **800-872-7245;** www.amtrak.com) has two trains departing daily from New York. That's the good news. The bad news: They take as long as 30 hours to reach Miami, and prices often aren't much cheaper than airfare (and they're worse if you want a sleeper). See Chapter 4 for additional information on train travel in Florida, including Amtrak's Auto Train.

Orienting Yourself in Miami

Most of western Miami-Dade County is undeveloped, but areas east of I-75 — especially the coastal zone — are so saturated that the county has had to go to ten-digit dialing for local calls. (That means you need to dial the 305 or 786 area code followed by the seven-digit local number.)

Miami's modest herd of high-rises lies in the heart of the city, and you can see them from a wide radius, making them a good reference point. The airport is west; the beaches are east; Coconut Grove and the Keys are south.

The mainland — some parts of Miami lie on islands, which are connected to the mainland by causeways — is cut into quadrants: Northeast, Northwest, Southeast, and Southwest. The quadrants converge at the intersection of Flagler Street and Miami Avenue. Street numbering, in most cases, is reasonably simple. Leaving that intersection, you progress through First Street, Second Street, Third Street, and so on. A *NE, NW, SE,* or *SW* designation following the street number tells you which quadrant you're in. The same holds true for avenues, boulevards, terraces, places, and lanes. Also note that most streets run east–west, while avenues run north–south.

Miami Beach's layout is simpler. First Street is on its southern tip, and the street numbers progress north. Collins Avenue, alias *A1A*, runs north–south the length of the island. As on the mainland, it's one of several thoroughfares that has more than one name or number. (If cases like this come up in hotel or attractions listings, I'll give you both names and/or numbers.)

One other point: Numbers on the mainland and island do not match up with each other. For instance, the 79th Street Causeway coming from the mainland reaches across Biscayne Bay to 71st Street on the beach.

Introducing the neighborhoods

Miami-Dade County is a huge area that includes Miami, Miami Beach, Coconut Grove, Coral Gables, Aventura, Hialeah, and a number of other cities. (Skip ahead to the "Miami at a Glance" map.) The sprawling metropolis is confusing at best for those who've never set foot in Miami and almost as baffling for those who've been here before. The street signs include both names and numbers to help you find your way, but they don't always lead you in a straight line because Miami is full of canals, causeways, parks, and other obstacles. Getting lost here is easier than acquiring a suntan on the beach.

We've broken the county into eight geographical regions that should help you navigate, or at least identify where you are when your trip to the beach somehow lands you in a swamp.

Coconut Grove

The Grove used to be quite groovy, a haven for hippies, intellectuals, and artists. Today, it's an enclave of Americana with stores like the Gap and Banana Republic. In addition to chain stores, the neighborhood's major streets — Grand Avenue, Main Highway, and McFarlane Road — boast theme restaurants, and a casual, mostly collegiate crowd that makes for some rowdy behavior, especially at night. The architecture here is schizophrenic — a cross between old-world Bahamian and prefabbed Mediterranean. Past all the stores and elements of commercialism, you'll find Bahamian-style frame homes along Charles Street built by early settlers from the Islands. The Coconut Grove Goombay Festival (in early June), a street party, celebrates that island heritage.

Miami at a Glance

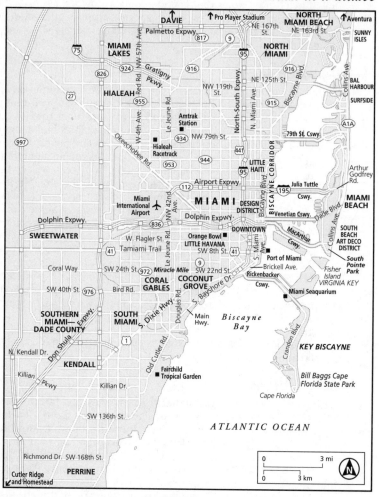

Don't stray far from the major tourist strips in this neighborhood at night.

Coral Gables

"The City Beautiful," created by George Merrick in the early 1920s, is one of Miami's first planned developments in which even the newspaper boxes have to conform to certain standards of beauty. This is not Levittown: The houses here were built in a Mediterranean style along lush tree-lined streets that open onto beautifully carved plazas, many with centerpiece fountains. The best architectural examples of the era have Spanish-style tiled roofs and are built from Miami *oolite,* a native limestone commonly called "coral rock." Once sleepy and outdated, **Miracle Mile** is a block in downtown Coral Gables that is undergoing a slow renaissance. It offers pricey furniture stores, cafes, wedding dress stores, and boutiques. Coral Gables also has landmark hotels, great golfing, upscale shopping, and some of the city's best restaurants.

Downtown Miami

Miami's downtown boasts one of the world's most beautiful cityscapes. Unfortunately, that's about all it offers. During the day, a vibrant community of students, businesspeople, and merchants make their way through the bustling streets. Vendors sell fresh-cut pineapples and mangos while young consumers on shopping sprees lug bags and boxes. However, at night, downtown is desolate (except for the burgeoning nightlife scene — only on NE 11th Street at the moment) and not a place in which you'd want to get lost. The downtown area does have a mall (**Bayside Marketplace,** where many cruise passengers come to browse), some culture (**Metro-Dade Cultural Center),** and a few decent restaurants, as well as the **American Airlines Arena.** An exclusive residential and commercial offshoot of Brickell Avenue, **Brickell Key** is accessible by bridge and perched pristinely on Biscayne Bay overlooking the magnificent city skyline. Additionally, a downtown revitalization project is in the works, in which a cultural arts center, among other things, is expected to bring downtown back to life and less reminiscent of the chapter in *Bonfire of the Vanitie,* in which taking a wrong turn in the wrong part of town was a big mistake.

This neighborhood is not the kind of place safety-conscious people hang around after dark.

Design District

With restaurants springing up between galleries, and furniture stores galore, the Design District is, as locals say, the new South Beach, adding a touch of New York's SoHo to an area formerly known as downtown Miami's "Don't Go." The district, which is a hotbed for furniture-import companies, interior designers, architects, and more, has also become a player in Miami's ever-changing nightlife, with rotating gallery parties that have become hipster central for South Beach expatriates and artsy bohemian types. In anticipation of its growing popularity, the district has also banded together to create an up-to-date Web site, www.design miami.com, which includes a calendar of events and is full of information. The district is loosely defined as the area bounded by NE Second Avenue, NE Fifth Avenue East and West, and NW 36th Street to the South.

Biscayne Corridor

From downtown near Bayside to the 70s, where trendy curio shops and upscale restaurants are slowly opening, Biscayne Boulevard is aspiring to reclaim itself as a safe thoroughfare where tourists can wine, dine, and shop. Previously known for sketchy, dilapidated 1950s- and '60s-era hotels that had fallen on hard times, residents fleeing the high prices of the beaches in search of affordable housing are renovating Biscayne block by block, trying to make this once-again-famous boulevard worthy of a Sunday drive. With the trendy Design District immediately west of 36th and Biscayne by two blocks, there is hope for the area.

Greater Miami

This zone encompasses everything from North Miami Beach to a large hunk of **Everglades National Park, Biscayne National Park,** and the **Florida Keys National Marine Sanctuary.** Although many of these are pristine areas, towns such as Hialeah, Miami Springs, and Homestead tend to be congested with condos and shopping malls. None are particularly visitor-oriented, though I make a few stops here later on in this chapter and the next.

Key Biscayne

Locals call it the Key, and technically, Key Biscayne is the northernmost island in the Florida Keys even though it is located in Miami. Situated south of Miami Beach, off the shores of Coconut Grove, Key Biscayne is protected from the troubles of the mainland by the long Rickenbacker Causeway and its $1 toll. Largely an exclusive residential community, with million-dollar homes and sweeping water views, Key Biscayne also offers visitors great public beaches, some top (read: pricey) resort hotels, and several good restaurants.

Little Havana

If you've never been to Cuba, just visit this small section of Miami and you'll come pretty close. The sounds, tastes, and rhythms are very reminiscent of Cuba's capital city. Some even jokingly say you don't have to speak a word of English to live an independent life here — even street signs are in Spanish and English. Cuban coffee shops, tailor and furniture stores, and inexpensive restaurants line **Calle Ocho** (pronounced *Ka*-yey *O*-choh), SW Eighth Street, the region's main thoroughfare. Salsa and merengue beats ring loudly from old record stores while old men in guayaberas (loose shirts) smoke cigars over their daily game of dominoes. The spotlight focused on the neighborhood during the Elian Gonzalez situation in 2000, but the area was previously noted for the groups of artists and nocturnal types who have moved their galleries and performance spaces here, sparking a culturally charged neobohemian nightlife.

As much as I love it, this is another area you'd best leave when the sun does.

Miami Beach

In the fabulous '50s, Miami Beach was America's true Riviera. The stomping ground of choice for celebrities such as Frank Sinatra and the Rat Pack, as well as notorious mobsters (Al Capone was a one-time habitué), its huge self-contained resort hotels were vacations unto themselves, providing a full day's worth of meals, activities, and entertainment. Then, in the 1960s and 1970s, people who fell in love with Miami began to buy apartments rather than rent hotel rooms. Tourism declined, the Rat Pack and *Sopranos* types decamped to Vegas, and many area hotels fell into disrepair. However, since the late 1980s and South Beach's renaissance, Miami Beach (24th Street and up) has experienced a tide of revitalization. Beach hotels are finding their niche with new international tourist markets and are attracting large convention crowds. New generations of Americans are discovering the qualities that originally made Miami Beach so popular, and they're finding out that the sand and surf now come with a thriving international city.

North Miami Beach and Aventura

A residential area, North Miami Beach has shopping and dining, but it's not much of a tourist stop. **Aventura Mall** is the area's biggest attraction, with an impressive selection of boutique, department, and chain stores located within the mostly residential, upscale NMB enclave of Aventura. Unlike its southern cousin, North Miami Beach is on the mainland.

South Beach: The Art Deco District

Though many monikers are used to describe Miami's publicity darling — Glitter Beach, SoBe, America's Riviera, Hollywood South, Manhattan South — South Beach is a uniquely surreal, Dalí-esque cocktail of cosmopolitan influences with a splash of saltwater thrown in to remind you that you're not in a concrete jungle anymore. South Beach's 10 miles of beach are alive with a frenetic, circuslike atmosphere and are center stage for a motley crew of characters, from eccentric locals, senior citizens, snowbirds, and college students to gender benders, celebrities, club kids, and curiosity-seekers. Individuality is as widely accepted on South Beach as Visa and MasterCard. Bolstered by a Caribbean-chic cafe society and a sexually charged, hip nightlife, people watching on South Beach (from 1st to 23rd streets) is almost as good as a front-row seat at a Milan fashion show. Sure, the beautiful people do flock here, but the models aren't the only sights worth drooling over. The thriving Art Deco District within South Beach contains the largest remaining concentration of 1930s architecture in the world. In 1979, much of South Beach was listed in the National Register of Historic Places. The pastel-hued structures are supermodels in their own right — only these models improve with age.

Finding information after you arrive

I urge you to plan in advance. Contact the visitor-information folks listed here and in the Appendix.

The **Greater Miami Convention and Visitors Bureau,** 701 Brickell Ave., Suite 2700, Miami, FL 33131 (☎ **800-933-8448** or 305-539-3063; www. tropicoolmiami.com), is the best source of information about Miami.

Even if you don't have a specific question, call ahead to request its free vacation planner, *TropiCool Miami,* which includes easy-to-use maps and useful contact numbers. The office is open weekdays from 9 a.m. to 5 p.m.

The local chambers of commerce also offer good information. The **Greater Miami Chamber of Commerce,** 420 Lincoln Rd., no. 20, Miami Beach, FL 33139 (☎ **305-350-7700;** www.greatermiami.com) can provide a neighborhood map and tourist information, as can the **Coral Gables Chamber of Commerce,** 50 Aragon Ave., Coral Gables, FL 33134 (☎ **305-446-1657;** www.gableschamber.org), and **Coconut Grove Chamber of Commerce,** 2820 McFarlane Rd., Miami, FL 33133 (☎ **305-444-7270**).

If you're hooked into the Internet, surf over to www.miami.com. It provides a vast array of information on accommodations, dining, and entertainment options throughout Miami and South Florida. You can also check out Miami-Dade County's official Web site at www.co.miami-dade.fl.us, which offers up-to-date information on county parks, sports, and attractions, such as the Miami Metrozoo, and cultural events. The **Miami Design Preservation League,** 1234 Washington Ave., Suite 207, Miami Beach (☎ **305-672-2014**), has an informative guide on South Beach's Art Deco District. It's open from 10 a.m. to 7 p.m., Monday through Saturday. The **Greater Miami and the Beaches Hotel Association,** 407 Lincoln Rd., Miami Beach (☎ **800-531-3553** or 305-531-3553) has information about accommodations and tours.

Getting around Miami

A car is your best option for getting around the city, as long as you have a reliable map (see the "Fast Facts" in Chapter 10). Taxis are a distant second — economical only if you're in a group of four or five people. Public transportation is plodding, and, except for South Beach and the shopping and dining meccas of Coconut Grove and Coral Gables, Miami isn't much of a walker's paradise.

By car

Most streets on the mainland and beaches are numbered, so finding your way around is fairly easy if you have a reliable map. (You can get one from one of the information sources listed under "Fast Facts" in Chapter 10, from AAA if you're a member, or from your car-rental agency.) Miami's attractions, beaches, restaurants, and hotels are spread out, making a car almost essential if you want to explore in a timely, cost-effective manner. If, on the other hand, you plan to camp at a resort or on South Beach and do your sightseeing by guided tour, you won't need a car. (Don't forget to allow time in your schedule for delays caused by traffic congestion and, if you're going to or from the beaches, drawbridge openings.)

Generally, there are plenty of parking spaces throughout Miami-Dade County (a major exception is South Beach), but parking can be expensive. Keep your pocket or wallet filled with quarters to feed the hungry meters or be prepared for fines of $20 or more. You can find parking garages and valet service in some areas. The going rate for valet parking at restaurants and hotels is $3 to $20 depending on how much they think you need them. (If you're in South Beach and don't mind losing a little shoe leather, there are parking garages at 17th Street and Washington Avenue, Seventh Street between Washington and Collins avenues, and 13th Street between Collins Avenue and Ocean Drive. The cost is $1 an hour or $8 a day.)

See the Appendix for contact information about rental-car agencies.

By taxi

Unless you can fill the cab (five passengers), this isn't a cheap way to travel, especially when you add a tip. However, a taxi is usually quick and direct, with fixed rates between certain points. Usually it's $1.50 to start the meter and $2 for each mile. The county's main cab companies are **Central** (☎ 305-532-5555), **Metro** (☎ 305-888-8888), and **Yellow** (☎ 305-444-4444).

By bus

Miami's public transit system offers little to recommend it. Bus routes almost universally are designed for commuters, not visitors. Even if buses go your way, they're slow, making too many stops and often requiring transfers and more time. For the record, the **Metro-Dade Transit System** (☎ 305-770-3131; www.co.miami-dade.fl.us/transit) operates the county's bus line. Fares are $1.25 plus 25¢ for each transfer.

By rail

The **Metro-Dade Transit System** (☎ 305-770-3131; www.co.miami-dade.fl.us/transit) also operates two trains in the county. **Metrorail,** the city's modern high-speed commuter train, is a 21-mile elevated line that travels north–south between downtown Miami and the southern suburbs. Locals like to refer to this semiuseless rail system as Metro*fail.* If you're staying in Coral Gables or Coconut Grove, you can park your car at a nearby station and ride the rails downtown. However, that's about it. There are plans to extend the system to service Miami International Airport, but until those tracks are built, these trains don't go most places tourists go, with the exception of Vizcaya in Coconut Grove. Metrorail operates daily from about 6 a.m. to midnight. The fare is $1.25. **Metromover,** a 4.4-mile elevated line, circles the downtown area and connects with Metrorail at the Government Center stop. This is a good way to get to Bayside (a waterfront marketplace, see Chapter 10) if you don't have a car. Riding on rubber tires, the single-car train winds past many of the area's most important attractions and shopping and business districts. You may not go very far, but you'll get a beautiful perspective from the towering height of the suspended rails. System hours are daily from about 6 a.m. to midnight. The fare is 25¢.

Staying in Style

The following listings reflect the city's best choices in various price categories. In general, you can expect to pay the highest prices for the more upscale digs, as well as those in or near the beaches.

Note that although rates in this chapter are per-night double occupancy, this is a kid-friendly state. Many accommodations let kids under 12 and in some cases under 18 stay free with parents or grandparents as long as you don't exceed the maximum occupancy of the room. Just to be safe, ask when booking your room.

The height of tourist season — the priciest period — is winter. Rates will be highest from November through March. The off season is generally considered to run from mid-May through August, and rates are discounted by as much as 30 to 50 percent. If you're a beach buff, you can also save by staying at a hotel a few blocks off the water.

If you don't like dealing directly with hotels or haggling over rates, you can contact several reservations services in the area, including **Central Reservation Service** (☎ 800-555-7555; www.reservation-services. com), **Florida Hotel Network** (☎ 800-538-3616; www.floridahotels. com), and the **Greater Miami and The Beaches Hotel Association** (☎ 800-733-6426; www.gmbha.org).

Don't forget to allow for taxes. The combined sales, local option, and hotel bed taxes can add as much as 12.5 percent to your bill.

One last note: This is Florida. That means every hotel listed here has air-conditioning and either has a pool or is on the ocean. These hotels also have television (most have cable and many have in-room movies) and telephones. Many also have hair dryers, coffeemakers, and in-room safes.

Miami's best hotels

The Biltmore Hotel
$$$$ Coral Gables

Old-world glamour and rich history permeate the Biltmore as much as the pricey perfume of the guests who stay here. Built in 1926, it's the oldest Coral Gables hotel and a National Historical Landmark — one of only two operating hotels in Florida to receive that designation. Rising above the Spanish-style estate is a majestic 300-foot, copper-clad tower, modeled after the Giralda bell tower in Seville and visible throughout the city. Over the years, the Biltmore has passed through many incarnations (including a post–World War II stint as a VA hospital), but it's now back to its original splendor. More intriguing than scary is the rumor that ghosts of wounded soldiers and even Al Capone, for whom the Everglades Suite is nicknamed, roam the halls here. But don't worry. The hotel is far from a haunted house. It's warm, welcoming, and extremely charming. Always a popular

South Beach Accommodations

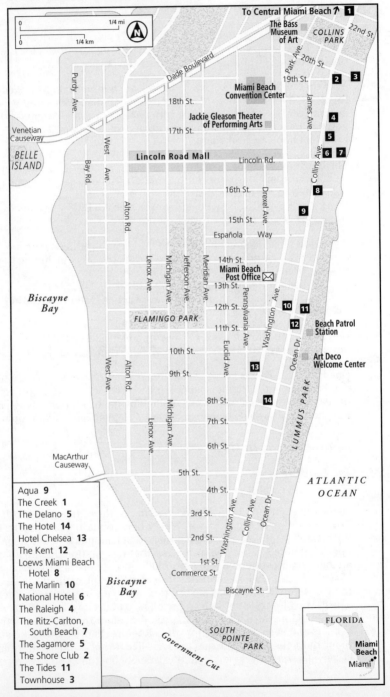

To Central Miami Beach ↑ **1**

The Bass Museum of Art

COLLINS PARK

22nd St.

Park Ave.

20th St.

19th St. **2** **3**

Dade Boulevard

Miami Beach Convention Center

18th St.

Jackie Gleason Theater of Performing Arts

James Ave. **4**

17th St. **5**

Purdy Ave.

West Ave.

Venetian Causeway

BELLE ISLAND

Bay Rd.

Lincoln Road Mall Lincoln Rd. Collins Ave. **6** **7**

16th St.

Drexel Ave. **8**

Alton Rd.

15th St. **9**

Española Way

Lenox Ave.

Michigan Ave.

Jefferson Ave.

Meridian Ave.

14th St.

Miami Beach Post Office ✉

13th St.

Pennsylvania Ave.

12th St. **10** **11**

Biscayne Bay

FLAMINGO PARK

Washington Ave. **12**

11th St. Beach Patrol Station

10th St.

Ocean Dr.

Art Deco Welcome Center

West Ave.

Alton Rd.

Euclid Ave.

9th St. **13**

8th St. **14**

Lenox Ave.

Michigan Ave.

7th St.

6th St.

LUMMUS PARK

MacArthur Causeway

5th St.

ATLANTIC OCEAN

4th St.

Aqua **9**
The Creek **1**
The Delano **5**
The Hotel **14**
Hotel Chelsea **13**
The Kent **12**
Loews Miami Beach Hotel **8**
The Marlin **10**
National Hotel **6**
The Raleigh **4**
The Ritz-Carlton, South Beach **7**
The Sagamore **5**
The Shore Club **2**
The Tides **11**
Townhouse **3**

Washington Ave.

Collins Ave.

Ocean Dr.

3rd St.

2nd St.

1st St.

Commerce St.

Biscayne Bay

Biscayne St.

SOUTH POINTE PARK

Government Cut

FLORIDA

Miami Beach

Miami

destination for golfers, including former President Clinton (who stays in the Al Capone suite), the Biltmore is situated on a lush, rolling 18-hole course that is as challenging as it is beautiful. The spa is fantastic, and the enormous winding pool is legendary — it's where a pre-*Tarzan* Johnny Weissmuller broke the world's swimming record.

See map p. 95. 1200 Anastasia Ave., 1 mile west of LeJeune Road/42nd Avenue. ☎ *800-727-1926 or 305-445-8066. Fax: 305-913-3159.* www.biltmorehotel.com. *To get there: From I-95, take U.S. 1/South Dixie Highway southwest to LeJeune, go right to Anastasia, left to hotel. Valet parking: $14. Rack rates: Apr–Sept $259–$379, Oct–Apr $339–$509. AE, CB, DISC, JCB, MC, V.*

The Creek
$ **South Beach**

This funky and arty hostel-like hotel, formerly known as the Banana Bungalow, is cheap, campy, and quintessentially Miami Beach. Popular with the MTV set, The Creek is a redone 1950s two-story motel that's loaded with amenities and where it's always spring break. There are three types of rooms: The Waterway Standard, no frills rooms which face a narrow canal where motorboats and kayaks are available for a small charge; the noisier Cabana Room, which opens to the pool deck (which boasts a serious sound system that the hotel turns off around midnight); and the Signature Rooms, 18 "altered living spaces" designed by artists and on the second floor facing the pool deck. I highly recommend the Signature Rooms that are facing the Intracoastal Waterway in terms of decor and privacy, something you won't have if you face out onto the buzzing pool deck. Shared rooms are available for the uber budget conscious.

See map p. 90. 2360 Collins Ave. ☎ *800-746-7835 or 305-538-1951. Fax: 305-531-3217.* www.thecreeksouthbeach.com. *To get there: Take Collins Avenue north to 23rd Street. Hotel is on the left-hand side, on the Indian Creek. Parking: Free. Rack rates: Mid-Dec–Apr $18–$104, May–Sept $16–$60, Oct–mid-Dec $70–$110. AE, DC, DISC, MC, V.*

David William Hotel
$$–$$$$ **Coral Gables**

At this sister hotel to the Biltmore, you get many of the same amenities for a lower price. Guests can even take a shuttle to the Biltmore to play a round of golf, enjoy the health club and spa, play tennis, or take a dip in the pool. The luxurious one- and two-bedroom suites are extremely spacious and have eat-in kitchens for extended stays. For a spectacular view of Miami, go up to the roof and have a drink by the pool. The hotel, which has undergone a recent exterior renovation, is directly across the street from the Granada Golf Course, less than 5 miles from the airport, and only 20 minutes from Miami Beach. Carmen The Restaurant, the culinary brainchild of chef Carmen Gonzalez, features Post-New-American Cuisine, a sexy spin on New American Cuisine steeped in exotic Hispanic/Latino influences. If you want luxury without the price, this is your best alternative in the Gables.

See map p. 95. 700 Biltmore Way. ☎ *800-757-8073 or 305-445-7821. Fax: 305-913-1943.* www.davidwilliamhotel.com. *To get there: Take I-95 south to U.S. 1, make a right on SW 17th Avenue and a left onto Coral Way. Turn left on Cardena Street and take a quick right onto Biltmore Way. Parking: Valet $9. Rack rates: Apr–Sept $99–$399, Oct–Mar $179@nd$479. AE, DISC, MC, V.*

The Delano
$$$$ South Beach

Today, the Delano, a place where smiles from staffers were once as rare as snow in Miami, is kinder and gentler to its guests (with an emphasis on B- and C-list celebrities and tourists not entirely in tune with the times), which for some, takes away the whole caché of staying here. But it certainly still is amusing to look at — with 40-foot, sheer, white, billowing curtains hanging outside, mirrors everywhere, Adirondack chairs, and faux fur–covered beds. The rooms are done up sanitarium style: sterile, yet terribly trendy, in pure white save for a perfectly crisp, green Granny Smith apple in each room — the only freebie you're going to get here. A bathroom renovation recently took place in all the rooms — but they remain small and spartan.

See map p. 90. 1685 Collins Ave. ☎ *800-555-5001 or 305-672-2000. Fax: 305-532-0099.* www.ianschragerhotels.com. *To get there: Take Alton Road and go east on 17th Street to Collins Avenue. The hotel is on the corner of 17th and Collins. Parking: $20. Rack rates: Oct–Mar $425–$675, Apr–Sept $255–$425. AE, DC, DISC, MC, V.*

Fontainebleau Hilton Resort
$$$–$$$$ Miami Beach

In many ways, this is the quintessential Miami Beach hotel. Designed by Morris Lapidus, who oversaw an expansion in 2000, this grand monolith symbolizes Miami decadence. Since its opening in 1954, the Fontainebleau has hosted presidents, pageants, and movie productions, including the James Bond thriller *Goldfinger.* This is where all the greats, including Sinatra and his pals, performed in their prime. Club Tropigala is reminiscent of Ricky Ricardo's Tropicana and features a Las Vegas–style floor show with dozens of performers and two orchestras. Rooms are luxurious and decorated in various styles from 1950s to ultramodern; bathrooms are done up in Italian marble. In 2001, the hotel underwent a $10 million renovation of its restaurants, introducing the massive, cruiseship-esque, 150-seat Bleu View Mediterranean restaurant and cocktail lounge. Meanwhile, the 7,000-square-foot Cookie's World water park brings a bit of Disney to Deco-land, complete with a water slide and river-raft ride. Along with supervised children's activities, the water park is geared to (though not reserved for) the little ones.

The hotel's size tends to cause problems. The staff is overworked, and lines in the lobby area are frequently long.

4441 Collins Ave./A1A, just south of 46th Street Park. ☎ *800-445-8667 or 305-538-2000. Fax: 305-531-9274.* www.fontainebleau.hilton.com. *To get there: From mainland, take Julia Tuttle Causeway to the island and Arthur Godfrey Road to Collins,* *turn left; hotel is oceanside. Parking: $13. Rack rates: Mid-Dec–Apr $209–$329, May–Sept $289–$459, Oct–mid-Dec $209–$459. AE, DC, DISC, MC, V.*

Loews Miami Beach Hotel
$$$ South Beach

The Loews Hotel is one of the largest beach hotels to arrive in South Beach in almost 30 years, consuming an unprecedented 900 feet of oceanfront. This 800-room behemoth is considered an eyesore by many, an architectural triumph by others. However you perceive it, you can't miss the hotel's cone-shaped, 18-story tower perched high above the rest of South Beach. Rooms are a bit boxy and bland — nothing to rave about — but they're clean and have new carpets and bedspreads to erase signs of early wear and tear from the hotel's heavy traffic. If you can steer your way through all the name-tagged businesspeople in the lobby, you can escape to the pool (with an undisputedly gorgeous, landscaped entrance that's more Maui than Miami), which is large enough to accommodate families and conventioneers alike. The Loews Loves Kids program features special menus, tours, welcome gifts for children under 10, supervised programs, and free accommodations for children under 18; in addition, the Generation G program offers perks for grandparents and grandkids traveling together. Adults can indulge in fun activities such as Dive in Movies at the pool, salsa lessons, and bingo. In November 2003, star chef Emeril Lagasse opened Miami's first-ever Emeril's restaurant here, making the Loews a bigger focal point for seeing and being seen than ever before.

See map p. 90. 1601 Collins Ave./A1A, just north of Lummus Park. ☎ **800-235-6397** *or 305-604-1601. Fax: 305-531-8677.* www.loewshotels.com. *To get there: From mainland, take MacArthur Causeway across Biscayne Bay and continue on Fifth Street to Ocean Drive, turn left; hotel is on left. Parking: Valet $19, self $17. Rack rates: Oct–Mar from $229, Apr–Sept from $189. AE, DC, DISC, MC. V.*

Mandarin-Oriental
$$$$ Brickell Key/Downtown Miami

The swank Mandarin Oriental is, hands down, the city's best. The waterfront view of the city is the hotel's best asset, but the service isn't too shabby either. Much of the hotel's staff was flown in from Bangkok and Hong Kong to demonstrate the hotel's unique brand of superattentive, Asian-inspired service. The hotel's two restaurants, the high-end Azul and the more casual Café Sambal, are up to Mandarin standards and are both wonderful, as is the 15,000-square-foot spa in which traditional Thai massages and Ayurvedic treatments are your tickets to nirvana.

See map p. 95. 500 Brickell Key Drive. ☎ **866-888-6780** *or 305-913-8288. Fax: 305-913-8300.* www.mandarinoriental.com. *To get there: Brickell Avenue to Brickell Key Drive. Drive over the bridge and stay to the right. Parking: Valet $24. Rack rates: from $575. AE, CB, DC, DISC, JCB, MC, V.*

The Raleigh
$$$–$$$$ South Beach

It's the Raleigh's romantic Deco lure that has people skipping over from the chillier, more sterile Delano a few blocks up for much needed warmth. Even more an incentive to stay here is the fact that hip hotelier André Balazs of LA's Chateau Marmont and Standard hotels fame is the new owner of the place. And he dates Uma Thurman. Rooms are small, but cozy, and celeb chef Eric Ripert of NYC's Le Bernadin is the hotel's newly appointed "directeur de cuisine." Even if you don't stay here, check out the legendary pool, where, on Sundays, the who's who of the chic elite bask in the fabulous Raleigh glow at a party known as Sunday Soiree.

See map p. 90. 1775 Collins Ave.. ☎ 800-848-1775 or 305-534-6300. Fax: 305-538-8140. www.raleighhotel.com. To get there: Take Alton Road and go east on 17th Street to Collins Avenue. Parking: Valet $20. Rack rates: Apr–Sept $209–$609, Oct–Apr $339–$769. AE, DISC, MC, V.

The Ritz-Carlton, South Beach
$$$$ South Beach

The lushly landscaped Ritz-Carlton has restored the landmark Morris Lapidus–designed 1950s DiLido Hotel to its original Art Moderne style and filled it with the hotel's signature five-star service. Also alluring are an elevated pool that provides unobstructed views of the Altantic, an impressive stretch of sand with a fabulous beach club run by Michael Capponi, Miami Beach's most popular promoter, an oceanfront Ritz Kids pavilion, and a world-class 13,000-square-foot spa and wellness center.

See map p. 90. 1 Lincoln Rd. ☎ 800-241-3333 or 786-276-4000. Fax: 786-276-4100. www.ritzcarlton.com. To get there: Take 17th St. east to Washington Avenue; turn left on Lincoln Road. The hotel is at the dead end on the left. Parking: Valet $30. Rack rates: Apr–Sept $245–$545, Oct–Apr $450–$720. AE, DISC, MC, V.

The Sagamore
$$$–$$$$ South Beach

The Sagamore, quietly fabulous in its own right, with an ultramodern lobby-cum–art gallery that's infinitely warmer than your typical pop art exhibit at the Museum of Modern Art, features all-suite, apartment-like rooms that are full of all the cushy comforts of home and then some.

See map p. 90. 1671 Collins Ave.. ☎ 87/SAGAMORE or 305-535-8088. Fax: 305-535-8185. www.sagamorehotel.com. To get there: 17th Street to Collins Avenue south. Hotel is on the left. Parking: Valet $18. Rack rates: Apr–Sept $215–$1,050, Oct–Apr $436–$1,072. AE, DC, DISC, MC, V.

Runner-up hotels

If your favorites are full or you can't find one in the previous listings to satisfy your tastes and budget, here are a few more places to consider:

Accommodations Elsewhere in Miami

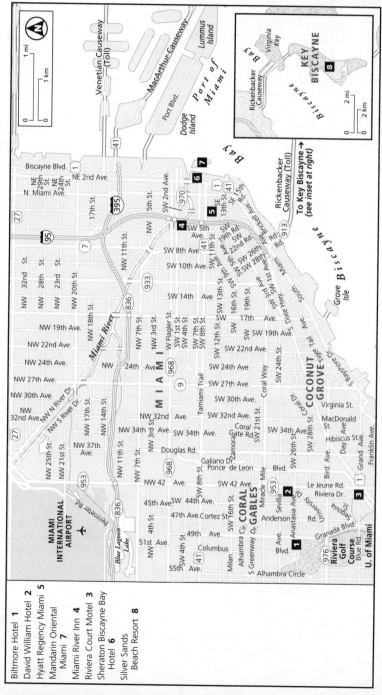

Aqua

$$ **South Beach** It's been described as The Jetsons meets Jaws, but the Aqua isn't all Hollywood. Animated, yes, but with little emphasis on special effects and more on a friendly staff, Aqua is definitely a good catch for those looking to stay in style without compromising their budget. *See map p. 90. 1530 Collins Ave.* ☎ *305-538-4361.* www.aquamiami.com.

The Hotel

$$$ **South Beach** Kitschy fashion designer Todd Oldham whimsically restored this 1939 gem (formerly the Tiffany Hotel) as he would have a vintage piece of couture. *See map p. 90. 801 Collins Ave.* ☎ *877-843-4683 or 305-531-2222.* www.thehotelofsouthbeach.com.

Hotel Chelsea

$$ **South Beach** With decor based on the Japanese art of Feng Shui, this boutiquey hotel offers the utmost in relaxation, with complimentary breakfast, beach yoga classes, free sake at happy hour, and, in case you've had enough relaxation, free passes to South Beach's hottest nightclubs. *See map p. 90. 944 Washington Ave. (at Ninth Street).* ☎ *305-534-4069.* www.thehotelchelsea.com.

Hyatt Regency Miami

$$$ **Downtown Miami** A room here comes with a nice view of the Miami River, and the hotel is just a few steps from the Brickell Avenue business district and the shops at Bayside Marketplace. *See map p. 95. 400 SE Second Ave.* ☎ *800-633-7313 or 305-358-1234.* www.hyatt.com.

The Kent

$$ **South Beach** This kitschy-chic hotel is a haven for budget-conscious hipsters. All rooms were recently made over, to the tune of $1 million, and feature wood floors and ultramodern steel furnishings and accessories, which surprisingly aren't cold, but rather inviting and whimsical. *See map p. 90. 1131 Collins Ave.* ☎ *800-OUTPOST or 305-604-5000.* www.islandlife.com.

The Marlin

$$$ **South Beach** Don't be surprised if you hear guitar riffs upon entering the Marlin. This rock-'n-roll hotel, owned by Chris Blackwell, founder of Island Records, also houses South Beach Studios, a recording and mixing facility, which has been put to use by Aerosmith and U2, among others. *See map p. 90. 1200 Collins Ave.* ☎ *800-OUTPOST or 305-672-5254.* www.islandoutpost.com.

Miami River Inn

$$ **Downtown Miami** Listed on the National Register of Historic Places, this is a quaint country-style hideaway (Miami's *only* bed-and-breakfast!) consisting of four cottages smack in the middle of downtown Miami. *See* map p. 95. 118 SW South River Dr. ☎ **800-468-3589** or 305-325-0045. www.miami riverinn.com.

National Hotel

$$$ **South Beach** This throwback to the 1940s is steeped in Deco, but you'll want to steep yourself in the hotel's magnificent, 205-foot swimming pool. See map p. 90. 1677 Collins Ave. ☎ **800-327-8370** or 305-532-2311. www. nationalhotel.com.

Riviera Court Motel

$ **Coral Gables** The Riviera is a basic but clean mom-and-pop motel that's near the University of Miami. See map p. 95. 5100 Riviera Dr. ☎ **800-368-8602** or 305-665-3528.

Sheraton Biscayne Bay Hotel

$$ **Downtown Miami** A short drive away from the best Miami has to offer, the hotel has 598 comfortable rooms overlooking the pool or the downtown skyline. See map p. 95. 495 Brickell Ave. ☎ **800-321-2323** or 305-373-6000. www.sheraton.com.

The Shore Club

$$$$ **South Beach** Spotting a celeb here is a sure thing, but you're going to pay for the privilege. The Shore Club has the requisite attitude, mod decor, the terminally trendy Skybar, and Florida's only branch of the swank sushi joint, Nobu. See map p. 90. 1901 Collins Ave. ☎ **877-640-9500** or 305-695-3100. www.shoreclubsouthbeach.com.

Silver Sands Beach Resort

$$ **Key Biscayne** The most affordable place on Key Biscayne, its 56 roomy rooms date to the 1950s but were remodeled after Hurricane Andrew in 1992. See map p. 95. 301 Ocean Dr. ☎ **305-361-5441**. www.silver sandsmiami.com.

The Tides

$$$$ **South Beach** This 12-story, all-suite, Art Deco masterpiece is reminiscent of a gleaming ocean liner, with porthole windows and lots of stainless steel and frosted glass. It's also the chicest place to stay on Ocean Drive. See map p. 90. 1220 Ocean Dr. ☎ **800-OUTPOST** or 305-604-5000. www. islandoutpost.com.

Townhouse

$$ **South Beach** The charm of this hotel is found in its clean and simple yet chic design with quirky details: exercise equipment that stands alone in the hallways, free laundry machines in the lobby, and waterbeds on the rooftop. See map p. 90. 150 20th St. ☎ **877-534-3800 or 305-534-3800**. www. townhousehotel.com.

South Beach Dining

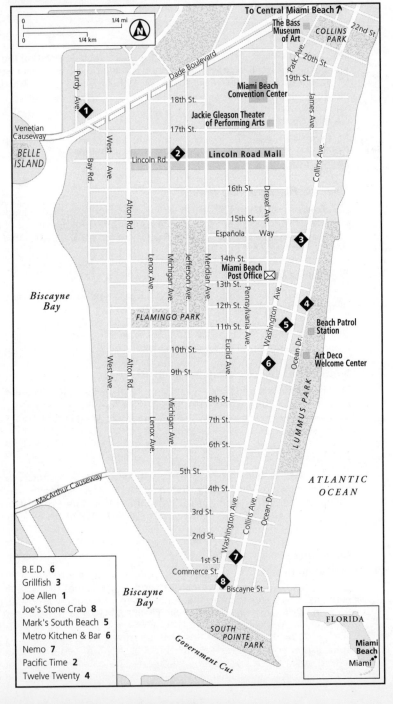

B.E.D. **6**
Grillfish **3**
Joe Allen **1**
Joe's Stone Crab **8**
Mark's South Beach **5**
Metro Kitchen & Bar **6**
Nemo **7**
Pacific Time **2**
Twelve Twenty **4**

Dining Out

Despite the plethora of toned, buff-body beautifuls, Miami is a foodie's paradise. People really do eat here. In fact, dining out is as much a pastime as inline skating on Ocean Drive or seeing and being seen in the clubs. A dizzying and mouthwatering array of cuisines awaits, from home-cooked Floribbean and Cuban to froufrou fusion fare. However, competition is so stiff that some places don't last three months — don't be surprised if your number-one choice on these pages has disappeared by the time you land. Some great kitchens can't stand the heat.

Smokers take note: All Florida restaurants and food-serving bars are smoke-free.

Keep in mind that you won't be the only one looking to eat at the hottest restaurants in town. To save yourself from headaches and an empty stomach, make reservations at the restaurants you want to sample. Otherwise, you may end up waiting several hours — and in the best of the best, several days — for a table.

Miami's best restaurants

Azul
$$$ **Brickell Key/Downtown Miami   GLOBAL FUSION**

Azul is a tour de force of international cuisine, inspired by Caribbean, French, Argentine, Asian, and homegrown American flavors. Although the restaurant itself is stunning — waterfront views, high ceilings, walls burnished in copper, and silk-covered chairs — the real jewel is the food. The hamachi carpaccio appetizer sumptuously arranges yellowtail (imported from Japan), shaved fennel, mixed greens, and cucumber. Entrees, or "Plates of Resistance" as they're called here, include braised open-faced ravioli with langoustine; ginger-lemongrass-glazed Chilean sea bass served with black rice, kimchi, and Napa cabbage; and chicken with red Thai curry. Desserts range from fruity to chocolatey and shouldn't be skipped.

See map p. 104. At the Mandarin Oriental, 500 Brickell Key Dr. ☎ 305-913-8254. Reservations strongly recommended. To get there: From I-95, take the Brickell Avenue exit and make a right onto Brickell Avenue, continuing over the bridge until you reach SE Eighth Street. Make a left and continue over the bridge. Hotel is on the right. Main courses: $24–$38. AE, DC, DISC, MC, V. Open: Mon–Fri noon–3 p.m.; Mon–Sat 7–11 p.m.

B.E.D.
$$$$ **South Beach   FRENCH FUSION**

Beverage, Entertainment, Dining is what B.E.D. stands for, but don't laugh: You will literally take your food lying down — sort of — as platform beds substitute for traditional tables at this nouveau, highly gimmicky haute spot. When you walk inside, you'll feel as if you've entered a Buddhist temple. An array of inviting mosquito-netted beds awaits diners. You'll rest your head against soft cushiony pillows. A deejay spins Euro mood music and some techno. You'll have no problem appreciating the taste and aroma of the exquisite (and exquisitely priced) cuisine, featuring dishes such as pan-seared foie gras with caramelized mango and cranberry with French toast, and Florida Red Snapper with garlic mash, matchstick asparagus (a fancy way of saying thin asparagus), and a choice of caper beurre noisette or Vermouth cream sauce. For dessert, try the Ménage à Trois — three sorbets including champagne, sour cherry, and mango — or indulge in some Fire and Ice — molten chocolate cake with rum vanilla ice cream and caramel sauce.

See map p. 98. 929 Washington Ave. ☎ 305-532-9070. Reservations required, accepted only on the day you plan to dine here. Main courses: $32–$40. AE, DC, MC, V. Open: Wed–Sun: first lay (no actual seats) 8:30 p.m. (opens at 8 p.m.); second lay 10:30 p.m. Lounge 11 p.m.–3 a.m.

Big Fish
$$ **Downtown Miami   SEAFOOD**

Hard to locate, but well worth the search, Big Fish lures diners with a sweeping view of the Miami skyline and some of the freshest catch around. The spectacular setting is also a draw, right on the Miami River where freighters, fishing boats, dinghies, and sometimes yachts slink by. Originally a traditional seafood spot, Big Fish added some Italian options to its all-seafood menu in the hopes of attracting more people, but the pasta is mainly a starchy diversion. Beware of Friday nights, when Big Fish hooks up with a big happy-hour scene.

See map p. 104. 55 SW Miami Avenue Rd. ☎ 305-373-1770. To get there: Cross the Brickell Avenue Bridge heading south and take the first right on SW Fifth Street; the road narrows under a bridge, and the restaurant is just on the other side. Main courses: $15–$28. AE, DC, MC, V. Open: Daily 11 a.m.–11 p.m.

Caffé Abbracci
$$ **Coral Gables   ITALIAN**

Abbracci's staff serves delightfully prepared food in a fun — if somewhat loud — setting. The menu changes periodically but may include snapper grilled with shiitake mushrooms or *frutti di mare* — an assortment of seafood — in tomato sauce served over linguine. Try the salmon or tuna carpaccio for starters. This place gets really packed on weekends.

See map p. 104. 318 Aragon Ave., Aragon at Salzedo. ☎ 305-441-0700. Reservations required. To get there: Take LeJeune Road/42nd Avenue south from airport, then east on Aragon. Main courses: $16–$28. AE, CB, DISC, MC, V. Open: Mon–Fri 11:30 a.m.–3 p.m. and 6–11:30 p.m.; Sat–Sun 6–11:30 p.m.

Chef Allen's
$$$ **North Miami Beach   AMERICAN CONTEMPORARY**

Foodies flock here for some of the best new-world cuisine in South Florida. And although chef-owner Allen Susser is certainly a star in the culinary world, the food is in the spotlight. Among the standouts are the goat cheese–crusted lamb chops with lentils and roasted peppers, and mesquite-grilled soft-shell crabs with pineapple salsa. Bottom line: Chef Allen's 16-year-old eatery stands out in a place where restaurants get flattened like wildlife on an interstate.

See map p. 102. 19088 NE 29th Ave., just east of U.S. 1/Biscayne Boulevard at 191st Street. ☎ *305-935-2900. Reservations suggested. To get there: Take U.S. 1 north to 191st Street; turn right. Main courses: $24–$35, also $52 prix-fixe menu. AE, DISC, MC, V. Open: Sun–Thurs 6–10:30 p.m.; Fri–Sat 6–11 p.m.*

The Forge
$$$ Miami Beach   AMERICAN

Although this restaurant looks like a leftover set from *Dynasty*, it actually hails way back to the days of Al Capone and his hungry mobsters. The caviar- (Beluga, naturally) and escargot-eating money crowd stops in here regularly, although the atmosphere is more elegant than stuffy. When it comes to entrees, red meat rules at The Forge — from prime rib and the award-winning Super Steak to veal, rack of lamb, buffalo, and venison. There's an impressive wine list, and, if you ask nicely, you'll be able to tour the restaurant's massive wine cellar, where, perhaps, Geraldo Rivera should have looked first when searching for Capone's tomb.

See map p. 102. 432 Arthur Godfrey Rd., ½ mile west of Collins Avenue/A1A. ☎ *305-538-8533. Reservations suggested. To get there: From mainland, take the Julia Tuttle Causeway into its merger with Arthur Godfrey Road. Main courses: $24–$40. AE, DISC, MC, V. Open: Sun–Thurs 6 p.m.–midnight, Sat–Sun 6 p.m.–1 a.m.*

Grillfish
$ South Beach   SEAFOOD

Grillfish manages to pay the exorbitant South Beach rent with the help of a loyal local following who come for fresh, simple seafood in a relaxed but upscale atmosphere. The servers are friendly and know the menu well. The barroom seafood chowder is full of chunks of shellfish, as well as some fresh whitefish filets, all in a tomato broth. The small ear of corn, included with each entree, is about as close as you'll get to any type of vegetable offering besides the pedestrian salad. Still, at these prices, it's worth a visit to try some local fare including mako shark, swordfish, tuna, marlin, and wahoo.

See map p. 98. 1444 Collins Ave. (corner of Espanola Way). ☎ *305-538-9908. Reservations for six or more only. Main courses: $9–$26. AE, DC, DISC, MC, V. Open: Daily 11:30 a.m.–4 p.m. and 5:30 p.m.–midnight.*

Hy-Vong
$ Little Havana   VIETNAMESE

An unlikely spot for a Vietnamese restaurant, Little Havana lucked out big time with this place, where Vietnamese cuisine combines the best of Asian and French cooking with spectacular results. Food at Hy-Vong is elegantly simple and superspicy. Appetizers include small, tightly packed Vietnamese spring rolls and kimchi, a spicy, fermented cabbage. Star entrees include

Miami Beach Dining

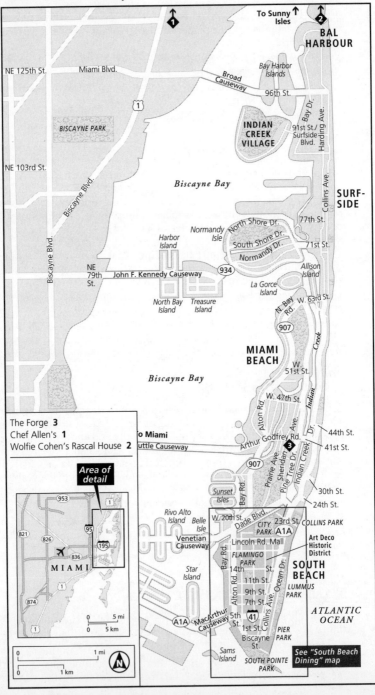

The Forge **3**
Chef Allen's **1**
Wolfie Cohen's Rascal House **2**

pastry-enclosed chicken with watercress cream-cheese sauce and fish in tangy mango sauce. Even though the service stinks and a flight to Vietnam seems shorter than the wait for a table, Hy-Vong should be high on your list of must-eats.

See map p. 104. 3458 SW Eighth St. (between 34th and 35th avenues). ☎ *305-446-3674. Reservations accepted for parties of five or more. To get there: Take 836 West toward the airport and exit at NW 37th Avenue. Take 37th Avenue to NW 14th Street and turn left onto North Douglas Road. Turn left onto SW Eighth Street; the restaurant is on the left. Main courses $9–$19. AE, MC, DISC, V. Open: Tues–Sun 6–11 p.m. Closed two weeks in Aug.*

Joe Allen
$$ Miami Beach AMERICAN

An offshoot of the Manhattan theater-district favorite, Joe Allen's is located on the bay side of the beach, nestled in an unassuming building conspicuously devoid of neon lights, valet parkers, and fashionable pedestrians. Inside, however, one discovers a hidden jewel: a stark yet elegant interior and no-nonsense, fairly priced, ample-portioned dishes such as meatloaf, pizza, fresh fish, and salads. The scene has a homey feel favored by locals looking to escape the hype without compromising quality.

See map p. 98. 1787 Purdy Ave./Sunset Harbor Dr. (3 blocks west of Alton Road), ☎ *305-531-7007. Reservations recommended, especially on weekends. Main courses: $15–$25. MC, V. Open: Mon–Fri 11:30 a.m.–11:30 p.m.; Sat–Sun noon–11:30 p.m.*

Joe's Stone Crab Restaurant
$–$$$$ South Beach SEAFOOD

What a clubby steakhouse is to Chicago, Joe's Stone Crab is to Miami. An institution of maddening proportion, Joe's is possibly the one restaurant in town to get away with accepting no reservations and making people wait upwards of three — that's right, three — hours for a table. Some say Joe's has a monopoly on the best, most succulent stone crabs out there, and we'd venture to agree they're right. For any seafood fan, Joe's is an absolute must.

See map p. 98. 11 Washington Ave. (at Biscayne Street, just south of First Street). ☎ *305-673-0365, or 305-673-4611 for takeout. Reservations not accepted. To get there: Take MacArthur Causeway to Washington Avenue; go right. Market price varies but averages $62.95 for a serving of jumbo crab claws, $38.95 for large claws; other entrees start at under $10. AE, DC, DISC, MC, V. Open: Mid-Oct–mid-May Tues–Sat 11:30 a.m.–2 p.m.; Mon–Thurs 5–10 p.m.; Fri–Sat 5–11 p.m.; Sun 4 p.m.–10 p.m.*

Mark's South Beach
$$$ South Beach MEDITERRANEAN

Located in the basement of the classy Hotel Nash, Mark's provides a shining example of how to run a haute restaurant without turning it into a Studio 54 wannabe. Star chef (and owner) Mark Militello is part of Miami's so-called Mango Gang — the chefs responsible for crafting and perfecting New World Floribbean cuisine. Although his menu changes nightly, what never varies is the consistency and freshness of the restaurant's exquisite

Dining Elsewhere in Miami

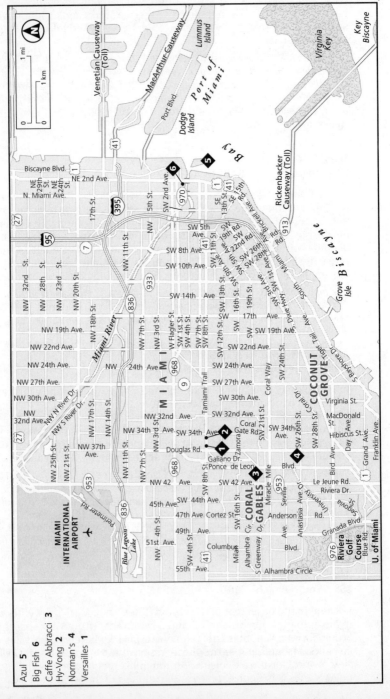

Azul **5**
Big Fish **6**
Caffe Abbracci **3**
Hy-Vong **2**
Norman's **4**
Versailles **1**

New World/Mediterranean dishes. The roasted rack of Colorado lamb with semolina gnocchi is exceptional and worth every bit of cholesterol it may have. Crispy-skin yellowtail snapper with shrimp, tomato, black olives, oregano, and crumbled feta cheese is in a school of its own. Desserts, including an impressive cheese cart, are outrageous, especially the pistachio cake with chocolate sorbet.

See map p. 98. In the Hotel Nash, 1120 Collins Ave. ☎ *305-604-9050. Reservations recommended. To get there: Take the MacArthur Causeway over Biscayne Bay and onto Fifth Street. Turn left on Collins Avenue, and the hotel is on the left. Main courses: $16–$38. AE, DC, DISC, MC, V. Open: Sun–Thurs 7–11 p.m., Fri–Sat 7 p.m.–midnight.*

Metro Kitchen + Bar
$$$ South Beach   FUSION

Metro definitely looks as if it belongs in a metropolis. So does the smart-looking crowd. The cuisine, created by Chef Rob Boone, formerly of Bambu, is a combination of modern American, Asian, French, and Italian cuisines. For dinner, do not miss the tomato tartlette appetizer with Majorero cheese and aged sherry vinegar. For a main course, choose from strip steak with truffle fries — the best fries you'll ever eat, pan-cooked snapper with udon noodles, or duck breast with grilled apples and fresh spinach. On Tuesday nights, Metro becomes a big scene as local luminaries convene here for cocktails, kibitzing, and star spotting.

See map p. 98. In the Hotel Astor, 956 Washington Ave. ☎ *305-672-7217. Reservations recommended. Main courses: $26–$29. AE, DC, DISC, MC, V. Open: Daily 11:30 a.m.– 2:30 p.m.; Sun–Thurs 7 p.m.–midnight; Fri–Sat 7 p.m.–1 a.m.*

Nemo
$$$ South Beach   PAN ASIAN

A funky, high-style eatery, Nemo features an open kitchen and an outdoor courtyard canopied by trees and lined with an eclectic mix of model types and bona-fide foodies. Among the reasons to eat in this restaurant (whose name is actually *omen* spelled backward): grilled Indian spiced pork chop, grilled local mahi with citrus and grilled sweet onion salad, kimchi glaze, basil and crispy potatoes, and an inspired dessert menu by Hedy Goldsmith that's not for the faint of calories.

See map p. 98. 100 Collins Ave. ☎ *305-532-4550. Reservations recommended. To get there: MacArthur Causeway to Fifth Street and make a right on Colllins Avenue. Restaurant is on the right. Main courses: $22–$36; Sun brunch $26. AE, MC, V. Open: Mon–Fri noon–3 p.m. and 7 p.m.–midnight, Sun 11 a.m.–3 p.m. and 6–11 p.m. Valet parking $10.*

Norman's
$$$–$$$$ Coral Gables   NEW WORLD

Owner Norman Van Aken is a perennial award winner, with trophies or at least kudos from *Bon Appétit, Condé Nast Traveler, Food & Wine, Gourmet,*

GQ, the James Beard Foundation, *Wine Spectator,* and Zagat. His restaurant features an open kitchen, a professional staff, and a tasteful atmosphere. The Asian- and Caribbean-inspired dishes definitely delight, including a pork tenderloin served with browned Haitian grits, and venison au poivre. And don't skimp on the front end here, the appetizers — a gazpacho-and-crab cocktail with Grey Goose vodka, for example — are excellent.

See map p. 104. 21 Almeria Ave., 3 blocks south of Miracle Mile, just west of Douglas Road. ☎ 305-446-6767. Reservations recommended. To get there: From the airport, take LeJeune Road/42nd Avenue south to Coral Way/Miracle Mile, go left to 37th Avenue/Douglas, turn right, go 3 blocks to Almeria, turn right. Main courses: $26–$46. AE, CB, DISC, MC, V. Open: Mon–Thurs 6–10 p.m.; Fri–Sat 6–10:30 p.m.

Pacific Time
$$$ South Beach   PACIFIC RIM

Although the Asian-fusion menu at this award-winning establishment often changes, you may find delicacies such as ginger-stuffed catfish tempura, honey-roasted Peking duck, Mongolian lamb salad, and grouper infused with sake and served on a bed of shredded shallots. For dessert, the chocolate bombe is sinfully explosive. There's an extensive wine list.

See map p. 98. 915 Lincoln Rd., between Jefferson and Michigan Avenue. ☎ 305-534-5979. Reservations suggested. To get there: From the mainland, take Venetian Causeway to Alton Road and go right, then left on Lincoln. Main courses: $17–$35. AE, DISC, MC, V. Open: Sun–Thurs 6–11 p.m.; Fri–Sat 6 p.m.–midnight.

Twelve Twenty
$$$ South Beach   AMERICAN PROGRESSIVE

Prepare to shell out a pretty penny for the very haute twist on American and international cuisine that rolls out of this kitchen in the high and mighty Tides Hotel. The air of elegance (perhaps pickled by the scent of money) mixes with the fragrances of dishes such as the blue prawn risotto with black trumpet mushrooms and curry, and warm maple and bourbon smoked salmon. Save room for dessert because you'll want to try the Baked Jamaica — a luscious concoction of coffee and banana macadamia ice creams, English toffee fudge, cinnamon meringue, and dark rum crème anglaise.

See map p. 98. In the Tides Hotel, 1220 Ocean Dr. ☎ 305-604-5130. Reservations recommended. To get there: Take MacArthur Causeway to Fifth Street. Make a left onto Ocean Drive. The hotel is on the left. Main courses: $26–$35. AE, MC, V. Open: Sun–Thurs 7–11 p.m., Fri–Sat 7 p.m.–midnight.

Versailles
$–$$ Little Havana   CUBAN

Versailles is the meeting place of Miami's Cuban power brokers, who get together daily over *cafe con leche* to discuss their exiled destiny. A glorified diner, the place sparkles with glass, chandeliers, murals, and mirrors meant to evoke the French palace. There's nothing fancy here — nothing French, either — just straightforward food from the home country. The menu includes Cuban specialties such as Moors and Christians (flavorful black beans with white rice), *ropa vieja* (a stew with flank steak), and fried whole fish, plus a side helping of Cuban kitsch.

See map p. 104. 3555 SW Eighth St. ☎ 305-444-0240. To get there: Take 836 West toward the airport. Exit at NW 37th Avenue and merge onto NW 14th Street. Turn left on North Douglas Road and left onto SW Eighth Street. Restaurant is on your left. Main courses: $5–$20. DC, DISC, MC, V. Open: Mon–Thurs 8 a.m.–2 a.m., Fri 8 a.m.–3:30 a.m., Sat 8 a.m.–4:30 a.m., Sun 9 a.m.–1 a.m.

Wolfie Cohen's Rascal House
$ Miami Beach/Sunny Isles   DELI

Open since 1954 and still going strong, this historic, nostalgic delicatessen extravaganza is one of Miami Beach's greatest traditions. Scooch into one of the ancient vinyl booths — which have hosted many a notorious bottom, from Frank Sinatra's to mob boss Sam Giancana's — and review the huge menu that's loaded with authentic Jewish staples. Consider the classic corned beef sandwich, stuffed cabbage, brisket, or potato pancakes. If you're lucky, the snarky waitress will give you a wax-paper doggy bag to wrap up the leftover rolls and Danish from your breadbasket.

See map p. 102. 17190 Collins Ave. ☎ 305-947-4581. To get there: Take I-95 to Ives Dairy Road. Make a right on Ives Dairy and go east on the William Lehman Causeway. Turn right onto Collins Avenue, and the restaurant is on the right. Main courses: $8–$30. AE, MC, V. Open: Daily 7 a.m.–1 a.m.

Chapter 10

Exploring Miami

$\bullet$ $\bullet$

In This Chapter

▶ Visiting must-see attractions and sights

▶ Playing and watching your favorite sports

▶ Taking a guided tour

▶ Shopping your way through Miami

▶ Having some after-dark fun

$\bullet$ $\bullet$

After you've had a chance to catch your breath and suck down some calories, it's time to start soaking in the sun and, the inevitable, turning turnstiles. In this chapter, I start with the day shift, exploring some of Miami's top attractions, museums, and parks. I also give you some shopping pointers. Then, as the sun sinks into the Everglades, I start painting the town whatever color suits you.

Seeing the Top Sights

Miami offers a lot more than sunny stretches of sand and silicone. No matter how you want to spend your day — touring museums or strolling through gardens of exceptional beauty — you'll find something here that will hold your attention. (Check out the "Central Miami Attractions" map if you want to see where the sights are in relation to each other.)

Biscayne National Park

Mangroves, coral reefs, and tiny keys form this 181,000-acre refuge, located 30 miles south of Miami. Hikers can take advantage of 1½- and 7-mile trails through Elliott Key's hardwood hammocks and mangroves, but you have to hitch a boat ride ($26) from the park's concessionaire, **Biscayne National Underwater Park** (☎ **305-230-1100**). Other possibilities include renting a canoe ($9 an hour, $24 a half-day), taking a glass-bottom boat tour ($24.45 adults, $19.45 seniors, $16.45 kids under 12; 10 a.m. and 1 p.m. daily), going on a snorkeling trip ($35 including gear, 1:30 and 5:30 p.m.), and going scuba diving ($54 for a two-tank dive including tanks, 8:30 a.m.). Reservations are recommended for boat tours. With the time it takes to

Attractions in South Miami–Dade County

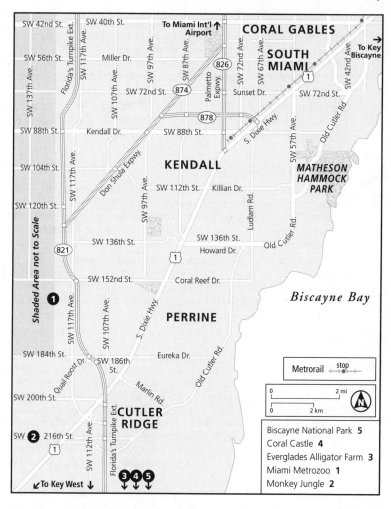

reach the park, allow all day to see it. If you really want to commune with nature, camping fees are $15 per night.

See map p. 109. 9700 SW 328th St., Convoy Point Visitor Center. ☎ **305-230-7275** *or 305-230-1100.* www.nps.gov/bisc *and* www.biscayne.national-park.com. *To get there: Take the Florida Turnpike and its Homestead extension south to Exit 6 (Speedway Boulevard), go left to SW 328th/North Canal Drive, go left again and continue about 5 miles to the entrance on the left. Admission: Free, but there are concession fees (see preceding information). Open: Daily 8 a.m.–5:30 p.m*

Coral Castle

There's plenty of competition, but Coral Castle is probably the strangest attraction in Florida. In 1923, the story goes, a 26-year-old crazed Latvian, suffering from unrequited love of a 16-year-old who left him at the altar, immigrated to South Miami and spent the next 25 years of his life carving huge boulders into a prehistoric-looking roofless "castle." Plan to spend 1½ to 2 hours and make sure to hum along to Billy Idol's "Sweet Sixteen," inspired by this very bizarre place.

See map p. 109. 28655 S. Dixie Hwy./U.S. 1. ☎ *305-248-6344.* www.coralcastle. com. *To get there: Take U.S. 1 south to SW 286th Street. Admission: $9.75 adults, $6.50 seniors 62 and older, $5 kids 7–11. Open: Daily 7 a.m.–9 p.m.*

Everglades Alligator Farm

Take a noisy airboat tour of a spread that's home to more than 3,000 creepy, surprisingly sedate specimens that seem to live off a diet of Lithium. Don't miss the "Weird Animal Show," starring freaks of reptilian nature. Allow 4½ to 5 hours including the 2-hour round-trip drive from downtown Miami.

See map p. 109. 40351 SW 192nd Ave., 2 miles west of Florida Turnpike. ☎ *305-247-2628.* www.everglades.com. *To get there: Follow U.S. 1 south to Palm Drive/SW 344th Street, go west/left to SW 192nd Avenue, left to entrance. Admission: $17 adults, $10 kids 4–10 ($5 less if you don't want to ride the airboat). Open: Daily 9 a.m.–6 p.m.*

Miami Metrozoo

This 290-acre, sparsely landscaped complex (it was devastated by Hurricane Andrew) is about 45 minutes from Miami proper and the beaches but worth the trip. Isolated and never really crowded, its also completely cageless — animals are kept at bay by cleverly designed moats. Favorite denizens include the Komodo dragons and white Bengal tiger. This is a fantastic spot to take younger kids — the older ones seem bored and unstimulated here. For the touchy-feely set, there's a wonderful petting zoo and play area, and the zoo offers several daily programs designed to educate and entertain. At a comfortable pace, you can see the zoo in about four hours.

See map p. 109. 12400 SW 152nd St., at 124th Avenue. ☎ *305-251-0400.* www.miami metrozoo.com. *To get there: Take U.S. 1 south to 152nd Street/Coral Reef Drive, go right/west past the Florida Turnpike to 124th. Admission: $12 adults, $7 kids 3–12. Open: Daily 9:30 a.m.–5:30 p.m.*

Miami Museum of Science and Space Transit Planetarium

This is the final — and only — frontier for sci-fi fans, with more than 140 hands-on exhibits that explore mysteries of the universe. Live demonstrations and collections of rare natural-history specimens make a visit here enjoyable and informative. Many of the demos involve audience participation, which can be lots of fun for kids and adults alike. There is also a Wildlife Center with more than 175 live reptiles and birds of prey. At the adjacent Space Transit Planetarium, astronomy and laser shows pulsate to the tune of the Dave Matthews Band and Pink Floyd. Call, or visit their Web site, for a list of upcoming exhibits and laser shows. Allow three to four hours, depending on how long you want to play.

See map p. 114. 3280 S. Miami Ave./Bayshore Dr., south of Rickenbacker Causeway. ☎ *305-646-4200 or 305-646-4420 (planetarium show times).* www.miamisci.org. *To get there: It's on South Miami/Bayshore, just south of the Rickenbacker Causeway. Admission: $10 adults, $8 seniors and students, $6 kids 3–12, half-price after 4:30 p.m. Open: Daily 10 a.m.–6 p.m.*

Miami Seaquarium

If you've been to Orlando's SeaWorld, you may be disappointed with Miami's version, which is considerably smaller and not as well maintained. You'll need at least three hours to tour the 35-acre oceanarium and see all four daily shows starring a number of showy ocean mammals. You can cut your visit to two hours if you limit your shows to the better, albeit corny, Flipper Show and Killer Whale Show. The highly regarded Water and Dolphin Exploration Program (WADE) allows visitors to touch and swim with dolphins in the Flipper Lagoon. The program costs $140 per person and is offered twice daily, Wednesday through Sunday. Children must be at least 52 inches tall to participate. Reservations are necessary for this program. Call ☎ **305-365-2501** in advance for reservations.

See map p. 114. 4400 Rickenbacker Causeway, in Biscayne Bay. ☎ **305-361-5705.** www.miamiseaquarium.com. *To get there: Take the causeway from U.S. 1 near Little Havana and go east halfway across Biscayne Bay. Admission: $24.95 adults, $19.95 kids 3–9. An annual pass is just $5 more per person. Open: Daily 9:30 a.m.–6 p.m.*

Monkey Jungle

Ever see a monkey in heat? You will here. You'll also see rare Brazilian golden lion tamarins and Asian macaques. No cages restrain the primates as they swing, chatter, and play their way into your heart — and nose (see the following paragraph). Screened-in trails wind through acres of "jungle," and daily shows feature the park's most talented pupils. People who go here are not monkeying around — many of the park's frequent visitors are scientists and anthropologists.

This place is not for the faint of smell, but if primates are your thing, you'll be in paradise here. If you're forced here against your will, bring nose plugs. Allow two and a half hours to see the park.

See map p. 109. 14805 SW 216th St., between South Miami and Homestead. ☎ *305-235-1611.* www.monkeyjungle.com. *To get there: Take U.S. 1 south to Cutler Ridge and head west 2 miles on 216th Street. Admission: $15.95 adults, $12.95 kids 4–12. Open: Daily 9:30 a.m.–5 p.m.*

Parrot Jungle Island

This Miami institution took flight from its lush, natural South Miami environment and headed north in the winter of 2003 to a new, overly fabricated, disappointing $46 million home on Watson Island, along the MacArthur Causeway near Miami Beach. While the island doubles as a protected bird sanctuary, the jungle's former digs in the heart of South Miami in a circa-1900 coral rock structure were a lot more charming and kitschier. The new, overpriced 19-acre park features an Everglades exhibit, a petting zoo, and several theaters, jungle trails, and aviaries. Watch your heads because flying above are hundreds of parrots, macaws, peacocks, cockatoos, and flamingos. But it's not all a loss. Be sure to check out the Crocosaurus, a 20-foot-long saltwater crocodile who hangs out in the park's Serpentarium, which also houses the park's reptile and amphibian collection. You can see it all in three to four hours.

See map p. 114. 1111 Parrot Jungle Trail, Miami. ☎ *305-2JUNGLE.* www.parrot jungle.com. *To get there: Take McArthur Causeway toward the beaches, follow signs. Admission: $23.95 adults, $21.95 kids 3–10. Open: Daily 9:30 a.m.–6 p.m.*

Villa Vizcaya Museum and Gardens

Sometimes referred to as the "Hearst Castle of the East," this magnificent villa was built in 1916 as a winter retreat for James Deering, cofounder and former vice president of International Harvester. Packed with European antiques and art from the 16th to the 19th centuries, the ornate mansion took 1,000 artisans five years to complete. Most of the original furnishings, including dishes and paintings, are still intact. You will see very early versions of a telephone switchboard, central vacuum cleaning system, elevators, and fire sprinklers. A free guided tour of the 34 furnished rooms on the first floor takes about 45 minutes. The second floor, which consists mostly of bedrooms, is open to tour on your own. Outside, lush formal gardens, accented with statuary, balustrades, and decorative urns, front an enormous swath of Biscayne Bay. Definitely take the tour of the rooms, but immediately thereafter, you'll want to wander and get lost in the resplendent gardens. Allow two to two and a half hours, more if you're really into art and architecture.

See map p. 114. 3251 S. Miami Ave./Bayshore Dr. ☎ *305-250-9133. To get there: It's on South Miami/Bayshore, south of the Rickenbacker Causeway. Admission: $12 adults, $5 kids 6–12. Open: Daily 9:30 a.m.–5 p.m.*

Finding More Cool Things to See and Do

For those who prefer to opt out of the Crocodile Hunter mode of sightseeing, there's an army of things to do in Miami that are less expensive and more leisurely. Some of these appeal to folks who have special interests — whether that means being an art buff, a golfer, an avid fisherman, or a pro-sports fan.

Visiting museums, gardens, parks, and more

Some of Miami's best museums and parks not only provide you with a wonderful day's entertainment and education, they do it for much less than many of the city's more popular attractions.

✔ **Barnacle State Historic Site,** 3485 Main Hwy., Coconut Grove (☎ **305-448-9445;** www.floridastateparks.org/thebarnacle), was built in 1891 as the home of naval architect Ralph Munroe and is now a museum in the heart of Coconut Grove. It's the oldest house in Miami and rests on its original foundation, which sits on 5 acres of hardwood and landscaped lawns. The house's quiet surroundings, wide porches, and period furnishings illustrate how Miami's first snowbird lived in the days before condo-mania and luxury hotels. Enthusiastic and knowledgeable state park employees offer a wealth of historical information to those interested in quiet, low-tech attractions like this one. Call for details on the fabulous monthly moonlight concerts during which folk, blues, or classical music is presented and picnicking is encouraged. It's open Friday through Monday from 9 a.m. to 4 p.m.; admission is $1. See map p. 114.

✔ At **Bill Baggs Cape Florida State Park,** 1200 S. Crandon Blvd., Key Biscayne (☎ **305-361-5811;** www.floridastateparks.org/cape florida), at the southern tip of Key Biscayne about 20 minutes from downtown Miami, you can explore the unfettered wilds and enjoy some of the most secluded beaches in Miami. There's also a historic lighthouse that was built in 1825, which is the oldest lighthouse in South Florida. A rental shack leases bikes, hydro-bikes, kayaks, and many more water toys. It's a great place to picnic, and a newly constructed restaurant serves homemade Latin food, including great fish soups and sandwiches. Bill Baggs has been consistently rated as one of the top ten beaches in the U.S. for its 1¼ miles of wide, sandy beaches and its secluded, serene atmosphere. Admission is $5 per car with up to eight people (or $3 for a car with only one person; $1 to enter by foot or bicycle). It's open daily from 8 a.m. to sunset. Tours of the lighthouse are available every Thursday through Monday at 10 a.m. and 1 p.m. Arrive at least an hour early to sign up — there's only room for ten people on each. See map p. 114.

✔ **Holocaust Memorial,** 1933 Meridian Ave., Miami Beach (☎ **305-538-1663**), stands out with Kenneth Triester's *Sculpture of Love and Anguish,* depicting victims of the concentration camps crawling up a giant, yearning hand. Along the reflecting pool, marble slabs relate the story of the Holocaust. At the center of the memorial, a tableau provides a solemn and moving tribute to the millions of Jews who lost their lives. You can walk through an open hallway lined with photographs and the names of concentration camps and their victims. From the street, you'll see the outstretched arm, but do stop and tour the sculpture at ground level. Open daily from 9 a.m. to 9 p.m. Admission is free. See map p. 114.

Central Miami Attractions

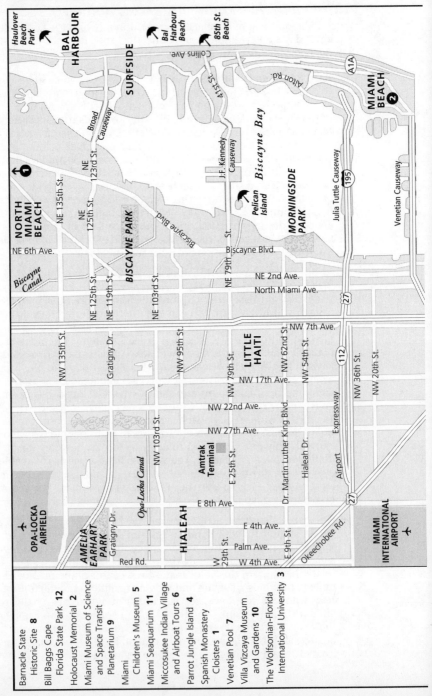

Barnacle State
Historic Site **8**
Bill Baggs Cape
Florida State Park **12**
Holocaust Memorial **2**
Miami Museum of Science
and Space Transit
Planetarium **9**
Miami
Children's Museum **5**
Miami Seaquarium **11**
Miccosukee Indian Village
and Airboat Tours **6**
Parrot Jungle Island **4**
Spanish Monastery
Cloisters **1**
Venetian Pool **7**
Villa Vizcaya Museum
and Gardens **10**
The Wolfsonian–Florida
International University **3**

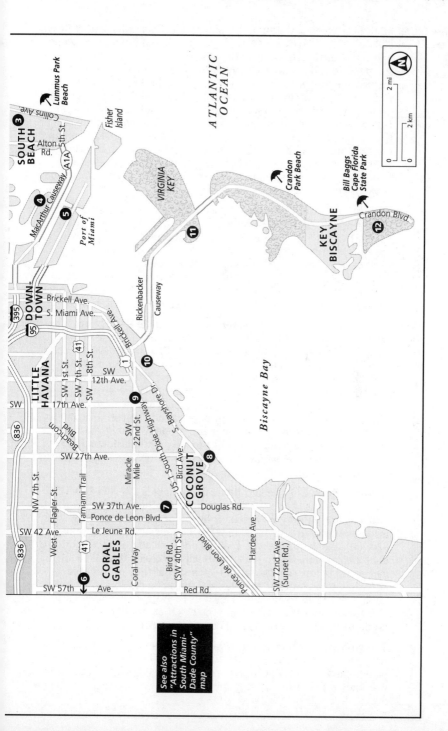

ATLANTIC OCEAN

Lummus Park Beach

SOUTH BEACH ❸

Collins Ave.

5th St.

Alton Rd.

A1A

MacArthur Causeway ❹

❺

Fisher Island

Port of Miami

VIRGINIA KEY

Crandon Park Beach

Bill Baggs Cape Florida State Park

KEY BISCAYNE

Crandon Blvd. ⓬

❶❶

395

DOWN-TOWN

Brickell Ave.

S. Miami Ave.

95

Rickenbacker

Causeway

Biscayne Bay

Brickell Ave.

41

LITTLE HAVANA

SW 1st St.

SW 7th St.

SW 8th St.

SW 12th Ave.

❶ ⓾

SW 17th Ave.

SW

❾

SW 22nd St.

836

Beacom Blvd.

SW 27th Ave.

Miracle Mile

US-1 South Dixie Highway

S. Bayshore Dr.

Bird Ave.

COCONUT GROVE ❽

NW 7th St.

Flagler St.

Tamiami Trail

SW 37th Ave.

Ponce de Leon Blvd.

❼

Douglas Rd.

Hardee Ave.

SW 42 Ave.

Le Jeune Rd.

Ponce de Leon Blvd.

836

41

CORAL GABLES

Coral Way

Bird Rd. (SW 40th St.)

Red Rd.

SW 72nd Ave. (Sunset Rd.)

❻

SW 57th Ave.

2 mi

2 km

0

0

See also "Attractions in South Miami-Dade County" map

✔ **Miami Children's Museum,** 980 MacArthur Causeway, Miami Beach (☎ **305-373-5437**; www.miamichildrensmuseum.org), this brand-new museum, located across the MacArthur Causeway from Parrot Jungle Island, is a modern, albeit odd-looking, Swiss-cheese inspired facility. Kids-only activities and exhibitions related to the arts, culture, community, and communication include a miniature Bank of America and Publix Supermarket and a re-creation of the NBC 6 television studio. There's also a re-creation of a Carnival Cruise ship and even a port stop in a re-created Brazil. Perhaps the coolest thing of all is the World Music Studio, in which aspiring Britneys, Justins, and Lenny Kravitzes can lay down a few tracks and play instruments. Open daily from 10 a.m. to 6 p.m. Admission is $8 for adults and children. See map p. 114.

✔ **Miccosukee Indian Village and Airboat Tours,** U.S. 41, 30 miles west of Miami (☎ **305-223-8380**; www.miccosukeeresort.com/mivillage.html), offers airboat rides, guided tours, alligator-wrestling demonstrations, and Native American arts and crafts exhibits. And because the village lies on a reservation, you'll also find cheap cigarettes and legal gambling. Open daily from 9 a.m. to 5 p.m. Admission is $10 for adults, $7 for children 7 to 14; kids under age 6 are free. Airboat rides are $10 per person. See map p. 114.

✔ The **Spanish Monastery Cloisters,** 16711 W. Dixie Hwy., North Miami Beach (☎ **305-945-1461**), is allegedly the oldest building in the Western Hemisphere, dating back to 1133. Erected in Segovia, Spain, the cloisters were eventually purchased by newspaper magnate William Randolph Hearst who brought them to America in pieces. The carefully numbered stones were quarantined for years until they were finally reassembled on the present site in 1954. It has often been used as a backdrop for movies and commercials and is a very popular tourist attraction. Open Monday through Saturday 10 a.m. to 4 p.m. and Sunday from 1 to 5 p.m. Admission is $5 for adults, $2.50 for seniors 55 and older, and $2 for kids 11 and under. See map p. 114.

✔ **Venetian Pool,** 2701 DeSoto Blvd., Coral Gables (☎ **305-460-5356**; www.venetianpool.com), lets you follow in the strokes of Esther Williams and Johnny Weissmuller by taking a dip in this pool, which is fed by underground artesian wells. During summer, the pool's 820,000 gallons of water are drained and refilled nightly, ensuring a cool, *clean* swim. Hours vary seasonally so check their Web site or call ahead before you go, but be warned that they're sometimes *very* slow to answer the telephone. Admission is $6.25 to $9.50 for adults, and $3.25 to $5.25 for kids 3 to 12. *Note:* Kids under 3 are not allowed to enter the facility, and the Venetian pool does not accept credit or debit cards (cash and check only). See map p. 114.

✔ The **Wolfsonian-Florida International University,** 1001 Washington Ave., Miami Beach (☎ **305-531-1001**; www.wolfsonian.fiu.edu), boasts the eclectic collection of pack rat Mitchell Wolfson, Jr., who was known to horde everything from controversial Nazi propaganda to King Farouk of Egypt's match collection. Also thrown in the diverse mix are zany works from great modernists such as Charles Eames and Marcel Duchamp. Open Tuesday and Friday through Saturday from 11 a.m. to 6 p.m., Thursday from 11 a.m. to 9 p.m., and Sunday from noon to 5 p.m. Admission is $5 adults, $3.50 students and seniors. See map p. 114.

Golfing

Golf is everywhere in Miami, and you can channel your inner Tiger Woods at a number of excellent courses. For golfing information online, haul your clubs over to www.golf.com and www.floridagolfing.com. If you like surfing the old-fashioned way, request course information from the **Florida Sports Foundation** (☎ 850-488-8347) or from **Florida Golfing** (☎ 877-222-4653). Here are just a few of the courses you can play while in Miami:

- ✔ **Don Shula's Golf Club,** 7601 Miami Lakes Dr., Miami Lakes (☎ 305-820-8106; http://golf.donshulahotel.com), has a flat course with plenty of water and tight, tree-lined fairways. It's a par-72. Greens fees are $40 to $145 in winter, $40 to $65 in summer.

- ✔ **Doral Resort Silver Course,** 5001 NW 104th Ave., Miami (☎ 305-477-1906; www.doralgolf.com/golf/courses.asp), is a par-71 that tests all facets of your game with bunkers, lakes, and trees. The "Island Hole" is the course's signature. Greens fees are $115 and up in winter, $45 to $65 during the summer.

- ✔ **Doral Resort Gold Course,** 4400 NW 87th Ave., Miami (☎ 305-592-2030; www.doralgolf.com/golf/courses.asp), is the home of the challenging "Blue Monster." It's a par-70. Greens fees are $115 and up in winter, $70 to $85 in the summer.

- ✔ **Golf Club of Miami,** 6801 Miami Gardens Dr., Miami (☎ 305-829-8449), offers a course designed by Robert Trent Jones, Sr., that may be Miami's best value. Greens fees are $66 to $85 in winter, under $25 in the summer.

- ✔ **Melreese International Links,** 1802 NW 37 Ave., Miami (☎ 305-633-4583), has 97 bunkers and 6 acres of water. Fairways have rolling hills and lots of sand. Greens fees are $66 to $85 during winter, $25 to $40 in the summer.

- ✔ Fairmont **Turnberry Isle Resort & Club,** 19999 W. Country Club Dr., Aventura (☎ 305-932-6200; www.fairmont.com/turnberryisle/), has a pair of Robert Trent Jones, Sr.–designed courses (par-70 and -72) and a reputation as a golfer's paradise. Greens fees are $95 to $130 and up winter, $25 to $65 summer.

Watching the big-league teams

The Miami area has franchises in each of the major sports. The line-up is as follows:

✔ **Florida Marlins:** Pro Player Stadium, 2269 NW 199th St., Miami (☎ **305-623-6100;** www.flamarlins.com). The Sunshine State's lovable worst-to-first-to-worst-to-first Major League Baseball team was assembled, and then dismantled by founding owner Wayne Huizenga. The Marlins won the '97 World Series, only to find Big Wayne shedding the huge payroll he amassed to win it, which left the team sucking cellar lint. They then showed him who's boss by beating the NY Yankees in 2003. It's a fun roller coaster ride, to say the least. The Marlins play their regular season home games here from April to September. Tickets cost $2 to $45.

✔ **Florida Panthers:** National Car Rental Center, One Panther Parkway, Fort Lauderdale (☎ **954-835-8275;** www.flpanthers.com). What do Miami and ice hockey have in common? Nothing. The team doesn't even play in the city proper. But that's close enough for Miamians to think it's theirs. The National Hockey League season runs November to April. It will set you back $14 to $65 to cheer from the stands.

✔ **Miami Dolphins:** Pro Player Stadium, 2269 NW 199th St., Miami (☎ **305-623-6100;** www.miamidolphins.com). It's been a long time since 1972's perfect season, but fan support remains high — high enough that it's hard to get tickets to the eight regular-season home games (Sept–Jan) or the preseason. And it isn't cheap either: A ticket costs $27 and up — way up!

✔ **Miami Heat:** American Airlines Arena, 601 Biscayne Blvd., Miami (☎ **305-577-4328;** www.nba.com/heat). The Heat hoopsters entered the National Basketball Association in the 1988–89 season and spent the first two years digging out of the cellar. By their tenth season they had 50 wins in an 82-game schedule and their second Atlantic Division title. In 2004, the Heat acquired their biggest win by scoring **Shaquille O'Neal,** whose celebrity has made a Heat ticket one of Miami's, uh, hottest. The season runs November through May. Tickets run from $14 to $150.

Fishing

Several saltwater species are common to all South Florida, including trout, snook, Spanish and king mackerel, sailfish, grouper, and snapper.

Charters for small groups (up to four people) begin at about $225 per half-day and $400 for eight hours of inshore fishing and about double that for deep-sea excursions. Rates on large party boats usually start at $25 ($40 for all day). Here are a couple places where you can get a guide for your fishing expedition:

✔ Internet users can get plenty of information at **Florida Charter Captains** online (www.fishfla.com), which breaks the state into several regions and profiles guides in each area.

✔ The cheekily titled **Sea Vous Play** in the Crandon Park Marina on Key Biscayne (☎ 305-361-7600) will take you out on various fishing charters with expert guides.

Laying down some bets

You can wager your hard-earned money on the athletic ability of humans or animals at several places. There is live and simulcast action at:

✔ **Calder Race Course** (☎ 305-625-1311), 2269 NW 199th St., Miami. Horse racing.

✔ **Flagler Greyhound Track** (☎ 305-649-3000), 401 NW 38th Court, Miami. Dog racing.

✔ **Gulfstream Park** (☎ 305-931-7223), at U.S. 1 and Hallandale Beach Boulevard, North Miami Beach. Horse racing.

✔ **Miami Jai Alai Fronton** (☎ 305-633-6400), 3500 NW 37th Ave., Miami. Looks like lacrosse, but it's called jai alai (pronounced hi-a-*lie*).

Seeing Miami by Guided Tour

If you want to leave decision-making to someone else, Miami has several organized tour options.

Bus tours

The oldest and arguably one of the most reliable operators is **Miami Nice Excursions,** 18430 Collins Ave., Miami Beach (☎ 305-949-9180). The company offers knowledgeable guides and will pick you up from your hotel. Minibus tours range from city sightseeing ($29–$95 for adults, $25 for kids 4–12) to longer and more expensive ones that travel to Key West, the Everglades, and the Kennedy Space Center. Beware, however, that your tour is only as good as your guide and, truth be told, Miami Nice has been known to hire a few that aren't so, uh, nice.

The best tour for the morbidly curious, however, is the **Murder, Mystery, and Mayhem Bus Tour,** Miami-Dade Cultural Center, 101 W. Flagler St., Miami (☎ 305-375-1621), in which you'll play witness to Miami's most celebrated crimes. From the killing spree of the Ashley Gang to the murder of designer Gianni Versace, historian Paul George conducts a fascinating tour of scandalous proportions. Tickets are $37 and advance reservations are strongly suggested.

Walking tours

The **Biltmore Hotel Tour,** 1200 Anastasia Ave., Coral Gables, is a free guided overview (Sundays only at 1:30, 2:30, and 3:30 p.m.) of the history, mystery and, yes, ghosts, attached to this wonderful old hotel. You must make a reservation by calling ☎ 305-445-1926.

A really quacky tour

It's not exactly a luxury yacht like JLo's or Puffy's, but that's okay because it's fun. The **Miami Duck Tours,** in which massive "vesicles" — part car, part boat — in the shape of ducks tool up to 49 passengers around Miami on land and sea. The ducks are actually cooler than your average yacht because they drive on land and sail in the water. Tickets are $24 adults, $21 seniors, and $17 children. Reserve your seat on the, uh, duck, by calling ☎ **877-DUCKTIX.**

The **Miami Design Preservation League,** 1001 Ocean Dr., South Beach (☎ **305-672-2014**), conducts 90-minute guided tours of the Art Deco District on Thursdays at 6:30 p.m. and Saturdays at 10:30 a.m. ($10). If a self-guided tour is more your speed, the league offers an audiotape tour seven days a week for a cost of $10.

Boat tour

The *Heritage of Miami II* topsail schooner, Bayside Marketplace Marina, 401 Biscayne Blvd., Miami (☎ **305-442-9697**), will sail you around the city for two hours, passing by Villa Vizcaya, Coconut Grove, and Key Biscayne and putting you in sight of Miami's spectacular skyline and million-dollar waterfront homes. Tickets for day tours are $20 adults, $15 children 12 and under. September through May only. Tours leave daily at 1:30, 4, and 6:30 p.m., and Friday through Sunday also at 9, 10, and 11 p.m.

Shopping

What to do in Miami when it rains? Go to a mall! With a dozen malls and a crush of other retail centers, Miami is a shopping mecca for Florida, the Southeast, and the Caribbean. Best of all, the area offers more than tourist trinkets. The 10 million people who visit every year lug home everything from hand-rolled cigars to electronics to imports from the Caribbean.

Before I outline Miami's neighborhoods and the shops you can find in them, here are a few basic ground rules:

✔ Most stores are open from 10 a.m. to 6 p.m. Monday through Saturday and noon to 5 p.m. Sunday. Those in malls and major shopping centers keep their doors open as late as 9 or 10 p.m. except on Sunday. Stores on South Beach run on their own, wacky schedules, usually not opening before 11 a.m. and closing near midnight.

✔ The state and local sales taxes add 6.5 percent to all purchases except food and medicine.

> ✔ If you don't want to haul it home with you, most stores will ship your purchase for you, though I recommend using some discretion. If you don't know the store, it's safer to make your own arrangements through a carrier such as UPS (☎ **800-742-5877**), or the post office (skip ahead to "Fast Facts" for more on mailing packages).

Burning some bucks

When you feel the urge to splurge on a shopping spree, here are the best places to empty your wallet:

- ✔ **Aventura:** All shopaholics need to know about Aventura is that it's home to the mammoth **Aventura Mall** (see "Crawling through the malls," later in this chapter).

- ✔ **Calle Ocho:** Little Havana's main shopping district is **"Eighth Street"** between SW 27th and SW 12th avenues. In addition to tantalizing smells, you can find everything from hand-rolled cigars to traditional Cuban shirts known as *guayaberas* to Latin CDs and tapes.

- ✔ **Coconut Grove:** The Grove's roomy sidewalks, particularly **along Main Highway and Grand Avenue,** are very shopper-friendly. You can find them lined with cafes as well as hippy and hipster boutiques, mass-marketed clothiers à la the Gap and Banana Republic, and import stores for shopping or browsing. The Grove is also the home of **CocoWalk** (see the following section on malls).

- ✔ **Coral Gables/Miracle Mile:** Actually, it's the Miracle Half-Mile, and it's peppered with not-so-trendy men's and women's clothing stores. Your best bet here is to browse the cool furniture shops and then spend your money on one of the area's excellent restaurants.

- ✔ **Downtown Miami:** If you like to bargain, **Flagler Street** west of Biscayne Boulevard is a good place to try your luck finding watches and jewelry, luggage, shoes, and other leather goods. But it's also a place where you can get hustled if you're not careful.

- ✔ **South Beach:** Some hip clothing stores (Von Dutch, Barneys Co-Op, Urban Outfitters, Armani Exchange, Benetton, and others) line **Collins and Washington avenues** between Sixth and Ninth streets, which also are good places to see Art Deco architecture. The seven-block **Lincoln Road Mall** offers a dizzying array of cafes and clone-producing chain shops (Gap, Banana, Victoria's Secret, bebe, and so on).

Crawling through the malls

Because most of Miami's shopping gets done in malls that could qualify as neighborhoods in and of themselves, here are a few of the best in town:

- ✔ **Aventura Mall:** This mega mall — 250 stores fill up 2.3 million square feet — is home to retail giants such as Bloomingdale's, Macy's, and Lord & Taylor as well as smaller local outfits. Stock up some energy at the mall's plethora of restaurants, or let your kids run down their batteries inside the mall's playground. The complex also has a 24-screen movie theater. Biscayne Boulevard and 196th Street, Aventura (☎ 305-935-1110; www.shopaventuramall.com).

- ✔ **Bal Harbour Shops:** The Rodeo Drive of Miami, Bal Harbour's headliners include Neiman Marcus, Saks Fifth Avenue, Cartier, Prada, Dolce & Gabbana, Chanel, Armani, Christian Dior, Gucci, and Tiffany. It's worth a look even if you can't afford the lofty prices. 9700 Collins Ave., Bal Harbour (☎ 305-866-0311; www.balharbour shops.com).

- ✔ **Bayside Marketplace:** This waterside shopping à la New York City's South Street Seaport area features all the mall regulars, including Sam Goody, Speedo Fitness, and Sharper Image. 401 Biscayne Blvd., Miami (☎ 305-577-3344; www.baysidemarketplace.com).

- ✔ **CocoWalk:** In addition to such name tenants as Banana Republic and Victoria's Secret, this mini outdoor mall has specialty stores selling cigars, books, cutlery, clothing, fragrances, and more. It also has a movie theater and several outdoor cafes. 3015 Grand Ave., Coconut Grove (☎ 305-444-0777; www.cocowalk.com).

- ✔ **The Falls:** This outdoor mall is worth the hike if you're going south and are in the market for Macy's, Bloomingdale's, Coach, and The Disney Store. If not, they're flanked by 100 other shops, a few restaurants, and a movie theater. 8888 SW 136th St., Miami (☎ 305-255-4570; www.thefallsshoppingcenter.com).

- ✔ **Village of Merrick Park:** This mammoth upscale outdoor shopping complex features Nordstrom, Neiman Marcus, Armani, Gucci, Jimmy Choo, and Yves St. Laurent, to name a few. 4425 Ponce de León Blvd. (between Ponce de León Boulevard and Le Jeune Road, just off the Mile), Coral Gables. (☎ 305-529-0200; www.villageof merrickpark.com).

You can find scores of other places to test your credit line or liquidate your traveler's checks at **Miami International Mall,** State Road 836 at NW 107th Avenue. (☎ 305-593-1775), and **Dadeland Mall,** Kendall Drive at U.S. 1 (☎ 305-655-6226).

Living It Up After Dark

After the sun goes down, Miami really raises the decibel level, the disco ball, and the night owls. You can boogie down, rhumba and samba, or just swill and chill. For an up-to-date scorecard, see the *Miami Herald's* "Weekend" section on Fridays. Tickets for specific events, concerts, plays, and other performances can be booked through **Ticketmaster** (☎ 305-358-5885; www.ticketmaster.com).

Toasting the town

If a mixed drink is more your style than mixing it up on the dance floor, you can find many bars waiting to launch you on alcoholic adventure.

- ✔ The **Clevelander Hotel,** 1021 Ocean Dr., South Beach (☎ **305-531-3485**), has the quintessentially South Beach bar with swimming pool, neon, glass blocks, plastic cups, out-of-towners, a beachy feel, and (best of all) no cover charge. Drinks are half-price from 5 to 7 p.m., Monday through Friday.

- ✔ **The Forge,** 432 41st St., Miami Beach (☎ **305-538-8533**), is an opulent, Dynasty-esque restaurant/bar known for its fabulous people watching, especially on Wednesday, which is "models" night. Call well in advance if you want a table so you can gawk while you eat. There's no cover.

- ✔ **Mac's Club Deuce,** 222 14th St., Miami Beach (☎ **305-673-9537**), is the quintessential dive bar, with cheap drinks and a cast of characters ranging from your typical barfly to your atypical drag queen. It's got a well-stocked jukebox, friendly bartenders, a pool table, and best of all, it's an insomniac's dream, open daily from 8 a.m. to 5 a.m.

- ✔ **Mynt,** 1921 Collins Ave., Miami Beach (☎ **786-276-6132**), is nothing more than a huge living room in which models, celebrities, and assorted hangers-on bask in the green glow to the beats of very loud lounge and dance music. If you want to dance — or move, for that matter — this is not the place in which to do so. It's all about striking a pose in here.

- ✔ **The Room,** 100 Collins Ave., Miami Beach (☎ **305-531-6061**), is an intimate, candlelit beer and wine bar with vintages and brews hailing from all over the world. The crowd is laid back, mature, and decidedly local.

- ✔ **Rose Bar at the Delano,** 1685 Collins Ave., South Beach (☎ **305-672-2000**), is one of the hottest of the many beach bars. The in crowd and its wannabes hang at the Rose or on its deck. The drinks are rather pricey, but there's no cover.

- ✔ **Tobacco Road,** 626 S. Miami Ave., Miami (☎ **305-374-1198**), is small and gritty and meant to be that way. Escape the smoke and sweat in the backyard patio, where air is a welcome commodity. Live music, cheap drinks, good food, and interesting characters are what make this, the owner of Miami's very first liquor license, one of the city's favorite bars.

Clubbing

South Beach, and, lately, downtown Miami, offer some of the hottest — and often snootiest — dance clubs in America. To get past the velvet rope, dress hip (such as wearing black) and arrive before midnight. Check out the following:

- ✔ **Club Space,** 142 NE 11th St., Miami (☎ 305-577-1007), is a cavernous, converted warehouse consisting of over 30,000 square feet of, uh, its namesake, in which you can twirl around all night — literally (it has an all-night liquor license) — to the tunes of the planet's hottest dance, techno, and electronic DJs. Cover ranges from free to $20.

- ✔ **Crobar,** 1445 Washington Ave., South Beach (☎ 305-531-8225), has raised the bar on South Beach nightlife with crazy theme nights, top-name DJs, and the occasional celebrity appearance. On Sunday, the club hosts an extremely popular gay night known as Anthem. Cover ranges from $15 to $25.

- ✔ **La Covacha,** 10730 NW 25th St., Miami (☎ 305-594-3717), is the hottest Latin joint in the city. Sunday features the best in Latin rock, with local and international acts. But the shack is really jumping on weekends when it stays open until 5 a.m. Friday is *the* night here.

- ✔ **Mansion,** 1235 Washington Ave., South Beach (☎ 305-532-1525), is the newest member of the Opium (see below) group of hauter than thou nightclubs in which a multilevel uber lounge complete with wood flooring and brick walls draws the who's who of gossip columns and *Access Hollywood*. Cover ranges from $20 to $30.

- ✔ **Nikki Beach Club,** 101 Ocean Dr., South Beach (☎ 305-538-1111), is an outdoor oasis that seems very Brady Bunch goes to Hawaii, with a sexy tiki hut/Polynesian theme, albeit rated R. The Sunday afternoon beach party is almost legendary and worth a glimpse — that is, if you can get in. Cover ranges from $10 to $20.

- ✔ **Opium Garden,** 136 Collins Ave., South Beach (☎ 305-531-5535), is a highly addictive nocturnal habit for those looking for a combination of sexy dance music, scantily clad dancers, and, for masochists, an oppressive door policy in which two sets of velvet ropes are set up to keep those deemed unworthy out of this open-air, see-and-be-scenery den of inequity. Cover ranges from $10 to $30.

- ✔ **Rumi,** 330 Lincoln Rd., South Beach (☎ 305-672-4353), is a very good restaurant with an even better late-night scene that's home to hipsters, celebs, and lounge lizards. No cover.

Pursuing splashes of culture

It may be more acclaimed for its clubs and bars, but Miami does have a respectable number of cultural institutions. If Beethoven and Bach have more appeal than technoelectronica, you won't have a problem finding a place to hear a little night music.

The **Concert Association of Florida,** 555 17th St., South Beach (☎ 305-532-3491; www.concertfla.org), is always up to speed on upcoming performances. Season after season, world-renowned dance companies and seasoned virtuosi (Itzhak Perlman, Andre Watts, and Kathleen Battle, to name a few) punctuate its schedules.

Miami is also home to three excellent symphonic orchestras:

- ✔ The **Florida Philharmonic Orchestra,** 1243 University Dr., Miami (☎ 800-226-1812), is the best of its kind in South Florida.

- ✔ The **Miami Chamber Symphony,** 5690 N. Kendall Dr., Kendall (☎ 305-672-0552; www.miamisymphony.org), features international soloists.

- ✔ The **New World Symphony,** 541 Lincoln Rd., South Beach (☎ 305-673-3331; www.nws.org), is under the direction of Michael Tilson Thomas, who leads the gifted young musicians in performances, many of which are free.

The **Florida Grand Opera,** 1200 Coral Way, Miami (☎ 800-741-1010 or 305-854-1643; www.fgo.org), will open a new headquarters in mid-2005. The respected company features top singers from America and Europe.

The highly acclaimed **Miami City Ballet,** Ophelia and Juan Js. Roca Center (2200 Liberty Ave.), Miami Beach (☎ 305-929-7000; www.miamicity ballet.org), runs through a repertoire of more than 60 ballets in a given season.

Fast Facts

Area Code

Miami's two area codes are **305** and **786**. All local calls made inside Miami-Dade County require ten-digit dialing: the area code plus the seven-digit local number. Calls from Miami to the Keys (see Chapter 11), which are in the 305 area code, require a 1 + 305 or 0 + 305 preceding the seven-digit number. Those will be billed as long distance.

Hospitals

HealthSouth Doctors' Hospital, 5000 University Drive in Coral Gables (☎ 305-666-2111) has a 24-hour emergency department.

Mail

U.S. post offices are located at 2200 NW 72nd Ave., Miami (west of the airport); 1300 Washington Ave., South Beach; and 3191 Grand Ave., Coconut Grove. To locate other postal offices, call ☎ 800-275-8777.

Maps

The information sources listed in the previous section are great ones to hit up for maps before or after you land. (Trust me: Good maps are necessities because getting lost in Miami is easy, and this city's bad neighborhoods are no place to get lost in.) Rental-car agencies are another good source (including those at the airport) and so are convenience stores, which sell maps for $3 to $5.

Newspapers

The *Miami Herald* (www.herald.com) is the major daily, and visitors shouldn't miss the paper's "Weekend" entertainment guide, which comes out on Friday. There's also a Spanish-language paper, *El Nuevo Herald* (www.elherald.com).

Safety

Miami is a large city and has all the crime that you would normally associate with a major metropolis. I don't recommend walking alone after dark; be wary about driving anywhere in downtown Miami. Stick to well-lit and known tourist areas, and even then, be aware of your surroundings. Keep your eyes peeled for bright-orange sunbursts on highway exit signs; they will direct you to tourist-friendly zones. Use a map (see preceding information on maps) to familiarize yourself with the city and make sure you know where you're going and your route before driving anywhere. Never stop on a highway and get out of your car if you can avoid it, and always keep your doors locked. Some car-rental agencies will rent you a cellphone for the duration of your trip; this way you can get immediate assistance if you need it.

Taxes

The sales and local-option taxes throughout Miami-Dade County add 6.5 percent to most purchases except medicines and groceries.

The hotel and restaurant taxes push the total to between 9.5 and 12.5 percent.

Taxis

It's $1.50 to $3 to start the meter and $2 for each mile. See Chapter 9 for details.

Transit Info

For Metrorail and Metromover schedule information call ☎ 305-770-3131 or visit www.co.miami-dade.fl.us/transit. See Chapter 9 for more transit information.

Weather Updates

For a recording of current conditions and forecast reports, call the local office of the National Weather Service at ☎ 305-229-4522, or check out the national office's Web site at www.nws.noaa.gov. You can also get information by watching the Weather Channel (www.weather.com).

Chapter 11

Unlocking the Keys

In This Chapter

▶ Orienting yourself with the Keys
▶ Snorkeling and diving for sunken treasure in Key Largo
▶ Fishing for snapper, grouper, and marlin in Islamorada
▶ Swimming with dolphins in Marathon
▶ Getting back to nature in the Lower Keys
▶ Visiting Hemingway's retreat in Key West

S outh Florida has two kinds of conchs: those that land in chowder and those that land where they please. The latter — Florida Keys natives — are born with a birthright to go against the grain and indulge in a little wacky behavior — traits that are carried out to the *n*th degree in the Keys' southernmost city, Key West.

The most famous of Florida's islands, Key West has threatened to secede from the Union and establish a Conch Republic three times (and counting). The top pastimes in Key West are fishing and getting fried (in a Bacardi sense), and not necessarily in that order. It's a city whose melting-pot character has long made Key West a home for pirates, preachers, gun runners, and gays, all of whom live more or less peacefully on a 3½-mile sandbar some locals call "paradise."

Of course, paradise isn't for everyone, including those Conchs (pronounced *konks*) who settled to the north in towns and on islands with far less razzle-dazzle but an equal amount of charm.

In this chapter, I show you the many faces of the Keys, including those where the only action is diving after a 300-year-old shipwreck, landing a tarpon, or swimming with dolphins.

Getting There

Most folks fly into the Keys because flying is convenient and usually economical. However, if you'll also be sightseeing elsewhere in Florida (especially the Miami area, which is about four hours from Key West), the scenic, albeit oftentimes trafficky, drive on U.S. 1/the Overseas Highway can become part of your travel experience as well.

By plane

If you're visiting the Upper or Middle Keys, your best bet is to book a flight to **Miami International Airport** (☎ **305-876-7000;** www.miami-airport.com) and then rent a car to drive to Key Largo, Islamorada, or Marathon. The airport is served by more than 100 airlines, including 42 foreign carriers, and virtually every car-rental agency in the U.S. (see the Appendix for rental-agency telephone numbers and Web sites; see Chapter 9 for more airport information).From Miami International Airport, it's a three- to four-hour drive to the Lower Keys and Key West, depending on the traffic. If you want to avoid the long commute, lock onto a commuter flight from Miami International Airport to **Key West International** (☎ 305-296-7223), which is about 25 minutes south of the Lower Keys. This airport is served by about a half-dozen major carriers or their partners, as well as Avis, Hertz, Budget, and Dollar. (See the Appendix for rental-agency telephone numbers and Web sites.)

By car

From the Florida/Georgia border to Key Largo is 500 miles. From the north, take the Florida Turnpike south along the East Coast. Just after Fort Lauderdale, take Exit 4 — the Turnpike Extension, which is marked for Homestead/Key West. This goes to U.S. 1 in Florida City, the only road into the Keys.

From the West Coast, come across I-75 (Alligator Alley) to the Miami exit and go south to the Turnpike Extension.

Alligator Alley is not the best of roads, so make sure to check your tires and fill up your tank before you get on it. Cellphone reception here is slim to none, so be sure to have all necessary equipment available in the event of a flat tire. Also, if at all possible, drive it during daylight hours only. You wouldn't want to get stuck here at night — there are no lights and no gas stations, and the only watering holes around are those that are populated by alligators and assorted swamp-life.

The drive from Miami to the Keys is a scenic, yet often congested, three to four hours. From Miami International Airport, take LeJeune Road south to Highway 836 West and the Turnpike Extension; then go south to U.S. 1 and the Keys.

By train

Even rail fans find that train travel to the Keys is time-consuming. **Amtrak** (☎ **800-872-7245;** www.amtrak.com) has two trains leaving daily from New York — that's the good news. The bad news: They take 30 hours to reach Miami (the furthest south they go); you'll then have to get on a bus to reach the Keys. In addition, rail prices aren't much cheaper than airfare (and they cost more if you want a sleeper). Amtrak's Miami station is 5 miles from the airport, which is where you'll find the best rental-car options.

Getting a Clue about the Keys

Although 400 islands are spread across this 150-mile chain, only a few dozen are inhabited, and fewer yet are developed into something a mainstream tourist would want to see. I subdivided them into five miniregions: Key Largo, Islamorada, Marathon, the Lower Keys, and Key West. You'll find them in the same sequence if you drive from the mainland, traveling from Florida City on U.S. 1. Skip ahead to the map of the Florida Keys for an overview of the area.

Getting Around

Think car. Trains, public transit, and taxis that travel the entire length of the islands are nonexistent in the Keys. With the possible exception of Key West, the only way to get around is by car or on one of those you-have-to-go-where-we-want-to-go tours. See Chapter 4 for more on package tours.

After you exit the mainland, U.S. 1 (the Overseas Highway) is the only route through the island chain — the Keys' version of Main Street. Given one highway and the liberal use of mile markers for addresses and reference points (skip ahead to the next paragraph in this section for more information), it's next to impossible to get lost driving in the Keys, unless — due to the Mob, the IRS, or your ex-spouse — you *want* to get lost. The speed limit throughout the Keys is no higher than 55 mph, and there are occasional passing lanes. Reaching the Upper Keys from Miami is a piece of cake, but if you're going farther south, driving gets tedious, sometimes aggravating. If you have the time and budget and you want to drive down U.S. 1, consider taking two days to travel from one end to the other.

The best way to find something in the Keys is to know the mile marker (MM) that's nearest that destination. Often used in place of addresses, the little green mile-marker signs adorn the roadside every mile, starting south of Florida City with MM 127 and running south to MM 1 in Key West. For a general guide to the Mile Marker system, see Table 12-1.

Table 12-1	The Keys' Mile-Marker Guide		
City	*Mile Marker*	*Miles from Miami*	*Driving Time from Miami*
Key Largo	110–87	58	1½ hours
Islamorada	86–66	76	2 hours
Marathon	65–40	111	2½ hours
Lower Keys	39–9	128	3 hours
Key West	8–0	159	4 hours

The Florida Keys

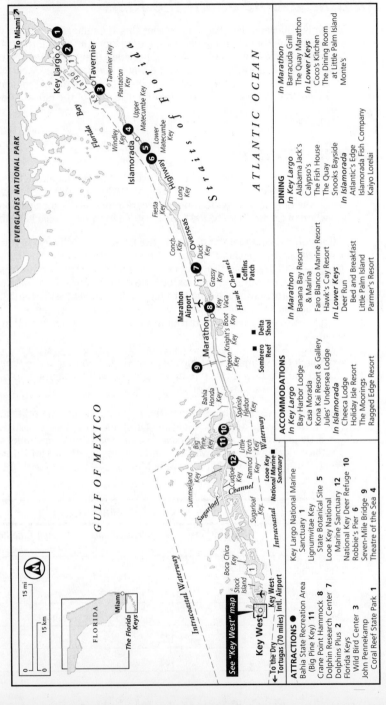

DINING

In *Marathon*
Barracuda Grill
The Quay Marathon
In *Lower Keys*
Coco's Kitchen
The Dining Room
   at Little Palm Island
Monte's

In *Key Largo*
Alabama Jack's
Calypso's
The Fish House
The Quay
Snooks Bayside
In *Islamorada*
Atlantic's Edge
Islamorada Fish Company
Kaiyo Lorelai

ACCOMMODATIONS

In *Key Largo*
Bay Harbor Lodge
Casa Morada
Kona Kai Resort & Gallery
Jules' Undersea Lodge
In *Islamorada*
Cheeca Lodge
Holiday Isle Resort
The Moorings
Ragged Edge Resort

In *Marathon*
Banana Bay Resort
   & Marina
Faro Blanco Marine Resort
Hawk's Cay Resort
In *Lower Keys*
Deer Run
   Bed and Breakfast
Little Palm Island
Parmer's Resort

ATTRACTIONS ●
Bahia State Recreation Area
   (Big Pine Key) **11**
Crane Point Hammock **8**
Dolphin Research Center **7**
Dolphins Plus **2**
Florida Keys
   Wild Bird Center **3**
John Pennekamp
Coral Reef State Park **1**

Key Largo National Marine
   Sanctuary **1**
Lignumvitae Key
   State Botanical Site **5**
Looe Key National
   Marine Sanctuary **12**
National Key Deer Refuge **10**
Robbie's Pier **6**
Seven-Mile Bridge **9**
Theatre of the Sea **4**

Key Largo

The Upper Keys are a refuge for many South Floridians who love the region's laid-back lifestyle and lack of congestion. Convenient to Miami but heavily built up, Key Largo is a favorite of saltwater fishermen and scuba divers, with many outfitters, motels, and restaurants catering to their needs.

Spending the night

The first and largest Florida Key, Key Largo offers a wide variety of accommodations, from chain hotels to full-scale resorts. Most hotels are right off U.S. 1 or on the waterfront. Since the accommodations generally combine a laid-back atmosphere with extensive facilities, you can do as much or as little as you want. Unless otherwise noted, all listings include air-conditioning, televisions, a pool, and free parking. As with much of coastal Florida, winter (Dec–Apr) is peak season. And don't forget to add an additional 11.5 percent room tax to your hotel rate.

Bay Harbor Lodge
$-$$ Key Largo

A small, simple retreat that's big on charm, the Bay Harbor Lodge is an extraordinarily welcoming place. The motel rooms are small and ordinary in decor, but even the least expensive is recommendable. The efficiencies are larger motel rooms with fully equipped kitchenettes. Larger still, the oceanfront cottages have full kitchens and represent one of the best values in the Keys. The 1½ lush acres of grounds are planted with banana trees and have an outdoor heated pool and several small barbecue grills. A small beach is ideal for quiet sunning and relaxation, and guests can use the rowboats, paddleboats, canoes, kayaks, and snorkeling equipment. Bring your own beach towels.

See map p. 130. 97702 Overseas Hwy., MM 97.7. ☎ *800-385-0986 or 305-852-5695.* www.thefloridakeys.com/bayharborlodge. *To get there: Bayside. Rack rates: Dec–Apr $55–$195; May–Nov $75–$135. MC, V.*

Casa Morada
$$$-$$$$ Key Largo

This 16-suite boutique hotel is tucked away off a sleepy street and radiates serenity and style in an area where serenity is aplenty but style elusive. Originally built in the 1950s, Casa Morada sits on 1.7 acres of prime bay-front land, which was upgraded with gorgeous landscaping, a limestone grotto, a freshwater pool, a waterside terrace for breakfast, lunch, and poolside beverage service, and a bocce ball court. Each of the cool rooms features either a private garden or terrace — request the one with the open air Jacuzzi that faces the bay. While the decor is decidedly island, think St. Barts rather than, say, Gilligan's. Although the hotel doesn't have a restaurant, a complimentary breakfast is served daily, and if you order out from one of the area's excellent restaurants, the hotel will replate the food on Casa Morada china.

See map p. 130. 136 Madeira Rd., MM 82.2. ☎ ***888-881-3030*** *or 305-664-0044. Fax: 305-664-0674.* www.casamorada.com. *To get there from U.S. 1 S, at MM 82.2, turn right onto Madeira Road, and continue to the end of the street. Hotel is on your right. Rack rates: Dec–Apr $199–$419; May–Nov $179–$349. AE, DISC,MC, V.*

Kona Kai Resort & Gallery
$$–$$$ Key Largo

The quintessential Keys retreat, this 11-unit resort overlooks the Gulf and sits on 2 beautifully landscaped acres — the antidote to your typical mass-marketed chain hotel. Lounge chairs, hammocks, a Jacuzzi, and a compact beach are available for those who just want to relax (no phones in the rooms make relaxing imperative), while the owners will organize excursions to the Everglades, the backcountry, or wherever for the more adventurous. All the rooms are very private and simply furnished; bathroom amenities are fabulous, with lotions, soaps, and shampoos made from tropical fruits. An art gallery featuring work by American and international painters, photographers, and sculptors doubles as the property's office and lobby. *Note:* Children under age 16 are not permitted.

See map p. 130. 97802 Overseas Hwy.., MM 97.8. ☎ ***800-365-7829*** *or 305-852-7200. Fax: 305-852-429.* www.konakairesort.com. *To get there: Go towards the bay on Ocean Drive. Rack rates: Dec–Apr $149–$259; May–Nov $159–$192. AE, DISC, MC, V.*

Jules' Undersea Lodge
$$$$ Key Largo

Staying here is certainly an experience of a lifetime — if you're brave enough to take the plunge. Originally built as a research lab in the 1970s, this small underwater compartment (which rests on pillars on the ocean floor) now operates as a two-room hotel. As expensive as it is unusual, Jules' is most popular with diving honeymooners. To get inside, guests swim 21 feet under the structure and pop up into the unit through a 4-by-6-foot "moon pool" that gurgles soothingly all night long. The 30-foot-deep underwater suite consists of two separate bedrooms that share a common living area. Room service will deliver your meals, daily newspapers, even a late-night pizza in waterproof containers at no extra charge.

See map p. 130. 51 Shoreland Dr., MM 103.2 (oceanside). ☎ ***305-451-2353.*** *Fax: 305-451-4789.* www.jul.com. *Rack rates: $295–$395 per person. Rates include breakfast, dinner, equipment, and diving. AE, DISC, MC, V.*

Dining locally

This is a seafood lover's destination. During the season, many restaurants offer Florida lobster. The local favorites also include grouper, trout, swordfish, tuna, mahimahi, and crab. If you're not a seafood lover, don't worry: All restaurants offer meat and poultry entrees. And don't forget to try a slice of Key lime pie — it's almost a mandatory dessert in the Keys. *Note:* All Florida restaurants and food-serving bars are smoke-free.

Calypso's
$ **Key Largo** SEAFOOD

The awning still bears the name of the former restaurant, Demar's, but the food here is all Todd Lollis's, an inspired young chef who looks like he may be more comfortable at a Grateful Dead concert than in a kitchen, but who turns out inventive seafood dishes in a casual and rustic waterside setting. The prices are surprisingly reasonable, but the service can be a little more laid back than you're used to.

See map p. 130. 1 Seagate Blvd., MM 99.5. ☎ *305-451-0600. To get there: Turn towards the bay at the blinking yellow lights near MM 99.5 to Ocean Bay Drive and then turn right. Look for the blue vinyl-sided building on the left. Main courses $9–$18. MC, V. Open: Wed–Mon 11:30 a.m.–10 p.m.; Fri and Sat until 11 p.m.*

The Fish House
$–$$ **Key Largo** SEAFOOD

This fun spot serves up great local seafood. Conch (in a salad, floating in chowder, or fried) is one headliner. So are oysters, shrimp, and yellowtail snapper. Keep your eye on the back door to see what local fisherman are bringing in for the day. The service is fast and the atmosphere relaxed, even whimsical, making it a good spot to bring the kids. If you want to bring the catch of the day back home with you, there's a fish market on premises.

See map p. 130. 102401 U.S. 1/Overseas Hwy., MM 102.4 (oceanside). ☎ *888-451-4665 or 305-451-4665. Reservations aren't accepted. Main courses: $5–$14 lunch, $9–$27 dinner; kids' menu $5–$10. AE, DISC, MC, V. Open: Daily 11:30 a.m.–10 p.m.*

The Quay
$$–$$$ **Key Largo** SEAFOOD/STEAKS

This waterfront restaurant offers dining with a spectacular view of the Keys' famous sunsets. You can chow down on seafood (broiled lobster tails, blackened swordfish) or meat dishes (prime rib) in the air-conditioned indoor dining room. Outside, the Dockside Bistro offers conch, prawns, and steaks.

See map p. 130. 102050 U.S. 1/Overseas Hwy., MM 102 (bayside, just past the Holiday Inn). ☎ *305-451-0943. Reservations accepted. Main courses: $12–$31 ($11–$15 dockside). AE, DISC, MC, V. Open: daily 4–10 p.m.*

Snooks Bayside
$$ Key Largo AMERICAN

Snooks daily menu and Sunday brunch feature seafood, steaks, chicken, and veal, complemented by a nice wine list. The dining room has a view of Florida Bay, and an outdoor terrace accommodates fresh-air fans. The casual atmosphere makes it a kid-friendly kind of place.

See map p. 130. 99470 U.S. 1/Overseas Hwy., MM 99.9. ☎ *305-453-3799. Reservations suggested. To get there: Look for it at Key Largo's only traffic light, by Marina Del Mar Bayside. Main courses: $15–$28. AE, DISC, MC, V. Open: Mon–Sat 11:30 a.m.–10:30 p.m., Sun 10 a.m.–10:30 p.m.*

Exploring Key Largo

Much of the doings here are related to water — Florida Bay to the west and the Atlantic Ocean to the east.

Dolphins Plus
Key Largo

One of a few swim-with-the-dolphins programs around the Keys, Dolphins Plus gives you a briefing before you get into the water. This is a dolphin-contact sport. You need to be a good swimmer (despite the flotation vest that you're required to wear) and comfortable in water that's taller than you are. There are three swims daily at 8:30 a.m., 12:45 p.m. and 3 p.m. If dolphins aren't your thing, a sea lion swim program is offered seven days a week at 9:15 a.m. and 1:15 p.m. for anyone 7 years or older. If you just want to watch, you can do it from high and dry. Allow two hours.

See map p. 130. 31 Corinne Place. ☎ *305-451-1993.* www.dolphinsplus.com. *To get there: Go towards the ocean at the stoplight at MM 99.9, go 1 block, take the first right, go another block, then left on Ocean Shores Drive, and go several blocks to a bridge, turning right just before it. Admission: dolphin swim $160 (minimum age: 10); sea lion swim $75 (minimum age 7); $10 to observe either swim ($5 for kids 7 and older). Open: Daily 9 a.m.–5 p.m.*

Florida Keys Wild Bird Center
Tavernier

Wander through lush canopies of mangroves on narrow wooden walkways to see the large variety of native birds, including broad-wing hawks, great blue and white herons, roseate spoonbills, white ibis, cattle egrets, and pelicans. A not-for-profit center, it serves as a hospital for birds that have been injured by accident or disease. Visit at feeding time, usually about 3:30 p.m., when you can watch the dedicated staff feed the hundreds of hungry beaks. Allow 30 to 60 minutes; more if there's a photographer in your group.

See map p. 130. 93600 U.S. 1/Overseas Hwy., MM 94 (bayside). ☎ *305-852-4486.* www.fkwbc.org. *To get there: The bird sculptures will point the way. Admission: Donation. Open: Daily 8:30 a.m.–6 p.m.*

John Pennekamp Coral Reef State Park

The first underwater preserve in the country, this 188-square-mile sanctuary protects part of the only living coral reef in the continental United States. Start off at the visitor center, which has a large saltwater aquarium that re-creates a reef ecosystem. At the adjacent dive shop, you can rent snorkeling and diving equipment, and join one of the boat trips that depart for the reef throughout the day. Along the reef, much of the water is shallow enough that snorkelers can easily see its 40-something varieties of coral, 650 species of fish, and *Christ of the Deep,* a 9-foot, 4,000-pound bronze sculpture that stands in 25 feet of water. Not getting wet is a shame, but if you insist on staying dry, take the glass-bottom boat tour. Boaters will also enjoy exploring the blue-green waters, with rentals of 19- to 28-foot motorboats offered by the hour ($27–$50), half-day ($90–$185), and full-day ($160–$325). For most visitors, this is an all-day outing.

See map p. 130. U.S. 1/Overseas Highway, MM 102.5 (oceanside, just a tad south of where U.S. 1 comes from the mainland). ☎ *305-451-1202 or 305-451-1621.* www.pennekamp.com. *Admission: $4 for a vehicle plus 50¢ per passenger; $1.50 for foot soldiers or bicyclists. Open: Daily 8 a.m.–5 p.m.*

Touring the waters

Arguably, the Keys offer some of the finest underwater fun anywhere in the United States. Even if you're not a certified scuba diver or lack the time to get certified here, you can still enjoy it. All it takes is a mask, snorkel, and fins. **John Pennekamp Coral Reef State Park** (described in the preceding section) and **The Key Largo National Marine Sanctuary** (☎ **305-451-1621;** www.fknms.nos.noaa.gov) are Key Largo's signature underwater sights. The sanctuary is heaven for divers, who'll love Molasses Reef's abundant sea life and the Elbow, which has several shipwrecks.

In addition to the dive shop at John Pennekamp, other area outfitters include **Conch Republic Divers,** MM 90.3 (☎ **800-274-3483** or 305-852-1655; www.conchrepublicdivers.com), and **Keys Diver Snorkel Tours,** MM 100 (☎ **888-289-2402** or 305-451-1177; www.keysdiver.com). Prices vary, but snorkel tours start at $35, and dive tours, at $65.

Boaters should also head for **John Pennekamp Coral Reef State Park,** described earlier in this chapter. Call ☎ **305-451-1202** or 305-451-6325 for details.

Fishing is another favorite Keys pastime. Sport fish, such as bonefish, tarpon, and marlin, are plentiful here, as are tasty treats such as grouper, yellowtail snapper, and red snapper. Inshore rates generally are $225 for a half-day and $400 for eight hours. Double that price for deep-sea expeditions. Charter operators include **Back Country Adventures** (☎ **305-451-1247**) and **Sailor's Choice** (☎ **305-451-1802**).

Shopping for local treasures

Unless you're looking to stock up on T-shirts and cheesy souvenirs, don't come to Key Largo to shop, with the following exceptions:

✔ **Key Lime Products,** 95231 U.S. 1/Overseas Hwy., MM 95 oceanside (☎ **305-853-0378**), sells some funky items made from the namesake fruit. The shelves are lined with the usual (pies, jellies, and candy), as well as more unusual gifts (hair- and skin-care products, pasta, cheesecakes, salsa, and soap).

✔ For a real Keys-style shopping experience, head for the **weekend flea market** held Saturday and Sunday at MM 103.5 (☎ **305-664-4615**). Dozens of vendors sell a wide variety of merchandise — antiques, T-shirts, shoes, books, among others — from 9 a.m. to 5 p.m.

Living it up after dark

Folks tend to party here at any hour, acting under the premise that it's 5 p.m. somewhere on the planet. Most of the action is at motel bars. Other options include **Snapper's Waterfront Saloon & Raw Bar,** 139 Seaside Ave., MM 94.5 oceanside (☎ **305-852-5956**), which is open nightly and usually has a band on weekends. **Snook's Bayside** (see the listing under "Dining locally" earlier in this chapter) has a guitar player on Thursday night and combos on Friday and Saturday.

Islamorada

The next major key south of Key Largo is not going to dethrone Walt Disney World as the top tourist draw, but Islamorada ("the purple island") has a lot of daytime fun and even a few places to keep you entertained at night. The unofficial capital of the Upper Keys, it has the area's best atmosphere, food, and lodging. You can find more fishing boats per square mile here than in any other vacation destination. Oh yes, it's pronounced *eye*-lah mor-*ah*-dah.

Spending the night

Sport fishing rules in Islamorada, and the hotels and resorts cater to the anglers who come to participate in annual fishing events or to just kick back and enjoy the emerald waters. Depending on your budget, you can choose from several accommodations options in Islamorada, including camping, guesthouses, bed-and-breakfast inns, and resorts.

Unless otherwise noted, all listings include air-conditioning, televisions, a pool, and free parking. As with much of coastal Florida, winter (Dec–Apr) is peak season. Also, remember to add an additional 11.5 percent room tax to your hotel rate.

Cheeca Lodge
$$–$$$$ Islamorada

Opened in 1949, the lodge remains one of the better places to turn out the lights in the Keys. Located on 27 acres of beachfront property (the 1,100-foot palm-lined beach is truly idyllic), this rambling resort is known for its excellent sports facilities, including one of the only golf courses in the Upper Keys. All rooms are spacious and have small balconies. For adults, there's the state-of-the-art Avanyu health spa and fitness center, and for kids, their own customized vacation with Camp Cheeca's organized activities and events. Most recently the lodge added brand-new beach bungalows with private balconies.

See map p. 130. U.S. 1/Overseas Highway at MM 82 (oceanside). ☎ *800-327-2888 or 305-664-4651. Fax: 305-664-2893.* www.cheeca.com. *Rack rates: May–Nov $129–$1,225; Nov–May $149–$1,600. AE, CB, DC, DISC, MC, V.*

Holiday Isle Resort
$$–$$$$ Islamorada

One of the biggest resorts in the Keys, the Holiday Isle attracts a spring-break kind of crowd year-round. The huge complex encompasses five restaurants, several lounges, a large marina, many retail shops, and four distinct (if not distinctive) hotels. Its Tiki Bar claims to have invented the rumrunner drink (151-proof rum, blackberry brandy, banana liqueur, grenadine, and lime juice), and there's no reason to doubt it. Hordes of partiers are attracted to the resort's nonstop merrymaking, live music, and beachfront bars. As a result, some of the accommodations can be noisy. Rooms can be bare-bones budget to oceanfront luxury, as the broad range of prices reflects. Even the nicest rooms could use a good cleaning. El Captain and Harbor Lights, two of the least-expensive hotels on the property, are both austere. Like the other hotels here, rooms could use a thorough rehab. Howard Johnson's, another Holiday Isle property, is a little farther from the action and a tad more civilized. If you plan to stay a few days, choose an efficiency or a suite; both have kitchenettes.

See map p. 130. U.S. 1 at MM 84 (oceanside). ☎ *800-327-7070 or 305-664-2321. Fax 305-664-2703.* www.holidayisle.com. *Rack rates: Nov–May $130–$420; May–Nov $110–$410. AE, DISC, MC, V.*

The Moorings
$$$–$$$$$ Islamorada

Staying at The Moorings is more like residing at a secluded beach house than at a hotel. You'll never see another soul on this 18-acre resort if you choose not to. There isn't even maid service unless you request it. The romantic whitewashed units, from cozy cottages to three-bedroom houses, are spacious and modestly decorated. All have full kitchens, and most have washers and dryers. Some have CD players and VCRs; ask when you book. The real reason to come to this resort is to relax on the more than

1,000-foot beach (one of the only real beaches around). This is a place for people who like each other a lot. Leave the kids at home unless they are extremely well behaved and not easily bored.

See map p. 130. 123 Beach Rd. near MM 81.5 (oceanside). ☎ *305-664-4708. Fax: 305-664-4242.* www.themooringsvillage.com. *Rack rates: Nov–May $185–$475; May–Nov $200–$375. MC, V.*

Ragged Edge Resort
$–$$ Islamorada

This small oceanfront property's 11 units are spread out along more than half a dozen gorgeous, grassy waterfront acres. All are immaculately clean and comfortable, and most are outfitted with full kitchens and tasteful furnishings. There's no bar, restaurant, or staff to speak of, but the retreat's affable owner, Jackie Barnes, is happy to lend you bicycles or good advice on the area's offerings. A large dock attracts boaters and a good variety of local and migratory birds.

See map p. 130. 243 Treasure Harbor Rd. near MM 86.5 (oceanside). ☎ *800-436-2023 or 305-852-5389.* www.ragged-edge.com. *Rack rates: Nov–May $79–$199; May–Nov $49–$142. AE, MC, V.*

Dining locally

Seafood isn't the only show in town, but passing up the chance to have it so fresh is a shame. Also, if you want to increase your dining choices, shop for restaurants in Key Largo, which is discussed earlier in this chapter, and Marathon, coming up a bit later. **Don't forget:** All Florida restaurants and food-serving bars are smoke-free.

Alabama Jack's
$ Key Largo SEAFOOD

On its own, there's not much to the waterfront shack that is **Alabama Jack's.** The bar serves beer and wine only, and the restaurant specializes in delicious, albeit, greasy bar fare. But this quintessential Old Floridian dive, located in a historic fishing village called Card Sound, located between Homestead and Key Largo, is a colorful must on the drive south, especially on Sundays, when bikers mix with line dancers and Southern belles who look as if they just got off the *Hee Haw* set in all their fabulous frill.

See map p. 130. 5800 Card Sound Rd. (U.S. 1 turns off to Card Sound Road at Homestead and Key Largo). ☎ *305-248-8741. Main courses: $5–$10. AE, DC, DISC, MC V. Open: Mon–Fri 11 a.m.–7 p.m., Sat 2 p.m.–5 p.m., Sun 2 p.m.–7 p.m.*

Atlantic's Edge
$$$ Islamorada SEAFOOD

This may be the fanciest restaurant in the Keys, but that's relative — a sports jacket for men may even be a bit too much. Steaks, chicken, pasta, and rack of lamb keep landlubbers happy, but seafood rules this ocean-front restaurant's menu. Specialties include mahimahi and Thai-spiced snapper. Everything is fresh, and the service is professional. The chef will cook the fish you caught that afternoon for $15 per person.

See map p. 130. 81801 U.S. 1/Overseas Hwy. at MM 82 in the Cheeca Lodge. ☎ *305-664-4651. Reservations suggested. Main courses: $20–$36. AE, CB, DC, DISC, MC, V. Open: Daily 6–10 p.m.*

Islamorada Fish Company
$–$$ Islamorada SEAFOOD

The original Islamorada Fish Company has been selling seafood out of its roadside shack since 1948. It's still the best place to pick up a cooler of stone crab claws in season (mid-Oct–Apr). Also great are the fried-fish sandwiches, served with melted American cheese, fried onions, and coleslaw. A few hundred yards up the road (at MM 81.6) is Islamorada Fish Company Restaurant & Bakery, a newer establishment. Although it looks like an average diner, it serves fantastic seafood and pastas. It's also the place for breakfast. Locals gather for politics and gossip as well as delicious grits, oatmeal, omelets, and homemade pastries.

See map p. 130. U.S. 1 at MM 81.5 (bayside). ☎ *800-258-2559 or 305-664-9271.* www.islamoradafishco.com. *Reservations not accepted. Main courses $8–$27; appetizers $4–$7. DISC, MC, V. Open: Sun–Thurs 11 a.m.–9 p.m., Fri–Sat 11 a.m.–10 p.m.*

Kaiyo
$$$ Key Largo SUSHI

Don't get smart and try to catch your own sushi in the Keys. Just come here, to the best — and only — sushi joint in the Lower Keys, whose kitchen is presided over by star chef Dawn Sieber, formerly of Atlantic's Edge. Signature sushi rolls such as the Spicy Volcano Conch roll and the Key Lime Lobster roll are outstanding, as are the farm-raised raw oysters and farmed baby conch tempura.

See map p. 130. 81701 Old Highway, MM 82 (oceanside). ☎ *305-664-5556. Reservations recommended. Main courses: $11.50–$15, sushi $4.50–$$11.50. AE, DC, MC, V. Open: Mon– Sat noon–10 p.m.*

Lorelai
$$ Key Largo SEAFOOD

This big old fish house and bar with the massive mermaid sign out front is a great place for a snack, a meal, or a beer. Excellent views of the bay remind you that you are in a very primitive, pristine form of civilization. Inside, a good-value menu focuses mainly on seafood. When in season, lobsters are the way to go. For $20, you can get a good-size tail — at least a 1 pounder — prepared any way you like. Other fare includes the standard clam chowder, fried shrimp, and doughy conch fritters. The outside bar has live music every evening, and you can order snacks and light meals from a limited menu that is satisfying and well priced.

See map p. 130. U.S 1, MM 82 (bayside). ☎ *305-664-4656. Reservations aren't required. Main courses: $12–$24 AE, DISC, MC, V. Open: Daily 7 a.m.–10:30 p.m.*

Exploring Islamorada

Islamorada is a small, but splashy hub for water sports, diving, and boating.

Lignumvitae Key State Botanical Site
Lignumvitae Key

If you want to see the Keys as they used to be, head for this 280-acre island, which you can only get to by boat. But Lignumvitae (named after a rare tree) is worth a trip. In addition to its namesakes, this place is home to mahogany, strangler fig, and gumbo-limbo trees. The lush hammocks also shelter several bird species, but bring mosquito repellent. Because of a limit on visitors, call ahead for reservations. Due to the ferry schedule, it's a half-day event.

See map p. 130. Leave from Robbie's Pier, MM 77.5 (see the next entry). ☎ *305-664-9814.* www.abfla.com/parks/LignumvitaeKey/lignumvitaekey.html. *To get there: Look for the Hungry Tarpon sign, just past the Indian Key channel. Admission: Robbie's runs a ferry twice a day (9:30 a.m. and 1:30 p.m.; arrive 30 min. before departure time) for $15 per person. Reservations are a good idea. Open: Dawn till dusk.*

Robbie's Pier
Islamorada

One of the best — and definitely one of the cheapest — attractions in the Upper Keys is the famed Robbie's Pier. Here, the fierce steely tarpons, a prized catch for backcountry anglers, have been gathering for the past 20 years. You may recognize these prehistoric-looking giants that grow up to 200 pounds; many are displayed as trophies and mounted on local restaurant walls. But here at Robbie's Pier, they're alive, and tens and sometimes hundreds of these behemoths circle the shallow waters waiting for you to feed them a $2 bucketful of fish. Kayak tours promise an even closer glimpse. Allow an hour if you come early or late.

See map p. 130. U.S. 1 at MM 77.5 (oceanside). ☎ *305-664-9814.* www.robbies.com. *To get there: Under Hungry Tarpon sign just past Indian Key channel. Admission: $1 (free if you take the Lignumvitae ferry). Open: Daily 8 a.m.–5 p.m.*

Theater of the Sea
Islamorada

Established in 1946, the Theater of the Sea is one of the world's oldest marine zoos. Recently refurbished, with newly paved walkways, landscaping, and an on-site photo service, the park's dolphin and sea lion shows are entertaining and informative, especially for children, who will also love seeing the sharks, sea turtles, and tropical fish. If you want to swim with dolphins and you haven't booked well in advance, you may be able to get in with just a few hours, or days, notice as opposed to the more rigid Dolphin Research Center in Marathon. Expect to spend two hours here (three if you do the swim).

See map p. 130. 84721 Overseas Hwy., MM 84.5 (oceanside). ☎ *305-664-2431.* www.theaterofthesea.com. *Admission: $19.50 adults, $12 kids 3–12; dolphin swim $140. Open: Daily 9:30 a.m.–5:45 p.m.*

Pursuing outdoor delights

If you're a skipper, you can rent a boat and chart your course from **Robbie's Pier,** located on U.S. 1/Overseas Highway at MM 77.5. (☎ **305-664-9814;** www.robbies.com), where 16- to 18-footers rent for $70 to $205 half-day, $90 to $295 full-day. Rental Boat Company at **Bud N' Mary's Marina** (☎ **305-664-0091**) has outdoor and pontoon boat rentals for $100 to $160 per half-day and $140 to $300 for a full day.

The diving magnet for this region is a sunken Spanish galleon, *The Eagle,* dating to 1733. Little is left, but the galleon is still a favorite of divers. Curators have added many authentic touches, including seven concrete cannon replicas and a ship's anchor from the 18th century. The ship, nearly a football field long in 110 feet of water, is a magnet for grouper, tarpon, and jack.

The **Holiday Isle Dive Shop,** 84001 Overseas Hwy. (☎ **305-664-DIVE;** www.diveholidayisle.com), is a full-service PADI shop with daily dive trips and private or group instruction. Snorkel and dive prices range from $10 to $55. Instruction runs from $165 to $495.

The rod-and-reel crowd will find catching bonefish, tarpon, and marlin a thrill. Plus, grouper, yellowtail snapper, and mahimahi make great meals. Inshore rates are generally $225 a half-day, $400 for eight hours; double that for deep-sea excursions. **Robbie's Pier,** 84500 U.S. 1/Overseas Hwy. (☎ **877-664-8498** or 305-664-9814; www.robbies.com) and **Reef Runner,** 176 Coral Rd. (☎ **305-852-3660**), are two reliable outfitters and offer a number of expeditions.

Living it up after dark

You haven't lived until you've experienced Big Dick and the Extenders at **Woody's Saloon and Restaurant,** MM 81.5 (☎ **305-664-4335**). Big is a large, often profane Native American whose shtick is particularly stinging if you climb into a front table. His band takes the stage at about 10 p.m. and holds court until 4 a.m., Wednesday through Saturday. Dick appears in time for an adult comedy show at 11 p.m. The **Lorelei Restaurant,** MM 82 (☎ **305-664-4338**), features nightly guitar and other music at its Cabana Bar. The restaurant is open from 6 a.m. to 10:30 p.m. daily; the bar stays open until 2 a.m.

Marathon

Marathon is another sleepy hollow where motels are a bit thin, and restaurants are thinner. But there's a bright side: Marathon has one of the better dolphin-swim programs. See "Exploring Marathon," later in this chapter for further details.

Spending the night

Marathon, in the heart of the Keys, offers the modern conveniences of a bustling commercial community and has a number of resort hotels. Even though Marathon is growing, it still retains its 19th-century fishing-village charm, so you'll also find some guesthouses and bed-and-breakfasts.

Unless otherwise noted, all listings include air-conditioning, televisions, a pool, and free parking. As with much of coastal Florida, winter (Dec–Apr) is peak season. And don't forget to add an additional 11.5 percent room tax to your hotel rate.

Banana Bay Resort & Marina
$$–$$$ Marathon

It doesn't look like much from the sign-cluttered Overseas Highway, but when you enter the lush grounds of Banana Bay, you'll realize you're in one of the most bucolic and best-run properties in the Upper Keys. Built in the early 1950s as a place for fishermen to stay during extended fishing trips, the resort is a beachfront maze of two-story buildings hidden among banyans and palms. The rooms are moderately sized, and many have private balconies where you can enjoy your complimentary coffee and newspaper every morning. Recent additions to the hotel include a recreational activity area with horseshoe pits, a bocce court, picnic areas with barbecue grills, and a giant lawn chessboard. The hotel's kitschy restaurant serves three meals a day, indoors or poolside. A surprising amenity is Pretty Joe Rock, the hotel's private island, which is available for long weekends and weekly rentals. The island has a Keys-style two-bedroom, two-bathroom cottage that's ideal for romantic escapes (contact the resort for rates). This resort is family-friendly, but if you're looking for an adults-only resort, there's also a Banana Bay Resort in Key West (☎ 305-296-6925) that doesn't allow children.

See map p. 130. U.S. 1/Overseas Highway at MM 49.5 (bayside). ☎ 800-226-2621 or 305-743-3500. Fax: 305-743-2670. www.bananabay.com. *Rack rates: Jan–May $135–$225, June–Dec $95–$175; $15 per child over 5. AE, DC, DISC, MC, V.*

Faro Blanco Marine Resort
$–$$$$ Marathon

Spanning both sides of the Overseas Highway and all on waterfront property, this huge, two-shore marina and hotel complex offers something for every taste. A far cry from the local Holiday Inn, Faro Blanco offers a full

Keys experience, with rooms available in houseboats, a lighthouse, or, if you prefer, a quaint cottage.

See map p. 130. 1996 Overseas Hwy./U.S. 1 at MM 48.5 (bayside). ☎ ***800-759-3276*** *or 305-743-9018. Fax: 305-866-5235. Rack rates: Winter $89–$150 cottage, $109–$200 houseboat, $185 lighthouse, $267–$327 condo; off season $79–$119 cottage, $99– $178 houseboat, $145 lighthouse, $215–$263 condo. AE, DISC, MC, V.*

Hawk's Cay Resort
$$$$ Duck Key/Marathon

Located on its own 60-acre island in the Middle Keys, this resort has a relaxed and casual island atmosphere. If it's recreation you're looking for, Hawk's Cay is far superior to the more luxurious Cheeca Lodge. It offers an impressive array of activities — sailing, fishing, snorkeling, and water-skiing, to name a few — plus the opportunity to swim in a special pool with dolphins. (You need to reserve the dolphin swim well in advance — there's a waiting list.) Large and recently renovated, rooms feature island-style furniture; each accommodation opens onto a private balcony with ocean or tropical views (pricing varies depending on the view). The large bathrooms are well appointed and have granite countertops. You can also book one of the hyper posh villas — there are 295 of them — with full kitchen, washer/dryer, and living rooms with water or garden views modeled after the kitschy 1950s concept of the "boatel." The 7,000-square-foot Indies Spa offers stellar treatments and a blissful Eucalyptus steam room that'll clear even the most stubborn of sinuses. In addition to a lagoon and several pools for families, the resort boasts a secluded pool for adults only. Organized children's activities, including special marine- and ecologically inspired programs, will keep your little ones busy while you relax.

See map p. 130. U.S. 1/Overseas Highway at MM 61 (oceanside). ☎ ***888-443-6393*** *or 305-743-7000.* www.hawkscay.com. *Fax: 305-743-5215. Rack rates: Winter $260– $410 double, $460–$1,100 suite; off season $220–$340 double, $380–$1,000 suite. Packages available. AE, DC, DISC, MC, V.*

Dining locally

As in the rest of the Keys, the cuisine in Marathon revolves around seafood. Fish, crabs, lobsters, and scallops are your best bets, although you'll also find basic burgers, poultry, and the like. If you want to increase your dining options, you can also look for places to eat in nearby Islamorada and the Lower Keys, which are also discussed in this chapter. ***Remember:*** All Florida restaurants and food-serving bars are smoke-free.

Barracuda Grill
$$ Marathon   BISTRO/SEAFOOD

This small, casual spot serves excellent seafood, steaks, and chops, but unfortunately, it's only open for dinner. Some of the favorite dishes are the Caicos gold conch, and mangrove snapper and mango. Try the Tipsy Olives appetizer, marinated in gin or vodka, to kick-start your meal. Fans of spicy food should try the red-hot calamari. Decorated with barracuda-themed art, the restaurant also features a well-priced American wine list with lots of California vintages.

See map p. 130. U.S. 1/Overseas Highway at MM 49.5 (bayside). ☎ *305-743-3314. Reservations aren't necessary. Main courses: $10–$26. AE, DISC, MC, V. Open: Wed–Sat 6–10 p.m.*

The Quay Marathon
$$–$$$ Marathon   STEAK/SEAFOOD

This Quay Marathon isn't related to the restaurant of the same name in Key Largo, but it has a nice selection of mahimahi, grouper, yellowtail snapper, shrimp, and lobster as well as steaks, veal, and chicken. You can dine indoors or out.

See map p. 130. U.S. 1/Overseas Highway at MM 54 (bayside). ☎ *305-289-1810. Reservations suggested. Main courses: $13–$33. AE, CB, DC, DISC, MC, V. Open: Sun–Thurs 11:30 a.m.–10 p.m., Fri–Sat 11:30 a.m.–11 p.m.*

Exploring Marathon

The options here are lean in terms of numbers, but Marathon will help you discover your inner Flipper at its famous Dolphin Research Center. If you want to take a tour of the area, **Latigo Yacht Charters,** in the Marathon Marina, 1021 11th St. (☎ **305-289-1066;** www.latigo.net) offers several excursions aboard a 56-foot motor yacht, including a "bed-and-breakfast cruise" ($490 per couple) that includes dinner, beer, wine, champagne, breakfast, and snorkeling.

Crane Point Hammock
Marathon

This is a little-known but worthwhile stop, especially for those interested in the rich botanical and archaeological history of the Keys. Privately owned, the 64-acre nature area contains what is probably the last virgin thatch-palm hammock in North America as well as a rain-forest exhibit and an archaeological dig site with pre-Columbian and prehistoric Bahamian artifacts. Allow three to four hours.

Also headquarters for the Florida Keys Land and Sea Trust, the hammock's impressive nature museum has simple, informative displays of the Keys' wildlife, including a walk-through replica of a coral-reef cave and life-size dioramas with tropical birds and Key deer. Here, kids can participate in art projects, see 6-foot-long iguanas, climb through a scaled-down pirate ship, and touch a variety of indigenous aquatic and landlubbing creatures.

See map p. 130. 5550 U.S. 1/Overseas Hwy. (bayside). ☎ *305-743-9100. Admission: $7.50 adults, $6 seniors 65 and older, $4 kids 6 and older, free for kids under 6. Open: Mon–Sat 9 a.m.–5 p.m., Sun noon–5 p.m.*

Dolphin Research Center
Marathon

This is number one: No other dolphin experience is as organized and informative. The center's primary goal is caring for the animals, and several experiences are interactive. Dolphin Encounter, the hands-down favorite, allows you to swim with bottlenose beauties. The cost is $155 for ages 5 and older; reservations and English comprehension are required. Dolphin Splash lets you get in the door without a dolphin swim. The price is $80, kids under 3 get in free. Hands on Training puts you behind the scenes to see training techniques and touch a dolphin. The cost is $50. Guided tours can also give you the basics about the mammals. Allow two to three hours.

A height requirement of 44 inches is enforced, and an adult must hold up children under the required height.

See map p. 130. U.S. 1 at MM 59 (bayside; look for the 30-foot dolphin statue). ☎ *305-289-1121 or 305-289-0002 (reservations).* www.dolphins.org. *Reservations must be made six weeks in advance. Admission: Guided tours $17.50 adults, $14.50 seniors, $11.50 kids 4–12. For special programs, see the preceding paragraph. Open: Daily 9:30 a.m.–4 p.m.*

Seven-Mile Bridge
Marathon

The bridge is not your typical tourist attraction, but you can't avoid a peek. It takes nine minutes to cross, and there's nothing else to do but gawk and marvel. Opened in 1982, the architectural wonder cost $45 million. Its crowning achievement is the fact that the Seven-Mile Bridge apex is the highest point in the Keys. Some people may recognize the remnants of the old bridge from the Arnold Schwarzenegger film *True Lies.* Don't worry that a wrong turn may lead you onto the old bridge instead of the new one. The old span is closed to cars and has been transformed into the world's longest fishing pier, also used for hiking and watching the sunset.

See map p. 130. Between MMs 40 and 47. To get there: It's south of Marathon.

Outdoor pursuits

Boaters should try **R&R Watersports,** 13201 U.S. 1/Overseas Hwy. (☎ **305-743-9385;** www.rrwatersports.com), which rents pontoons ($100–$140 for a half-day) and WaveRunners ($75 per hour).

Popular diving sites include the ***Adelaide Baker,*** a wrecked steamer whose twin stacks lie in 25 feet of water; ***Thunderbolt,*** a 188-foot wreck at a depth of 115 feet; and **Coffin's Patch,** a series of six reefs brimming with coral and fish.

Prices vary by outfitter, but snorkel tours usually begin at $25 and dive tours at $60. Marathon's charter fleet includes **Marathon Divers,** 12221 U.S. 1/Overseas Hwy. (☎ **800-724-5798** or 305-289-1141), and **Capt.**

Hook's Marina & Dive Centers, 11833 U.S. 1/Overseas Hwy. (☎ 800-278-4665).

As in the rest of the Keys, the fish are always biting in Marathon. Thanks to offshore depths that reach up to 1,100 feet, this area has more than its share of blue and white marlin, mako shark, and blackfin tuna; you'll also find many common in-shore species. Local charters include **The Bounty Hunter,** 15th Street at Burdine's Marina, Marathon (☎ 305-743-2446), which offers full- and half-day outings. For 28 years, Captain Brock Hook's huge sign has boasted, "no fish, no pay": You're guaranteed to catch something, or your money back! Choose your prey from shark, barracuda, sailfish, or whatever else is running. Prices are $400 for a half-day, $500 for three-quarters of a day, and $600 for a full day. Rates are for groups of no more than six people.

The Lower Keys

If you want to be near but not in the middle of zany Key West, the Lower Keys is the place. Despite proximity to party central, Big Pine, Summerland, and Sugarloaf Keys remain largely quiet and natural.

Spending the night

The 50 or so islands that make up the Lower Keys are largely undeveloped, with just a few small properties and one or two resorts — and no national chains. Most accommodations here are vacation rental homes, generally offering two- to three-bedroom units, some with oceanfront views.

In the following listings, I only tell you about air-conditioning, pools, televisions, and free parking if a property doesn't have them. And, as always, don't forget to tack on the 11.5 percent room tax to your hotel rate.

If a back-to-nature experience appeals to you, the area also offers some great camping. **Bahia Honda State Recreation Area** (see the listing for the park, later in this chapter), which features 80 camping sites, is loaded with facilities and outdoor activities. A site costs $26 for a maximum of four people and includes electricity. Cabins hold up to eight people. Equipped with linens, kitchenettes, and utensils, the cabins run from $50 to $110 depending on the season. For more information, or to reserve a site, call ☎ 305-872-2353.

Deer Run Bed and Breakfast
$$ Little Torch Key

Located directly on the beach, Sue Abbott's small, homey, smoke-free B&B is a real find. One upstairs and two downstairs guest rooms are comfortably furnished with queen-size beds, good closets, and touch-sensitive lamps. Rattan and 1970s-style chairs and couches furnish the living room, along with 13 birds and 3 cats. Breakfast, which is served on a pretty, fenced-in porch, is cooked to order by Sue herself. The wooded area around the property is full of Key deer, which often wander the beach as well. There's no pool, but a hot tub overlooking the ocean is especially nice. Ask to use one of the bikes to explore nearby nature trails.

See map p. 130. Long Beach Drive (P.O. Box 431), Big Pine Key. ☎ ***305-872-2015.*** *Fax: 305-872-2842.* http://thefloridakeys.com/deerrun. *To get there: From U.S. 1, turn towards the ocean at the Big Pine Fishing Lodge (MM 33); continue for about 2 miles. Rack rates: Winter from $110 double; off season from $95 double. Rates include full American breakfast. No credit cards.*

Little Palm Island
$$$$ Little Torch Key

This exclusive island escape — host to presidents and royalty — is not just a place to stay while in the Lower Keys; it is a destination all its own. Built on a private 5-acre island, it's accessible only by boat. Guests stay in thatched-roof duplexes amid lush foliage and flowering tropical plants. Many villas have ocean views and private sundecks with rope hammocks. Inside, the romantic suites have all the comforts and conveniences of a luxurious contemporary beach cottage but without telephones, TVs, or alarm clocks. As if its location weren't idyllic enough, a new full-service spa recently opened on the island. Note that on the breezeless south side of the island, mosquitoes can be a problem, even in the winter, so bring bug spray and lightweight, long-sleeved clothing. Leave kids under 16 at home — they'd be bored here anyway.

See map p. 130. 28500 U.S. 1/Overseas Hwy. at MM 28.5 (oceanside; look for the Little Palm Island Ferry Service sign). ☎ ***800-343-8567*** *or 305-872-2524. Fax: 305-872-4843.* www.littlepalmisland.com. *Rack rates: Winter $795–$1,695 per couple; off season $695–$1,595. Rates include transportation to and from the island and unlimited (nonmotorized) water sports. Meal plans include two meals daily for an additional $125 per person per day, three meals at $140 per person. AE, DC, DISC, MC, V.*

Parmer's Resort
$–$$ Little Torch Key

A fixture for more than 20 years, Parmer's is well known for its charming hospitality and helpful staff. This downscale resort offers modest but comfortable cottages, each of them unique. Some are waterfront, many have kitchenettes, and others are just a bedroom. Room 26 (also known as Wahoo), a one-bedroom efficiency, is especially nice, with a small sitting area that faces the water. Room 6, a small efficiency, has a kitchenette and an especially large bathroom. Recently updated, rooms are consistently very clean. Many can be combined to accommodate large families. The hotel's waterfront location almost makes up for the fact that you must pay extra for maid service.

See map p. 130. Barry Avenue (P.O. Box 430665), near MM 28.5. ☎ ***305-872-2157.*** *Fax 305-872-2014.* www.parmersresort.com. *To get there: From U.S. 1, turn bayside* *onto Barry Avenue. Resort is a half-mile down on the right. Rack rates: Winter $85–$150 double, from $105 efficiency; off season $65–$105double, $85–$150 efficiency. Rates include continental breakfast. AE, DISC, MC, V.*

Dining locally

Unfortunately, the Lower Keys don't have many dining options. Aside from the following eateries, your best restaurant bet is to try the one with the most cars parked in front of it. ***Don't forget:*** All Florida restaurants and food-serving bars are smoke-free.

I can tell you from experience that if a storm rears up during hurricane season, every establishment shuts up tight. You may want to keep a few snacks in your room.

Coco's Kitchen

$ Big Pine Key   CUBAN/NICARAGUAN

This tiny storefront has been dishing out black beans, rice, and shredded beef to fans of Cuban cuisine for more than ten years. The owners, who are actually from Nicaragua, cook not only superior Cuban food but also some local specialties, as well as Italian and Caribbean dishes. Favorites include fried shrimp, whole fried yellowtail, and Cuban-style roast pork (available only on Sat). The best bet is the daily special, which may be roasted pork or fresh grouper, served with rice and beans or salad and crispy fries. Top off the huge, cheap meal with a rich caramel-soaked flan.

See map p 130. 283 Key Deer Blvd., in the Winn-Dixie shopping center at MM 30.5. ☎ *305-872-4495. Reservations aren't necessary. To get there: Turn towards the bay at the traffic light and stay in the left lane. Main courses: $6–$15. No credit cards. Open: Mon–Sat 7 a.m–7:30 p.m.*

The Dining Room at Little Palm Island

$$$$ Little Palm Island   FRENCH/FLORIBBEAN

If you aren't keeping track of your dining budget, go dressy casual, grab the island ferryboat, and head to this resort restaurant. Choose from a menu that leans toward French and Floribbean (that's Florida and Caribbean flavors colliding). The menu changes, but it may include pan-seared snapper with lobster dumplings, crab cakes with vegetables, or roast chicken in a tarragon-Riesling sauce. The wine list is extensive.

See map p. 130. 28500 U.S. 1/Overseas Hwy. at MM 28.5 (oceanside; look for the Little Palm Island Ferry Service sign). ☎ *800-343-8567 or 305-872-2524. Fax: 305-872-4843.* www.littlepalmisland.com. *Main courses: $30–$43. AE, CB, DC, DISC, MC, V. Open: Daily 7:30–10 a.m., 11:30 a.m.–2:30 p.m., and 6:30–10 p.m.*

Monte's

$ **Summerland Key**   **SEAFOOD**

Certainly nobody goes to this restaurant/fish market for its atmosphere: Plastic place settings rest on plastic-covered picnic-style tables in a screen-enclosed dining patio. But Monte's doesn't need great atmosphere because it has survived for more than 20 years on its very good and incredibly fresh food. The day's catch may include shark, tuna, lobsters, stone crabs, or shrimp.

See map p. 130. Just off U.S. 1 at MM 25 (bayside). ☎ ***305-745-3731.*** *Reservations aren't necessary. Main courses: $13–$17. No credit cards. Open: Mon–Sat 9 a.m.– 10 p.m., Sun 11 a.m.–9 p.m.*

Exploring the Lower Keys

This is outdoorsville — the place to be if you want to commune with nature in a tranquil and relatively unspoiled setting. Unlike their neighbors to the north and Key West to the south, the Lower Keys are devoid of spring-break crowds and have little nightlife. Unless you drive to Key West, you won't even be able to find a tourist trap.

Bahia Honda State Recreation Area
Big Pine Key

The only state park in the Lower Keys, Bahia Honda also has the only natural beach in the entire chain. Its 524 acres are made of dunes, coastal mangroves, and hammocks. The white-sand beach has deep water close to shore, making this venue good for diving and snorkeling. (You may find starfish floating only 3 feet below the surface of the water.) Snorkel trips to **Looe Key Reef** depart two to three times daily, and the cost is $24.95 for adults, $19.95 for kids under 18, and $5 for equipment rental. (See Looe Key National Marine Sanctuary later in this chapter under "Taking it to the water.") While you're here, climb aboard what's left of Henry Flagler's rail line and treat yourself to a panorama of the nearby keys. For information about camping here, see "Spending the night" in the section "The Lower Keys, " earlier in this chapter.

See map p. 130. 36850 U.S. 1/Overseas Hwy. at MM 37. ☎ ***305-872-2353.*** *For diving/ snorkeling trips, call* ☎ ***305-872-3210.*** www.bahiahondapark.com. *Reservations recommended for snorkeling. Admission: $5 per couple and 50¢ for each additional person. Open: Daily 8 a.m.–sunset.*

National Key Deer Refuge
Big Pine Key

Key deer — no larger than medium-sized dogs — are making a last stand on this isle. Due to pollution, vanishing habitats, and speeding cars, only 300 deer are left. The deer sanctuary has a marked trail (Watson Hammock) where you may get a glimpse of a deer if you come early or late in the day. *Important note:* Please don't feed the deer — the animals' tiny bodies aren't built for people food.

See map p. 130. No address. ☎ 305-872-2239. To get there: Weekdays, go to the ranger station at MM 30.5 in the Winn-Dixie plaza. Otherwise, go to Big Pine Key's lone traffic light and take Key Deer Boulevard back, then take the left fork. Admission: free. Open: The ranger station is open Mon–Fri 8 a.m.–5 p.m. The refuge is open daily, during daylight hours.

Taking it to the water

Divers will find that the **Looe Key National Marine Sanctuary,** located off Bahia Honda State Recreation Area (see earlier information and map p. 130) boasts dramatic reefs due to a ban on spear fishing as well as coral and shell collecting. You can see barracuda, tarpon, and moray eels at a depth of less than 35 feet, and some of the marine life swims right up to your mask. Prices begin at $35 for snorkelers and $45 for divers. **Looe Key Reef Resort and Dive Center,** U.S. 1/Overseas Highway, at MM 27.5, Ramrod Key (☎ 305-872-2215), is one of the area's better diving operators.

Fishermen love a fight. The Keys' favorite contenders are bonefish (3–15 pounds), tarpon (usually 40–50 pounds but as big as 200), and permit (up to 25 pounds). **Back Country Guide Service,** 472 Sands Rd., Big Pine Key (☎ 800-663-5780 or 305-872-9528) charges $275 per half-day and $375 for a full day aboard an 18-footer with little sun relief. **Grouch Charters,** MM 24.5, Summerland Key (☎ 305-745-1172), takes $350 for four people per half-day, and $475 for a full day on an offshore boat.

Key West

Paradise? That may be stretching things when you describe Key West. There's traffic, prices are high, it's hot, the decibel level can split an oak, and franchises have usurped Hemingway's hideaway. Did I mention that cruise ships dock here?

But Key West does combine some of the natural treasures of the Keys (fishing and other water sports) with some of the rum-and-then-some fun of a destination that also has bars, restaurants, weird shows, and weirder people. (See an overview of "Key West" coming up.) And the gay lifestyle of many residents and tourists is openly accepted, which makes Key West one of the more progressive cities east of the Mississippi.

The island is small, and there are enough transportation options that you won't need a car, unless you're planning on touring some of the other Keys. Taxis from the airport to town run $3.50 to $7 per person for two or more, depending on your destination. **Five Sixes Taxi** (☎ 305-296-6666) and **Friendly Cab Co.** (☎ 305-295-5555) are two of the regulars. Rates are $2 for the first 0.2 mile and 50¢ for each additional 0.2 mile.

Key West

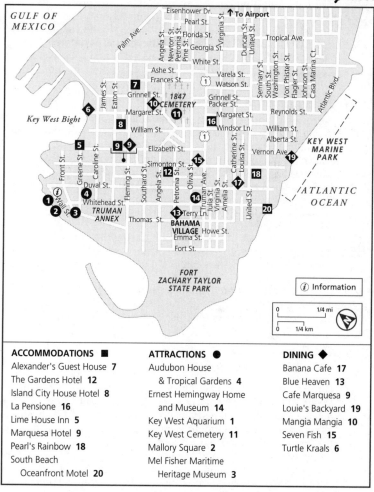

ACCOMMODATIONS ■

Alexander's Guest House **7**
The Gardens Hotel **12**
Island City House Hotel **8**
La Pensione **16**
Lime House Inn **5**
Marquesa Hotel **9**
Pearl's Rainbow **18**
South Beach
   Oceanfront Motel **20**

ATTRACTIONS ●

Audubon House
   & Tropical Gardens **4**
Ernest Hemingway Home
   and Museum **14**
Key West Aquarium **1**
Key West Cemetery **11**
Mallory Square **2**
Mel Fisher Maritime
   Heritage Museum **3**

DINING ◆

Banana Cafe **17**
Blue Heaven **13**
Cafe Marquesa **9**
Louie's Backyard **19**
Mangia Mangia **10**
Seven Fish **15**
Turtle Kraals **6**

Although Key West is a tiny island, it's broken up into four distinct "neighborhoods": Old Town, South Beach, the Port Area, and North End. **Old Town** is where you'll find most of the mainstream hotels, restaurants, bars, and, of course, Duval Street. North of Duval Street is the aptly named **North End,** where you'll find the best sunsets in the world and famous **Mallory Square.** On the Atlantic side of Old Town is **South Beach,** named for its location at the southern end of Duval Street. It is exactly what it says it is — a beach. The **Port Area,** officially known as the Historic Seaport at Key West Bight, is located east on Caroline Street. What you'll find there besides boats are restaurants and, yes, bars.

Key West's downtown parking and traffic are annoying, however, so your best bet for getting around may lie on two wheels. If you're staying in Key West, consider renting a bike (from $8 a day and $30 a week) or moped ($30 and $100, respectively) from **Moped Hospital,** 601 Truman Ave. (☎ **305-296-3344**). **Tropical Bicycles & Scooters,** 1300 Duval St. (☎ **305-294-8136**), rents bikes for $8 a day and $40 a week; scooters are $29 and $129, respectively.

Spending the night

Here's a city with a melting-pot character that permits a large, liberal base to mingle with crusty natives, called Conchs (pronounced *konks*), and with Miami wheeler-dealers. The wealth of places to stay in Key West ranges from bed-and-breakfasts to hotel chains and upscale resorts. **Vacation Key West** (☎ **800-595-5397** or 305-295-9500; www.vacationkw. com) is a hotel reservation service that can often get you discounts of 20 to 30 percent at some of the major chains on the island and also offers car-rental discounts. They also represent a few guesthouses.

Keep in mind that prices skyrocket during the holidays, high season (Dec–Apr), and for the island's special events. Reserve well in advance because rooms become scarce and many places require minimum stays.

Unless otherwise noted, all listings include air-conditioning, televisions, a pool, and free parking. Key West assesses an additional hotel tax of 11.5 percent, so budget for this when selecting your accommodations.

The Gardens Hotel
$$$–$$$$ **Key West/Old Town**

Once a private residence, The Gardens Hotel is hidden amidst the exotic Peggy Mills tropical botanical gardens. What lies behind the gardens is a luxurious, Bahamian-style hideaway featuring 17 lavishly appointed accommodations including two suites, two historic rooms in the main house (which is listed in the National Register of Historic Places), 12 garden and courtyard rooms, and one uber secluded cottage. A gorgeous freeform swimming pool is right in the middle of the courtyard, with an adjacent tiki bar to serve up whatever libation you desire. Winding brick pathways leading to secluded seating areas in the private gardens make for an idyllic romantic getaway that's the quintessence of paradise.

See map p. 151. 526 Angela St. (at Simonton Avenue). ☎ *800-526-2664 or 305-294-2661. Fax: 305-292-1007.* www.gardenshotel.com. *Rack rates: Dec–Apr $220–$320, May–Nov $155–$595. AE, DC, MC, V.*

Island City House Hotel
$$–$$$ **Key West/Old Town**

This small resort's 24 rooms have kitchens and share a junglelike courtyard that is home to a Jacuzzi. Rooms facing this courtyard are the best of the bunch. The wraparound verandas on the main building are great for casual strolls or kicking back. Most rooms (from studios to two-bedroom suites, some dating to 1880) have king-size beds and antique furnishings. A complimentary continental breakfast is served in the garden.

See map p. 151. 411 Williams St. (at Eaton Street). ☎ *800-634-8230 or 305-294-5702. Fax: 305-294-1289.* www.islandcityhouse.com. *Parking: On street only. Rack rates: Dec–May $145–$175 studios, $180–$240 1-bedroom suites, $230–$315 2-bedroom suites; June–Nov $115 studios, $120–$185 1-bedroom suite, $195–$220 2-bedroom suites. AE, CB, DC, DISC, MC, V.*

La Pensione
$$ Key West/Old Town

This Classic Revival mansion's nine rooms are pretty intimate. The bed-and-breakfast was built in 1891, and the comfortable rooms all have king-size beds and private baths. Some rooms have French doors that open onto verandas, where you can enjoy a made-to-order breakfast (included). Room Nine is the largest in the house. Telephones and televisions are lacking, but the service is friendly and first-rate. Kids aren't welcome.

See map p. 151. 809 Truman Ave. (between Windsor and Margaret streets). ☎ *800-893-1193 or 305-292-9923. Fax: 305-296-6509.* http://lapensione.com. *Rack rates: May–Dec from $108, Dec–May $168–$178. AE, DC, DISC, MC, V.*

Marquesa Hotel
$$$ Key West/Old Town

Oversize furnishings, four-poster beds, and marble baths complement this 40-room inn, a perennial award winner. Rooms and suites are scattered throughout four buildings; some have living areas and private porches. Two pools and two waterfalls help you forget the rush-hour traffic back home, and Cafe Marquesa serves dinner nightly. The hotel provides a free daily newspaper, wine on your arrival, and a Saturday night cocktail party.

See map p. 151. 600 Fleming St. (at Simonton). ☎ *800-669-4631 or 305-292-1919. Fax: 305-294-2121.* www.keywest.com/marquesa.html. *Rack rates: Dec–Apr $275–$410, May–June and Sept–Nov $220–$320, June–Aug $170–$285. AE, DC, MC, V.*

South Beach Oceanfront Motel
$$ Key West/South Beach

View the ocean or walk to Duval Street from this motel but don't expect many frills. (Only two rooms have a view of the ocean; the rest overlook the pool.) Three of the 47 rooms are efficiencies, which offer shaded balconies. An on-site dive shop offers scuba and snorkeling lessons.

See map p. 151. 508 South St. (on the ocean at Duval). ☎ *800-354-4455 or 305-296-5611. Fax: 305-294-8272.* www.oldtownresorts.com/southbeach.htm. *Rack rates: Jan–Apr $169–$230, May–Dec $99–$179. AE, MC, V.*

Dining locally

You can find a tempting array of food choices on Key West, with many different cuisines represented. If your tastes run more toward food of the fast variety, many national chains have franchises along Roosevelt Boulevard. Fresh fish and seafood, as in the rest of Florida, are usually your best bets on a menu, and don't visit here without trying a slice of authentic Key lime pie. *Note:* Quality Key lime pie will be pale yellow, not green.

Restaurants, for the most part, offer a relaxed and casual atmosphere. Many offer outdoor dining so patrons can get a good look at the Key West sunsets. Note, however, that many don't offer on-site parking, and don't forget that all Florida restaurants and food-serving bars are smoke-free.

Banana Café
$–$$ Key West/Old Town   FRENCH

Like many of Key West's restaurants, this eatery is situated in a century-old house that was built near the end of the island's maritime heyday. The entrees include sliced duck breast in green peppercorn sauce; rack of lamb in sautéed apples and Madeira wine sauce; and shrimp, mussels, scallops, and fish in Provençal tomato sauce served over saffron fettuccine. A jazz band plays here on Thursday nights.

See map p. 151. 1211 Duval St. (at Louisa Street). ☎ *305-294-7227. Reservations suggested. Main courses: $$5–$20. AE, DC, DISC, MC, V. Open: Daily 8 a.m.–3 p.m. and 7–11 p.m.*

Blue Heaven
$–$$$ Key West/Old Town   CARIBBEAN

This little hippie-run gallery and restaurant has become the place to be in Key West — and with good reason. Be prepared to wait in line. The food here is some of the best in town, especially for breakfast. You can enjoy homemade granola, huge tropical-fruit pancakes, and seafood Benedict. Dinners are just as good and run the gamut from fresh-caught fish dishes to Jamaican-style jerk chicken, curried soups, and vegetarian stews. But if you're a neat freak, don't bother. Some people are put off by the dirt floors and roaming cats and birds, but frankly, it adds to the charm.

See map p. 151. 305 Petronia St. (at Thomas Street). ☎ *305-296-8666. Reservations suggested. Main courses: $5–$30. DISC, MC, V. Open: Daily 8 a.m.–11:30 a.m., noon–3 p.m., and 6–10:30 p.m.*

Café Marquesa
$$$ Key West/Old Town   AMERICAN

Fine wine, formal service, and sinfully delicious seafood are the headliners at this hotel restaurant. The theater-style kitchen here produces such hits as pan-seared yellowfin tuna dusted in peppercorns, and Florida lobster tail and scallops in Thai basil sauce and Asian vegetables.

See map p. 151. 600 Fleming St. (at Simonton, in the Marquesa Hotel). ☎ **800-869-4631** *or 305-292-1919. Reservations suggested. Main courses: $21–$31. AE, DISC, MC, V. Open: Daily 7–11 p.m.*

Louie's Backyard
$$$–$$$$ Key West/South Beach   CARIBBEAN/AMERICAN

Nestled amid blooming bougainvillea on a lush slice of the Gulf, Louie's remains one of the most romantic restaurants on earth. Famed chef Norman Van Aiken of Norman's in Miami brought his talents farther south and started what has become one of the finest dining spots in the Keys. As a result, this is one of the hardest places to score a reservation: Either call way in advance or hope that your hotel concierge has some pull. After dinner, sit at the dockside bar and watch the waves crash, almost touching your feet, while enjoying a cocktail at sunset.

See map p. 151. 700 Waddell Ave. (at Vernon Street). ☎ **305-294-1061.** *Reservations suggested. Main courses: $25–$45. AE, DC, MC, V. Open: Daily11:30 a.m.–3 p.m., 6:30–10 p.m.*

Mangia Mangia
$ Key West/near Old Town   ITALIAN

Locals appreciate that they can get good, inexpensive food here in a town filled with tourist traps. Off the beaten track, in a little corner storefront, this great Chicago-style pasta place serves some of the best Italian food in the Keys. The family-run restaurant offers superb homemade pastas of every description, including one of the tastiest marinaras around. The simple grilled chicken breast brushed with olive oil and sprinkled with pepper is another good choice, as is the Picadillo Pasta — black-bean pasta shells smothered in a Cuban-inspired sauce with meat, tomatoes, olives, capers, and spices. You wouldn't know it from the glossy glass-front room, but there's a fantastic little outdoor patio dotted with twinkling pepper lights and lots of plants.

See map p. 151. 900 Southard St. (at Margaret Street). ☎ **305-294-2469.** *Reservations not necessary. Main courses: $9.50–$15.50. AE, MC, V. Open: Daily 5:30–10 p.m.*

Seven Fish
$$ Key West/North End   SEAFOOD

Simple, good food is Seven Fish's motto, but this hidden little secret is much more than simple. One of the most popular locals' restaurants, Seven Fish is a chic seafood spot serving some of the best fish dishes on the entire island. Crab and shiitake mushroom pasta, seafood pasta, sea scallops, fish of the day, and gnocchi with blue cheese and sautéed fish are among the dishes to choose from. Try the tropical shrimp salsa for starters, and for dessert, don't miss the Key lime cake over tart lime curd with fresh berries. Be sure to make reservations well in advance, as seating is extremely limited.

See map p. 151. 632 Olivia St. (at Elizabeth). ☎ *305-296-2777. Reservations suggested. Main courses: $12–$23 AE, MC, V. Open: Wed–Mon 6–10 p.m. Closed Tues.*

Turtle Kraals

$ Key West/North End   SOUTHWESTERN/SEAFOOD

Built on the site of an old turtle cannery, Turtle Kraals attracts lots of locals to a converted waterfront warehouse that serves up Southwestern dishes and excellent seafood. Specials include Bahamian seafood stew (shrimp, scallops, and fish in a garlic-and-tomato sauce), grilled chicken enchiladas, and mango crab cakes. When stone crabs are in season (mid-Oct–Apr), do order them. They're fantastic and not nearly as exorbitantly priced as they are up in Miami. Blues bands play here on most nights.

See map p. 151. 213 Margaret St. (at Caroline Street). ☎ *294-2640. Reservations not necessary. Main courses: $7–$16. DISC, MC, V. Open: Daily 11 a.m.–10 p.m.*

Exploring Key West

In addition to the attractions mentioned here, Key West throws two grand parties (and nightly mini ones) during the year. The first is **Hemingway Days** (☎ **305-294-4440;** www.hemingwaydays.com), which is held each July and includes festivities ranging from Papa look-alike contests to a fishing tournament and literary events. **Fantasy Fest** (☎ **305-296-1817;** www.fantasyfest.net) covers the ten days leading up to Halloween. Activities include balls, parades, a celebrity look-alike contest, and beach and toga parties.

Now, on with the rest of the show.

Audubon House & Tropical Gardens
Key West/Old Town

Painter and bird fancier John James Audubon didn't own the place, but he spent a few nights here in 1832. Rare Audubon prints and antiques are joined by a self-guided audio tour that takes about 30 minutes. You can also wander the grounds, which contain orchid and herb gardens.

See map p. 151. 205 Whitehead St. (between Greene and Caroline streets). ☎ *877-281-2473 or 305-294-2116.* www.audubonhouse.com. *Admission: $9 adults, $5 kids 6–12. Open: Daily 9:30 a.m.–5 p.m.*

Ernest Hemingway Home and Museum
Key West/Old Town

In this case, the namesake did live here and probably would roll over in his grave if he saw what happened to one of his favorite cities, as well as his image. Papa is the biggest celebrity to hit Key West, with his mug plastered on everything from T-shirts to beer mugs. This Spanish-colonial house dates to 1851, 80 years before the author landed. Descendants of his six-toed cats rule the grounds. A self-guided tour of the house and grounds takes about an hour.

See map p. 151. 907 Whitehead St. (between Truman Avenue and Olivia Street). ☎ *305-294-1136.* www.hemingwayhome.com. *Admission: $10 adults, $6 kids 6–12. Open: Daily 9 a.m.–5 p.m.*

Key West Aquarium
Key West/Port Area

Born in 1934, Key West Aquarium is the oldest continuous attraction on the island. A touch tank contains sea cucumbers and anemones. Watch the daily shark and turtle feedings (not to each other, of course). A large aquarium sports eels, barracudas, tarpons, and more. Allow three hours.

See map p. 151. 1 Whitehead St. (at Mallory Square). ☎ *800-868-7482 or 305-296-2051.* www.keywestaquarium.com. *Admission: $8 adults, $4 kids 4–12. Open: Daily 10 a.m.–5:30 p.m.*

Key West Cemetery
Key West/Old Town

As strange and crowded as the city it serves, this final resting place underscores the notion that Key Westers keep their senses of humor even in death. Epitaphs include such parting thoughts as: "His beautiful little spirit was a challenge to love," for a Yorkshire terrier buried beside his mistress; "Now I know where he's sleeping at night," for a wayward husband deserving a proper send-off from his wife; "I told you I was sick," for a woman who apparently had trouble getting her friends and physician to listen; and "The buck stops here," for a native whose spirit pretty much epitomizes the local lifestyle. Allow one to three hours depending on your interest in the dead.

See map p. 151. At Margaret and Angela streets. ☎ *305-294-8380 for tours. Admission: Free; 90-minute tours are $20. Open: Daily dawn to dusk.*

Mel Fisher Maritime Heritage Museum
Key West/Old Town

The namesake treasure hunter has gone to that great salvage yard in the sky, but his life's work remains on display. Exhibits include some of the treasure he recovered from shipwrecked Spanish galleons, such as the *Nuestra Senora de Atocha,* which sank in 1622. Artifacts are priceless, with gold and silver bars, jewels, and emeralds that would make Elizabeth Taylor green with envy. This is a good stop if you're into pirates and treasure hunting. Most folks stay one to two hours.

See map p. 151. 200 Greene St. (at Whitehead Street). ☎ *305-294-2633.* www.melfisher.org/home.htm. *Admission: $7.50 adults, $4 students, $3.75 kids under 6. Open: Daily 9:30 a.m.–5 p.m.*

Seeing Key West by guided tour

You can see Key West in an organized fashion in several ways. **Sharon Wells' Biking & Walking Guide to Key West** (☎ 305-294-8380; www. seekeywest.com) offers plenty of touring choices in the $20 to $25 range. Themes include architecture, the Key West Cemetery, and an island overview.

The **Conch Train** (☎ 800-868-7482 or 305-296-6688) is one of two island tours operated by Historic Tours of America. It's tacky and touristy (a Jeep disguised to look like a locomotive pulls you around), but enduring this 90-minute special is almost required by the Tourists' Honor Code. The narrative (usually tongue-in-cheek) provides an overview of Key West sights. Catch it at Mallory Square or the Welcome Center near U.S. 1/Overseas Highway and North Roosevelt; the tours depart every half-hour from 9 a.m. to 4:30 p.m. daily. The cost is $20 for adults, $10 for kids between 4 and 12. The **Old Town Trolley** (☎ 800-868-7482 or 305-296-6688) offers the same sort of humorous tours at the same prices, but you can get off and reboard at any of the trolley's 14 stops. Choose the trolley if you're staying at one of the hotels along the trolley route, or in the case of bad weather — the Conch Train doesn't have a roof.

Ghost Walk (☎ 305-294-9255; www.hauntedtours.com), is a 90-minute, 1-mile hike through the city's historic district offered by the Key West Tour Association. The spooky but fun experience costs $20 for adults (you can find $3-off coupons everywhere; if you can't, the staff discounts the cost anyway) and $10 (no discount) for kids 3 to 12. The tour leaves nightly at 8 p.m. from the Holiday Inn La Concha at 430 Duval St., Old Town. Getting there 15 minutes early is smart; so are day-before reservations.

Several local vessels offer short sightseeing excursions, and some go to **Fort Jefferson** in nearby **Dry Tortugas National Park.** Known as the "Gibraltar of the Gulf," the fort was built in the mid-19th century to give the United States control of navigation in the Gulf of Mexico. The walls are 8 feet thick and 50 feet high. Its main claim to fame, though, was as a Civil War prison for the Union Army. The fort's most famous inmate was Dr. Samuel Mudd, the Maryland surgeon who unwittingly set the broken leg of John Wilkes Booth, President Lincoln's assassin. Today, it's a favorite of bird-watchers. (Tens of thousands of orioles, swallows, and terns pass through each spring.) Divers and snorkelers may see leatherback, green, and Atlantic Ridley sea turtles. For more information, call the **National Park Service** (☎ 305-242-7700).

The catamaran **Sunny Days** (☎ 305-296-5556; www.sunnydayskeywest. com) makes runs to the Dry Tortugas from its dock at the end of Elizabeth and Greene streets (arrive by 7:30 a.m.). The 8½-hour excursion includes continental breakfast, lunch, soft drinks, snorkeling gear, and a guided tour. The ride costs $100 for adults, $95 for seniors and students, $70 for kids under 6. **Yankee Freedom** (☎ 800-926-5332 or 305-294-7009; www.yankee-fleet.com) makes the same run from Key West Seaport, 240 Margaret St. The fare for this 100-foot catamaran is $125 for adults,

$115 for seniors and college students, and $83 for kids. The price includes continental breakfast, lunch, snorkeling gear, and a tour.

The 130-foot, 1939 schooner *Western Union* (☎ 305-292-1766; www.schoonerwesternunion.com) is the last tall ship built in Key West. Berthed at Schooner Wharf, 202 William St., the schooner is used for two-hour afternoon cruises ($44 per person, including beer, wine, and champagne) and sunset sails ($65 per person, including beer, wine, champagne, conch chowder, and live entertainment). The 74-foot schooner *Wolf* (☎ 305-296-9694; www.schoonerwolf.com) sails from 201 Williams St. Its two-hour day-trips ($30 per person) include soda. Sunset cruises ($40) include champagne, beer, soda, and music.

Seaplanes of Key West (☎ 800-950-2359 or 305-294-0709; www.seaplanesofkeywest.com) offers four- and eight-hour snorkeling/sightseeing excursions to the Dry Tortugas National Park. Rates are $179 per half-day and $305 for a full day, including snorkel equipment, sodas, and water. If you want lunch, bring your own. It's based out of Key West Airport.

Outdoor adventures

Key West continues the Florida Keys' strong water-sports theme. Key West also delivers the chain's only legitimate golf course.

Diving and snorkeling

The southernmost city has several good sites for diving and snorkeling. Resting 65 feet below the surface, **Joe's Tug** is a good place to see moray eels, barracudas, and jacks. At the **Nine-Foot Stake** reef you can encounter soft coral and juvenile marine life at 10 to 25 feet.

At The Water's Edge offers a reservations service (☎ 305-766-2240; http://hometown.aol.com/doitallman/keywest.html). Local outfitters include **No Wake Charters,** 201 William St., Key West (☎ 305-294-3912; www.nowakecharters.com), which uses a 31-foot sailboat for private half-day ($225 for two people) and full-day ($400 for two people) charters. The trip includes round-trip transportation from your hotel. **Southpoint Divers,** 714 Duval St. (☎ 800-891-3483 or 305-292-9778; www.southpointdivers.com), offers two-tank scuba trips for $59 if you have gear and $75 if you need to rent all your equipment.

Fishing

Bonefish, tarpon, and permit are some of the inshore fishing prizes. Grouper and snapper are common on reefs or around wrecks. Marlin, sailfish, blackfin tuna, wahoo, and dolphin are just a few of the creatures lurking in the depths. Party-boat rates average about $40 for a full day; charters that take four to six anglers are about $600.

Reservations can be arranged through **At The Water's Edge** (see listing under "Diving and snorkeling" above). You can also go straight to guides, such as **Key West Flats Fishing,** 903 Eisenhower, at the Harborside Motel

(☎ 305-294-7670; keywestflatsfishing.com), or **Lethal Weapon Charters,** 245 Front St., at the Key West Hilton Resort & Marina (☎ 305-296-6999; www.lethalweaponcharters.com).

There is a drought of good golfing in the Keys, but the **Key West Golf Club,** 6450 E. College Rd., MM 4.5, and then turn on College Road (☎ 305-294-5232; www.keywestgolf.com) can come to the rescue of desperate duffers. This 6,526-yard 18-holer was designed by Rees Jones and is open to the public. Mangroves and water spell many hazards. Greens fees are $55 to $80 from June to October, $80 to $140 from November to May.

Keeping a bit of the Keys for yourself

If you fall in love with local seafood, you can bring favorites home from **Key West Seafood,** 517 Duval St. (☎ 800-292-9853 or 305-292-4774; www.keywestseafood.com). It ships fresh stone crab claws (Oct–May only), lobster tails, shrimp, fish, and Key lime pie overnight. **Nellie & Joe's** (☎ 800-546-3743; www.keylimejuice.com) is Key West's oldest and best known bottler. Thirty years ago, the happy couple started pouring Key-lime juice into longneck beer bottles and corking them. Today, the selection also includes lemon juice and marinades. Although this wholesaler doesn't have its own storefront, you can find its products in local stores, or you can order by phone or online. **Peppers of Key West,** 291 Front St. and 602 Greene St. (☎ 800-597-2823; www.peppersofkeywest.com), has an exhaustive selection of hot sauces. The **Saltwater Angler,** in the Hilton Resort & Marina at 243 Front St. (☎ 800-223-1629 or 305-296-0700; www.saltwaterangler.com), features high-end fishing tackle as well as tropical clothes and gear. In addition to the aforementioned stores, most bars in town sell T-shirts and other trinkets bearing their logos.

Living it up after dark

According to some folks, **Captain Tony's,** 428 Greene St. (☎ 305-294-1838), is the original Sloppy Joe's of Hemingway's novels. Even if it isn't, Capt. Tony's is a delightful dive named for former owner/mayor Tony Tarracino. Folks get so caught up in the action here that many leave undergarments hanging from the ceiling.

The **Hog's Breath Saloon,** 400 Front St. (☎ 800-826-6969 or 305-292-2032; http://hogsbreath.com), comes with the motto: "Hog's Breath Is Better Than No Breath." Like most of the town, the saloon is raucous and sometimes raunchy. Expect such events as a homemade bikini contest where the combatants wear coconuts or water-filled plastic bags. The reigning **Sloppy Joe's,** 201 Duval St. (☎ 305-294-5717; www.sloppyjoes.com), has live music evenings and is often packed with tourists. The atmosphere is mellower but possibly the most touristy at **Jimmy Buffett's Margaritaville,** 500 Duval St. (☎ 305-292-1435; www.margaritaville.com), where parrot heads (Buffett fans) down tasty margaritas, but Jimmy doesn't. He left the place to the tourists years ago.

The **Sunset Celebration at Mallory Square,** behind the Clinton Street Market at the west end of Duval (near the cruise-ship docks), happens most days, even if it's a bit overcast. One of the island's most unusual theaters, Sunset Celebration is a show where dwarfs juggle fruit, aging hippies sing Janis Joplin's songs (sometimes a little off-key), and someone always swallows a flaming sword or walks a high wire. The performance is free, though handouts are widely solicited. For more information call ☎ **305-292-7700** or surf over to http://sunsetcelebration.org.

Coming out to enjoy the gay scene

Key West has a very active gay and lesbian social scene. Some of the best nightlife in town can be found in predominantly gay clubs that welcome anybody with an open mind. **Aqua** (☎ **305-292-8500**) at 711 Duval St., is the only real disco in town, playing eardrum-busting loud music and featuring a colorful assortment of folks boogying down. **One Saloon,** 514 Petronia St. (☎ **305-294-9349**), is another high-flying late-nighter among male partygoers. The same goes for the **801 Bourbon Bar** at 801 Duval (☎ **305-294-4737**), where nightly drag shows redefine your ideals of beauty. Considering the island's popularity with gay and lesbian travelers, it's no wonder that Key West boasts a number of hotels that cater specifically to gays and lesbians. Here are a few of the best in town:

- ✔ One of the city's best known and respected inns, **Alexander's Guest House,** 1118 Fleming St. (☎ **800-654-9919** or 305-294-9919; www.alexghouse.com; see map p. 151), has 17 rooms that have private baths, cable TV, and refrigerators. Some have full kitchens, verandas, and king-size beds. Rates at this award-winning guest-house ($150–$300 Dec–Apr, $90–$180 Apr–Dec) include continental breakfast (served poolside if the weather permits) and evening cocktails.

- ✔ **Pearl's Rainbow,** 525 United St. (☎ **800-749-6696** or 305-292-1450; www.pearlsrainbow.com; see map p. 151), is among Key West's better establishments catering solely to women. It offers rooms and suites, all with queen-size beds, TVs, telephones, and private baths. Pearl's Rainbow has two clothing-optional pools, a sun deck, and two hot tubs. Rates ($99–$169 May–December, $159–$249 Dec–Apr) include continental breakfasts.

Fast Facts: The Keys

Area Code

It's **305** throughout the Keys.

Hospitals

Mariners Hospital, Tavernier (☎ 305-852-4418). Lower Keys Health System, Key West (☎ 305-294-5531).

Information

For a free vacation kit, call the Florida Keys and Key West Visitors Bureau (☎ 800-352-5397 in U.S. and Canada, or 305-296-1552; www.fla-keys.com). You can write to the bureau at P.O. Box 1146, Key West, FL 33041, or when you're in town, stop in at 3406 N. Roosevelt Blvd., Suite 201.

Mail

Find the nearest post office location by dialing ☎ 800-275-8777.

Newspapers

The *Key West Citizen* (☎ 305-294-6641) is the Keys' only daily. Its "Paradise" section, published Thursdays, has things to do and see, mainly in the city but also in some of the other keys. The *Miami Herald* also circulates here, as does *USA Today.*

Taxes

The hotel tax is 11.5 percent, and there's a sales tax of 7.5 percent on most other items.

Weather Updates

For a recording of current conditions and forecast reports, call the local office of the National Weather Service at ☎ 305-229-4522, or check out the national Web site at www.nws.noaa.gov. You can also get information by watching the Weather Channel (www.weather.com).

Chapter 12

The Everglades

· ·

In This Chapter

▶ Hiking through cypress and swamp
▶ Biking to the bush and beyond
▶ Dining out in the Glades
▶ Viewing panthers, manatees, and crocodiles
▶ Experiencing outdoor adventures

· ·

"*There* are no other Everglades in the world. They are, they have always been, one of the unique regions of the earth, remote, never wholly known. Nothing anywhere else is like them: their vast glittering openness, wider than the enormous visible round of the horizon, the racing free saltiness and sweetness of their massive winds, under the dazzling blue heights of space," wrote the late Marjory Stoneman Douglas, whose crusade to preserve and protect the swampy splendor earned her the title of "mother of the Everglades." Some people, however, didn't think this mother knew best, calling the Everglades a worthless swamp. They were clearly wrong.

The Everglades, located just an hour's drive from the madness of Miami, are a magnet to naturalists, animal lovers, and those seeking peace and quiet.

Introducing the Everglades

Highways, agricultural runoff, and other fingerprints of civilization have partially destroyed Florida's largest wetland. Plants and animals have disappeared, the water has been poisoned, and habitats have been turned into subdivisions.

But parts of the Everglades remain untouched, leaving this spot, at least for now, primordial and unique. **Everglades National Park** is one of the most beautiful wildernesses in the continental United States. The park is basically a 40-mile-wide river, full of dense vegetation, which runs in super slo-mo; a gallon of water takes nearly a month to move from one end to the other. (Skip ahead to the map for an overview of "The Everglades.") High season for travel here is late November to May, when the weather is relatively cooler and less humid.

Everglades National Park lies in the southernmost part of mainland Florida, reaching from Everglades City on the west coast down to Cape Sable and a state of mind called Flamingo. Then, the park goes along the bottom of Florida to where the mainland gives way to the Keys. The park's supporting cast includes **Big Cypress Swamp** to the north and its namesake national preserve, **Fakahatchee Strand State Preserve,** and **Collier-Seminole State Park.** Combined, these four include the ancestral homes of the Seminole and Miccosukee Indians and the last habitats for scores of plant, tree, and animal species, including the Florida panther.

Although the area brims with natural wonders, it certainly is not a destination for everyone. But the Glades may be a good fit if you like places where:

- ✔ TV, a rare commodity, gets fuzzy reception.

- ✔ If you can find a newspaper, the front-page headline may be "Mayor Crowns Miss Speckled Perch."

- ✔ Bugs rule the day, the night, and the in between.

- ✔ Domino's doesn't deliver.

If these factors aren't enough to discourage you, consider also that it's hot in the winter, the sun in this part of Florida can cause a nasty burn, and bullfrogs' pickup lines are one of the few forms of nightlife.

Did I mention kids? Most children marvel when they see eagles, manatees, and river otters for the first time in the wild, but the magic wears off for many youngsters when they discover that video games and thrill rides (unless you consider the fact that airboat rides put virtual reality games to shame) don't exist here.

But if you consider all this and you're still psyched, then welcome to the Everglades!

Getting There

The Glades are just about as remote as Florida gets. Unless you come on a see-Florida-by-bus tour, you're going to need a rental car for the last leg of your journey. The best option is to fly into Miami (see Chapter 9 for airport information), rent a car, and then drive the 50 miles to the Glades. To get there from the airport, take I-95 south to the Dolphin Expressway/Highway 836; go west to the West Dade Expressway/Highway 821; then south to U.S. 41/Tamiami Trail, and then head west.

You can attack from the west, but **Southwest Florida International Airport** in Fort Myers is the only realistic landing zone (see Chapter 16 for more on the airport), and it's 70 miles from the western fringe of the Glades. If you opt for this route, after you're on the ground, take I-75 south to Naples and then head west to the Glades.

Getting Around

Without an airboat, a car is the only way around the Glades. That said, this is a wilderness region. Some of these roads, even the major highways, can be pretty remote, and signs of civilization are few and far between. A breakdown is the last thing you want to suffer on the more remote roads, especially if you're traveling at night. So have a solid plan if you're traveling by car. Don't take chances with your gas level, and skip the adventure routes or anything that could leave you stranded. My advice: Carry a cellphone in case of an emergency. Reception in the Glades is sketchy, but it's better than nothing — there are no pay phones in the area. Often, you can get a cellphone as an add-on to your rental car, so ask at the rental agency (see Chapter 5 for more on car rentals). Also, check — and then double-check — directions to activities, accommodations, and restaurants. Travel in daylight only. If a road looks suspicious, find another route or activity.

Looking at a regional road map (see the "Maps" entry in "Fast Facts" at the end of this chapter), you can see that straight paths from any given Point A to Point B are often nonexistent. So, make sure you allow enough time in your schedule. The major east–west roads are I-75/Alligator Alley (north end) and U.S. 41/Tamiami Trail central. The north–south roads are Highway 29 (west) and Highway 997 (east). Additionally, from Florida City south of Miami, take Highway 9336 and follow the signs to Everglades National Park and **Ernest F. Coe Visitor Center.** The highway continues southwest to the **Flamingo ranger station** on the park's south end. The other entrances include Everglades City (west) at U.S. 41/Tamiami Trail and **Shark Valley** (east) at U.S. 41/Tamiami Trail.

Staying in Style

Sparsely developed, the Everglades have only a meager smattering of places to stay. You won't find a Ritz-Carlton or even a Motel 6 here, unless you opt to stay on the park's outskirts. In addition to the following listings, check out the hotels in Miami (see Chapter 9) and those in Fort Myers and Naples (see Chapter 16) if you want more options. Also see the campgrounds listed under "Exploring the Everglades," later in this chapter.

Best Western Gateway to the Keys
$$ Florida City

This two-story, standard-style inn caters to a business clientele and has all the modern comforts. Suites have microwaves, coffeemakers, and small refrigerators. There's a Jacuzzi and a small pool. Local phone calls, a daily newspaper, and continental breakfast are included in the room rate. *Note:* A three-day stay is often required during high season; ask when you reserve.

The Everglades

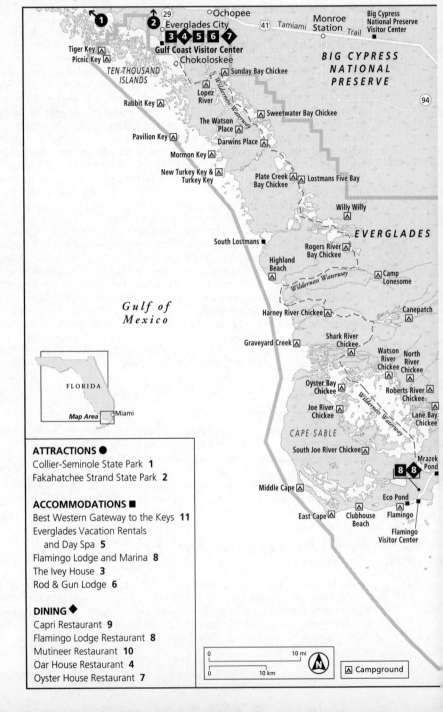

ATTRACTIONS ●
Collier-Seminole State Park **1**
Fakahatchee Strand State Park **2**

ACCOMMODATIONS ■
Best Western Gateway to the Keys **11**
Everglades Vacation Rentals
   and Day Spa **5**
Flamingo Lodge and Marina **8**
The Ivey House **3**
Rod & Gun Lodge **6**

DINING ◆
Capri Restaurant **9**
Flamingo Lodge Restaurant **8**
Mutineer Restaurant **10**
Oar House Restaurant **4**
Oyster House Restaurant **7**

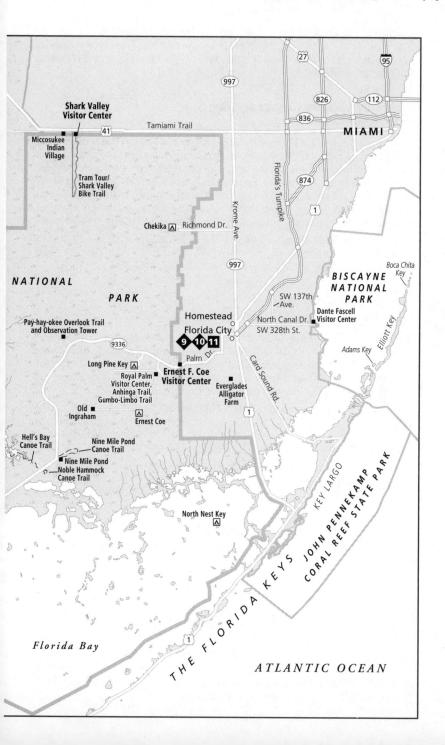

See map p. 166. 411 S. Krome Ave. ☎ *888-981-5100 or 305-246-5100. Fax: 305-242-0056.* www.bestwestern.com. *To get there: Just off U.S. 1, south of the Florida Turnpike. Rack rates: Dec–Apr $135–$150 (suites $144), May–Nov $109–$124 (suites $125). AE, DC, DISC, MC, V.*

Everglades Vacation Rentals and Day Spa
$ Everglades City

This very cute bed-and-breakfast, formerly known as On the Banks of the Everglades, is right on the money, as far as kitsch is concerned. It's a fabulous retreat from the lush greenery of the swampy Everglades to the even more lush greenery of money. Located in a building that was formerly the first bank established, in 1923, in Collier County, money is the premise this inn founds itself on but doesn't rob you of. A new day spa on the premises provides all the necessary pampering after a long day exploring the swamps.

See map p. 166. 201 W. Broadway. ☎ *888-431-1977. Fax: 941-695-3335.* www.banks oftheeverglades.com. *To get there: Off Highway 29, turn right on West Broadway. Rack rates: $100–$135. Closed: July–Oct. AE, DISC, MC, V.*

Flamingo Lodge and Marina
$–$$ Flamingo/Everglades National Park

If you want to commune with nature and stay inside the park, this resort is your only choice. Its 74 motel units and 24 cottages overlook Florida Bay. The cottages are larger and have kitchenettes, but they don't offer televisions. Choose from a host of outdoor activities. In many ways, the resort feels like a backwoods camp, and the scenery is great.

See map p. 166. 1 Flamingo Lodge Hwy. ☎ *800-600-3813 or 941-695-3101. Fax: 941-695-3921.* www.flamingolodge.com. *To get there: From Miami, head south on U.S. 1, turn right on Palm Drive/Highway 9336/SW 344th Street, and follow the signs. Rack rates: $68–$148. Closed: May–Oct. AE, DC, DISC, MC, V.*

The Ivey House
$–$$ Everglades City

Housed in what used to be a recreational center for the men who built the Tamiami Trail, the Ivey House offers three types of accommodations. In the original house (now a B&B), there are ten small rooms that share communal bathrooms (one each for women and men). One private cottage consists of two bedrooms, a full kitchen, a private bath, and a screened-in porch. The Ivey's new inn (opened in 2001) adds 17 rooms (with private bathrooms) that face a courtyard with a screened-in shallow "conversation" pool. During the summer, however, the mosquitoes are out in full force and a trip to the pool could leave you with multiple bites (screens or not). Bring bug spray!

See map p. 166. 107 Camellia St. ☎ *941-695-3299. Fax: 941-695-4155.* www.ivey house.com. *To get there: Off Highway 29, 1 block behind Circle K Convenience store. Rack rates: $70–$175 for the inn, which is open all year. Cottage is $125–$175 (open Nov–Apr); B&B is $50–$125 (open Nov–Apr). MC, V.*

Rod & Gun Lodge
$$ **Everglades City**

Sitting on the banks of the sleepy Barron River, the Rod & Gun Lodge was originally built as a private residence nearly 170 years ago, but Barron Collier turned it into a cozy hunting lodge in the 1920s. President Harry S. Truman flew in to sign Everglades National Park into existence in 1947 and stayed over as well. Other guests have included President Richard Nixon, Burt Reynolds, and Mick Jagger. But it's no Four Seasons. This rustic, old white clapboard house has plenty of history and all kinds of activities for sports enthusiasts, including a swimming pool, bicycle rentals, a tennis center, and nearby boat rentals and private fishing guides.

See map p. 166. Riverside Drive and Broadway. ☎ *941-695-2101. To get there: Off Highway 29 between Riverside Drive and Broadway. Rack rates: Winter $110; off season $95. No credit cards.*

Dining Out

As with places to stay, the Glades offer relatively few dining choices. If you're after some diversity, consider some of the Miami (Chapter 9) or Fort Myers/Naples (Chapter 16) dining options. *Note:* All Florida restaurants and food-serving bars are smoke-free.

Capri Restaurant
$ **Florida City   ITALIAN/AMERICAN**

The main attractions at this fortresslike restaurant — open since 1958 — are pasta, local seafood, beef, and salads. The reasonably large portions of Italian fare come at a moderate price.

See map p. 166. 935 N. Krome Ave. ☎ *305-247-1542. Reservations accepted. To get there: It's just west of U.S. 1 off Highway 997. Main courses: $7–$18. AE, MC, V. Open: Mon–Thurs 11 a.m.–10 p.m., Fri–Sat 11 a.m.–11 p.m.*

Flamingo Lodge Restaurant
$–$$ **Flamingo   SEAFOOD**

Located in Everglades National Park, the Flamingo Lodge Restaurant's views of Florida Bay complement a reasonably priced menu featuring shrimp scampi, steaks, chicken, pastas, and fresh fish served grilled, blackened, or fried. Sandwiches, salads, and conch chowder are the lighter luncheon fare.

See map p. 166. 1 Flamingo Lodge Hwy. ☎ *941-695-3101. Reservations suggested. To get there: From U.S. 1 south of Miami, turn right on Palm Drive/Highway 9336/SW 344th Street, and follow the signs to the park. Main courses: $11–$22. AE, DC, DISC, MC, V. Open: Daily 7–10 a.m., 11:30 a.m.–3 p.m., and 5:30–9 p.m.*

Mutineer Restaurant
$$ Florida City   SEAFOOD/STEAK

If you're a seafood freak, this is a good place to chow down before or after heading into the heart of the Everglades. Fresh marine cuisine, including stuffed grouper, blackened snapper, and frog legs sautéed in garlic fill the menu. You can also order steaks, chicken, and ribs. There's a lunch buffet ($7.50, 11 a.m.–3 p.m., Mon–Sat), a kids' menu, and, uh, a petting zoo.

See map p. 166. 11 SE First Ave./U.S. 1. ☎ 305-245-3377. Reservations aren't necessary. To get there: It's at the light just south of the Florida Turnpike. Main courses: $12–$27. AE, DC, DISC, MC, V. Open: Daily 11 a.m.–10 p.m.

Oar House Restaurant
$ Everglades City   SEAFOOD

This dinerlike establishment offers seafood baskets and regional specialties, including gator tail, turtle, and frog legs. If you're thirsty, the main dining room is equipped with a four-keg beer cooler. Reasonable prices, a selection of cardiac-friendly options, and waitresses who call everyone "hon" make this a good place to stop for a bite.

See map p. 166. 305 Collier Ave. ☎ 941-695-3535. Reservations are a good idea in winter. To get there: It's south of U.S. 41/Tamiami Trail off Highway 29. Main courses: $8–$18. MC, V. Open: Mon–Sat 6 a.m.–9 p.m., Sun 6 a.m.–2 p.m.

Oyster House Restaurant
$ Everglades City   SEAFOOD

Besides the fabulous hush puppies, the best thing about this quintessential seafood joint are the Kodak-moment views of the 10,000 Islands. Oh yeah, and if you eat too much and are too tired to go on, the restaurant has accommodations in the form of Cozy Cabins for $80 to $100 a night.

See map p. 166. Chokoloskee Causeway, Highway 29 South. ☎ 941-695-2073. To get there: Take Highway 29 to Everglades City. Turn right in Everglades City in front of Captains Table; go 1 block to traffic circle; ¾ of the way around, bear right. Go less than 1 mile. It's next door to Glades Haven, which is a two-story, gray building across from Everglades National Park. Main courses: $5–$17. MC, V. Open: Mon–Sat 6 a.m.–9 p.m., Sun 6 a.m.–2 p.m.

Exploring the Everglades

If you missed my hints earlier, glitter and glitz aren't expected to land in the Glades' region until Y3K. Just about everything to do in the Glades is natural or relates to nature. Although there are more places here to visit than most people realize, the headliner is Everglades National Park.

Top attractions

Everglades National Park

The park was dedicated by President Harry Truman in 1947, the same year Marjory Stoneman Douglas immortalized this corner of the world in her book, *The Everglades: River of Grass.* Douglas died in 1998 at 107, after dedicating her life to saving the Glades.

The park remains one of the few natural places to see endangered species such as American crocodiles, West Indian manatees, and, on an incredibly rare evening or early morning, Florida panthers. Unfortunately, many of the park's creatures are in severe decline elsewhere — fewer than 50 panthers are alive in the wild today — so a trip here may be your only opportunity to catch a glimpse of this kind of wildlife.

Just the facts

Here's all the information you'll need about the park:

- ✔ **Admission:** It's $10 per vehicle or $5 per person if you're on a motorcycle. Your admission pass is good for seven days. (Sorry, there's no shorter option.) Florida residents should consider getting an annual Everglades Park Pass ($25), and U.S. citizens 62 and over can snag a Golden Age Pass ($10) that's good for life.

- ✔ **Getting there:** Some of the park's northern reaches are accessible off U.S. 41/Tamiami Trail and Highway 29. You can get to its eastern and southern areas off State Road 9336, but much of the park has no easy access.

- ✔ **Information:** Write to **Everglades National Park,** 40001 Hwy. 9336, Homestead, FL 33034-6733 (☎ **305-242-7700;** www.everglades. national-park.com).

- ✔ **Peak season:** It runs from November through April.

- ✔ **Ranger programs:** More than 50 programs are conducted during peak season, and cost nothing more than the standard park admission. Regular walking tours include **Glades Glimpses,** a 50-minute outing discovering some of the area's flora and fauna, and **Anhinga Ambles,** a similar walking program that lasts 20 minutes. Check ahead for schedules unless you want to do the miles of hiking and biking trails on your own.

- ✔ **Visitor centers:** The park's five naturalist- and ranger-staffed centers are:

    - **Ernest F. Coe Visitor Center** (☎ **305-242-7700**), located at the main entrance to the park on Highway 9336, west of Florida City. It's open 8 a.m. to 5 p.m. daily.

    - **The Royal Palm Visitor Center** (☎ **305-242-7700**) is situated 4 miles west of the main entrance. It has a small nature museum and is open daily from 8 a.m. to 4 p.m.

- **The Flamingo Visitor Center** (☎ 941-695-3311), located 38 miles southwest of the main entrance on Highway 9336, offers interactive nature displays and exhibits. It's open daily from 8 a.m. to 5 p.m.

- **The Gulf Coast Visitor Center** (☎ 941-695-3311), at the western entrance to the park, in Everglades City off Highway 29, has exhibits on the local wildlife and offers information on boat tours. It's open daily from 7:30 a.m. to 5 p.m.

- **The Shark Valley Visitor Center** (☎ 305-221-8776), on U.S. 41/ Tamiami Trail, 15 miles west of Highway 997, is in the northern reaches of the park. The small center is open daily from 8:30 a.m. to 5:30 p.m.

Enjoying the park

Preparation is the key to a good experience in Everglades National Park. Here are a few things to keep in mind before you arrive:

✔ **Bike rentals:** You can rent bikes at **Shark Valley Tram Tours** (☎ 305-221-8455), adjacent to the Shark Valley Visitor Center (see "Just the facts" preceding this section), for $5.50 per hour.

✔ **Climate, clothing, and mosquitoes:** The Everglades are mild and pleasant from December through April, though *rare* cold fronts may bring you face to face with chilly, 58-degree conditions. Summers are wire-to-wire hot and humid — 90 degrees and 90 percent humidity *or worse!* Afternoon thunderstorms are common, and the mosquitoes are ferocious, so bring repellent. Wear comfortable sportswear in winter; loose-fitting pants, long-sleeved shirts, and plenty of sunscreen in summer.

✔ **Supplies:** Bring your own water and snacks (they're not available in most areas), but keep in mind that snacks aren't allowed on the interpretive trails, which are marked for self-guided hikers.

Camping out

If you really want to get back to nature, try camping overnight in the Everglades. Three campgrounds have tent and RV sites, restrooms, and water but no electrical hookups. (I hope you like your showers cold.) All three sites are open year-round. To make reservations, call ☎ 800-365-2267 (U.S. only), 301-722-1257, or 888-530-9796 with a TTY for the hearing-impaired. Reservations should be made at least 30 days in advance. Sites are $14 nightly for a maximum of eight people. Here's a rundown of your choices:

✔ **Long Pine Key Campground:** Seven miles from the main entrance, just off the main road, the campground has 108 drive-up sites for tents and RVs. There are restrooms, water, phones, a sewer dump station, and freshwater fills but no showers. A nearby picnic area has fire grates. The camp also has a fishing pond, an amphitheater for winter programs, and several hiking trails.

✔ **Flamingo Campground:** Located at the end of the main park road in Flamingo, the campground has 234 drive-in sites, including 55 with a view of the water. There are cold-water showers, two dump stations, picnic tables, grills, and a public telephone. Flamingo has an observation tower, hiking and canoe trails, and a store with limited groceries and camping supplies.

✔ **Chekika:** Located 6 miles west of Krome Avenue/Highway 997 on SW 168th Street, southwest of Miami, Chekika has 20 sites for RVs and tents, with water basins for filling jugs, a dump station with a freshwater fill, hot showers, and a fishing pond.

Big Cypress National Preserve

Not as well known as its national-park neighbor, this preserve is a part of the larger, 2,400-square-mile Big Cypress Swamp, and home to an incredible array of wildlife, including alligators, bald eagles, black bears, wood storks, and rare Florida panthers. Although a portion of the preserve is swampland, it also has dry prairies, marshes, sloughs, hardwood uplands, mangroves, and cypress forests. The preserve's name refers to the vast amount of cypresses that once blanketed the entire area. Loggers cut down most of the virgin trees in the 1930s and 1940s. Those that remain are mainly dwarf pond cypresses, but you can still find the occasional 700-year-old bald cypress within the 728,000-acre sanctuary.

Big Cypress was established as a northwest buffer to Everglades National Park and includes the ancestral home of the Seminole and Miccosukee Indians. It's accessible from either coast via I-75/Alligator Alley (north) and U.S. 41/Tamiami Trail (south).

You'll find Big Cypress rather lean on visitor amenities; this is true wilderness. So unless you're into roughing it, an afternoon of exploration will suffice.

Here is some information that will help make your visit more enjoyable:

✔ **Admission:** It doesn't get much cheaper than free.

✔ **Information:** Call ☎ 941-695-4111, write to **Big Cypress National Preserve Headquarters,** HCR 61, Box 110, Ochopee, FL 34141, or surf over to www.nps.gov/bicy. Request a map and specialized information on the preserve.

✔ **Lodging and camping facilities:** Eight primitive campgrounds are available to the public, seven of which are free: Bear Island, Midway, Burns Lake, Monument, Loop Road, Pinecrest, and Mitchell's Landing. None have water or restrooms. Dona Drive Campground ($4 per night) has an RV dump station. Call the preserve's headquarters for more information on camping here.

✔ **Oasis Visitor Center:** It's located 20 miles east of Ochopee (55 miles east of Naples) on U.S. 41/Tamiami Trail. There's a 15-minute film about the preserve as well as exhibits on its flora and fauna. Pick up a free trail map here before heading into Big Cypress. It's open daily from 8:30 a.m. to 4:30 p.m.

✔ **Programs and activities:** Ranger-led hikes, canoe trips, bike rides, and campfire programs at the campgrounds are offered during the winter season. If you go during the rainy season, prepare to hike through ankle-deep water on some of the trails.

✔ **Supplies:** Located far away from civilization, the preserve has no stores, gas stations, or restaurants. Make sure to pack plenty of snacks and water, and fill up your tank before you set off.

Fakahatchee Strand State Park

You may laugh at the name, but this park is serious business — especially for Hollywood types. Located in the area's southwest corner, this second preserve in the Big Cypress Swamp is something of a secret, but discovery may be just over the horizon. The Fakahatchee served as a location for the 2002 film *Adaptation,* based on the book *The Orchid Thief* about a man obsessed with poaching a rare flower.

For now, the park is about as far as you can get from Hollywood. While Everglades National Park gets more than 1 million visitors a year, some 130,000 motorists drive through the Fakahatchee, but only a few stop to enjoy it. Part of the blame rests with the swamp's inhospitable nature. It's wild and not easily accessible. To get here, the best route involves taking I-75/Alligator Alley from Naples or Fort Lauderdale, exiting on Highway 29 and going 14 miles south to the ranger station on Jane's Scenic Drive.

Those who come will find bald cypresses, the largest stand of royal palms in North America, and ghost orchids along the 11-mile Jane's Scenic Drive, an improved dirt road. Visits near dawn and dusk may give you a glimpse of a black bear, bobcat, or Everglades mink, but don't count on it. Fox squirrels, wood storks, roseate spoonbills, snowy white egrets, and great blue herons are commonly observed. Stay on the main road and don't be tempted by those dirt spur roads that go to the swamp's wilder areas.

Searching for skunk apes

The Everglades' answer to Bigfoot and Yeti, Skunk Apes are supposed to be big, hairy, and very aromatic (imagine rotten eggs and fresh dung with a trace of road-kill skunk). Legend has it that these man-apes live in abandoned alligator dens, which would account for the smell and their muddy-brown appearance. The 7-foot, 300-pound (or more) creatures supposedly love lima beans. If all this sounds fascinating to you, just ask one of the many willing storytellers, but so far there's little proof of them or their lima-bean fixation.

Considering the remoteness of the location, you won't find many visitor-oriented amenities here, but keep in mind the following:

- ✔ **Admission:** This is another freebie.

- ✔ **Information:** Call ☎ **941-695-4593,** write to P.O. Box 548, Copeland, FL 33926, or go to www.abfla.com/parks/FakahatcheeStrand/fakahatchee.html.

- ✔ **Programs and activities:** Although this preserve is self-guided, there's a 2,000-foot boardwalk meandering through virgin cypress trees at Big Cypress Bend, which is about 3 miles west of Highway 29 on U.S. 41. From November through February, rangers lead swamp walks at 10 a.m. the third Saturday of the month. They're limited to 15 people, and reservations are required; call ☎ **941-695-4593** for more information or to make a reservation.

- ✔ **Supplies:** This is the boonies — bring plenty of food and water, and top off your gas tank before you arrive.

Collier-Seminole State Park

In the early 1940s, Barron Collier, a wealthy advertising executive and developer, laid the framework for a park that went into the state ledger in 1947. It's named for him and the tribe that has long made the area its home. The park's 6,430 acres have rare royal palms, as well as salt marshes, mangrove and cypress swamps, and pine flatwoods. Wildlife includes wood storks, bald eagles, red-cockaded woodpeckers, American crocodiles, black bears, and fox squirrels. Panthers, the state animal, and manatees, the state marine mammal, may also be seen occasionally.

The park also has fishing, boating, picnicking, canoeing, and several hiking trails. To get here, head for the entrance, 17 miles east of Naples on U.S. 41/Tamiami Trail.

Unlike the nature preserves, the park offers a bit more for visitors to see and do. If you decide to visit, keep the following in mind:

- ✔ **Admission:** $4 per vehicle.

- ✔ **Information:** Call ☎ **941-394-3397** or write to Collier-Seminole State Park, 20200 U.S. 41 S., Naples, FL 33961. Information is available online at www.floridastateparks.org/collier-seminole/default.asp. Also, a Seminole-style log fort at the park's entrance houses a small information center.

- ✔ **Programs and activities:** A 6½-mile hiking trail winds through pine flatwoods and cypresses; a self-guided trail features a boardwalk system and observation platform overlooking the salt marsh. Rangers lead tours through the park from December to April. You can see plant and wildlife exhibits in the park's interpretive center. Boat tours down river ($10 for adults, $7.50 for kids 6–12 years) are available from a concessionaire.

Going outdoors in the Everglades

This isn't theme-park central, but there are plenty of outdoor activities in the Everglades to keep you occupied.

Cycling enthusiasts should head for **Shark Valley Tram Tours** (☎ 305-221-8455; www.nps.gov/ever/visit/tramroad.htm) in Everglades National Park (see the information on the Shark Valley Visitor Center in "Just the facts," earlier); it rents bikes for $4.25 per hour. The area has one of the top cycling venues in South Florida, a 15-mile loop that has no traffic except other peddlers and trams. Alligators are everywhere as you bike, so watch where you pedal! They don't pose a major danger, but obviously I suggest you just let them be and don't disturb them. Give yourself at least 3 hours to explore the entire trail. **Everglades City** has a 4-mile paved trail across the scenic causeway to Chokoloskee Island. You can rent wheels at **The Ivey House,** 107 Camellia St. (☎ 941-695-3299), for $3 an hour and $15 a day from November to May.

If you want to go canoeing, Everglades National Park has four marked trails, 4 to 22 miles long, with starting points from the Flamingo area. You can also take on all or parts of the 99-mile Wilderness Waterway from Flamingo to Everglades City. Visitor centers (see "Everglades National Park," earlier in this chapter) distribute maps. You can rent canoes at the **Flamingo Lodge and Marina** in Everglades National Park, at the southwest end of Highway 9336 (☎ 941-695-3101; www.flamingo lodge.com), for $8 an hour and $22 for a half-day ($12 and $30, respectively, for a family-size model). **North American Canoe Tours,** 107 Camellia St., at the Ivey House in Everglades City (☎ 941-695-4666), rents canoes for $25 a day (Nov–May). This outfitter also leads canoe tours starting at $40 a half-day and $50 a full day.

The Everglades is not renowned for fishing. There are few guide services; the coast is so remote that it discourages most surf fishermen. Because the Glades are shallow, freshwater fishing is often frustrating.

Flamingo Lodge and Marina is the exception (☎ 941-695-3101; www.flamingolodge.com) in Everglades National Park. Several guides go after redfish, snook, tarpon, and trout out of the marina. An excursion costs $250 per half-day for two people, $350 for a full day.

If you want a few more selections to choose from while you're in the Everglades area, I list some more fishing options in Chapter 15.

Taking a guided tour

Billie Swamp Safari, HC-61, Box 46, Clewiston, FL 33440 (☎ 800-949-6101 or 941-983-6101; www.seminoletribe.com/safari) is somewhat Disneyfied but nonetheless offers a unique way to see the landscape. The Seminole Tribe of Florida has opened some 2,000 acres of its Big Cypress Reservation to **eco-tours.** The tours include a ride in a *swamp buggy* (a big truck with monster tires) over hardwood hammocks, wetlands, and sloughs that are home to white-tailed deer, bison, wild hogs, bald eagles, and alligators ($20 for adults, $18 seniors, $10 for kids 4–12). You also can take an airboat ride ($12 adults) or watch a 40-minute snake-and-alligator show ($8 for adults, $4 for kids). To get there from Naples or Fort Lauderdale, take I-75 to Exit 14; then go north 19 miles to the Big Cypress Seminole Indian Reservation.

Flamingo Lodge and Marina, at the southwest end of Highway 9336 in Everglades National Park (☎ **941-695-3101;** www.flamingolodge.com), offers two-hour backcountry cruises ($16 for adults, $8 for kids 6–12) and 90-minute Florida Bay cruises ($10 for adults, $5 for kids 6–12), among other tours.

Fast Facts

Area Code
It's **305** to the east and **941** to the west.

Hospitals
The nearest are Homestead Hospital, 160 N.W. 13th St., Homestead (☎ 305-242-3535), and Naples Community Hospital, 350 Seventh St. N., Naples (☎ 941-436-5111).

Information
For information on the area, contact the Everglades Area Chamber of Commerce (☎ 941-695-3941; www.florida-everglades.com). Although not particularly well designed, the Web site offers some valuable advice, including maps, fishing tips, event listings, and a wildlife photo gallery.

Mail
U.S. post offices are located at 301 Collier Ave. in Everglades City and 333 W. Palm Dr. in Homestead. To find a post office location anywhere in the United States, call ☎ 800-275-8777.

Maps
Ask the Chamber of Commerce (see "Information" earlier in this section) for a detailed map, or, if you're renting a car, ask the rental agency for a map. You can also buy maps at some convenience stores for $3 to $5.

Newspapers
The Naples Daily News (☎ 941-262-3161; www.naplesnews.com) and the Miami Herald (☎ 305-350-2111; www.herald.com) are the two major papers.

Taxes
Florida's sales tax is 6 percent. Hotels here add another 3 percent.

Weather Updates
For a recording of current conditions and forecast reports, call the local office of the National Weather Service at ☎ 305-229-4522, or check out the Web site (www.nws.noaa.gov). You can also get information from the Weather Channel (www.weather.com).

Chapter 13

The Gold Coast

. . . .

In This Chapter

▶ Checking out the Gold Coast

▶ Relaxing on the beaches in Fort Lauderdale and Hollywood

▶ Shopping 'til you drop in Boca Raton and Palm Beach

. . . .

*I*t's easy to think that the Gold Coast earned its name because of the blue-haired ladies who have a fancy for gold lamé, or because people like Donald Trump have channeled the spirit of the Great Gatsby in an ostentatious recreation of the Gilded Age, but not so. Named for the gold salvaged from shipwrecks off its coastline, the Gold Coast shines for over 60 miles of Atlantic shoreline, from the pristine sands of Jupiter in Northern Palm Beach County to the legendary strip of beaches in Fort Lauderdale. Although the only gold you're likely to find on the 60 miles of beaches is skin tones and a few chains dangling from necks here and there, you'll encounter the requisite bodies straight out of *Baywatch* central casting as well as families (oh yeah — and some metal-detecting seniors hoping to strike it rich). Though the beaches aren't as rowdy as they used to be, there's always lots of amusement to be found on them.

And although this region maintains the gold standard when it comes to mansions, jewels, and Rolls-Royces, you don't need a 24-carat wallet to have a good time here, especially if you come during the off season, which runs from May through October.

Seeing the Gold Coast

The most popular areas in the Gold Coast are Fort Lauderdale, Boca Raton, and Palm Beach. While **Fort Lauderdale** is a favored beachfront destination, **Boca Raton** and **Palm Beach** are better known for their country-club lifestyles and excellent shopping. Farther north is the quietly popular **Jupiter,** best known for spring training at the Roger Dean Stadium. In between these better-traveled destinations are a few things worth stopping for, but not much.

Technically the Gold Coast begins with **Hallandale,** which is a sleepy condo community just north of North Miami Beach. Its main attractions are the Gulfstream Raceway and the fact that it leads to the rest of the

Gold Coast. **Hollywood** comes right after Hallandale, and it's gone through a renaissance of sorts. Popular with Canadian snowbirds, Hollywood's a low-key beach town with a touristy boardwalk and a "downtown" featuring cafes, clubs, and bars. Further north after Boca Raton are two burgeoning Gold Coast cities — **West Palm Beach** and **Delray Beach,** both of which are booming with development from modern loft buildings and luxe condos to chichi restaurants, bars, shopping, and nightlife in general.

The cities and towns on the Gold Coast are close enough together that you can mix and match many of the restaurants and attractions.

Driving north along the coastline is one of the best ways to fully appreciate what the Gold Coast is all about — it's a perspective you certainly won't find in a shopping mall.

The area also has 300 miles of **Intracoastal Waterway** — the aquatic "highway" that travels from Boston to Key West. Dotted with million-dollar houses and mega yachts, the Intracoastal includes Fort Lauderdale's Venetian-inspired canals. A boating excursion on its waters is the South Florida equivalent of a scenic drive through Beverly Hills.

Unfortunately, like its neighbors to the south, the Gold Coast can be prohibitively hot and buggy in the summer. The good news is that bargains are plentiful in the summer months (May–Oct), when many locals take advantage of package deals and uncrowded resorts.

Fort Lauderdale, Hollywood, and Beyond

When it comes to coastal development in Florida, the upper Gold Coast is second only to Miami. The beach highways (A1A/Ocean Boulevard/ Atlantic Boulevard) and U.S. 1 are well developed, offering many places to stay and eat, numerous things to do, and 23 miles of coast. On the more tranquil side, **Hollywood** is quaint but growing, sort of like Miami's South Beach without the tourist glut, parking fees, and attitude. **Lauderdale-by-the-Sea** also tends to be more serene and quiet.

Spring-break mayhem is a thing of the past in Fort Lauderdale, thanks to tough ordinances. People looking for rowdier action had best head down to South Beach or up to Daytona.

Getting there

Flying is the easiest, quickest, and most economical way to get here from most places. Florida highways and rail service make car and train travel good secondary options, but driving is time-consuming, and taking a train is virtually as expensive as flying.

By plane

Fort Lauderdale Hollywood International Airport (☎ 954-359-6100;
www.broward.org/fll.htm) is Florida's fourth largest airport, trans-
porting almost 14 million passengers per year. Thirty-three domestic,
foreign, and commuter airlines land here. In January 2005, the airport
debuted a fantastic Car Rental Center that houses ten rental companies
under one roof, making renting a car from the airport very convenient.
Levels 1 through 4 in the Rental Center will be the new home of Alamo,
Avis, Budget, Dollar, Enterprise, E-Z, Hertz, National, Royal, and Thrifty
(see the "Quick Concierge" in the back of this book for telephone numbers and Web sites). Levels 5 through 9 will provide 5,500 spaces for
public parking. Taxis and shuttles (see "Getting around," a little later
in this chapter) are on the same level. The same goes for **Tri-County
Airport Express** (☎ 800-244-8252 or 954-561-8888), which offers several
ride options, and limousine services, such as **Broward Limousine**
(☎ 954-791-3000) and **Elite Limousine** (☎ 954-563-2122).

Here are sample rates from the airport to Fort Lauderdale Beach:

- ✔ **Taxi:** $14 to $18 for up to five
- ✔ **Limousine:** $65 for up to eight
- ✔ **Shuttle:** $7 to $11 per person

If you want additional options, **Miami International Airport** (☎ 305-876-
7000; www.miami-airport.com) is only an hour's drive south of Fort
Lauderdale and welcomes more than 100 airlines, including 42 foreign
carriers (see "Getting there" in Chapter 9 for more on MIA). Sometimes
airfares are cheaper if you fly into one airport instead of another, so
check to see if you can reduce costs by flying into Miami instead of Fort
Lauderdale. All major airlines also fly to the **Palm Beach International
Airport,** at Congress Avenue and Belvedere Road (☎ 561-471-7400).

By car

If you're coming from Florida's west coast, I-75 and U.S. 41/Tamiami Trail
are your best choices. I-95 and Florida's Turnpike are the best routes to
drive on from the east coast; both require a 350- to 400-mile journey after
you cross the Florida/Georgia line. U.S. 1 (east coast) and U.S. 27 (west
coast) are additional options if you don't mind passing through small
towns.

By train

Amtrak (☎ 800-872-7245; www.amtrak.com) runs two trains a day out
of New York, but they take 28 to 30 hours to reach Fort Lauderdale.
Amtrak rides from other cities can take even longer. **Amtrak** has a terminal in West Palm Beach, at 201 S. Tamarind Ave. (☎ 561-832-6169).

Train travel in the United States doesn't cost much less than airfare. If you want a sleeper car, the price is usually higher. Unless your heart is set on a train trip, you can most likely do better traveling in the air than on the ground. See Chapter 4 for more Amtrak information.

Getting around

If you stick to the tourist-friendly coastal cities and the areas immediately adjacent to them, you can find a number of good transportation options.

By car

Less expensive than taking cabs and more efficient than public transit, driving is the best way to get around Fort Lauderdale. The main north–south routes are U.S. 1/Federal Highway, A1A/Ocean Boulevard on the beach side (for scenic reasons), and I-95 (for longer hauls). The primary east–west thoroughfares are I-595, Hallandale Beach Boulevard/Highway 858, Hollywood Boulevard/Highway 820, Sheridan Street/Highway 822, SW 24th Street/Highway 84, Griffin Road/Highway 818, Broward Boulevard/Las Olas/Highway 842, Sunrise Boulevard/Highway 838, Oakland Park Boulevard/Highway 816, and Commercial Boulevard/Highway 870.

If you plan on driving around, invest in a map (see "Maps" in "Fast Facts" at the end of this section on Fort Lauderdale). That said, the Fort Lauderdale grid is pretty simple to navigate; traffic, except during rush hour, isn't particularly nasty. Most streets have numbers, but names are given to the main thoroughfares, such as those that run from the west to the beaches and back. The exception is the 17th Street Causeway, which is the east–west road that leads to Port Everglades, a major shipping and cruise port, before turning north into A1A (the road that travels along the beach). All the major streets, except Broward, run across bridges over the Intracoastal Waterway.

Although numbered streets grow consecutively between named boulevards, you can find some exceptions. For the most part, however, Andrews Avenue divides the city between east and west, and Broward Boulevard divides north and south. Streets run east and west; avenues run north and south. Also, all addresses are assigned to one of four quadrant designations: NE, NW, SE, and SW. A street address that's NE is north of Broward Boulevard and east of Andrews Avenue.

By taxi

Taxi fares for up to five passengers are $2.50 for the first mile and $1.75 for each additional mile. The biggest cab company in the area is **Yellow Cab/Checker** (☎ **954-565-5400**).

Unless you happen to be at a major hotel, hailing a taxi can be next to impossible; so call ahead.

By water taxi

The upper Gold Coast is one of the few places in the United States where you can call a taxi and have a boat pick you up. The marine highway is the Intracoastal Waterway. In addition to sightseeing, the boat stops include boutiques and eateries along Las Olas Boulevard.

Water Taxi of Fort Lauderdale (☎ 954-467-0008; www.watertaxi.com) sells one-way tickets for $4 and an unlimited day pass for $5. Taking a water taxi is cheaper than renting a car, as long as you want to stay in its service area. Water taxis run from 10 a.m. until midnight on weekdays and until 2 a.m. on weekends.

By bus

Broward County Transit (☎ 954-357-8400; www.broward.org/bct/welcome.htm) has 250 buses covering 30 routes. The fare is $1 for adults, 50¢ for seniors and kids taller than 40 inches (bring exact change). Buses run daily from 4:45 a.m. to 12:35 a.m.

If you stay on the beach and limit your goings, you can get away with using public transportation. Like many other Florida transit systems, however, Broward County's is designed for commuters, not tourists. Unless you really don't want to rent a car, I can't recommend this public transit system as an efficient way to get around the area.

By train

Tri-Rail (☎ 800-874-7245 or 954-942-7245) is a 67-mile commuter line that connects Palm Beach, Broward, and Miami-Dade counties. As is often the case, this public-transit line isn't very tourist-friendly. Six commuter stations are located in the Greater Fort Lauderdale area. Round-trip fares range from $3.50 to $9.25.

Staying in style

Fort Lauderdale's beach zone is teeming with hotels and motels in every style, size, and price range. (See the "Fort Lauderdale" map later in this chapter.) If you're on a tight budget, look for a hotel in Hollywood, where rates are often cheaper. Many accommodations let kids under 12 (and sometimes under 18) stay free if you don't exceed the maximum-room occupancy. To be safe, though, ask when booking a room. Refer to Chapter 6 for general information about booking accommodations in Florida.

Sales and hotel taxes add 11 percent to your bill. Also note that winter (Dec–Apr) is peak season, and rates can be 50 percent higher than during the rest of the year.

If you're traveling during high season and can't find a room that you're happy with, or you don't want to deal directly with the hotels, you can choose from two good booking services. The **Central Reservation Service** (☎ 800-555-7555; www.reservation-service.com), and

Florida Hotel Network (☎ 800-538-3616; www.floridahotels.com) will make lodging arrangements after you tell them your needs.

The area's best hotels

Banyan Marina Resort
$$ Fort Lauderdale

Built around a stunning 75-year-old banyan tree, the Banyan Marina Resort is located directly on the active canals halfway between Fort Lauderdale's downtown and the beach. These fabulous waterfront apartments, located on a beautifully landscaped residential island, may have you vowing never to stay in a hotel again. They're intimate, charming, *and* reasonably priced.

See map p. 184. 111 Isle of Venice. ☎ *954-524-4430. Fax 954-764-4870.* www.banyan marina.com. *To get there: From I-95, exit Broward Boulevard East; cross U.S. 1 and turn right on SE 15th Avenue. At the first traffic light (Las Olas Boulevard), turn left. Turn left at the third island (Isle of Venice). Free parking. Rack rates: Winter $95–$250 apartment; off season $60–$170 apartment. MC, V.*

Lago Mar Resort and Club
$$–$$$ Fort Lauderdale Beach

Not to be confused with Donald Trump's home-turned–country club Mar a Lago, Lago Mar is an equal-opportunity hotel in which guests have access to the broadest and best strip of beach in the entire city, not to mention the picture-perfect bougainvillea-lined, 9,000-square-foot swimming lagoon. Lago Mar is very family oriented, with lots of facilities and supervised activities for children, especially during school holidays. For the adults, there's a full-service spa and 1,000-square-foot exercise facility.

See map p. 184. 1700 S. Ocean Dr./A1A. ☎ *877-524-6627 or 954-523-6511. Fax: 954-524-6627.* www.lagomar.com. *To get there: From 17th St. Bridge, go east to where A1A turns north along ocean. Free parking. Rack rates: Nov $125–$210 ($185–$480 suites), Dec–Apr $195–$295 ($305–$685 suites), May–Oct $115–$150 ($150–$380 suites). AE, CB, DISC, MC, V.*

Marriott's Harbor Beach
$$$–$$$$ Fort Lauderdale Beach

Everything in this place is huge — from the guest rooms and suites to the 8,000-square-foot swimming pool to the $8 million, 24,000-square-foot European spa. All rooms open onto private balconies overlooking either the ocean or the Intracoastal Waterway. Best of all, it's located on 16 secluded, oceanfront acres close enough — or far away enough, depending on your frame of mind — to/from the Fort Lauderdale "strip."

See map p. 184. 3030 Holiday Dr. ☎ *800-800-222-6543 or 954-525-4000. Fax 954-766-6193.* www.marriottharborbeach.com. *To get there: From I-95, exit on I-595 east to U.S. 1 N.; proceed to SE 17th Street; make a right and go over the Intracoastal bridge past three traffic lights to Holiday Drive; turn right. Valet parking: $10. Rack rates: Winter $259–$429; off season $179–$219. AE, DC, DISC, MC, V.*

Fort Lauderdale

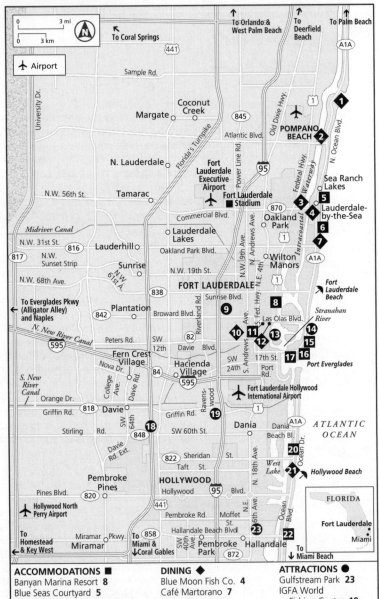

ACCOMMODATIONS ■
Banyan Marina Resort **8**
Blue Seas Courtyard **5**
Courtyard Villa on the Ocean **6**
Hyatt Regency Pier Sixty-Six **17**
Lago Mar Resort and Club **16**
Marriott's Harbor Beach **15**
Riverside Hotel **11**
Sea Downs
(and the Bougainvillea) **20**
Westin Diplomat Resort & Spa **22**

DINING ◆
Blue Moon Fish Co. **4**
Café Martorano **7**
Cap's Place
Island Restaurant **1**
Eduardo De San Angel **3**
Himmarshee Bar & Grill **10**
Mark's Las Olas **12**
Sunfish Grill **2**
Taverna Opa **21**

ATTRACTIONS ●
Gulfstream Park **23**
IGFA World
Fishing Center **19**
International Swimming
Hall of Fame **14**
Museum of Discovery
and Science **9**
Seminole Hard Rock
Hotel and Casino **18**
Stranahan House **13**

Riverside Hotel
$$–$$$$ Fort Lauderdale

There's no beach here, but the hotel, built in 1936, is located on the sleepy and scenic New River, capturing the essence of Old Florida. Out front, the New Orleans–style hotel faces Las Olas Boulevard, where the old meets the nouveau. The best rooms face the New River, but it's hard to see the water past the parking lot and trees. Twelve rooms offer king-size beds with mirrored canopies and flowing drapes. There are also seven elegantly decorated suites with wet bars and French doors that lead to private balconies.

See map p. 184. 620 E. Las Olas Blvd. ☎ *800-325-3280 or 954-467-0671. Fax 954-462-2148.* www.riversidehotel.com. *To get there: From I-95, exit onto Broward Boulevard; turn right onto Federal Highway (U.S. 1) and then left onto Las Olas Boulevard. Valet parking: $8–$10. Rack rates: Winter $179–$369 suite; off season $124–$339 suite. AE, DC, MC, V.*

Sea Downs (and the Bougainvillea)
$–$$ Hollywood

This bargain accommodation is often booked months in advance by returning guests who want to be directly on the beach without paying a fortune. Apartmentlike rooms have been redecorated here and exude a very Floridian, grandmotherly feel. For even more of a bargain, check out the hotel's sister property next door, the 11-unit Bougainvillea. Guests at both hotels share the Sea Downs's pool.

See map p. 184. 2900 N. Surf Rd. ☎ *954-923-4968. Fax 954-923-8747.* www.seadowns.com *or* www.bougainvilleahollywood.com. *To get there: From I-95, exit Sheridan Street East to Florida A1A, go south; drive ½ mile to Coolidge Street; turn left. Free parking. Rack rates: Winter $80–$135 daily, $511–$875 weekly; off season $52–$99 daily; $315–$651 weekly. No credit cards.*

Westin Diplomat Resort & Spa
$$$–$$$$ Hollywood

This 1,060-room, full-service beach resort is Hollywood's biggest hope for revitalization. The hotel's main building is a 39-story oceanfront tower (with adjacent conference center) surrounded by 8 acres of man-made lakes. A gorgeous bridged, glass-bottomed swimming pool with cascading waterfalls, private cabanas, and a slew of water sports and activities adds a tropical touch. Rooms are a cross between a subtle boutique hotel and an Art Deco throwback, with dark woods, hand-cut marble and, most impressive, the ten-layer Heavenly Bed, a Westin trademark with custom-designed mattresses and a very cushy down blanket (crank up the AC!). Dining options are resortlike in quantity and quality.

See map p. 184. 3555 S. Ocean Dr. (A1A). ☎ *800-327-1212 or 954-457-2000.* www.diplomatresort.com. *To get there: From I-95, take the Hallandale Beach Boulevard exit and go all the way east to A1A. Valet parking: $16. Rack rates: Winter $285–$370; off season $239–$325. AE, DC, DISC, MC, V.*

Runner-up hotels

If you can't find lodging in the preceding listings to satisfy your tastes and budget, here are a few more places to consider:

Blue Seas Courtyard

$ Lauderdale-by-the-Sea This 1940s motel will take you back to the days of Old Florida, thanks to a careful restoration and renovation. Rooms are large with full kitchen and massive bathroom. With the beach just a block away, this is a great bargain. *See map p. 184. 4525 El Mar Dr.* ☎ *877-225-8373 or 954-772-6337.* www.blueseascourtyard.com.

Courtyard Villa on the Ocean

$$ Lauderdale-by-the-Sea Once a private home, this eight-room hotel has been beautifully restored with 19th-century antique reproductions. It offers a romantic getaway right on the beach. *See map p. 184. 4312 El Mar Dr.* ☎ *800-291-3560 or 954-776-1164.* www.courtyardvilla.com.

Hyatt Regency Pier Sixty-Six

$$$ Fort Lauderdale This luxury resort offers 380 rooms with balconies, a full range of recreational activities and facilities, a spa, and a 142-slip marina on the Stranahan River. *See map p. 184. 2301 SE 17th St./A1A.* ☎ *800-633-7313 or 954-525-6666.* www.hyatt.com.

Dining out

Much like Miami, Broward County has virtually any kind of cuisine you can imagine. The largest collection of restaurants in town is along Las Olas Boulevard. Not surprisingly, seafood is a good bet in this area. *Note:* All Florida restaurants and food-serving bars are smoke-free.

Don't forget to add 6 percent local sales tax to your budget.

If you have a car, also try some of the Palm Beach–area restaurants described later in this chapter or the Miami restaurants in Chapter 9.

Blue Moon Fish Co.
$$ Lauderdale-by-the-Sea CONTINENTAL/SEAFOOD

Weather permitting, dine alfresco and watch the yachts glide by on the Intracoastal Waterway or eat in the Art Deco dining room of this casually elegant restaurant. The open kitchen dishes out excellent seafood, such as sea bass in a macadamia-nut crust, and oak-roasted swordfish. A raw bar and a nice wine list are available, too.

See map p. 184. 4405 W. Tradewinds Ave. ☎ *954-267-9888. Reservations suggested. To get there: On the Intracoastal, north of Commercial Boulevard. Main courses: $19–$29. AE, MC, V. Open: Daily 11:30 a.m.–3 p.m.; Sun–Thurs 6–10 p.m., Fri–Sat 6–11 p.m.*

Café Martorano
$$–$$$ **Fort Lauderdale ITALIAN**

This small storefront eatery doesn't win any awards for decor or location, but when it comes to food that's good enough to feed an entire Italian family, Café Martorano is one of the best, one that has people waiting for a table for upwards of two hours as the restaurant accepts no reservations and can get away with it. An almost-offensive sound system (playing disco tunes and Sinatra) has a tendency to turn many a diner off, but you don't go to Café Martorano for an intimate dinner. Eating here is like being in a big, fat, Italian wedding, where eating, drinking, and dancing are paramount. The colossal meatballs are sublime, as are all of the pasta dishes. Ingredients hail from all over Italy, including tomatoes grown in volcanic soil near Salermo. The menu changes daily, but regulars have the power to request special, off-the-menu items. If you don't ask, you don't get, so open your mouth. Also keep your eyes wide open for celebrities such as Liza Minelli, James Gandolfini, and Steven Van Zandt, among others, who make it a point to stop here for a meal while in town.

See map p. 184. 3343 E. Oakland Park Blvd. ☎ *954-561-2554. Reservations not accepted. Main courses: $13–$29. MC, V. Open: Daily 5–11 p.m.*

Cap's Place Island Restaurant
$$ **Lighthouse Point SEAFOOD**

Opened in 1928 by a bootlegger who ran in the same circles as gangster Meyer Lansky, this barge-turned-restaurant is one of South Florida's best-kept secrets. Although it's no longer a rum-running restaurant and gambling casino, its illustrious past (FDR and Winston Churchill dined here together, too) landed it a coveted spot on the National Register of Historic Places. To get there, you have to take a ferryboat, provided by the restaurant. And the food's good, too! Traditional seafood dishes such as Florida or Maine lobster, linguine with clams, clams casino, and oysters Rockefeller will take you back to the days when a soprano was thought to be just an opera singer.

See map p. 184. 2765 NE 28th Court. ☎ *954-941-0418. Reservations accepted. To get there: From I-95, exit at Copan's Road and go east to U.S. 1 (Federal Highway). At NE 24th Street, turn right and follow the double lines and signs to the Lighthouse Point Yacht Basin and Marina (8 miles north of Fort Lauderdale). From there, follow a Cap's Place sign pointing you to the shuttle. Main courses: $20–$25. MC, V. Open: Daily 5:30 p.m.–midnight.*

Eduardo De San Angel
$$–$$$ **Fort Lauderdale MEXICAN**

Gourmet Mexican is *not* an oxymoron, and for those who don't believe that, take one meal at the sublime Eduardo De San Angel and you'll see how true it is. Chef Eduardo Pria has a masterful way with food as seen in dishes such as Jaibas Rellenas, fresh Florida blue crab, plum tomatoes, onions, jalapeño peppers, and Spanish green olives baked in a shell with melted jack cheese au gratin and mole poblano, herb-oil-brushed grilled breast of chicken topped with the traditional mole from Puebla, toasted sesame seeds, and sliced avocado. And then there's the roasted poblano pepper filled with fresh Florida blue crab, pickled jalapeño peppers, green olives, and tomatoes over stewed sweet onions baked in a parchment-paper pocket. Fresh flowers and candlelight, not to mention the fact that the restaurant resembles an intimate hacienda, also drive home the fact that this isn't your mom's Old El Paso taco dinner.

See map p. 184. 2822 E Commercial Blvd. ☎ 954-772-4731. Reservations essential. Main courses: $18–$29. AE, DC, DISC, MC, V. Open: Mon–Thurs 11:30 a.m.–10:30 p.m., Fri–Sat 5:30–10:30 p.m.

Himmarshee Bar & Grille
$$ Fort Lauderdale AMERICAN

Located on a popular street of bars frequented by Fort Lauderdale's young professionals, Himmarshee Bar & Grille is known for its cool scene and its cuisine. A mezzanine bar upstairs is ideal for people watching; outdoor tables, if you can score one, are tight but strategically situated in front of all the street's action. On Friday and Saturday nights, in particular, it's difficult to get a table here. However, if you can deal with cramming into the bar, it's worth a cocktail or two. The wine list is particularly impressive, and the grilled sirloin burger with creamy basil Gorgonzola is a delicious meal in itself for only $7.50. Also try the wasabi-crusted salmon or the pan-roasted Baramundi (Australian sea bass). Check out Side Bar, the restaurant's very Colorado ski-lodgey bar next door featuring live music and a bustling crowd of young hipsters on the prowl.

See map p. 184. 210 SW 2nd St. (south of Broward Boulevard, west of U.S. 1). ☎ 954-524-1818. Reservations recommended. Main courses: $12–$24. AE, MC, V. Open: Mon–Fri 11:30 a.m.–2:30 p.m.; Sun–Thurs 6–10:30 p.m., Fri–Sat 6–11:30 p.m.

Mark's Las Olas
$$–$$$ Fort Lauderdale CONTEMPORARY CUISINE

The first chichi restaurant to hit Las Olas Boulevard, Mark's Las Olas certainly deserves its staying power, thanks to star chef Mark Militello. One standout specialty is the grilled spiny lobster, with applewood-smoked bacon-conch sauce, sweet plantain mash, and conch fritters. If the kitchen is out of it — they tend to run out quickly — everything else on the menu, from the tuna pizza to the wood-oven-roasted salmon, is delicious. Save room for a chocolate dessert — any one will do.

See map p. 184. 1032 E. Las Olas Blvd. ☎ 954-463-1000. Reservations suggested. To get there: From I-95, exit at #27, S.R. 84, turn left on South Andrews Avenue, and then right on Las Olas Boulevard. The restaurant is on the right. Main courses: $14–$30. AE, DC, MC, V. Open: Mon–Fri 11:30 a.m.–2:30 p.m.; Mon–Thurs 6–10:30 p.m., Fri–Sat 6–11 p.m., Sun 6–10 p.m.

Sunfish Grill
$$–$$$ **Pompano Beach SEAFOOD**

Forget fusion and prepare to douse your taste buds with the freshest fish
in town. The wildly talented chef, Anthony Sindaco, buys at local markets
and often from well-known local fishermen who appear at his back door
with their catches of the day.

*See map p. 184. 2771 E. Atlantic Blvd. ☎ 954-788-2434. Reservations accepted. To
get there: From I-95, exit at East Sunrise Boulevard. Turn left on North Atlantic
Boulevard and turn right on NE 27th Street. Main courses: $17–$28. AE, MC, V. Open:
Mon–Thurs 6–9:30 p.m., Fri–Sat 6–10:30 p.m. Closed Sun.*

Taverna Opa
$ **Hollywood GREEK**

This authentic Greek taverna offers delicious *meze* (appetizers) such as
souvlaki, spanakopita, and calamari — the idea here is to order lots of
dishes and share. Add in the fantastic water views plus the opportunity to
dance on tables and watch the waitstaff break plates, and you'll understand why this is the liveliest spot in Hollywood.

*See map p. 184. 410 N. Ocean Dr. ☎ 954-929-4010. Reservations accepted weekdays
only. To get there: Take I-95 to Hallandale Beach Boulevard. Turn right and continue
over the bridge to Ocean Drive. Turn left onto Ocean, and the restaurant is on the
left-hand side. They serve meze (appetizers) only, $2.95–$10. AE, DC, DISC, MC, V.
Open: Daily 4 p.m. "until the ouzo runs out."*

Exploring Fort Lauderdale, Hollywood, and beyond

Despite the upper Gold Coast's size and tenure as a tourist destination,
it has relatively few attractions. The beaches, however, more than make
up for the lack of sights.

Relaxing on the beaches

The southern part of the Gold Coast, Broward County, has the region's
most popular and amenities-laden beaches, which stretch for more than
23 miles. Most do not charge for access, though all are well maintained.
Here's a selection of some of the county's best from south to north.

Hollywood Beach, stretching from Sheridan Street to Georgia Street, is
a major attraction in the city of Hollywood, a virtual carnival with a
motley assortment of young hipsters, big families, and sunburned French
Canadians who dodge bicyclers and skaters along the rows of tacky
souvenir shops, T-shirt shops, game rooms, snack bars, beer stands,
hotels, and even miniature-golf courses. The 3-mile-long Hollywood
Beach **Broadwalk,** modeled after Atlantic City's legendary boardwalk, is
Hollywood's most popular beachfront pedestrian thoroughfare, a cement
promenade that's 30 feet wide and stretches along the shoreline. Popular
with runners, skaters, and cruisers, the Broadwalk is also renowned as a
hangout for thousands of retirement-age snowbirds who get together for

Turtle Trail

In June and July, the John U. Lloyd beach is crawling with nature lovers who come for the spectacular Sea Turtle Awareness Program. Park rangers begin the evening with a lecture and slide show while scouts search the beach for nesting loggerhead sea turtles. If a turtle is located — plenty of them usually are — a beach walk is conducted, where participants can see the turtles nesting and, sometimes, their eggs hatching. The program begins at 9 p.m. on Wednesdays and Fridays from mid-May through mid-July. Call ☎ 954-923-2833 for reservations. Comfortable walking shoes and insect repellent are recommended. The park entrance fee of $3 to $5 per carload applies.

frequent dances and shows at a faded outdoor amphitheater. Despite efforts to clear out a seedy element, the area remains a haven for drunks and scammers, so keep alert.

If you tire of the hectic diversity that defines Hollywood's Broadwalk, enjoy the natural beauty of the beach itself, which is wide and clean. There are lifeguards, showers, bathroom facilities, and public areas for picnics and parties.

The **Fort Lauderdale Beach Promenade,** along the beach, underwent a $26 million renovation and it looks fantastic. It's especially peaceful in the mornings when there's just a smattering of joggers and walkers. but even at its most crowded on the weekend, the expansive promenade provides room for everyone. Note, however, that the beach is hardly pristine; it is across the street from an uninterrupted stretch of hotels, bars, and retail outlets. Also nearby is a megaretail and dining complex, Beach Place on A1A, midway between Las Olas Boulevard and Sunrise Boulevard.

Just across the road, on the sand, most days you will find hard-core volleyballers, who always welcome anyone with a good spike, and an inviting ocean welcoming swimmers of any level. The unusually clear waters are under the careful watch of some of Florida's best-looking lifeguards. Freshen up afterward in any of the clean showers and restrooms conveniently located along the strip. Pets have been banned from most of the beach in order to maintain the impressive cleanliness not commonly associated with such highly trafficked public beaches; a designated area for pets exists away from the main sunbathing areas.

Especially on weekends, parking along the ocean-side meters is nearly impossible to find. Try biking, skating, or hitching a ride on the water taxi instead. The strip is located on A1A, between SE 17th Street and Sunrise Boulevard.

Dania Beach's **John U. Lloyd Beach State Park,** 6503 N. Ocean Dr., Dania (☎ **954-923-2833**), is 251 acres of barrier island between the Atlantic

Ocean and the Intracoastal Waterway, from Port Everglades on the north to Dania on the south. Its natural setting contrasts sharply with the urban development of Fort Lauderdale. Lloyd Beach, one of Broward County's most important nesting beaches for sea turtles, produces some 10,000 hatchlings a year. The park's broad, flat beach is popular for swimming and sunning. Self-guided nature trails are great for those who are too restless to sunbathe.

The top attractions (after the beaches, that is)

IGFA (International Game Fish Association) World Fishing Center
Dania Beach

It may smell a little fishy, but if you're one of America's 60 million rod-and-reelers, you'll think that you're in angler's heaven. The $32 million complex includes a Fishing Hall of Fame, an honor roll of folks who caught the really big ones, and a collection of vintage lures. Fishing fans will spend at least two hours here.

 If the World Fishing Center baits your hook, drop in next door at **Bass Pro Shops Outdoor World** (☎ 954-929-7710; www.outdoor-world.com), where a 160,000-square-foot showroom sells fishing, hunting, boating, and golfing goodies.

See map p. 184. 300 Gulf Stream Way. ☎ 954-927-2628. www.igfa.org. To get there: Go west of I-95 on Griffin Road to Anglers Avenue and south. Admission: $5 adults, $4 kids 6–12. Open: 10 a.m.–6 p.m. daily.

International Swimming Hall of Fame
Fort Lauderdale

This is a splashy tribute to aquatic heroes, including the definitive Tarzan, Olympian, and charter-member Johnny Weissmuller; seven-time (1972) Olympic champ Mark Spitz; and former lifeguard and collegiate swimming team captain, President Ronald Reagan. There's an interactive area, two swimming pools, a theater, photos galore, and artifacts dating to the 1500s. Allow one and a half to two hours.

See map p. 184. 1 Hall of Fame Dr. ☎ 954-462-6536. www.ishof.org. To get there: 1 block west of A1A, 1 block south of Las Olas. Admission: $5 families or $3 adults, $1 kids and seniors. Open: 9 a.m.–7 p.m. daily. Pool open daily 8 a.m.–4 p.m.

Museum of Discovery and Science

Fort Lauderdale

If studying the silicon on the beach isn't your idea of science, then hightail it to this informative and entertaining museum of science and (natural) substance. Allow three to four hours to see the museum's scientific playground, space-flight simulator, ecology area with living turtles and sharks, virtual volleyball game, Internet area, and five-story IMAX theater.

See map p. 184. 401 SW Second St. ☎ **954-467-6637.** www.mods.org. To get there: Take Broward Boulevard east to Fifth, right to the garage. Admission: $14 adults, $13 seniors, and $12 kids 3–12, including admission to one IMAX film. Open: Mon–Sat 10 a.m.–5 p.m., Sun noon–6 p.m.

Stranahan House
Fort Lauderdale

Built in 1901 as a trading post, Stranahan House is the city's oldest standing structure and an example of pre–cookie cutter, Florida-frontier architecture. This is a pleasant way to spend an hour or so if you're a museum or architecture buff; otherwise, skip it.

See map p. 184. 335 SE Sixth Ave. ☎ **954-524-4736.** www.stranahanhouse.com. To get there: It's on Sixth at Las Olas. Admission: $6 adults, $5 seniors, $3 kids under 12. Open: Wed–Sat 10 a.m.–4 p.m., Sun 1–4 p.m.

More cool things to see and do

Beyond the first tier, Fort Lauderdale offers many other sights, including some items that will appeal to folks with special interests.

Baseball and spring training

The **Baltimore Orioles** (☎ 954-776-1921; www.theorioles.com) train at Fort Lauderdale Stadium, 5901 NW 12th Ave. Tickets cost $6 to $12. Workouts begin in mid-February, and games are played during March. In the sport of ice hockey, the youngish Florida Panthers (☎ 954-835-7000) have already made history. In the 1994–95 season, they played in the Stanley Cup finals, and the fans love them. They play in Sunrise at the **Office Depot Center** at 2555 NW 137th Way (☎ 954-835-8000). Tickets range from $14 to $100. Call for directions and ticket information.

Fishing

The saltwater pickings are the same farther south: redfish, trout, snook, mackerel, sailfish, grouper, and snapper. Charters for small groups (up to four people) inshore begin at about $250 for a half-day, $450 for a full day; deep-sea excursions are about double that. Rates on large party boats start at $40 per half-day, $60 for a full day. **Action Sportfishing** (☎ 954-423-8700; www.actionsportfishing.com) and **Hillsboro Inlet Marina** (☎ 954-943-8222) are among the area's more notable outfitters.

Gambling

The **Seminole Hard Rock Hotel and Casino** in Hollywood (☎ 866-502-7529 or 954-327-7625; www.seminolehardrockhollywood.com) is one of South Florida's most popular destinations, a 24/7, Vegas-esque hot spot. The Hard Rock can be seen off the Florida Turnpike, and its stark, white minimalist façade is very deceiving. Beyond the façade, it's an 86-acre resort featuring a colossal 130,000-square-foot casino, a lush 4-acre lagoon area with a theme-park-style water slide, authentic Seminole Chickee poolside cabanas. There's also a massive European-style spa and fitness center, and Seminole Paradise, a 300,000-square-foot dining, shopping, and entertainment district. The gambling isn't exactly Vegas in that there are no games in which you bet against the house, so what you'll find is poker, lots of it, and video slot machines, even more of them. The complex is located on State Road 7 (U.S. Highway 441) just north of Stirling Road on the Seminole Indian Reservation.

Further south in Hallandale is the **Gulfstream Park,** at U.S. 1 and Hallandale Beach Boulevard (☎ **305-931-7223;** www.gulfstreampark. com), a South Florida institution for horse racing that at press time was undergoing a multi-million-dollar renovation and expansion. Large purses and important races are commonplace at this sprawling suburban course, and the track is typically crowded.

Golfing

More than 50 golf courses offer tee times to the public in the Fort Lauderdale area. For information on golfing in the region, surf over to www.golf.com and www.floridagolfing.com. You can also request course information from the **Florida Sports Foundation** (☎ **850-488-8347**) or **Florida Golfing** (☎ **877-222-4653**). Here is a small sampling of the courses available in the area:

- ✔ The **Carolina Club,** 3011 Rock Island Rd., Margate (☎ **954-753-4000**), has a par-72 course with tough water hazards and a lot of doglegs. Greens fees are $75 to $100 in the winter and $30 to $50 in the summer.

- ✔ The **Crystal Lake Country Club,** 3800 Crystal Lake Dr., Pompano Beach (☎ **954-943-2902**), offers a fun-but-forgiving course with narrow fairways. Greens fees are $50 to $75 during the winter and $30 to $50 in summer.

- ✔ **Hillcrest Golf Club,** 4600 Hillcrest Dr., Hollywood (☎ **954-983-3142**), is one of the area's prettiest courses and has an island green on the ninth hole. Greens fees are $50 to $75 during winter and $30 to $50 in summer.

Touring

Several companies offer waterfront cruises. **Jungle Queen,** 801 Seabreeze Blvd./A1A in Bahia Mar Marina, Fort Lauderdale (☎ **954-462-5596;** www. junglequeen.com), runs three-hour sightseeing ($13.50 adults, $9.25 children 12 and under) and four-hour dinner cruises ($31 adults, $17 kids 4–12) aboard a riverboat. **Water Taxi of Fort Lauderdale** (☎ **954-467-0008;** www.watertaxi.com) travels the Intracoastal Waterway. In addition to sightseeing, the water taxi stops at boutiques and eateries along Las Olas Boulevard. One-way tickets are $4, and an unlimited all-day pass is $5. You can call for pickup or hail one from 10 a.m. until midnight on weekdays, until 2 a.m. on weekends.

Shopping the local stores

Fort Lauderdale has the same kinds of shops and malls that you can find in most major cities. Most stores are open from 10 a.m. to 6 p.m. from Monday through Saturday and from noon to 5 p.m. on Sunday. Those shops located in malls and major shopping centers keep their doors open as late as 9 or 10 p.m. except on Sunday.

If you feel like shopping, here are some favorite places to browse in the Fort Lauderdale area:

- ✔ **Antique Row:** Hundreds of shops line Dania's *old stuff* district on Federal Highway/U.S. 1, just south of the airport. Most upscale shops are overpriced, but some smaller ones offer bargains.

- ✔ **Hallandale Beach Boulevard (also known as "Schmatta Row"):** You can find deep discounts on off-brand shoes, bags, and jewelry in a string of stores east of Dixie Highway and the railroad tracks.

- ✔ **Las Olas Boulevard:** This is arguably Fort Lauderdale's trendiest shopping area, but bargains are hard to find here. Hundreds of boutiques, galleries, and restaurants can keep you browsing and buying at least for a full day along Las Olas.

Mall shopping may very well be the favorite local sport, and a number of excellent places can bust your bank account. **Broward Mall,** 8000 W. Broward Blvd., Plantation (☎ 954-473-8100), has 120 stores with such anchors as Burdines, Sears, and J.C. Penney. **The Galleria,** 2414 E. Sunrise Blvd., Fort Lauderdale (☎ 954-564-1036), offers Neiman Marcus, Lord & Taylor, Saks, Dillard's, and 150 other shops. Bargain hunters should head for **Sawgrass Mills,** Flamingo Road at West Sunrise Boulevard in Sunrise (☎ 800-356-4557 or 954-846-2300). The largest outlet mall in the world, Sawgrass Mills sports 270 outlet stores, including Neiman Marcus, Ann Taylor, Saks, and DKNY.

Living it up after dark

If you're still hankering for some action after a day at the beach, you can find plenty after the sun goes down. Fort Lauderdale is home to hundreds of bars and clubs that cater to a wide range of tastes. In addition to the hot spots listed in the following sections, check out Friday's entertainment section in the local newspaper, the *Sun-Sentinel.* Tickets for specific events, concerts, plays, and other performances can be booked through **Ticketmaster** (☎ 954-523-3309; www.ticketmaster.com).

Bars

Most of the large, modern hotels have lounges that liven up after dark. A particularly good one is the **Pier Top Lounge** (☎ 954-525-6666) in the Hyatt Regency Pier Sixty-Six at 2301 SE 17th St. (A1A and 17th Street Causeway). Other popular Fort Lauderdale watering holes include **Rush Street,** 220 SW Second St. (☎ 954-522-6900); **The Parrot,** 911 Sunrise

Lane (☎ 954-563-1493); and **Elbo Room,** 241 S. Atlantic Blvd. (☎ 954-463-4615). **Riverwalk,** 200 E. Las Olas Blvd. (☎ 954-468-1541), is a dining and entertainment complex in downtown Fort Lauderdale with plenty of rowdy bars. In Pompano Beach, check out **Durty Harry's,** 3214 E. Atlantic Blvd./A1A (☎ 954-783-7060).

Clubs

O'Hara's Pub and Jazz Cafes, 722 E. Las Olas Blvd., Fort Lauderdale (☎ 954-524-1764), and 1903 Hollywood Blvd., Hollywood (☎ 954-925-2555; www.heatbeat.com/oharasjazzcafe.html), are moody clubs with live music. For the diehard clubber in you, **Karma Lounge,** 4 W. Las Olas Blvd., Fort Lauderdale (☎ 954-609-6369), has a resident DJ from the U.K. to spin you right round, baby. You pay anywhere from $3 to $12 as a cover.

Music venues

The **Broward Center for Performing Arts,** 201 SW Fifth Ave., Fort Lauderdale (☎ 800-564-9539 or 954-462-0222; www.browardcenter.org) has large and small theaters that feature everything from comedy and drama to jazz and opera.

Fast Facts

Area Code

The local area code is **954.**

American Express

There's an office at 3312 NE 32nd St., Fort Lauderdale (☎ 954-565-9481).

Doctors

You can get referrals from the Broward County Medical Association at ☎ 954-714-9477.

Hospitals

Florida Medical Center, 5000 W. Oakland Park Blvd., Fort Lauderdale (☎ 954-735-6000); Broward General Medical Center, 1600 S. Andrews Ave., Fort Lauderdale (☎ 954-776-6000); Memorial Regional Hospital, 3501 Johnson St., Hollywood (☎ 954-987-2000); University Hospital and Medical Center, 7201 N. University Dr., Tamarac (☎ 954-721-2200).

Information

Contact the Greater Fort Lauderdale Convention and Visitors Bureau, 1850 Eller Dr., Fort Lauderdale (☎ 800-227-8669, 800-356-1662, or 954-765-4466; www.sunny.org).

Internet Access

You'll find several listings in the Yellow Pages including Cybernation, 2635 E. Oakland Park Blvd., Fort Lauderdale (☎ 954-630-0223), and Hard Drive Cafe, 1942 Hollywood Blvd., Hollywood (☎ 954-929-3324).

Mail

U.S. post offices are located at 6240 W. Oakland Park Blvd., Fort Lauderdale, and 1801 Polk St., Hollywood. To find a location near your hotel, call ☎ 800-275-8777.

Maps

The Greater Fort Lauderdale Convention and Visitors Bureau (see "Information," earlier in this section) is a great place to hit up for maps before or after you land. Rental-car agencies are another good source (including those at the airport), and so are convenience stores, which sell maps for $3 to $5.

Newspapers

The *Sun-Sentinel* (☎ 954-356-4000; www.sun-sentinel.com) publishes its entertainment section on Friday.

Pharmacies

Local 24-hour pharmacies include Walgreen's, 2355 NE 26th St., Fort Lauderdale (☎ 954-561-3880), and Eckerd, 1701 E. Commercial Blvd., Fort Lauderdale (☎ 954-771-0660).

Taxes

State sales tax is 6 percent. Hotels add 5 percent for a total of 11 percent.

Taxis

Generally, the rates are $2.45 for the first mile, $1.75 per additional mile. The major company is Yellow Cab/Checker (☎ 954-565-5400).

Transit Info

Broward County Transit (☎ 954-357-8400; www.broward.org/bct/welcome.htm) charges $1 for adults, 50¢ for seniors and kids over 40 inches (bring exact change).

Weather Updates

For a recording of current conditions and forecast reports, call the local office of the National Weather Service at ☎ 305-229-4522, or check out its Web site at www.nws.noaa.gov. You also can get information by watching the Weather Channel (www.weather.com).

Boca Raton, Palm Beach, and West Palm Beach

The ritzy reputations of Palm Beach and Boca, the playgrounds of the Pulitzers, Rockefellers, and Kennedys, may be enough to scare away budget-conscious travelers. But these areas have changed a great deal in the last quarter of a century. Although the wealthy still winter here, they no longer own the franchise, and affordable places have grown up around them. As I show you in the next several pages, Palm Beach and Boca offer plenty of cool, and relatively cheap, things to do.

Getting there

 Flying here is your best bet, although modern interstate highways and rail lines make car and train travel viable options, if you don't mind a long ride.

By plane

Palm Beach International Airport (☎ 561-471-7412; www.pbia.org) welcomes 16 domestic carriers and Air Canada and serves about 6 million passengers a year. **Alamo, Avis, Budget, Dollar, Enterprise, Hertz,** and **National** rental-car agencies are stationed on Level 1. Hotel shuttles and taxis also depart from Level 1.

Fort Lauderdale-Hollywood International Airport (☎ 954-359-6100; www.co.broward.fl.us/fll.htm) is a second option and has about double the airlines that Palm Beach does. See the "By plane" section in "Fort Lauderdale, Hollywood, and Beyond" earlier in this chapter for details on the Fort Lauderdale airport. And check out the "Quick Concierge" in the back of the book for general information on airlines and rental-car companies.

By car

I-75 and U.S. 41 lead in from the west. I-95 and Florida's Turnpike are the best routes to use when driving in from the north. If you're on a tight budget, use I-95 because the turnpike's tolls are high. (You'll pay $9 driving here from Orlando.) U.S. 1 and U.S. 27 are options if you don't mind passing through small towns and traffic lights. It's 300 to 350 miles from the state line to here.

By train

Amtrak (☎ 800-872-7245; www.amtrak.com) has a station in West Palm Beach at 201 S. Tamarind Ave. (☎ 561-832-6169).

Getting around

Like its neighbors to the south — Broward and Miami-Dade counties — Palm Beach County is relatively easy to navigate because most of the development is along the coast. Traffic, although not quite as bad as in the Miami area, can be bad enough; you may want to leave the driving to someone else.

By car

The same roads that get you here are the primary north–south thoroughfares (I-95, A1A, and U.S. 1). Common east–west routes include Palmetto Park Road (Boca Raton), Atlantic Avenue/Highway 806 (Delray Beach), and Okeechobee Road/Highway 704 (West Palm and Palm Beach).

By taxi

Sunshine Cab (☎ 561-832-8500) in West Palm Beach and **Metro Taxi** (☎ 561-391-2230) in Boca Raton are two of several taxi companies in the area. It will cost you $1 to start the meter and $1.80 a mile thereafter.

By bus

Palm Tran (☎ 561-841-4200; www.co.palm-beach.fl.us/palmtran), runs routes throughout the county. The fare is $1 for adults and 50¢ for kids 3 to 18. It operates from 6 a.m. to 7 p.m. Monday through Friday, from 8 a.m. to 6 p.m. Saturday, and from 10 a.m. to 4 p.m. on Sunday. Free route maps are available by calling ☎ 561-233-4-BUS.

Free trolleys operate round-trip from City Place and Clematis Street in downtown West Palm Beach on weekdays from 11 a.m. to 9 p.m, and on weekends from 11 a.m. to 11 p.m. Look for the bright pink buses when you're downtown. For more information, call ☎ 561-833-8873.

By train

Tri-Rail (☎ 800-874-7245 or 954-942-7245) is a tourist-friendly commuter service running from Palm Beach County to Broward and Miami-Dade counties. Round-trip fares range from $3.50 to $9.25.

Staying in style

Palm Beach County tends to be pricey, with most accommodations falling into either the luxury or chain-hotel categories. (Skip ahead to the "Palm Beach and Boca Raton" map for an overview.) If you don't find anything that fits your budget in the listings that follow, check out the chain-hotel numbers and Web sites in the "Quick Concierge" at the back of this book.

Florida Hotel Network (☎ 800-538-3616; www.floridahotels.com) can take care of your hotel arrangements after you tell the folks there your specific needs. You can also try **Palm Beach Accommodations** (☎ 800-543-SWIM). This booking service specializes in long-term rentals, but it does represent other kinds of accommodations.

Many accommodations let kids under 12 (and sometimes under 18) stay free if you don't exceed the maximum occupancy. But, to be safe, ask when booking. Also, pools and air-conditioning are part of the deal unless otherwise noted.

Don't forget the 10 percent sales and hotel taxes.

The area's best hotels

Boca Raton Resort and Club
$$$$ Boca Raton

Welcome to the Hotel California of Boca Raton. Built in 1926 by Addison Mizner, the posh resort now comprises three oddly matched buildings: the original, more traditional building; the somewhat drab, pink, 27-story Tower; and the more modern, airier Beach Club, which is accessible by a water shuttle. Everything at this resort, which straddles the Intracoastal and encompasses over 350 acres of land, is fully at your fingertips; however, it sometimes requires a little effort to reach it. The amenities here cannot be beat. The resort features two 18-hole championship golf courses, a $10 million Tennis and Fitness Center, indoor basketball and racquetball courts, a 25-slip marina with full fishing and boating facilities, and a private beach with water-sports equipment for rent. With a choice

Palm Beach and Boca Raton

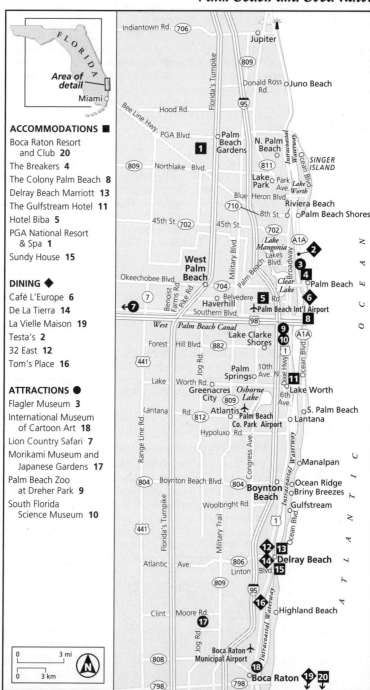

ACCOMMODATIONS ■

Boca Raton Resort
and Club **20**

The Breakers **4**

The Colony Palm Beach **8**

Delray Beach Marriott **13**

The Gulfstream Hotel **11**

Hotel Biba **5**

PGA National Resort
& Spa **1**

Sundy House **15**

DINING ◆

Café L'Europe **6**

De La Tierra **14**

La Vielle Maison **19**

Testa's **2**

32 East **12**

Tom's Place **16**

ATTRACTIONS ●

Flagler Museum **3**

International Museum
of Cartoon Art **18**

Lion Country Safari **7**

Morikami Museum and
Japanese Gardens **17**

Palm Beach Zoo
at Dreher Park **9**

South Florida
Science Museum **10**

of ten places to dine, five swimming pools, and an excellent children's program, the resort is ideal for families.

See map p. 199. 501 E. Camino Real. ☎ **800-327-0101** *or 561-395-3000. Fax 561-447-3183.* www.bocaresort.com. *To get there: From I-95 North, exit onto Palmetto Park Road East. Turn right onto Federal Highway (U.S. 1), and then left onto Camino Real to the resort. Rack rates: Winter $400–$750 double; off season $230–$460. AE, DC, DISC, MC, V.*

The Breakers
$$$$ Palm Beach

Speaking of Palm Beach without mentioning this extra-starchy, hoity-toity resort is impossible, but the royal-sized rates make it better for sightseeing than staying. The 1920s, Great Gatsby–style resort epitomizes Palm Beach luxury. Guest rooms range from 250-square-foot standards (ask for a corner room, which offers a bit more room for the same price) to ocean-front suites that are double that. All rooms have a full array of luxurious and modern amenities, including robes and PlayStations. The resort has 2 golf courses, 14 tennis courts, 7 restaurants, and 4 bars. A revamp of Florida's oldest existing golf course, led by Brian Silva, transformed The Breakers Ocean Course into a 6,200-yard, championship-level par 70. Also superb is the hotel's Family Entertainment Center, a fabulous 6,160-square-foot space filled with video games, skee ball, air hockey, board games, a children's movie room, computers and X-Box games, and several supervised camp programs designed for children.

See map p. 199. 1 S. County Rd. ☎ **888-273-2537** *or 561-655-6611. Fax: 561-659-8403.* www.thebreakers.com. *To get there: Okeechobee Boulevard east to South County Road; turn left. Parking: $17 valet; free self-parking. Rack rates: Jan–Apr $420–$3,000, May $270–$1,950, June–Dec $250–$1,750. AE, CB, DC, DISC, MC, V.*

Delray Beach Marriott
$$–$$$$ Delray Beach

Ever since Delray Beach came into its own as a dining and nightlife hot spot, this hotel has been hopping. Located halfway between Boca Raton and Palm Beach, this hotel — popular with business travelers — has 342 rooms and suites equipped with the usual array of modern amenities. The hotel overlooks the ocean and is within walking distance of boutiques, galleries, cafes, restaurants, and nightlife. You can skip a rental car if you aren't interested in seeing some of the area's outermost attractions; a car is a must, however, if you want to venture into the downtown or West Palm Beach area.

See map p. 199. 10 N. Ocean Blvd./A1A. ☎ **800-228-9290** *or 561-274-3200. Fax: 561-274-3202.* www.marriotthotels.com/PBIDR. *To get there: Just north of Atlantic Avenue on A1A. Parking: $8 valet, $6 self-parking. Rack rates: Jan–Apr $275–$390, May–Sept $110–$262, Oct–Dec $142–$390. AE, DISC, MC, V.*

Hotel Biba
$–$$ West Palm Beach

Hipsters finally have a place to rest their heads in Palm Beach County! Housed in a renovated 1940s motor lodge, the way-cool Hotel Biba has been remarkably updated on the inside by de rigueur designer Barbara Hulanicki and features a sleek and chic lobby with the requisite hotel bar, the Biba Bar, a gorgeous outdoor pool area with Asian gardens, and a reflecting pond.

See map p. 199. 320 Belvedere Rd. ☎ 561-832-0094. Fax 561-833-7848. www.hotel biba.com. *To get there: Take I-95 to Belvedere Road exit. Turn right on Belvedere. The hotel is on the right. Free parking. Rack rates: $99–$179. AE, DC, MC, V.*

PGA National Resort & Spa
$$$–$$$$ Palm Beach Gardens

This golfers' paradise (5 championship courses) also has 19 tennis courts, an excellent spa, a fitness center, a croquet complex, and 9 pools to help you burn off some of the calories you may pick up in its 9 restaurants. Standard rooms have marble foyers and large bathrooms. Suites come with patios or balconies. Cottages include two bedrooms, two baths, a living room, and kitchen.

See map p. 199. 400 Avenue of the Champions. ☎ 800-633-9150 or 561-627-2000. Fax: 561-622-0261. www.pga-resorts.com. *To get there: 2 miles west of I-95 exit 57. Parking: $10 valet; free self-parking. Rack rates: Dec–Apr $189–$1,400, May–Sept $99–$800, Oct–Nov $290–$1,200. AE, DC, DISC, MC, V.*

Sundy House
$$$ Delray Beach

Sundy House is the oldest residence in Delray Beach and is a bona fide 1902 Queen Anne house that has been restored to its full Victorian glory — on the outside, at least. Inside, however, the four one- and two-bedroom apartments are in a style that is best described as Caribbean funky, adorned in brilliant colors and with state-of-the-art audiovisual equipment, full modern kitchens, and laundry facilities. Six new guest rooms known as The Stables are equestrian chic, with more rustic appointments, including dark-wood furnishings and wooden floors. And while the rooms here are comfortable and gorgeous in their own rights, it's the surrounding property of the Sundy House that garners the most oohs and aahs. Set on an acre of lush gardens, the Sundy House is surrounded by more than 5,000 species of exotic plants, gently flowing streams, and colorful parrots, making an escape here seem more like something you'd find in Hawaii rather than South Florida. And going along with the whole nature theme is the hotel's swimming pond, literally that, in which guests can swim with the fish (in a good way!). The restaurant, De La Tierra, uses fresh herbs, fruits, and vegetables grown at the hotel's off-property farm.

See map p. 199. 106 S. Swinton Ave. ☎ 877-439-9601 or 561-272-5678. Fax: 561-272-1115. www.sundyhouse.com. *To get there: 2 miles east of I-95 exit 52. Parking: Free valet and self-parking. Rack rates: Dec–Apr $250–$500, May–Nov $175–$500. AE, DC, DISC, MC, V.*

Runner-up hotels

The Colony Palm Beach

$$–$$$ **Palm Beach** This British-flavored boutique hotel offers cheery rooms, luxurious suites, and a prime location only 100 yards from the beach. *See map p. 199. 155 Hammon Ave. ☎ 800-521-5525 or 561-655-5430.* www.thecolonypalmbeach.com.

The Gulfstream Hotel

$$ **Lake Worth** Ideally situated across the bridge from Palm Beach proper, this historic hotel offers comfortable rooms, friendly service, and an excellent restaurant that's a favorite with Palm Beachers looking to kick back in a relaxed, unstuffy atmosphere. *See map p. 199. 1 Lake Ave. ☎ 888-540-0669 or 561-540-6000.* www.thegulfstreamhotel.com.

Dining out

Palm Beach has some of the finest restaurants in Florida, and you'll pay royally to dine with the upscale types who winter here. The dress code is a tad more formal as well; most men wear blazers, and ladies sport classy dresses when dining out. Boca has its fair share of pricey seafood and steak joints, but the atmosphere is a bit more casual. *Note:* All Florida restaurants and food-serving bars are smoke-free.

If you have a car, you can easily get to the Fort Lauderdale and Hollywood restaurants mentioned earlier in this chapter.

Don't forget to allow for the 6 percent sales tax.

Café L'Europe
$$$ **Palm Beach** **CONTINENTAL**

This award-winning restaurant offers romantic dining and superb service. Seafood and steaks are your best bets. For deep-pocketed starters, there's a grand caviar bar ($16.50–$87). The main events include sea bass steamed en papillote with spinach, zucchini, and garlic; a grilled veal chop with potato cake; and a luscious cut of pan-seared sesame tuna in ginger vinaigrette.

See map p. 199. 331 S. County Rd. ☎ 561-655-4020. Reservations required. To get there: Okeechobee Boulevard over the Intracoastal to South County Road, right to Brazilian Avenue. Main courses: $22–$36. AE, DISC, MC, V. Open: Tues–Sat noon–3 p.m., daily 6–10 p.m.

De La Tierra
$$ **Delray Beach FLORIBBEAN**

This restaurant is a stunning experience that combines elegant indoor dining and lush tropical outdoor settings with gastronomic wizardry that's a product of the fresh fruits, vegetables, and spices grown on the hotel's 5-acre farm. Each dish is prepared with a palpable, edible precision. Consider the following: Smoked tomato soup is served with tiny grilled brie sandwiches and cilantro sour cream; leg of duck confit cakes are served with mango coleslaw; calamari is breaded with blue cornmeal, fried crispy, and plated with chipotle lime vinaigrette, red chili aioli, and tropical fruit salsa; diver scallops are caramelized and served with truffle-braised oyster mushrooms, corn broth, caviar, and microgreens; and chicken is marinated in pesto and served with mushroom risotto, truffled roasted chicken broth, baby carrots, and broccoli rapini. Save room for dessert, which includes a phenomenal American blueberry cobbler and mango and jackfruit shortcake. A decadent Sunday brunch buffet makes the day before going back to work infinitely more bearable. De La Tierra may mean "of the earth," but in my book, it's from the gods.

See map p. 199. 106 South Swinton Ave. ☎ *561-272-5678. Reservations essential. Main courses: $14–$26. AE, DC, DISC, MC, V. Open: Daily 11:30 a.m.–2:30 p.m. and 6–10 p.m.; Sun brunch 10:30 a.m.–2:30 p.m.*

La Vielle Maison
$$$$ **Boca Raton FRENCH**

La Vielle Maison is the place to go for froufrou French cuisine at its finest. The luxurious setting, a Mediterranean-inspired home filled with a variety of antique French furnishings and paintings, gives you the feeling of walking into a small chateau. It's difficult to choose from the many enticing entrees, which range from red snapper in black- and green-olive potato crust to medallions of beef, lamb, and venison over three sauces.

See map p. 199. 770 E. Palmetto Park Rd. ☎ *561-391-6701 or 561-737-5677. Reservations recommended. Main courses; $18–$50; fixed-price dinners $42 and $68. AE, DC, DISC, MC, V. Open: Daily 6–9:30 p.m. (call for seating times).*

Testa's
$$ **Palm Beach SEAFOOD**

Family owned and operated for 75 years (there's a Maine location, too), Testa's has indoor and alfresco dining and a menu loaded with south Florida staples (stone crabs and seared tuna) and a few novelties (almond-crusted prawns and a seafood marinara with lobster, mussels, shrimp, scallops, and fish). If you're here in season, the restaurant's massive omelet buffet, served 11 a.m. to 2 p.m. on Sundays, is a fantastic bargain at only $12.95. The laid-back atmosphere makes it very popular for families with young 'uns.

See map p. 199. 221 Royal Poinciana Way. ☎ *561-832-0992.* www.pbol.com/ testas. *Reservations required in winter. To get there: 4 blocks east of Flagler Memorial Bridge on A1A. Main courses: $14–$23. AE, CB, DC, DISC, MC, V. Open: Daily 7 a.m.–midnight (until 11 p.m. in summer).*

32 East
$$ Delray Beach AMERICAN

Eat indoors or out at this casual restaurant. Fish is front and center, but there's plenty for landlubbers as well. Menu standards include oak-roasted snapper with avocado salsa, roasted chicken breast in mustard-butter sauce, and grilled yellowfin tuna served with rice and a spring roll. The wine list is pretty extensive.

See map p. 199. 32 E. Atlantic Ave. ☎ *561-276-7868.* www.32east.com. *Reservations suggested. To get there: On mainland between Swinton Boulevard and SE First Avenue. Main courses: $14–$28. AE, DISC, MC, V. Open: Daily 5:30–10 p.m.*

Tom's Place
$ Boca Raton BARBECUE

The only place in Boca where it's acceptable to eat with your hands, Tom's Place is an institution of saucy proportions. Tom and Helen Wright's no-nonsense shack offers flawlessly grilled meats paired with well-spiced sauces. Beef, chicken, pork, and fish are served soul-food style, with your choice of two sides such as rice with gravy, collard greens, black-eyed peas, coleslaw, or mashed potatoes.

7251 N. Federal Hwy. ☎ *561-997-0920. Reservations not accepted. Main courses: $8–$15; sandwiches $5–$6; early-bird special $7.95. AE, MC, V. Tues–Thurs 11:30 a.m.–9:30 p.m., Fri 11:30 a.m.–10 p.m.; Sat noon–10 p.m.*

Exploring Palm Beach, West Palm Beach, and Boca Raton

Cartoons, critters, and museums provide much of the action in Palm Beach County, which also has some beautiful beaches, several parks, and the sport of kings — polo.

The top attractions

Flagler Museum
Palm Beach

This estate, billed as the "Taj Mahal of North America," was a gift from railroad and oil magnate Henry Flagler to his third wife. Built in 1902 to the tune of $4 million, the museum has a marble entry and 55 antiques-filled rooms, including a Louis XIV music room. Guided tours are available. Outside, you can look at The Rambler — Flagler's private rail car. Allow two hours.

See map p. 199. 1 Whitehall Way. ☎ 561-655-2833. www.flagler.org. *To get there: Go north on A1A, left on Worth Avenue, west to Coconut Row, right ⁹⁄₁₀ mile to the museum. Admission: $10 adults, $3 kids 6–12. Open: Tues–Sat 10 a.m.–5 p.m., Sun noon–5 p.m..*

International Museum of Cartoon Art
Boca Raton

For those who don't think it a laughing matter when someone tosses the funny pages in the trash, this museum is pure bliss. The works of artists from 50 countries are housed in a collection of 160,000 drawings that includes comics, gags, editorial cartoons, and more. A single artist's work — such as that of the late Charles Schultz, who created *Peanuts* — is usually featured for months at a time. There's also a toon-town hall of fame. The museum will keep you busy for two to four hours.

See map p. 199. 201 Plaza Real. ☎ 561-391-2200. www.cartoon.org. *To get there: On U.S. 1, 2 blocks north of Palmetto Park Road in Mizner Park. Admission: Donation requested. Open: Wed–Sun 10 a.m.–5 p.m.*

Lion Country Safari
Loxahatchee

The featured attractions are well fed. But just in case, convertibles and pets are not allowed, and you have to keep your car windows up as you drive through. You can rent cars for $8 per one and a half hours, and pets can stay in a kennel for a $5 refundable deposit. Park residents also include gibbons, wildebeests, rhinos, and elephants. There's also a walking tour, a cruise, and a kids' petting zoo (no meat-eaters here, of course). Allow at least two and as many as four hours to see everything.

See map p. 199. 2000 Lion Country Safari Rd. ☎ 561-793-1084. www.lioncountry safari.com. *To get there: It's 15 miles west of West Palm Beach on Southern Boulevard. Admission: $17.95 adults, $15.95 seniors, $12.95 kids 3–9. Open: Daily 10 a.m.–5:30 p.m.*

Palm Beach Zoo at Dreher Park
West Palm Beach

It seems that every city has to have a zoo of some sort, so here's Palm Beach's. A dainty, compact 22 acres, this zoo has 500 animals, including tigers, giant tortoises, kangaroos, and wallabies. There's an elevated boardwalk that allows you to see deer, shore birds, and plants. The kids' zoo gives little ones a chance to dirty their hands and clothing. The Zoo's newest attraction is the Tropics of the Americas, a 3-acre jungle path and complex that will immerse zoo guests into the animals, plants, and culture of a new-world rain forest. Figure on spending about one and a half to two and a half hours here, more if you walk like a sloth.

See map p. 199. 1301 Summit Blvd. ☎ *561-533-0887.* www.palmbeachzoo.org. *To get there: From I-95, take Summit Boulevard to Parker, right, then left on Summit. Admission: $7.50 adults, $6 seniors, $5 kids 3–12. Open: Daily 9 a.m.–5 p.m.*

Seeing and doing more cool things

If you're into museums, there are two excellent ones in the area.

Museums

The **Morikami Museum and Japanese Gardens,** 4000 Morikami Park Rd., Delray Beach (☎ **561-495-0233;** www.morikami.org; see map p. 199), was once home to a short-lived agricultural community. Today, it's the only U.S. museum dedicated to living Japanese culture and features gardens, trails, art, artifacts, and bonsai. It costs $9 for adults, $8 for seniors, and $6 for kids 6 to 18. The museum is open Tuesday through Sunday from 10 a.m. to 5 p.m.

The **South Florida Science Museum,** 4801 Dreher Trail N., West Palm Beach (☎ **561-832-1988;** www.sfsm.org/index.htm; see map p. 199), beckons with hands-on exhibits, laser shows, and a planetarium. Admission to the museum costs only $7 for adults, $5 for kids 3 to 17; if you add on a visit to the planetarium and a laser show, admission costs $11 for adults, $8 for kids 3 to 17. The museum is open Monday through Thursday from 10 a.m. to 5 p.m., Friday from 10 a.m. to 6 p.m., and Sunday from noon to 6 p.m.

Baseball and spring training

The **St. Louis Cardinals** and **Florida Marlins** (☎ **561-966-3309**) share Roger Dean Stadium at 4751 Main St. in Jupiter. Tickets run from $5 to $17 and sell out fast, so calling for them in advance is smart. Spring training workouts begin in mid-February; games are played through March.

Beaches

John D. MacArthur Beach State Park, 2 miles south of PGA Boulevard and U.S. 1 on A1A, North Palm Beach (☎ **561-624-6950**), has a 1,600-foot boardwalk running through 760 acres of submerged land, hammocks, and mangroves. Expect to see ibises, herons, and skittish fiddler crabs. Its nature center features displays and a video about this barrier island, and there's a footbridge to the dune area and the Atlantic Ocean. Take Blue Heron Boulevard across the Intracoastal and turn north on Ocean Boulevard. Admission is $4 per vehicle.

Other good beaches include:

- ✔ **Juno Beach:** On A1A, 1 mile north of the town. This is an undeveloped beach with lifeguards.

- ✔ **Carlin Park:** On A1A, south of Indiantown Road, Jupiter. Here you'll find 3,000 feet of rocky beach with lifeguards and trails.

> ✔ **Lantana Park:** State Road 12 and A1A, 1 mile east of Lantana. Lantana Park is an undeveloped beach with lifeguards.

> ✔ **Spanish River Park:** 3000 N. A1A, Boca Raton. This 46-acre park offers more than half a mile of beachfront manned by lifeguards.

Diving

Local favorites include **Breakers Reef,** a 45- to 60-foot dive that's usually packed with fish, and **Northwest Doubles,** an 80- to 90-footer where you'll find many tropicals and maybe some reef sharks. Tours begin at $40 per person for divers and snorkelers.

Charter operators include **Coral Island Charters** (☎ 888-889-3483 or 561-745-9286; www.coralislandcharters.com) in North Palm Beach, **SS Minnow** (☎ 561-848-6860; www.ssminnow.charters.com) in Palm Beach Gardens, and **Splashdown Divers** (☎ 561-736-0712) in Boynton Beach.

Fishing

The **Palm Beach County Fishing Club** (☎ 561-832-6780) is a good place to start. For $10, the club sends you a bunch of information on camps, charters, and tournaments. Call, or write to P.O. Box 468, West Palm Beach, FL 33402, but allow four weeks for delivery. If you want to be a bit more spontaneous, *Capt. Bob* (☎ 561-842-8823), in the Riviera Beach Marina at the foot of 13th Street, is a 65-foot party boat that offers four-hour trips twice a day except Wednesday. The cost is $30 for adults, $25 for kids 11 and under.

Golfing

On the Internet, go to www.golf.com and www.floridagolfing.com for a full list of local courses. You also can call **Florida Golfing** (☎ 877-222-4653). Three good places to play are the following:

> ✔ **Delray Beach Golf Club,** 2200 Highland Ave., Delray Beach (☎ 561-243-7380), has a course that is a bit long in the tooth (1923) but is still a challenge at 6,900 yards. Greens fees run under $25 in summer, $50 to $75 in winter.

> ✔ The **PGA National Resort & Spa,** 400 Avenue of the Champions, Palm Beach Gardens (☎ 561-627-2000; www.pga-resorts.com), has five courses and is home to the headquarters of the PGA. Greens fees run $95 to $120 in summer, $135 to $150 in winter.

> ✔ The **Village Golf Club,** 122 Country Club Dr., Royal Palm Beach (☎ 561-793-1400), offers a course that is rated one of the 20 toughest in south Florida. Greens fees run under $25 in summer, $41 to $65 in winter.

Watching polo matches
The **Palm Beach Polo & Country Club,** 11809 Polo Club Rd., Wellington, 10 miles west of I-95 off Forest Hills (☎ **561-798-7110;** www.palmbeach polo.com), puts on a pro season that peaks with the $100,000 World Cup in March. Matches take place at 3 p.m. on Sundays from January through April. Tickets cost $7 to $40.

Going on organized tours
Loxahatchee Everglades Airboat Tours, 15490 Loxahatchee Rd., Boca Raton (☎ **800-683-5873** or 561-482-6107), offers swamp tours on 6- to 20-passenger models. The cost is $25.50 for adults, $12.75 for kids 6 to 10, and free for children 5 and under.

Shopping the local stores
Palm Beach has some fabulous — and fabulously expensive — shopping, but pickings in this part of the Gold Coast are generally a little leaner than in Fort Lauderdale. Most shops, however, have the same kind of hours as that city: 10 a.m. to 6 p.m. Monday through Saturday and noon to 5 p.m. on Sunday. Stores inside malls and major shopping centers are open as late as 9 or 10 p.m., except on Sunday.

Even if you don't like shopping, visiting **Worth Avenue** is a Palm Beach tradition (☎ **561-659-6906**). Often referred to as "the Rodeo Drive of the South," it stretches four blocks from South Ocean Boulevard to Coconut Row and offers more than 200 upscale shops and boutiques. Although you won't find many bargains, the people watching is worth every minute. The same is true for Boca Raton's **Mizner Park** (☎ 561-362-0606), an outdoor mall with 45 specialty shops, seven good restaurants, and a multiplex. In West Palm, **CityPlace** (☎ 561-835-0862) is a $550 million, Mediterranean-style shopping, dining, and entertainment complex that's responsible for revitalizing what was once a lifeless downtown West Palm Beach.

Boynton Beach Mall, 801 N. Congress Ave. (☎ **561-736-7900**), houses 150 shops, including Macy's and Burdines. The **Gardens of the Palm Beaches Mall,** 3101 PGA Blvd., Palm Beach Gardens (☎ **561-775-7750**), has 180 tenants, including Saks, Bloomingdale's, and Macy's. **Town Center Mall** (☎ **561-368-6000**) in Boca Raton sports Bloomingdale's, Lord & Taylor, and Saks. It's west of I-95 on Glades Road between St. Andrews and Butts Road. One of the few places you can get a real bargain in Palm Beach County is **The Grand Bazaar,** 5700 Okeechobee Blvd., West Palm Beach (☎ **561-684-5700**), a flea-market-style shopping center.

Living it up after dark
From culture to classic rock, Palm Beach rivals Fort Lauderdale when it comes to after-dark offerings.

Cultural corner

Staffers at the **Palm Beach County Cultural Council,** 1555 Palm Beach Lakes Blvd., West Palm Beach (☎ **800-882-2787** or 561-471-2901; www. pbccc.org), can give you information on everything from museums to theater.

The **Palm Beach Opera,** 415 S. Olive Ave., West Palm Beach (☎ **888-886-7372;** www.pbopera.org) has a season running from October to April. The **Raymond F. Kravis Center for the Performing Arts,** 701 Okeechobee Blvd., West Palm Beach (☎ **800-572-8471** or 561-832-7469; www.kravis. org), is the big star on the local cultural scene. Its 2,500 indoor seats and amphitheater host more than 300 performances each year, from the **Doobie Brothers** to the 70-piece **Boca Pops.**

Bars

Café L'Europe, 331 S. County Rd. (☎ **561-655-4020**), has a piano bar in its bistro, which is open six nights a week; a jazz combo plays here on Friday and Saturday evenings. **Clematis Street,** in the heart of downtown West Palm Beach (☎ **561-833-8873;** www.downtownclematis.com), has a rocking street fest every Thursday night. Many of the street's storefronts offer live and canned music including **Respectable Street Café,** 518 Clematis (☎ **561-832-9999**); **Spanky's Sports Bar,** 500 Clematis (☎ **561-659-5669**); and **Rooney's Irish Pub,** 213 Clematis (☎ **561-833-7802**). For a more organized form of nightlife, downtown West Palm's **CityPlace,** with its inviting outdoor-mall format, is home to several bars.

Clubs

Hugh Jorgan's, 96 NE Second Ave., Delray Beach (☎ **561-272-7887**), is a rollicking dueling-piano bar that has shows at 8 p.m. Wednesday through Saturday. (A $5 to $10 cover is charged on Fri and Sat.) Look for it inside Love's Drugs. **Delux,** 16 E. Atlantic Ave., Delray Beach (☎ **561-297-4792**) is just one of many trendy bar/club/lounges on Atlantic Avenue, but unlike the rest, this one boasts an appearance by No Doubt's Gwen Stefani, who partied Delux-style after a concert.

Fast Facts

Area Code

The local area code is **561.**

Hospitals

JFK Medical Center, 5301 S. Congress Ave., Atlantis (☎ 561-965-7300); St. Mary's Hospital, 901 45th St., West Palm Beach (☎ 561-650-6126).

Information

For information, brochures, and maps, contact the Palm Beach County Convention and Visitors Bureau, 1555 Palm Beach Lakes Blvd., Suite 204, West Palm Beach, FL 33401 (☎ 561-471-3995; www.palmbeachfl.com).

Mail

U.S. post offices are located at 401 S. County Rd., Palm Beach, and 8185 Via Ancho Rd., Boca Raton. To find a location near your hotel, call ☎ 800-275-8777.

Maps

The information source in this section is a great one to hit up for maps before or after you land. (Trust us: Good maps are necessities because getting lost is easy in this part of the state.) Rental-car agencies are another good source (including those at the airport), and so are convenience stores, which sell maps for $3 to $5.

Newspapers

The *Palm Beach Post* (☎ 561-820-4100; www.palmbeachpost.com), publishes a weekly entertainment section on Friday.

Taxes

The sales tax is 6 percent; the hotel tax is an additional 4 percent.

Transit Information

Palm Tran (☎ 561-841-4200; www.co.palm-beach.fl.us/palmtran) operates routes throughout the county. The fare is $1 for adults and 50¢ for kids 3 to 18. It runs from 6 a.m. to 7 p.m. Monday through Friday, 8 a.m. to 6 p.m. Saturday, and 10 a.m. to 4 p.m. Sunday.

Weather Updates

For a recording of current conditions and forecast reports, call the local office of the National Weather Service at ☎ 305-229-4522, or check out the service's Web site at www.nws.noaa.gov. You also can get information by watching the Weather Channel (www.weather.com).

Part IV
The Gulf Coast

The 5th Wave   By Rich Tennant

In this part . . .

Contrary to popular belief, there's more to Tampa than Busch Gardens. So although I tell you all you need to know about Tampa's signature theme park and its fantastic attractions — including six stomach-churning roller coasters — I also fill you in on downtown Tampa and all that it has to offer. I then take you for a short jaunt across Tampa Bay to St. Petersburg and Clearwater where, if you can pull yourself away from the Gulf Coast's best beaches, you can experience the very surreal Salvador Dalí Museum. The area also chips in big-league baseball, football, and hockey.

Venturing south of Tampa Bay, I tell you about Sarasota's cultural offerings; the natural beauty of Sanibel, Captiva, and a ton of other islands; the rich history of Fort Myers; and the wealth of pristine Naples and Marco Island, which lie just on the fringe of the Everglades, attracting millions of visitors each year.

Chapter 14

Tampa

In This Chapter

▶ Making your way to Tampa
▶ Mapping out your itinerary beforehand
▶ Finding your way around Tampa
▶ Getting a hotel room and a great meal
▶ Roller-coasting through Busch Gardens and other great attractions
▶ Getting great shopping deals
▶ Finding fun after dark

*T*ampa and St. Petersburg, which are separated by 20 miles including Upper Tampa Bay, have at least one characteristic of sibling rivals: competitiveness, though it's more a case of one-upmanship than battling for the same prize. Although they have some things in common, including ultraflat terrain and Interstate 275, there are distinct differences. Tampa is more of a business center (although it is starting to make tourism more of its business lately) — whereas St. Petersburg relies heavily on its beaches and tourism — and is also one of the most built-up areas in Florida.

Despite its commercial character, Tampa attracts tourists in droves with its signature theme park, Busch Gardens, and exceptional sports venues. Real baseball (not just spring training) is the newest attraction in the area, with the Tampa Bay Devil Rays playing across the bay in St. Petersburg (see Chapter 15 for information). Tampa is also a growing port for cruise ships bound for the western Caribbean and Mexico. For an overview of things to do, see the "Tampa Attractions" map later in this chapter.

In this chapter, I take you to **Busch Gardens,** which rivals some of Orlando's larger theme parks. I also highlight the city's smaller attractions, including the **Florida Aquarium, Lowry Park Zoo,** and **Museum of Science and Industry.** And if you're the kind of person who truly comes alive when the sun goes down, I also take a look at the **Ybor City** club scene. Although this isn't the place to spend a week unless you include St. Petersburg in your itinerary, Tampa's premiere attractions definitely merit a look.

Getting to Tampa

As is the case with most Florida cities, arriving by air is the quickest and, in many cases, the most convenient way to get here. Train travel from the Northeast takes 25 to 28 hours, and if you're coming by car, you face a 4½- to 5-hour drive even after crossing the Florida-Georgia line.

By plane

Florida's third largest airport, **Tampa International Airport** (☎ 813-870-8700; www.tampaairport.com) handles about 16 million passengers a year, half the amount of second-ranked Orlando. More than 30 domestic and foreign lines land at TIA.

Hook up with ground transportation on Level 1, the baggage claim area, which has **SuperShuttle** vans (☎ 800-282-6817 or 727-572-1111, $9–$27 per person one-way throughout the Tampa area; www.supershuttle.com). **Tampa Yellow** (☎ 813-253-0121) and **United Cab** (☎ 813-253-2424) also serve TIA. The average fare from the airport to downtown Tampa is $14. Level 1 is also home to **Avis, Budget, Dollar, Hertz,** and **National** rental desks (see the "Quick Concierge" in the back of the book for telephone numbers); eight other rental agencies have shuttle service to offsite locations. Level 3 has ATMs, information booths, first-aid stations, currency exchanges, mail drops, and other services.

Much smaller than Tampa International, **St. Petersburg-Clearwater International Airport** (☎ 727-453-7800; www.fly2pie.com) handles flights from smaller airlines, including **American Trans Air** and **Southeast. Alamo, Avis, Budget, Enterprise, Hertz,** and **National** serve the airport. Cab fare from this airport to Tampa really is too costly to consider.

By car

Cruise along I-75, the primary north–south route, with I-275 being the spur that cuts through downtown Tampa and St. Petersburg. I-4 is an option if you're arriving from I-95 and the East Coast, though construction and overuse make for I-4 madness worse than in Orlando. Consider U.S. 301, 41, and 19 only if you want to take a marginally scenic route — and you have a strong tolerance for bumper-to-bumper traffic.

By train

Amtrak (☎ 800-872-7245; www.amtrak.com) has a station in Tampa at 601 Nebraska Ave. If you bring your car with you on your vacation, drive to Lorton, Virginia (four hours' driving time from New York, two hours from Philadelphia); then put yourself and your car on Amtrak's Auto Train out of Lorton. The train stops in Sanford, about 90 minutes east of Tampa. Fares begin at $368 for two passengers and an auto.

Orienting Yourself in Tampa

Most streets in Tampa have names, making the need for a map (see "Fast Facts" at the end of this chapter) reasonably important. Some of the most common streets found in this guide include Dale Mabry (west side), Fowler Avenue and Busch Boulevard (north side), Seventh Avenue and Broadway (Ybor City), and Kennedy Boulevard and Tampa and Ashley streets (downtown). For the most part, the downtown and its museums are dead center, with Busch Gardens due north on I-275, Ybor City's clubs and memories east on I-4, the airport and business areas west on I-275, and St. Petersburg, Clearwater, and their Gulf beaches an hour farther west, traffic willing.

Introducing the neighborhoods

Despite its business-destination character, Tampa has plenty of places to stay, eat, party, and play, including Busch Gardens, Florida Aquarium, Lowry Park Zoo, and Ybor City. Downtown also has a modern performing arts center, and the city has pro football and hockey franchises. Surrounding towns include Temple Terrace (north), Brandon and Plant City (east), and Riverview and Ruskin (south).

Finding information after you arrive

The **Tampa/Hillsborough Convention & Visitors Association,** 400 N. Tampa St. (☎ **800-448-2672** or 813-223-2752; www.gotampa.com) is your best bet for information. The association also operates an information center downtown at the Channelside Entertainment District, 701 Channelside Dr. The center is open from 9 a.m. to 5 p.m. daily. See the "Quick Concierge" at the back of the book for general Florida information sources.

The **Tampa Bay Visitor Information Center (☎ 813-985-3601**) is located near Busch Gardens at 3601 E. Busch Blvd. The privately owned center sells discounted attractions tickets and has many brochures regarding things to do in the area. The helpful staff will also book hotels and car rentals for you. It's open Monday through Saturday from 9:30 a.m. to 5 p.m., Sunday from 11 a.m. to 5 p.m.

Getting Around Tampa

The best way to get around the Tampa area is to drive because the city's public transportation system isn't ideal for traveling to the tourist spots.

Rush hour — the worst of which occurs from 7 to 9 a.m. and 4 to 6 p.m. weekdays — causes severe traffic backups on Dale Mabry, Kennedy Boulevard, I-4, I-275, and I-275's Howard Franklin Bridge (locals refer to it as the "Howard Frankenstein"), which leads to St. Petersburg. Because Dale Mabry and I-275 are common routes for exiting the airport, allow plenty of time to get to your hotel — or back to the airport if your flight is wrapped around either peak period.

By car

Tampa is in the crosshairs of I-4 and I-75/275. The latter two split north of town. I-75 goes around the city to the east toward Brandon and then south toward Sarasota (see Chapter 16). I-275 cuts through the heart of downtown and continues across Tampa Bay to St. Petersburg (Chapter 15). Tampa is laid out in a grid, but like many of Florida's cities, it relies on named streets. So if you'll be driving — either your own car or a rental — get a map (see "Fast Facts" at the end of this chapter). Major roads here include Florida Avenue, which separates the east and west portions of the city, and Kennedy Boulevard/Highway 60/Adamo Drive, which divides Tampa's north and south.

By taxi

You won't find many taxis cruising the streets, waiting to be hailed, but they usually line up at hotels, performance venues, and train stations. **United Cab** (☎ 813-253-2424) and **Yellow Cab** (☎ 813-253-0121) are the major taxi companies in Tampa. The meter starts at $1.45, and it's another $1.75 per mile. Fares are for up to five people.

By bus

HARTline, Tampa's public transportation system, serves the city and the suburbs. Fares are $1.30 for adults and 60¢ for seniors, children, and riders with disabilities (exact change is required). For information, call ☎ 813-254-4278 or check its Web site (www.hartline.org). As is often the case, city buses aren't the best choice to get to and from tourist areas.

Staying in Style

Although high season in Tampa runs from December to April, peak season rates here are lower than those at properties near the beaches. Downtown and the area near the airport are mostly commercial, so hotels in these areas — although close to many of Tampa's attractions — are usually filled with business types and convention attendees during the week. (See the map of "Tampa Accommodations and Dining.") You may also find a number of national chain hotels in these zones. See the "Quick Concierge" in the back of the book for a listing of chain hotel numbers and Web sites.

Because Tampa actively caters to business travelers, visitors can often get better deals on weekends, especially in the downtown area. And, if you plan on visiting Busch Gardens, ask whether a hotel offers special discount packages. Also, many accommodations let kids under 12 (and sometimes under 18) stay free if you don't exceed the maximum room occupancy. To be safe, though, ask when booking a room.

All the accommodations listed here offer free parking, air-conditioning, and pools, unless otherwise noted.

Sales and hotel taxes add 11.75 percent to your bill.

If you don't want to haggle, the **Florida Hotel Network** (☎ 800-538-3616; www.floridahotels.com) can take care of making accommodations arrangements for you.

Tampa's best hotels

Best Western All Suites
$$ North Side/Busch Gardens

This three-story all-suites hotel is the most beachlike vacation venue you'll find close to the park. Whimsical signs lead you around a lush tropical courtyard with heated pool, hot tub, and a lively, sports-oriented Tiki bar. They pride themselves on being "so close" to Busch Gardens that "the parrots escape to our trees," hence the hotel's nickname "that parrot place." The bar can get noisy before closing at 9 p.m., and ground-level units are musty, so ask for an upstairs suite away from the action. Suite living rooms are well equipped, and separate bedrooms have narrow screened patios or balconies. Great for kids, 11 "family suites" have bunk beds in addition to a queen-size bed for parents. Another 28 suites are especially equipped for business travelers (but are great for couples, too) with ergonomic chairs and big writing desks with speakerphones.

See map p. 218. 3001 University Center Dr. (at I-275 and Busch). ☎ *800-786-7446 or 813-971-8930. Fax: 813-971-8935.* www.bestwestern.com/prop_10296. *Rack rates: Dec–Apr $109–$159, May–Nov $89–139. AE, CB, DC, DISC, MC. V.*

Doubletree Guest Suites/Busch Gardens
$$ North Side/Busch Gardens

This property's 129 suites offer kitchenettes with refrigerators, sofa beds, and dataports. A continental breakfast and daily newspaper are also included in your rate. Located less than 1 mile from Busch Gardens, the hotel runs a free shuttle on mornings and afternoons to the theme park.

See map p. 218. 11310 N. 30th St. ☎ *800-222-8733 or 813-971-7690. Fax: 813-972-5525.* www.doubletree.com. *To get there: South of Fowler Avenue on 30th. Rack rates: Dec–Apr $99–$139, May–Nov $79–$119. AE, DISC, MC, V.*

Hyatt Regency
$$$ Downtown

Situated in the business district, near the Performing Arts and Convention Centers, this hotel caters to the corporate crowd. All 521 rooms have dataports, and minirefrigerators are available on request. The Hyatt also features a small fitness center, rooftop sundeck, lounge, and on-site restaurant.

See map p. 218. 2 Tampa City Center, ☎ *800-233-1234 or 813-225-1234. Fax: 813-204-3095.* www.tampa.regency.hyatt.com. *To get there: South from I-275 on Ashley*

Tampa Accommodations and Dining

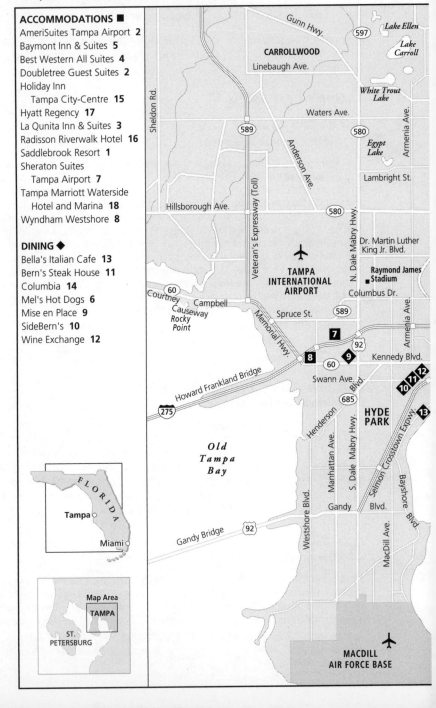

ACCOMMODATIONS ■
AmeriSuites Tampa Airport **2**
Baymont Inn & Suites **5**
Best Western All Suites **4**
Doubletree Guest Suites **2**
Holiday Inn
   Tampa City-Centre **15**
Hyatt Regency **17**
La Qunita Inn & Suites **3**
Radisson Riverwalk Hotel **16**
Saddlebrook Resort **1**
Sheraton Suites
   Tampa Airport **7**
Tampa Marriott Waterside
   Hotel and Marina **18**
Wyndham Westshore **8**

DINING ◆
Bella's Italian Cafe **13**
Bern's Steak House **11**
Columbia **14**
Mel's Hot Dogs **6**
Mise en Place **9**
SideBern's **10**
Wine Exchange **12**

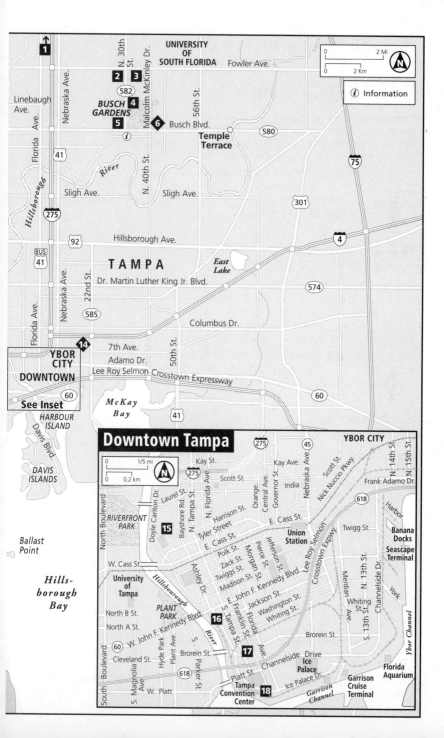

Linebaugh Ave.

Nebraska Ave.

Florida Ave.

1

N. 30th St.

Malcolm McKinley Dr.

2 **3**

582

BUSCH **4**
GARDENS

5 **6** Busch Blvd.

UNIVERSITY
OF
SOUTH FLORIDA

Fowler Ave.

56th St.

580

Temple
Terrace

i Information

0   2 Mi
0   2 Km

N

41

Hillsborough

River

N. 40th St.

Sligh Ave.

Sligh Ave.

301

75

275

92

BUS
41

Hillsborough Ave.

4

TAMPA

Nebraska Ave.

22nd St.

Dr. Martin Luther King Jr. Blvd.

*East
Lake*

574

Florida Ave.

585

Columbus Dr.

50th St.

60

14

7th Ave.

Adamo Dr.

Lee Roy Selmon Crosstown Expressway

60

41

**YBOR
CITY**

DOWNTOWN

60

See Inset

*HARBOUR
ISLAND*

Davis Blvd.

*McKay
Bay*

*DAVIS
ISLANDS*

*Ballast
Point*

*Hills-
borough
Bay*

Downtown Tampa

275

45

YBOR CITY

0   1/5 mi
0   0.2 km

N

Kay St.

275

Scott St.

Kay Ave.

India

Scott St.

Nebraska Ave.

Governor St.

Nick Nuccio Pkwy.

N. 14th St.

N. 15th St.

Frank Adamo Dr.

North Boulevard

*RIVERFRONT
PARK*

Doyle Carlton Dr.

Laurel St.

Bayshore Rd.

N. Tampa Ave.

N. Florida Ave.

Harrison St.

Tyler Street

E. Cass St.

Polk St.

15

Orange.

Central Ave.

E. Cass St.

618

Harbor

Union
Station

Twigg St.

Lee Roy Selmon Crosstown Expwy.

**Banana
Docks**

**Seascape
Terminal**

W. Cass St.

University
of
Tampa

Hillsborough

Ashley Dr.

Zack St.

Twiggs St.

Madison St.

Morgan St.

Pierce St.

Jefferson St.

E. John F. Kennedy Blvd.

Jackson St.

Washington St.

Whiting St.

N. 13th St.

Meridan Ave.

Whiting St.

Channelside Dr.

York.

*PLANT
PARK*

60

Hyde Park Ave.

Plant Ave.

W. John F. Kennedy Blvd.

S. Franklin St.

Florida

S. Tampa St.

16

North B St.

North A St.

River

Brorein St.

S. 13th St.

Ybor Channel

Cleveland St.

Brorein St.

17

Channelside Drive

**Ice
Palace**

**Florida
Aquarium**

South Boulevard

S. Magnolia Ave.

Parker St.

618

W. Platt

Platt St.

**Tampa
Convention
Center**

18

Ice Palace Dr.

*Garrison
Channel*

**Garrison
Cruise
Terminal**

to Jackson, east on Tampa Street. Parking: Valet $12. Rack rates: Dec–Apr $249–$275, May–Nov $165–$225. AE, DC, DISC, MC, V.

La Quinta Inn & Suites
$$ North Side/Busch Gardens

This property, located only 1½ miles from Busch Gardens, is a shade on the upscale side, but La Quinta's 105 rooms are still standard motel fare. The rooms have all the standard amenities, including dataports; a free continental breakfast is included in your rate.

See map p. 218. 3701 E. Fowler Ave. ☎ **888-729-7705** or 813-910-7500. Fax: 813-910-7600. www.flhotels.com/tampa/laquinta_977.html. To get there: Take the Fowler Avenue exit off I-275 east to the motel. Rack rates: Dec–Apr $105–$129, May–Nov $89–$119. AE, CB, DC, DISC, V.

Radisson Riverwalk Hotel
$$$ Downtown

The hotel sits on the banks of the not-so-scenic metro leg of the Hillsborough River, but the Radisson Riverwalk is a good option if you're after a central location. Set three blocks from the convention center, the hotel's 286 large rooms come with dataports and a free daily newspaper. Two restaurants, a bar, a fitness center, and a sauna are also on-site.

See map p. 218. 200 N. Ashley St. ☎ **800-333-3333** or 813-223-2222. Fax: 813-221-5292. www.radisson.com. To get there: Take Ashley Street exit off I-275. Parking: Valet $10. Rack rates: Dec–Apr $219–$279, May–Nov $169–$209. AE, CB, DC, DISC, MC, V.

Saddlebrook Resort
$$$ Far North

Set on 480 rolling acres of priceless countryside, Saddlebrook is off the beaten path (30 min. north of Tampa International Airport) and is a land-locked condominium development. If you're interested in spas, tennis, golf, or all of the above, I recommend this resort, which offers complete spa treatments, the Hopman Tennis Program (Jennifer Capriati pitches a tent here), and the Arnold Palmer Golf Academy. *Note:* The rates are per person, double occupancy, and include breakfast and dinner daily.

See map p. 218. 5700 Saddlebrook Way, Wesley Chapel, ☎ **800-729-8383** or 813-973-1111. Fax: 813-973-4504. www.saddlebrookresort.com. To get there: Off I-75 east on Hwy. 54. Rack rates: Jan–Apr $250–$320 rooms, $258–$378 suites; May–Sept $130 rooms, $130–$180 suites; Oct–Dec $175 rooms, $197–$259 suites;. AE, DC, DISC, MC, V.

Tampa Marriott Waterside Hotel & Marina
$$–$$$ Downtown

This luxurious 22-story hotel occupies downtown's most strategic location in the area's emerging Channel District — beside the river and between the Tampa Convention Center and the St. Pete Times Forum. Opening onto a riverfront promenade, the towering, three-story lobby is large enough to accommodate the many conventioneers drawn to the two neighboring venues and the hotel's own 50,000 square feet of meeting space. The third floor has a fully equipped spa, modern exercise facility, and outdoor heated pool. About half of the guest quarters have balconies overlooking the bay or city (choice views are high up on the south side). Although spacious, the regular rooms are dwarfed by the 720-square-foot suites. For those interested in boating the bay, there's also a 32-slip marina.

See map p. 218. 700 S. Florida Ave. (at St. Pete Times Forum Drive). ☎ **888-268-1616** *or 813-221-4900. Fax: 813-204-6373.* www.marriott.com. *Parking: Valet $14. Rack rates: Oct–Jan $119–$260, Feb–May $184–$244, June–Sept $149–$240. AE, DC, DISC, MC, V.*

Wyndham Westshore
$$$ West Side/Airport

Corporate and professional types usually patronize this Wyndham, which is located near the airport. The hotel's 324 rooms come with free coffee, dataports, and a free weekday newspaper. A business center, an 11-story atrium, and a restaurant are on-site.

See map p. 218. 4860 W. Kennedy Blvd. ☎ **877-999-3223** *or 813-286-4400. Fax: 813-286-4053.* www.wyndham.com. *To get there: It's on Kennedy, south of I-275 and west of Westshore. Rack rates: Dec–Apr $194–$234, May–Nov $174–$214. AE, DC, DISC, MC, V.*

Runner-up accommodations

Here are some more options. Most of these hotels (other than accommodations near Busch Gardens) usually cater to business travelers, meaning they may be a shade more expensive but are most likely upscale and have a good assortment of amenities.

AmeriSuites Tampa Airport

$$ West Side/Airport   Located near the airport, some of this hotel's 126 rooms and suites have kitchens. Rates include a free breakfast buffet, and the hotel has a fitness room. *See map p. 218. 4811 W. Main St.* ☎ **800-833-1516** *or 813-282-1037.* www.amerisuites.com.

Baymont Inn & Suites

$ North Side/Busch Gardens   A good place for the cost-conscious to rest their heads, this motel features spacious rooms, a free continental breakfast, and a great location near Busch Gardens. *See map p. 218. 9202 N. 30th Blvd.* ☎ **800-428-3438** *or 813-930-6900.* www.baymontinns.com.

Holiday Inn Tampa City-Centre

$$ Downtown   All rooms have dataports, some have microwaves and refrigerators, and upper floors overlook the Hillsborough River. *See map p. 218. 111 W. Fortune St.* ☎ ***800-513-8940*** *or 813-223-1351.* www.siscontinents hotels.com/holiday-inn.

Sheraton Suites Tampa Airport

$$ North Side/Busch Gardens   Newly renovated, this hotel's two-room suites offer numerous amenities, including refrigerators. It's near the airport and only ten minutes from the Buccaneers' Raymond James Stadium. *See map p. 218. 4400 W. Cypress St.* ☎ ***888-713-3330*** *or 813-873-8675.* www. sheraton.com.

Dining Out

Not exactly a culinary hotbed, Tampa touts a respectable number of good restaurants offering numerous types of cuisine in a wide range of prices. You'll also find plenty of fast-food joints, especially near Busch Gardens and along Dale Mabry and Kennedy Boulevard. *Note:* All Florida restaurants and food-serving bars are smoke-free.

Don't forget to add 6.75 percent local sales tax to your budget. And if you have a car, try some of the St. Petersburg–Clearwater restaurants in Chapter 15.

Bella's Italian Cafe

$$$ Midtown   ITALIAN

Creative dishes and very reasonable prices make this sophisticated yet informal cafe one of SoHo's (South Howard Ave.'s) most popular neighborhood hangouts. Although you can order the wood-fired pizzas and homemade pasta under traditional Bolognese or Alfredo sauces, the stars here feature the tasty likes of blackened chicken in a creamy tomato sauce over fettuccine, or shrimp and scallops in a roasted-tomato sauce over bow-tie pasta. Finish with the house version of tiramisu. Local professionals flock to the friendly bar during two-for-one happy hours nightly from 4 to 7 p.m. and from 11 p.m. until closing. The open kitchen provides only appetizers, salads, pizzas, and desserts after 11 p.m.

See map p. 218. 1413 S. Howard Ave. ☎ ***813-254-3355***. *Reservations not accepted. To get there: I-275 south on Armenia to Azeele, left a block to Howard, then left. Main courses: $7–$15. AE, DC, DISC, MC, V. Open: Mon–Tues 11:30 a.m.–11:30 p.m.; Wed–Thurs 11:30 a.m.–12:30 a.m.; Fri 11 a.m.–1:30 a.m.; Sat 4 p.m.–1:30 a.m.; Sun 4–11:30 p.m.*

Bern's Steak House
$$–$$$$ Midtown STEAKS

Long regarded as Tampa's premiere steakhouse, Bern's offers an atmos-
phere akin to that of an exclusive club or, as some say, a bordello because
of its ornate, over-the-top decor. Although the restaurant may have lost a
little luster over the years, it's still a favorite among travelers and locals.
Even if the menu includes seafood and chicken, ordering anything other
than the aged beef — sold in 62 cuts — is a sin. Bern's also features a huge
wine list — more than 6,900 labels are stored on the premises — and a
dessert room upstairs. *Note:* Also see SideBern's, later in the restaurant
listings.

See map p. 218. 1208 S. Howard Ave. ☎ *813-251-2421. Reservations required. To get
there: I-275 south on Armenia to Azeele, left a block to Howard, then left. Main
courses: $18–$60. AE, DC, DISC, MC, V. Open: Daily 5–11 p.m.*

Columbia
$$ Ybor City CUBAN/SPANISH

Built in 1905, the Columbia, with its frenetic flamenco dancers in the main
dining room to the ceramic-tile exterior, is truly a Latin legend and among
Tampa's finest restaurants. Ask to sit in the patio room for a bright time,
although it's tough to pass on those dancers who perform nightly Monday
through Saturday ($6 per person additional charge). The *paella* is a tradi-
tional dish of shrimp, scallops, squid, clams, fish, and mussels in a mound
of yellow rice. Served with black beans and rice, the *boliche* is a melt-in-
your-mouth-tender eye of round, stuffed with chorizo. Several newer
Columbia restaurants are located in other Florida cities, but none can
touch this one, which has to appease the city's fickle Latin diners.

Rumor has it that eating the Columbia's *boliche* while listening to the soul-
ful strains of flamenco can be a powerful aphrodisiac.

See map p. 218. 2117 E. Seventh Ave. ☎ *813-248-4961. Reservations recommended.
To get there: From I-4 go south on 21st Street, then left on Seventh. Main courses:
$14–$28 AE, DC, DISC, MC, V. Open: Mon–Thurs 11 a.m.–10 p.m., Fri–Sat 11 a.m.–
11 p.m., Sun noon–9 p.m.*

Mel's Hot Dogs
$ North Side/Busch Gardens AMERICAN

Few guidebooks are bold enough to offer a hot-dog stand as a top dog, but
few stands can match Mel's. Roll up your sleeves up and join some of
Tampa's movers, shakers, and hot-dog makers at this compact red-and-
white cottage. Most of the hot-dog selections are served with french fries
and a choice of coleslaw or baked beans. Mel also sells burgers,
bratwursts, and more.

See map p. 218. 4136 E. Busch Blvd. ☎ *813-985-8000. Reservations? Ha! To get there:
From I-275 go east 2 miles and look away from Busch Gardens. Main courses: $4–$9.
Credit cards? Ha, again! Open: Daily 11 a.m.–8 or 9 p.m.*

Mise en Place
$$ Downtown FLORIDA/CARIBBEAN

Chef Marty Blitz uses the freshest of ingredients to put together a creative, award-winning menu that changes weekly. Main courses often include fascinating choices such as grainy mustard–pecan-crusted rack of lamb with bourbon shallot demiglace, cayenne onion rings, and tarragon white-cheddar grits; and Creole-style mahimahi served with chili cheese grits and a ragout of black-eyed peas, andouille sausage, and rock shrimp.

See map p. 218. 442 W. Kennedy Blvd. ☎ 813-254-5373. Reservations suggested. To get there: Take I-275 Ashley Street exit south, turn right on Kennedy. It's two blocks west of the Hillsborough River. Main courses: $15–$26; tasting menu $50. AE, DC, DISC, MC, V. Open: Tues–Fri 11:30 a.m.–2:30 p.m.; Tues–Thurs 5:30–9:45 p.m., Fri–Sat 5:30–10:45 p.m.

SideBern's
$$ Midtown ASIAN/FLORIBBEAN

This child of Bern's Steak House (see review earlier in this section) has tried out and discarded several menus styles. It's finally settled on something the management calls "One World Cuisine," which is actually a mix of Pacific Rim, African, Asian, and (I hate the word) Floribbean. Try such delicacies as Szechuan-glazed grouper, lemon confit organic chicken, or chorizo-scaled sea bass. Casually elegant, the restaurant offers indoor seating in a light and airy dining room, as well as covered outdoor seating.

See map p. 218. 2208 W. Morrison St. (at Howard Street). ☎ 813-258-2233. Reservations suggested. To get there: I-275 south on Armenia to Azeele, left a block to Howard, then left and around the corner from Bern's. Main courses: $14–$26. AE, DC, DISC, MC, V. Open: Mon–Thurs and Sun 6–10 p.m., Fri–Sat 6–11 p.m.

Wine Exchange
$$ Downtown MEDITERRANEAN

This Tampa hot spot is a wine lover's dream come true, in which each dish is paired with a particular wine available by the bottle or glass. While the menu is rather simple, featuring pizzas, pastas, salads, and sandwiches, the daily specials are more elaborate, including grilled Delmonico steak, blackened pork tenderloin, or dijon-crusted salmon. The outdoor patio is a great place to sit, that is, if there's room. There's almost always a wait at this buzzworthy eatery.

See map p. 218. 1611 W. Swan Ave. ☎ 813-254-9463. Reservations not accepted. Main courses: $10–$22. AE, DC, DISC, MC, V. Open: Mon–Fri 11:30 a.m.–10 p.m.; Sat 11 a.m.–11 p.m., Sun 11 a.m.–9 p.m.; brunch on Sat and Sun 11 a.m.–3 p.m.

Exploring Tampa

Although St. Petersburg–Clearwater has the five-star beaches (find them in Chapter 15), Tampa wins when it comes to the number of attractions available.

The top attraction: Busch Gardens

This Tampa park grew out of a brewery. In the 1960s, the main (and only) attractions at Busch Gardens were a parrot show and free beer. (You may be thinking, who could ask for anything more?) Today, however, although there still are birds and free beer, Busch Gardens is among Florida's top theme parks. Two things set it aside from Disney's Animal Kingdom (see Chapter 18) in nearby Orlando: its roller coasters and its better view of critters.

Busch Gardens has six — count 'em, six! — roller coasters to keep your adrenaline rising and stomach dropping. The newest is **SheiKra,** the nation's first dive coaster, which carries riders up 200 feet at 45 degrees and then hurtles them 70 miles per hour back at a 45-degree angle. Yikes. Then there's **Gwazi,** a wooden wonder named for a fabled African lion with a tiger's head. This $10 million ride slowly climbs to 90 feet before turning, twisting, diving, and *va-rrroommming* to speeds of 50 mph — enough to give you air time (also known as weightlessness). These twin coasters, the Lion and the Tiger, provide 2 minutes and 20 seconds of thrills and chills, steep-banked curves, and bobsled maneuvers. At six different points on the ride, you feel certain you're going to slam the other coaster as you hit 3.5 Gs. (That's science's way of saying that if you weigh 100 pounds, your body will feel like 350.) There's a 48-inch height minimum.

Smaller than an airline seat, Gwazi's 15-inch seat is a tight squeeze for thin folks and close to misery for larger models.

Busch's other four roller coasters are made of steel. **Kumba** covers 4,000 feet of track at 60 mph. The 143-foot-high roller coaster jerks you with sudden turns (54-inch height minimum). On **Montu,** speeds exceed 60 mph while the G-force keeps you plastered to your seat (54-inch minimum). **The Python,** a tad tamer, runs through a double spiraling corkscrew and a 70-foot plunge (48-inch minimum). **The Scorpion** offers a high-speed 60-foot drop and 360-degree loop (42-inch minimum).

Busch's wildlife has fewer places to hide and, therefore, is easier to see than the denizens at Animal Kingdom (Chapter 18). **Edge of Africa** and the **Serengeti Plain** allow views of white rhinos, lions, hippos, crocodiles, hyenas, and other animals that seem to roam free. (In the Serengeti, Busch encourages the 300 animals to wander closer to the tourist-carrying trains by placing food, cool shade, and water misters nearby.)

For an extra $29.95 over the admission price, you and 19 others can join a guide on a 30- to 40-minute **Serengeti Safari Tour** that gives you an

Tampa Attractions

Adventure Island **5**

Busch Gardens **4**

Florida Aquarium **12**

Henry B. Plant Museum **8**

Legends Field **1**

Lowry Park Zoo **3**

Museum of Science
and Industry **6**

Raymond James
Stadium **2**

Tampa Museum of Art **9**

Tampa Theatre **10**

Visitor Information
Center **11**

Ybor City State Museum **7**

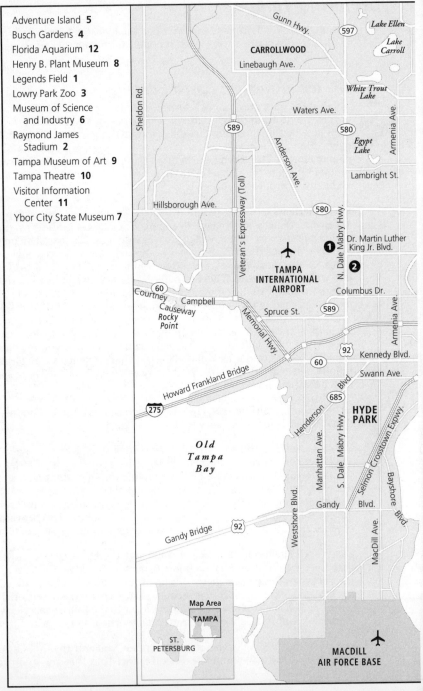

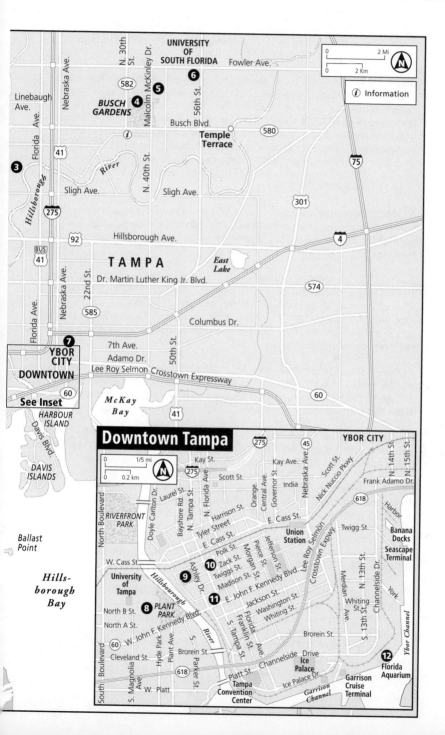

ultraclose look at animals and a chance to feed giraffes, gazelles, and more. (Tours are limited; advance reservations are suggested, and children must be at least 5 years old.)

Rhino Rally starts off as an off-road safari ride in real Land Rovers that take guests as close as 15 feet to elephants, white rhinos, crocodiles, cape buffalo, and other animals (riders must be at least 39 inches tall and 3 years old). After a few adventures, the Rovers drive over a shaky pontoon bridge that's washed out by a mock flash flood. The vehicles and passengers spiral downriver in what amounts to a raft ride. *Note:* The "raft" portion of this ride is often shut down, turning an 8-minute adventure into a 4-minute waste of time if the wait to board is longer than 15 minutes.

Nairobi's Myombe Reserve is home to gorillas and chimpanzees, that sometimes nap or pose in front of a Plexiglass wall. **The Congo** features rare white Bengal tigers. For a good view, try the sky ride and Serengeti Railway.

The park's three water rides provide welcome relief from the summer heat. **Tanganyika Tidal Wave** is a peaceful boat ride interrupted by a 55-foot plunge (48-inch height minimum). **Stanley Falls** is a log flume ride with a 40-foot drop (46-inch height minimum). **Congo River Rapids** is a raft ride very similar to Kali River Rapids in Animal Kingdom (42-inch height minimum).

In addition to the animals, your kids will love the three-story treehouse, slides, rides (56-inch height maximum), and the Captain Kangaroo Show in **Land of the Dragons,** as well as the sandy dig site in the re-created **King Tut's Tomb** and the friendly lorikeets of **Lory Landing.**

To avoid long lines, buy your tickets in advance at the Tampa Bay Visitor Information Center (see "Finding information after you arrive," earlier in this chapter), across Busch Boulevard from the park's entrance.

Busch Gardens recently began offering guests a **Rain Guarantee Program:** If it rains at all during your visit, no matter how much, you can ask for a free pass to return for a second day in the next seven days at no extra cost.

Did I mention **free beer** if you're 21 or older? You can sample Anheuser-Busch products at the Hospitality House.

Busch Gardens is located at 3000 E. Busch Blvd. at McKinley Drive/N. 40th Street (see map p. 226). From Orlando, take I-4 west to U.S. 41 (Exit 3), go right (north) to Busch Boulevard, then right (east). The route to the park is well marked, and it's 90 minutes from Orlando. From downtown Tampa, take I-275 to Busch Boulevard/Highway 580 (Exit 50) and go east. Park hours are usually at least 10 a.m. to 6 p.m. daily; however, the park sometimes opens as early as 9 a.m. and closes as late as 8 p.m.

Admission costs $56 for adults, $46 kids 3 to 9, excluding tax. FlexTicket pricing is $225 for adults, $190 for kids for a five-park pass good for 14 days that also includes unlimited admission to Universal Studios Florida, Islands of Adventure, SeaWorld, and Wet 'n Wild in Orlando. Parking is $7 for cars and motorcycles, $11 for trucks and campers. Call ☎ **866-353-8622** or 813-987-5082 or visit its Web site at www.buschgardens.com for more information.

Seeing other top sights

Busch Gardens may be Tampa's top attraction, but several other city sights are worthy of your attention, and most of them won't empty your wallet as fast as the theme park will.

Adventure Island
North Side/Busch Gardens

This Busch-owned water park offers 36 acres of wet fun. The A-list attractions here include the **Key West Rapids,** a 700-foot tube run; **Tampa Typhoon,** a seven-story, adrenaline-pumping water slide and freefall; and **Gulf Scream,** a 210-foot body slide that's guaranteed to give most folks a wedgie. This all-day affair also has picnic areas and a volleyball complex.

See map p. 226. 10001 McKinley Dr. ☎ *813-987-5600.* www.adventureisland.com. *To get there: It's on the east side of Busch Gardens. Admission: $32.95 adults, $30.95 kids 3–9. Parking: $5. Open: March–Oct daily at least 10 a.m.–5 p.m., sometimes later. Closed: Nov–Feb.*

Florida Aquarium
Downtown

Its 4,300 animals and plants include 550 of Florida's native species. The galleries explore wetlands, bays, beaches, coral reefs, the sea, and the creatures that live in them. Numerous interactive exhibits, including a 600-gallon touch pool, make this a great place to take younger children, who can also watch divers feed sharks and other marine life. Audio tours are available in English and Spanish. Allow two to four hours to see everything.

Certified scuba divers who pay a $150 fee in addition to admission can swim with a variety of sharks, including nurse, sand tiger, and black tip, all of which are 6 feet or less in length. The program has an hour-long orientation on policies and an educational presentation about sharks. The dive begins in a cage with two dive chaperones, and then the guests can move into the open, 13-foot-deep tank.

See map p. 226. 701 Channelside Dr. ☎ *813-273-4000.* www.flaquarium.org. *To get there: Take Kennedy Boulevard to 13th Street, turn right and follow the signs. Admission: $18 adults, $15 seniors, $12 kids 3–12. Parking: $5. Open: Daily 9:30 a.m.–5 p.m.*

Lowry Park Zoo
North Side

Dating to the early 1930s, Lowry Park faced extinction 20 years ago, but park lovers got Tampa's oldest zoo on track. Today's version is rated among the top small zoos in the nation. The zoo's 1,500 residents include manatees, Komodo dragons, river otters, Persian leopards, sloth bears, Indian rhinos, and Sumatran tigers. The park has a free-flight aviary, birds-of-prey show, kids' petting zoo, and hands-on discovery center. Home to one of Florida's three manatee hospital and rehabilitation centers, it's also a sanctuary for Florida panthers and red wolves. It takes four to six hours to enjoy the zoo.

See map p. 226. 7530 N. Blvd. ☎ *813-935-8552.* www.lowryparkzoo.com. *To get there: Exit I-275 on Sligh Avenue and follow the signs 1 mile west. Admission: $15 adults, $14 seniors, $10.50 kids 3–11. Free parking. Open: Daily 9:30 a.m.–5 p.m.*

Museum of Science and Industry
North Side

The Amazing You lets you explore the body; Diplodocus Dinosaurs offers a close look at our earliest giants; and Flight Avionics Flight Simulator in Our Place in the Universe takes 15 fliers on a five-minute adventure (for an extra charge of $3.50). You also can pedal a bicycle balanced on a 1-inch steel cable, suspended 30 feet above the ground (you're harnessed into the bike for the 98-foot journey). The museum has 450 hands-on, minds-on exhibits, including a hurricane simulator, a planetarium, an IMAX Theater, and several traveling exhibits. Plan to stick around for three to four hours.

See map p. 226. 4801 Fowler Ave. ☎ *813-987-6300.* www.mosi.org. *To get there: 2 miles east of I-275 on Fowler. Admission: $16 adults, $14 seniors, $12 kids 2–13. Free parking. Open: Daily 9 a.m.–5 p.m.*

Ybor City
East of downtown

The liveliest section in Tampa and the epicenter of the city's Latin culture, Ybor City was born in 1885 when Cuban exile Don Vicente Martinez Ybor (pronounced *ee*-bore) moved his cigar business from Key West to a palmetto patch east of Tampa. Hailed as the cigar capital of the world until the industry high-tailed it to South and Latin America 60 years ago, Ybor City is still a good spot to pick up a hand-rolled stogie. The **Ybor City State Museum,** 1818 Ninth Ave. (☎ 813-247-6323; www.ybormuseum.org; admission: $3; open: 9 a.m.–5 p.m. daily; see map p. 226), tells the story of Cuban exiles and spans half a block, including a restored worker's home and the historic **Ferlita Bakery.**

The district is loaded with excellent restaurants, shopping, and nightlife. Just west of 21st Street, there's a wall-to-wall run of clubs, cafes, and galleries. If you come after dark, however, stick to well-lit and well-traveled areas. Allow two to four hours to hit the major spots.

The National Historic District stretches for 110 red-brick blocks, but most of the action happens along a 12-block stretch of Seventh Avenue/East Broadway (I-4 east to 21st Street, south to Broadway). The best way to see this charming slice of yesterday is on foot. Parking spaces are available on Broadway. There's also a lot south of Broadway near the west end.

More cool things to see and do

Some of these attractions and activities appeal to people with special interests — whether you're an art buff, a golfer, or a pro-sports fan.

Taking in some culture: Museums and more

Here are three options for visitors who are culturally inclined:

✔ **Henry B. Plant Museum:** Now on the University of Tampa campus, the museum is in part of what used to be the Tampa Bay Hotel. Although the building is the highlight of a visit, don't skip its contents: art and furnishings from Europe and the Orient; and exhibits that explain the history of the original railroad resort, Florida's early tourist industry, and the hotel's role as a staging point for Theodore Roosevelt's Rough Riders during the Spanish-American War. It's at 401 W. Kennedy Blvd. (☎ 813-254-1891; www.plantmuseum.com; see map p. 226). Admission costs $5 for adults, $2 for kids under 12.

✔ **Tampa Museum of Art:** Permanent and changing exhibits are housed in eight galleries, with 6,000 to 7,000 pieces displayed. Classical and Mediterranean antiquities and 20th-century American art are its specialties. The museum is located at 600 N. Ashley Dr. (☎ 813-274-8130; www.tampamuseum.com; see map p. 226). Admission is $7 for adults, $6 for seniors, and $3 for kids over 6.

✔ **Tampa Theatre:** Architecture is the big draw of this 1926 classic, but it also presents films and concerts during the year. It has balconies, replicas of Roman sculptures, and one of those ghostly Wurlitzers. Speaking of ghosts, this old house is said to be haunted by Foster Finley, a projectionist who worked here for 35 years. Tours are usually available at noon Tuesday and Saturday for $5 per person. Movie tickets usually are $5, too. The theater is at 711 Franklin St. (☎ 813-274-8982; www.tampatheatre.org; see map p. 226).

Playing around: Sports and more

Major-league baseball has arrived, courtesy of the Tampa Bay Devil Rays, who play across the bay in St. Petersburg (see Chapter 15). You can also catch the New York Yankees playing their spring-training games at **Legends Field** on North Dale Mabry Highway (☎ 813-879-2244 or 813-287-8844), where tickets will set you back $10 to $16.

If you prefer sports other than the national pastime, you'll find an abundance of options open to you, including the following:

✔ **Fishing:** My best advice for anglers is to head across the bay to St. Petersburg–Clearwater (Chapter 15), where you can find several saltwater guides at **Hubbard's Marina.**

✔ **Football:** The **Tampa Bay Buccaneers** rose from the ashes of two decades of frustration to win Super Bowl XXXVII under new coach Jon Gruden. They play preseason games in August and eight regular-season games in the fall and early winter at Raymond James Stadium at 4201 N. Dale Mabry Hwy. (☎ 813-879-2827; www.buccaneers.com). Tickets are hard to come by, but you can almost always find them advertised under the tickets category of *The Tampa Tribune* classified ads.

✔ **Golf:** You'll find loads of tee-time options on the Internet at www.golf.com and www.floridagolfing.com. If you prefer to do your research the old-fashioned way, request course information from the **Florida Sports Foundation** (☎ 850-488-8347) or **Florida Golfing** (☎ 866-833-2663). Some of the more popular courses here are:

- **Saddlebrook,** north of Tampa (☎ 813-973-1111; www.saddlebrookresort.com), has two Arnold Palmer–designed courses. Greens fees: $70 to $130.

- **Summerfield,** in Riverview (☎ 813-671-3311), a moderately priced, par-71 course for long-ball hitters. Greens fees: Under $25.

- **Tournament Players Club,** in Tampa (☎ 813-949-0091; www.tpc.com), a challenging course best saved for golfers with low handicaps. Greens fees: $41 to $110.

Guided tours

If you're a foot soldier, there are several good walking tours around town. You can join a twice-weekly, one-hour guided tour of the **Tampa Theatre.** The tour costs $5 (☎ 813-274-8982). For a spooky time, try **Centro Ybor Ghost Walks** (☎ 813-242-4660; www.centroybor.com). The 75-minute walks are $10 per person. **J.B. Starkey's Flatwoods Adventures** offers a 90-minute swamp buggy-style bus trek through a cattle ranch and the ecosystem around it. Tours are $15.75 for adults, $8.75 for kids 3 to 12 (☎ 813-926-1133; www.flatwoodsadventures.com).

Shopping the Local Stores

Although Florida isn't known as a paradise for shoppers, Tampa does offer a couple of funky areas that are worth browsing. Malls are generally open from 10 a.m. to 9 p.m. (noon–6 p.m. Sun); individual shops are usually open from 10 a.m. to 6 p.m. Monday through Saturday.

Tampa's best shopping areas

Whether you're looking for handmade cigars or discounts at factory outlets, here are the top places to find them:

- ✔ **Ybor City:** You may encounter an aged craftsman or -woman hand-rolling cigars in the string of clubs, restaurants, and shops that run through the core area (a 12-block stretch of Seventh Avenue/East Broadway). You can find Caribbean trinkets at the open-air market. **Centro Ybor**, a 7-acre shopping, entertainment, and restaurant area is located on Eighth Avenue (☎ **813-242-4660;** www.the centroybor.com).

- ✔ **Prime Outlets:** This outlet mall is at 5461 Factory Shops Blvd. in Ellenton, which is southeast of Tampa. Stores include Anne Klein, Banana Republic, Danskin, Izod, Liz Claiborne, and Polo (☎ **888-260-7608;** www.primeoutlets.com).

- ✔ **Old Hyde Park Village:** Located south of downtown at 748 S. Village Circle (☎ **813-251-3500**), this landing zone has a collection of 60-some shops and eateries in an old-world, outdoor setting. Standouts here include Ann Taylor, Brooks Brothers, and Gap Kids.

Hitting the malls

The newest player in town is the upscale **International Plaza** near Tampa International Airport, where the headliners include Neiman Marcus, Nordstrom, and Lord & Taylor (☎ **813-342-3790;** www.shop internationalplaza.com). **Brandon TownCenter,** 459 Brandon TownCenter (☎ **813-661-5100;** www.shopbtc.com), has 120 stores including Burdines, Abercrombie & Fitch, Dillard's, and Banana Republic. **Citrus Park Town Center,** 8021 Citrus Park Town Center (☎ **813-926-4644;** www.citrusparktowncenter.com) has an equal number of shops led by Burdines, Dillard's, The Disney Store, and Eddie Bauer. **Westshore Plaza,** 250 Westshore Plaza (☎ **813-286-0790;** www.westshoreplaza. com), has 100 stores, including FAO Schwarz and Saks Fifth Avenue.

Living It Up After Dark

Although bars and clubs are scattered throughout the Tampa Bay area, Ybor City has the biggest concentration. Along Seventh Avenue between 15th and 20th streets, a host of stylish clubs cater to the 20s-and-under set. In addition, the city has several cultural venues. To find out what's playing where, don't forget to peruse a copy of the "Friday Extra" section in *The Tampa Tribune* (www.tampatrib.com). You can get the latest arts information, 24 hours a day, from **Artsline** at ☎ **813-229-2787.**

Bars

Four Green Fields, at 205 Platt St./Downtown (☎ **813-254-4444;** www.fourgreenfields.com) is a friendly thatched-roof pub with friendlier

Irish music nights, Thursday through Saturday. **Centro Ybor,** a 7-acre shopping, entertainment, and restaurant district on Eighth Avenue (☎ 813-242-4660; www.thecentroybor.com) has a handful of places to wet your whistle, including **Barley Hopper's** (☎ 813-242-6680) and **Big City Tavern** (☎ 813-247-3000).

Clubs

The **Columbia Restaurant's** flamenco dancers perform nightly, Monday through Saturday. The show is $6 plus the cost of dinner. The restaurant is located at 2117 E. Seventh Ave., Ybor City (☎ 813-248-4961; www.columbiarestaurant.com). **Improv Comedy Club** at Centro Ybor (☎ 813-864-4000; www.tampaimprov.com) has shows most nights of the week ($5–$40). **Side Splitters Comedy Club** showcases stand-up Tuesday through Sunday. It's at 12938 N. Dale Mabry Hwy. (☎ 813-960-1197; www.sidesplitterscomedy.com). Cover is $5 to $14. **Club Hedo,** 1510 E. Seventh Ave. in Ybor City, has DJs and theme nights including "Kill the Keg Bikini" and ladies' nights (☎ 813-248-2336; www.clubhedo.com; cover usually $5 and under).

Cultural centers

The **Tampa Bay Performing Arts Center,** 1010 MacInnes Place (☎ 800-955-1045 or 813-229-7827; www.tampacenter.com) is a four-theater complex that stages Broadway plays, concerts, operas, and other special events. The **Florida Orchestra** (☎ 800-262-7286 or 813-286-1170; www.floridaorchestra.org) presents a series of operas, concerts, and more from fall into spring.

Fast Facts

Area Code
The local area code is 813.

Hospitals
Hospitals servicing the area are: St. Joseph's Hospital, 3001 Martin Luther King Blvd. (☎ 813-870-4000); Tampa General Hospital, 2 Columbia Dr. (☎ 813-844-7000); and University Community Hospital, 3100 Fletcher Ave. (☎ 813-971-6000).

Information
The Tampa/Hillsborough Convention & Visitors Association, 400 N. Tampa St., (☎ 800-448-2672 or 813-223-2752; www.gotampa.com), is your best bet for tourist information.

Mail
U.S. post offices are located at 9748 N. 56th St., Temple Terrace, and 5201 W. Spruce St., Tampa Airport. Call ☎ 800-275-8777.

Maps
The preceding information sources listed earlier in this section are great organizations to hit up for maps before or after you land. (Trust us: Good maps are necessities because getting lost in Tampa is easy.) Rental-car agencies and motor clubs such as AAA are another good source, and so are convenience stores, which sell maps for $3 to $5.

Newspapers

The Tampa Tribune (☎ 813-259-7711;
Internet www.tampatrib.com) publishes a useful weekly entertainment section called "Friday Extra."

Safety

Tampa has all the crime that's associated
with a large city. I don't recommend walking alone after dark, and you should be
wary about driving in the downtown area.
Stick to well-lit and known tourist zones,
and even then, be aware of your surroundings. Never stop on a highway and get out
of your car if you can avoid it. Always keep
your doors locked.

Taxes

The sales and local-option taxes equal
6.75 percent in Hillsborough County. Hotels
add another 5 percent for a total of
11.75 percent.

Taxis

Generally, getting into a taxi costs $1.45
and it's $1.75 per mile after that. The major
companies in Tampa are United Cab
(☎ 813-253-2424) and Yellow Cab
(☎ 813-253-0121).

Transit Information

Hillsborough Area Regional Transit or
HARTline (☎ 813-254-4278; Internet www.
hartline.org) runs buses throughout
the county, although routes are not very
tourist-friendly. Bus fare is $1.25.

Weather Updates

For a recording of current conditions and
forecast reports, call the local office of the
National Weather Service at ☎ 813-645-
2506.

Chapter 15

St. Petersburg, Clearwater, and the Beaches

. . . .

In This Chapter

▶ Sunning along the Pinellas coast
▶ Fishing for grouper, amberjack, and sea bass
▶ Going insane on the primary north–south highway
▶ Swimming with manatees

. . . .

*U*nlike Tampa, across the bay, St. Petersburg can never be described as a business center. The city was built with visitors in mind and it shows, especially if you're looking for sunny escape. This 28-mile-long stretch of shoreline and barrier islands along Florida's Gulf Coast is *beachville,* with free public strands (although you have to pay for parking at most) virtually from one tip of Pinellas County to the other. In addition to sun, sand, and sea, the area has one very surreal reason for attracting visitors: the Salvador Dalí Museum.

The warm, calm waters of the Gulf are prone to the following annoyances that can put a damper on your beach time:

✔ **The Jellyfish Jitterbug:** These translucent critters are common on the Gulf beaches. Although their sting is far from deadly, it's painful enough, and their washed-up carcasses can ruin the moment. If they sting you, meat tenderizer helps relieve the pain.

✔ **The Stingray Shuffle:** Rays love to snooze on the bottom of the ocean. Most folks who get hit by the poisonous spines on the creatures' tails step directly down on them. If you shuffle your feet as you walk through the water, stingrays usually skedaddle.

✔ **The Red Tide Hide:** All you can do is hide when the marine blight known as the *red tide* comes to the beach. This phenomenon occurs when a microscopic marine algae — appearing as red patches in the water — begins to multiply at a higher rate than normal, poisoning fish. The stink from the dead fish washing up on the beach is monstrous. If red tide lands, forget beach time. The Florida Marine Research Institute maintains a Web site that includes current areas, if any, that have red tide. It's at www.floridamarine.org.

Okay, now that you've been warned, I'll get to the introductions.

Searching the Suncoast: What's Where?

Pinellas County is a narrow peninsula. The sun-drenched beaches on the west side of the county — a zone nicknamed the Suncoast — are an especially popular tourist draw. With a handful of exceptions, much of this region's action takes place along or near the Gulf Coast.

St. Petersburg was conceived and built a century ago primarily for tourists and wintering snowbirds. Here you can find one of the most picturesque and pleasant downtowns of any city in Florida, with a waterfront promenade, and the famous, inverted pyramid-shaped Pier offering great views across the bay, plus quality museums, interesting shops, and a few good restaurants. Thanks to an urban redevelopment program, St. Pete has awoken from its slumber and is starting to actually resemble a city that could be considered "hip," with renewed, restored streetscapes full of punk'd-out skateboarders, clubs, bars, and a vibrancy that goes well beyond the excitement surrounding Bingo night at the "adult communities" in town.

For sun and sand, there's plenty on the 28 miles of barrier islands skirting the Gulf shore and the Pinellas Peninsula. **St. Pete Beach** is the granddaddy of the area's resorts, but a more gentle lifestyle begins on the 3½ mile **Treasure Island.** Over the bridge is **Clearwater Beach,** whose silky sands attract active families and couples.

St. Petersburg and Its Beaches

The southern half of Pinellas County is the west coast's biggest tourist zone, mainly due to the beaches on the Gulf of Mexico. As you travel around, you may run into a few interior areas, such as Kenneth City and Pinellas Park (north), Seminole (northwest), and South Pasadena and Gulfport (south). But I concentrate on the most popular zones downtown or along the coast: **St. Pete Beach, Treasure Island, Madeira Beach, Redington Shores,** and **Indian Rocks Beach.**

Getting there

Your only convenient option to get directly to St. Petersburg or its beaches is by plane, although driving is a possibility.

By plane

St. Petersburg–Clearwater International Airport (☎ 727-453-7800; www.fly2pie.com) courts small airlines, including American Trans Air, Pan Am, and Southeast. Alamo, Avis, Budget, Enterprise, Hertz, and National serve the airport. You can also get a ride from **Yellow Cab** (☎ 727-799-2222). Standard rates are $2 to start the meter and $1.60 per mile; a trip from the airport costs about $5 and takes between 5 and 10 minutes.

If you want more options, consider flying into **Tampa International Airport** (☎ 813-870-8700; www.tampaairport.com), which is only 20 miles from St. Petersburg. (See Chapter 14 for more information.)

By car

If you're a highway hero, you have three choices by car:

- ✔ **U.S. 19:** This highway, also known as Instant Insanity, is a constantly clogged artery down most of Florida's lower Gulf Coast.

- ✔ **I-75/275:** This road brings you across the Florida/Georgia border and down the state's midsection. North of Tampa, take the I-275 option (it bears right, through Tampa and then into St. Petersburg).

- ✔ **I-95/I-4/I-275:** I-95 gets you into the state along the east coast, where you can pick up I-4 in Daytona Beach and ride it onto I-275, and from there into Tampa and St. Petersburg.

Getting around

When you consider that St. Petersburg was designed with tourists in mind, it should come as no surprise that this is one of the easiest cities in Florida to navigate. Thank city planners who keep things simple.

By car

St. Petersburg is easy to navigate because, with only a few exceptions, street numbers are used rather than names. Think of Central Avenue as the bull's-eye. Avenues run east to west. They grow (First, Second, and so on) in either direction from Central. Streets go north–south; numbers go higher as they move west from downtown. You'll find a few exceptions, most notably the northeast and southeast addresses that are on the city's east side, which are numbered in reverse of the preceding street procedure. In some cases, the beaches use St. Petersburg's street-numbering system; in others, they use names. The main beach road is Gulf Boulevard/Highway 699.

By taxi

In general, it costs $2 to get into a cab and $1.60 a mile thereafter. **Yellow Cab** (☎ 727-799-2222) is the main company in St. Petersburg.

By trolley

The tourist-friendly **Suncoast Beach Trolley** (☎ 727-530-9911), serves St. Pete Beach and Treasure Island and runs every 30 minutes from 5 a.m. to 10 p.m. daily, until midnight Friday and Saturday. Rides cost $1.25 per person.

By bus

The **Pinellas Suncoast Transit Authority** (☎ 727-530-9911; www.psta.net) serves the entire county. The fare is $1.25 per ride for adults, 75¢

Downtown St. Petersburg

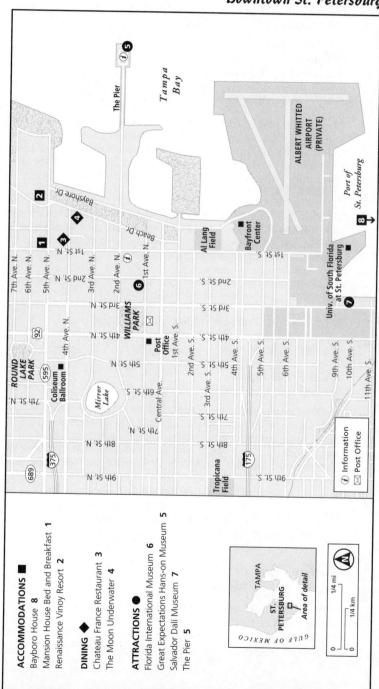

ACCOMMODATIONS ■
Bayboro House **8**
Mansion House Bed and Breakfast **1**
Renaissance Vinoy Resort **2**

DINING ◆
Chateau France Restaurant **3**
The Moon Underwater **4**

ATTRACTIONS ●
Florida International Museum **6**
Great Expectations Hans-on Museum **5**
Salvador Dali Museum **7**
The Pier **5**

for students, and 60¢ for seniors. Exact change is required. Unless you don't mind a slow pace, skip it.

Staying in style

St. Petersburg has a wide range of accommodations. Numerous chain motels lie along U.S. 19. The high season runs from January to April, and many hotels offer significant off-season discounts.

The **St. Petersburg/Clearwater Convention and Visitors Bureau,** 14450 46th St. N., Clearwater (☎ **727-464-7200;** www.floridasbeach.com), publishes a brochure listing members of its Superior Small Lodgings program, all of which have been inspected and certified for cleanliness and value. Visitors can also call the bureau's free reservations service at ☎ **800-345-6710.**

You can also book a hotel room through the **Florida Hotel Network** (☎ **800-538-3616;** www.floridahotels.com), but be advised that on the Web site you need to click "More" under "Other Cities" to find lodgings in St. Petersburg and St. Pete Beach.

All the accommodations listed here offer free parking, air-conditioning, and pools, unless otherwise noted.

Sales and hotel taxes add 11 percent to your bill.

The top hotels

Alden Beach Resort
$$–$$$$ St. Pete Beach

Located on the beach near the south end, this resort's 140 one-bedroom suites have fully equipped kitchenettes and separate living areas with sofa beds. Some suites have private balconies overlooking the Gulf. The resort has numerous recreational facilities, including two lighted tennis courts, a game room, and two whirlpools. Free coffee and newspaper are included in the rates.

See map p. 249. 5900 Gulf Blvd. ☎ *800-237-2530 or 727-360-7081. Fax: 727-360-5957.* www.aldenbeachresort.com. *To get there: 1½ miles north of Pinellas Bayway/Highway 682. Rack rates: Feb–Apr $185–$265, May–Sept and Dec–Jan $133–$187, Sept–Nov $115–$169. AE, CB, DC, DISC, MC, V.*

Bayboro House
$$–$$$ St. Pete Beach

A huge departure from the area's monstrous resorts, this Victorian mansion located along the shore of Tampa Bay is a well-kept secret preserved by innkeepers Antonia and Gordon Powers, who managed to preserve the home's early-1900s ambience with heart-of-pine flooring, wooden mantelpiece, fireplace, and 1926 player piano.

See map p. 239. 1719 Beach Dr. S.E. ☎ **877-823-4955** *or 727-823-4955. Fax: 727-823-1644.* www.bayborohousebandb.com. *To get there: 1.2 miles north of Pinellas Bayway. Rack rates: Nov–May $149–$285, June–Oct $129–$275. AE, DC, DISC. MC, V.*

Beach Haven

$–$$ St. Pete Beach

Here's a 1950s-style beachfront property that offers family warmth and a modernized interior. It's also a member of Superior Small Lodgings I mentioned a bit earlier. There are five motel rooms (with shower-only bathrooms), as well as tropically decorated one- and two-bedroom efficiencies. The property has a large beach deck, barbecue grills, and a coin-operated laundry and is near several restaurants.

See map p. 249. 4980 Gulf Blvd. ☎ **727-367-8642**. *Fax: 727-360-8202.* www.beachhavenvillas.com. *To get there: 1.2 miles north of Pinellas Bayway. Rack rates: Feb–Apr $90–$147, Dec–Jan $80–$122, May–Aug $68–$110, Sept–Dec $58–$95. MC, V.*

Don CeSar Beach Resort and Spa

$$$$ St. Pete Beach

Opulent and *pink* are the best ways to describe the Don, St. Pete Beach's most famous landmark since its first guest signed the register in 1928. Dubbed the "Pink Palace" because of its color and architecture, it offers 347 rooms, suites, and guesthouses overlooking the Gulf of Mexico or Boca Ciega Bay. A full-scale spa, fitness center, and restaurant are available on-site. Even if it's beyond your budget, the Don's worth a stop as a tourist attraction.

Note: Rates don't include a $10-per-person per-night resort fee.

See map p. 249. 3400 Gulf Blvd. ☎ **800-637-7200** *or 727-360-1881. Fax: 727-367-3609.* www.doncesar.com. *To get there: At 34th Avenue and the Pinellas Bayway. Rack rates: Feb–Apr $251–$1,800 Jan, Apr–May, and Oct–Dec $234–$1,250; June–Sept $212–$1,100. Parking: $10 valet; free self-parking. AE, DISC, MC, V.*

Renaissance Vinoy Resort

$$$–$$$$ Downtown St. Petersburg

This old beauty rests on Tampa Bay and is even more of a showpiece than the Don. Built in 1925 and restored in 1992, the Vinoy is on the National Register of Historic Places and has 360 luxuriously appointed rooms, many offering bay views. The resort features graceful arches, marble floors, a marina, an 18-hole golf course, 12 tennis courts, 5 restaurants, and a health club and spa.

See map p. 239. 501 Fifth Ave. NE. ☎ **800-468-3571** *or 727-894-1000. Fax:: 727-822-2785.* www.renaissancehotels.com. *To get there: 2 miles east of I-375 (off I-275) on Fourth Avenue, north to Beach Drive, go left, then right on Fifth. Rack rates: Jan–Apr $299–$359, Oct–Dec $249–$319, May $239–$299, June–Sept $199–$259. Parking: $13 valet; $9 self-parking. AE, DC, DISC, MC, V.*

Tradewinds Sandpiper Hotel & Suites
$$ St. Pete Beach

Located on the beach, the Sandpiper is one of three connecting Tradewinds properties. (The others are Tradewinds Island Grand and Tradewinds Sirata Beach Resort.) The hotel's 56 standard rooms have refrigerators, wet bars, toasters, and dishware; the 103 suites offer separate bedroom and living areas as well as full kitchens. There's a fitness center and kids' program to keep the little ones from ruining your tan. *Note:* An additional $12 to $17 per day is charged to cover the cost of self-parking, telephone calls, and the use of recreational and other amenities.

See map p. 249. 5500 Gulf Blvd. ☎ *800-237-0707 or 727-562-1212. Fax: 727-562-1222.* www.tradewindsresort.com. *To get there: 2 miles north of the Pinellas Bayway. Rack rates: Feb–Apr $159–$795, May–Dec $129–$695, Jan $119–$595. AE, CB, DC, DISC, MC, V.*

Runner-up hotels

Here are a few other places to park yourself while you're in the area. You can also check out the major hotel chains listed in the "Quick Concierge" in the back of this book.

Buccaneer Beach Resort

$ Treasure Island Here's a 40-something-year-old property on the beach with 70 rooms (some with kitchens and multiple bedrooms) and pocket-friendly rates. *See map p. 249. 10800 Gulf Blvd.* ☎ *800-826-2120 or 727-367-1908.* www.bucbeachresort.com.

Island's End Resort

$$ St. Pete Beach Situated right off the beach, this small hideaway offers five one-bedroom cottages with kitchens at an excellent value plus a three-bedroom home with private pool. *See map p. 249. 1 Pass-A-Grille Way.* ☎ *727-360-5023.* www.islandsend.com.

Mansion House Bed and Breakfast

$$ Downtown St. Petersburg This inn's twin romantic houses date to 1901 and 1912. The headliner room, the Pembroke, has a four-poster bed with mosquito netting and a whirlpool in a screened hut. *See map p. 239. 105 Fifth Ave. NE.* ☎ *800-274-7520.* www.mansionbandb.com.

Schooner Motel

$ Madeira Beach Although far from fancy, the motel's rooms have refrigerators, microwaves, and coffeemakers and are located on the beach. Efficiencies are available, and pets are welcome for a fee, usually $15 to $25. *See map p. 249. 14500 Gulf Blvd.* ☎ *800-573-5187 or 727-392-5167.* www.schoonermotel.com/index.html.

Thunderbird Beach Resort

$ **Treasure Island** This 1950s-style motel has a lush pool area, a location right on the Gulf, and well-equipped rooms and efficiencies. *See map p. 249. 10700 Gulf Blvd.* ☎ *800-367-2473 or 727-360-2800.* www.gotampabay.com/thunderbird.

Dining out

The Suncoast is another destination made for seafood lovers, and you can find fresh fish dishes on almost every menu. Carnivores won't go hungry; plenty of menus brim with meat and poultry items, too. Families and those on a tight budget can find many national chain restaurants and fast-food joints along the major thoroughfares. *Note:* All Florida restaurants and food-serving bars are smoke-free.

If you have a car, try some of the ones listed later in this chapter under "Clearwater." And don't forget to add 7 percent sales tax to your budget.

Chateau France Restaurant

$$ **Downtown St. Petersburg** **TRADITIONAL FRENCH**

This romantic Victorian house (circa 1910) tempts with a kitchen and chef that turn out treats such as homemade pâté, Dover sole meunière, coq au vin, and lamb filet mignon with cognac, herbs, and garlic. The wine list is excellent, and desserts such as chocolate soufflé are sinful. Make sure to ask for the Eiffel Tower salad, which will have you drooling every time you see the Parisian version.

See map p. 239. 136 Fourth Ave. NE. ☎ *727-894-7163. Reservations recommended. To get there: Take Central Avenue east to First Street Northeast, go north to Fourth Avenue, then east. Main courses: $20–$29. AE, DC, DISC, MC, V. Open: Daily 5–11 p.m.*

Crabby Bills

$–$$ **St. Pete Beach** **SEAFOOD**

This member of a small local chain sits right on the beach in the heart of the hotel district. There's an open-air rooftop bar, but big glass windows enclose the large dining room. They offer fine water views from picnic tables equipped with rolls of paper towels and buckets of saltine crackers, the better with which to eat the blue, Alaskan, snow, and stone crabs that are the big draws here. The crustaceans fall into the moderate price category or higher, depending on the market, but most other main courses, such as fried fish or shrimp, are inexpensive — and they aren't overcooked or overbreaded. The creamy smoked fish spread is a delicious appetizer, and you'll get enough to whet the appetites of at least two people. This is a very good place to feed the entire family.

See map p. 249. 5300 Gulf Blvd. (at 53rd Avenue), St. Pete Beach. ☎ *727-360-8858. Main courses: $10–$24, market price for lobster and stone crab claws; sandwiches $5.50–$8. AE, MC, V. Open: Mon–Thurs 11:30 a.m.–10 p.m., Fri–Sat 11:30 a.m.–11 p.m., Sun noon–10pm.*

Hurricane Seafood Restaurant
$ Pass-a-Grille/St. Pete Beach   SEAFOOD

A favorite haunt of locals and tourists, the Hurricane, situated just across from Pass-a-Grille Beach, offers a large selection of fish (served blackened, jerk style, and more), shellfish, and a belly-busting Class 5 Hurricane platter (flounder, shrimp, crab cake, clam strips, and scallops). The rooftop bar features magnificent views at sunset.

See map p. 249. 807 Gulf Way. ☎ *727-360-9558. Reservations not accepted. To get there: From the Bayway, go south on Gulf Boulevard to 22nd Avenue, turn right, then left on Gulf Way and go 12 blocks. Main courses: $8–$18; sandwiches $7–$9. AE, MC, V. Open: Daily 8 a.m.–1 a.m.*

The Moon Under Water
$ Downtown St. Petersburg   INDIAN/ECLECTIC

Offering a change of pace, this restaurant serves the cuisines of former British outposts. Eat on the outdoor verandah or inside the British-colonial dining room. Entrees range from pot pies to minced spiced beef and fiery Indian curries. Wash your meal down with an Irish, English, or Australian beer. There's live music on weekends.

See map p. 239. 332 Beach Dr. ☎ *727-896-6160. Reservations recommended for six or more. To get there: Central Avenue east to Beach, then north 3 blocks. Main courses: $10–$17; sandwiches under $9. AE, DC, DISC, MC, V. Open: Daily 11:30 a.m.–11 p.m.*

Ted Peters' Famous Smoked Fish
$ South Pasadena   SEAFOOD

This open-air eatery has been an institution since the 1950s. Some folks bring the fish they caught for the staff to smoke ($1.50 a pound), others figure fishing is a waste of time and come right to Ted's table for mullet, mackerel, salmon, and other fish slowly cooked over red oak. Enjoy the smell and sip a cold one while you wait for your order.

See map p. 249. 1350 Pasadena Ave. ☎ *727-381-7931. Reservations not accepted. To get there: Central Avenue west to Pasadena, then 1 mile south. Main courses: $8–$18. No credit cards. Open: Wed–Mon 11 a.m.–7:30 p.m.*

The Wine Cellar
$$–$$$ North Redington Beach   CONTINENTAL

An elegant family-run restaurant, this makes a good destination for a special evening out, with an intimate atmosphere, professional service, and — surprise! — a great wine list. Entrees include rainbow trout sautéed in butter and crushed pecans, beef Wellington, veal scallopini, and Dover sole filleted at your table. The menu also includes rack of lamb for two ($58.50) and a five-course special that changes daily ($69.50 per couple).

See map p. 249. 17307 Gulf Blvd. ☎ 727-393-3491. www.thewinecellar.com. *Reservations recommended. To get there: 2½ miles north of Madeira Beach Causeway at 173rd Avenue. Main courses: $10–$39. AE, DC, MC, V. Open: Daily 4:30–11:00 p.m. daily; buffet with limited menu on Mon.*

Exploring St. Petersburg

You won't find theme parks or roller coasters, but there are some dandy beaches and many other things to see and do in St. Petersburg, especially if you have a car and can visit Tampa (see Chapter 14) and Clearwater.

The top attractions

Florida International Museum
Downtown St. Petersburg

This excellent museum attracted 600,000 visitors from around the world when it opened its first exhibition in 1995, and the success has continued. Its outstanding exhibit on the Cuban Missile Crisis features a full-size fallout shelter and a Soviet SA-2 missile and is well worth your visit even if the two temporary exhibits don't catch your fancy. On the other hand, they very well could, since the museum is associated with the Smithsonian Institution in Washington, D.C. Allow two to three hours to take in the exhibits. A new cafe opened at the museum in February 2005.

See map p. 239. 100 Second St. N. ☎ 800-777-9882 or 727-822-3693. www.florida museum.org. *To get there: 1 block north of Central Avenue on Second Street. Admission: $10 adults, $8 seniors, $5 kids 6 and over. Open: Mon–Sat 10 a.m.–5 p.m., Sun noon–5 p.m.*

Great Explorations Hands-On Museum
Downtown St. Petersburg

Although this isn't on the same level as Tampa's Museum of Science and Industry (see Chapter 14), it's user-friendly and geared to kids. Children can don lab coats and pretend they're vets, get familiar with spiders and snakes, or dabble in a ton of other hands-on experiments. Allow two to three hours to see the museum.

See map p. 239. 800 Second Ave. NE. ☎ 727-821-8992. www.greatexplorations. org. *To get there: On the third floor of The Pier. Admission: $8 adults, $7 seniors and children 3–11. Open: 10 a.m.–8 p.m. Mon–Sat, 11 a.m.–6 p.m. Sun.*

Salvador Dali Museum
Downtown St. Petersburg

Wow, did this guy have a *different* perspective of Spaceship Earth! St. Petersburg, of all places, has the world's largest collection of what George Carlin would call Dalí's "stuff" — including a melting clock. The museum offers tours and has a little shop of oddities for souvenirs. Unless you're a Dalí fanatic, spending two or three hours here is plenty.

See map p. 239. 1000 Third St. S. ☎ *727-823-3767.* www.salvadordalimuseum. org. *To get there: It's on Third Street, 10 blocks south of Central Avenue. Admission: $13 adults, $10 seniors, $6 students over 10. Open: Mon–Sat 9:30 a.m.–5:30 p.m., Thurs 9:30 a.m.–8 p.m., Sun noon–5:30 p.m.*

More cool things to see and do

You'll find many things, beyond the city's first-tier attractions, to occupy your time. Best of all, some are free for the taking:

- ✔ **Baseball:** The **Tampa Bay Devil Rays** play their 81-game, regular-season home schedule (Apr–Oct) at Tropicana Field, 16th Street at 4th Avenue South (☎ **866-225-6457** or 727-825-3137; www.tampa bay.devilrays.mlb.com). Tickets run $5 to $75; parking is $4 to $10. The Rays also play spring-training games in March at nearby Florida Power Park at Al Lang Field (☎ **727-825-3137**; $6–$15).

  Prices at concession stands and restaurants under the dome at St. Petersburg's **Tropicana Field** are anything but civilized. Expect to pay up to $8 for a burger, $10 to park in the same time zone, $5 or more if you want this Bud to be for you, and $5 for those Cracker Jacks. Heck, it's only $6 for sushi — yes, you heard right, *sushi* at a ballpark.

  The average price for a family of four is about $145 for admission, parking, and food. In fairness, though, that ranks about in the middle of the Major League. And you can find bargains. If you're not affected by altitude sickness, you can shag $5 seats in the outfield for some games. You can use the water fountain instead of the beer or soda carts. And there's free parking — 1 mile away — if you don't mind riding a shuttle.

- ✔ **Beaches:** Southern Pinellas County is lined with public beaches from one end of Gulf Boulevard/Highway 699 to the other. **Pass-a-Grille** and **St. Pete Beach,** in the south, near the Pinellas Bayway, are popular among families and water-sports enthusiasts; therefore, they're crowded. The same goes for **Treasure Island,** in the middle, a west extension of Central Avenue and the Treasure Island Causeway. **Madeira Beach,** on the northern end, is more laid back, meaning there are fewer services, also fewer access points. The beaches are free, but they do have metered parking, so bring a reasonable number of quarters (the average parking charge is about $1 an hour). Information on all the Gulf beaches can be found on the Web at www.gulfbeaches-tampabay.com.

- ✔ **Fishing:** Hubbard's Marina at John's Pass Village and Boardwalk, between Treasure Island and Madeira Beach (☎ **800-755-0677** or 727-393-1947; www.hubbardsmarina.com), offers half-day ($40) and full-day ($72) charters aboard party boats as well as 12-hour ($83) and overnight ($203–$230) charters. The best bet is a sunset cruise with free beer for $12! Grouper, amberjack, sea bass, and red snapper are among the rewards.

✔ **Golf:** If you want to get out your clubs while on vacation, information on courses in the area is available on the Internet at www.golf.com and www.floridagolfing.com. If you prefer to do your research the old-fashioned way, request course information from the **Florida Sports Foundation** (☎ 850-488-8347), or **Florida Golfing** (☎ 877-222-4653). See some of the more popular courses later in this chapter under North Pinellas and Beaches golf options.

✔ **Parks: Fort DeSoto Park,** 3500 Pinellas Bayway (☎ 727-866-2484), on Mullet Key, is a 900-acre county park with a neat old Spanish-American War–era fort (its cannons were never fired in anger). Fort DeSoto is a good place for the kids to explore, but bring insect repellent. The park also has playgrounds, picnic shelters, and 7 miles of beach. There's an 85¢ toll to drive into the park. A concessionaire, known as the Camp Store, rents canoes for $16 an hour or $35 for a full day (☎ 727-864-1991).

Going on a guided tour

Hubbard's Marina at John's Pass Village and Boardwalk, halfway between Treasure Island and Madeira Beach (☎ 800-755-0677 or 727-393-1947; www.hubbardsmarina.com) offers a two-hour dolphin-watch and sightseeing cruise. It costs $12 for adults, $6 for kids 11 and under. There's also a three-hour shelling tour ($20 for adults, $10 for kids).

Shopping the local stores

Haslam's Book Store, 2025 Central Ave., St. Petersburg (☎ 727-822-8616; www.haslams.com), is a great place to browse. Dating to 1933, its collection has grown to more than 350,000 volumes, making Haslam's Florida's largest bookstore.

John's Pass Village and Boardwalk, 12901 Gulf Blvd., Madeira Beach (☎ 727-394-0756) is a new, made-to-look-old shopping area that features restaurants, galleries, saloons, and boutiques — most of which are overpriced. It's a nice place for a stroll and a little browsing though. A ton of other souvenir shacks lining Gulf Boulevard peddle T-shirts, shells, and other trinkets.

On the mall front, the area's most notable is **Tyrone Square Mall,** 6901 22nd Ave. N., St. Petersburg (☎ 727-345-0126), which has 150 stores anchored by Macy's and Dillard's.

Living it up after dark

In addition to the following listings, you can get up-to-the-minute entertainment information each Thursday in the "Weekend" section of the *St. Petersburg Times* (www.sptimes.com).

Bars

Ever since St. Pete started coming into its own as far as the hipster quotient is concerned, cool bars started appearing as quickly as Madonna changes her accent. Among them, **A Taste for Wine,** 241 Central Ave. (☎ 727-895-1623), an upscale spot with polished woods and a granite bar offering terrific by-the-glass vintages, appetizers, and a gorgeous outdoor balcony; the **Haymarket Pub,** 8308 4th St. N. (☎ 727-577-9621), the gay-friendly Cheers of St. Pete, where audible conversation and reasonably priced drinks aren't implausible demands; **Janus Landing,** 200 1st Ave. N. (☎ 727-896-1244), a fantastic outdoor concert venue and bar where mostly alternative and rock bands perform; **Ringside Café,** 2742 4th St. N. (☎ 727-894-8465), a laid-back jazz and blues bar; and **Martini Bar,** 131 2nd Ave. N. (☎ 727-895-8558), where a crowd that looks as if it stepped off the set of *Sex and the City* convenes for some serious seeing and being seen.

Performing arts

The **Bayfront Center** and the **Mahaffey Theater,** 400 First St. S., St. Petersburg (☎ **727-892-5767** or 727-892-5700; www.stpete.org/mahevent.htm or www.stpete.org/bayfront.htm), present a variety of Broadway plays, ice shows, and concerts including performances by the Florida Orchestra.

North Pinellas and Its Beaches

The North Pinellas area isn't Grand Tourist Central, but its beaches do a jam-up business in summer (with families) and winter (with snowbirds). Inland, the major cities include Clearwater, Dunedin, Largo, and Palm Harbor. On the coast, you come across **Bellair Beach, Clearwater Beach,** and **Sand Key.** (See the "St. Pete and Clearwater Beaches" map, later in this chapter.) The Greek community of **Tarpon Springs** anchors the north end.

Getting there

Like St. Petersburg, reaching Clearwater by the sky is best. For details on flying in, see "Getting there" in the "St. Petersburg" section of this chapter.

If you're coming by car, you have a choice of three routes:

  ✔ **U.S. 19:** The traffic on this route is beyond frustrating.

  ✔ **I-75/275:** This highway cuts through the center of the state from the Florida/Georgia border, and then runs into Tampa and Pinellas County.

  ✔ **I-95/I-4/I-275:** I-95 gets you into the state along the east coast, where you can pick up I-4 in Daytona Beach and ride it onto I-275, which takes you through Tampa into North Pinellas.

St. Pete and Clearwater Beaches

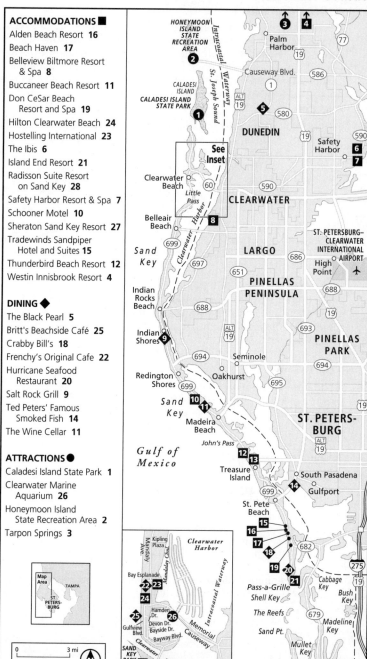

ACCOMMODATIONS ■

Alden Beach Resort **16**

Beach Haven **17**

Belleview Biltmore Resort & Spa **8**

Buccaneer Beach Resort **11**

Don CeSar Beach Resort and Spa **19**

Hilton Clearwater Beach **24**

Hostelling International **23**

The Ibis **6**

Island End Resort **21**

Radisson Suite Resort on Sand Key **28**

Safety Harbor Resort & Spa **7**

Schooner Motel **10**

Sheraton Sand Key Resort **27**

Tradewinds Sandpiper Hotel and Suites **15**

Thunderbird Beach Resort **12**

Westin Innisbrook Resort **4**

DINING ◆

The Black Pearl **5**

Britt's Beachside Café **25**

Crabby Bill's **18**

Frenchy's Original Cafe **22**

Hurricane Seafood Restaurant **20**

Salt Rock Grill **9**

Ted Peters' Famous Smoked Fish **14**

The Wine Cellar **11**

ATTRACTIONS ●

Caladesi Island State Park **1**

Clearwater Marine Aquarium **26**

Honeymoon Island State Recreation Area **2**

Tarpon Springs **3**

Getting around

Clearwater and the beaches primarily use a named street system, so navigating isn't as easy as in St. Petersburg. This is, however, a smaller area, so getting lost is difficult. If you do take a wrong turn, remember that the water is to the west. If you're driving, pick up a map (see "Fast Facts" at the end of this chapter), and you shouldn't have a problem.

By car

U.S. 19 (known to the locals frequently ensnared in its traffic tie-ups as #%$#!! 19) is the main north–south highway. Highway 611 runs the same route to the far east, Alt. U.S. 19 does it to the west, and Gulf Boulevard does it on the beach. East Bay Drive/Highway 686 (Largo), Gulf to Bay Boulevard/Highway 60 (Clearwater), and Curlew Road/Highway 586 (Dunedin) are the primary east–west roads.

By taxi

In general, it costs $2 to get into a cab and $1.60 a mile thereafter. **Yellow Cab** (☎ 727-799-2222) is the main company in North Pinellas.

By trolley

The tourist-friendly **Suncoast Beach Trolley** (☎ 727-530-9911), serves St. Pete Beach and Treasure Island and runs every 30 minutes from 5 a.m. to 10 p.m. daily, until midnight Friday and Saturday. Rides cost $1.25 per person.

By bus

The **Pinellas Suncoast Transit Authority** (☎ 727-530-9911; www.psta.net) serves the entire county. The fare is $1.25 per ride for adults, 75¢ for students, and 60¢ for seniors. Exact change is required. Unless you don't mind a slow, often nontourist pace, skip it.

Staying in style

Because the beaches tend to be crowded much of the year, making hotel reservations early is wise. You can get discount packages during the summer, so ask when you reserve your room.

The **Florida Hotel Network** (☎ 800-538-3616; www.floridahotels.com) will make accommodations arrangements for you, if you don't want the hassle of haggling with motel clerks.

All the accommodations listed here offer free parking, air-conditioning, and pools, unless otherwise noted.

Don't forget to add 11 percent in sales and hotel taxes to your bill.

The top hotels

The Ibis
$$ Safety Harbor

The rooms in this charming, modernish bed-and-breakfast have beach, river, or lake themes and all have private baths. A daily buffet breakfast, wine, and snacks are included in the rates. The inn is within walking distance of parks and shops, but it doesn't have a pool.

See map p. 249. 856 Fifth St. S. ☎ **727-723-9000.** www.ibisbb.com. *To get there: From Highway 60, turn right at Bayshore, left on Seventh Street in Safety Harbor, and right on Ninth Avenue. It's on the corner of Fifth Street and Ninth Avenue. Rack rates: Year-round $99–$129. MC, V.*

Safety Harbor Resort and Spa
$$–$$$ Safety Harbor

This Mediterranean-style, 22-acre resort sits above natural mineral springs originally thought to be Ponce de León's fabled Fountain of Youth when Hernando de Soto stumbled upon them west of Tampa Bay. All 189 rooms offer dataports and most have views of the grounds or Tampa Bay; the deluxe rooms have balconies and dressing areas. The resort has numerous recreational facilities, a full-service spa offering 60 treatments, and fitness programs. Spa packages are available.

See map p. 249. 105 N. Bayshore Dr. ☎ **800-458-5409** *or 727-726-1161.* www.safety harborspa.com. *To get there: Highway 60 east to Bayshore, left 3 miles. Rack rates: Dec–May $119–$235, June–Sept $139–$159, Oct–Nov $250–$375. AE, DC, DISC, MC, V.*

Sheraton Sand Key Resort
$$–$$$ Sand Key/Clearwater Beach

One of this resort's best virtues is its location, away from the tourist glitz. Located next to Sand Key Park, the 10-acre resort has a large, white-sand beach and is popular with water-sports enthusiasts. All rooms have coffeemakers, balconies with a view of the Gulf or Bay, and Nintendo. Its summertime **Kids Camp** program (ages 5–12, 9 a.m.–2 p.m. weekdays) costs $18 per child the first day and $15 per day thereafter. Other facilities include a restaurant, fitness and tennis centers, and an on-site store.

See map p. 249. 1160 Gulf Blvd. ☎ **800-325-3535** *or 727-595-1611. Fax: 727-596-8488.* www.sheratonsandkey.com. *To get there: Gulf to Bay/Highway 60 west to the roundabout, go right to southwest corner, follow the beach road across the Sand Key Bridge. Rack rates: Jan–Apr $165–$259, May–Dec $165–$336. AE, DC, DISC, MC, V.*

Westin Innisbrook Resort
$$$–$$$$ Palm Harbor

Golf Digest, Golf, and other magazines pick this as one of the country's best places to play (provided you stay here, of course). Situated off U.S. 19

between Palm Harbor and Tarpon Springs, this 1,000-acre, all-condominium resort has 90 holes on championship courses that are more like the rolling links of the Carolinas than the usually flat courses found in Florida. Kids and golf widows will love the $3.4 million **Loch Ness Monster Pool and Spa.** Golf and tennis packages are available.

See map p. 249. 36750 U.S. 19 N. ☎ *877-752-1480 or 727-942-2000. Fax: 727-942-5576.* www.westin-innisbrook.com. *To get there: It's about 3 miles north of Highway 584 on U.S. 19. Rack rates: Jan–Apr $209–$485, Mar–May and Sept–Dec $225–$359, June–Aug $145–$289. AE, DC, DISC, MC, V.*

Runner-up hotels

In addition to the following listings, don't overlook the restaurants in Tampa (Chapter 14) and St. Petersburg (earlier in this chapter), which are all within driving distance of the beaches.

The Belleview Biltmore Resort & Spa

$$ Clearwater   A 292-room Victorian palace with creaking wood floors, the Biltmore has a championship golf course and a full-service spa and beach club laid out in a 19th-century setting. *See map p. 249. 25 Belleview Blvd.* ☎ *800-237-8947 or 727-373-3000.* www.belleviewbiltmore.com.

Hilton Clearwater Beach

$$ Clearwater Beach   This 10-acre beachfront resort has 425 rooms decorated in Hilton's modern though impersonal style. For $12 a day, the Hilton Clearwater Beach's Resort Activities pass will give you unlimited use of of an off-site fitness center, bike rental, and a 10 percent discount on fitness classes and water sports. *See map p. 249. 400 Mandalay Ave.* ☎ *800-445-8667 or 727-461-3222.* www.clearwaterbeachresort.com.

Hostelling International

$ Clearwater Beach

Located two blocks from the Gulf, this youth hostel has 33 beds including four private rooms. Guests get free use of canoes and can rent bicycles. *See map p. 249. 606 Bay Esplanade.* ☎ *727-443-1211.* www.hiayh.org.

Radisson Suite Resort on Sand Key

$$$ Clearwater Beach

An all-suite resort, the Radisson offers two-room waterfront suites with balconies, microwaves, and coffeemakers; a kids' program; and a 35-foot waterfall cascading into the pool. *See map p. 249. 1201 Gulf Blvd.* ☎ *800-333-3333 or 727-596-1100.* www.radissonsandkey.com.

Dining out

Seafood is the name of the game when dining in the Clearwater area, but you can find plenty of other choices if marine cuisine doesn't make your mouth water. Budget-minded travelers can find a host of fast-food joints and chain restaurants in the tourist zones and off the main highways that lead to the beaches. *Note:* All Florida restaurants and food-serving bars are smoke-free.

Don't forget to add 7 percent sales tax to your meal budget.

The Black Pearl
$$–$$$ Dunedin   INTERNATIONAL

A creative menu is headlined by treats such as wild-mushroom ragout ignited with Jack Daniels, cedar-plank salmon with an herb rub and lemon horseradish sauce, Maryland lump crabmeat imperial, and veal medallions in a vanilla-bean sauce with shiitake and crimini mushrooms. Desserts such as black-licorice ice cream with raspberry trimmings are definitely out of the ordinary from your typical vanilla dining experience.

See map p. 249. 315 Main St. ☎ 727-734-3463. Reservations recommended. To get there: Take Alt. U.S. 19 north to Main, then east to the restaurant. Main courses: $14–$30. AE, MC, V. Open: Daily 5–10 p.m., Sun brunch 10 a.m.–2 p.m.

Britt's Beachside Café
$ Clearwater Beach   SEAFOOD

Britt's is a casual place offering indoor and outdoor seating with a great view of the Gulf. The tasty cuisine features wraps (blackened-chicken Caesar), seafood (grouper Dijon and spinach-and mushroom-stuffed salmon), and a good jambalaya. Most items are under $15.

See map p. 249. 201 S. Gulfview Blvd. ☎ 727-461-5185. Reservations accepted. To get there: Take Gulf to Bay/Highway 60 across the causeway, go left as you enter the beach, then right at the next light and veer around the curve (in the Beach Towers Hotel). Main courses: $7–$24, sandwiches $5–$8. MC, V. Open: Mon–Fri 11 a.m.– 2 a.m., Sat–Sun 8:30 a.m.–2 a.m.

Frenchy's Original Cafe
$ Clearwater Beach   SEAFOOD

Popular with locals and visitors in the know since 1981, this casual pub makes the best grouper sandwiches in the area and has all the awards to prove it. The sandwiches are fresh, thick, juicy, and delicious. The atmosphere is pure Florida casual style. There can be a wait during winter and on weekends year-round. For a similarly relaxed setting, directly on the beach, **Frenchy's Rockaway Grill,** at 7 Rockaway St. (☎ 727-446-4844), has a wonderful outdoor setting, and it keeps a charcoal grill going to cook fresh fish.

See map p. 249. 41 Baymont St. ☎ 727-446-3607. Sandwiches and burgers: $5–$7.50. AE, MC, V. Open: Mon–Thurs 11:30 a.m.–11 p.m., Fri–Sat 11:30 a.m.–midnight, Sun noon–11 p.m.

Salt Rock Grill
$$ **Indian Shores** STEAKS/SEAFOOD

Affluent professionals and the so-called beautiful people pack this water-front restaurant, making it *the* place to see and be seen on the beaches. The big, urbane dining room is built on three levels, thus affording every table a view over the creeklike waterway out back. And in warm, fair weather you can dine out by the dock or slake your thirst at the lively Tiki bar (bands play out here Sat–Sun during the summer). Anything from the wood-fired grill is excellent. Thick, aged steaks are the house specialties. Pan-seared peppered tuna and salmon cooked on a cedar board lead the seafoods.

See map p. 249. 19325 Gulf Blvd. ☎ 727-593-7625. Reservations accepted. To get there: It's ¼ mile north of the Highway 694/Park Boulevard bridge. Main courses: $9–$36. AE, DC, DISC, MC, V. Open: Mon–Thurs 4–10 p.m., Fri–Sat 4–11 p.m.

Exploring Clearwater

The beaches are the main draw in this area. If you tire of the surf and sand, however, several other attractions can help fill your time. Keep in mind that this area's major showstoppers are of the natural variety. So if you prefer hanging out in museums, head into St. Petersburg.

Touring the top sights

Caladesi Island State Park
Dunedin

This 3-mile island's résumé includes sea grasses, dunes, and a variety of birds, including blue herons. If you're lucky, you may see some wild dolphins performing off the beach, and in summer you can probably see the crawl marks left by nesting loggerhead turtles. Cars and trucks aren't allowed, so noise and carbon dioxide are minimal. The park is only accessible by boat, and there's a four-hour maximum stay.

See map p. 249. 3 Causeway Blvd. ☎ 727-469-5918. www.floridastate parks.org/caladesiisland. *To get there: Use the ferry ($8 adults, $4.50 kids 3–12, no credit cards; ☎ 727-734-5263) from Honeymoon Island State Recreation Area (see listing later in this section). Admission: No charge beyond the $5 for Honeymoon Island. Open: Ferry runs hourly 10 a.m.–4:30 p.m.*

Clearwater Marine Aquarium
Clearwater Beach

This aquarium is dedicated to rehabilitating or providing a permanent home for injured marine mammals (including dolphins and otters), as well as sea turtles. On Sundays and Mondays visitors can participate in a four-and-a-half-hour trainer-for-a-day program. The program is limited to one person per day and costs $125. Otherwise, allow two to three hours to see all the exhibits.

See map p. 249. 249 Windward Passage. ☎ *888-239-9414 or 727-441-1790.* www.cm aquarium.org. *To get there: Highway 60 west to Island Way, right to Windward. Admission: $8.75 adults, $6.25 kids 3–12. Open: Mon–Fri 9 a.m.–5 p.m., Sat 9 a.m.– 4 p.m., Sun 11 a.m.–4 p.m.*

Tarpon Springs: Sponge-ing up some history

Tarpon Springs calls itself "the Sponge Capital of the World." Greek immigrants from the Dodecanese Islands settled here in the late 19th century to harvest sponges, which grew in abundance offshore. By the 1930s, Tarpon Springs was producing more sponges than any other place in the world. A blight ruined the business in the 1940s, but the descendants of those early immigrants stayed on. Today they comprise about a third of the population, making Tarpon Springs a center of transplanted Greek culture.

Sponges still arrive at the historic **Sponge Docks,** on Dodecanese Boulevard. With a lively, carnival-like atmosphere, the docks are a great place to spend an afternoon or early evening, poking your head into shops selling sponges and other souvenirs while Greek music comes from the dozen or so family restaurants purveying authentic Aegean cuisine. You can also venture offshore from here because booths on the docks hawk sightseeing and fishing cruises. Make your reservations as soon as you get here; then go sightseeing ashore or grab a meal at one of the multitudinous Greek restaurants and bakeries facing the dock while waiting for the next boat to shove off.

You also can visit the tin-roofed **Spongeorama** (510 Dodecanese Blvd.; no phone; open daily 10 a.m.–5 p.m.), a museum dedicated to sponges and sponge divers that sells a wide variety of sponges (they'll ship your purchase home) and shows a 30-minute video several times a day about sponge diving. Admission is free. A scuba diver feeds sharks three times a day in the **Konger Tarpon Springs Aquarium** (850 Dodecanese Blvd.; ☎ 727-938-5378; open Mon–Sat 10 a.m.–5 p.m., Sun noon–5pm), at the western end of the boulevard. Admission is $4.75 adults, $4 seniors, $2.75 for children 3–11, free for kids under 3.

South of the docks, the **Downtown Historic District** sports turn-of-the-last-century commercial buildings along Tarpon Avenue and Pinellas Avenue (Alt. U.S. 19). On Tarpon Avenue west of Pinellas Avenue, you'll come to the Victorian homes overlooking **Spring Bayou.** This creek-side area makes for a delightfully picturesque stroll.

The **Tarpon Springs Chamber of Commerce,** 11 E. Orange St., Tarpon Springs, FL 34689 (☎ 727-937-6109; www.tarponsprings.com), has an information office on Dodecanese Boulevard at the Sponge Docks, which is open Tuesday through Sunday from 10:30 a.m. to 4:30 p.m.

To get to Tarpon Springs from Tampa or St. Petersburg, take U.S. 19 north and turn left on Tarpon Avenue (C.R. 582). From Clearwater Beach, take Alt. U.S. 19 north through Dunedin. The center of the historic downtown district is at the intersection of Pinellas Avenue (Alt. U.S. 19) and Tarpon Avenue. To reach the Sponge Docks, go 10 blocks north on Pinellas Avenue and turn left at Pappas' Restaurant onto Dodecanese Boulevard.

Honeymoon Island State Recreation Area
Dunedin

Although it's not as appealing as neighboring Caladesi Island (see earlier listing), this public park features ospreys, mangroves, and dunes as well as swimming, fishing, picnic areas, and bathhouses for changing. If you add a side trip to Caladesi, this can be an all-day affair.

See map p. 249. 3 Causeway Blvd. ☎ *727-469-5942.* www.floridastateparks. org/honeymoonisland. *To get there: From Clearwater go north on U.S. 19, then west on Curlew Road, which ends at the park. Admission: $5 per vehicle. Open: Daily 8 a.m.–dusk.*

More cool things to see and do

Most folks come to this region to sample an old Florida attraction — the shore. North Pinellas beaches are just as attractive as those in the southern part of the county, but they are fewer in number. The star is **Clearwater Beach,** the place to go if you want to see or be seen, or if you're seeking an abundance of water sports.

If you can't go on vacation without hitting the greens at least once, or if you yearn to watch the Boys of Summer get into shape, here are a few of your options:

✔ **Golf:** If you want to take out your clubs while on vacation, information on courses in the area is available on the Internet at www.golf. com and www.floridagolfing.com. If you prefer to do your research the old-fashioned way, request course information from the **Florida Sports Foundation** (☎ 850-488-8347), or **Florida Golfing** (☎ 877-222-4653). Some of the more popular courses here are:

  • **Bardmoor Golf Club,** 7979 Bayou Club Blvd., Largo (☎ 727-392-1234; www.bardmoorgolf.com). Greens fees: $35 to $54 summer, $35 to $95 winter.

  • **Belleview Biltmore Golf Club,** 1501 Indian Rocks Rd., Clearwater (☎ 727-581-5498; www.belleviewbiltmore. com). Greens fees: $25 to $100 year-round.

  • **Lansbrook Golf Club,** 4605 Village Center Dr., Palm Harbor (☎ 727-784-7333; www.lansbrook-golf.com). Greens fees: $19 to $65 year-round.

✔ **Spring training:** The **Philadelphia Phillies** play at Jack Russell Stadium, 800 Phillies Dr., Clearwater (☎ 727-442-8496; www. phillies.com). Tickets costs $7 to $13. The **Toronto Blue Jays** make camp at Grant Field, 311 Douglas Ave., Dunedin (☎ 727-733-0429; www.bluejays.com). Tickets run $12.50 to $15. Workouts begin in mid-February; games run through March.

Taking a guided tour

Starlite Cruises, 25 Causeway Blvd., Clearwater Beach (☎ **800-444-4814** or 727-462-2628; www.starlitecruises.com), runs two- to three-hour sightseeing, lunch, dinner, and dancing cruises out of the Clearwater City Marina. Prices run from $12 to $40.

Captain Memo's Pirate Cruise also runs out of the Clearwater Marina (☎ **727-446-2587;** www.captainmemo.com), using a replica of a pirate ship for sightseeing and champagne cruises that are often escorted by dolphins. The cruises cost from $28 to $30 for adults, $23 for teens and seniors, and $18 for kids. A $2 discount is offered if you book online.

Shopping

This is not a major shopping zone, so if you came to exercise your credit card, go elsewhere. If you're desperate enough, **Countryside Mall,** U.S. 19 and Highway 580, Clearwater (☎ **727-796-1079**), houses 180 stores, including Dillard's, Burdines, and Sears.

Living it up after dark

Many of the beach's restaurants offer some form of entertainment when the sun goes down, including **Britt's Beachside Café** (see listing under "Dining out" earlier in this chapter), and you can find many bars in the same area.

Up on the northern tip of Treasure Island, **Gators on the Pass** (☎ **727-367-8951**) claims to have the world's longest waterfront bar, with a huge deck overlooking the waters of John's Pass. The complex also includes a nonsmoking sports bar and a three-story tower with a top-level observation deck for panoramic views of the Gulf of Mexico. There's live music, from acoustic and blues to rock, most nights.

In Clearwater Beach, the **Palm Pavilion Grill & Bar,** on the beach at 18 Bay Esplanade (☎ **727-446-2742**), has live music Tuesday through Sunday nights during winter and on weekends in the off-season. Nearby, **Frenchy's Rockaway Grill,** at 7 Rockaway St. (☎ **727-446-4844;** www.frenchysonline.com/rockaway.html), is another popular hangout.

Club-wise, check out two of the most popular nightspots:

- ✔ **Club Liquid Blue,** 22 N. Fort Harrison, Clearwater (☎ **727-446-4000;** www.clubliquidblue.com), is a dance, martini, and cigar venue that features DJs and, on some nights, live radio.

- ✔ **Shephard's Tiki Bar,** 601 S. Gulfview Blvd., Clearwater Beach (☎ **727-442-5107**), features live reggae, rock 'n' roll, and more, with a cover of $7 to $15.

On the performing-arts front, **Ruth Eckerd Hall,** 1111 McMullen Booth Rd., Clearwater (☎ **727-791-7400;** www.rutheckerdhall.com), ranks as one of the state's finest centers, with music, dance, and other varied performances during the year.

For more information on cultural offerings, the *St. Petersburg Times* (☎ **727-893-8111;** www.sptimes.com) puts out an entertainment and dining guide called "Weekend" each Thursday.

Day-Tripping to Weeki Wachee, Homosassa Springs, and Crystal River

Kitschy, old Florida is alive and well in these parts.

Weeki Wachee Springs (☎ **877-469-3354;** www.weekiwachee.com) opened in 1947 and still features its "mermaid" shtick. It's a sight to see the mermaids doing their dances in waters that come from one of America's most prolific freshwater springs, pouring some 170 million gallons of 72°F (22°C) water a day into the river. There's more than mermaids here; you can take a Wilderness River Cruise across the Weeki Wachee River and send the kids on the flume ride at Buccaneer Bay, the water-park part of the attraction. The springs are open to scuba divers, too. Weeki Wachee is at U.S. 19 and Highway 50, 45 miles north of Clearwater, and is open from 10 a.m. to 3 p.m. in winter (until 6 p.m. in summer) daily. Admission costs $20 for adults, $16 for kids 3 to 10.

Just 15 miles north of Weeki Wachee, **Homosassa Springs State Wildlife Park,** 4150 U.S. 19 (☎ **352-628-5343;** www.citrusdirectory.com/hsswp), lets you see manatees without getting wet. A permanent home and rehabilitation center for injured manatees, the park also has an underwater observatory where you get another angle on the marine mammals as well as thousands of fish. Nature trails wind through the habitats of several other permanent residents, including eagles, owls, red-tailed hawks, river otters, and a black bear. The park is open from 9 a.m. to 5 p.m. daily. Admission includes a 30-minute narrated boat ride and costs $9 for adults, $5 for kids 3 to 12.

If you want to take a swim with some manatees, you can do so in **Crystal River,** 7 miles north of Homosassa Springs. Its warm springs and federal sanctuaries attract these slow-moving, endangered marine mammals every winter, from November to March. Manatees also reside in some of the local rivers during the warmer months. A number of dive shops on U.S. 19 in Crystal River offer sightseeing and snorkeling tours beginning at $25 or $30. They also rent fins, masks, and wet suits.

If you choose to do only one of the preceding activities, you can do it in a long day-trip from St. Petersburg, lasting from five to seven hours. You can get information by calling ☎ **800-587-6667** or logging onto www.visitcitrus.com. You can also contact the **Citrus County Chamber of Commerce,** 28 NW Highway 19, Crystal River (☎ **352-795-3149**).

Fast Facts

Area Code

The local area codes are **727** and **352.**

Hospitals

Area hospitals include Bayfront Medical Center, 701 Sixth St. S., St. Petersburg (☎ 727-823-1234), and Morton Plant Hospital, 300 Pinellas St., Clearwater (☎ 727-462-7000).

Information

For advance information on the area, contact the St. Petersburg/Clearwater Convention and Visitors Bureau, 14450 46th St. N., Clearwater (☎ 727-464-7200; www.floridasbeach.com).

Mail

U.S. post offices are located at 1299 66th St. N., St. Petersburg; 250 Corey Ave., St. Pete Beach; and 1281 S. Lincoln Ave., Clearwater. To locate a post office near your hotel, call ☎ 800-275-8777.

Maps

The St. Petersburg/Clearwater Convention and Visitors Bureau (see "Information" earlier in this section) a great place to hit up for maps before or after you land. Rental-car agencies are another good source (including those at the airport), and so are convenience stores, which sell maps for $3 to $5.

Newspapers

The *St. Petersburg Times* (☎ 727-893-8111; www.sptimes.com) is the local paper and puts out an entertainment and dining guide called "Weekend" each Thursday.

Taxes

A sales tax of 7 percent is assessed on almost everything except groceries and medicine. The hotel tax raises the tax total to 11 percent on rooms.

Taxis

Taxis cost $2 to get in and $1.60 per mile. Yellow Cab (☎ 727-799-2222) is the major cab company in the area.

Transit Info

The Pinellas Suncoast Transit Authority (☎ 727-530-9911) operates the region's public bus system. The fare is $1.25 for adults, 75¢ for students, and 60¢ for seniors.

Weather Updates

For a recording of current conditions and forecast reports, call the local office of the National Weather Service at ☎ 813-645-2506, or check out www.nws.noaa.gov. You also can get information by watching the Weather Channel (www.weather.com).

Chapter 16

Sarasota, Fort Myers, and Naples

. . . .

In This Chapter

▶ Encountering tigers and a 12-foot-long python in Naples

▶ Seeing showstopping museums: From Ringling to Imaginarium

▶ Retreating to the beaches in the Land of 10,000 Islands

. . . .

*H*ave you ever heard about the green flash? It's a brief, brilliant flare that occurs as the last tip of the sun disappears beneath the horizon. Although they're very rare, you may be able to see one when you visit the southwestern coast of Florida. Meteorologists say that a green flash requires just the right atmospheric brew (heavy on the greens, light on the reds) for the setting sun to ignite this explosion of color. It also takes a flat horizon and cloudless sky. If everything adds up, a green flash probably will steal your breath.

But even if you don't see a flash, you can still find plenty to write home about. The Sarasota–Fort Myers–Naples region of Florida is called the Land of 10,000 Islands. That may be a stretch, but there are a lot of them, and most have never met a bulldozer. If you like civilization, well, don't fret about that, either. You can find plenty to fill your date book here.

Southwest Florida: What's Where?

Down south, Florida's Collier County, which includes Naples and Marco Island, woos more millionaires per capita than any other county east of the Mississippi. While you're in town, you can cruise **Millionaire's Row** in Olde Naples, as well as some of the boutiques and galleries that keep the rich from getting too idle.

Thirty miles north, Fort Myers and Fort Myers Beach are as quiet and quaint as they were when **Thomas Edison** and **Henry Ford** built their winter homes here. Just offshore, **Sanibel** and **Captiva** are two of the region's island gems.

Sarasota, which is the home of the **Asolo Theatre** and **Ringling Museum,** is this region's largest city. Offshore, more than 40 miles of gloriously white beaches fringe a chain of barrier islands that stretch from Sarasota to Tampa Bay, including St. Armands, Longboat, and Lido keys.

On the downside, the Sarasota–Fort Myers–Naples region is spread far and wide. Very few activities take up an entire day, and you'll occasionally have to drive for a spell before reaching your next stop.

Sarasota and Bradenton

Sarasota caters to its residents with a wide variety of cultural attractions and events. Thanks to its theaters and performing-arts centers, the city has grown into an upscale retirement community, similar to Marco Island and, to a lesser degree, Naples to the south. (Skip ahead to the map for an overview of "Sarasota and Bradenton.") Bradenton, Sarasota's often-overlooked neighbor, remains more of a casual fishing village and blue-collar town.

Getting there

The cities' location on the south side of Tampa Bay means that coming here is best by air, but I also give options for people who prefer to leave their feet on the ground.

By plane

Sarasota-Bradenton International Airport (☎ 941-359-2770; www.srq-airport.com) 3 miles (a $5 cab ride) north of downtown off University Parkway between U.S. 41 and U.S. 301, is served by a half-dozen major airlines or their partners, including **Continental, Delta, Northwest, TWA,** and **US Airways. Alamo, Avis, Budget, Dollar, Hertz,** and **National** have rental counters in the terminal.

Another option is to fly into **Tampa International** (☎ 813-870-8700; www.tampaairport.com), which is about one and a half to two hours north of Sarasota. Because Tampa International offers more arrival and departure choices (see Chapter 14 for more information), you often get a better airfare — and cheaper car-rental prices — here.

By car

I-75 is the primary route into Sarasota from the north, and it's about five to six hours from the Florida-Georgia line to Sarasota. If you prefer I-95, take it to Daytona Beach and then follow I-4 to I-75 before heading south.

Getting around

Start by getting a map, which you can get from the information sources listed in "Fast Facts" at the end of this chapter.

Sarasota and Bradenton

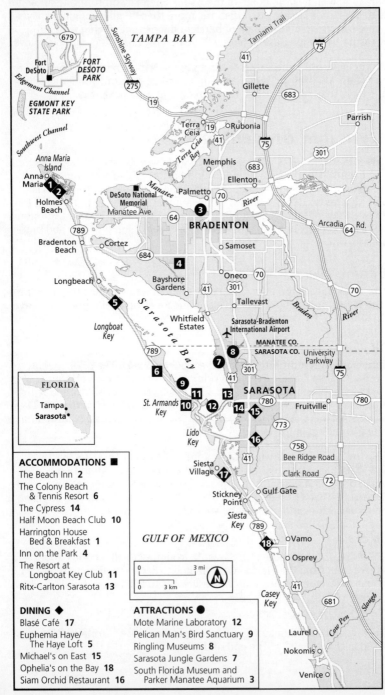

ACCOMMODATIONS ■
The Beach Inn 2
The Colony Beach
    & Tennis Resort 6
The Cypress 14
Half Moon Beach Club 10
Harrington House
    Bed & Breakfast 1
Inn on the Park 4
The Resort at
    Longboat Key Club 11
Ritz-Carlton Sarasota 13

DINING ◆
Blasé Café 17
Euphemia Haye/
    The Haye Loft 5
Michael's on East 15
Ophelia's on the Bay 18
Siam Orchid Restaurant 16

ATTRACTIONS ●
Mote Marine Laboratory 12
Pelican Man's Bird Sanctuary 9
Ringling Museums 8
Sarasota Jungle Gardens 7
South Florida Museum and
    Parker Manatee Aquarium 3

By car

U.S. 301 and U.S. 41/Tamiami Trail are the major north–south arteries on the mainland; the Gulf-to-Mexico Drive (Highway 789) is the main island road. The largest east–west thoroughfares in Sarasota are Highway 72 (Stickney Point Road), Highway 780, University Parkway, and (to the islands) Ringling Causeway, which deposits you on Lido Beach. Highway 70 (53rd Avenue), Highway 684 (Cortez Road), and Highway 64 (Manatee Avenue) are the main roads in Bradenton.

By taxi

Taxi companies include **Yellow Cab** (☎ 941-955-3341), **Green Cab** (☎ 941-922-6666), and **Diplomat Taxi** (☎ 941-359-8294). The standard fare is $2.10 plus $1.50 per mile.

By public transit

Sarasota County Area Transit, or SCAT (☎ 941-316-1234), runs regularly scheduled bus service. A 50¢ fare will take you to stops in the city and St. Armands, Longboat, and Lido keys. It runs from 6 a.m. to 7 p.m. Monday through Saturday. It's not NYC-caliber public transportation, but it works and it's cheap.

Staying in style

The beaches in this area are loaded with condominiums, but you can find a number of other lodging options. In downtown Sarasota and on U.S. 41, just south of the airport, you can find several modern chain hotels. See the "Quick Concierge" at the back of the book for hotel reservation numbers and Web sites.

You can leave the reserving to someone else by contacting the **Florida Hotel Network** (☎ 800-538-3616; www.floridahotels.com). You can also call the free reservation service operated by the **Bradenton Area Convention and Visitors Bureau** at ☎ 800-4-MANATEE.

High season here runs from January to April, but rates along the beaches remain high year-round, so if you're looking for a bargain, stick to the downtown area.

Don't forget Sarasota's 10 percent and Bradenton's 9 percent hotel tax.

The top hotels

The Cypress
$$–$$$ **South Sarasota**

The Cypress is a two-story, tin-roofed inn tucked away amidst giant mango trees and hovering palms, among other lush forms of vegetation. Best of all, it overlooks the bay. You can't get much better than this, with antiques, a grand piano, and rooms with private baths, queen-size beds, hardwood floors, ceiling fans, and Oriental rugs.

See map p. 262. 621 Gulfstream Ave. ☎ **941-955-4683.** *Fax: 941-906-8952.* www. cypressbb.com. *To get there: From 1-75, take Exit 210, go west on Fruitville Road for about 6 miles, take the Tamiami Trail south into downtown Sarasota. Go through the light at Ringling Boulevard, turn left onto Palm Avenue and then a left into the Cypress parking lot. Free parking. Rack rates: Dec–Apr $210–$230, May–Nov $150–$180. AE, DISC, MC, V.*

The Colony Beach & Tennis Resort
$$$$ Longboat Key

If you can stand the sticker shock, this beachside resort offers modern and luxurious one- and two-bedroom suites, lanais, and beach houses. All accommodations have kitchens with microwaves, refrigerators, and dishwashers; baths have whirlpools. The resort has 21 hard- and soft-surface tennis courts (court time is included in your rate), a fitness center and spa, and programs for kids 3 to 13 (also included in the price of your room).

See map p. 262.1620 Gulf of Mexico Dr. ☎ **800-282-1138** *or 941-383-6464. Fax: 941-383-7549.* www.colonybeachresort.com. *To get there: 1 mile north of the Ringling Causeway. Free parking. Rack rates: Feb–Apr and Oct–Nov $395–$1,395, Jan and May $275–$1,125, June–Sept $195–$1,100.*

Half Moon Beach Club
$$ St. Armands Key/Lido Beach

All rooms, efficiencies, and suites in this beachfront motel come with a patio or balcony, refrigerator, and coffeemaker. Some of the spacious rooms have kitchenettes with a microwave, and a few rooms sport Gulf views. The Art Deco property also has an on-site restaurant and a guest laundry.

See map p. 262. 2050 Ben Franklin Dr. ☎ **800-358-3245** *or 941-388-3694. Fax: 941-388-1938.* www.halfmoon-lidokey.com. *To get there: Ringling Causeway to Lido Beach, south to Ben Franklin. Free parking. Rack rates: $139–$269 Feb–Apr, $119–$189 May–Jan. AE, DC, DISC, MC, V.*

Inn on the Park
$$ Bradenton

Set in a three-story building that wraps around the courtyard/pool area, the spacious rooms are rich in amenities; some have Jacuzzis. A free continental breakfast is served. There's an on-site pub where guests can chug complimentary cocktails from 5 to 7 p.m., and numerous restaurants are a short walk away. The inn is 6 miles from Bradenton Beach.

See map p. 262. 4450 47th St. W. ☎ **941-795-4633.** *Fax: 941-795-0808.* www.parkinn clubbradenton.com. *To get there: Manatee Avenue/Highway 64 west to 43rd, left to Cortez Road, right to 47th, left to inn. Free parking. Rack rates: Jan–Apr $109–$149, May–Dec $94–$124. AE, CB, DISC, MC, V.*

Ritz-Carlton Sarasota
$$$–$$$$ **Sarasota**

The Ritz occupies the bottom ten floors of an 18-story, Mediterranean-style building (the top floors are private residencies). It sits perpendicular to the bay, so most of the spacious guest units have views looking across the water to the keys and the Gulf. The rooms are luxuriously appointed in typical Ritz-Carlton fashion, including marble bathrooms. The elegantly appointed lobby opens to a bay-side courtyard with a heated pool. There is no beach on-site, but a shuttle will take you to Lido Key, where the hotel debuted its own private beach club in January 2004. There's also a full-service spa and fitness center on site.

See map p. 262. 1111 Ritz-Carlton Dr. ☎ **800-241-3333** *or 941-309-2000. Fax: 941-309-2100.* www.ritzcarlton.com. *To get there: At Tamiami Trail/U.S.41. Parking: $20. Rack rates: Feb–Apr $215–$535, May–Jan $395–$695. AE, DC, DISC, MC, V.*

Runner-up hotels

In addition to my top picks, here are a few more equally good options for your snoozing pleasure.

The Beach Inn

$$ **Holmes Beach**   This small inn features six clean and comfortable units. *See map p. 262. 101 66th St.* ☎ **800-823-2247** *or 941-778-9597.* www.thebeachinn.com.

Harrington House Bed & Breakfast

$$ **Holmes Beach**   This cozy inn still exudes the ambience of the year it was built, 1925. *See map p. 262. 5626 Gulf Dr.* ☎ **888-828-5566** *or 941-778-5444.* www.harringtonhouse.com.

The Resort at Longboat Key Club

$$$ **Longboat Key**   This upscale resort offers 232 luxurious rooms and suites, 45 holes of golf, 38 tennis courts, and 500 feet of private beach. *See map p. 262. 301 Gulf of Mexico Dr.* ☎ **800-237-8821** *or 941-383-8821.* www.longboatkeyclub.com.

Dining out

A veritable bounty of upscale restaurants caters to the tastes of Sarasota locals, but there are also plenty of places to dine that won't put a king-size dent in your budget. As in most Florida cities, your best bet is to stick to local seafood, which is almost always fresh and well prepared. *Note:* All Florida restaurants and food-serving bars are smoke-free.

Don't forget to allow for the 7 percent sales tax.

Blasé Café

$–$$ Siesta Key   INTERNATIONAL

Tongue in cheeky, to say the least, this restaurant doesn't take itself seriously, hence the ironic and oxymoronic name. One of Florida's most unusual restaurants, Ralph and Cindy Cole's supercasual establishment has tables indoors and a few under the cover of the Village Corner shopping center's walkway, but most are alfresco, on a wooden deck built around a palm tree in the center's asphalt parking lot. This is Siesta Key's best breakfast spot, offering Italian- and Louisiana-flavored frittatas as well as plain old bacon and eggs. Lunch sees burgers, big salads, and platters such as chicken Alfredo and Florentine crepes with shrimp. At night, Ralph puts forth the likes of pan-seared, sushi-quality yellowfin tuna with tangy wasabi and pickled ginger. You can while away the rest of the evening in the wine bar, where the Coles have installed the original bar from the Don CeSar Beach Resort & Spa in St. Pete Beach. There's also live music in there on weekends.

See map p. 262. 5263 Ocean Blvd. ☎ **941-349-9822.** *Reservations recommended. To get there: In the Village Corner at Calle Miramar. Main courses: $10–$23; breakfast and lunch $5–$9. MC, V. Open: Mon–Thurs 8:30 a.m.–9:30 p.m., Fri–Sat 8:30 a.m.– 10 p.m. Closed Mon June–Nov.*

Euphemia Haye/The Haye Loft

$$–$$$ Longboat Key   CONTINENTAL

FYI: A Euphemia Haye isn't a chichi culinary creation, but, rather, the grandmother of the restaurant's founder. Another highly praised establishment, this restaurant combines a great menu (peppered and pan-fried steak, snapper baked in a pistachio crust), an incredible ambience, and an extensive wine list. Whatever you do, do not miss Euphemia Prime Peppered Steak (whose famous sauce is now available for purchase). If all this sounds sweet, wait until you go upstairs to The Haye Loft, the casual dessert bar. Up here you can take your pick from fabulous pies topped with thick whipped cream or Ben & Jerry's ice cream. You can also sample the kitchen's offerings, for the loft has its own light-fare menu, including soups, appetizers, small pizzas, and sandwiches.

See map p. 262. 5540 Gulf of Mexico Dr. ☎ **941-383-3633.** *Reservations suggested. To get there: Take Highway 789 7.8 miles north of New Pass Bridge. Main courses: $18–$39. CB, DISC, MC, V. Open: Sun–Thurs 5–10 p.m., Fri–Sat 5–10:30 p.m.*

Michael's on East

$$–$$$ Sarasota   CONTINENTAL

Michael Klauber's chic bistro is one of Sarasota's top places for fine dining and is the locals' favorite after-theater haunt. Huge cut-glass walls create three intimate dining areas, one a piano bar for pre- or after-dinner drinks. Prepared with fresh ingredients and a creative flair, the offerings here will tempt your taste buds. House specialties are the Dungeness crab cakes, pan-seared Chilean sea bass with couscous and artichoke hearts in a thyme-accented tomato coulis, and grilled duck breast with Bermuda onion, shiitake fondue, and pecan risotto.

See map p. 262. 1212 East Ave. S. ☎ *941-366-0007. Reservations recommended. To get there: On U.S. 41/Tamiami Trail in Midtown Plaza at junction of Bahia Vista Drive. Main courses: $18–$36. AE, DISC, MC, V. Open: Mon–Fri 11:30 a.m.–2 p.m., nightly 5:30–10 p.m.*

Ophelia's on the Bay
$$–$$$ Siesta Key   AMERICAN

Casually elegant, Ophelia's continues this area's string of award-winners. The glass-walled dining rooms offer a romantic atmosphere and wonderful views of the bay, or you can dine on an outside patio. The staff is thoroughly professional, and there's a good wine list. The menu offers modern American options, such as mango-and-rum-glazed breast of duck and pistachio-crusted prawns.

See map p. 262. 9105 Midnight Pass Rd. ☎ **941-349-2212**. *Reservations suggested. To get there: 3 miles south of Stickney Point Road. Main courses: $15–$32. AE, DC, DISC, MC, V. Open: Daily 5–10 p.m.*

Siam Orchid Restaurant
$–$$ Sarasota   THAI

This 15-year-old Thai restaurant offers an exotic atmosphere, friendly service, and a good wine list. House specials include *goong tod* (well-seasoned fried shrimp) and shrimp, mussels, and lobster tail on stir-fried noodles. Many entrees cost under $15, such as the *pad talay* (mixed seafood with vegetables).

See map p. 262. 4141 Tamiami Trail/U.S. 41. ☎ **941-923-7447**. *Reservations suggested. To get there: Go south on U.S. 41 to Robinhood Street, then make a right and head into the 4141 Plaza. Main courses: $9–$24. AE, DISC, MC, V. Open: Mon–Fri 11 a.m.–2 p.m., daily 5–9:30 p.m.*

Exploring Sarasota and Bradenton

Visitors won't find any theme parks here, but there is a nice mix of things to do for plant, animal, and art lovers.

The top attractions

Mote Marine Laboratory
Longboat Key

Stare into a shark's eye or count a barracuda's teeth. Meet manatees named Hugh and Buffett, enjoy a 30-foot touch tank, and find out a lot about nature in the river and estuary displays. Don't forget to stick your head around the corner to see the marine mammal hospital or the brand-new sea turtle and aquaculture exhibits. Allow two to four hours to see everything.

See map p. 262. 1600 Ken Thompson Pkwy. ☎ 941-388-4441. www.mote.org. *To get there: From St. Armands Circle, go north toward Longboat Key and follow the signs. Admission: $12 adults, $8 kids 4–17. Open: Daily 10 a.m.–5 p.m.*

Pelican Man's Bird Sanctuary
Sarasota

Dale Shields started this MASH unit for feathered patients in 1989, and today the 2-acre sanctuary in Ken Thompson Park has 200 walking-wounded birds. There's a viewing area, hospital, recovery and rehabilitation areas, and a gift shop. You can adopt a pelican for $25. When you go, the pelican stays (but you get a picture). Allow an hour.

See map p. 262. 1708 Ken Thompson Pkwy. ☎ 941-388-4444. www.pelicanman.org. *To get there: From St. Armands Circle, go north and follow the signs. Admission:$6 adults, $2 kids 18 and under. Open: Daily 10 a.m.–5 p.m.*

Ringling Museums
Sarasota

This 60-acre showstopper, once the home of showman John Ringling, is Sarasota's Big Top. Combined, the **Baroque Art Gallery, Museum of the Circus,** and the Ringling residence, **Ca'd'Zan,** house a ton of European and American art, including works by Rubens, Van Dyck, and Poussin. The Circus Museum exhibits artifacts such as 19th- and early 20th-century posters, costumes, beautifully carved parade wagons, and more. Ca'd'Zan (House of John) itself is a grand terra-cotta palace of stained glass, whimsical carvings, and personal mementos of John and Mable Ringling. Plan on spending about four hours if you want to see everything.

See map p. 262. 5401 Bayshore Rd. ☎ 941-359-5723 or 941-351-1660 (recording). www.ringling.org. *To get there: U.S. 41 north to University Parkway and follow the signs. Admission: $15 adults, $12 seniors 55 and over, kids 12 and under free. Open: Daily 10 a.m.–5:30 p.m.*

Sarasota Jungle Gardens
Sarasota

Jungle trails meander through 240 species of trees, plants, and flowers at this exotic attraction. Rounding out the menu are bird and reptile shows, a kids' jungle (a petting area and energy-burning playground), and flamingos that will eat from your hand. Plan to spend three to four hours here.

See map p. 262. 3701 Bayshore Rd. ☎ 877-861-6547 or 941-355-1112. www.sarasota junglegardens.com. *To get there: Take U.S. 41 north to Myrtle and turn left. Admission: $11 adults, $10 seniors 62 and over, $7 kids 3–12. Open: Daily 9 a.m.–5 p.m.*

South Florida Museum and Parker Manatee Aquarium
Bradenton

Snooty, the oldest captive-born manatee in our galaxy, headlines this attraction. Born in 1948, the Snootster and his sidekick, Mo, live in the 60,000-gallon aquarium. The complex also has astronomy, natural history, and cultural exhibits; a hands-on room; and laser-light shows in the planetarium. (Fire recently damaged the museum's Bishop Planetarium, which is now closed.) Allow four hours to explore the total experience.

See map p. 262. 201 10th St. W. ☎ *941-746-4131.* www.southfloridamuseum. org. *To get there: Take Manatee Avenue/Highway 64 west to 10th Street and turn right. Open: Tues–Sat 10 a.m.–5 p.m., Sun noon–5 p.m. Admission: $9.50 adults, $7.50 seniors, $6 kids 5–12.*

More cool things to see and do

If you have special interests or just want to work on your tan, you can find many other options for occupying your time. Here are some ideas:

- ✔ **Baseball:** The **Pittsburgh Pirates** (☎ **941-747-3031;** www.pittsburgh pirates.com), use McKechnie Field, 17th Avenue and Ninth Street West, for training camp. Tickets cost $6 to $9. The **Cincinnati Reds** (☎ **941-954-4464** or 941-334-3309; www.cincinnatireds.com) pitch their tents at Sarasota's Ed Smith Stadium, 2700 12th St. Tickets run $5 to $12. Workouts begin in mid-February, and games are played through March.

- ✔ **Beaches:** Swim in several places located along the barrier islands, from Holmes Beach to Casey Key. Although Sarasota's **Siesta Beach** is just a quarter of a mile long, it's also 500-feet wide. The sand granules are soft and squeaky under your toes, and the Gulf's waters soothe. Go west on Highway 72 over U.S. 41 and the Intracoastal Waterway to the end at Midnight Pass, and then turn right. The beach is free; although there are 800 free parking spots, they go fast, so get here early.

- ✔ **Fishing:** The **Flying Fish Fleet** (☎ **941-366-3373;** www.flyingfish fleet.com), at Marina Jack's, U.S. 41 at Island Circle, Sarasota, offers half-day rates of $30 for adults and $18 for kids under 15 on big boats, and $395 for private charters (up to six people).

- ✔ **Gardens: Selby Botanical Gardens,** 811 South Palm Ave., Sarasota (☎ **941-366-5731;** www.selby.org), has been called a "supernova in the constellation of botanical gardens." The star attraction is the collection of more than 6,000 orchids. In addition. the 11-acre complex has an open-air museum of some 20,000 colorful plants. Admission costs $12 for adults and $6 for kids 6 to 11. The gardens are open 10 a.m. to 5 p.m. daily.

- ✔ **Golf:** The **Bobby Jones Golf Complex,** 1000 Circus Blvd., Sarasota (☎ **941-365-4653**), is a 45-hole municipal course where greens fees run under $25 year-round. The **Legacy Golf Club,** 8255 Legacy Blvd.,

Bradenton (☎ 941-907-7067; www.legacygolfclub.com), has
sand and water hazards on all 18 of its holes. Greens fees run $$40
to $99. **Tatum Ridge Golf Links,** 421 Tatum Rd., Sarasota (☎ 941-
378-4211), has 18 holes set among wetlands. Greens fees here run
under $25 in summer, and $25 to $40 during the winter.

Shopping

Although the area offers little in terms of unique merchandise, Sarasota
does have a unique shopping district. **St. Armands Circle** on St. Armands
Key is a fun place to window-shop or splurge a little (more like a lot —
you pay more here than in other areas). An outdoor zone of 150 trendy
shops, art galleries, and cafes, the circle is on a par with Worth Avenue
in Palm Beach and Park Avenue in Winter Park. To get there, follow
Highway 780 across the Ringling Causeway until you see the circle. For
more information, call ☎ 941-388-1554.

Living it up after dark

In addition to the following listings, the *Sarasota Herald-Tribune* (☎ 941-
953-7755; www.newscoast.com/xwelcome.cfm) publishes a Friday
entertainment edition called "Ticket." The *Bradenton Herald* (☎ 941-
748-0411; bradenton.com) features "The Weekender" on Friday.

Bars and clubs

The HayeLoft atop the Euphemia Haye restaurant, 5540 Gulf of Mexico
Dr., Longboat Key (☎ 941-383-3633; www.euphemiahaye.com), offers
live jazz Friday through Tuesday and blues on Wednesday and Thursday.
You can find plenty of music to dance to on the mainland at **Sarasota
Quay,** the downtown waterfront dining-shopping-entertainment complex
on Tamiami Trail (U.S. 41), a block north of John Ringling Causeway. Just
walk around this brick building and your ears will take you to the action.
The laser sound-and-light crowd gathers at **In Extremis** (☎ 941-954-2008),
where a high-energy DJ spins Top 40 tunes for 20-somethings. Michael's
Mediterranean Grill turns into **Anthony's After Dark** rocking disco at
10:30 p.m. An older but still energetic crowd dances to contemporary
jazz at the **Downunder Jazz Bar** (☎ 941-951-2467). In Siesta Key Village,
The Old Salty Dog, 5023 Ocean Blvd. (☎ 941-349-0158), offers a fabu-
lous selection of British ales and a lovely outdoor patio.

Performing arts

The **FSU Center for the Performing Arts,** 5555 N. Tamiami Trail/U.S. 41,
Sarasota (☎ 800-361-8388 or 941-351-8000; www.asolo.org), is the
home of the **Asolo Theatre,** Florida's official state theater. The center's
large and small stages present various performances throughout the
year. There's also an actors-in-training program. Tickets to performances
run from $13 to $39.

The **Van Wezel Performing Arts Center,** 777 N. Tamiami Trail/U.S. 41,
Sarasota (☎ 941-953-3366; www.vanwezel.org), commands the bay-

front skyline with a seashell-shaped hall. The acoustics here are great, and year-round programs range from ballet to jazz and musical comedy. The **Sarasota Ballet** (☎ 941-351-8000; www.sarasotaballet.org) performs at the center from October to April, and it also stages performances at the FSU Center. Tickets cost $11 to $45.

Fort Myers, Sanibel, Naples, and Marco Island

Marco Island and, to a lesser degree, Naples can stake a legitimate claim to being west Florida's wealthiest areas per capita. Meanwhile, Fort Myers Beach and its island neighbors — Sanibel and Captiva — are among the area's most popular tourist magnets. Tough zoning laws and efforts to protect the local ecology should help keep the area's natural wonders, if not untouched, then certainly unspoiled. Don't come here looking for beach-blanket bacchanalia, à la spring break in Daytona. But for ample sun, R&R, and places that close well before midnight, this is *the* place. Travels in this half of the chapter stay close to the coast. (See the "Fort Myers, Sanibel, and Naples" map in this chapter.)

If you're interested in heading farther south to see the **Everglades,** check out Chapter 12.

Getting there

Most out-of-state visitors opt to fly here. **Southwest Florida International Airport** in Fort Myers (☎ 941-768-4700; www.swfia.com) is served by about two dozen American, Canadian, and European airlines or their partners, including **Continental, Delta, Northwest/KLM, TWA, US Airways, Air Canada,** and **LTU International** (see the "Quick Concierge" at the back of this book for telephone-number and Web-site information). **Alamo, Avis, Budget, Dollar, Hertz,** and **National** have desks at the airport. **Superior Airport Shuttle** (☎ 888-397-9571 or 941-267-4777; www.superiorairportshuttle.com) can get you to most southwest Florida destinations from the airport. Here are a few one-way rates for up to three passengers: Fort Myers, $16 to $35; Sanibel and Captiva, $37 to $56; Naples, $38 to $56; and Marco Island, $56 to $70.

If you do decide to come by car (and I can't recommend it), expect a seven- to eight-hour drive from the Florida-Georgia state line. I-75 is the primary route from the north. If you prefer to drive in from the East Coast, take I-95 to Daytona Beach; then take I-4 to I-75 and head south. (See the "Fort Myers, Sanibel, and Naples" map, in this chapter.)

Getting around

Top to bottom, this area is about 60 miles long, though the tourist zones pretty much hug the coastline and barrier islands. Unless you're going to be relatively stationary, you need to have a car.

Fort Myers, Sanibel, and Naples

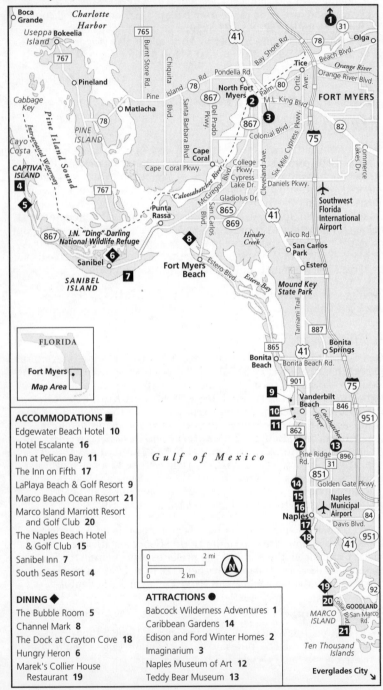

ACCOMMODATIONS ■
Edgewater Beach Hotel **10**
Hotel Escalante **16**
Inn at Pelican Bay **11**
The Inn on Fifth **17**
LaPlaya Beach & Golf Resort **9**
Marco Beach Ocean Resort **21**
Marco Island Marriott Resort
and Golf Club **20**
The Naples Beach Hotel
& Golf Club **15**
Sanibel Inn **7**
South Seas Resort **4**

DINING ◆
The Bubble Room **5**
Channel Mark **8**
The Dock at Crayton Cove **18**
Hungry Heron **6**
Marek's Collier House
Restaurant **19**

ATTRACTIONS ●
Babcock Wilderness Adventures **1**
Caribbean Gardens **14**
Edison and Ford Winter Homes **2**
Imaginarium **3**
Naples Museum of Art **12**
Teddy Bear Museum **13**

By car

U.S. 41/Cleveland Avenue/Tamiami Trail is the primary north–south road on the mainland. Highway 865/Estero Boulevard runs between Fort Myers Beach and Bonita Beach. Highway 78/Pine Island Road connects that island with North Fort Myers, while Highway 867/McGregor Boulevard leads the way from Fort Myers to Sanibel and Captiva.

You definitely need a map to navigate the area. Good maps are available from the sources listed in "Fast Facts" at the end of this chapter.

By taxi

Yellow Cab (☎ 941-332-1055 in Fort Myers and ☎ 941-262-1312 in Naples) is the major taxi company in the area. Fares cost $2.75 to $3.75 for the first mile and $1.50 per mile thereafter (for up to five passengers).

By trolley

The **Naples Trolley** (☎ 941-262-7300) makes 25 stops in the downtown and the beach area and allows riders to get on and off the trolley throughout the entire day. Fares run $17 for adults and $7 for kids 3 to 12.

By bus

Buses should be used only as a last resort because in most cases they cater to commuters, not tourists. **Lee Tran** (☎ 941-275-8726), operates buses in the Fort Myers and beach areas from 6 a.m. to 9:45 p.m. Monday through Saturday. The fare is $1 for adults, 50¢ for seniors, and kids under 42 inches get on free.

Staying in style

As with the rest of South Florida, room rates are highest in the winter, and even motels far removed from the beaches charge premium rates from mid-December through April (although Jan sees somewhat lower rates in Sanibel and Captiva). Rates drop by as much as 50 percent during the off season, so if you're on a tight budget, the timing of your vacation is crucial.

Also, keep in mind that hotels can pack in the crowds during high season, so make sure to reserve a room well in advance.

Accommodations in southwest Florida range from small motels to condominiums to major resorts. Fort Myers is home to a branch of seemingly every chain hotel on the planet, Sanibel offers a host of old-fashioned cottages and condominiums, and Naples has some of the most expensive resorts in the region, such as the hyperswank Ritz-Carlton Golf Resort featuring the Greg Norman–designed Tiburon golf course (www.ritz carlton.com), and the revamped LaPlaya Beach and Golf Resort (www. laplayaresort.com).

Several reservation services can help get you decent rates or find you a hotel room during a particularly busy time of year. The **Lee Island Coast Visitor and Convention Bureau** operates a free reservation service (☎ 800-237-6444) that covers lodging in the Fort Myers and Sanibel areas. **Sanibel and Captiva Central Reservations, Inc.** (☎ 800-325-1352; www. sanibel-captivarents.com) can book you into condos and cottages on the islands. **Florida Hotel Network** (☎ 800-538-3616; www.florida hotels.com) can make arrangements for you in many locations in Southwest Florida.

Remember: Sales and hotel taxes add 9 percent to your bill.

The top hotels

Hotel Escalante
$$–$$$$ **Naples**

The closest thing to Italy that you'll find in Naples, *Florida,* this 71-room Mediterranean villa–style hotel is only blocks away from the beach and worlds away from the hustle and bustle of the real world, ensconced in 4 acres of lush, private gardens. A swimming pool, Jacuzzi, spa and workout room are enough to distract you from walking around the corner and spending money on swanky Fifth Avenue. Although there's no on-site restaurant, the hotel will be happy to suggest one of the 15 restaurants located within walking distance.

See map p. 272. 290 Fifth Ave. S. ☎ *877-485-3466. Fax: 239-262-8748.* www.hotel escalante.com. *To get there: Take I-75 west towards Naples. Exit at #15 (CR-951) and go left. Turn right onto Davis Boulevard and then right onto East Fifth Avenue South. Hotel is ½ mile up on the left. Free parking. Rack rates: Oct–Apr $195–$655, May–Sept $165–$400. AE, DISC, MC, V.*

The Inn on Fifth
$$–$$$$ **Old Naples**

This former bank building still exudes that old-money, old-world European charm, but it's hardly stuffy. Located on the somewhat happening Fifth Avenue South, The Inn features 87 large guest rooms elegantly decorated with rich, warm tones—the antithesis of Florida decor, frankly. French doors opening to a balcony or terrace may not reveal the ocean, but you will see either the lovely pool or "action" on the Avenue. The one drawback of this place is that it's six blocks away from the beach, but that's hardly a big deal. McCable's Irish Pub downstairs is a hotbed of activity, featuring live music, a fabulous beer selection, and a youngish contingency of revelers.

See map p. 272. 699 Fifth Ave. S. ☎ *888-403-8778 or 941-403-8777. Fax: 941-403-8778.* www.naplesinn.com. *To get there: Pine Ridge Road to U.S. 41, south 5 miles to Fifth, go right 2½ blocks. Free valet and self-parking. Rack rates: Winter $250–$300; off season $130–$180. AE, CB, DC, DISC, MC, V.*

LaPlaya Beach & Golf Resort
$$$–$$$$ **Naples**

There is certainly no dearth of beach resorts in Naples, but what is conspicuously missing — that is until now — has been a more intimate beach resort, directly on the beach, in which you don't feel underdressed or socially inappropriate when walking through the lobby in a bathing-suit cover-up. Located on pristine Vanderbilt Beach, LaPlaya Beach & Golf Resort has filled the void with plush, beautifully decorated rooms overlooking the Gulf and bay (all have a private balcony), a spectacular 4,500-square-foot spa, and a sprawling, scenic, and challenging Bob Cupp–designed golf club and the David Leadbetter Golf Academy for the novices. But let's get back to the rooms for a minute. The French-country decor and goose-down pillows are hardly what you'd expect at a beach resort, but there's the rub! You'll find none of that cookie-cutter, as-seen-in-*Martha-Stewart-Living* stuff here.

See map p. 272. 9891 Gulf Shore Dr.. ☎ **800-237-6883** *or 239-597-3123. Fax: 239-597-6278.* www.laplayaresort.com. *To get there: Take I-75 south to Exit 111. Turn right off the Interstate onto Immokalee Road and head west. Cross U.S. 41. Road will change name to 111th Avenue and then to Bluebill. Follow to the end and turn left at the stop sign (just after the bridge) onto Gulf Shore Drive. The resort will be on the right. Valet parking: $15. Rack rates: Winter $395–$695, off season $159–$359. AE, MC, DC, V.*

Marco Island Marriott Resort and Golf Club
$$$–$$$$ **Marco Island**

Marco Island is far from Disney World, so if you plan to bring your kids while you experience the utmost in R&R, the Marco Island Marriott will help entertain them with a summer camp's worth of activities, from water sports and Everglades excursions to bingo and "dive-in" movies in the pool. Parents can play, too, or they can opt for the hotel's convenient nanny service. A $55 million renovation has spruced up the 735 guest rooms and 8 restaurants and lounges and added a par-72 golf course located seven minutes away, as well as a 24,000-square-foot Balinese-style spa.

See map p. 272. 400 South Collier Blvd. ☎ **941-394-2511.** *Fax: 941-642-2672.* www.marriotthotels.com. *To get there: From U.S. 41/Tamiami Trail, turn south/west onto Florida 92, which will become San Marco Road. Turn left onto South Collier Boulevard. The hotel is on the right. Free valet and self-parking. Rack rates: Mid-Dec–mid-Jan $280–$1,250, mid-Jan–mid-May $335–$1,250, mid-May–Sept $200–$815, Oct–mid-Dec $235–$1,075. AE, CB, DC, DISC, MC, V.*

The Naples Beach Hotel & Golf Club
$$–$$$$ **Naples**

This hospitable, beachy-keen resort is unique — family-owned since 1946. Despite its modern amenities, the hotel is decidedly retro-looking, impervious to the sterile minimalism that has invaded most hotels today. Its 318 tropically decorated rooms are large and comfortable, sporting dataports, minibars, and balconies. Set on 125 acres, the resort has a spa that's a lot more modern than the fabulous '50s-esque ambience of the hotel itself, a kids' club that offers free activities for children ages 5 to 12, and a front-row view of the Gulf of Mexico that's usually standing room only on Sunday afternoons when the hotel's pool bar turns into a happening happy-hour spot.

See map p. 272. 851 Gulf Shore Blvd. N. ☎ **800-237-7600** *or 941-261-2222. Fax:: 941-261-7380.* www.naplesbeachhotel.com. *To get there: From Pine Ridge Road, go south on U.S. 41/Tamiami Trail 4 miles and, at the resort's golf club, turn right on South Golf Drive. Free parking. Rack rates: Dec–Apr $165–$545, May–Nov $135–$310. AE, CB, DISC, MC, V.*

Sanibel Inn
$$$–$$$$ Sanibel

Look for hummingbirds and butterflies in the gardens on this 8-acre resort set on a nature preserve. Accommodations here include standard rooms, efficiencies, and one- and two-bedroom apartments. Rattan furnishings match the islandy motif, and all rooms have a microwave, a refrigerator, and a screened balcony or patio. An on-site restaurant, recreational programs, and two tennis courts are also available.

See map p. 272. 937 E. Gulf Dr. ☎ **800-965-7772** *or 941-472-3181. Fax: 941-481-4947.* www.sanibelinn.com. *To get there: McGregor Boulevard/Highway 867 Causeway to East Gulf Drive and the inn. Free parking. Rack rates: Jan–Apr $329–$539, May–Dec $175–$275. AE, DISC, MC, V.*

South Seas Resort
$$$$ Captiva

This 330-acre resort is set on 2½ miles of beach that provide some of Florida's finest shelling. South Seas has 18 tennis courts, a 9-hole golf course, a fitness center, 5 restaurants, a sailing school, and a marina where you may see manatees and loggerhead turtles. The comfortable accommodations here range from standard hotel rooms to luxurious three-bedroom villas, and all come with balconies or porches. Rates don't include the $8-per-person daily service charge.

See map p. 272. 5400 South Seas Plantation Rd. ☎ **800-965-7772** *or 941-481-3636. Fax: 941-481-4947.* www.ssrc.com *or* www.south-seas-resort.com. *To get there: Follow Highway 869 across the Sanibel Causeway and continue 16 miles to the resort. Free parking. Rack rates: Jan–Apr $350–$1,800, May–Sept $260–$1,300, Oct–Dec $260–$2,000. AE, DISC, MC, V.*

Runner-up hotels

In addition to the following, check out the chains listed in the Appendix in the back of this guide for more lodging possibilities.

Edgewater Beach Hotel

$$$ **Naples** This all-suite resort on Millionaire's Row is a bit more elegant — and stuffier — than the Naples Beach Hotel & Golf Club (see listing above). *See map p. 272. 1901 Gulf Shore Blvd. N.* ☎ **800-821-0196** *or 941-403-2000.* www.edgewaternaples.com.

Inn at Pelican Bay

$$ **Naples** This modern six-story, upscale motel is just a few blocks from the Gulf of Mexico — a good location if most of your visit will be spent in Naples but you also want to be near the Miromar Outlets and Fort Myers. *See map p. 272. 800 Vanderbilt Beach Rd.* ☎ **800-597-8770** *or 941-597-8777.* www.naplesinn.com.

Marco Beach Ocean Resort

$$$ **Marco Island** Making up for the lack of a Ritz-y resort on Marco is this posh, all-suite hotel and spa in which a dress code (no T-shirts, shorts, tank tops, or casual hats in the lobby) is loosely enforced. *See map p. 272. 480 S. Collier Blvd.* ☎ **800-715-8517** *or 941-393-1400.* www.marcoresort.com.

Sandpiper Gulf Resort

$$ **Fort Myers Beach** A clean, family feel is evident in this resort's Gulf-side rooms, which have kitchens and convertible sofas. *5550 Estero Blvd.* ☎ **800-584-1449** *or 941-463-5721.* www.sandpipergulfresort.com.

Dining out

The good news is that restaurants in the affluent areas of Southwest Florida — especially the islands — couldn't afford to stay in business if they didn't churn out good food. So if fine dining tickles your fancy, your luck runneth over. And you don't need to be a millionaire to feast like one, although a bulging wallet certainly helps. Those travelers on very tight budgets, or in search of that must-have Big Mac, can find chain restaurants and fast-food joints strung along U.S. 41 from Fort Myers all the way to Naples. *Note:* All Florida restaurants and food-serving bars are smoke-free.

Don't forget to allow for the 7 percent sales tax.

The Bubble Room
$$–$$$ **Captiva STEAK/SEAFOOD**

Imagine Walt Disney on acid and you'll understand where the Bubble Room is coming from. The kitschiest restaurant you'll probably ever find, the Bubble Room's tongue-in-cheeky American cuisine is complemented by a decor that's filled with Christmas and Hollywood memorabilia from the '30s, '40s, and '50s. Distracting, to say the least — but in a very good way. The Bubble Room makes it hard to decide which is cooler, the Henny Young-One boneless breast of young chicken, the prime ribs Weissmuller, or the thousands of movie stills, puppets, antique jukeboxes, or toy trains. *Note:* Readers have complained about the "awful" food here, but I still think The Bubble Room is fun, with good (though admittedly not fabulous) food and a great atmosphere.

See map p. 272. 15001 Captiva Rd. (at Andy Rosse Lane). ☎ **239-472-5558.** *Reservations not accepted, but call for preferred seating. Main courses: $17–$30. AE, DC, DISC, MC, V. Open: Daily 11:30 a.m.–2:30 p.m. and 5–10 p.m.*

Channel Mark
$$–$$$ Fort Myers Beach   SEAFOOD

Try this waterfront restaurant for a scenic lunch or a romantic evening out. Every seat in the house has a view of Hurricane Bay and its passing boats. In fact, most people come here by boat, lured by the locally caught seafood and northern Italian fare. (Don't worry, you can still drive here, too.) The menu offers creative twists on seafood dishes. House specialties include a scrumptious grouper topped with shrimp and poached in parchment paper, and honey-and-bacon grilled shrimp. But whether you've come by land or by sea, the surf and turf, with filet mignon and lobster tail, is the reason to make your mark here.

See map p. 272. 19001 San Carlos Blvd. ☎ **941-463-0117.** *Reservations not accepted. To get there: On San Carlos, just before the bridge to Estero Island. Main courses: $11–$32. AE, DC, DISC, MC, V. Open: Sun–Thurs 11 a.m.–10 p.m., Fri–Sat 11 a.m.–11 p.m.*

The Dock at Crayton Cove
$–$$ Olde Naples   SEAFOOD/FLORIBBEAN

If you're in the mood for a locals' joint, this is arguably the best place in town. Visitors and locals frequent the casual waterfront restaurant, which serves Floribbean-inspired seafood. Options also include a crispy rum-and-molasses barbecued duck and an assortment of sandwiches, including a crab-salad BLT. The bar features daily happy hours and makes a great margarita.

See map p. 272. 1200 Fifth Ave. S. ☎ **941-263-2734.** *Reservations not accepted. To get there: It's on 12th Avenue at Naples Bay (at the City Dock). Main courses: $8.50–$20. AE, DISC, MC, V. Open: Daily 11 a.m.–midnight.*

Hungry Heron
$ Sanibel   AMERICAN/SEAFOOD

This colorful family restaurant — Sanibel's most popular — has a whimsical tropical decor and a menu bursting with nearly 300 items, including 35 for kids. Disney movies and cartoons play on multiple screens while families chow down on big sandwiches, pasta, and shellfish. All-you-can-eat specials (prime rib, gulf shrimp, and so on) are featured throughout the week.

See map p. 272. 2330 Palm Ridge Rd. ☎ **941-395-2300.** *Reservations not accepted. To get there: It's at Palm Ridge and Periwinkle Way (in Palm Ridge Plaza). Main courses: $7–$16. AE, DISC, MC, V. Open: Daily 11 a.m.–9:30 p.m.*

Marek's Collier House Restaurant
$$–$$$ Marco Island CONTINENTAL

Both the indoor and veranda dining rooms of this restaurant — Marco Island's finest — offer relaxed-but-refined dining. Chef-owner Peter Marek, a triple gold-medal winner at the World Culinary Olympics, has cooked for Queen Elizabeth, and you'll dine royally at his home base. House specials include shrimp stuffed with spicy crabmeat and wrapped in filo, and rack of lamb with garlic and rosemary. There's an extensive wine list.

See map p. 272. 1231 Bald Eagle Dr. ☎ 941-642-9948. Reservations suggested. To get there: It's 1 mile north of Collier Boulevard/Highway 951. Main courses: $18–$32.50. AE, MC, V. Open: Daily 5:30–9:30 p.m. Closed Sept 15–Nov 30.

Exploring Fort Myers, Sanibel, Naples, and Marco Island

You may not find many major attractions in this area of Florida, but if you like old things, animals, and the great outdoors, you can still find plenty to do.

The top attractions

Babcock Wilderness Adventures
Punta Gorda

One of the easiest and most informative ways to see Southwest Florida's abundant wildlife is on Babcock's "swamp buggy" ride. Experienced naturalists lead 90-minute tours through the Babcock Ranch, the largest contiguous cattle operation east of the Mississippi River and home to countless birds and wildlife (including panthers and alligators) as well as domesticated bison and quarter horses. Unlike most wildlife tours in the region, this one covers five different ecosystems, from open prairie to cypress swamp. If you'd rather tour the area using pedal power, three-hour off-road bicycle tours are also offered. **Note:** Advance reservations are required for all tours. Allow two-plus hours in addition to driving time. (It's 45 minutes north of Fort Myers.)

See map p. 272. 8000 Hwy. 31. ☎ 800-500-5583. www.babcockwilderness.com. To get there: On Highway 31 off Highway 80, east of I-75. Admission: $18 adults, $11 kids 3–12. Bicycle tours: $35 adults, $30 kids 10–14. Open: Nov–May daily 9 a.m.–3 p.m., June–Oct mornings only (call for times).

Caribbean Gardens
Naples

The only zoo in Florida to feature rare Indochinese tigers, it also has a cast of lions, leopards, spotted hyenas, and African wild dogs. At Safari Canyon, ocelots, water monitors, and more star in a show supplemented by video presentations about the animals and their habitats. The zoo also offers boat rides, primate islands, and close encounters with kangaroos, alligators, and a 12-foot-long python. You can fill three to four hours if you like animals.

See map p. 272. 1590 Goodlette-Frank Rd. ☎ **941-262-5409.** www.napleszoo.com. *To get there: South on U.S. 41 to entrance sign just before Golden Gate Parkway. Admission: $16 adults, $10 kids 4–15. Open: Daily 9:30 a.m.–5 p.m.*

Edison and Ford Winter Homes
Fort Myers

Who knew that Fort Myers was such a hotbed of industrial geniuses? Thomas Edison and Henry Ford had winter homes here, and were both neighbors *and* friends. Edison spent winters in what he dubbed "Seminole lodge" from 1886 to 1931. The 14-acre riverfront estate includes his lab, garden, vintage cars, and 200 phonographs. Ford arrived at his 3-acre estate in 1916. His home, known as "Mangoes," has a 1914 Model T and a 1917 Model T Truck. Guided and self-guided tours are available. Plan to spend two to three hours here.

See map p. 272. 2350 McGregor Blvd. ☎ **941-334-7419.** www.edison-ford-estate. com. *To get there: West on Colonial to McGregor; turn right and continue to the houses. Admission: $15 adults, $8.50 kids 6–12 including guided tour. Open: Mon–Sat 9 a.m.–5:30 p.m., Sun noon–5:30 p.m.*

Imaginarium Hands-On Museum
Fort Myers

This cool, hands-on aquarium and museum lets you stand in a Florida thunderstorm without getting wet, watch Elvis the eel slither through coral, get blown away in the Hurricane Experience, and get lost in the Amazing Maze. Allow two hours to see all the exhibits.

See map p. 272. 2000 Cranford Ave. ☎ **941-337-3332.** www.cityftmyers.com/ attractions/imaginarium.htm. *To get there: Just east of downtown. Admission: $7 adults, $4 kids 3–12. Open: Mon–Sat 10 a.m.–5 p.m., Sun noon–5 p.m.*

Naples Museum of Art
Naples

If anything demonstrates the emerging sophistication of a sleepy seaside town, it's this three-story, 30,000-square-foot art museum, attached to the Naples Philharmonic Center for the Arts. The first full-scale art museum in Southwest Florida, the Naples Museum of Art features 15 different galleries with paintings, sculptures, and drawings. Major permanent collections concentrate on American modern and ancient Chinese art, while touring shows and exhibitions bring welcome eclecticism to the museum. The structure is a dramatic work of art itself, with 14-foot entrance gates and a 90-x-45-foot glass dome. Tuesdays through Saturdays October through May, the museum offers free guided tours at 11 a.m. and 2 p.m.

See map p. 272. 5833 Pelican Bay Blvd. (at West Boulevard). ☎ 941-597-1900. www. thephil.org. *Admission: $6 adults, $3 students. Tues–Sat 10 a.m.–4 p.m., Sun noon–4 p.m. Closed mid-July–Sept.*

Olde Naples
Naples

This city grew up around a beach and boat pier. Some of the homes built by well-to-do Northerners in the early part of the 20th century remain today. **Millionaire's Row,** a long, palm-studded block of these fabulous houses, runs from Gulf Shore Boulevard to the beach. In addition to its rich architecture, the tree-lined district offers clubs, shops, restaurants and sidewalk cafes, boutique hotels, a 1,000-foot fishing pier, and a sugar-sand beach. Some of the area's highlights include **Palm Cottage,** 137 12th Ave. S. (☎ **941-261-8164**), built in 1895 and now the home of the Collier County Historical Society, which maintains it as a museum filled with authentic furniture, paintings, photographs, and other memorabilia and offers tours (winter only) Monday through Friday from 1 to 3:30 p.m. (adults $5, kids 12 and under free); and **Old Marine Marketplace at Tin City,** 1200 Fifth Ave. S., an old oyster-processing plant that's now the home of 40 or so shops and restaurants. Plan to spend four to six hours here, depending on your tolerance for browsing and, of course, the heat factor.

Olde Naples reaches north from 12th Avenue South to Central and west from Ninth Street to the Gulf of Mexico.

Teddy Bear Museum
Naples

In addition to 4,000 stuffed bears from around the globe, this museum has a gift shop if you feel the urge to bring home something huggable. Unless you're a teddy fanatic, you can see everything in about 90 minutes.

See map p. 272. 2511 Pine Ridge Rd. ☎ 941-598-2711. www.teddymuseum.com. *To get there: On Pine Ridge/Highway 896 east of Airport Road. Admission: $8 adults, $6 seniors 60 and older, $3 kids 4–12. Open: Tues–Sat 10 a.m.–5 p.m.*

More cool things to see and do
Here are some more ways to fill your days, especially if you're a sports or outdoors enthusiast:

- ✔ **Baseball:** The **Texas Rangers** play at Charlotte County Stadium in Port Charlotte, 2300 El Jobean Rd. (☎ **941-625-9500;** www.texas rangers.com). Tickets cost $7 to $9. The **Boston Red Sox** take the field at City of Palms Park, 2201 Edison Ave., Fort Myers (☎ **941-334-4700;** www.bostonredsox.com), and seeing a game sets you back $10 to $11. The **Minnesota Twins** play at Hammond Stadium in the Lee County Sports Complex, 14100 Six Mile Cypress Pkwy., Fort Myers (☎ **800-338-9467;** www.minnesotatwins.com), and tickets run $9 to $12. Workouts begin in mid-February, with games played through March.

✔ **Beaches, parks, and preserves:** Rare plants and animals, as well as miles of plush sands, are the big attractions here:

- The **Corkscrew Swamp Sanctuary,** 375 Sanctuary Rd., Naples (☎ 941-348-9151), is an 11,000-acre preserve with a 2¼-mile boardwalk running through the prairie and hammock homes of wild orchids, wood storks, and virgin bald cypresses, some of which are 500 years old. Admission costs $10 adults, $6 kids 6 to 18.

- The beach at **Delnor-Wiggins Pass State Recreation Area,** 11100 Gulf Shore Dr., Naples (☎ 941-597-6196; www.florida stateparks.org/delnor-wiggins), has been listed among America's top ten stretches of sand. The swimming is good, but stay out of the pass to avoid undertows. The park's boardwalks lead to nature areas that boast flora and fauna that other parts of Florida have lost: sea oats, sea grapes, cabbage palms, wading birds, manatees, and loggerhead turtle nests. Rangers provide nature tours throughout the year, with the most interesting during the loggerhead nesting season from June to October (call or check the Web site for schedules). Admission is $4 per car.

- **J.N. "Ding" Darling National Wildlife Refuge,** 1 Wildlife Dr., Sanibel (☎ 941-472-1100), is Sanibel Island's finest hour, a 6,000-acre preserve that offers 2 miles of footpaths through sea grapes, sabal palms, and mangroves that provide homes to spoonbills, mangrove cuckoos, alligators, and a few American crocodiles. You can also view nature from your car by taking a one–way, 5-mile Wildlife Drive. The visitor center sells Wildlife Drive maps and shows videos about the park's wildlife. Admission is $5 for vehicles.

✔ **Fishing:** The main event happens in mid-July, when hundreds of anglers arrive in Boca Grande for the **World's Richest Tarpon Tournament** (☎ 941-964-2283) and a shot at the $100,000 grand prize. Small party charter rates start at about $250 per half-day and $450 for a full day (for up to six people). You can find guides through the **Boca Grande Fishing Guides Association** (☎ 941-964-1711), **Jensen's Marina** on Captiva Island (☎ 941-472-5800), **Naples City Boat Dock** in Olde Naples (☎ 941-434-4693), and **Cedar Bay Marina** on Marco Island (☎ 800-906-2628 or 941-394-9333).

✔ **Golf:** With more than 90 golf courses in the Collier County area, you won't have to look far for a fore-some. You can find local golf information on the Web at www.golf.com and www.florida golfing.com, or request information from the **Florida Sports**

Foundation (☎ 850-488-8347) or **Florida Golfing** (☎ 877-222-4653). Some options are

- **Cypress Woods,** 3525 North Brook Dr., Naples (☎ 239-592-7860), with hills and tree-lined fairways. Greens fees: $25 to $40 in the summer, and $41 to $65 during winter.

- **Eagle Ridge,** 14589 Eagle Ridge Dr., Fort Myers (☎ 941-768-1888), offering big greens and water on 17. Greens fees: Under $25 in the summer, and $41 to $65 in the winter.

- **Marriott's Golf Club,** 400 S. Collier Blvd., Marco Island (☎ 941-793-6060), which has water hazards on 16 holes and well-bunkered greens. Greens fees: $25 to $40 summer, and $86 to $110 during the winter.

Going on a guided tour

Several tour companies offer visitors a chance to explore Naples and its surroundings. Some of the sightseeing options in this corner of Florida also give you a chance to experience the Everglades, but for a deeper look at this wonderful wilderness, see Chapter 12.

By air

Casablanca Air in Naples (☎ 941-431-1133; www.casablancaair.com) offers biplane tours out of **Naples Municipal Airport,** 160 Aviation Blvd., including one where you get to take the controls. Tours cost $70 to $205. There are also tours, which run $300 to $650, for up to six people in a modern plane. All these tours last 15 to 30 minutes; destinations include the Gulf of Mexico and the Everglades.

By airboat and van

Fossil Expeditions of Fort Myers (☎ 800-304-9432 or 941-368-3252; www.fossilexpeditions.com) offers six-hour, hands-on, fossil-collecting tours in the Everglades that include an airboat ride. Tours run $60 for adults, $50 for kids 12 and under. The company also offers a four-and-a-half-hour Everglades Eco-Tour by van that includes a pickup at most Sanibel or Fort Myers Beach motels; it runs $60 for adults, and $55 for kids 12 and under.

By trolley

Naples Trolley Tours (☎ 941-262-7300; www.naples-trolley.com) provide an often humorous, narrated introduction to the city, including Olde Naples and some of its century-old estates. The trolleys make 22 stops at area shops, restaurants, and hotels. You can get on and off at stops at your leisure. It costs $17 for adults, and $7 for kids 3 to 12 for all-day passes.

Shopping

Shoppers will find the same theme in this region as in the rest of Florida: We have few unique products other than seashells, T-shirts, and other cheap trinkets.

A two-block stretch of **3rd Street South,** at Broad Avenue, aspires to be the Rodeo Drive of Naples but with the conspicuous absence of Gucci, Prada, and Tiffany and Co. remains just an ordinary, albeit lovely, pricey place for window-shopping. This glitzy collection of jewelers, clothiers, and art galleries may be too rich for many wallets, but the window-shopping here is unmatched.

Nearby, the **5th Avenue South** shopping area, between 3rd and 9th streets south, has seen a renaissance in recent years and is now Naples's hottest wining and dining spot, complete with requisite Starbucks, though the avenue is longer and a bit less chic than 3rd Street South, with stockbrokerages and real-estate offices thrown into the mix of boutiques and antiques dealers. In Olde Naples (see the "The Top Attractions" following "Exploring Fort Myers, Sanibel, Naples, and Marco Island," earlier in this chapter). The **Old Marine Marketplace at Tin City,** 1200 Fifth Ave. S. (☎ 239-262-4200), an oyster-processing plant in a past life, now houses 40 or so shops, plus restaurants, boat charters, and tours.

Finding the second-best shopping spots

North of Naples, the **Miromar Outlets Mall** (☎ 941-948-3766; www.miromar.com) has Big Dog Sportswear, Off Fifth, Polo, Cole Haan, Dansk, and dozens more. To get there, take I-75 north from Naples or south from Fort Myers to Exit 19 (Corkscrew Road) and follow the signs. Remember my standard outlet warning: Know what the retail price is so you can tell if you're really getting a bargain.

In the south, **Coastland Center Mall,** U.S. 41 between Golden Gate Parkway and Fleischmann (☎ 941-262-2323), is anchored by Sears, JCPenney, Macy's, and Dillard's. The **Village at Venetian Bay,** 4200 Gulf Shore Blvd. N., Naples (☎ 941-261-6100), features 50 canal-side shops, including clothiers and art galleries.

Buying special souvenirs

Okay, you may be dying to put a shell next to your ear and pretend to hear the ocean. Here's your shot. **The Shell Factory,** 2787 N. Tamiami Trail/U.S. 41, North Fort Myers (☎ 800-474-3557 or 941-995-2141), is tacky, touristy, free, and crammed with 5 million shells, sponges, pieces of coral, and fossils.

Living it up after dark

Keep in mind that in these parts, the most vibrant nightlife will probably be found in your dreams. But for sunset cocktails that last until, say, midnight at the latest, you'll find plenty of places. In addition to the listings in this section, get entertainment updates from the local newspapers: The

News Press in Fort Myers (☎ **941-335-0200;** http://news-press.com) and the *Naples Daily News* (☎ **941-262-3161;** www.naplesnews.com). Also, most hotels on the beaches and coast offer live or canned music at night; so do clubs sprinkled around **Olde Naples.**

Bars

Named for the legendary flare sometimes caused by the setting sun, the **Green Flash Restaurant,** Sanibel-Captiva Road, Captiva Island (☎ **941-472-3337**), has a ten-seat bar. (But because the restaurant faces east, you'll have to sip your beer out back to watch the sunset.) **The Beached Whale,** 1249 Estero Blvd., Fort Myers Beach (☎ **941-463-5505**), has bands four or five nights a week. **Stan's Idle Hour Seafood Restaurant,** 221 West Goodland Dr., Goodland (☎ **941-394-3041**), is famous — well, within local circles — for its sideshows. There's a little song (Stan and others are not quite ready for prime time), a little dance (the **Buzzard Lope Queens,** a mondo bizarro feathery fiasco), and a little seltzer in your pants (the **Goodland Mullet Festival,** always held the weekend before the Super Bowl in conjunction with crowning a Buzzard Lope Queen).

Performing arts

The **Barbara B. Mann Performing Arts Hall,** 8099 College Pkwy. SW, Fort Myers (☎ **800-440-7469** or 941-481-4849; www.bbmannpah.com), stages concerts and Broadway-style shows. The **Philharmonic Center for the Arts,** 5833 Pelican Bay Blvd., Naples (☎ **800-597-1900** or 941-597-1900; www.naplesphilcenter.org), offers Broadway, country, dance, jazz, and pop performances.

Fast Facts

Area Code

The local area code is **941.**

Hospitals

The major area hospitals are Sarasota Memorial Hospital, 1700 S. Tamiami Trail/U.S. 41 (☎ 941-917-9000); Columbia Blake Medical Center, 2020 59th St. W., Bradenton (☎ 941-792-6611); Lee Memorial Hospital, 2776 Cleveland Ave., Fort Myers (☎ 941-437-5211); and Naples Community Hospital, 350 Seventh St. N., Naples (☎ 941-436-5000).

Information

For the Sarasota-Bradenton area, contact the Sarasota Convention and Visitors Bureau, 655 N. Tamiami Trail/U.S. 41 (☎ 800-522-9799 or 941-957-1877; www.sarasotafl.org), or the Bradenton Area Convention and Visitors Bureau (☎ 800-462-6283 or 941-729-9177; www.floridaislandbeaches.org). Both bureaus offer maps, brochures, and tourist information.

Your best sources of information for Naples and the surrounding territory are the Lee Island Coast Visitor and Convention Bureau, 2180 W. First St., Suite 100, Fort Myers (☎ 800-237-6444 or 941-338-3500; www.leeislandcoast.com), and The Naples Area Chamber of Commerce, 895 Fifth Ave. S., Naples (☎ 941-262-6141; www.naples-online.com).

Other good resources are the Greater Fort Myers Chamber of Commerce (☎ 800-366-3622 or 941-332-3624; www.fortmyers. org), the Sanibel-Captiva Islands Chamber of Commerce (☎ 941-472-1080; www. sanibel-captiva.org), and Visit Naples (☎ 800-605-7878; www.visit-naples.com).

Mail

U.S. post offices are located at 1661 Ringling Blvd., Sarasota; 815 Fourth Ave. W., Bradenton; 1200 Goodlette Rd. N., Naples; and 1350 Monroe St., Fort Myers. For branches near your hotel, call ☎ 800-275-8777.

Maps

The information sources listed in the previous section can provide maps. Rental-car agencies are another good source, as are local convenience stores, which sell good maps for $3 to $5.

Newspapers

The *Sarasota Herald-Tribune* (☎ 941-953-7755; www.newscoast.com/xwelcome. cfm), the *Bradenton Herald* (☎ 941-748-0411; bradenton.com), the *News Press* in Fort Myers (☎ 941-335-0200; http:// news-press.com), and the *Naples Daily News* (☎ 941-262-3161; www.naples news.com) are the four major papers.

Taxes

The sales tax in Sarasota and Bradenton is 7 percent on almost everything except groceries and medicine. Sarasota adds on another 3 percent for a total of 10 percent on hotel rooms. That total is 9 percent in Bradenton.

Fort Myers and Naples assess a standard 6 percent state sales tax on most goods

except groceries and medicine. Both add 3 percent for a total of 9 percent tax on hotel rooms.

Taxis

Generally, in Sarasota and Bradenton it's $2.10 to get in the cab, plus $1.50 per mile thereafter. The fleet includes Yellow Cab (☎ 941-955-3341), Green Cab (☎ 941-922-6666), and Diplomat Taxi (☎ 941-359-8294).

Cab fare in the rest of the region costs $2.75 to $3.75 for the first mile and $1.50 per mile thereafter (up to five passengers). Yellow Cab (☎ 941-332-1055 in Fort Myers and ☎ 941-262-1312 in Naples) is the major taxi company in the area.

Transit Info

Sarasota County Area Transit, or SCAT (☎ 941-316-1234), runs buses in the city and St. Armands, Longboat, and Lido keys. The fare is 50¢. Buses run from 6 a.m. to 7 p.m. Monday through Saturday.

Lee Tran (☎ 941-275-8726) operates buses in the Fort Myers and beach areas. The fare is $1 adults, 50¢ seniors, kids under 42 inches free. Naples Trolley (☎ 941-262-7300) makes 25 stops in the downtown and beach area. An all-day pass costs $17 adults, $7 kids 3 to 12.

Weather Updates

For a recording of current conditions and forecast reports for Sarasota, call the local office of the National Weather Service at ☎ 813-645-2323. For conditions in and around Naples, call the Miami office of the National Weather Service at ☎ 305-229-4522, or check out the Web site (www. nws.noaa.gov).

Part V
Visiting Central Florida: Mickey Mania

The 5th Wave · By Rich Tennant

In this part . . .

If you know only one thing about Florida's geography, it's probably that Orlando and Walt Disney World are smack-dab in the middle of the bull's-eye.

These locations are worlds unto themselves, especially Mickeyville, which includes 47 square miles of real estate. When you add Universal Orlando, SeaWorld, and several wannabes to the mix, there are more options than there are turrets on Cinderella Castle.

Fear not: In this part I help you divide and conquer this area. In the first chapter I tell you how to get you here, help you find a bed, and suggest a few dining options. I devote the second chapter to Orlando's major shrines — the theme parks. Finally, in the third chapter I tell you all about the city's smaller attractions, shopping, and nightlife.

Chapter 17

Settling into Walt Disney World and Orlando

*W*elcome to Orlando, a land ruled by a king-size mouse who turned it into a modern utopia to many of the young and young at heart. To the tens of millions who make the pilgrimage here — a group that includes Super Bowl champs, princes, eccentric pop stars and regular folks — it's a national shrine. And it's a crowded shrine at that.

Walt Disney's Florida legacy is still growing almost 40 years after his death and even includes two mega cruise ships. At current count, Orlando has eight major theme parks (see Chapter 18), 80 or so smaller attractions nearby (see Chapter 19), some 111,000 hotel and motel rooms, and an avalanche of restaurants.

In this chapter, I get you into town, tell you how to get around, outline the best places for you to lay your head at the end of the day, and give you options for dining out. Making choices in this town doesn't require a doctorate in dodging dilemmas, but deciding a few things before the landing gear lowers allows you to spend more time cozying up to the Magic Mickey and the wannabes.

Getting There

A majority of travelers have limited vacation time — that's why most people fly to Orlando. Because you may have a little more leisure time, I also give information about driving and taking the train.

By plane

Using the aerial route, you'll most likely fly into **Orlando International Airport** (☎ 407-825-2001; www.orlandoairports.net). Located just 25 minutes from Walt Disney World, Orlando International has direct or non-stop service from 70 American and 25 international cities. Forty scheduled airlines, and as many charters, feed 30 million people or more into these terminals annually. The most frequently used carriers include **Delta, American, America West, British Airways, Air Canada, Continental, Jet Blue, Midway, Northwest, Southwest,** and **US Airways.** (See the "Quick Concierge" in the back of the book for the telephone numbers and Web sites of the major air carriers.)

The way to baggage claim is clearly marked. (You land at Level 3, take a shuttle to the terminal, and then go to Level 2.)

If you need cash, ATMs are located in the arrival and departure terminals near each pod of gates (1 to 29, 30 to 59, and so on). ATMs are also located where the shuttles deposit you in the main terminal. If you need to convert your pounds, euros, and so on to U.S. dollars, you can find currency exchanges (open 10 a.m.–9 p.m.) opposite the ATMs at gate pods 1 to 29 and 60 to 99 in the air terminal. In the main terminal, they're located where shuttles arrive from gates 1 to 29.

All major car-rental companies are located at the airport (on Level 1) or nearby. Check out the "Quick Concierge" in the back of this book for the toll-free numbers of the major rental companies. You can find other car-rental companies online at the airport's Web site (www.orlando airports.net).

At Orlando International Airport, arriving passengers can find information at The Magic of Disney and Disney's Flight of Fantastic, two shops located in the A and B terminals, respectively. They sell Disney multiday park tickets, make dinner-show and hotel reservations, and provide brochures. They're open 7 a.m. to 8 p.m. daily. The **Universal Orlando** and **SeaWorld** stores in the airport offer similar services and hours.

The airport is a 25-minute hop, skip, and long jump from **Disney World** and 20 minutes from Universal Orlando.

If you're traveling with at least one other person or you simply want to avoid the hassle of a crowded shuttle bus, taxis are a good choice for getting to your hotel. The rates for **Ace Metro** (☎ 407-855-0564) and **Yellow Cab** (☎ 407-699-9999) are $2 for the first mile and $1.75 a mile thereafter. The one-way charge from the airport to **Disney** for up to five people in a cab or seven in a van is about $50. A trip to International Drive is $30; to downtown, it's $25. Vans and taxis load on the ground level of the airport.

Mears Transportation (☎ 407-423-5566; www.mearstransportation. com) provides shuttle service to and from area hotels and the airport with vans running 24 hours a day and departing every 15 to 25 minutes. Round-trip fares are $25 to $29 adults and $18 to $21 children ages 4 to 11 (actual price depends on the location you're going to); children 3 and under ride free.

QuickTransportation/Orlando (☎ **888-784-2522** or 407-354-2456; www. quicktransportation.com) offers shuttle or limo service that is a bit more personal. Employees greet you at the airport's baggage claim (with a sign bearing your name). This company is more expensive than Mears unless you have a big group (upwards of $130 roundtrip for up to seven people), but it comes for you, not a full load of tourists, and it only goes to your resort. This is a reasonable option for groups of five or more.

 Some hotels offer free shuttle service to and from the airport, so make sure to ask when booking your room.

By car

Driving to Orlando is a less expensive and potentially more scenic option, unless the distance is so great that making the road trip eats up too much of your vacation.

Here's how far several cities are from Orlando: Atlanta, 436 miles; Boston, 1,312 miles; Chicago, 1,120 miles; Cleveland, 1,009 miles; Dallas, 1,170 miles; Detroit, 1,114 miles; New York, 1,088 miles; and Toronto, 1,282 miles.

Folks coming from the West and Midwest usually connect with I-10 in north Florida, go east, and follow I-75 south to the Florida Turnpike. From inland eastern cities, take I-75 into Florida. For the coastal route, take I-95 to Daytona Beach and then I-4 west to Orlando.

By train

Amtrak trains (☎ **800-872-7245**; www.amtrak.com) pull into two central stations: 1400 Sligh Blvd., between Columbia and Miller streets in downtown Orlando, and 111 Dakin Ave., at Thurman Street in Kissimmee. Amtrak's Auto Train allows you to bring your car to Florida without having to drive it all the way. The service begins in Lorton, Virginia — about a four-hour drive from New York, two hours from Philadelphia — and ends at Sanford, Florida, about 23 miles northeast of Orlando. The Auto Train departs Lorton and Sanford daily at 4 p.m., arriving at the other end of the line the next day at about 8:30 a.m. Fares for the Auto Train vary according to season and schedule, but fares for two passengers and a car begin at $398.

 Amtrak offers money-saving packages to Orlando, including accommodations (some at Walt Disney World resorts), car rentals, tours, and so on. For package information, call ☎ **800-321-8684.**

Orienting Yourself in Orlando

Orlando's major artery is Interstate 4, which runs diagonally across the state from Tampa to Daytona Beach. Locals call it I-4 or that #@$*%^#!! #$^#$% because it crawls at a snail's pace, especially during the daily rush hours (7–9 a.m. and 4–6 p.m.). Exits from I-4 — they're mostly well marked — lead to all **Walt Disney World** properties, **Universal Orlando, SeaWorld,** International Drive, U.S. 192, Kissimmee, Lake Buena Vista, downtown Orlando, and Winter Park. (Skip ahead to the "Orlando Neighborhoods" map.)

The Florida Turnpike crosses I-4 and links with I-75 to the north. U.S. 192, a major east–west artery, reaches from Kissimmee to U.S. 27, crossing I-4 near the southern Walt Disney World entrance road. Farther north, the BeeLine Expressway toll road (or Florida 528) goes east from I-4, past Orlando International Airport to Cape Canaveral and the Kennedy Space Center. The East-West Expressway (also known as Florida 408) is a downtown toll road that bypasses the tourist meccas.

Introducing the neighborhoods

We've broken Orlando into seven geographical areas:

- ✔ **Walt Disney World:** The area is big, and its tourist parks, resorts, restaurants, shops, and trimmings are scattered across 30,500 acres. Oh, and Disney isn't in Orlando — it's southwest of the city, off I-4 on west U.S. 192. Stay here and discover that convenience has its price — room rates can be double those in nearby Kissimmee.

  A major section of Walt Disney World, **Downtown Disney** is the name that Disney gives to its two nighttime entertainment areas, **Pleasure Island** and **West Side,** plus its shopping complex, **Downtown Disney Marketplace.** The area is filled with restaurants, shops, and dance clubs of all types and prices. Downtown Disney is actually in Lake Buena Vista, although it's a part of **Walt Disney World.**

- ✔ **Lake Buena Vista:** This Disney next-door neighbor is where you can find *official* (Disney-approved but not Disney-owned) hotels. It's close to Downtown Disney and Pleasure Island. This charming area has manicured lawns, tree-lined thoroughfares, and free transportation throughout the realm. The major north–south road is Highway 535, or Apopka-Vineland Road, which becomes Highway 435 north of Palm Parkway.

- ✔ **Celebration:** Imagine if Disney World were responsible for the remake of *The Stepford Wives.* Scary, isn't it? Celebration is an attempt to re-create a Mickey-magic town. It has thousands of residents living in Disney homes, which start at about $220,000. Celebration's downtown area is, however, designed for tourists and there is a proposal to add 1,000 more hotel rooms on the south side of this community. The town square has some first-rate, if pricey, shops and restaurants. Celebration is located off U.S. 192.

Orlando Neighborhoods

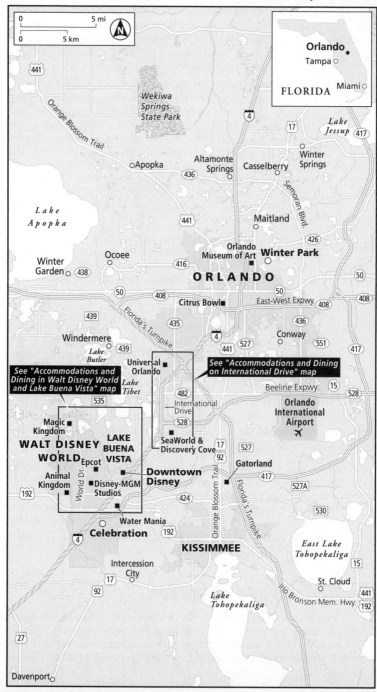

0   5 mi
0   5 km

Orlando •
Tampa ○
FLORIDA   Miami ○

441

Wekiwa Springs State Park

4

17

Lake Jessup   417

Orange Blossom Trail

Altamonte Springs   Casselberry   Winter Springs
○Apopka   436

Semoran Blvd.

Lake Apopka

441

Maitland

426

Orlando Museum of Art   **Winter Park**
Winter Garden ○   Ocoee ○   416   ○
438   **ORLANDO**   50

50   408   **Citrus Bowl**■   East-West Expwy   408   408

439   435   436   Conway   551   417

Florida's Turnpike   4   527
Windermere ○   441
Lake Butler   439   Universal Orlando ■

See "Accommodations and Dining in Walt Disney World and Lake Buena Vista" map   *Lake Tibet*   See "Accommodations and Dining on International Drive" map

Beeline Expwy.   15   528

482
International Drive   **Orlando International Airport** ✈

535
528

Magic Kingdom ■
WALT DISNEY   **LAKE BUENA**   SeaWorld & Discovery Cove ■   17   527
WORLD Epcot ■   **VISTA**   92   Gatorland ○
Animal   World Dr.   417   527A
Kingdom ■   ■Disney-MGM   **Downtown Disney**
192   Studios ■   424   530

Orange Blossom Trail   Florida's Turnpike

Water Mania ■
4   ● **Celebration** ○   192
East Lake Tohopekaliga   15

KISSIMMEE
St. Cloud
Intercession City ○   17
92   *Lake Tohopekaliga*   Irlo Bronson Mem. Hwy.   441   192

27

Davenport ○

✔ **Kissimmee:** This area has a tacky side, loaded with T-shirt shops and every burger barn known to Western civilization. But Kissimmee is just 10 to 15 miles from the Wizard of Disney (beware of perpetual road construction), and, with plenty of modest motels, it's a good choice for those on a budget. The town centers on U.S. 192/Irlo Bronson Memorial Highway.

✔ **International Drive (Highway 536):** Oozing with T-shirt and souvenir shops, not to mention chain motels and fast-food joints, I-Drive is a euphemism for "tourist trap." This neon-lit, always open area extends 7 to 10 miles north of the Disney kingdom, between Highway 535 and the Florida Turnpike. The north end is truly tacky. From bungee jumping to dozens of themed restaurants, this stretch of road is *the* tourist strip in Central Florida. I-Drive also offers some upscale hotels and shopping areas in its central and southern regions. It's the home of the Orange County Convention Center and offers easy access to **SeaWorld** and **Universal Studios.** The road runs north–south.

✔ **Downtown Orlando:** Right off I-4 East, Downtown Orlando, located 12 miles north of Disney, is the home of hotels, restaurants, bars, and cultural offerings patronized by locals but only a sprinkling of tourists. Dozens of shops line **Antique Row** on Orange Avenue near Lake Ivanhoe.

✔ **Winter Park:** Just north of downtown Orlando, Winter Park offers **Park Avenue,** a collection of upscale shops and restaurants, along a cobblestone street. Winter Park has little if any kid-appeal, and it's too far north (about 20 miles) to use as a home base, if you plan on spending much time at the Disney parks.

Finding information after you arrive

After you've landed, one of the best places for up-to-date information is the concierge or the front desk at your hotel (and they're even better if you're staying at a Disney property).

If you're in the International Drive area, stop at the official **Orlando/ Orange County Convention & Visitors Bureau** (☎ **407-363-5872;** www. Orlandoinfo.com), 8723 International Dr. (four blocks south of Sand Lake Road), for information. Friday's "Calendar" section in the *Orlando Sentinel* (www.orlandosentinel.com) also includes a lot of tourist-friendly information on dining and entertainment. See "Fast Facts" at the end of Chapter 19 for additional information sources.

Getting Around Orlando

Tens of millions of people visit Orlando's theme parks yearly, and the city's tourism czars want to make going from Point A to Point B as easy as 1-2-3. That's because the faster you can get around, the more time (and money) you can spend in the parks, attractions, and restaurants.

Still, unless you spend your entire vacation inside Walt Disney World or Universal, you're going to have to deal with slow-downs, such as rush hour (7–9 a.m. and 4–6 p.m. daily) and peak-period crowds (weekends and summers are the worst).

One way you shouldn't travel around Orlando is on foot. This city isn't conducive to strolling. Within the safe confines of the theme parks, you'll have no problems getting around (in fact, most folks are on their feet quite a bit), but walking anywhere outside the theme parks is a thrills-and-chills experience that most people want to avoid. Wide roads that are designed to move traffic quickly and a shortage of sidewalks, streetlights, and crosswalks are to blame.

Here are some of the more conventional ways of getting around.

By the Disney transportation system

If you're going to stay at a **Walt Disney World** resort or official hotel (see "Staying in Style," later in this chapter) and spend the majority of your time in Disney parks, then you can skip a rental car. A free transportation network runs throughout Disney World. Buses, ferries, water taxis, and monorails operate from two hours prior to the Disney parks' opening until two hours after closing. There's also service to various Disney shopping areas, nightclubs, and smaller attractions.

In addition to being free, the system saves you the cost of a rental car, gas, and/or the $8 daily parking charge at the attractions. But you're at the mercy of Disney's schedule. Sometimes you have to take a ferry to catch a bus to get on the monorail to reach your hotel. Reaching a place that's right across the lagoon from you can take an hour or more.

By trolley

The **I-Ride Trolley** on International Drive (☎ **866-243-7883;** www.iride trolley.com) runs every 15 minutes, 8 a.m. to 10:30 p.m. (75¢ for adults, 25¢ for seniors, kids under 12 ride free). Due to I-Drive's bumper-to-bumper traffic, this is the best way to get around if you're staying in this area or at least spending the day.

By car

If you're flying here on an extended stay — more than a week — you probably want to rent a car for at least a day or two to venture beyond the tourist areas. (Yes, there *is* life beyond the theme parks.) See the "Quick Concierge" at the back of this book for toll-free numbers of various car-rental agencies. For navigational tips, check out "Orienting Yourself in Orlando," earlier in this chapter.

By bus

Lynx (☎ **407-841-2279;** www.golynx.com) bus stops are marked with a paw print. The buses serve **Disney, Universal,** and **International Drive** as well as the downtown ($1.25 for adults, 50¢ for kids 8–18), but their routes are not always visitor-oriented.

By taxi

 Yellow Cab (☎ 407-699-9999) and **Ace Metro** (☎ 407-855-0564) are among the taxi companies serving the Orlando area. But for day-to-day travel to and from the attractions, cabs are expensive, unless your group has five or more people. Rates are $2 for the first mile, and $1.75 per mile thereafter.

By shuttle

Mears Transportation Group (☎ 407-423-5566) operates shuttle buses to all major attractions, including **Cypress Gardens, Kennedy Space Center, Universal Orlando,** and **SeaWorld,** among others. Rates vary by destination.

Staying in Style

Unlike the less competitive areas of Florida, almost every hotel in Orlando (at least each listed here) has been built or renovated in the past 20 years, so you can expect reasonably modern trimmings. (You don't need rabbit ears to see what's on the tube.) Most places in Orlando also try to make kids feel like Mickey's personal guests. However, deciding where to stay isn't all that easy because Orlando's more than 111,000 rooms come in many different flavors: hotels, motels, bed-and-breakfasts, and so on.

The best bet is to first determine which attractions you want to visit during your stay, and then book a hotel close to those areas. For example, if you're visiting **Walt Disney World,** stay in a Disney resort, if you don't mind paying a little extra; on Highway 535/Apopka-Vineland Road, if you want to save a few bucks; or U.S. 192, if you want to save even more.

Beyond the obvious proximity to the parks, there are other benefits to staying in an official WDW hotel. Perks often include extended hours in parks for hotel guests, special discount passes to parks and, of course, the ability to dine with Mickey and Minnie at character-themed meals within the hotel restaurants.

Although not Disney-owned, official Disney hotels in Lake Buena Vista offer some of the privileges Disney resort guests enjoy, often for less money than the better Disney resorts. If you're planning your trip around **Universal Orlando,** consider one of its hotels or, as is the case with SeaWorld fans, one of those along International Drive. To orient yourself, see the "Accommodations and Dining in Walt Disney World and Lake Buena Vista" map, later in this chapter.

Many accommodations let kids under 12 (and in many cases under 18) stay free with parents or guardians, as long as you don't exceed the room's capacity. But to be sure, ask when booking your room.

All the accommodations listed here offer free parking, air-conditioning, and pools, unless otherwise noted.

 Don't forget to allow for taxes. The combined sales, local-option, and hotel taxes will increase your bill by 11 percent to 12 percent, depending on where you choose to stay.

If you're considering booking a room at a Disney resort, be sure to ask, when calling the **Central Reservations Office** (☎ **407-934-7639**); www. disneyworld.com), about any discounts available to members of AAA or other auto clubs, AARP, frequent-flier programs, or other groups. Also, ask about meal plans that could save you money or packages that include your room, tickets, and airfare.

If you don't like dealing with hotels or haggling over rates, the **Florida Hotel Network** (☎ **800-538-3616;** www.floridahotels.com) will make your reservations for you.

The top hotels

 ### Best Western Lake Buena Vista
$$ Lake Buena Vista/Official WDW Hotel

This 18-story high-rise is a great place to view the Disney fireworks ($15 more per night for a room with a view) without braving the crowds in the parks. The 325-unit lakefront hotel is located on prime property along Hotel Plaza Boulevard and is within walking distance of **Downtown Disney Marketplace.** The rooms are large, and some come with balconies and views of the lake. Amenities include Nintendo, coffeemakers, free local calls, an on-site restaurant, several pools, a playground, baby-sitting service, and free shuttles to Disney parks.

*See map p. 300. 2000 Hotel Plaza Blvd. ☎ **800-348-3765** or 407-828-2424. Fax:: 407-828-8933.* www.orlandoresorthotel.com. *To get there: Located between Buena Vista Drive and Apopka-Vineland Road/Highway 535, across from Doubletree Hotel. Free parking. Rack rates: $99–$159; $199–$399 suite. AE, DC, DISC, JCB, MC, V.*

Celebration Hotel
$$–$$$ Celebration

Located in the Disney-created town of Celebration, this hotel has a three-story, wood-frame design straight out of 1920s Florida. All rooms have TVs with Nintendo, speaker phones with voice mail and dataports, ceiling fans, safes, hair dryers, and makeup mirrors. Suites and studios have refrigerators and wet bars. Other amenities include a Jacuzzi and fitness center. You can walk to shops and restaurants. An 18-hole golf course is nearby.

See map p. 302. 700 Bloom St. ☎ 888-499-3800 or 407-566-6000. Fax: 407-566-6001. www.celebrationhotel.com. *To get there: Take I-4 to the U.S. 192 exit, go east to the second light, then right on Celebration Avenue. Parking: $10 valet, free self-parking. Rack rates: $139–$219; $289–$470 suite. AE, DC, DISC, MC, V.*

Disney's All-Star Movies Resort
$–$$ **Walt Disney World**

Kids aren't the only ones amazed by the, uh, aesthetics of this resort. When did you last see architecture as inspiring as Goliath-size Dalmatians leaping from balconies? And the low (by Mickey standards) rates will thrill some parents. The All-Star resort in the "Runner-up accommodations" listings, later in this chapter, is pretty much the same — expect small rooms and postage-stamp-size bathrooms. But you're still "on property," and you're enjoying the lowest prices your Mouse bucks can buy. There's a food court that serves pizza, pasta, sandwiches, and family-dinner platters.

Note: Disney has two additional All-Star resorts — the All-Star Sports-Resort and the All-Star Music resort — both identical to the Disney's All-Movies Resort where it counts (like room size and layout). The only major difference is the change in theme: One offers musical themes ranging from jazz to Calypso, and the other features movies (of the Disney variety of course). All three of the All Star resorts are located out in the Disney boonies, and the closest park is Animal Kingdom.

See map p. 300. 1991 W. Buena Vista Dr. ☎ 407-934-7639 or 407-939-7000. Fax: 407-939-7111. www.disneyworld.com. *To get there: Located close to Animal Kingdom, Blizzard Beach, and Winter Summerland. Free parking. Rack rates: $77–$126. AE, DC, DISC, JCB, MC, V.*

Disney's BoardWalk Inn & Villas
$$$$ **Walt Disney World**

Overlooking a village green and lake, this 1920s "seaside" resort appeals to couples and singles looking for a sliver of yesterday. The standard accommodations have two queen-size beds, a child-size daybed, a midsize bathroom, dataports, hair dryers, and balconies. Recreational facilities include tennis, fishing, boating, bike rental, and even a moonlight cruise. Hang onto your swimsuit if you hit the pool's famous — or infamous, depending on how you look at it — 200-foot "keister coaster" water slide. The villas sleep up to 12 and some have kitchens, washer-dryers, and whirlpool baths. After the sun goes down, there's plenty to do because the resort has a quarter-mile boardwalk that offers shops, restaurants, and street performers. There are two restaurants. **Note:** Rooms overlooking the Boardwalk have the best views, but they tend to be noisier, thanks to the action below.

See map p. 300. 2101 N. Epcot Resorts Blvd. ☎ 407-934-7639 or 407-939-5100. Fax: 407-934-5150. www.disneyworld.com. *To get there: Located north of Buena Vista Drive, on Epcot Resorts Boulevard. Parking: Valet $7, free self-parking. Rack rates: $289–$675; $289–$1,915 villa. AE, DC, DISC, JCB, MC, V.*

Disney's Coronado Springs Resort
$$ Walt Disney World

This moderate-priced resort has an American Southwest theme and a slightly more upscale feel than the others in this class. Rooms are housed in four- and five-story hacienda-style buildings with palm-shaded courtyards. Some overlook the 15-acre Golden Lake; the better your view, the higher the price. Rooms feature two double beds (the decor differs in each section, but the layout is the same) with coffeemakers, hair dryers, and dataports. Ninety-nine rooms are specially designed to accommodate travelers with disabilities, and nearly three-fourths of the rooms are nonsmoking.

See map p. 300. 1000 Buena Vista Dr. ☎ 407-934-7639 or 407-939-1000. Fax: 407-939-1003. www.disneyworld.com. *To get there: It's near Disney's Blizzard Beach off Buena Vista Drive. Free parking. Rack rates: $133–$209; $278–$1,050 suite. AE, DC, DISC, JCB, MC, V.*

Disney's Fort Wilderness Resort and Campground
$–$$$ Walt Disney World

This woodsy, 780-acre resort is a camper's dream come true, but it's quite a hike from most of the Disney parks except the **Magic Kingdom.** Even so, there's more than enough to keep you busy here. Guests enjoy extensive recreational facilities, ranging from a riding stable to a nightly campfire. The 784 secluded campsites for RVs and tents offer 110/220-volt outlets, barbecue grills, picnic tables, and kids' play areas. There are also 408 wilderness cabins (actually, they're trailers) that can sleep up to six people; they also have living rooms, fully equipped eat-in kitchens, coffeemakers, hair dryers, and barbecue grills. Nearby Pioneer Hall hosts the rambunctious *Hoop-Dee-Doo Musical Revue* (see listing under "Disney character dining," later in this chapter) nightly.

See map p. 300. 3520 N. Fort Wilderness Trail. ☎ 407-934-7639 or 407-824-2900. Fax: 407-824-3508. www.disneyworld.com. *To get there: Located off Vista Boulevard, on Fort Wilderness Trail. Free parking. Rack rates: $35–$82 campsites; $229–$329 cabins. AE, DC, DISC, JCB, MC, V.*

Disney's Grand Floridian Resort & Spa
$$$$ Walt Disney World

You won't find a more luxurious address than this 40-acre *Great Gatsby*–era resort on the shores of the Seven Seas Lagoon. It's a great choice for couples seeking a bit of romance, especially honeymooners who aren't on a tight budget. The Grand Floridian is **Walt Disney World's** upper-crust flagship, and it's as pricey as it is plush. The opulent, five-story domed lobby hosts afternoon teas accompanied by piano music. In the evenings, an orchestra plays big-band tunes. Most rooms overlook a garden, pool, courtyard, or the lagoon. The hotel is one of three on the Disney monorail line. The resort also has a first-rate health club and spa, as well as five restaurants, including the ultrapricey Victoria & Albert's.

Accommodations and Dining in Walt Disney World and Lake Buena Vista

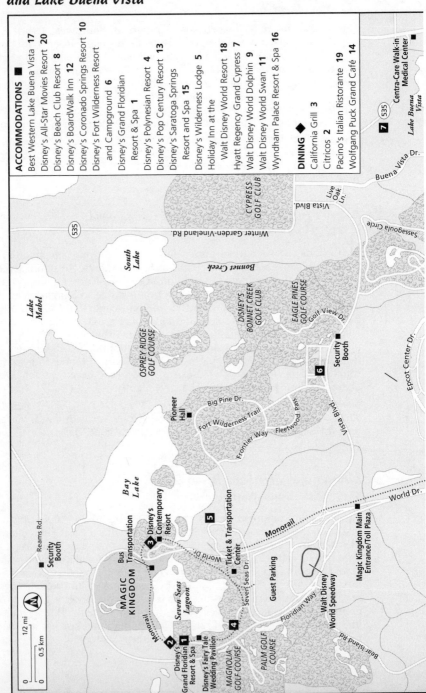

ACCOMMODATIONS ■

Best Western Lake Buena Vista **17**
Disney's All-Star Movies Resort **20**
Disney's Beach Club Resort **8**
Disney's BoardWalk Inn **12**
Disney's Coronado Springs Resort **10**
Disney's Fort Wilderness Resort
and Campground **6**
Disney's Grand Floridian
Resort & Spa **1**
Disney's Polynesian Resort **4**
Disney's Pop Century Resort **13**
Disney's Saratoga Springs
Resort and Spa **15**
Disney's Wilderness Lodge **5**
Holiday Inn at the
Walt Disney World Resort **18**
Hyatt Regency Grand Cypress **7**
Walt Disney World Dolphin **9**
Walt Disney World Swan **11**
Wyndham Palace Resort & Spa **16**

DINING ◆

California Grill **3**
Citricos **2**
Pacino's Italian Ristorante **19**
Wolfgang Puck Grand Café **14**

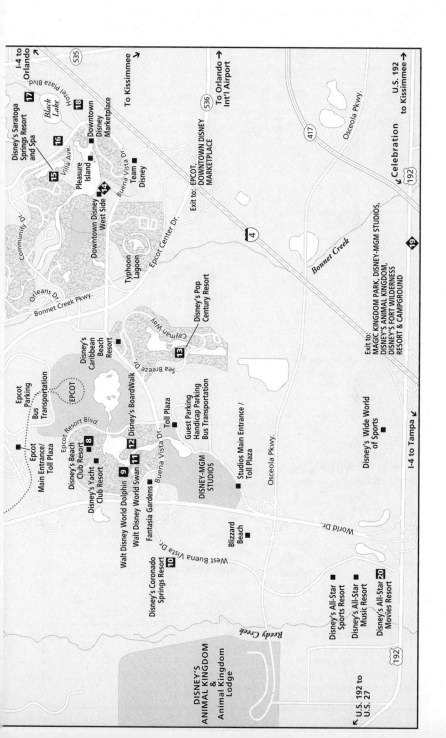

I-4 to Orlando

535

Hotel Plaza Blvd.

17

18

Black Lake

Downtown Disney Marketplace

To Kissimmee

Disney's Saratoga Springs Resort and Spa

16

Villa Ave.

15

Pleasure Island

14

Team Disney

Buena Vista Dr.

536

Exit to: EPCOT, DOWNTOWN DISNEY MARKETPLACE

To Orlando Int'l Airport

417

Osceola Pkwy.

Celebration

U.S. 192 to Kissimmee

192

Community Dr.

Downtown Disney West Side

Orleans Dr.

Bonnet Creek Pkwy.

Typhoon Lagoon

Epcot Center Dr.

4

Bonnet Creek

19

Disney's Pop Century Resort

Cayman Way

Exit to: MAGIC KINGDOM PARK, DISNEY-MGM STUDIOS, DISNEY'S ANIMAL KINGDOM, DISNEY'S FORT WILDERNESS RESORT & CAMPGROUND

Disney's Caribbean Beach Resort

Sea Breeze Dr.

13

Epcot Parking

Bus Transportation

EPCOT

Epcot Resort Blvd.

Disney's BoardWalk

Toll Plaza

Guest Parking Handicap Parking Bus Transportation

I-4 to Tampa

Epcot Main Entrance/ Toll Plaza

Disney's Beach Club Resort

8

12

Disney's Yacht Club Resort

9

Walt Disney World Dolphin

11

Walt Disney World Swan

Buena Vista Dr.

Studios Main Entrance / Toll Plaza

DISNEY-MGM STUDIOS

Osceola Pkwy.

Fantasia Gardens

10

Disney's Coronado Springs Resort

West Buena Vista Dr.

Blizzard Beach

World Dr.

Disney's Wide World of Sports

Reedy Creek

DISNEY'S ANIMAL KINGDOM & Animal Kingdom Lodge

Disney's All-Star Sports Resort

Disney's All-Star Music Resort

20 Disney's All-Star Movies Resort

192

U.S. 192 to U.S. 27

Other Orlando Area Accommodations and Dining

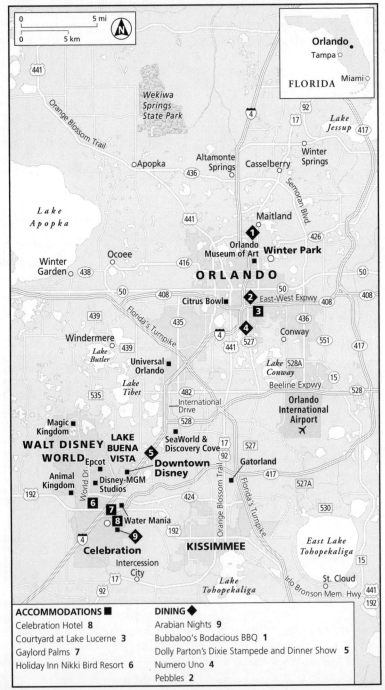

ACCOMMODATIONS ■

Celebration Hotel **8**

Courtyard at Lake Lucerne **3**

Gaylord Palms **7**

Holiday Inn Nikki Bird Resort **6**

DINING ◆

Arabian Nights **9**

Bubbaloo's Bodacious BBQ **1**

Dolly Parton's Dixie Stampede and Dinner Show **5**

Numero Uno **4**

Pebbles **2**

See map p. 300. 4401 Floridian Way. ☎ 407-934-7639 or 407-824-3000. Fax: 407-824-3186. www.disneyworld.com. To get there: At the northwest corner of the WDW property, north of the Polynesian Resort. Parking: Valet $7, free self-parking. Rack rates: $339–$840; $885–$2,450 suite. AE, DC, DISC, JCB, MC, V.

Disney's Polynesian Resort
$$$$ Walt Disney World

Just south of the Magic Kingdom, the 25-acre Polynesian is the third resort on the monorail line. Its extensive play areas and themed swimming pools make it a good choice for those traveling with kids. Public areas have canvas cabanas, hammocks, and big swings overlooking a 200-acre lagoon. Lush landscaping gives it a true island feel. Rooms are average size, and all but a few can accommodate up to five people.

See map p. 300. 1600 Seven Seas Dr. ☎ 407-934-7639 or 407/824-2000. Fax: 407-824-3174. www.disneyworld.com. To get there: Take I-4 to the Hwy. 536/Epcot Center Drive exit and follow the signs. Parking: $7 valet; free self-parking. Rack rates: $299–$560; $390–$675 concierge-level; $680–$2,490 suite. AE, DC, DISC, MC, V.

Disney's Pop Century Resort
$–$$ Walt Disney World

More for the parents than for the kids, this resort pays homage to prominent members of pop culture including the 8-track tape and the Rubik's Cube with larger-than-life replicas of them and other kitschy memorabilia. Although the rooms and bathrooms here are smaller than the blow-up Rubik's Cube, it's worth a stay here just for the kitsch factor alone, not to mention the opportunity to explain to the kids how cool you once were.

See map p. 300. 1050 Century Dr. ☎ 407-938-4000 or 407-939-6000. Fax: 407-938-4040. www.disneyworld.com. To get there: Located near the Wide World of Sports Complex. Free parking. Rack rates: $77–$126. AE, DC, DISC, JCB, MC, V.

Disney's Saratoga Springs Resort and Spa
$$$$ Walt Disney World

The newest of the Disney vacation club resorts opened in May 2004 and transports guests back in time to the heyday of upstate New York's 19th-century resorts. The small resort town of Saratoga Springs is evoked through lavish gardens, Victorian architecture, bubbling springs, and a country setting. The resort's main pool brings to mind its namesake's natural springs, with "healing" waters spilling over the rocky landscaping. The renowned spa at the now-closed Disney Institute has been incorporated into this resort. Accommodations resemble those of the other Disney vacation properties and range from studios that sleep four to grand villas that can sleep up to 12 people quite comfortably.

See map p. 300. Lake Buena Vista. ☎ 407-827-1100 or 407-939-6244. Fax: 407-827-1151. www.disneyworld.com. To get there: Located in the Downtown Disney area of the park. Free parking. Rack rates: $254–$329 studio; $340–$1,310 villa. AE, DC, DISC, MC, V.

Disney's Wilderness Lodge
$$–$$$$ Walt Disney World

The surrounding tall timbers, spouting geyser and hot springs, mammoth stone hearth, and bunk beds for the kids give the Wilderness Lodge an old-time national-park feel, making it a favorite of families and couples alike. Standard rooms sleep four, and if a view is important to you, those with woods views are the best. The restaurants located at this resort offer some of the most spectacular views in the park. While the nearest park is Magic Kingdom, the resort, in keeping with its theme, is in a fairly remote area.

See map p. 300. 901 W. Timberline Dr. ☎ *407-934-7639 or 407-938-4300. Fax: 407-824-3232.* www.disneyworld.com. *To get there: Located on the southwest shore of Bay Lake just east of the Magic Kingdom. Free parking. Rack rates: $194–$515 lodge; $350–$475 concierge-level; $720–$1,155 suite; $279–$955 villa. AE, DC, DISC, MC, V.*

Hard Rock Hotel
$$$ International Drive Area/Universal Orlando

You can't get rooms closer to **CityWalk, Islands of Adventure,** or **Universal Studios Florida** than those at this hotel. Rooms come with two queens or one king, and feature safes, irons, and hair dryers. Unfortunately, although the rooms are pretty soundproof, a few notes of music seep through the walls, so ask for a room that's away from the lobby. There's free transportation to the **Universal** and **SeaWorld** parks. As for **Disney,** you're on your own. The biggest perk: Guests get no-line access to almost all rides at Universal's theme parks.

See map p. 306. 5000 Universal Blvd. ☎ *888-232-7827 or 407-363-8000. Fax: 407-224-7118.* www.universalorlando.com. *To get there: Take I-4 to the Kirkman Road/Highway 435 exit and follow signs to Universal Orlando. Parking: Valet $12, $6 self-parking. Rack rates: $209–$359; $345–$1,675 suite. AE, CB, DC, DISC, MC, V.*

Holiday Inn in The Walt Disney World Resort
$–$$ Lake Buena Vista/Official WDW Hotel

Formerly known as The Courtyard by Marriott, this official WDW hotel is a moderately priced landing pad on Hotel Plaza Boulevard, close to **Downtown Disney Marketplace's** shops and restaurants. Rooms have coffeemakers and hair dryers; most have balconies. Rooms on the west side, floors 8 to 14, have a view of the Magic Kingdom and Disney fireworks. The hotel has a 14-story atrium, a full-service restaurant, and two lounges. There's free transportation to **WDW** parks, transportation for a fee to others.

See map p. 300. 1805 Hotel Plaza Blvd. ☎ *877-465-4329 or 407-828-8888. Fax: 407-827-4623.* www.holiday-inn.com. *To get there: Between Lake Buena Vista Drive and Apopka-Vineland Road/Highway 535, close to the Hilton Royal Plaza Hotel. Free parking. Rack rates: $86–$199. AE, CB, DC, DISC, JCB, MC, V.*

Hyatt Regency Grand Cypress
$$$–$$$$ Lake Buena Vista

A resort destination in and of itself, this is a great place to escape the Disney crowd frenzy, but be just a mile away from the park itself. You need deep pockets to stay here, but the reward is a palatial resort with a Thai theme. The hotel's 18-story atrium has inner and outer glass elevators, which provide a unique thrill. The beautifully decorated rooms offer minibars, safes, irons, dataports, and hair dryers. Recreational facilities include 45 holes of golf, 12 tennis courts (5 lighted), 2 racquetball courts, a spa, an adjoining equestrian center, and more. The property's half-acre, 800,000-gallon pool has caves, grottoes, and waterfalls. There's free transportation to WDW, and hotel personnel can arrange shuttle service for a fee to go elsewhere.

See map p. 300. 1 N. Jacaranda. ☎ *800-233-1234 or 407-239-1234. Fax: 407-239-3837.* www.hyattgrandcypress.com. *To get there: Take Highway 535 north, one light past Disney's Lake Buena Vista entrance or Hotel Plaza Boulevard and turn left. Parking: valet $12, free self-parking. Rack rates: $239–$585, $395–$1,575 suite. AE, CB, DC, DISC, JCB, MC, V.*

Portofino Bay Hotel
$$$–$$$$ International Drive Area/Universal Orlando

Can you say swanky? This romantic, upscale resort is designed to look like the village of Portofino, Italy, complete with a harbor and canals that lead you via boat to the theme parks. The rooms sleep up to five and have beds with Egyptian-woven sheets and pillows so soft you'll want to take them home. Ask for a view overlooking the piazza and "bay" area. The Portofino doesn't just have swimming pools; its beach pool has a fort with a water slide, and the villa pool offers several cabanas with laptop hookups for the perfect mix of business and pleasure. The resort's Mandara Spa features a state-of-the-art fitness center and full-service spa. The drawbacks: There are stairs everywhere you turn, and the sheer size of the resort can make it difficult to find your way around. There's free transportation to **Universal** and **SeaWorld** parks, but (they're not stupid!) not the **Disney** ones. Guests get no-line access to almost all rides at Universal's theme parks.

See map p. 306. 5601 Universal Blvd. ☎ *888-322-5541 or 407-503-1000. Fax: 407-224-7118.* www.universalorlando.com. *To get there: Off I-4, take Apopka-Vineland Road west to Universal Orlando. Parking: Valet $12, $6 self-parking. Rack rates: $249–$359; $450–$2,100 suite. AE, CB, D, DC, MC, V.*

Renaissance Orlando Resort at SeaWorld
$$–$$$ International Drive

Large rooms, good service, and luxurious surroundings are this hotel's calling cards. Its most valuable feature, however, is a location that's perfect if you're going to **SeaWorld** (it's right across the street), **Universal,** and to a lesser degree, the second-tier I-Drive attractions. The comfortable rooms offer marble baths, safes, dataports, and Sony PlayStations. The Renaissance has four lighted tennis courts, a health club, spa and

Accommodations and Dining on International Drive

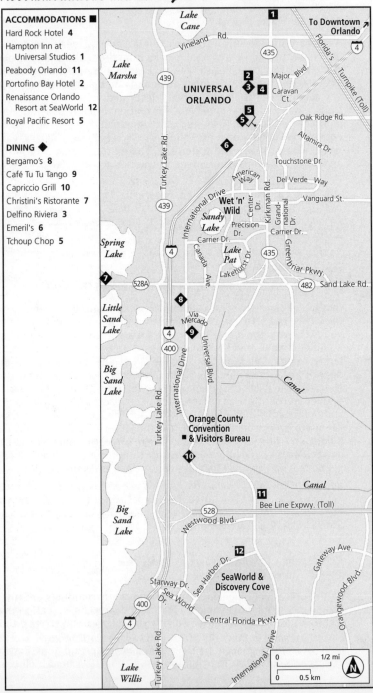

ACCOMMODATIONS ■

Hard Rock Hotel **4**

Hampton Inn at
  Universal Studios **1**

Peabody Orlando **11**

Portofino Bay Hotel **2**

Renaissance Orlando
  Resort at SeaWorld **12**

Royal Pacific Resort **5**

DINING ◆

Bergamo's **8**

Café Tu Tu Tango **9**

Capriccio Grill **10**

Christini's Ristorante **7**

Delfino Riviera **3**

Emeril's **6**

Tchoup Chop **5**

sauna, two restaurants, and arguably the best Sunday brunch in Orlando. Transportation to the parks is available for a fee, though most can walk to SeaWorld, which is available for your eyes to behold if you book an east-side room from the sixth floor up.

See map p. 306. 6677 Sea Harbour Dr. ☎ *800-327-6677 or 407-351-5555. Fax: 407-351-1991.* www.renaissancehotels.com. *To get there: From I-4 follow signs to SeaWorld; the hotel is across from the attraction. Parking: Valet $10, free self-parking. Rack rates: $149–$249. AE, DISC, DC, MC, V.*

Walt Disney World Dolphin/Walt Disney World Swan
$$$$ **Walt Disney World/Official WDW Hotels**

These two resorts, located on a single property and connected by a walkway, are close to Downtown Disney. They offer a chance to stay on Magic Mickey's property without being bombarded by rodent decor. Both hotels have larger-than-life statues (you can't miss them) of swans and dolphins on the roofs. The luxurious rooms are fairly large, with two queen-size beds and first-class amenities; some of the units come with balconies. (The Swan's rooms are a bit smaller.) Guests are encouraged to dine at both resorts, which share a Body by Jake health club.

See map p. 300. Dolphin: 1500 Epcot Resorts Blvd. ☎ *800-227-1500 or 407-934-4000. Fax: 407-934-4884.* www.swandolphin.com. *To get there: Located off Buena Vista Drive, next to Walt Disney World Swan. Parking: Valet $8, free self-parking. Rack rates: $325–$519; $465–$3,100 suite. AE, CB, DC, DISC, JCB, MC, V.*

See map p. 300. Swan: 1200 Epcot Resorts Blvd. ☎ *800-248-7926 or 407-934-3000. Fax: 407-934-4499.* www.swandolphin.com. *To get there: Located off Buena Vista Drive, next door to the Walt Disney World Dolphin. Parking: Valet $8, free self-parking. Rack rates: $325–$495; $485–$3,150 suite. AE, CB, DC, DISC, JCB, MC, V.*

Wyndham Palace Resort & Spa
$$–$$$$ **Lake Buena Vista/Official WDW Hotel**

The hotel's spacious accommodations — most with lake-view balconies or patios — are within walking distance of Downtown Disney Marketplace. It's ideal for honeymooners or those looking for a romantic getaway. The appealing rooms are equipped with bedroom and bathroom phones, safes, and ceiling fans. Other accommodations include one- and two-bedroom suites that have living and dining rooms, 65 hypoallergenic rooms, and 20 rooms equipped for travelers with limited mobility. Rates include free transportation to Disney; you pay a fee for transportation to the other theme parks. The massive, European-style spa offers over 60 luxe treatments to relax tired park-hoppers, including massage therapy, body treatments, and rejuvenating facials. There's also a fitness center, private lap pool, and whirlpool.

See map p. 300. 1900 Buena Vista Dr. ☎ *800-327-2990 or 407-827-2727. Fax: 407-827-6034.* www.wyndham.com/palaceresort. *To get there: Off Highway 535, turn in the entrance to Downtown Disney Marketplace; the hotel is on Hotel Plaza Boulevard. Parking: Valet $10, free self-parking. Rack rates: $179–$398 double; $289–$749 suite. AE, CB, DC, DISC, MC, V.*

Runner-up hotels

Something in the preceding list of accommodations didn't catch your fancy or finances? No problem. Here are some others that may.

Courtyard at Lake Lucerne

$$ **Downtown Orlando** This B&B hideaway is comprised of several historic buildings dating as far back as 1833. All rooms have private baths, and rates include a continental breakfast. *See map p. 302. 211 N. Lucerne Circle* ☎ *800-444-5289 or 407-648-5188.* www.orlandohistoricinn.com.

Disney's Beach Club Resort

$$$$ **Walt Disney World** The Beach Club has a Victorian Cape Cod theme and a 3-acre, free-form swimming pool called Stormalong. *See map p. 300. 1800 Epcot Resorts Blvd.* ☎ *407-934-7639 or 407-934-8000.* www.disneyworld.com.

Gaylord Palms

$$$$ **Kissimmee** Even if you don't stay in this massive, Mall of America–esque, thousand-plus rooms hotel slash city within a city, you must do a walk-through. *See map p. 302. 6000 Osceola Pkwy.* ☎ *877-677-9352 or 407-586-0000.* www.gaylordpalms.com.

Hampton Inn at Universal Studios

$ **International Drive** It isn't fancy, but it's close (3 blocks) to Universal Orlando, 1 mile from the heart of International Drive's tourist traps, and 4 miles from SeaWorld. *See map p. 306. 5621 Windhover Dr.* ☎ *800-426-7866 or 407-351-6716.* www.hamptoninn.com.

Holiday Inn Nikki Bird Resort

$$ **Kissimmee** Just minutes from Downtown Disney, this family favorite lets children eat free at a buffet breakfast. *See map p. 302. 7300 Irlo Bronson Memorial Hwy./U.S. 192.* ☎ *800-206-2747 or 407-396-7300.* www.holidayinnsofcentralflorida.com.

Hosteling International

$ **Kissimmee** Some of these bargain-basement rooms are private and all have baths. The site has Internet access and free use of paddle boats. *4840 W. Irlo Bronson Memorial Hwy./U.S. 192.* ☎ *800-909-4776 or 407-396-8282.* www.hiorlando.org.

Peabody Orlando

$$$$ **International Drive** Home to the renowned marching mallards that frolic in the lobby fountain, this hotel's upscale, relaxing ambience extends to both its restaurants and guest rooms. *See map p. 306. 9801 International Dr.* ☎ *800-732-2639 or 407-352-4000.* www.peabodyorlando.com.

Royal Pacific Resort

$$ Universal Orlando   This moderately priced (by Universal standards) resort is part of a complex that includes two theme parks, the CityWalk nightclub-and-restaurant district and two other Loews hotels. *See map p. 306. 4500 Universal Blvd.* ☎ *800-232-7827 or 407-363-8000.* www.universal orlando.com.

Dining Out

Hungry yet? You can pick and choose from almost 4,000 restaurants in Orlando. Because you may spend a lot of time in the Walt Disney World area, I give special attention to dining choices there.

Unless otherwise noted, parking is free.

All sit-down restaurants inside the Disney parks require park admission, with one exception: the Rainforest Café at Animal Kingdom. If you spend all day in the parks, you may find eating inside at one of the WDW restaurants more convenient, but you'll probably pay an average of 25 percent more than you would in the outside world. Also, keep in mind that alcohol isn't served in the Magic Kingdom. *Note:* All Florida restaurants and food-serving bars are smoke-free.

The Disney restaurants don't take typical reservations. Instead, all Walt Disney World eateries have *priority seating*. Priority seating *isn't* a reservation. You will get priority over any others waiting for a table at the time you schedule. There may still be a wait, but it will generally be shorter than it would be if you didn't have one. And if you don't use priority seating, especially for the most popular restaurants such as Cinderella's Table, you may miss out all together as these popular restaurants are usually booked well in advance, leaving little or no room at all for the guests who decide to just show up for a table. To make a priority seating, call ☎ **407-939-3463.** If you're staying on Disney property, you can arrange priority seating right at your resort. At Epcot, you can do it at the WorldKey interactive terminals at Guest Relations near Innoventions East, the WorldKey Information Service on the main concourse to the World Showcase, as well as at the restaurant of your choice.

Don't forget to allow for the 6 to 7 percent sales tax when estimating your dining budget.

Bergamo's
$$–$$$ International Drive Area   NORTHERN ITALIAN

Bergamo's is almost always packed, and the singing waiters here are nearly as much fun as the food. For example, you may find Broadway show tunes and opera mixed with roasted veal and steamed mussels, among other treats. Even if you don't eat, this is a good spot to enjoy the show over cocktails.

See map p. 306. 8445 International Dr. ☎ 407-352-3805. To get there: Take the I-4 Sand Lake Road exit east to International Drive and head south; it's in the Mercado shopping center off Universal Boulevard. Reservations recommended. Main courses: $20–$30. AE, DC, MC, V. Open: Sun–Thurs 5–10 p.m., Fri–Sat 5–11 p.m.

Bubbaloo's Bodacious BBQ
$ **Near North**   **BARBECUE**

Smoke billows from the chimney of this real-pit barbecue joint. The atmosphere is informal, but watch the sauces. Even the mild may be too hot for tender palates; the killer sauce comes with a three-alarm warning — it's meant only for those with asbestos taste buds and a ceramic-lined tummy. The pork platter with fixins is a deal and a half. It comes with beans and slaw. Monday through Friday you'll find daily specials that include chicken, meat loaf, turkey, and open-face roast-beef sandwiches with gravy and vegetables. And, it wouldn't be a barbecue without plenty of brew on hand.

See map p. 302. 1471 Lee Rd. ☎ 407-295-1212. To get there: From I-4, take the Lee Road exit; the restaurant is on left, next to a dry cleaner. Reservations not accepted. Main courses: $4–$13. AE, MC, V. Open: Sun–Thurs 10 a.m.–9:30 p.m., Fri–Sat 10 a.m.–10:30 p.m.

Café Tu Tu Tango
$ **International Drive**   **TAPAS**

This colorful eatery features treats from Latin America, Asia, the Caribbean, the Middle East, and the United States. It's an ideal spot for sampling; every order comes in a miniature size. Try the Cajun-style egg rolls filled with blackened chicken, pepper-crusted seared tuna sashimi with rice noodles, or alligator bites in pepper sauce. The sangria here is potent, so beware. While you eat or wait for your table, you may be entertained by a belly dancer, a magician, or a couple doing a tango. *Note:* Ordering several tapas (even those with small appetites will want two or three) and drinks can turn this into a $$$ restaurant.

Food from around the world

Epcot's World Showcase has some of the best dining options inside the WDW theme parks, thanks to the cultural cuisine of its 11 nation pavilions. Although many consider a meal here an essential part of the experience, I must point out that the food (as in all the parks) is priced higher than comparable fare in the free world.

Chow on red meat in Canada, dine on Yorkshire pudding in the U.K., have more than french fries in France, do a kebab in Morocco, teriyaki in Japan, pasta in Italy, and, well, you get the picture.

See map p. 306. 8625 International Dr. ☎ **407-248-2222.** *To get there: Just west of the Mercado shopping center. Reservations recommended. Main courses: Tapas $4–$11. AE, DC, DISC, MC, V. Open: Sun–Thurs 11:30 a.m.–11 p.m.; Fri–Sat 11:30 a.m.–midnight.*

California Grill
$$–$$$ **Disney's Contemporary Resort   NEW AMERICAN**

The 15th-floor views of the **Magic Kingdom** and environs are stunning, and the food is pretty good, too. You can sit by the show kitchens and talk to the chefs as they work magic before your eyes. Not necessarily catering to kids, the menu features choices ranging from seafood and sushi to steaks, with highlights such as roasted striped bass and grilled pork tenderloin with balsamic-smothered mushrooms. In addition, the Grill sports a grand wine list and has a nice sushi menu (Dungeness crab, eel, tuna, and more), ranging from appetizers to large platters.

See map p. 300. 4600 World Dr. ☎ **407-939-3463** *or 407-824-1576. Priority seating recommended. Main courses: $20–$34; sushi $10–$25. AE, DC, DISC, MC, V. Open: Daily 5:30–10 p.m.*

Capriccio Grill
$$–$$$$ **International Drive   TUSCAN/NORTHERN ITALIAN/ STEAKHOUSE**

The decor is chic and elegant, but the showcase is an exhibition kitchen. Main events may include bucatini tossed with chunks of mesquite-grilled chicken and mushrooms in a slightly garlicky herbed white-wine/pesto sauce or pan-seared tuna with braised fennel and radicchio served with lentil flan and a buttery citrus sauce. Chefs also make pizzas and breads in mesquite-burning ovens. There's an extensive wine list.

See map p. 306. 9801 International Dr. ☎ **407-345-4540.** www.peabodyorlando. com. *To get there: In the Peabody Orlando, across from the Orange County Convention Center. Reservations recommended. Main courses: $20–$40; most pizzas under $15. AE, CB, DC, DISC, JCB, MC, V. Open: Tues–Sun 6–11 p.m.*

Christini's Ristorante
$$–$$$$ **International Drive   ITALIAN**

Awards on the walls attest to Chris Christini's standard of service. The fact that he's been around since 1984 shows he's a survivor. Count on great service and a possible peek at celebs like Michael Douglas, Michael Jordan, and Tiger Woods, among others. A tender veal chop seasoned with sage and served with applesauce is one of the headliners. Other acts include pan-seared Chilean sea bass over shrimp-and-lobster risotto, or the shrimp flamed with brandy and vodka, then simmered in a spicy sauce and served with linguine. The wine list is definitely a winner. The dress code leans toward jackets for men and dressy dresses for women.

See map p. 306. 7600 Dr. Phillips Blvd. ☎ **407-345-8770.** www.christinis.com. *To get there: From I-4, take Exit 74A, Sand Lake Road/Highway 528, west to Dr. Phillips*

Boulevard, turn right, then left into the Marketplace Shopping Plaza. Reservations suggested. Main courses: $18–$45 (many under $27). AE, CB, DC, DISC, MC, V. Open: Daily 6 p.m.–midnight.

Citricos
$$$–$$$$ Disney's Grand Floridian Resort & Spa   NEW FRENCH

The chef of this bright and airy 190-seat restaurant makes a statement with French, Alsatian, and Provençal cuisine with California and Florida touches. (Whew!) Depending on when you visit, the menu may include basil-crusted rack of lamb or grilled salmon with fennel ravioli and Swiss chard. The dining room includes a show kitchen and views of the Seven Seas Lagoon and Magic Kingdom fireworks. Add a three-course wine offering for $25.

See map p. 300. 4401 Floridian Way. ☎ *407-939-3463 or 407-824-3000. Priority seating recommended. Main courses: $25–$45. AE, DC, DISC, MC, V. Open: Wed–Sun 5:30–10 p.m.*

Delfino Riviera
$$–$$$ Universal Orlando   ITALIAN

The atmosphere is pretty romantic in this ristorante, located above a piazza overlooking the rest of the Portofino Bay Hotel. It's the resort's signature eatery and includes strolling musicians and crooners. The chef's table has eight seats, and 20 more can dine on a balcony that offers a view of the commoners sitting below. There's also a terrace for outdoor dining. Menu highlights include savory lobster-champagne risotto or black-olive pasta with monkfish. Meat-eaters should consider veal roasted with porcini mushrooms. Delfino's wine list is second only to Emeril's (see next listing) among Universal Orlando's restaurants.

See map p. 306. 5601 Universal Studios Blvd. ☎ *407-503-3463. To get there: In the Portofino Bay Hotel. Reservations recommended. Main courses: $30–$42. AE, MC, V. Open: Tue–Sat 6–10 p.m.*

Emeril's
$$–$$$ Universal Orlando   NEW ORLEANS

Get a mouthful and eyeful in this ultramodern showplace operated by Emeril Lagasse, star of *Emeril Live* on cable TV's Food Network. This two-story restaurant looks like an old warehouse, with a 12,000-bottle wine gallery on the second floor. If you want a show, I highly recommend trying to get one of the eight counter seats where you can watch the chefs working their Creole magic, but to get one you'll need to make reservations *excruciatingly* early — at least six weeks in advance.

Best bets include andouille-crusted redfish with pecan-and-vegetable relish and quail served with vegetables and cornmeal-crusted oysters. Jackets are recommended for gents at dinner, though you'll find many diners, fresh out of the Universal theme parks, far less dressy. *Note:* This place isn't geared toward kids.

See map p. 306. 6000 Universal Studios Blvd. ☎ 407-224-2424. To get there: In CityWalk. Reservations far in advance are a must. Parking: $7 (free after 6 p.m.). Main courses: $18–$28 lunch, $18–$45 dinner. AE, DISC, MC, V. Open: Daily 11:30 a.m.–2:30 p.m. and 5:30–10 p.m. (until 11 p.m. Fri–Sat).

Numero Uno
$ Downtown Orlando   CUBAN

Some see this family-run Cuban eatery as a hole in the wall, but you won't notice the decor after the *paella* hits your table. Selections also include *ropa vieja* (literally "old clothes" because the beef is so tender), and *arroz con pollo* (chicken and rice). The trimmings include Latin treats, such as plantains.

See map p. 302. 2499 S. Orange Ave. ☎ 407-841-3840. To get there: From I-4, take Highway 50/Colonial Drive east to Orange, then turn right and go 2 blocks. Reservations recommended. Main courses: $6–$18. AE, DC, DISC, MC, V. Open: Mon–Fri 11 a.m.–3 p.m. and 5–9:30 p.m., Sat noon–10 p.m.

Pacino's Italian Ristorante
$$ South Orlando   ITALIAN

The ceiling of this restaurant contains fiber optics that create an aura of dining under the stars, but there's also a patio if you want the real thing. Some servers can be a little aloof, but the price and taste make up for it. Pacino's serves veal chops that are usually fork tender, a challenging 32-ounce porterhouse steak, and *frutti di mare* (shrimp, calamari, clams, and scallops sautéed with white wine and herbs and heaped onto a mound of linguine).

See map p. 300. 5795 W. Hwy. 192/Irlo Bronson Memorial Pkwy. ☎ 407-396-8022. To get there: 2 miles east of I-4. Reservations accepted. Main courses: $13–$26 (most are under $20); pizza $9–$11. AE, MC, V. Open: Daily 4–10 p.m.

Pebbles
$$ Downtown Orlando   AMERICAN

This is as close as Orlando gets to a hometown chain. Classy and casual, Pebbles features a menu that ranges from a create-your-own burger (price negotiable) to filet mignon and honey-roasted spareribs. Owner Manny Garcia offers affordability in the Pebbles line with entrees such as duck, lamb, and pasta dishes as well as tapas (appetizers) and soups. Many entrees come with three-cheese mashed potatoes and zucchini wedges. The restaurant has a respectable wine list (order by the glass) and fun atmosphere.

Pebbles has other locations, including at 2110 W. Hwy. 434 (☎ 407-774-7111) and 12551 Hwy. 535 (☎ 407-827-1111).

See map p. 302. 17 W. Church St. ☎ 407-839-0892. To get there: Just south of Highway 50/Colonial Drive. Reservations not accepted. Main courses: $10–$18. AE, DC, DISC, MC, V. Open: Sun–Thurs noon–11 p.m., Fri–Sat 11 a.m.–11 p.m.

Restaurant Akershus
$$ World Showcase at Epcot's Norway pavilion   NORWEGIAN

This eatery is a re-created 14th-century castle where you can sample a 40-item smorgasbord of *smavarmt* (hot) and *koldtbord* (cold) dishes. The reasonably good entrees usually include such dishes as venison stew, roast pork, gravlax, smoked mackerel, and mustard herring.

In the Norway pavilion at World Showcase in Epcot. ☎ *407-939-3463. Priority seating recommended. Lunch buffet: $14 adults, $7 kids 4–9; dinner buffet: $20 adults, $9 kids. AE, DC, DISC, MC, V.*

Tchoup Chop
$$ Universal's Royal Pacific Hotel   POLYNESIAN/ASIAN FUSION

Can you say BAM!? Pronounced "chop chop," Emeril Lagasse's second restaurant in Orlando is named for the location of his original restaurant, Tchoupitoulous Street in New Orleans. The exhibition kitchen offers a look at chefs making Polynesian- and Asian-influenced entrees such as Kona coffee–glazed duck breast with duck and vegetable chow mein, and grilled rib-eye steak with garlic mashed potatoes, fried Maui onions, teriyaki sauce, and stir-fried vegetables.

See map p. 306. 6300 Hollywood Way, in Universal's Royal Pacific Hotel. ☎ *407-503-2467. To get there: From I-4, take the Kirkman Rd./Hwy. 435 exit and follow the signs to Universal. Reservations strongly recommended. Main courses: $15–$24. AE, DISC, MC, V. Open: Daily 11:30 a.m.–2 p.m.; Sun–Thurs 5:30–10 p.m.; Fri–Sat 5:30–11 p.m.*

Wolfgang Puck Café
$$–$$$ Downtown Disney   AMERICAN/CALIFORNIA

My favorite stop is the copper-and-terrazo sushi bar, one of the best in Orlando. You also can eat gourmet pizza, with thin crusts and exotic toppings, inside or on an outdoor patio. Upstairs, the main dining room offers a seasonally changing menu that may feature grilled rack of lamb with mushroom-infused mashed potatoes or a refreshing smoked duck Napoleon with Boursin cheese, mango, and papaya between veggie wontons. The lower level can be noisy, so conversation may be difficult. Puck's also has a grab-and-go express restaurant that has sandwiches, pizzas, desserts, and more.

1482 Buena Vista Dr. ☎ *407-938-9653. To get there: In Disney's West Side. Reservations in dining room. Free parking. Dining room main courses: $26–$38; $8–$25 pizza and sushi. AE, DC, DISC, MC, V. Open: Daily 11 a.m.–1 a.m.*

Disney character dining

The 8-and-under crowd usually gets starry-eyed when Mickey, Pluto, Cinderella, and friends show up to sign autographs and pose for photos. Characters turn out at mealtimes at several Disney parks, attractions, and resorts. These get-togethers are incredibly popular. Translation: One-on-one interaction is somewhat brief.

You may not find a seat if you show up to a character meal unannounced, so make priority-seating reservations (these reservations don't lock down a table, but they do give you the next available table after you arrive) by calling ☎ **407-939-3463.**

Prices vary, but generally expect breakfast (most serve it) to be $17 to $20 for adults, $9 to $10 for kids 3 to 11; those that serve dinner charge $21 to $24 for adults and $10 to $11 for kids.

Although I mention specific characters here, be advised that *WDW frequently changes its lineups,* so don't promise the kids a specific character or you may get burned. Also, keep in mind that you'll have to *add the price of admission* to meals that are held inside the theme parks.

That said, here are a few of the choices.

Chef Mickey's

Here, you can encounter your favorite cartoon characters twice a day: at buffet breakfasts (eggs, bacon, sausage, pancakes, fruit, and other items) and dinners (entrees change daily and are joined by a salad bar, soups, vegetables, and ice cream with toppings). **Mickey and various pals** are there to meet and mingle.

In Disney's Contemporary Resort, 4600 North World Dr. Character breakfast: $16.99 adults, $8.99 children 3–11. Character dinner: $23.99 adults, $12.99 children 3–11. Open: Daily 7–11:30 a.m. and 5–9:30 p.m.

Cinderella's Royal Table

This castle — the focal point of the park — is the setting for daily character breakfasts. The menu has standard fare: eggs, bacon, Danish, and fresh breads. Hosts vary, but **Cinderella** always makes an appearance. This is one of the most popular character meals in the park, so reserve far in advance. This meal is a great way to start your day in the **Magic Kingdom.**

You must make priority-seating reservations backed by a credit card for this breakfast; it will cost you $10 per adult and $5 per child if you cancel.

In Cinderella Castle, The Magic Kingdom. $15.99 adults, $8.99 children 3–11. Open: Daily 8–10 a.m.

Liberty Tree Tavern

This colonial-style, 18th-century pub offers character dinners hosted by **Minnie, Goofy, Pluto,** and **Chip 'n' Dale.** Family-style meals include salad, roast turkey, ham, cornbread, and dessert.

Food-wise, this is the best character meal in the **World.**

In Liberty Square, The Magic Kingdom. Dinner: $20.99 adults, $9.99 children 3–11. Open: Daily 4 p.m. to park closing.

1900 Park Fare

The elegant Grand Floridian resort hosts character breakfasts (eggs, French toast, bacon, and pancakes) and dinners (prime rib, pork loin, fish, and more) in the festive, exposition-themed 1900 Park Fare. Big Bertha — a 100-year-old French band organ that plays drums, cymbals, the xylophone, and more — provides music. **Mary Poppins, Alice in Wonderland, and friends** appear at breakfast; **Pooh and friends** star at dinner.

In Disney's Grand Floridian Beach Resort, 4401 Floridian Way. Breakfast: $16.99 adults, $9.99 children 3–11. Dinner: $25.99 adults, $10.99 children 3–11. Open: Daily 7:30–11:30 a.m. and 5:15–9 p.m.

Dinner shows

Disney and Orlando have a reasonably busy dinner-show scene, but their offerings aren't like what you'll find in New York or London. Here, productions offer fun, not critically acclaimed drama, and focus on entertaining the most important VIPs — kids. The shows serve meals that are a cut above a TV dinner, but don't come expecting a primo dining experience. The admission prices listed below include dinner.

Arabian Nights

If you're a horse fan, this show is a winner. It stars many of the most popular breeds, from chiseled Arabians to hard-driving quarter horses to beefcake Belgians. They giddy-up through performances that include Wild West trick riding, chariot races, a little slapstick comedy, and bareback daredevils. Locals rate it number one among Orlando dinner shows. Usually, the performance opens with a ground trainer working one-on-one with a black stallion. The dinner, served during the two-hour show, includes salad, prime rib, or a vegetarian entree such as lasagna, plus vegetables, potatoes, and dessert.

See map p. 302. 6225 W. Irlo Bronson Memorial Hwy./U.S. 192. ☎ 800-553-6116 or 407-239-9223. www.arabian-nights.com. *To get there: East of I-4. Reservations recommended. Shows held daily, times vary. Admission: $39.59 adults, $20.33 kids 3–11.*

Dolly Parton's Dixie Stampede and Dinner Show

Heee-haw, this is fun! And even if you or the kids aren't fans of the buxom country star, no worries, as she has little to do with this show besides owning it. Horses, buffalo, and patriotic performers put on quite the show while a feast of rotisserie chicken, hickory smoked barbecue pork loin, biscuits, corn on the cob, potatoes, soup and all the Pepsi you can drink make for a bombastic affair, to say the least.

See map p. 302. 8251 Vineland Ave. ☎ 866-443-4943. www.dixiestampede.com. *To get there: South of International Drive, past Sea World. Turn right into Vineland Village. Reservations recommended. Shows held daily, times vary. Admission: $46.99 adults, $19.99 kids 3–11.*

Hoop-Dee-Doo Musical Revue

This is Disney's most popular show, so make reservations early. The reward: You feast on an all-you-can-eat barbecue (fried chicken, smoked ribs, salad, corn on the cob, baked beans, bread, strawberry shortcake, and your choice of coffee, tea, beer, wine, sangria, or soda). While you stuff yourself silly in Pioneer Hall, performers in 1890s garb lead you in a hand-clapping, high-energy show that includes jokes you haven't heard since second grade.

If you catch one of the early shows, consider sticking around for the Electrical Water Pageant at 9:45 p.m., viewed from the Fort Wilderness Beach.

Be prepared to join in the fun, or the singers and the rest of the audience will humiliate you.

3520 N. Fort Wilderness Trail. ☎ ***407-939-3563.*** www.disneyworld.com. *To get there: At WDW's Fort Wilderness Resort and Campground. Reservations required. Shows: 5 and 7:15 p.m.; sometimes a later show, too. Admission: Adults $49, kids 3–11 $25 including tax and gratuity.*

Polynesian Luau Dinner Show

Although not quite as much in demand as the Hoop-Dee-Doo, the Polynesian presents a delightful two-hour show that's a favorite among kids, all of whom are invited onto the stage. A colorfully costumed cast of entertainers from Hawaii, New Zealand, Tahiti, and Samoa perform hula, warrior, love, and fire dances on a flower-filled stage. It takes place five nights a week in an open-air theater (dress for nighttime weather) with candlelit tables, red-flame lanterns, and tapa-bark paintings on the walls. Arrive early for the preshow highlighting Polynesian crafts and culture (lei making, hula lessons, and more).

The all-you-can-eat meal includes island fruits, roasted chicken and pork ribs, shrimp fried rice, vegetables, red and sweet potatoes, pull-apart cinnamon bread, tropical ice-cream sundaes, coffee, tea, beer, wine, and soda.

1600 Seven Seas Dr. ☎ ***407-939-3463.*** www.disneyworld.com. *To get there: At Disney's Polynesian Resort. Reservations required. Shows: Tues–Sat 5:15 and 8 p.m. Admission: $49.01 adults, $24.81 kids 3–11 including tax.*

Chapter 18

Touring the Theme Parks

. . . .

In This Chapter

▶ Purchasing tickets and passes

▶ Enjoying the theme-park thrill rides

▶ Seeing all-star parades, fireworks, and shows

. . . .

*F*inally, we're off to the parks — Disney's Fab Four (**Magic Kingdom, Epcot, Disney–MGM Studios,** and **Animal Kingdom**), Universal Orlando's Dynamic Duo (**Universal Studios Florida** and **Islands of Adventure**) plus the marine scene at **SeaWorld** and **Discovery Cove.**

You know you won't be alone. But do you know how much company you're going to have? In a typical year, these eight theme parks combined attract more than *60 million* visitors — 40 million of whom invade the four Disney parks. And, all these folks are bent on riding the same rides and eating at the same restaurants as you. You can have much more fun at all the theme parks in Orlando if you arrive knowing which parks and attractions suit your tastes and which you should avoid. So, you can discover how to rank them in this chapter.

Each of these parks takes at least a full day to see.

Walt Disney World: An Overview

Disney's main theme parks line the western half of this 30,500-acre world. (Skip ahead to the "Walt Disney World" map.) The **Magic Kingdom** is the original attraction. With more than 15 million visitors in a normal year, it's busier than any other U.S. park. **Epcot** is the third busiest, welcoming about 10 million visitors a year, followed by **Disney–MGM Studios,** at 8 million, and **Animal Kingdom,** with just under 8 million visitors a year.

Thrill-ride junkies end up finding many of the rides in the Disney parks disappointing compared to Universal's Islands of Adventure. However, 9 of the 14 major rides at Islands have height restrictions, making it less attractive to those traveling with smaller children.

All theme parks consider everyone 10 and older an adult, and the prices I give you don't include the 6 percent sales tax.

Walt Disney World

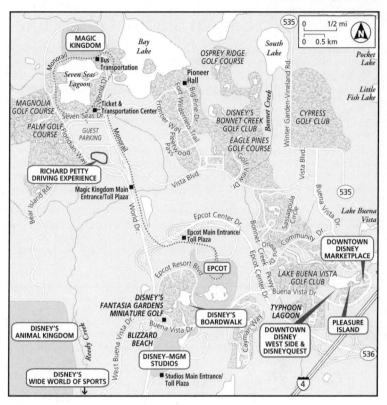

Pricing theme parks

At the time this book was published, Disney's single-day, single-park admission was $59.75 for adults and $48 kids 3 to 9. **Multiday tickets** allow you to visit *one park per day*. A 7-day ticket costs $199 for adults, $160 for kids. A **Park Hopper** add-on ($35 *per ticket*, per person*) allows visitors unlimited admission to Disney's major parks for the length of their ticket. A 1-day adult Park Hopper ticket costs $94.75, while the 7-day version costs $234—making the latter a far better deal. **Premium Passes** are Park Hopper tickets that also allow visitors their choice of two to five admissions to Typhoon Lagoon, Blizzard Beach, Pleasure Island, Disney-Quest, or Disney's Wide World of Sports. Prices range from an obscene $139.95 for a 1-day adult pass to $268 for a 7-day pass (a very good deal). Get more information on the parks and on prices for Disney's tickets by calling ☎ **407-934-7639** or checking out www.disneyworld.com.

If you're driving to the Disney parks, parking costs $8 per day. In the Size XXXL Magic Kingdom lot, you probably want to ride the tram to the gate. Trams are also available at Epcot, Disney–MGM Studios, and Animal Kingdom, though many energetic guests hoof it to those gates.

FASTPASSing to the front of the line

Don't want to stand in line as long as other guests? Disney parks have installed a ride-reservation system called **FASTPASS** where you go to the primo rides, feed your theme-park ticket stub into a small slot, and get an assigned time to return. When you do, you get into a short line and climb aboard. FASTPASS is free. Here's how it works:

Hang onto your ticket stub when you enter and go to the hottest ride on your dance card. If it's a FASTPASS attraction (they're noted in the handout guide map), feed your stub into the waist-level ticket taker. Retrieve your ticket stub and the FASTPASS stub that comes with it. Look at the two times stamped on the latter. You can return during that one-hour window and enter the ride with almost no wait. In the meantime, you can do something else until the appointed time. *Remember:* Each person in your group has to get his or her own FASTPASS ticket to get in the quickie line for a ride.

Note: Early in the day, your one-hour window may begin 40 minutes after you feed the FASTPASS machine, but later in the day it may be hours. Initially, Disney only allowed you to do this on one ride at a time. Now your FASTPASS ticket gives you a time you can return to sign up for a second FASTPASS, even if you haven't used your first reservation yet.

Make a note of your parking area and row. After a day spent standing in line, listening to screaming kids, and being tapped out by cash registers, you may have a hard time remembering where you parked.

Enjoying Walt Disney World

Most of the parks open at 9 a.m. throughout the year. They remain open at least until 6 p.m., and often as late as 11 p.m. or midnight during peak periods. The exception is Animal Kingdom, which usually opens at 8 a.m. and closes at 6 p.m. (slightly later during summer).

Ride and show lines at Disney can be incredibly long and irritating. A 20-minute wait is considered short, and 45 minutes to 1 hour or more is common at primo rides. Consider getting a **FASTPASS** (see the "FASTPASSing to the front of the line" sidebar later in this chapter) ticket to shorten your line time.

Here are a few other ways to beat the lines:

- ✔ Come during off periods: mid-October through November (except Thanksgiving week), the first two weeks of December, and mid-April to late May. The worst times to visit are during holidays, spring break, and school summer vacations.

- ✔ Arrive early and head straight for your number-one ride, preferably one that's away from the entrance. Most people stop at the first ride they see.

- ✔ If you don't like the parades held each afternoon in the various parks, skip them and get on rides instead. Lines are shorter when most visitors are lining the parade route.

- ✔ Pay attention to the signs at most attractions telling you how long you have to wait.

- ✔ Ask or read the health and height restrictions for the rides before you get in line, to avoid wasting time on one that isn't for you.

- ✔ Get a show schedule as soon as you enter the park. You can find them in the guide maps at the turnstiles and in park shops. The rides are nonstop, but shows run at specific times.

If you want to know all there is to know about Central Florida and its parks, purchase a copy of *Walt Disney World & Orlando For Dummies* (Wiley Publishing, Inc.).

The Magic Kingdom

Even newer additions to the park, such as Stitch's Great Escape and Splash Mountain, fall short of the 3-D and high-tech dynamics that you'll find at some other parks, but the kingdom is still the fairest of them all.

Main Street, U.S.A.

Though it's considered one of the kingdom's lands, Main Street is an entry zone. **Main Street Cinema** is one of its few attractions (we call it that in the loosest sense). You don't have to pay admission to watch the theater's cartoons, including vintage ones like 1928's *Steamboat Willie*. But you do have to stand — there are no seats. You also can catch the **Walt Disney World Railroad** here. This steam-powered train makes a 15-minute loop around the park, with stops in Frontierland and Mickey's Toontown Fair.

We recommend passing through Main Street quickly when you arrive, unless you hop the train. You have to return this way at the end of the day, and if you're inclined to visit the shops, you can do it then.

Tomorrowland

Thanks to *Star Wars* director George Lucas and others, today's version of the future is high-tech. Here are some of the headliners:

- ✔ **Astro Orbiter:** Astronaut wannabes, especially those who are 6 years old and under, love whirling high into the galaxy in colorful rockets that circle a hub while rising and falling. Unfortunately, the orbiter has ridiculously long lines, so skip it if you're on a tight timetable.

✔ **Buzz Lightyear's Space Ranger Spin:** On this ride, you embark on an interactive space adventure in which you help Buzz defend the Earth's supply of batteries from the evil Emperor Zurg. You fly an XP-37 space cruiser armed with twin lasers and a joystick that's capable of spinning the craft. (Space Rangers who get motion sickness should sit this attraction out.) While you cruise through space, you collect points by blasting anything that smells remotely like Zurg. Your hits trigger light, sound, and animation effects. Together, you and Buzz save the galaxy.

✔ **Space Mountain:** Imagine a roller coaster. Then imagine it in the dark. This ride, Big Thunder Mountain Railroad (later in this chapter), and Splash Mountain (also later) are the four **Magic Kingdom** attractions that teens and other thrill junkies bolt for first. So get here early or save it for the off hours, such as lunch or parade time. Space Mountain, a classic coaster, spins and plunges plenty (though it seems faster, it never tops 28 mph). Grab a front seat for the best ride. *Note:* Modern coaster crazies may find it a bit lame. *The ride has a 44-inch height minimum.*

✔ **Stitch's Great Escape:** Gone is the ultrascary *ExtraTERRORestrial Alien Encounter,* and in its place is this ostensibly family-friendly attraction based on the Disney hit film *Lilo & Stitch.* The story line is a prequel to the movie, showing the mischief caused by rascally Experiment 626 (aka Stitch) when he was originally captured. Unfortunately, the ride is something of a disappointment both technically and thematically — and some of its scarier effects mean it's not all that kid-friendly either.

✔ **The Timekeeper** is hosted by a robot/mad scientist (Robin Williams) and his assistant, 9-EYE, a flying, camera-headed droid that moonlights as a time-machine test pilot. In this jet-speed escapade, the audience hears Mozart as a young prodigy playing for French royalty, watches da Vinci work, and floats in a hot-air balloon over Red Square. It's more for adults than kids.

✔ **Tomorrowland Indie Speedway:** Kids ages 4 to 9 like slipping into these Indy-car knockoffs; but older children, teens, and adults find the lines and the steering less than stellar — especially those who are used to go-karts. The top speed is 7 mph, and a thick iron bar separates your tires; so you're pretty much kept on track. *You have to be a minimum of 52 inches tall to drive alone.*

Mickey's Toontown Fair

Head off cries of "Where's Mickey?" by taking young kids (ages 2–8) to this 2-acre site as soon as you arrive. **Toontown** gives kids a chance to meet Disney characters, including Mickey, Minnie, Donald Duck, Goofy, and Pluto. The **Magic Kingdom**'s smallest land is set in a whimsical collection of candy-striped tents. Here are some of Toontown's highlights:

✔ **The Barnstormer at Goofy's Wiseacre Farm** is a mini roller coaster designed to look and feel like a crop duster that flies slightly off course and right through the Goofmeister's barn. It has a *35-inch height minimum,* and its tight turns and small dips even give some adults a rush.

✔ **Donald's Boat (The S.S. Miss Daisy)** is an interactive play area with fountains and water snakes that win squeals of joy (and relief on hot days).

✔ **Mickey's & Minnie's Country Houses** provide a lot of visual fun and some interactive areas for youngsters, though they're usually crowded and the lines flow like molasses. Mickey's place features garden and garage playgrounds. Minnie's lets kids play in her kitchen, where popcorn goes wild in a microwave and the utensils strike up a symphony of their own.

✔ **Toontown Hall of Fame** offer continuous meetings with Disney characters and a large assortment of Disney souvenirs.

Fantasyland

The rides and attractions in **Fantasyland** are based on the Disney movies you grew up with way back when and some of the more recent additions to the Disney treasure chest of films. Young kids want to spend lots of time here, and the seemingly endless lines ensure that you will. Here's a list of attractions in *Fantasyland:*

✔ **Cinderella Castle:** Modeled on several French chateaux, the fairytale Gothic-style castle sits at the end of *Main Street* in the center of the park, and its hard to miss the 189-foot landmark and its 18 towers. It's a favorite photo op, and if you land at the right time, you can meet Cinderella and other characters at the Forecourt Stage. Otherwise, the castle is mainly a visual attraction. The interior corridor has lovely murals and some exquisite mosaics depicting the story of Cinderella. The castle is also home to Cinderella's Royal Table restaurant (see Chapter 17).

Though the exterior appears to be made of bricks, the castle's structure is actually composed of fiberglass and steel. But nobody will be blowing this house down anytime soon — it's designed to withstand 90 mph winds.

✔ **Cinderella's Golden Carousel:** This old beauty was built in 1917 by the Philadelphia Toboggan Company and served tours in Detroit and New Jersey before it was discovered in the late 1960s by Disney Imagineers and brought to the **Magic Kingdom.** A patriotic red, white, and blue in its first incarnation, it was restored and re-themed in time for the park's opening and now tells the tale of Cinderella in 18 hand-painted scenes set above magnificent antique horses. It's a delight for kids and carousel lovers of all ages. The organ plays — what else? — Disney classics such as "When You Wish Upon a Star" and "Heigh Ho."

✔ **Dumbo the Flying Elephant:** This attraction doesn't do much for adrenaline-addicted older kids — or line-hating parents — but it's a favorite of kids ages 2 through 6. Dumbo's ears keep them airborne for a gentle, circular flight with some little dips. Except for the Disney theme, it's not all that different from the kiddie rides at most local carnivals. Most kids older than 6 are humiliated if you even suggest they ride it. If your little ones are dying to ride Dumbo, get here early — wait times are brutal, and it doesn't have FASTPASS!

This ride is designed for the young ones, so plus-sized parents may have trouble getting their elephant to fly, and the taller among you may feel somewhat cramped.

✔ **It's a Small World:** Young kids and most parents love this attraction; teens and most other adults find it a real gagger. Nevertheless, pay your dues — it's an initiation rite every Disney visitor needs to undergo, and the line isn't usually too long. You glide around the world in small boats, meeting Russian dancers, Chinese acrobats, and French cancan girls — and every one of them sings a tune that eats its way into your brain and refuses to stop playing for months.

This attraction, one of the original few that opened with the park in 1971 (it was originally built by Walt Disney for the 1964 World's Fair), underwent a major renovation in 2004 that included painting and repairing the animatronics figures, as well as replacing the sound system and lights.

✔ **Mad Tea Party:** You make this tea party wild or mild, depending on how much you choose to spin the steering wheel of the teacup that serves as your chariot. The ride is suitable for ages 4 and older. Teens and older kids seem to enjoy this ride's potential for turning unwary passengers green. The woozy mouse who pops out of a big teapot in the center of the platform would no doubt sympathize with those left spinning.

✔ **The Many Adventures of Winnie the Pooh:** Pooh inadvertently created a small storm of protest when Disney used this ride to replace the popular *Mr. Toad's Wild Ride* in 1999. *The Many Adventures of Winnie the Pooh* features the cute-and-cuddly little fellow along with Eeyore, Piglet, and Tigger. You board a golden honey pot and ride through a storybook version of the Hundred Acre Wood, keeping an eye out for Heffalumps, Woozles, blustery days, and the Floody Place. This ride has become a favorite of kids 2 to 8 and their parents, so use a FASTPASS to avoid a long wait.

✔ **Mickey's PhilharMagic:** This show stars Mickey, Donald, Ariel, Aladdin, and others in an animated enhanced 3-D adventure projected on a 150-foot screen — the largest wraparound screen on the planet. Like *Jim Henson's Muppet*Vision 3-D* (later in this chapter), the show combines music, animated film, puppetry, and special effects that tickle several of your senses. Kids love the effects, and if you're a sucker for the classic Disney films, you will absolutely adore it.

The show marks the first time the classic Disney characters have ever been rendered in 3-D. In order to add nostalgic flavor, Donald's dialogue was created using a classic performance by Clarence "Ducky" Nash, the character's original voice.

✔ **Peter Pan's Flight:** Another popular ride among visitors younger than 8, it begins with a nighttime flight over London (the only plus for adults) in search of Captain Hook, Tiger Lily, and the Lost Boys. It's one of the old glide rides dating back to the limited technology that was available when the **Magic Kingdom** was born. This ride often has long lines, so I recommend a FASTPASS.

✔ **Snow White's Scary Adventure:** Your journey takes you to the dwarfs' cottage and the wishing well, ending with the prince's kiss to break the evil spell. This version of the Grimms' fairy tale is much less grim than it was years ago, when the focus was inexplicably on the wicked witch. Snow White now appears in several friendly scenes, though kids younger than 4 still may get scared. I can't recommend it if your time schedule is tight; it's very tame and most find it a waste of time.

Liberty Square

Located between *Fantasyland* and *Frontierland,* **Liberty Square** is a re-creation of Revolutionary War–era America that infuses you with Colonial spirit. Younger guests may not appreciate the historical touches (such as the 13 lanterns symbolizing the original 13 colonies), but they'll delight in the chance to pose for a picture while locked in the stocks. You may also encounter a fife-and-drum corps marching along the cobblestone streets. Here are some other features of *Liberty Square:*

✔ **Liberty Belle Riverboat:** A steam-powered sternwheeler called the *Liberty Belle* departs Liberty Square for scenic cruises along the Rivers of America. The passing landscape resembles the Wild West. It makes a restful interlude for foot-weary park-stompers.

✔ **Hall of Presidents:** American-history buffs ages 10 and older most appreciate this show, which can be a real squirmer for younger children. The Hall is an inspiring production based on painstaking research, right down to the clothes — each president's costume reflects his period's fashion, fabrics, and tailoring techniques. The show begins with a film on the importance of the Constitution projected on an immense 180-degree screen, and then the curtain rises on America's leaders, from George Washington through George W. Bush. Pay special attention to the roll call of presidents. The animatronic figures are incredibly lifelike: They fidget, whisper, and talk to the audience.

✔ **Haunted Mansion:** Although this attraction has changed little through the years, and the Eddie Murphy flick bombed at the box office, the mansion continues to be a favorite and has a cult following. (My editor makes a pilgrimage here every time she hits the park.) It has detailed special effects (this was one of the last rides Walt Disney actually had a hand in designing) and an atmosphere that's more fun than creepy. You may chuckle at the corny tombstones lining the entrance before you hop aboard your Doom Buggy and are whisked past a ghostly banquet and ball, a graveyard band, weird flying objects, and more. And don't forget the 999 spirits of the house, one of whom may try to hitch a ride home with you.

The ride doesn't get much scarier than spooky music, eerie howling, and things that go bump in the night. It's best for those ages 6 and older. FASTPASS is recommended as this attraction always has a line.

Frontierland

Frontierland is located behind *Adventureland* and the rough-and-tumble Old West architecture runs to log cabins and rustic saloons, while the landscape is Southwestern scrubby with mesquite, cactus, yucca, and prickly pear. Attractions in *Frontierland* include the following:

✔ **Big Thunder Mountain Railroad:** The lines don't lie: This rocking railroad is a favorite in the **Magic Kingdom.** *Thunder Mountain* bounces you around an old mining site, where you dodge floods, a bridge collapse, rock slides, and other mayhem. The ride is something of a low-grade roller coaster with speed and a lot of corkscrew action. It has enough of a reputation that even first-time visitors make a beeline for it. So if you can't get to it as soon as the park opens, FASTPASS is your best bet. Or give it a try late in the day or when a parade pulls most visitors away from the rides.

Most Disney coaster veterans maintain the ride is at its best after dark. The ride can be too intense for kids younger than 6 (and for those with neck problems); *riders must be at least 40 inches tall.*

✔ **Country Bear Jamboree:** The stars of this 15-minute animatronic show are bears that croon country-and-western tunes. The Jamboree is a park standard — a show that's been around since Disney invented dirt — but it's still a hit with Disney buffs and little kids. The audience gets caught up in the hand-clapping, knee-slapping, foot-stomping fun as Trixie laments lost love as she sings "Tears Will Be the Chaser for Your Wine." Teddi Beara descends from the ceiling in a swing to perform "Heart, I Did All That I Could," and Big Al moans "Blood in the Saddle."

Unless you have an affinity for all things Disney or have younger children, this might be best saved for those really hot days when you need a break inside. Most teens, young adults, and repeat visitors won't want to do it, even then.

✔ **Frontierland Shootin' Arcade:** Combining state-of-the-art electronics with a traditional shooting-gallery format, this arcade offers 97 targets (slow-moving ore cars, buzzards, and gravediggers) in an 1850s boomtown scenario. If you hit a tombstone, it may spin around and mysteriously change its epitaph. Coyotes howl, bridges creak, and skeletal arms reach out from the grave. To keep things authentic, newfangled electronic firing mechanisms with infrared bullets are concealed in genuine buffalo rifles. When you hit a target, you set off sound and motion gags. Fifty cents fetches 25 shots.

✔ **Splash Mountain:** If I had to pick one ride as the **Kingdom's** most popular, *Splash Mountain* would be it. It's on par with **SeaWorld's** *Journey to Atlantis* (later in this chapter), though half a click below *Jurassic Park River Adventure* at **Islands of Adventure** (later in this chapter). Still, *Splash Mountain* is a nifty voyage through the world of Disney's classic film *Song of the South,* past 26 colorful scenes that include backwoods swamps, bayous, spooky caves, and waterfalls. You ride in a hollow-log flume as Brer Fox and Brer Bear chase the ever-wily Brer Rabbit and end your journey with a 52-foot, 45-degree, 40-mph finish, with a rather high splash factor (around 200 megatons worth of wet). If you're lucky enough to have some real heavyweights in the front seat, look for a little extra explosion on the five-story downhill.

In summer, this ride can provide sweet relief from the heat and humidity, but in cool weather, parents may want to protect their kids (and themselves) from a chill. *Splash Mountain* is recommended for ages 8 and older. *Riders must be at least 40 inches tall.*

On warmer days, the ride shoots out a spray of water onto the viewing bridge in front of the big drop. If you want to catch your friends unaware for a good soaking, count the log drops: Every third one emits the spray.

✔ **Tom Sawyer Island:** Board Huck Finn's raft for a two-minute float across a river to this densely forested island, where kids can explore *Injun Joe's Cave* (complete with such scary sound effects as whistling wind) and navigate a swinging bridge. Narrow, winding dirt paths lined with oaks, pines, and sycamores create an authentic backwoods atmosphere. It's easy to get briefly lost and stumble upon some unexpected adventure. It's a good place for kids to lose a little energy and for moms and dads to relax and maybe indulge in lunch or a snack at Aunt Polly's, which overlooks the river.

Adventureland

Adventureland is a left turn off the end of *Main Street*. Kids can engage in swashbuckling behavior while walking through dense tropical foliage (complete with vines) or marauding through bamboo and thatch-roofed huts. The architecture here is a combination of the Caribbean, Southeast Asia, and Polynesia. Walt Disney wanted this section of the park to exude romance, mystery, and (duh!) adventure. There's plenty of the latter here, especially for kids, though you may have trouble finding the first two. Here are some of the most popular attractions in *Adventureland:*

✔ **Enchanted Tiki Room:** Upgraded over the years, the show's newest cast member is Iago of *Aladdin* fame. This attraction is set in a Polynesian-style building with thatched roof, bamboo beams, and tapa-bark murals. Other players include 250 tropical birds, chanting totem poles, and singing flowers that whistle, tweet, and warble. The show runs continuously throughout the day. Young children are most likely to appreciate this one but so will nostalgic adults. Otherwise, consider this only as a respite from the heat.

✔ **Jungle Cruise:** You give Disney 10 minutes, they'll give you four famous rivers on three different continents. This narrated voyage on the Congo, Amazon, Mekong, and Nile rivers offers glimpses of animatronic animals, tropical and subtropical foliage (most of it real), a temple-of-doom-type camp, and lots of surprises. The ride passes animatronic pygmies, pythons, elephants, rhinos, gorillas, and hippos that pop threateningly out of the water and blow snot — well, it could've been snot if they weren't robots — on you. This exhibit is about 30 years old, which means it's pretty hokey sometimes, but it's still a nice way to relax if the lines don't stretch too long (though the waiting area for this ride does offer some amusing moments — check out the prop menus on the walls).

✔ **Magic Carpets of Aladdin:** The first major ride added in Adventureland since 1971 delights wee ones and some older kids. Its 16 four-passenger carpets circle a giant genie's bottle while camels spit water at riders in much the same way riders are spritzed at *One Fish, Two Fish* at **Islands of Adventure** (later in this chapter). The fiberglass carpets spin and move up, down, forward, and back.

If the lines are too long at *Dumbo* (see the "Fantasyland" section, earlier in this chapter), this is a good alternative as the rides are similar and the lines here aren't as sluggish.

✔ **Pirates of the Caribbean:** This oldie but goodie is another cult favorite (a Disney archivist confessed to me that it's still his favorite and this is another ride that Walt Disney had a hand in creating). After walking through a long grotto, you board a boat headed into a dark cave and are warned that "dead men tell no tales." Therein, elaborate scenery and hundreds of incredibly detailed (some of Disney's best) animatronic figures re-create an almost refreshingly non-P.C. Caribbean town overrun by buccaneers. To a background of cheerful yo-ho-ho music, the sound of rushing waterfalls, squawking seagulls, and screams of terror, passengers pass through the line of fire into a raging raid and panorama of almost fierce-looking pirates swigging rum, looting, and plundering. This ride is another great place to cool off on a hot day.

Kids ages 5 and younger may find a pirate's life a bit too scary, especially with the small drop in the dark. Most kids 6 or older, though, will enjoy it. The recent Oscar-nominated film based on the ride (alas, there's no Johnny Depp to be found here) has made it even more popular with the young and teen set, who have fun spotting the scenes appropriated by the movie.

Offer a tip of your head to the parrot that sits above the ride's entrance plaza, and you may get a hearty greeting in response.

✔ **Swiss Family Treehouse:** The story of the shipwrecked Swiss Family Robinson (via the 1960 Disney film of the same name) comes alive in this attraction made for swinging, exploring, and crawling fun. The "tree," designed by Disney Imagineers, has 330,000 polyethylene leaves sprouting from a 90-foot span of branches; although it isn't real, it's draped with actual Spanish moss. It's simple and void of all that high-tech stuff that's popular in today's parks.

Be prepared to stand in a slow-moving line on busy days. The attraction is also hard for travelers with limited mobility to navigate. Though little kids like it, I couldn't get either of my borrowed offspring to give it a try — they wanted the big-ticket thrill rides.

Parades and fireworks

Disney excels at producing fanfare, and its parades and fireworks displays are among the best of their kind in the world. Note, however, that some productions are staged only on a limited basis or during certain times of the year. Grab a guide map when you arrive. It includes an entertainment schedule that lists special goings-on for the day, including concerts, encounters with characters, holiday events, and other major happenings. If you want to know whether a specific parade or fireworks show will be staged when you're in town, consult the calendar at www.disneyworld.com or call ☎ 407-934-7639.

During fireworks and parades, Disney ropes off designated viewing spots for travelers with disabilities and their parties. Consult your park map or a park employee at least an hour before the parade or you may have trouble making it through the crowds to get to the designated spots. Additionally, if there are two showings of a parade, the later one is usually less crowded.

If nobody in your party is a huge parade fan, these are the best times to ride some of the more popular attractions — while everyone else is lined up along the parade route. You can also use the *Walt Disney Railroad* (mentioned earlier in the chapter) to navigate around the various areas of the park when the parade route has blocked off most major routes through the park.

Here are Disney's best parades and fireworks displays:

✔ **Wishes:** This explosive display debuted in fall 2003 and is touched off nightly at closing except during the summer and on holidays when extended park hours allow for the fireworks to be shown between two scheduled showings of *SpectroMagic* (see next in this list). Before the display, Tinker Bell flies magically from *Cinderella Castle.* Then as a cacophony of intricately choreographed fireworks fills the skies, and Jiminy Crickett narrates, images are projected onto the castle in time to the medley of Disney songs being broadcast park-wide. Suggested viewing areas are *Liberty Square, Frontierland,* and *Mickey's Toontown Fair.* Disney hotels close to the park (the Grand Floridian, Polynesian, Contemporary, and Wilderness Lodge) also offer views, as the fireworks display is rather large. This show can make even the most blasé fireworks watcher say "wow!"

✔ **SpectroMagic:** This after-dark parade combines fiber optics, holographic images, clouds of liquid nitrogen, old-fashioned twinkling lights, and a soundtrack featuring classic Disney tunes. Mickey, dressed in an amber-and-purple grand magician's cape, makes an appearance in a confetti of light. You'll also see the SpectroMen atop the title float, and Chernabog, *Fantasia*'s monstrous demon, who unfolds his 38-foot wingspan. It takes the electrical equivalent of seven lightning bolts (enough to power a fleet of 2,000 trucks) to bring the show to life.

SpectroMagic plays only *on limited nights,* when park closing extends past dusk (generally during busy periods and on weekends). When park hours are extended to 10 p.m. or later, there are often two chances to view the parade. Check your show schedule to determine availability.

✔ **Share a Dream Come True Parade:** This parade honors the 100th anniversary of Uncle Walt's birth (which has come and gone though the parade lives on). Loads of characters (over 110 cast members take part) march up *Main Street* and into *Frontierland* daily. The parade was still going strong at press time, but it's future status is up in the air, so it may be gone by the time you arrive in Orlando.

Epcot

Grab a big pot. Stir in equal measures of theme park and museum, and then add movies and cultural exhibits. What do you have? **Epcot.** Think of Epcot as a trip around the world — without the jet lag, though some say it's just as draining if you try to experience it in one day.

Walt Disney wanted this "Experimental Prototype Community of Tomorrow" to be a high-tech city of 20,000 residents. But, when it was built 15 years after his death, it was more theme park than community. Epcot is divided into two sections. **World Showcase** lets you experience exotic, far-flung lands without a passport, or you can sit in a sidewalk cafe, munching some of the best pastries this side of Paris. In **Future World,** you can ride deeper into the third millennium aboard thrill rides or inside exhibits that use cutting-edge technology.

Of all the Disney parks, this one appeals least to younger children; it's better suited to the imaginations of older children and adults.

Future World

Most visitors enter **Epcot** through Future World, the northern section of the park (although it appears on the bottom of your guide map). Spaceship Earth, that thing that looks like a giant, silver golf ball, is at the center of Future World. Exhibits focus on scientific achievements, and technology, spanning areas from energy to undersea exploration.

Innoventions

The crescent-shaped buildings to your right and left, just beyond Spaceship Earth, showcase cutting-edge technology and future products. The headliner in the building to the left **(Innoventions East)** as you enter the park is House of Innoventions, which has a preview of tomorrow's smart house (including a refrigerator that can itemize and order groceries, and a picture frame that can store and send photos to other "smart frames"). There's also an exhibit on Future Cars. Across the way at **Innoventions West,** Sega is the major player, sponsoring dozens of stations at Video Games of Tomorrow. Nearby, Medicine's New Vision goes behind the scenes with exhibits such as 3-D body imaging.

The fountains inside Innovention Plaza, the courtyard that separates Innoventions East from West, perform water ballets to various Disney and New Age (think John Tesh and Yanni) musical selections every 15 minutes or so. At night, the streams of water are illuminated by more than 1,000 colored lights.

Imagination

Even the fountains in front of this pavilion are magical — shooting water snakes through the air. (The fountains are popular with kids, who like to try to catch the water snakes.)

The **Journey into Imagination** exhibit features *Figment*, a crazy-but-lovable purple dragon. Things begin with an open house at the Imagination Institute, with Dr. Nigel Channing (played by Monty Python's Eric Idle) taking you on a tour of the labs that demonstrate how the senses capture and control one's imagination. Figment arrives at each of the areas to prove it's far, far better to set your imagination free. He invites you to his upside-down house, where a new perspective enhances your imagination.

After you disembark from the ride, head for the **"What If"** labs, where your kids can burn lots of energy while exercising their imaginations at a number of interactive stations that allow them to conduct music and experiment with video.

The pavilion's main attraction is the 3-D **Honey I Shrunk the Audience** ride, based on the Disney film *Honey I Shrunk the Kids.* Inside, mice terrorize you and, after you're shrunk, a large cat adds to the trauma; then a giant 5-year-old gives you a good shaking. Vibrating seats and tactile effects enhance the 3-D action. Finally, everyone returns to proper size — but not the dog, who offers up one final surprise.

The Land

The Land is Future World's largest pavilion (a whopping 6 acres) and showcases the wonders of food and the environment. *Living with the Land,* a 14-minute boat ride through a simulated rain forest, an African desert, and the Great Plains may be a tad too dry for visitors not interested in agriculture. New farming methods and experiments ranging from hydroponics to plants growing in simulated Martian soil are showcased in real gardens.

A 45-minute *Behind the Seeds* walking tour for gardeners and others who want a more detailed agricultural lesson is offered daily and costs $8 for adults and $6 for kids 3 to 9. Sign up at the Green Thumb Emporium near the Sunshine Season Food Fair.

Live footage and animation mix in *Circle of Life,* a 15-minute, 70mm motion picture based on *The Lion King.* The story line has Timon and Pumbaa building a monument to the good life called Hakuna Matata Lakeside Village, but their project, as Simba points out, is damaging the savanna for other animals. It's a fun but pointed environmental message.

The long-running *Food Rocks* production was recently closed to make room for the new *Soarin'* ride. Borrowed from Disney's California Adventure park, where it's one of the more popular rides, the experience combines cinematic artistry and state-of-the-art motion technology as guests are seated in mock-gliders and lifted 40 feet inside a giant projection-screen dome. Completely surrounded with the beauty and wonder of the state of California, their elevated seats take them on a scenic tour over the Golden Gate Bridge, the Redwood forests, Napa Valley, Yosemite, and more. Guests can even feel the sweeping winds and smell fragrant orange blossoms and pine trees around them. It's definitely a one-of-a-kind experience and should not be missed, though the lines for this one can get *very* long. One has to wonder, though, why Disney isn't creating a Florida version of this ride because . . . well, Epcot *is* in Florida.

The Living Seas

The Living Seas pavilion has a 5.7-million-gallon aquarium filled with more than 4,000 sharks, barracudas, rays, dolphins, and other reef fish. It starts with a film, *The Seas,* demonstrating the formation of the Earth and the seas as a means to support life. You also can see other exhibits such as a diving barrel used by Alexander the Great in 332 B.C. and Sir Edmund Halley's first diving bell (1697). After the films, you enter "hydrolators" (a hokey elevator ride) and descend to the simulated ocean floor and Sea Base Alpha. The two-level base displays numerous exhibits dealing with various aspects of marine science and technology, and — most important of all — you get close-up views through acrylic windows of real denizens of the deep as they swim amidst a man-made coral reef. Both kids and adults enjoy visiting the rescued manatees (sea cows), which reside on the second level.

Be sure to check out the adorable **Turtle Talk with Crush,** which debuted at The Living Seas in late 2004. Crush (from *Finding Nemo*), chitchats with passersby from behind his undersea movie screen, engaging them in conversation and telling a joke or two. This is a first-of-its-kind attraction using digital projection and voice-activated animation to create a real-time experience. Your kids will get a huge kick out of it; you will, too.

Epcot's DiveQuest program enables certified adult divers to participate in a three-hour program that includes a 30-minute dive in the Living Seas aquarium. The program costs $140. Call ☎ **407-939-8687** for details. Keep in mind, however, that you get more for your money at **Discovery Cove** (later in this chapter) if you want to swim with the dolphins.

Test Track

Test Track is a $60 million marvel of a ride that combines GM engineering and Disney Imagineering. You can wait in line an hour or more during peak periods, so use FASTPASS. During the last part of your wait, you snake through displays about corrosion, crash tests, and more. The five-minute ride follows what looks to be an actual highway. It includes braking tests, a hill climb, and tight S-curves in a six-passenger "convertible." The left front seat offers the most thrills as the vehicle moves through the curves. There's also a 12-second burst of speed that's heart pumping to the tune of 65 mph on the straightaway (with no traffic!). It's the best thrill ride in Epcot.

Universe of Energy

Ellen's Energy Adventure, a 32-minute ride, features comedian Ellen DeGeneres as an energy expert tutored by Bill Nye (the Science Guy) to be a *Jeopardy!* contestant. An animated movie depicts the Earth's molten beginnings, its cooling, and the formation of fossil fuels. You then tour a 275-million-year-old, storm-wracked Earth where giant AudioAnimatronic dragonflies, pterodactyls, dinosaurs, earthquakes, and streams of molten lava surround you. The show ends with a vision of an energy-abundant future and Ellen as a new *Jeopardy!* champion.

Wonders of Life

The focus of the **Wonders of Life** pavilion (you can't miss the giant DNA strand that marks its entrance) is on health and biology.

The entire *Wonders of Life* pavilion began opening on a limited schedule (mostly during peak crowds to alleviate long lines on other rides) in January 2004, prompting speculation that a new exhibit may be installed here within the next few years.

The *Making of Me,* starring Martin Short, is a 15-minute film combining live action with animation and spectacular in utero photography to create a sweet introduction to the facts of life. Brief travels take visitors back in time to witness his parents as children, their meeting at a college dance, their wedding, and their decision to have a baby. Alongside Short, *Making of Me* visitors view his development inside his mother's womb and witness his birth.

The presentation may prompt some pointed questions from young children; therefore, I recommend it for ages 10 and older.

Didn't get your fill of being shrunk at *Imagination?* Haven't been shaken up enough on a simulator? Try *Body Wars,* where you're reduced to the size of a cell for a rescue mission inside a human's immune system (it reminds many sci-fi fans of the Isaac Asimov classic novel *Fantastic Voyage,* and the story line isn't all that different). This motion-simulator takes you on a wild ride through gale-force winds in the lungs and pounding heart chambers. It's nowhere near as cool as the similar *Star Tours* attraction at **Disney–MGM Studios** (later in this chapter), but is still fun.

Engineers designed this ride from the last row of the car, so that's the best place to sit to get the most bang for your buck.

In the hilarious *Cranium Command,* Buzzy, an animatronic brain-pilot-in-training in the Cranium Commando Squad, is charged with the daunting task of controlling the brain of Bobby, a 12-year-old boy, during adolescent traumas that include meeting a girl and a run-in with the principal. The audience is seemingly seated inside Bobby's head as Buzzy guides him through his day — and gets chewed out every now and then by his animated C.O., General Knowledge. Well-known actors and comedians, including Charles Grodin, Jon Lovitz, and Dana Carvey, play the boy's body parts. This must-see attraction has a very loyal fan following and is good for all ages.

Don't skip the very funny preshow film at this attraction as it sets up the action that happens inside. At *The Fitness Fairgrounds,* you can have your tennis, golf, or baseball swing analyzed by experts. You can also get a computer-generated evaluation of your health habits.

World Showcase

Adults and older kids with an appreciation of world history and cultural shows enjoy **World Showcase.** Its 11 miniature nations open at 11 a.m. daily and surround a 40-acre lagoon. All the showcase's countries have authentically indigenous architecture, landscaping, background music, restaurants, and shops. The nations' cultural facets are explored in art exhibits, song and dance performances, and innovative rides, films, and attractions. And all the employees in each pavilion are natives of the country represented.

Most of these nations offer some kind of live entertainment throughout the day. You may see acrobats, bagpipers, mariachi bands, storytellers, belly dancers, and stilt walkers. Characters regularly appear in the Showcase Plaza. Check your guide map/show schedule when you enter the park. You can also find schedules posted near the entrance to each country.

Those with kids should grab a copy of the *Epcot Kids' Guide* at *Guest Relations* upon entering the park; it uses a "K" in a red square to note **Kidcot Fun Stops** inside the **World Showcase.** These play and learning stations are for the younger set and allow them to stop at various World Showcase countries, do crafts, get autographs, have Kidcot passports stamped (these are available for purchase in most Epcot stores and make a great souvenir), and chat with cast members native to those countries. Your kids get the chance to learn about different countries and make a souvenir to bring home. For more information, stop in at *Guest Relations* when you get into the park. The stations open at 1 p.m. daily.

Finally, excellent shopping and dining opportunities are available at all the pavilions. For details on dining inside the **World Showcase,** see Chapter 17.

Canada

The pavilion's highlight attraction is *O Canada!* — a dazzling, 18-minute, 360-degree CircleVision film that shows our northern neighbor's scenic wonders, from sophisticated Montréal to the thundering flight of thousands of snow geese departing the St. Lawrence River.

The theater has no seats, and you stand for the entire production (though there are lean rails).

The architecture and landscape in **Canada** include a mansard-roofed replica of Ottawa's 19th-century Château Laurier (here called the Hôtel du Canada) and an Indian village complete with 30-foot replicas of Ojibwa totem poles. The Canadian wilderness is reflected by a rocky mountain (really made of concrete and chicken wire); a waterfall cascading into a white-water stream; and a miniforest of evergreens, stately cedars, maples, and birch trees. Don't miss the stunning floral display inspired by Victoria's world-renowned Butchart Gardens. *Off Kilter* entertains visitors with New Age Celtic music.

China

You enter **Epcot**'s version of **China** through a triple-arched ceremonial gate inspired by the Temple of Heaven in Beijing, a summer retreat for Chinese emperors. Passing through the gate, you'll see a half-size replica of this ornately embellished red-and-gold circular temple, built in 1420 during the Ming dynasty. Gardens simulate those at Suzhou, with miniature waterfalls, lotus ponds, and bamboo groves.

Inside the temple, you can watch *Reflections of China,* a 20-minute, 360-degree CircleVision film (it debuted in spring 2003) that explores the culture and landscapes in and around seven Chinese cities. Shot over a two-month period in 2002, it visits Beijing, Shanghai, and the Great Wall (begun 24 centuries ago!), among other places.

Like Canada, the theater here has no seats, and you stand for the entire production (though there are lean rails).

Land of Many Faces is an exhibit that introduces China's ethnic peoples, and entertainment is provided daily by the amazing *Dragon Legend Acrobats.*

France

This pavilion focuses on **France**'s Belle Époque (Beautiful Age) — the period from 1870 to 1910 — when art, literature, and architecture ruled. You enter via a replica of the beautiful cast-iron Pont des Arts footbridge over the Seine and find yourself in a park with bleached sycamores, Bradford pear trees, flowering crape myrtle, and sculptured parterre flower gardens inspired by Seurat's painting *A Sunday Afternoon on the Island of La Grande Jatte.* The grounds also include a ¹⁄₁₀-scale model of the Eiffel Tower, which was built from Gustave Eiffel's original blueprints.

The premiere attraction here is *Impressions de France.* Shown in the palatial *Palais du Cinema,* a sit-down theater à la Fontainebleau, this 18-minute film is a journey through diverse French landscapes projected on a vast, 200-degree wraparound screen and enhanced by the music of French composers. Outside, grab a yummy French pastry and watch the antics of *Serveur Amusant,* a comedic waiter, or the visual comedy of *Le Mime Roland.*

Germany

Enclosed by castle walls, **Germany** offers 'wursts, oompah bands, and a rollicking atmosphere. The clock tower in the central *platz* (plaza) is embellished with a glockenspiel that heralds each hour with quaint melodies. The Biergarten was inspired by medieval Rothenberg, while 16th-century building façades replicate a merchant's hall in the Black Forest and the town hall in Frankfurt's Römerberg Square.

If you're a model-train fanatic or visiting with young kids, don't miss the exquisitely detailed version of a small Bavarian town, complete with working train station, located between *Germany* and *Italy.*

Italy

Italy lures visitors over an arched stone footbridge to a replica of Venice's intricately ornamented pink-and-white Doge's Palace. Other architectural highlights include the 83-foot *Campanile* (bell tower) of St. Mark's Square, Venetian bridges, and a piazza enclosing a version of Bernini's Neptune Fountain. A garden wall suggests a backdrop of provincial countryside, and citrus, cypress, pine, and olive trees frame a formal garden. Gondolas are moored on the lagoon.

In the street-entertainment department, the seemingly lifeless forms of *Imaginum, A Statue Act* fascinate visitors young and old daily, and the hilarious *World Showcase Players,* who, at press time, were seen spoofing Shakespeare's Italian-set *Taming of the Shrew* here.

Japan

A flaming-red *torii* (gate of honor) on the banks of the lagoon and the graceful blue-roofed Goju No To pagoda, inspired by an 8th-century shrine built at Nara, welcome you to the **Japan** pavilion, which focuses on Japan's ancient culture. If you have some leisure time, enjoy the exquisitely cultivated Japanese garden — it's a haven of tranquility in a place that's anything but, and 90 percent of the plants you see are actually native to Japan. The Shishinden is inspired by the ceremonial and coronation hall found in the Imperial Palace grounds at Kyoto, and the *Bijutsu-kan Gallery* offers rotating exhibits ranging from 18th-century Bunraki puppets to Japanese baseball.

Make sure that you include a performance of traditional Taiko drumming by *Matsuriza,* which entertains guests daily. Japanese storytellers offer up native tales every now and then.

Mexico

The music of mariachi bands greets you at **Mexico's** festive showcase, fronted by a Mayan pyramid modeled on the Aztec temple of Quetzalcoatl (God of Life) and surrounded by dense Yucatán jungle landscaping. Just inside the pavilion's entrance, a museum exhibits rare Oaxacan wood sculptures. Also inside the pyramid is *El Rio del Tiempo* (River of Time), an eight-minute cruise through Mexico's past and present (the audio-animatronic dolls you encounter en route may remind you of those in the Magic Kingdom's *It's a Small World*). Along the river route, passengers get a close-up look at the Mayan pyramid and the erupting Popocatepetl volcano.

Mariachi Cobre, a 12-piece mariachi ensemble, performs Tuesday through Saturday.

Morocco

A replica of the world-famous Koutoubia Minaret, the prayer tower of a 12th-century mosque in Marrakesh, overlooks the very atmospheric pavilion of **Morocco,** featuring the architectural styles of several cities inside the North African kingdom. The exotic ambience is enhanced by geometrically patterned tile work, hand-painted wood ceilings, and brass lighting fixtures. The *Medina* (old city), entered via a replica of an arched gateway in Fez, leads to a traditional Moroccan home and the narrow, winding streets of the *souk,* a bustling marketplace where authentic handicrafts are on display. The Medina's courtyard centers on a replica of the ornately tiled Najjarine Fountain in Fez.

 King Hassan II of Morocco took a personal interest in the pavilion when it was built and dispatched royal artisans to assist in its construction. Note the imperfections left in each mosaic tile; they were put there on purpose in accordance with the Muslim belief that only Allah is perfect.

The *Gallery of Arts and History* contains ever-changing exhibits of Moroccan art. A guided tour of the pavilion, *Treasures of Morocco,* runs three times daily. (Check your show schedule.) Speaking of shows, the band *Mo'Rockin'* kicks things up with Arabian rock music on traditional instruments.

Norway

The **Norway** pavilion's stave church, located off a charming cobblestone plaza and styled after the 13th-century Gol Church of Hallingdal, features changing exhibits focusing on Norwegian art and culture. A replica of Oslo's 14th-century Akershus Castle is the setting for the pavilion's restaurant. Other buildings simulate the red-roofed cottages of Bergen and the timber-sided farm buildings of the Nordic woodlands.

Norway includes a two-part attraction. *Maelstrom,* a boat ride in a dragon-headed Viking vessel, travels Norway's fjords and mythical forests to the music of *Peer Gynt.* Along the way, you see polar bears prowling the shore and are turned into frogs by trolls that cast a spell on your boat. The watercraft crashes through a narrow gorge (two small separate drops) and spins into the North Sea, where a storm is in progress. (Don't worry — this is a relatively calm ride, though some of the thunder elements may frighten the very young.) The storm abates, a princess's kiss turns you into a human again, and you disembark to a 10th-century Viking village to view the 70mm film *Norway,* highlighting history and culture (you can proceed through the theater to the exit if you don't want to watch the film).

United Kingdom

The **United Kingdom** pavilion evokes Merry Olde England through its *Britannia Square* — a London-style park complete with copper-roofed gazebo bandstand, a stereotypical red phone booth (it really works!), an old-fashioned pub, a thatched cottage, and a statue of the Bard. Four centuries of architecture — from the Tudor era all the way through the English Regency period — line cobblestone streets. In the horticulture department, there's a formal garden with low box hedges in geometric patterns, and the flagstone paths and a stone fountain replicating the landscaping of 16th- and 17th-century palaces.

Don't miss *The British Invasion,* a group that impersonates the Beatles; vivacious pub pianist Pam Brody; and Jason Wethington, a pub magician who offers up Disney magic of the sleight-of-hand variety.

U.S.A.: The American Adventure

This flagship pavilion's main building is a 108,000-square-foot Georgian mansion and occupies the central spot in the **World Showcase.** Notable U.S. landmarks that inspired Disney's Imagineers in the design of the building include Independence Hall, Monticello, and Colonial Williamsburg. The action takes place in an elegant, colonial-style, 1,024-seat theater loaded with Corinthian columns, chandeliers, elegant fabrics, and 12 marble statues symbolizing the 12 "Spirits of America." The flags you pass under as you enter the theater — 44 in all — include every one that has flown over the United States throughout its history.

The actual production, a 29-minute CliffsNotes version of U.S. history, features rousing music and a large cast of lifelike audio-animatronic figures, including narrators Mark Twain and Ben Franklin. You follow the voyage of the *Mayflower,* watch Jefferson writing the *Declaration of Independence,* and witness Matthew Brady photographing a family that the Civil War is about to divide. You can also witness Pearl Harbor and the *Eagle* going to the moon. Teddy Roosevelt discusses the need for national parks; Susan B. Anthony speaks out on women's rights; Frederick Douglass discusses slavery; and Chief Joseph talks about the plight of Native Americans. It's one of Disney's best historical productions.

Entertainment includes the *Spirit of America Fife & Drum Corps* and the *Voices of Liberty* a cappella group, which sings patriotic songs in the lobby of the main theater between shows. Large-scale outdoor productions are often staged in the *America Gardens Theatre,* a 1,800-seat outdoor venue across from the main pavilion building.

Ending your day at Epcot

Epcot's end-of-day celebration, **IllumiNations,** is a moving blend of fireworks, lasers, and fountains in a display that's signature Disney. The show is worth the crowds that flock to the parking lot when it's over (just be sure to keep a firm grip on young kids).

 You can find tons of good viewing points around the lagoon (one excellent spot is the terrace at the Rose & Crown Pub in the United Kingdom pavilion). That said, it's best to stake your claim to a primo place a half-hour or so before show time, which is listed in your entertainment schedule.

Disney–MGM Studios

Anyone who loves movies will enjoy wandering the realistic streets, shops, sets, and back lots of this 110-acre combination theme park and working studio. Filming is done here throughout the year, so you never know whether you're seeing slapstick or an actual taping. Stroll the neighborhoods, which include Hollywood and Sunset boulevards, where Art Deco movie sets recall the golden age of Hollywood. New York Street is lined with miniature renditions of the Empire State and Chrysler buildings. It's also an impromptu stage for street performers.

Checking out the best of Disney–MGM

Unlike the Magic Kingdom and Epcot, you can pretty much see **Disney–MGM**'s 110 acres of attractions in one day if you arrive early. Here's a rundown of the best Disney–MGM has to offer:

- ✓ **Backstage Pass:** This uses sets from occasionally changing shows and movies to give you a 25-minute, yawn-able tour of a production facility. It's a good one to skip if time is a factor.

- ✓ *Beauty and the Beast Live on Stage:* A 1,500-seat, covered amphitheater provides the stage for this 25-minute, live Broadway-style production of *Beauty and the Beast* adapted from the movie version. Musical highlights include the rousing "Be Our Guest" opening number and the poignant title song, featured in a romantic waltz-scene finale. Arrive early to get a good seat.

- ✓ **Disney–MGM Studios Backlot Tour:** This 35-minute behind-the-scenes tour starts on foot and then you board a tram for a ride through Disney's costume department, sets from popular (and not-so-popular) TV shows and movies, and the domain of special-effects wizards. The best comes when you reach Catastrophe Canyon, where an "earthquake" causes a tanker truck to explode, rocking the tram. Then a very large, *very wet* wave throws 70,000 gallons of water at you — some people do get doused.

- ✓ **The Great Movie Ride:** A slow journey down MGM's memory lane, it uses animatronic versions of Jimmy Cagney, John Wayne, and Clint Eastwood to re-create some of their most memorable roles. Live bandits then show up and blow up the bank on the set. One of the bad guys kidnaps you and your mates, but he runs into the space thing from *Alien.* Younger children could be frightened, and older teens will be bored with this ride.

- ✓ *Honey, I Shrunk the Kids* **Movie Set:** An 11,000-square-foot playground where everything is larger than life, it has a 30-foot-tall thicket of grass, three-stories-high mushroom caps, and a friendly ant that makes a suitable seat. Play areas include a 52-foot garden hose with leaks, cereal loops that are 9-feet wide and cushioned for jumping, and a waterfall that cascades from a leaf to a dell of fern sprouts. It's great for small children.

- ✓ *Indiana Jones Epic Stunt Spectacular: Spectacular* is a good word for this 30-minute extravaganza, *guaran-double-teed* to keep you on the edge of your seat. The show is held in a big, open-air pavilion and uses some adult volunteers. It begins with Indy rappelling down from the rafters, and the nifty special effects soon have him dodging spikes, falling into a pit of molten something-or-other, and then outrunning fire, steam, and a large boulder that nearly flattens him — all before the first commercial break. It may be a little intense for kids under 6.

✔ ***Jim Henson's Muppet*Vision 3-D:*** This in-your-face, 25-minute spectacle allows the humor of the late Jim Henson to live on through Miss Piggy, Kermit, and the gang. A delight for all ages, this production mixes 3-D effects and sensory gags with puppets and live-action characters. You'll encounter flying Muppets, cream pies, and cannonballs, as well as high winds, fiber-optic fireworks, bubble showers, and even an actual spray of water.

✔ **The Magic of Disney Animation:** Disney characters come alive at the stroke of a brush or pencil as you tour glass-walled animation studios. Walter Cronkite and Robin Williams explain what's going on via video monitors. They also star in a very funny eight-minute Peter Pan–themed film about the basics of animation. The 35-minute tour, recommended for ages 8 and up, also includes a grand finale of magical moments from classic Disney films.

✔ **Lights, Motors, Action! Extreme Stunt Show:** Inspired by the popular *Stunt Show Spectacular* at Disneyland Paris, this high-octane stunt show features specially designed cars, motorcycles and jet skis, plus special effects — with audience members pulled into the fun. Insiders will reveal show secrets, detailing how stunts are created, designed, and filmed for the movies. Filmed images are revealed on an oversized screen, illustrating how the use of different camera angles can add drama to filmed scenes. It's entertaining and certainly offers its share of thrills, but it's not as engaging as the Indiana Jones production unless you're a car buff. The new show is part of a larger redevelopment of the back-lot area of Disney–MGM Studios, which has added new cityscapes for Chicago and San Francisco to the existing New York City skyline.

✔ ***Playhouse Disney — Live on Stage!*** Younger audiences (2 to 8 years old) love this 20-minute show, where they meet characters from *Bear in the Big Blue House, The Book of Pooh,* and other stories. The show encourages preschoolers to dance, sing, and play along with the cast. Check your show schedule for times.

✔ **Rock 'n' Roller Coaster:** Wow! This inverted roller coaster — the fastest off the line in Orlando — is one of the best thrill rides that Walt Disney World has to offer and is certainly not for younger kids or folks with neck or back problems, faint hearts, or a tendency toward motion sickness. Fast and furious, this indoor ride puts you in a 24-passenger stretch limo, outfitted with 120 speakers that blare Aerosmith at 32,000 watts. Faster than you can scream, "Stop the music!" (around 2.8 seconds, actually), you shoot from 0 to 60 mph and into the first inversion at 5 Gs. *Riders must be at least 48 inches tall.*

Sounds Dangerous Starring Drew Carey: Drew Carey (on film) provides laughs while dual audio technology provides some incredible hair-raising effects during a 12-minute mixture of movie and live action at ABC Sound Studios. You feel like you're right in the middle of the action of a TV pilot featuring undercover police work and plenty of amusing mishaps. Even when the picture disappears, you continue the chase via headphones that demonstrate "3-D" sound effects such as a roomful of angry bees, a herd of galloping elephants, and a deafening auto race.

Most of the show takes place in total darkness, so you may want to think twice before bringing really young children here.

✔ **Star Tours:** Your journey to a place far, far away begins with a winding walk (a line) through a bunch of *Star Wars* 'droids and a preride warning about high turbulence, sharp drops, and sudden turns. Star Tours is a virtual ride where you go nowhere, but you feel like you do. The ride starts kind of slow, but it finishes fast, as you soar through space in a good-guy fighter, with R2-D2 and C-3PO helping you make passes through the canals of Lord Vader's mother ship. *Riders must be at least 40 inches tall.*

✔ *The Twilight Zone* **Tower of Terror:** If you like leaving your stomach at several levels, you'll love this ride. Its legend says that during a violent storm on Halloween night 1939, lightning struck the Hollywood Tower Hotel, causing an entire wing and an elevator full of people to disappear. And you're about to meet them as you star in a special episode of *The Twilight Zone.* After various spooky adventures, the ride ends in a dramatic climax: a terrifying, 13-story free-fall into *The Twilight Zone!* At 199-feet, it's the tallest Walt Disney World attraction. *You must be 40 inches tall to ride.*

✔ *Voyage of the Little Mermaid:* Hazy lighting helps paint a picture of an underwater world in a 17-minute show that combines live performances, movie clips, puppetry, and special effects. Sebastian sings "Under the Sea," Ariel performs "Part of Your World," and the evil, tentacled Ursula, 12 feet tall and 10 feet wide, belts out "Poor Unfortunate Soul."

✔ *Who Wants to Be a Millionaire* — **Play It:** Forget about winning $1 million — it ain't happening here — but contestants earn points for prizes ranging from collectible pins to a trip to New York to meet Regis Philbin. Based on Disney-owned ABC TV's game show, the theme-park version features lifelines (such as asking the audience or calling a stranger on two phones set up in the park). Contestants get a shot at up to 15 multiple-choice questions in the climb to the top. Games run continuously in the 600-seat studio. Audience members play along on keypads. The fastest to answer qualifying questions become contestants.

Parades and fireworks

It's hard not to be in awe of the choreography, laser lights, and fireworks that are the core of **Fantasmic!,** a 25-minute extravaganza. Shooting comets, great balls of fire, and animated fountains are among the special effects that really amaze the audience. The cast includes 50 performers, a giant dragon, a king cobra, and 1 million gallons of water — most of it orchestrated by a sorcerer mouse who looks very familiar. The ample amphitheater holds 9,000 souls. If you want to avoid a real traffic jam after the show, arrive up to an hour early and sit on the right (the theater empties right to left).

A dinner package available at The Hollywood Brown Derby, Mama Melrose's Italian Ristorante, and Hollywood & Vine Café allows you preferred seating at Fantasmic! There's no extra charge — just eat entrees at one of the restaurants before the show, and you can wiggle into a reserved seating area right up until ten minutes before show time, though it's not a specific seat. You can only make arrangements for the package at Guest Relations in the park or at a Disney resort, and you must tell the reservation taker you want the Fantasmic! package.

Animal Kingdom

The biggest knock against Disney's fourth theme park is that seeing the animals is sometimes difficult. Because the park is as animal-friendly as it is people-friendly, the wildlife can escape the heat, and your view, if they choose. However, if your timing is right, you'll see African lions, giraffes, cheetahs, white rhinos, lowland gorillas, and hippos. You'll also bump into some that may be new to you, such as bongos (the antelopes, not the drums) and naked mole rats.

Your best bet for animal viewing is to arrive in time for the park's opening (usually 8 a.m., but sometimes an hour earlier) or to come here around closing or during winter cold spells. Like Magic Kingdom, this park has several areas, or *lands.*

The Oasis

Your introduction to Animal Kingdom, The Oasis is one of the better places to see animals early in the day. The lush vegetation, streams, grottoes, and waterfalls on either side of the walkway are good places to spot wallabies, miniature deer, anteaters, sloths, iguanas, tree kangaroos, otters, and macaws.

Discovery Island

After you pass through The Oasis, head straight onto Discovery Island, which is the hub for Animal Kingdom's five lands. This is another animal-viewing area, where you may see wood ducks, flamingos, kangaroos, and small-clawed otters.

Here are a couple of the highlights in this section of the park:

✔ **It's Tough to Be a Bug!** Take the walkway through the Tree of Life's 50-foot base, grab a pair of 3-D glasses, and settle into a sometimes creepy-crawly seat. Based on the Disney-Pixar film, *A Bug's Life,* the special effects in this multimedia adventure are pretty impressive. Although it may not be a good choice for kids under 4 (it's dark and loud) or bug haters, this attraction is a fun and sometimes-poignant look at life from a smaller perspective. The stars include ants, beetles, spiders, and — oh, no! — a stinkbug.

✔ **Tree of Life:** Fourteen stories tall, this man-made tree and its carved animals are the work of Disney artists, who worked for over a year on its carved, free-form animal sculptures. It's impressive, with 8,000 limbs, 103,000 leaves, and 325 mammals, reptiles, amphibians, bugs, birds, dinosaurs, and Mickeys carved into its trunk, limbs, and roots.

Camp Minnie-Mickey

Youngsters love this place. It's a favorite hangout for several Disney characters from the forest and jungle, including Simba from *The Lion King* and Baloo from *The Jungle Book.* Mickey, Minnie, Goofy, Pluto, Donald, Daisy, and a variety of other stars also make appearances from time to time around this woody retreat, which resembles an Adirondack summer camp. The big guns here are as follows:

✔ *Festival of the Lion King:* Held at the Lion King Theater, this rousing 28-minute show is the best in Animal Kingdom and one of the top three shows in all of Orlando's theme parks. The several-times-per-day extravaganza celebrates nature's diversity with a talented, colorfully attired cast of singers, dancers, and life-size critters that lead the way to an inspiring sing-along. The action takes place onstage and around the audience.

✔ *Pocahontas and Her Forest Friends:* The wait to see *Pocahontas and Her Forest Friends* can be nightmarish, and the 15-minute show isn't close to the caliber of *Festival of the Lion King* and *Tarzan Rocks!* (later in this chapter). In this show, Pocahontas, Grandmother Willow, and some forest creatures hammer home the importance of treating nature with respect.

Africa

Enter through the town of Harambe, which means "coming together" in Swahili. Costumed employees greet you as you enter the buildings. The whitewashed structures, built of coral stone and thatched with reed brought from Africa, surround a central marketplace, rich with local wares and colors. The best attractions here include the following:

✔ **Kilimanjaro Safaris:** This attraction is one of the few rides and the best animal-viewing venue in this kingdom. But remember what I told you about the animals being scarce during the middle of the day, especially in the heat of summer. After you hit the end of the line, you board a large truck, and then you're off on a bouncy ride through what pretends to be Africa. The animals are real and include black rhinos, hippos, Nile crocodiles, zebras, wildebeests, and lions.

Arrive early! Lines can be an hour long or worse. Definitely consider using FASTPASS, unless you can get there within 15 minutes of the park's opening.

✔ **Pangani Falls Exploration Trail:** You can get a pretty good look at birds and the ever-active mole rats along the trail, but the gorillas — including a silverback with his family — are the main event. Lines that grow to three or more people deep, when animals do materialize, can also make viewing difficult.

✔ **Rafiki's Planet Watch:** This area of Africa includes Conservation Station, which offers a look at how Disney cares for animals inside the park. You'll walk past a series of nurseries and veterinarian stations. The problem is that these facilities need staff in order to be interesting and there is no guarantee that anyone will be working when you visit. Affection Section gives you a chance to cuddle some friendly animals (including goats and pot-belly pigs), while Habitat Habit! is home to some smaller animals, such as cotton-top tamarinds.

Asia

Disney's Imagineers have outdone themselves in creating the mythical kingdom of Anadapour. The intricately painted artwork at the front is appealing, and it also helps make the lines seem to move a little faster. Also, watch for (with little prior announcement) the appearance of local youngsters performing Asian dances. Here is a list of the top attractions:

✔ *Flights of Wonder:* Mixing live-animal action with a Disney character show, *Flights of Wonder* has undergone several transformations since the park opened. It's a low-key break that has a few laughs, but it's not much by bird-show standards.

✔ **Kali River Rapids:** White-water fanatics will scoff, but for a theme-park raft ride, it's pretty good — slightly better, than Congo River Rapids at Busch Gardens (see Chapter 14), but not as good as Popeye & Bluto's Bilge-Rat Barges in Islands of Adventure (later in this chapter). Its churning water mimics real rapids, and optical illusions make you wonder if you're about to go over the falls. You *will* get wet. And lines are frequently long. *This ride has a 38-inch height minimum.*

✔ **Maharajah Jungle Trek:** Disney keeps its promise to provide up-close views of animals with this exhibit. If you don't show up in the midday heat, you'll see Bengal tigers through the thick glass. Nothing but air divides you from dozens of giant fruit bats hanging in what appears to be a courtyard. (If you have a phobia, you can bypass this area, but the bats are harmless.) Komodo dragons, gibbons, and other monkeys might also be on view.

Dinoland U.S.A.

Here's Disney's attempt to capitalize on the dinosaur craze inspired by *Jurassic Park* and other films. To enter this area, you pass under Olden Gate Bridge, a 40-foot-tall Brachiosaurus reassembled from excavated fossils. Until late summer 1999, *Dinoland* had three paleontologists working on the very real skeleton of *Sue,* a monstrously big Tyrannosaurus rex unearthed in the Black Hills of South Dakota in 1990. The paleontologists patched and assembled the bones here, mainly because **Disney** helped pay for the project. Alas, *Sue* has moved to her permanent home at The Field Museum in Chicago, but a cast replica of her 67-million-year-old bones, called *Dino-Sue* on the handout guide maps, is on display.

Here are Dinoland's best attractions:

✔ **The Boneyard:** Kids love this play area, and it's a great place for parents to catch a second wind. Little ones can slide and climb over a simulated paleontology site, and they can squeeze through the fossils and skeletons of a triceratops and a brontosaurus.

✔ **Dinosaur:** This ride hurls you through darkness in a CTX Rover time machine, past snarling dinosaurs that are a little hokey. It's far from a smooth ride, and some kids may find the dinosaurs and darkness frightening. However, Dinosaur is as close as Animal Kingdom comes to a thrill ride — a herky-jerky, twisting-turning ride in which you and 20 other passengers try to save the last dinosaur worth saving. *Riders must be at least 40 inches tall.*

✔ **Primeval Whirl:** Although this twin, carnival-style coaster doesn't have inversions, it does have a lot of spinning action in rider-controlled cars that whirl by asteroids and dinosaurs that pop up along the track. The ride has tight loops, short dips, and a final spin that sends you into the gaping jaws of a fossilized dinosaur. *Primeval Whirl has a 48-inch height minimum.*

✔ *Tarzan Rocks!* This 28-minute, several-times-per-day show pulses with music and occasional aerial theatrics. Phil Collins's movie soundtrack supports a cast of 27, including tumblers and in-line skating daredevils who really get the audience into the act. The costumes and music are spectacular, second in Animal Kingdom only to *Festival of the Lion King* in Camp Minnie-Mickey (earlier in this section).

✔ **Triceratops Spin:** The principle is pretty much the same as The Magic Carpets of Aladdin and Dumbo the Flying Elephant at WDW's Magic Kingdom (earlier in this chapter). In this case, cars that look like cartoon dinosaurs are attached to arms that circle a hub while moving up and down and all around. Most children age 2 to 6 love it.

Universal Orlando: An Overview

Team Universal's original park, **Universal Studios Florida,** is similar to Disney–MGM Studios in that it spends a ton of time and money to plug its movies and characters. Here, that means visitors get a healthy dose of *Earthquake, Terminator, Back to the Future, Jaws, E.T.,* and more. Its second park, **Islands of Adventure,** rules Orlando in thrill rides, thanks to Dueling Dragons, Incredible Hulk Coaster, Jurassic Park River Adventure, and Dudley Do-Right's Ripsaw Falls.

Single-day tickets cost $59.75 for adults, $48 for kids 3 to 9. That total doesn't include the 6 percent sales tax or, if you're driving to the park, the $8 parking charge. For more information on tickets and on Universal's multiday passes call ☎ **800-711-0080** or 407-363-8000 or visit www.universal orlando.com on the Web.

One multiday, multi-park option is the **FlexTicket.** This is the most economical way to see the various "other-than-Disney" parks. With the FlexTicket, you pay one price to visit any of the participating parks during a 14-day period. A four-park pass to Universal Studios Florida, Islands of Adventure, Wet 'n' Wild, and SeaWorld is $184.95 for adults and $150.95 for children 3 to 9. A five-park pass, which adds Busch Gardens in Tampa, is $224.95 for adults and $189.95 for kids.

Universal Express is a line-beating program for guests staying at Universal Orlando resorts. Under the three-tiered system, guests of the **Portofino Bay, Hard Rock,** and **Royal Pacific** hotels (see Chapter 17) only need to show their room keys to get at or near the front of the line for most rides. Multiday ticket buyers can go to special kiosks in the two parks and make reservations on up to three rides at a time, getting two windows of time in which to return for each. Guests can make more reservations when those are used or expire. Single-day ticket holders can make one reservation at a time.

Universal Studios Florida

Universal matches Disney stride for stride, and in some cases is a half-step ahead, when it comes to cutting-edge rides. Real as well as virtual thrills, terrific special effects, mammoth screens, and 3-D action are part of its successful mix. The rides and shows at Universal are located in six zones: Hollywood, New York, Production Central, San Francisco/Amity, Woody Woodpecker's KidZone, and World Expo.

Hollywood

This area is to the right of the Front Lot, where you enter. The main streets are Rodeo Drive, Hollywood Boulevard, and Sunset Boulevard. Here's a list of the best that Hollywood has to offer:

- ✔ **Terminator 2: 3-D Battle Across Time:** This attraction is billed as "the quintessential sight and sound experience for the 21st century!" Live actors and six giant Cyborgs interact with Arnie, who appears onscreen (actually there are three huge screens). The 3-D effects are among the best in Orlando. (When liquid mercury falls from the screen, cold water hits your legs.) It's a must-see, but little kids may find it a bit intense. *This show is rated PG-13.*

- ✔ **The Gory, Gruesome & Grotesque Horror Make-up Show:** At this show, you'll get a behind-the-scenes look at how monster makeup is done, including the transformation scenes from such movies as *The Fly. This show is rated PG-13.*

- ✔ **Lucy: A Tribute:** If you loved Lucille Ball, you'll adore viewing these exhibits, which include classic shows, costumes, scripts and even rare home movies.

New York

New York is near the back of the park and includes rides and shows along 42nd and 57th streets, Park Avenue, and Delancy Street. The premiere attraction in this section is **Twister — Ride It Out.** The curtain rises in the movie town of Wakita, where Universal engineers have created a five-story funnel cloud by injecting 2 million cubic feet of air per minute (enough to fill four full-size blimps). Power lines spark and fall, an oak splits, and the storm rumbles at a rock-concert level as cars, trucks, and a cow fly about, while the audience watches from just 20 feet away. In the finale, the floor begins to buckle at your feet. *This show is rated PG-13.*

The Big Gorilla has lost out to a mummy. Park favorite **Kongfrontation,** a ride that had been at Universal since its opening, closed in 2003 to make room for *Revenge of the Mummy,* an indoor roller coaster based on The Scorpion King from *The Mummy Returns.* Billed as a "psychological thrill ride," the $40 million indoor roller coaster relies on speed, pyrotechnics, and robotics to induce screams as riders hurtle through Egyptian sets, passageways, and tombs in cars that move forward and in reverse. Even the preshow for the waiting victims — riders, I mean riders — lends to the ominous atmosphere and includes several surprise interactive areas and a story line that plays out as you get closer to boarding the ride.

The five-minute journey aims to prey on one's inner phobias via encounters with overhead flames, pitch black darkness, insects. and a skeletal warrior that hops aboard your coaster.

Production Central

Production Central is directly behind and to the left of the Front Lot. Its main thoroughfares are Nickelodeon Way and Seventh and Eighth avenues. Here are some of the area's highlights:

✔ **Nickelodeon Studios:** Tour the soundstages where Nick shows are produced, see concept pilots, visit the kitchen where Gak and green slime are made, and try new Sega video games. This 45-minute behind-the-scenes tour is a fun escape, and there's a lot of audience participation. One child volunteer always gets slimed.

The tour usually doesn't open until at least 11 a.m., sometimes noon.

✔ **Shrek 4-D:** In this fractured, 4-D fairytale you will be able to see, hear, and smell the adventure thanks to motion simulators, OgreVision glasses, and other special effects, including spritzes of water. The attraction picks up where the movie left off, letting you join Shrek and Princess Fiona on their honeymoon. The preride features the ghostly return of the vertically challenged Lord Farquaad.

✔ **Jimmy Neutron's Rocket Ride:** This spinning, careening adventure has you battling Yokians — evil, egg-shaped aliens — on a journey in which you also encounter cartoon favorites such as SpongeBob SquarePants and the Rugrats.

San Francisco

This L-shaped zone faces the waterfront, and its attractions line The Embarcadero and Amity Avenue. Here are some highlights:

✔ **Earthquake — The Big One:** Sparks fly shortly after you board a BART train. The whopper — 8.3 on the Richter scale! — hits as you pull into the Embarcadero Station, and you're trapped as a propane truck bursts into flames, a runaway train comes hurtling at you, and the station floods (65,000 gallons of water cascade down the steps, but not onto passengers).

✔ **Jaws:** As your boat heads into a 7-acre, 5-million-gallon lagoon, an ominous dorsal fin appears on the horizon. What follows is a series of attacks from a 3-ton, 32-foot-long, mechanical great white shark that tries to sink its urethane teeth into your hide — or at least into your boat's hide. A 30-foot wall of flame, caused by burning fuel, surrounds the boat in this loud, $45-million attraction.

✔ *The Wild, Wild, Wild West Stunt Show:* Stunt people demonstrate falls from three-story balconies, gun and whip fights, dynamite explosions, and other Wild West staples. This is a well-performed, lively show that's especially popular with foreign visitors who have celluloid visions of the American West.

Woody Woodpecker's KidZone

This section of the park contains rides and attractions sure to please the littlest members of your party. If you're traveling with a number of youngsters, plan on spending a lot of time here. Here's an A-list list of kid-friendly attractions:

✔ *A Day in the Park with Barney:* Set in a parklike theater-in-the-round, this 25-minute musical stars the Purple One, Baby Bop, and BJ. It uses song, dance, and interactive play to deliver an environmental message. This show can be the highlight of your youngster's day. Next door, the playground has treehouses to explore plus lots of other things to intrigue little visitors.

✔ *E.T. Adventure:* Soar with E.T. on a mission to save his ailing planet, traveling through the forest and into space aboard a star-bound bicycle. You also meet some new characters Steven Spielberg created for the ride, including Botanicus, Tickli Moot Moot, Horn Flowers, and Tympani Tremblies.

✔ **Woody Woodpecker's Nuthouse Coaster:** This is the top attraction in the KidZone. Sure, it's a kids' ride, but the Nuthouse Coaster will thrill some moms and dads, too. Although it's only 30 feet at its peak, it offers quick, corkscrew turns while you sit in a miniature steam train. It's the same kind of ride as the Barnstormer at Goofy's Wiseacre Farm in the Magic Kingdom.

The ride only lasts 50 seconds, and waits can be 30 minutes, but few kids will let you miss it.

If you're looking for more to do in Woody Woodpecker's KidZone, **Fievel's Playland** is a wet, Western-themed playground with a house to climb and a small water slide. **Curious George Goes to Town** has water- and ball-shooting cannons plus a huge water tower that empties (after an alarm), drenching anyone who doesn't run for cover. Nearby, *Animal Planet Live!* offers an amusing 20-minute, behind-the-scenes look at the Animal Planet Network with a heart-warming multimedia show starring a host of furry actors (many of them rescued from shelters or pounds before getting their big break).

World Expo

The smallest zone in Universal Studios Florida offers a lot of punch in its two rides. World Expo is on Exposition Boulevard, between San Francisco/Amity and KidZone. The dual highlights are as follows:

✔ *Back to the Future — The Ride:* This attraction offers a chance at time travel in a simulator that looks like a DeLorean. Six to eight of you are packed into a car, after a video briefing from Christopher Lloyd, also known as Dr. Emmett Brown. Biff the Bully has stolen a similar vehicle, and you have to catch him. The fate of the universe is in your hands. The huge screen makes this ride very intense, but if you begin to feel a little woozy, just stick your neck out of your car — literally. You can see the other cars, lending the very true perspective that you're really only in a theater. *This ride has a 40-inch height minimum.*

✔ *Men in Black:* **Alien Attack:** Board a six-passenger cruiser, and you'll buzz the streets of New York, using laser tag–style guns to splatter 80 kinds of bug-eyed invaders. This four-minute ride relies on 360-degree spins rather than speed for its thrill factor. At the ride's conclusion, a giant roach swallows you, and you must then blast your way out (getting doused with bug guts — warm water) for your efforts. Will Smith rates you as galaxy defender, atomically average, or bug bait. *This ride has a 42-inch height minimum.*

Islands of Adventure

Universal's second park opened in 1999 with a collection of fast, fun rides wrapped in a 110-acre package. Roller coasters thunder above its pedestrian walkways, water rides careen through the center of the park, and theme restaurants are camouflaged to match their surroundings. The $1 billion park is divided into six areas: the **Port of Entry,** where you'll find shops and eateries, and the themed sections: **Seuss Landing, Toon Lagoon, Jurassic Park, Marvel Super Hero Island,** and **The Lost Continent.** Islands of Adventure has a large menu of thrill rides and coasters, plus a growing stable of play areas for younger guests.

Nine of the 14 major rides at Islands of Adventure have minimum heights (40–54 inches), so if you have very young children, you're better off at another park.

Port of Entry

Think of this as the starting line. Designed to resemble a marketplace that you'd find in *Indiana Jones,* Port of Entry is where the park pushes stuff like junk food, souvenirs, and other completely unnecessary items while you're still suffering from ticket shock. From here, you can walk to the five other islands dotting the lagoon.

Seuss Landing

The main attractions in Seuss Landing, a 10-acre island, are aimed at the younger set, though anyone who loved the good Doctor as a child will enjoy some nostalgic fun on the colorful rides. Here are some of the attractions you'll find:

- ✔ **Caro-Seuss-El:** This not-so-ordinary carousel replaces the traditional wooden horses with seven whimsical Seussian characters (54 total mounts), including Cowfish, Elephant Birds, and Mulligatawnies. They move up and down, as well as in and out. Pull the reins to make their eyes blink or heads bob as you twirl through the riot of color surrounding the ride.

- ✔ **The Cat in the Hat:** All aboard the couch! In this case, they're six-passenger futons that steer 1,800 people an hour through 18 show scenes. Any Seuss fan will recognize the giant candy-striped hat looming over the entrance and probably many of the scenes from the chaotic journey inside. It's one of the signature experiences of Islands of Adventure, though you may find it tame.

✔ **If I Ran the Zoo:** If I Ran the Zoo is an interactive playland for kids who enjoy everything from flying water snakes to getting a chance to tickle the toes of a Seussian animal. The 19 play stations are a nice place to let your kids burn off some excited energy.

✔ **One Fish, Two Fish, Red Fish, Blue Fish:** On this attraction, your controls allow you to move your funky fish up or down 15 feet, as you spin around on an arm attached to a hub. Watch out for squirt posts, which spray unsuspecting riders who don't follow the ride's rhyme scheme (and sometimes the ones who do follow it). *Riders must be 48 inches or taller to ride **without** an adult; smaller children can ride when accompanied.*

Marvel Super Hero Island

Thrill junkies love the twisting, turning rides on this island that's filled with building-tall murals of Marvel Super Heroes. Children can meet some of their favorite heroes in front of The Amazing Adventures of Spider-Man. Spidey's ride is just one of the highlights on this island, which includes the following attractions:

✔ **The Amazing Adventures of Spider-Man:** A primo ride, it combines moving vehicles, filmed 3-D action, and special effects themed around the original webmaster. The script: While you're touring the *Daily Bugle* newspaper — *yikes!* — the boys in black hats steal the Statue of Liberty. Your mission is to help Spidey get it back. Passengers wearing 3-D glasses squeal, and computer-generated objects fly toward their 12-person cars, which spin and soar through this comic-book universe. There's also a simulated 400-foot drop that feels an awful lot like the real thing. *This ride has a 40-inch height minimum.*

✔ **Dr. Doom's Fearfall:** Look! Up in the sky! Uh-oh, it's you falling 200 feet, if you're courageous enough to climb aboard. This towering metal skeleton provides screams that you can hear far into the day and night. The plot line: You're touring a lab when something goes horribly wrong as Doctor Doom tries to cure you of fear. You're fired to the top of the ride, with feet dangling, and dropped in intervals, leaving your stomach at several levels. The fall feels like the Tower of Terror at Disney–MGM Studios (earlier in this chapter) but with the additional sensation of hanging free. *This ride has a 52-inch height minimum.*

✔ **Incredible Hulk Coaster:** Get ready to rocket from a dark tunnel into the sunlight while accelerating from 0 to 40 mph in two seconds. Although it's only two-thirds the speed of Disney–MGM's Rock 'n' Roller Coaster (earlier in this chapter), this ride is in broad daylight and you can see the asphalt! After launching, you spin upside down 128 feet from the ground, feel weightless, and careen through the center of the park over the heads of other visitors. Coaster lovers will be pleased to know that this ride, which lasts 2 minutes and 15 seconds, includes seven rollovers and two deep drops. *It has a 54-inch height minimum.*

✔ **Storm Force Accelatron.** This ride is little more than a 22nd-century version of the Magic Kingdom's Mad Tea Party and its spinning teacups. While aboard, you and the *X-Men*'s Storm try to defeat the evil Magneto by spinning faster and faster. In addition to creating upset stomachs, your motion creates a thunderstorm of sound and light, which gives Storm all the power she needs.

Toon Lagoon

More than 150 life-size, sculpted cartoon images let you know you've entered Toon Lagoon, dedicated to your favorite Sunday funnies. Here's what you can find:

✔ **Comic Strip Lane:** Beetle Bailey, Hagar the Horrible, and Dagwood and Blondie are just a few of the 80 characters in this comic-strip neighborhood. Although this attraction is fun for visuals and passive moments, skip it if you're on a tight schedule.

✔ **Dudley Do-Right's Ripsaw Falls:** On this splashy flume ride that drops 75 feet at 50 mph, your task is to save Nell from Snidely Whiplash. The boats take you around a 400,000-gallon lagoon and plunge you 15 feet below the water's surface, but this is mainly hype — the water is contained on either side of you. *Note:* You will get very wet, despite the contained water. *This ride has a 44-inch height minimum.*

✔ **Me Ship, The Olive:** This three-story boat is a family-friendly playland with dozens of interactive activities from bow to stern. Kids can toot whistles, clang bells, or play the organ. Kids 6 and up love Cargo Crane, where they can drench riders on Popeye & Bluto's Bilge-Rat Barges (see the next listing).

✔ **Popeye & Bluto's Bilge-Rat Barges:** Here's a turning, twisting raft ride with the same kind of vehicle as Kali River Rapids at Disney's Animal Kingdom (earlier in this chapter), but this one's faster and bouncier. You'll get wet from the rapids as well as the water cannons fired by guests at Me Ship, The Olive (see the previous listing). The 12-passenger rafts bump and dip their way along a course lined with villains, most notably Bluto and Sea Hag, and a twirling octopus boat wash. *This ride has a 42-inch height minimum.*

Jurassic Park

All the basics from Steven Spielberg's wildly successful films and some of the high-tech wizardry are incorporated into this lushly landscaped tropical locale that includes a replica of the visitor center from the movie. Expect long lines at the River Adventure and pleasant surprises at the Discovery Center, both described in the following list of attractions:

✔ **Camp Jurassic:** Designed along the same lines as The Boneyard in Disney's Animal Kingdom (earlier in this chapter), this play area has everything from lava pits to a rain forest. Watch out for the spitters (you'll get wet) that lurk in dark caves. The multilevel area offers lots of places for kids to crawl, explore, and lose a little steam. Keep a close eye on young children; it's easy to get turned around inside the caverns.

✔ **Discovery Center:** Relax while you discover something new. The center has life-size dinosaur replicas and some interactive games, including a sequencer that lets you combine your DNA with a dinosaur's. The Beasaur exhibit gives you a chance to see and hear as the dinosaurs did. For the highlight, watch a tiny, animatronic velociraptor hatch in the lab.

✔ **Jurassic Park River Adventure:** Although this attraction begins slowly, it soon throws you into a world of stormy skies and five-story dinosaurs, including a T-Rex, one of the most fearsome bullies on the planet. To escape, you take a heart-stopping 85-foot plunge in a flume that's quick enough to leave your fingerprints embedded in the restraining bar's padded foam. Did I mention that you'll get soaked? *This ride has a 42-inch height minimum.*

✔ **Pteranodon Flyers:** Unlike the traditional gondolas in sky rides, on Pteranodon Flyers, your feet hang free from the two-seat, skeletal flyers and there's little but a restraining belt between you and the ground. Now that I've scared you, this is a kiddie ride — *single passengers must be between 36 and 56 inches tall;* adults can board *only* when accompanying someone that size.

✔ **Triceratops Discovery Trail:** Meet a "living" dinosaur and find out about the care and feeding of the 24-foot-long, 10-foot-high animatronic Triceratops from its trainers. The creature's responses to touch include realistic blinks, breathing, and leg movements.

The Lost Continent

Although the millennia are mixed — ancient Greece with medieval forest — Universal has done a good job creating a foreboding mood in this section of the park.

✔ **Dueling Dragons:** Although this puppy only takes two and a half minutes, it comes with the usual health warnings and a scream factor of 11 on a 10-point scale. True coaster crazies love this intertwined set of leg-dangling racers that climb to 125 feet, invert five times, and on three occasions come within 12 inches of each other as the two dragons battle. The Fire Dragon can reach speeds of up to 60 mph, while the Ice Dragon only makes it to 55 mph. *This ride has a 54-inch height minimum.*

✔ *The Eighth Voyage of Sindbad:* The mythical sailor Sindbad is the star of a stunt demonstration that takes place in a 1,700-seat theater decorated with blue stalagmites and eerie shipwrecks. The show includes water explosions and pyrotechnic effects including a 10-foot circle of flames. It doesn't, however, come close to the *Indiana Jones* stunt show at Disney–MGM Studios (described earlier in this chapter).

✔ **The Flying Unicorn.** This small roller coaster is similar to Woody Woodpecker's Nuthouse Coaster at Universal Studios Florida (see earlier in this chapter) and The Barnstormer at Goofy's Wiseacre Farm in the Magic Kingdom (also earlier). That means a fast, corkscrew run sure to earn squeals but probably not superterrifying. The ride travels through a mythical forest next to Dueling Dragons. *Riders must be at least 36 inches tall.*

✔ **The Mystic Fountain:** This interactive "smart" fountain delights younger guests. It can see and hear, leading to a lot of kibitzing with those who stand before the stone fountain, suitably named "Rocky." If you get close enough, you may even get a surprise shower. It's a real treat for 3- to 8-year-olds.

✔ *Poseidon's Fury:* This is the park's best show. That said, it's one of the park's only shows. You pass through a 42-foot vortex — where 17,500 gallons of water swirl around you, barrel style — and then get a front-row seat in a battle royale, where Zeus and the evil Darkenon hurl 25-foot fireballs at each other. But if the lines are long and you're on a tight schedule, skip it.

Children younger than 7 may find the flaming fireballs, explosive sounds, and rushing water a little too intense.

SeaWorld

Though it's a distant seventh (out of eight) in Orlando's theme-park wars, SeaWorld still manages to attract 4.7 million visitors a year by delivering a more relaxed pace with several animal encounters. This modern marine park focuses more on discovery than on thrill rides, though it offers its share of excitement with Journey to Atlantis, a steep flumelike ride, and Kraken, a floorless roller coaster.

Park prices

Single-day admission is $59.75 for adults, $48 for kids 3 to 9, plus the 6 percent sales tax and $8 parking.

You also can buy a **FlexTicket.** This is the most economical way to see the various "other-than-Disney" parks. With the **FlexTicket,** you pay one price to visit any of the participating parks during a 14-day period. A four-park pass to Universal Studios Florida, Islands of Adventure, Wet 'n' Wild, and SeaWorld is $184.95 for adults and $150.95 for children 3 to 9. A five-park pass, which adds Busch Gardens in Tampa, is $224.95 for adults and $189.95 for kids.

SeaWorld attractions

SeaWorld combines wildlife-conservation awareness with laid-back fun. Although close encounters with marine life are the major draw, you'll also find some excellent shows and thrill rides. Here are the highlights:

- *Cirque de la Mer:* Other than costumes, there's little aquatic about it, but a cast of acrobats, mimes, dancers, musicians, and comics provide a show that's at times artistic and funny (and always entertaining). The sets and costumes focus on Peru's folklore and Incan past and there's a small amount of audience participation.

- *Clyde & Seamore Take Pirate Island:* A lovable sea lion–and-otter duo, with a supporting cast of walruses and harbor seals, stars in this fish-breathed comedy that comes with a swashbuckling conservation theme. The show is corny, but it's a refreshing break from all the high-tech rides and shows at the other theme parks.

- *Intensity Games Water Ski Show:* It's hard to top this show, a crowd-pleaser for more than 15 years. The hypercompetition stars some of the most skilled athletes on water. The 20-person team includes world-class skiers, wake-boarders, and stunt men and women from across the United States performing aquabatics.

- **Journey to Atlantis:** Taking a cue from Disney's Imagineers, SeaWorld came up with a flume ride that carries the customary surgeon-general's warning about heart problems, neck or back ailments, pregnancy, seizures, dizziness, and claustrophobia. The story line of this attraction involves a battle of good versus evil, but what really matters is the drop — a wild plunge from 60 feet with lugelike curves and a shorter drop thrown in for good measure. *The ride carries a 46-inch height minimum.*

- **Key West at SeaWorld:** A tree- and flower-lined Caribbean-esque village, it offers island food, entertainers, and street vendors. It has three animal habitats: **Stingray Lagoon,** where you get a hands-on encounter with harmless rays; **Dolphin Cove,** a habitat for bottlenose dolphins set up for visitor interaction; and **Sea Turtle Point,** home to endangered and threatened species. Shortly after this area opened, the dolphins loved to tease visitors by swimming just out of arm's reach. But they soon discovered there are advantages to human interaction — namely smelt. Speaking of smelt, you can buy them to feed the dolphins, and it's real easy to spend a bundle to reward the dolphins' begging.

- *Key West Dolphin Fest:* At the partially covered, open-air Whale and Dolphin Stadium, Atlantic bottlenose dolphins perform flips and high jumps, swim at high speeds, do the backstroke, and give rides to trainers. Some false killer whales (*Pseudocra crassidens*) also make an appearance, accompanied by calypso music. The tricks are impressive, but if you've seen a traditional tourist-park dolphin show, you already know the plot.

✔ **Kraken:** SeaWorld's deepest venture into thrill rides is named for a massive, mythological, underwater beast kept caged by Poseidon. This 21st-century version involves floorless, open-sided 32-passenger coasters that plant you on a pedestal high above the track. When the monster breaks loose, you climb 151 feet, fall 144 feet, reach 65 mph, go underground three times (spraying bystanders with water, and make seven loops over a 4,177-foot course. It may be the longest 3 minutes, 39 seconds of your life. *This ride has a 54-inch height minimum.*

✔ **Manatees: The Last Generation?** This exhibit is as close as most people get to the endangered West Indian manatees. Underwater viewing stations, innovative cinema techniques, and interactive displays combine for a tribute to these gentle marine mammals.

✔ **Marine Mammal Keeper Experience:** Expect to invest a sizable chunk of your day and budget in this eight-hour program (it runs from 6:30 a.m. to 3:30 p.m., so you'll also need to be an early riser). You get to work side by side with a trainer, preparing meals and feeding the animals, learning basic training techniques, and sharing lunch. It costs $389, which also includes seven days of consecutive admission to SeaWorld, lunch, a souvenir photo, and a T-shirt. The program is limited to two people per day, so make the required reservations very early. You must be 13 or older, at least 52 inches tall, able to climb, and able to lift and carry 15 pounds of vittles. Call ☎ **407-432-117**8 for more information.

✔ **Penguin Encounter:** The Penguin Encounter transports you, via a moving sidewalk, through Tuxedoville. The stars of the show are on the other side of a Plexiglas shield. You get a glimpse of them as they preen, socialize, and swim at bullet speeds in a 22-degree habitat. You can also see puffins and murres in a similar area.

✔ *Pets Ahoy!* Eighteen cats, 12 dogs, three pot-bellied pigs, and a horse are joined by birds and rats to perform comic relief in a 25-minute show held several times a day. Almost all the stars were rescued from animal shelters.

✔ *The Shamu Adventure:* Everyone comes to SeaWorld to see the big guy, and he and his friends really dive into their work! Extremely well choreographed, the show is carried out by very good trainers and very smart orcas. The fun builds until the video monitor flashes an urgent "Weather Watch" and one of the trainers utters the warning: "Uh-oh!" Hurricane Shamu is about to make landfall. At this point, many folks remember the splash-area warnings, posted throughout the grandstand. Those who didn't pay attention when they arrived get one last chance to flee. The orcas then race around the edge of the pool, creating huge waves of icy water that profoundly soak everything in range.

✔ **Shamu's Happy Harbor:** This 3-acre play area has a four-story tower with a 35-foot crow's-nest lookout, water cannons, remote-controlled vehicles, and a water maze. It's one of the most extensive play areas at any park and a great place for kids to unwind. Bring extra clothes for the tots (or for yourself) because the Harbor isn't designed to keep you dry.

✔ **Shark Encounter:** This attraction is actually home to some 220 species of marine predators. Pools out front have small sharks and rays (feeding isn't allowed). The interior aquariums have big eels, beautiful lionfish, hauntingly still barracudas, and the fat, bug-eyed pufferfish.

This tour isn't for the claustrophobic: You walk through a Plexiglas tube beneath hundreds of millions of gallons of water. Also, small children may find the sharks too much to handle.

✔ **Whale Encounter:** This program allows four guests per day to get in the water with false killer whales, which are a cousin of Atlantic bottlenose dolphins but at 1,300 pounds are up to two or three times their size. The $200, two-hour encounter includes 30 minutes in waist-deep water with one of the park's four critters, lunch, a T-shirt, souvenir photo, and one week's admission to SeaWorld. *Note:* This experience lets you touch but not swim with pseudorcas. *It has a 52-inch minimum height requirement.* Call ☎ **407-370-1382** for details.

✔ *Wild Arctic: Wild Arctic* combines a high-definition adventure film with flight-simulator technology to evoke breathtaking Arctic panoramas. After a hazardous flight over the frozen north, visitors emerge at a series of interior aquariums that are the homes of polar bears, seals, walruses, and white beluga whales. Kids may find the bumpy ride a little much, but there's a separate line for those who want to skip the thrill-ride section.

Discovery Cove

SeaWorld's second theme park opened in summer 2000. Its $100-million construction cost is one-tenth the sticker price of Universal's Islands of Adventure (earlier in this chapter), but Discovery Cove's admission price is more than four times higher. You have two options: $229 to $259 per person plus 6 percent sales tax if you want to swim with a dolphin (minimum age 6), or $129 to $159 if you can skip that luxury.

Discovery Cove provides plenty of elbow room — there's a limit of 1,000 guests per day. The all-inclusive nature of the park means that prices include almost everything you'll need, from lunch (with choices such as fajitas, salmon, and pesto chicken), to your towel and locker, to swimming/snorkeling gear, and your activities. The fun includes:

✔ Swimming near (but on the other side of Plexiglas from) black-tip sharks and barracudas.

✔ Snorkeling around a huge pool containing a coral reef with brightly colored tropical fish and another area with gentle rays.

✔ Feeding 300 exotic birds in an aviary hidden under a waterfall.

✔ Cooling off under foaming waterfalls.

✔ Soaking up the sun on the beaches.

✔ Enjoying the park's pools and rivers (freshwater and saltwater).

✔ Seven days of unlimited admission to SeaWorld.

To get to Discovery Cove, follow the directions to SeaWorld, earlier in this chapter. For up-to-the-minute information on this park, call ☎ **877-434-7268** or go to www.discoverycove.com.

Chapter 19

Exploring the Rest of Orlando

*1*n addition to the eight major parks I listed in Chapter 18, a ton of other attractions will help you take a break from the Mouse ears. These are places where you can spend two to six hours but, in most cases, not a small fortune at the ticket window. Considering Disney's corner on the Orlando market, it's not surprising that many of the most popular small attractions in town are at WDW. If, however, you prefer to leave Walt's wonderland for something a little more peaceful, intellectual, or cultural, numerous attractions that are far from Mickey-Mouse operations await you.

Seeing the Top Smaller Attractions

I start with the Disney attractions and then get into some of the other things that you can do in less than a day in and around O Town.

The never-ending world of Disney

Destination Disney never seems to run out of things to do. It's really a well-planned plot to corner more of your dough, instead of having to share it with others. To the tune of "When You Wish Upon a Star," I offer the next level.

Blizzard Beach
Near Disney–MGM Studios

Blizzard Beach is a 66-acre "ski resort" situated in the midst of a tropical lagoon (there's also some faux snow). Attractions include Cross Country Creek, a 2,900-foot tube ride around the park; Ski-Patrol Training Camp, a preteen area with a rope swing and slides; Meltaway Bay, a 1-acre, relatively calm wave pool; and Teamboat Springs, Walt Disney World's longest white-water raft ride (1,200 feet of rushing waterfalls).

But the headliner is Summit Plummet. Read every speed, motion, vertical-dip, wedgie, and hold-onto-your-breastplate warning, and then — as a warm-up — test your bravado in a bullring, a space shuttle, or any other death-defying hobby. This puppy starts pretty slow, with a ski-lift ride (even in Florida's 100-degree dog days) to the 120-foot summit, where you board the world's fastest body slide. Can you say *natural enema?* You can easily spend the day in this park.

See map p. 319. On World Drive. ☎ *407-560-3400.* www.disneyworld.com. *To get there: Located just north of the All-Star Sports and Music resorts. Admission: $34 adults, $28 kids 3–9. Open: Daily 10 a.m–5 p.m., extended to 9 a.m.–8 p.m. during peak times, such as summer.*

DisneyQuest
Downtown Disney West Side

Meet the world's most interactive video arcade, with everything from virtual rides to old-fashioned pinball with a new-fangled twist. Here are the best:

- ✔ **Aladdin's Magic Carpet Ride** puts you astride a motorcycle-like seat while you fly through the 3-D Cave of Wonders.

- ✔ If you have an inventive mind (and a steel stomach), stop in at **Cyberspace Mountain,** where Bill Nye the Science-Turned-Roller-Coaster Guy helps you create the ultimate loop-and-dipster, which you then can ride in a very real-feeling simulator. It's a major hit with the coaster-crazy crowd. (I know some adrenaline junkies who spent hours here constructing, then riding, one heart-stopper after another.) Bring your own motion-sickness medicine (though you can choose slow, medium, or quick death).

- ✔ **Invasion: An ExtraTERRORestrial Alien Encounter** takes you on an intense mission to save colonists from intergalactic bad guys. One player flies the module while up to three others fire an array of weapons. (Just try to work all in sync — after a minute it's a free-for-all shooting fest.) This was an offshoot of the now-defunct **Magic Kingdom** attraction, but there's not much of a connection other than the preshow video.

- ✔ **Mighty Ducks Pinball Slam** is an interactive, life-size game in which the players ride platforms and use body English to score points.

✔ **Pirates of the Caribbean: Battle for Buccaneer Gold** outfits you and up to three mates in 3-D helmets so you can battle pirate ships virtual-reality style. One of you volunteers to be the captain, steering the ship, while the others assume positions behind cannons to blast the black hearts into oblivion — maybe. Each time you do, you're rewarded with some doubloons, but beware of sea monsters that can gobble you and your treasure.

✔ **Animation Academy** provides some quiet time for those who need it, by way of a minicourse in Disney cartooning.

There are also snack and food areas. A typical theme-park meal and drink at the food areas runs about $12 per person. There's no specific children's menu, but the servings are plentiful and can easily be enough for two. *Note:* Crowds are heaviest here after dark.

See map p. 319. Off of Buena Vista Dr. ☎ *407-828-4600.* www.disneyworld.com. *To get there: Located adjacent to Pleasure Island and Downtown Disney. Admission: $34 adults, $28 kids 3–9 for unlimited play. Open: Daily 11:30 a.m.–11 p.m. (until midnight Fri–Sat).*

Disney's Wide World of Sports
South of Disney–MGM Studios

This 200-acre complex has several baseball and softball fields, 6 basketball courts, 12 lighted tennis courts, a golf driving range, and 6 sand volleyball courts. **The Multi-Sports Experience** challenges guests with a variety of activities, covering many sports: football, baseball, basketball, hockey, soccer and volleyball. It's open on select days. Depending on your stamina, interest, and the size of the crowds, the experience can last 45 minutes to several hours.

See map p. 319. South Victory Way, just north of U.S. 192. ☎ *407-828-3267.* www.disneyworld.com. *To get there: Take the I-4 U.S. 192 exit west to World Drive. Make a right onto the Osceola Parkway, then another right at Victory Way. Admission: Prices vary by venue; general admission including the Multi-Sports Experience is $10 adults, $7.50 kids 3–9. Open: Daily, but hours vary by venue.*

Richard Petty Driving Experience
Walt Disney World Speedway

This is your chance to race in a 600-horsepower NASCAR Winston-Cup racecar. How real is it? You must sign a two-page waiver with words like DANGEROUS and UPDATE YOUR WILL before getting into a car. At one end of the spectrum, you can ride shotgun for two laps at 145 mph ($90). At the other end, you can spend anywhere from three hours to two days learning how to drive the car yourself and racing other daredevils for 8 to 30 laps of excitement (for a cool $403–$1,330). You must be 18 years old to ride in the car.

See map p. 319. Located on World Drive at Vista Boulevard just off U.S. 192. ☎ 800-237-3889. To get there: Take I-4 to the Epcot Center Drive exit and head west to World Drive. Make a right onto the Osceola Parkway and follow it 5 miles to the speedway. Adults only. Open: Varies by seasons and hours, so call ahead.

Typhoon Lagoon
Near Downtown Disney

The fantasy setting for this water park is a storm-ravaged tropical island strewn with tin-roofed structures, surfboards, and other wreckage left by a typhoon. Headline attractions include **Castaway Creek,** a 2,100-foot raft and tube venue; **Ketchakiddie Creek,** an area for the under-4-foot set; **Shark Reef,** where you can snorkel with fish that live on a simulated coral reef; **Typhoon Lagoon,** the signature wave pool that offers waves every 90 seconds; and **Humunga Kowabunga,** a snaking water-slide area. You can spend all day here.

The creative minds at Disney have added a way for you to learn how to catch a wave and "hang ten" at the Typhoon Lagoon water park. Tuesdays and Fridays, instructors from **Carroll's Cocoa Beach Surfing School** show up for an early-bird session in the namesake lagoon, which has a wave machine capable of 8-footers. The two-and-a-half-hour session is held before the park opens to the general public. It's limited to 14 people. Minimum age is 8. The $125 cost doesn't include park admission, which you have to pay if you want to hang around after the lesson (☎ 407-939-7529).

See map p. 319. 1195 East Buena Vista Dr. ☎ 407-560-4141. www.disneyworld.com. *To get there: It's west of Downtown Disney and south of Lake Buena Vista Drive, between the Disney Village Marketplace and Disney–MGM Studios. Admission: $34 adults, $28 kids 3–9. Open: Daily 10 a.m.–5 p.m., extended to 9 a.m.–8 p.m. during peak periods.*

Beyond Disney

Believe it or not, some folks escape the theme parks *and* Disney. (Skip ahead to see the "More Orlando Attractions" map.) Here are a few of the options.

Flying Tigers Warbird Restoration Museum
Kissimmee

Tom Reilly, the founder and owner of this museum, restores vintage warplanes from World War II through Vietnam. His guided tours go through hands-on exhibits and a lab where his restorers perform magic before your eyes. The outdoor showroom has a Corsair, MIG-21, P-38 Lightning, and three dozen others planes. Allow two to four hours to see the museum.

See map p. 364. 231 N. Hoagland Blvd., south of U.S. 192. ☎ 407-933-1942. www.warbirdmuseum.com. *To get there: Take U.S. 192 east of Disney to Kissimmee, turn right on Hoagland Boulevard. Free parking. Admission: $9 adults, $8 children 6–12 and seniors 60 and over. Open: Daily 9 a.m.–5 p.m.*

More Orlando Attractions

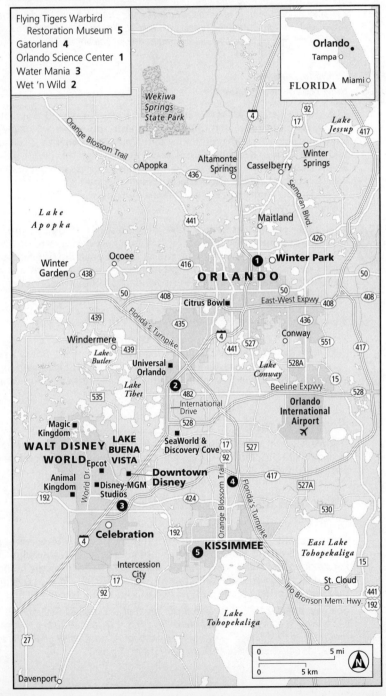

Flying Tigers Warbird
    Restoration Museum **5**
Gatorland **4**
Orlando Science Center **1**
Water Mania **3**
Wet 'n Wild **2**

Gatorland
South Orlando

Founded in 1949 with a handful of alligators living in huts and pens, Gatorland today features thousands of alligators and crocodiles on 70 acres. Breeding pens, nurseries, and rearing ponds are scattered throughout the park, which also displays monkeys, snakes, birds, Florida turtles, and a Galápagos tortoise. There are three shows — *Gator Wrestlin'*, which is more of an environmental awareness program; the *Gator Jumparoo*, in which one of the big reptiles lunges 4 or 5 feet out of the water to snatch a long-dead chicken from a trainer's hand; and *Jungle Crocs of the World*, which showcases the toothy reptiles. The park has an open-air restaurant where you can feast on smoked gator ribs and nuggets. Younger guests enjoy the park's water play area, train ride, and petting zoo with baby llamas and goats. Allow four to five hours to see everything, a full day if you add an adventure tour (see the following paragraph).

Gatorland offers several **Adventure Tour** programs ($38–$190). Options include being a trainer for a day (you actually get to wrestle an alligator), day and night airboat rides, sea turtle watches, and alligator-egg-collecting expeditions (a seasonal option, generally in mid- to late spring).

See map p. 364. 14501 S. Orange Blossom Trail/U.S. 441 (between Osceola Parkway and Hunter's Creek Boulevard, Orlando). ☎ *800-393-5297 or 407-855-5496.* www. gatorland.com. *Admission: $19.95 adults, $9.95 kids 3–12. Free parking. Open: Daily 9 a.m.–6 p.m., sometimes later.*

Orlando Science Center
North of Orlando

This four-story center has ten halls that allow visitors to explore everything from the swamps of Florida to the arid plains of Mars. The **Dr. Phillips CineDome** is a 310-seat theater that uses the latest technology to present large-format films as well as planetarium and laser shows. In **KidsTown,** little folks wander in a miniature version of the world around them. One section has a pint-sized community that includes a construction site, park, and wellness center. **Science City,** located nearby, has a power plant, suspension bridge, and the **Inventor's Workshop,** a garage-like station for creative play. Children stopping by **123 Math Avenue** work on puzzles and play with math-based toys that teach as they entertain. Plan to spend three to four hours.

See map p. 364. 777 E. Princeton St. (between Orange and Mills in Loch Haven Park). ☎ *407-514-2000 or 888-672-4386.* www.osc.org. *Admission: $15 adults, $14 seniors 55 and older, $10 kids 3–11; additional fee for CineDome and planetarium. Parking: $3.50 in a garage across the street. Open: Tues–Thurs 9 a.m.–5 p.m., Fri–Sat 9 a.m.–9 p.m., Sun noon–5 p.m.*

Water Mania
Kissimmee

This 36-acre water park isn't on a Disney scale, but it offers a variety of aquatic thrill rides and attractions. You can boogie board or body surf in continuous-wave pools, float lazily along an 850-foot river, enjoy a white-water tubing adventure, and plummet down spiraling water slides and steep flumes. Plan on about four hours.

See map p. 364. 6073 W. Irlo Bronson Memorial Hwy./U.S. 192. ☎ 800-527-3092 or 407-396-2626. www.watermania-florida.com. *To get there: Take the I-4 U.S. 192 exit west 2 miles; turn left on Old Lake Wilson Road/Highway 545; the park is 1 mile ahead on left. Admission: $24 adults, $20 kids 3–9. Parking: $6. Open: Daily 10 a.m.–5 p.m. Mar–Sept.*

Wet 'n Wild
International Drive

Unlike Water Mania (see the preceding listing), this 25-acre Universal-owned water park is in the same league as Disney's Typhoon Lagoon and Blizzard Beach (see Chapter 18). It has several first-rate water rides, including **Fuji Flyer,** a six-story, four-passenger toboggan ride packing 450 feet of banked curves; **The Surge,** which offers 580 feet of slippery curves and is billed as the fastest tube ride in the Southeast; and **Black Hole,** where two-person rafts shoot through 500 feet of twisting, sometimes dark passages. *All three require that kids 36 to 48 inches have an adult with them.* **Raging Rapids** is a simulated white-water run with a waterfall plunge; **Blue Niagra** has 300 feet of loops and dips (*48-inch height minimum*); **Knee Ski** is a cable-operated knee-boarding course only open in warm weather (*56-inch height minimum*); and **Mach 5** has a trio of twisting, turning flumes. The park also has a large kids' area with miniature versions of some of the grown-up rides.

See map p. 364. 6200 International Dr., at Universal Blvd. ☎ 800-992-9453 or 407-351-9453. www.wetnwild.com. *To get there: Take I-4 east to Exit 75A and follow the signs. Parking: Cars $5, RVs $6. Admission: $33 adults, $27 kids 3–9, $14.48 seniors 55 and older. Tube, towel, and locker rentals are $9 plus a $2 refundable deposit. A 14-day* **Flexticket** *— good for admission to Wet 'n' Wild, Universal Studios Florida, Islands of Adventure, and SeaWorld — is available for $214.95 for adults, $179.95 for kids 3–9. Open: Daily, but hours vary seasonally; call before you go.*

More Cool Things to See and Do

Now, I get into things that have more of a special-interest flavor. (And, this is another area where you'll discover I was stretching the truth a wee bit when I suggested you were escaping Disney.)

✔ **Baseball:** The **Atlanta Braves** play 18 spring-training games at the Disney Wide World of Sports stadium during a one-month season that begins in early March. (Workouts begin in mid-February.)

Game tickets for the stadium's two seating areas are $11.50 and $19.50. For information, call ☎ **407-828-3267.** You can order tickets through Ticketmaster at ☎ **407-839-3900** or online at www.atlanta braves.com.

✔ **Golf:** The Magic Mickey has five 18-hole, par-72 golf courses and one 9-hole, par-36 walking course. All have pro shops, equipment rentals, and instruction. Rates range from $105 to $170 per 18-hole round for resort guests; the fee is $5 more if you're not staying at a Walt Disney World property. For tee times and information, call ☎ **407-824-2270** up to seven days in advance (up to 30 days in advance for Disney-resort and official-property guests). Call ☎ **407-934-7639** for information about golf packages.

If you want more golfing options, or want to get out of Disney for a bit, three excellent sources of information and tee-time reservations are **Golfpac** (☎ **888-848-8941** or 407-260-2288; www.golfpacinc.com), **Florida Golfing** (☎ **866-833-2663;** www.floridagolfing.com), and **Tee Times USA** (☎ **888-465-3356;** www.teetimesusa.com).

✔ **Miniature golf:** Normally, I wouldn't list this category, but Diz makes it something special. **Winter Summerland,** off Buena Vista Drive, north of Osceola Parkway (☎ **407-560-3000;** $10 adults, $8 kids 3–9), and **Fantasia Gardens,** Buena Vista, east of World Drive (☎ **407-560-8760;** $9.76 adults, $7.78 kids 3–9) each have two 18-hole, ton-of-fun courses.

Shopping

Orlando is far from paradise for shoppers, but it has a fair number of places where you can wear out your credit card.

Orlando's best shopping areas

Orlando doesn't have a central shopping district. Instead, it has tourist areas that are best avoided unless you want cheap goods at high prices, as well as neighborhood retail locations, such as malls, where locals shop. The following is a list of some of the more frequented shopping zones:

✔ **Celebration:** Think *Pleasantville* with a Mickey touch. This Disney-created town of 5,000 is more of a diversion than a shopper's paradise. The downtown area has a dozen pricey shops and galleries. The shops offer some interesting buys for those with deep pockets, but the real plus is the *Pleasantville* atmosphere. To get to Celebration from Disney, take U.S. 192 east 5 miles, a little beyond Interstate 4. The entrance is on the right (☎ **407-566-2200**).

✔ **Downtown Disney Marketplace:** This Size XXXL shopping hub on Buena Vista Lagoon is a colorful place to browse, people watch, have lunch, and maybe buy a trinket. Stores include the **Lego**

Imagination Center, where kids can play in a free Lego-building area outside while their parents browse inside; EUROSPAIN, which sells products that crystal and metal artists make before your eyes; and the Art of Disney, a store that can dent your bank account if you crave original Disney art (www.disneyworld.com).

✔ **Downtown Disney West Side:** This venue on Buena Vista Drive has many specialty stores where you can find unique gifts and souvenirs. **Guitar Gallery** tempts string-strokers and wannabes with custom jobs and rare collectibles, and **Sosa Family Cigars** beckons with a tradition reaching back to yesterday's Cuba. The **Virgin Megastore** is a movie, music, and multimedia gold mine (www.disneyworld.com).

✔ **Behind-the-Scenes Disney:** Held six times a year, WDW's backlot auctions feature a lot of castoff and surplus merchandise, from theme-park props to pots and pans to over-the-hill maintenance equipment, such as lawn mowers. They're always held on a Thursday, when Disney workers get paid. Call ☎ 407-824-6878 for dates, directions, and information. For bigger trinkets, check out Disney auctions on eBay (www.disneyauctions.com).

✔ **Kissimmee:** Southeast of the Disney parks, Kissimmee straddles U.S. 192/Irlo Bronson Memorial Highway — a sometimes tacky strip lined with budget motels, smaller attractions, and every fast-food restaurant known to the Western world. Kissimmee's shopping merit is negligible unless you're looking for a cheap T-shirt or a white elephant gift. (Seashells, anyone?)

✔ **International Drive:** This tourist magnet extends 7 to 10 miles north of the Disney parks between Highway 535 and the Florida Turnpike. The southern end has a little elbowroom, but the northern part is a tourist strip crowded with small-time attractions (there's bungee jumping for those who have a death wish), fast fooderies, and souvenir shacks. The main shopping draw is **Pointe Orlando,** which is listed later in this chapter under "Malls."

✔ **Winter Park:** Just north of downtown Orlando, Winter Park began life as a haven for Yankees escaping from the cold. Today, Winter Park's centerpiece is **Park Avenue,** a collection of upscale shops, restaurants, and art galleries along a cobblestone street. For more information on Winter Park, call ☎ 407-644-8281.

Searching for shopping hot spots

Orlando has the usual collection of outlets and malls. Except for Disney, Universal, and SeaWorld souvenirs, though, it has few products of its own.

Factory outlets

In the last decade, the tourist areas in Orlando have bloomed with places where shoppers can find name-brand bargains — maybe. Smart shoppers always know suggested-retail prices before going to outlet stores, so they can tell what is — and *isn't* — a bargain.

✔ **Belz Factory Outlet World,** 5401 W. Oak Ridge Rd., at the north end of International Dr. (☎ **407-354-0126;** www.belz.com), is the grand-daddy of all Orlando outlets. It has 180 stores, including 18 shoe stores (Bass, Nike, and Rockport), 14 housewares stores (Fitz & Floyd, Corning, Oneida, and Mikasa), and more than 60 clothing shops (London Fog, Guess Jeans, Harvé Benard, Calvin Klein, and Anne Klein). You can also buy books, toys, electronics, sporting goods, jewelry, and so on.

✔ **Orlando Premium Outlets,** 8200 Vineland Ave., just off the southern third of I-Drive (☎ **407-238-7787;** www.premiumoutlets.com) bills itself as Orlando's only upscale outlet. The 110 tenants include Coach, Polo/Ralph Lauren, and Tommy Hilfiger. Some of the best buys here are at Banana Republic, where many items are half the price of those at other BR stores.

Malls

The Orlando area has several traditional shopping malls. Like tenants in malls everywhere, these merchants pay a hefty rent, so good buys are elusive. Arguably, the best bargain is the people watching, which is free.

✔ **Mall at Millenia** (www.mallatmillenia.com), is a 1.3-million-square-foot shoppers' paradise in the sprawling Millenia development near Universal Orlando (at Conroy Road and I-4). Its anchors are Bloomingdale's, Macy's, and Neiman Marcus, and it has 200 specialty stores, including Tiffany & Co., Gucci, Cartier, and Louis Vuitton.

✔ **Florida Mall** (☎ **407-851-6255;** www.shopsimon.com) offers Lord & Taylor, Dillard's, Saks, Macy's, JCPenney, Sears, an Adam's Mark Hotel, and more than 200 specialty stores, restaurants, and entertainment venues. It's located at 8001 S. Orange Blossom Trail at Sand Lake Road, 4 miles east of International Drive.

✔ Although **Pointe Orlando** is set up like a mall, this complex's two levels of stores, restaurants, and a 21-screen IMAX theater aren't under one roof. It's currently undergoing renovations that will add more retail shops to its current collection of 80 stores. Pointe Orlando is located at 9101 International Dr. (☎ **407-248-2838;** www.pointeorlandofl.com).

Living It Up After Dark

If you have the energy to go out after a day in the theme parks, Orlando has plenty for you to do when the sun goes down.

Disney after dark

A few years back, the Disney folks — never the type to pass up a new opportunity to rake in some bucks — built several haunts where night owls can dance, drink, and play to their hearts' content. In general,

Disney's venues are far more family-friendly than Orlando's other evening entertainment zones, but keep in mind that distinction is relative; even some of Disney's clubs lock out the under-21 crowd.

Pleasure Island

This 6-acre, sometimes gated, entertainment district is the home of several nightspots. Admission to the island is free from 10 a.m. to 7 p.m. Admission is $19.95 from 7 p.m. to 2 a.m., when the clubs are open. The Pleasure Island admission is included if you have a Park Hopper Plus or Ultimate Park Hopper ticket (see Chapter 18 for information on Disney admission passes). Self-parking is free. For complete information on all the Pleasure Island clubs, including entertainment schedules, call the Downtown Disney Tonite! hotline at ☎ **407-939-2648,** or check out Disney's Web site at www.disneyworld.com. Here's a list of the best that Pleasure Island has to offer:

- ✔ **Mannequins Dance Palace,** a high-energy club with a big, rotating dance floor, is the main event on Pleasure Island. Because it's a local favorite, it's hard to get into, so arrive early, especially on weekends. Three levels of bars and mixing space are adorned with elaborately dressed mannequins. The DJ plays contemporary tunes loud enough to wake the dead. You must be 21 to enter.

- ✔ **The Adventurers Club** almost defies description — it needs to be experienced. According to Walt Disney World legend, it was designed to be the library and archaeological trophy room for Pleasure Island founder and explorer, Merriweather Adam Pleasure. Pleasure's zany band of globetrotting friends and servants, played by skilled actors, interact with guests, while staying in character. Improvisational comedy and cabaret shows are performed in the library. You can easily hang out here all night.

- ✔ If you're a fan of the BET Cable Network, you'll probably love **BET Soundstage** (☎ 407-934-7666), which offers traditional R&B and the rhyme of hip-hop. You can dance on an expansive floor or kick back on an outdoor terrace. Cover charge for the Soundstage is included in the Pleasure Island pass except for major concerts.

- ✔ The Who, What, and Warehouse Players are the main event at the **Comedy Warehouse.** The group performs 45-minute improvisational shows based on audience suggestions. They do five shows a night.

- ✔ Disco and polyester rule at **8Trax,** a 1970s-style club where 50 TV screens air diverse shows and videos over the dance floor. A DJ plays everything from "YMCA" to "The Hustle."

- ✔ **Motion** features Top-40 tunes and alternative rock. It's a hyperactive club that appeals to younger and young-at-heart partiers. Moody blue lighting helps you pretend you're dancing the night away in deep space.

Disney West Side

Immediately adjacent to Pleasure Island, Disney West Side is a slightly newer district, where you'll find clubs, restaurants, and **DisneyQuest** (see earlier in this chapter).

✔ Singer Gloria Estefan and her husband, Emilio, created **Bongo's Cuban Café** (☎ 407-828-0999; www.bongoscubancafe.com), which serves up loud salsa music and second-rate Cuban fare. Come for the Latino atmosphere, rather than the food (which will run you $10–$26). The Café is open daily from 11 a.m. to 2 a.m. and doesn't take reservations. You can find plenty of free self-parking.

✔ **Cirque du Soleil** doesn't have any lions, tigers, or bears; but you won't feel cheated. The "Circus of the Sun's" 64 performers deliver nonstop energy on trampolines, the trapeze, and a high wire in a five-star show called *La Nouba*. The two ticket categories are $85 for adults and $59 for kids 3 to 9 (plus tax) for center-of-the-theater seats, and $73 and $49, respectively, to the right and left of the stage. Shows are held at 6 and 9 p.m. Thursday through Monday. For information, call ☎ 407-939-7600, or visit its Web site at www.cirquedusoleil.com.

✔ The rafters in the **House of Blues** literally shake with rhythm and blues. The House is decorated with folk art, and the patio has a view of the bay. If you like spicy food, offerings such as jambalaya and gumbo ($9–$25) are respectable. Sunday's Gospel Brunch ($30 for adults and $15 for kids 3–12) has foot-stomping music served with so-so food (omelets, beef, jalapeño smashed potatoes, cheese grits, and sausage). Brunch is the only time you can make reservations. Guests dining before attending a show that night are often eligible for early admission, which is handy during the general admission shows. Ask your server for details, call ☎ 407-934-2583, or go to www.hob.com. House of Blues is open daily from 11 a.m. to 2 a.m. and offers free self-parking.

Disney's Boardwalk

The Boardwalk (☎ 407-939-3492; www.disneyworld.com) is a great place for a quiet stroll or more. Street performers sing, dance, juggle, and make a little magic most evenings. **Atlantic Dance** features Top-40 and '80s dance hits. The rustic, saloon-style **Jellyrolls** offers dueling pianos ($5 cover). If you need a game fix, **ESPN Sports** has dozens of TV screens, a full-service bar, food, and a small arcade, all without a cover charge.

Universal after dark

Universal's answer to Pleasure Island is **CityWalk**, a two-level collection of clubs and restaurants located between its two theme parks (☎ 407-363-8000; www.universalorlando.com). It's open from 11 a.m. to 2 a.m. daily. There's no admission, but several clubs have cover charges after 5 or 6 p.m., and some aren't open earlier than that. CityWalk offers **party**

passes. A pass to all clubs is $9.95 per night; for $13 you can add a movie at Universal Cineplex (☎ **407-354-5998**). Universal also offers free club access to those who buy certain multiday tickets. Parking is $8 before 6 p.m., free afterwards. Here's what you'll find:

- **Bob Marley — A Tribute to Freedom** (☎ **407-224-2262**) has architecture said to replicate Marley's home in Kingston. Local and national reggae bands perform, and light Jamaican fare is served under umbrellas. Hours are 4 p.m. to 2 a.m. There's a $5 cover after 8 p.m.; cover prices increase when there are special concerts. You must be 21 or older to party after 10 p.m.

- The collection of memorabilia at the **Downbeat Jazz Hall of Fame** at **CityJazz** (☎ **407-224-2189**) ranges from Buddy Rich to Ella Fitzgerald. The adjoining **Thelonious Monk Institute of Jazz** is a performance venue that's also the site of workshops. You can browse through 500 pieces of memorabilia marching through Dixieland, swing, bebop, and modern jazz. Nationally acclaimed acts sometimes perform. It's open from 7 or 8 p.m. to 1 or 2 a.m. daily. Cover charge is $5 (more for special events).

- **the groove** (☎ **407-363-8000**) is CityWalk's answer to Pleasure Island's Mannequins, though it's not as crowded. The sound system is guaranteed to blow your hair back, and the dance floor is in a room gleaming with chrome. Music-wise, the groove features hip-hop, jazz fusion, techno, and alternative music. You must be at least 21 to enter, and it will cost you $5 for the privilege. The club is open from 9 p.m. to 2 or 3 a.m. daily.

- CityWalk's **Hard Rock Cafe** (☎ **407-351-5483**) is the largest in the world, and the adjoining **Hard Rock Live** is the first concert hall to bear the name. There's also a free exhibit area in the cafe, where you can browse through displays of rock memorabilia, including the platform heels, leather jumpsuits, and tongue-action photos of KISS. Cover charge varies by act. The cafe is open daily from 11 a.m. to 2 a.m.

- Canned music is piped through **Jimmy Buffett's Margaritaville** (☎ **407-224-2155**), with a Jimmy sound-alike strumming on the back porch. Bar-wise, you have three options. **The Volcano** erupts (we're not kidding) margaritas; the **Land Shark** has fins swimming around the ceiling; and the **12 Volt,** is, well, a little electrifying. Margaritaville is open from 11 a.m. to 2 a.m., and there's a $5 cover after 10 p.m.

- Just like the original version in New Orleans's French Quarter, drinking is the highlight at **Pat O'Brien's** (☎ **407-363-8000**). You can enjoy dueling pianos and a flame-throwing fountain while you suck down the signature drink — the Hurricane. No one under 21 is permitted after 7 p.m. Hours are 4 p.m. to 2 a.m., and there is a $5 cover charge after 9 p.m.

Other nighttime venues

8 Seconds, 100 W. Livingston Ave., downtown (☎ **407-839-4800;** www.
8-seconds.com; $5 cover for 21 and older, $7 for 18–21; open 8 p.m.–
2 a.m. Fri–Sat), is a honky-tonk with a huge dance floor where you can
get free line-dancing lessons early in the evening. If you go on Saturday,
take the side-trip to the parking lot for "Buckin' Bull Nights," when cow-
boys provide some extra entertainment in the ring. On Fridays, you can
find monster-truck pulls in the back lot. Country stars sometimes perform outside the ring.

Howl at the Moon Saloon, 55 W. Church St., downtown (☎ **407-841-9118;**
www.howlatthemoon.com; $2–$4 cover; open daily 6 p.m.–2 a.m.), is a fun
bar, and the fun hits its peak on a full moon — even if you're too shy to
cock your head back and hooowlllll with the best of them. **Sak Comedy
Lab,** 380 W. Amelia St., downtown (☎ **407-648-0001;** www.sak.com; $5–$12
admission; shows are usually at 8 and 10 p.m., plus midnight on Sat), is a
200-seat club where locals perform in eight to ten shows weekly (usually
Tues and Thurs–Sat). Favorites include Duel of Fools, where two teams
face off in improvised scenes based on suggestions from the audience,
and Lab Rats, where students play in improv formats.

Side-tripping to John F. Kennedy Space Center

Explore the history of manned flights at **Kennedy Space Center** (☎ **321-
449-4444;** www.kennedyspacecenter.com), beginning with the wild ride
of Alan Shepard (1961) and Neil Armstrong's 1969 moonwalk. The center
has dual five-and-a-half-story, 3-D Imax theaters that reverberate with
special effects. The shows are *L5: First City in Space,* a fictional look at a
space colony; and *The Dream Is Alive,* a rousing past-and-present focus
on the Space Shuttle program. The Visitor Complex has real NASA rockets and exhibits that look at plans for space exploration well into this
millennium. There are also hands-on activities for kids, a chance to meet
a real astronaut, several dining venues, and a shop selling a variety of
space memorabilia and souvenirs.

Bus tours (rent the audio tape for $5) run continuously. You can get off
at the Vehicle Assembly Building, where shuttles are prepared for
launch; the LC-39 Observation Gantry, which has a 360-degree view of
shuttle launch pads; and the Apollo/Saturn V Center, which includes artifacts, photos, interactive exhibits, and a 363-foot-tall Saturn V rocket.
Note: The last bus tour usually departs about two hours before closing
time. Call for schedules.

This is an all-day attraction. To get to the Kennedy Space Center from
Orlando, take the BeeLine Expressway east to Highway 407, turn left, and
then turn right at Highway 405. Directions to the center are well marked
along the roadside. The Space Center is located at NASA Parkway/

Highway 405, 6 miles east of Titusville, about a half mile west of Highway 3. Admission is $26 adults, $16 kids 3 to 11, and the center is open from 9 a.m. to dusk daily.

On launch days, the center is closed at least part of the day. These aren't good days to see the center, but they're great days to observe history in the making. For $15 per person ($36.50 adults and $26.50 kids if you decide to buy center admission, too), you can go on at least a two-hour excursion to NASA Parkway to see the liftoff. You must pick up tickets, available five days prior to the launch, on-site.

If you're staying in Orlando and don't have a car, you can arrange a trip to the center through Mears Transportation by calling ☎ 407-423-5566. From **WDW,** it's $19 per person round-trip (kids under 4 are free). Shuttles run only on Monday, Wednesday, and Friday. Mears does *not* run buses on launch days.

Side-tripping to Cypress Gardens

FDR was in his first term when this foundation theme park opened in 1936. After a brief closure several years ago, the park reopened in 2004, adding a plethora of new rides to its already famous gardens and shows.

The 200-acre attraction continues to showcase 8,000 kinds of plants, ancient cypress trees, ponds, lagoons, waterfalls, classic Italian fountains, bronze sculptures, and manicured lawns. **Southern belles** still stroll the manicured grounds or sit on benches under parasols in idyllic tree-shaded nooks. In late winter and early spring, more than 20 kinds of bougainvilleas, 40 types of azaleas, and hundreds of varieties of roses burst into bloom. Crape myrtles, magnolias, and gardenias perfume the air, while hibiscuses and jasmines brighten the summer landscape.

But years of transformation have turned Cypress Gardens into a less passive, more-than-just-visual park. Kids love the **Boardwalk Carousel,** an ornate turn-of-the-20th-century-style carousel. The adjoining **Jubilee Junction** features an elaborately landscaped model railroad that travels 1,100 feet of track with up to 20 trains, visiting miniature landmarks including New Orleans and Mount Rushmore. **Electric boats** navigate a maze of canals in the botanical gardens area. In order to compete with the thrills available at other Orlando parks, Cypress Gardens has installed a number of roller coasters, including the 5-story-high **Inverter,** the wooden **Triple Hurricane,** and the 80-miles-an-hour **Pharaoh's Fury.**

Splash Island Park (open late spring through summer) lets kids cool off in a pint-size pool, and everyone get a rush on the six flumes. For a water-based thrill, brave the 60-foot-drop on the park's **Storm Surge** or tackle the twists and turns of the **Wave Runner. Nature's Way** features ring-tailed lemurs, colorful macaws, Nile crocodiles, wallabies, and a jaguar.

On the water, Cypress Gardens's celebrated skiers (called the Top Fun Ski Academy) keep a legendary tradition going with standards such as ramp jumping, the aqua-maid ballet line, the human pyramid, and the flag line — all with a little slapstick thrown in for good measure. Shows change periodically. There's some frozen water, too: *Cypress Gardens on Ice* is an ice-skating show starring world-class performers.

Wings of Wonder is a conservatory with more than 1,000 brilliant butterflies (50 species) in a Victorian-style, climate-controlled, free-flight aviary. This man-made rain forest features lush foliage, miniwaterfalls, and iguanas. There's also a hatching display that shows the various stages of butterfly metamorphosis.

The **Birdwalk Aviary** has 40 to 50 hand-raised lories and lorikeets that welcome you by landing on your shoulders. The young Australian parrots are brilliantly colored and very inquisitive. They share the sanctuary with pheasants, ducks, and muntjacs (the smallest deer species in the world).

Cypress Gardens is located at 2641 S. Lake Summit Dr., Highway 540 at Cypress Gardens Boulevard, 40 miles southwest of Disney World, Winter Haven (☎ **800-282-2123;** www.cypressgardens.com). It's open from 9:30 a.m. to 5 p.m. daily, sometimes later. Admission is $34.95 for adults, $29.95 for children 6 to 9. Parking costs $7.

Fast Facts

Area Code

The local area codes are **407** and **321**.

Hospitals

Sand Lake Hospital, 9400 Turkey Lake Rd. (☎ 407-351-8550), is about 2 miles south of Sand Lake Road. Celebration Health (☎ 407-303-4000), located in the Disney-owned town of Celebration, is at 400 Celebration Place.

Information

To receive local telephone information, call ☎ 411. The other most common sources of information are Walt Disney World, Box 10000, Lake Buena Vista, FL 32830-1000 (☎ 407-934-7639; www.disneyworld.com), and the Orlando/Orange County Convention and Visitors

Bureau, 8723 International Dr., Suite 101, Orlando, FL 32819 (☎ 407-363-5872; www.orlandoinfo.com).

Mail

Orlando's main post office (☎ 800-275-8777) is located at 1040 Post Office Blvd. Lake Buena Vista's main post office (☎ 800-275-8777) is at 12133 S. Apopka-Vineland Rd.

Newspapers

You can find a lot of bargains in the major daily, the *Orlando Sentinel* (www.orlandosentinel.com) throughout the week. The paper's Friday "Calendar" section is a gold mine for current information about the area's accommodations, restaurants, nightclubs, and attractions.

Safety

Don't let the aura of Mickey Mouse allow you to lower your guard. Orlando has a crime rate that's comparable to other major U.S. cities. Stay alert and remain aware of your immediate surroundings. Renting a locker is always preferable to leaving your valuables in the trunk of your car, even in the theme-park lots. Be cautious and avoid carrying large amounts of cash.

Taxes

Expect to add 11 or 12 percent to room rates and 6 to 7 percent on most everything else — except groceries and medicines.

Taxis

Yellow Cab (☎ 407-699-9999) and Ace Metro (☎ 407-855-0564) are among those cabs serving the area. Rates are $2.50 for the first mile and $1.50 per mile thereafter.

Transit Info

Lynx (☎ 407-841-2279; www.golynx. com) bus stops are marked with a paw print. The buses serve Disney, Universal, and International Drive ($1.25 for adults, 50¢ for kids and seniors; $10 for an unlimited weekly pass), but they're not very tourist-oriented.

Weather

Call ☎ 321-255-0212 to get forecasts from the National Weather Service. When the phone picks up, punch in 412 from a Touch-Tone phone, and you'll get the Orlando forecast. Also check with The Weather Channel if you have cable television or go to its Web site at www.weather.com.

Part VI
The Great North

"We've been snow-birds for six years now. We try to get down to Florida around October, just before Darlene starts to molt."

In this part . . .

No Miami Vice. No Orlando Mice.

And in spite of that, Florida's top half has plenty to keep you
busy. I start you off at Daytona Beach, which is the closest
this region gets to glitzy tourism, and you can find plenty of
it there. Even historic St. Augustine sports a tourist-trap
atmosphere — if you buy that Fountain of Youth hype, I've
got a bridge to sell you. But I help you look past the bottled
Fountain of Youth Water to find some serious Euro-style old
world charm. Up in Jacksonville I tell you about a city on the
move — especially after hosting the Super Bowl. Finally, I
take you off the metro-path, to Fernandina Beach and Amelia
Island — two of Florida's most sublime stunners. With the
exception of such vacation hot spots as Panama City, Destin,
and Fort Walton Beach (not reviewed in this book for reasons
of space), this part of Florida is wide-open territory, showcas-
ing dune-lined beaches and vast pine forests.

Chapter 20

Daytona Beach

· ·

In This Chapter

▷ Driving with the pros at Daytona International
▷ Sunbathing at Daytona, Ormond, and Ponce Inlet beaches
▷ Dining and staying over in Daytona: Restaurants and hotels
▷ Partying the night away

· ·

*L*ocal tourism types call it the "World's Most Famous Beach." That's a much disputed claim, of course, but Daytona does court tens of thousands of snowbirds in winter, families in summer, college kids during spring break, and bikers during Bike Week and Biketoberfest — a series of races, parties, and games (mainly of the drinking variety). They are all wooed by sun, sand, surf, and the chance to drive on the beach. (What they don't tell you are the side effects of beach driving: auto-pedestrian run-ins, carbon monoxide highs, 10 mph traffic jams, and paint and body corrosion when you park too close to the surf and take a nap on an incoming tide.)

For some travelers, especially older ones or those seeking a quieter, less glitzy beach experience, Daytona Beach is a complete waste of time. Daytona appeals more to the college crowd, young families, or aging Barbie and Ken types who want to exhibit what they have left. The core area around the boardwalk is lined with bars, T-shirt shacks, suntan-oil stands, and souvenir shops. It leans toward sleazy or rowdy, even with the recent redevelopment. However, Daytona remains pretty affordable for a prime beach destination and visitors continue to flock here.

If you want less clutter, look to Ormond Beach, New Smyrna Beach, Ponce Inlet (all discussed later in this chapter) or Indian Shores or Caladesi Island State Park (both in Chapter 15). If you decide to pitch your tent in Daytona itself, well, come expecting one big, noisy party.

After suffering a brutal 2004 hurricane season, Daytona Beach was the victim of severe beach erosion. The worst of the erosion was found in the New Smyrna Beach area — officials estimated the loss of sand from hurricanes Frances and Jeanne was between 7 and 9 feet of vertical elevation of beach, with higher losses in some areas. At press time, the county was seeking emergency sand replacement from the Federal Emergency Management Agency to provide beachfront berms, or mounds of earth.

Getting There

Air travel is the perennial favorite for getting to Daytona because it saves time and, in most cases, isn't prohibitively expensive. But the airport only has two primary carriers. Also, because Daytona lies in North Florida, it's a little easier to reach by car or train than most Florida destinations, should you prefer to travel on land.

By plane

Daytona Beach International Airport, on U.S. 92 (☎ 386-248-8069; http://flydaytonafirst.com), is served by **Delta** and **Continental Connection. Alamo, Avis, Budget, Dollar, Enterprise, Hertz,** and **National** have rental counters at the airport. **Yellow Cab** (☎ 386-255-5555) will take you from the airport to most places in the area for $8 to $18 for up to four people.

If you want a greater selection of airlines to choose from, **Orlando International Airport** (☎ 407-825-2001; www.state.fl.us/goaa) is about 90 minutes southwest of Daytona by car (see Chapter 17) and is serviced by a number of major carriers.

By car

I-95 is the best route when driving to Daytona from the north or south. U.S. 1 is an option, but plan on traffic lights and stop signs as you pass through tiny towns. U.S. A1A is the scenic beach route, but it's even slower. I-4 will get you to Daytona from Orlando. From the west, take I-10 to I-95; from the Midwest, follow I-75 to I-10, and then onward to I-95.

By train

Amtrak (☎ 800-872-7245; www.amtrak.com) offers scheduled service to Deland (the county seat, located about 25 miles southwest of the ocean) at 2491 Old New York Ave.

Orienting Yourself in Daytona Beach

Center stage is the Daytona Beach Boardwalk and the Main Street Pier, located (appropriately enough) just east of Main Street and U.S. A1A, and just north of the eastern end of Volusia Avenue/U.S. 92. Ormond Beach is north of Daytona; New Smyrna Beach and Ponce Inlet are south. The mainland and the rest of Volusia County are to the west. (See the "Daytona Beach" map in this chapter.)

Introducing the neighborhoods

Here is a rundown of the neighborhoods in Daytona and its surrounding area that are of interest to visitors. Most of these spots are pretty close to the coast:

Daytona Beach

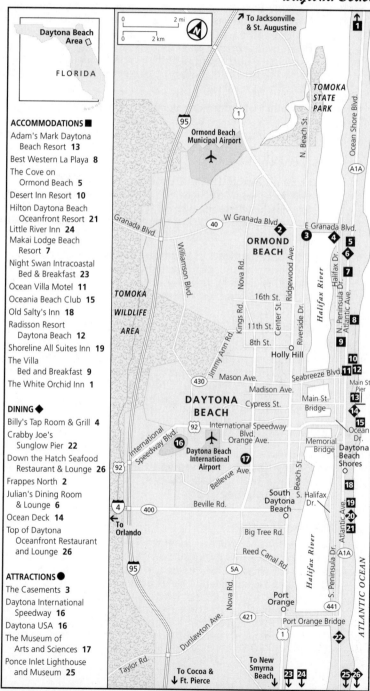

ACCOMMODATIONS ■

Adam's Mark Daytona
  Beach Resort **13**
Best Western La Playa **8**
The Cove on
  Ormond Beach **5**
Desert Inn Resort **10**
Hilton Daytona Beach
  Oceanfront Resort **21**
Little River Inn **24**
Makai Lodge Beach
  Resort **7**
Night Swan Intracoastal
  Bed & Breakfast **23**
Ocean Villa Motel **11**
Oceania Beach Club **15**
Old Salty's Inn **18**
Radisson Resort
  Daytona Beach **12**
Shoreline All Suites Inn **19**
The Villa
  Bed and Breakfast **9**
The White Orchid Inn **1**

DINING ◆

Billy's Tap Room & Grill **4**
Crabby Joe's
  Sunglow Pier **22**
Down the Hatch Seafood
  Restaurant & Lounge **26**
Frappes North **2**
Julian's Dining Room
  & Lounge **6**
Ocean Deck **14**
Top of Daytona
  Oceanfront Restaurant
  and Lounge **26**

ATTRACTIONS ●

The Casements **3**
Daytona International
  Speedway **16**
Daytona USA **16**
The Museum of
  Arts and Sciences **17**
Ponce Inlet Lighthouse
  and Museum **25**

✔ **Daytona Beach:** The spot where most tourists come to play, Daytona Beach has the greatest selection of hotels and restaurants in the area, as well as a few attractions. This sector is bordered by Highway 400/Beville Road in the south and by A1A in the east, and it stretches northward to within 1 mile of Highway 40. It's connected to the mainland by the Memorial, Seabreeze Boulevard, and Main Street bridges.

✔ **Daytona Mainland:** Although not as popular with tourists as the beach side, the mainland has some prime attractions, including Daytona International Speedway and Daytona USA. Visitors can also find some restaurants and motels on U.S. 1 and U.S. 92/International Speedway Boulevard.

✔ **Ormond Beach:** This town is a step quieter than Daytona, though it has become more congested in the last 15 years. Its beach, centered just east of where Highway 40 hits A1A/Atlantic Avenue, is its main attraction. Most of the city's motels and restaurants are strung along A1A, south of Highway 40.

✔ **New Smyrna Beach:** The south coast is quieter still. It has some nice beaches and less glitz, although, like most of the county's east side, this area has shoulder-to-shoulder development, including many motels and restaurants.

Finding information after you arrive

On weekdays, you can contact the **Daytona Beach Convention and Visitors Bureau** at 126 E. Orange Ave. (☎ **800-554-0415;** www.daytona beach.com) from 9 a.m. to 5 p.m. Staff members can give you advice on attractions, accommodations, dining, and special events.

Getting Around Daytona

With the exception of the speedway area, most of the prime tourist zone is set along A1A/Atlantic Avenue, so finding the places where you need to be is easy. Keep in mind, however, that the highway occasionally has some very frustrating traffic.

By car

Daytona is primarily a driver's town, so a car is a good idea. The major east–west roads in Daytona are U.S. 92, which is called International Speedway Boulevard inside the city, and Highway 430/Mason Avenue, which links the mainland to the beaches. Highway 40 is the main east-to-west road in Ormond Beach, whereas it's Highway 44 for New Smyrna Beach. The main north–south roads are U.S. 1/Ridgewood Avenue, Riverside Drive, and Beach Street on the mainland. A1A/Atlantic Avenue and Halifax Avenue are the primary north–south beach routes.

By taxi

Yellow Cab (☎ 386-255-5555) is the main taxi franchise. Fares are $2.60 for the first mile and $1.60 per additional mile.

By bus

VOLTRAN (☎ 386-756-7496), Volusia County's public transit system, runs buses and trolleys throughout the area. Fares are $1 for adults and 50¢ for seniors, kids, or riders with disabilities.

There's also a **free tram** to the beach if you park in the $5-per-day lot at Earl Street and Atlantic Avenue, near Adventure Landing (☎ 386-756-7496). Trams run every 15 minutes from 9 a.m. to 11 p.m. daily.

Staying in Style

Most folks who come to this area want to stay on Daytona Beach, so that's the area I emphasize.

The good news for bargain hunters is that Daytona offers some of the most affordable digs in Florida, provided you don't arrive during a major event or at the height of the spring break. Rates during those periods skyrocket, hotel rooms become a *very* scarce commodity, and most establishments require you to stay for at least two or three nights.

Although major chains operate in the area, hundreds of the hotels lining Atlantic Avenue along the beach are family-owned and -operated. The **Daytona Beach Convention and Visitors Bureau,** 126 E. Orange Ave. (☎ 800-554-0415; www.daytonabeach.com), distributes a list of "Superior Small Lodgings" (75 rooms or fewer) in the area, all of which have passed muster with the bureau.

All the accommodations listed here offer free parking, air-conditioning, and pools, unless otherwise noted.

Note: The following are year-round rates and don't include the county's 11.5 percent hotel tax.

The top hotels

Adam's Mark Daytona Beach Resort

$$ Daytona Beach

Right in the middle of all the beach action, this hotel in 2002 finished a $53 million expansion that nearly doubled its size to 746 rooms, cabanas, and suites, some of which offer scenic views of the Atlantic Ocean. The standard rooms come with a sofa and coffee table and are equipped with dataports, voice mail, desks, and minibars. Cabanas are decorated in bright floral fabrics and have a sofa, small table, and chairs. Guests can use the health club, complete with a sauna, steam room, whirlpools, and massage and tanning services. The resort offers up numerous recreational activities and six restaurants and lounges.

See map p. 381. 100 N. Atlantic Ave./A1A. ☎ *800-444-2326 or 386-254-8200. Fax: 386-253-8841.* www.adamsmark.com. *To get there: From I-95, exit east on International Speedway Boulevard/U.S. 92, cross the Intracoastal Waterway to the beaches and A1A/Atlantic Avenue, and go north. Rack rates: $115–$185. Parking: $10 valet, $6.50 self-parking. AE, DC, DISC, MC, V.*

Best Western La Playa
$$ Daytona Beach

This large, modern high-rise is located right on the beach. The rooms — ranging from standard units to efficiencies and suites — are decorated with tropical prints, and all come with microwaves, refrigerators, coffeemakers, and balconies. The hotel has an on-site restaurant, a lounge, and an indoor spa, whirlpool, and sauna.

See map p. 381. 2500 N. Atlantic Ave./A1A. ☎ *800-874-6996 or 386-672-0990. Fax: 386-677-0982.* www.staydaytona.com. *To get there: Take I-95 to International Speedway Boulevard/U.S. 92, head east to A1A, turn north and go 3 miles. Rack rates: $99–$199. AE, CB, DC, DISC, MC, V.*

The Cove on Ormond Beach
$$ Ormond Beach

This six-story beachfront lodge offers studios and one- to two-bedroom units that, like many newer and less-expensive Florida beachfront properties lack warmth. Studios sleep up to four, with a Murphy bed and sleeper sofa; they also have full kitchens. The two-bedroom units have room for six and come with kitchens. All rooms have balconies that offer a view of the ocean.

See map p. 381. 145 S. Atlantic Ave./A1A. ☎ *386-677-1446. Fax: 386-677-2834.* www.islandone.com/ior/rjorb.html. *To get there: Take International Speedway Boulevard/U.S. 92 to A1A and turn north. Rack rates: $91–$199. AE, DISC, MC, V.*

Desert Inn Resort
$$ Daytona Beach

This property delivers comfortable rooms, a friendly atmosphere, plus recreational activities such as a health club, volleyball courts, and Ping Pong tables. Most of the oceanfront resort's accommodations sport balconies and views of the beach. The large deluxe rooms come with microwaves and refrigerators; free rollaway beds are available. Efficiencies offer two double beds and a kitchenette. Suites have one or two bedrooms and full kitchens; a few have Jacuzzis.

See map p. 381. 900 N. Atlantic Ave./A1A (1 mile north of the boardwalk on A1A). ☎ *800-826-1711 or 386-258-6555. Fax: 386-238-1635.* www.desertinnresort.com. *To get there: From I-95, exit east on International Speedway Boulevard/U.S. 92 and head to the beaches and A1A, then go north. Rack rates: $89–$300. AE, DC, DISC, MC, V.*

Hilton Daytona Beach Oceanfront Resort
$$–$$$ Daytona Beach Shores

Far enough south to escape the maddening crowds at Main Street, the 3½ acre Hilton is among the best choices here. It welcomes you in an elegant terra-cotta-tiled lobby with comfortable seating areas, a fountain, and potted palms. The large guest rooms are grouped in pairs and can be joined to form a suite; only one of each pair has a balcony. Oceanfront rooms are preferable, but all have sea and/or river views. A few also have kitchenettes. While the hotel sustained some exterior damage during Hurricane Frances and was closed for a few months, all damages have been repaired.

See map p. 381. 2637 S. Atlantic Ave./A1A. ☎ *800-774-1500 or 386-767-7350. Fax: 386-760-3651.* www.hilton.com. *To get there: Take I-95, exit east on International Speedway Boulevard/U.S. 92 and go to A1A, head south to Daytona Beach Shores. Rack rates: $116–$359. AE, DC, DISC, MC, V.*

Night Swan Intracoastal Bed & Breakfast
$$ New Smyrna Beach

Built in 1906, this property has a wraparound porch with swings and a view of passing sailboats and, occasionally, dolphins in the Indian River. All 16 rooms have private baths and several have whirlpool tubs. A full breakfast is included daily or you can order a continental breakfast delivered by room service. *Note:* Smoking is prohibited, and the inn doesn't have a pool.

See map p. 381. 512 Riverside Dr. (at Anderson Street). ☎ *800-465-4261 or 386-423-4940. Fax: 386-239-0068.* www.nightswan.com. *To get there: From I-95, take Highway 44 east 4 miles and turn right on Live Oak, go 1 block and turn left on Andrews, go 2 blocks and turn right on Riverside. Rack rates: $95–$200 AE, DISC, MC, V.*

Ocean Villa Motel
$ Daytona Beach

All the rooms, efficiencies, and suites here feature refrigerators and face either the ocean (more expensive) or a courtyard. The property's large suites, equipped with living rooms, balconies, bedrooms, and sofa beds as well as full baths, kitchens, and vanities, make this a good choice for larger families. Kids flock to the property's 60-foot water slide.

See map p. 381. 828 N. Atlantic Ave./A1A. ☎ *800-225-3691 or 386-252-4644. Fax: 386-255-7378.* www.ocean-villa.com. *To get there: Take I-95 to International Speedway Boulevard/U.S. 92, go east to A1A, and head north. Rack rates: Year-round $60–$85; $115–$165 suite. AE, DC, DISC, MC, V.*

Old Salty's Inn
$ Daytona Beach Shores

The most unusual of the many mom-and-pop beachside motels here, Old Salty's is a lush tropical enclave carrying out a *Gilligan's Island* theme, with old motors, rotting boats, life preservers, and a Jeep lying about. The TV series' main characters are depicted in big murals painted on the buildings. The two-story wings flank a courtyard festooned with palms and banana trees (you can pick yourself a banana for breakfast). Facing this vista, the bright rooms have microwaves, refrigerators, and front and back windows allowing for good ventilation. The choice units have picture windows overlooking the beach. Gas grills and rocking chairs furnish a gazebo near a heated beachside swimming pool.

See map p. 381. 1921 S. Atlantic Ave./A1A. ☎ *800-417-1466 or 386-252-8090. Fax: 386-947-9980.* www.visitdaytona.com/oldsaltys. *To get there: From U.S. 192, head south on A1A for 1.4 miles. Rack rates: $53–$71 rooms; $63–$93 efficiency; $75–$121 suite. AE, DISC, MC, V.*

The Villa Bed and Breakfast
$$–$$$ Daytona Beach

You'll think you're in Iberia upon entering this 70-plus-year-old Spanish mansion's great room with its fireplace, baby grand piano, terra-cotta floors, and walls hung with Mediterranean paintings. A sunroom equipped with a TV and VCR, a formal dining room, and a breakfast nook are also located downstairs. The lush backyard surrounds a swimming pool and a covered, four-person Jacuzzi. Upstairs, the nautically themed Christopher Columbus room has a vaulted ceiling and a small balcony overlooking the pool. The largest quarter here is the King Carlos suite, the original master bedroom with a four-poster bed, entertainment system, refrigerator, rooftop deck, dressing area, and bathroom equipped with a four-head shower. No children allowed.

See map p. 381. 801 N. Peninsula Dr. ☎ *and fax 386-248-2020.* www.thevilla bb.com. *To get there: At Riverview Boulevard. Rack rates: $125–$250. AE, MC, V.*

The White Orchid Inn
$$–$$$ Flagler Beach

Located on the ocean about 15 minutes north of Ormond Beach, The White Orchid has sleek Art Deco decor. Here, you can watch the breakers roll in off the Atlantic while you enjoy a full breakfast or munch afternoon appetizers with wine. All of the ten rooms have refrigerators; most offer Jacuzzis. The inn also has a full spa (treatments $10–$110, spa packages $135–$285). No smoking.

See map p. 381. 1104 S. Oceanshore Blvd./A1A. ☎ *800-423-1477 or 904-439-4944. Fax: 904-439-4946.* www.whiteorchidinn.com. *To get there: It's on A1A, ½ mile south of Highway 100. Rack rates: $99–$229. AE, DISC, MC, V.*

Runner-up hotels

Sometimes the first team doesn't make the earth move for you, or you were unable to get a reservation at the above locations. If that's the case, here are more options.

Little River Inn

$$ **New Smyrna Beach** This stately old home sits on the Indian River Lagoon, which, along with the Ponce Inlet Lighthouse, is visible from some of the six rooms, most of which have private baths. There is no pool. *See map p. 381. 532 N. Riverside Dr.* ☎ *888-424-0102 or 386-424-0100.* www.little-river-inn.com.

Makai Lodge Beach Resort

$$ **Ormond Beach** A 1960s-style Florida motel, this location offers tropically themed rooms and efficiencies, right off one of the area's more popular beaches. *See map p. 381. 707 S. Atlantic Ave./A1A.* ☎ *800-799-1112 or 386-677-8060.* www.makailodge.com.

Oceania Beach Club

$$ **New Smyrna Beach** This resort offers two-bedroom, two-bath condos, most with an ocean view. Rates are reasonable for this type of property, mainly because it's south of the action. *See map p. 381. 412 S. Atlantic Ave./A1A.* ☎ *800-874-1931 or 386-423-8400.*

Shoreline All Suites Inn

$$ **Daytona Beach Shores** Situated right off the beach, this cool little complex of 30 (very small) cottages dates back to 1927. *See map p. 381. 2435 S. Atlantic Ave./A1A.* ☎ *800-293-0653 or 386-239-0653.* www.daytonashoreline.com.

Dining Out

If you like fast food, you'll feel right at home in Daytona Beach, but if you prefer fine dining, you'll probably be disappointed. Nevertheless, the area does offer a nice mix of cuisine, headlined by seafood, which is one of the blessings of Daytona Beach's coastal location. *Note:* All Florida restaurants and food-serving bars are smoke-free.

Billy's Tap Room & Grill

$$ **Ormond Beach** SEAFOOD

This 80-year-old restaurant still has a congenial 1920s atmosphere and serves great seafood in a mahogany-paneled dining room filled with antiques. Notable entrees include Maryland-style jumbo lump crab cakes, sautéed shrimp, shrimp scampi, and a seafood casserole (shrimp, scallops, white fish, and crabmeat) topped with cheese. Have a drink before dinner at the solid-maple bar.

See map p. 381. 58 East Granada Blvd. ☎ *386-672-1910. To get there: Located on Granada/Highway 40, just west of the beach area. Reservations not required. Main courses: $12–$27. AE, MC, V. Open: Mon–Fri 11:30 a.m.–10 p.m., Sat 5–10 p.m.*

Crabby Joe's Sunglow Pier
$ Daytona Beach   SEAFOOD

There's nothing crabby about this fun waterfront hangout. Located on the south end of the beach, this informal restaurant offers indoor/outdoor dining and a fantastic view of the ocean. Joe's serves a respectable blackened or grilled grouper sandwich (made more respectable by the $5 price). The sandwich menu also includes an oyster po'boy on Cuban bread. Heartier appetites can tackle crab cakes, fried shrimp, and, if you want to get even with Jaws, shark bites. The portions are large and the price is right.

See map p. 381. 3701 S. Atlantic Ave. ☎ *386-788-3364. To get there: U.S. 92/International Speedway Boulevard east to A1A, then south. Reservations not accepted. Main courses: $4–$14. Credit cards not accepted. Open: Daily 11 a.m.–10 p.m.*

Down the Hatch Seafood Restaurant & Lounge
$–$$ Ponce Inlet   SEAFOOD

Watch the world glide by this seafood-serving, fishing lodge–style eatery on the Halifax River. You can start with oysters (on the half shell, steamed, or raw) and then go on to entrees such as lobster and fried fish. The family-oriented restaurant also offers a kids' menu and a few selections for those counting their calories.

See map p. 381. 4894 Front St. ☎ *386-761-4831. To get there: A1A/Atlantic Ave. south to Ponce Inlet, at four-way stop turn right and go to the river. Reservations not accepted. Main courses: $8–$28. AE, MC, V. Open: Daily 8 a.m.–9 p.m.*

Frappes North
$$ Ormond Beach   FUSION

Several chic dining rooms — one has beams extending like spokes from a central pole — set the stage for an inventive, ever-changing "Menu of the Moment" fusing a multitude of styles. Ingredients are always fresh, and the herbs come from the restaurant's garden. You may run into treats such as organically groovy chicken with goat cheese, prosciutto, shiitake mushrooms, and Madeira wine sauce or maple-glazed crispy duck.

See map p. 381. 123 W. Granada Blvd. ☎ *386-615-4888. To get there: From the beaches, drive 4 miles north on Fla. A1A to left on Granada Boulevard (Fla. 40); cross Halifax River to restaurant on right. Reservations suggested. Main courses: $15–$25. AE, MC, V. Open: Mon–Fri 11:30 a.m.–2:30 p.m. and 5–9 p.m. (until 10 p.m. Fri–Sat).*

Julian's Dining Room & Lounge
$$ Ormond Beach   AMERICAN

This family-owned and -operated restaurant has catered to locals and tourists since 1967, offering a casual atmosphere and friendly service. Unlike most eateries in this area, it specializes in prime Western beef, but the seafood is far from second fiddle. Choices include salmon, Maine lobster, and deviled crab.

See map p. 381. 88 S. Atlantic Ave. ☎ *386-677-6767.* www.juliansrest.com. *To get there: Just south of Highway 40, on the west side of A1A. Reservations suggested. Main courses: $8–$26. AE, DC, MC, V. Open: Daily 4–11 p.m.*

Ocean Deck
$ **Daytona Beach   SEAFOOD**

Known by spring-breakers, bikers, and other beachgoers as Daytona's best "beach pub" since 1940, the Ocean Deck is also the best restaurant in the busy area around the Main Street Pier. Opening to the sand and surf, the downstairs reggae bar is as sweaty, noisy, and packed as ever (a band plays down there nightly from 9 p.m.–2:30 a.m.). The upstairs dining room can be noisy, too, but you can come here for some good food, reasonable prices, and great ocean views. You can choose from a wide range of seafood, chicken, sandwiches, and the best burgers on the beach, but don't pass up the mahimahi.

See map p. 381. 127 S. Atlantic Ave./A1A. ☎ *386-253-5224. To get there: Go north from International Speedway Boulevard on A1A to first right (next to the Mayan Inn). Reservations not required. Main courses: $9–$18. AE, DISC, MC, V. Open: Daily 11 a.m.–2 a.m.*

Top of Daytona Oceanfront Restaurant and Lounge
$$ **Daytona Beach   AMERICAN/CONTINENTAL**

Located 29 floors above sea level in a circular high-rise, this restaurant's view is almost worth the price you pay for a meal. The menu isn't up to the scenery, but the chow is respectable. Pastas are some of the featured attractions. Nonpastafarians can ponder chicken, steaks, seafood, and surf-and-turf platters. All kids' meals (pasta, chicken, beef, and shrimp) cost $7.

See map p. 381. 2625 S. Atlantic Ave./A1A. ☎ *386-767-5791. To get there: South of International Speedway Boulevard on A1A. Reservations suggested. Main courses: $13–$28. AE, DISC, MC, V. Open: Tues–Thurs and Sun 4–9 p.m., Fri–Sat 4–10 p.m.*

Exploring Daytona Beach

Years ago, you could drive on most of Volusia County's 500-foot-wide, 23-mile-long beach. Today, only 9 miles are open to cars and only during the day. Car-pedestrian collisions — some fatal — were an issue, but endangered sea turtles were one of the biggest factors in the decision to close most of the beach to vehicles. The turtles nest here in April and May, and their young, after they've hatched and begun heading for the water, don't stand much of a chance against cars.

For beach driving, cars enter at well-marked locations, and even regular vehicles can navigate on the hard-packed sand. The speed limit is 10 mph. The daily cost for vehicle access is $5 February 1 through November 30.

The top attractions

The Casements
Ormond Beach

Visit the winter home of the late billionaire John D. Rockefeller, who built The Casements in 1912 when he discovered that he was being charged more than the other guests at the nearby Ormond Hotel. After he moved into his new digs, the townies dubbed him "Neighbor John." Today, his restored Queen Anne–style home features art exhibits, a museum of the city, a Rockefeller-period room, and Boy Scout exhibits. Guided tours are conducted Monday through Saturday. Allow one to two hours to see everything.

See map p. 381. 25 Riverside Dr. ☎ 386-676-3216. To get there: It's on Highway 40 at the Granada Boulevard Bridge (Halifax River). Admission: Donations. Open: Mon–Fri 9 a.m.–5 p.m., Sat 9 a.m.–noon; tours Mon–Fri 10 a.m.–2:30 p.m., Sat 10–11:30.

Daytona International Speedway
Daytona Beach Mainland

The speedway and its new adjoining tourist attraction, Daytona USA (see the listing later in this section), are second only to the beach in visitor magnetism. Built in 1959, the speedway is the home of the Daytona 500 (Feb), Pepsi 400 (July), Speed Week (Feb), Biketoberfest (Oct), and several other excuses to drive fast and get rowdy. Tickets for major events start at $35. Even when there isn't something going on at the track, you can take a 30-minute guided tour of the World Center of Racing at Daytona USA, climbing into a tram to see the speedway's garages, pit area, and 31-degree banked turns. Plans for a multimillion-dollar renovation project were underway at press time and should be completed by the time you read this.

See map p. 381. 1801 W. International Speedway Blvd./U.S. 92. ☎ 386-253-7223 (tickets) or 386-254-7200 for tours. www.daytonaintlspeedway.com. *To get there: Take I-95's International Speedway Blvd. exit, then head east. The huge grandstand is really hard to miss. Nonrace admission: Free. (Who pays to look at an empty track and stands?) Open: Daily 9 a.m.–5 p.m.*

Daytona USA
Daytona Beach Mainland

This state-of-the-art, interactive attraction gives you a chance to beat the pros' record at a NASCAR Nextel Cup pit stop, design and test your own race car, compete with other aficionados in a trivia game, and call the final laps of a race from the broadcast booth. You can also see the Stanley Steamer, a steam-powered racer that set the World Land Speed Record in 1906, and a modern stock car that comes apart, section by section, to show visitors how a race car is built. For an extra few bucks, you can tour the speedway in a tram or drive a simulator against the computer. A snack bar serves hamburgers and hot dogs. You can spend four to six hours here, depending on whether you're a gearhead.

While you're at Daytona USA, you can take three laps on the storied speedway at 150 mph in a real racecar. The bad news: It costs $106 and you have to leave the driving to a pro, but the cost includes admission to Daytona USA and the speedway tour.

See map p. 381. 2909 W. International Speedway Blvd./U.S. 92. ☎ 386-947-6800. www. daytonausa.com. *To get there: It's next to the speedway, 4 miles west of A1A. Admission: $16 adults, $8 kids 6–12; combined Daytona USA visit and Daytona International Speedway tour $20 adults, $14 kids 6–12, $5 extra for a driver and passenger in Acceleration Alley simulator. Open: 9 a.m.–6 or 7 p.m., later in summer.*

The Museum of Arts and Sciences
Daytona Beach

Trace Florida's history from prehistoric times to the present. Exhibits include the skeleton of a 13-foot-tall, 130,000-year-old giant ground sloth that was found near the museum in 1974. The museum also features changing art exhibits and a planetarium with a computer-animated program that shows star systems and what early Earth may have looked like were it seen from space. Allow one to two hours to take in everything.

See map p. 381. 1040 Museum Blvd. ☎ 386-255-0285. www.moas.org. *To get there: Take International Speedway Boulevard/U.S. 92 to Nova Road, go south, then west on Museum Boulevard. Admission: $7 adults, $2 kids and students; planetarium shows: $3 adults and $2 kids. Show times: Tues–Fri 2 p.m., Sat–Sun 1 and 3 p.m. Open: Tues–Fri 9 a.m.–4 p.m., Sat–Sun noon–5 p.m.*

Ponce Inlet Lighthouse and Museum
Ponce Inlet

This structure is one of only a handful of Florida lighthouses that has managed to keep its brick torso. Built in 1887, it stayed in service for 83 years and then was reactivated by the Coast Guard in 1982. If you're up for a 203-step climb, the 175-foot sentinel offers a great view of this bitty burg and the ocean. The keeper's house is the museum; the assistant's house is maintained as it would have appeared in 1890. The site has a lens exhibit, a display of lights from around the world, and a 46-foot tugboat that was built in 1938 and served until a few years ago. Allow one to two hours, and then hit the bar across the street.

See map p. 381. 4931 S. Peninsula Dr. ☎ 386-761-1821. www.ponceinlet.org. *To get there: It's at the south end of the county, off A1A/Atlantic Boulevard. Admission: $5 adults, $1.50 kids 11 and under. Open: Daily 10 a.m.–5 p.m., till 9 p.m. in summer.*

More cool things to see and do
Here's where I give visitors with varied interests a few more-specialized options for their Daytona vacation:

 ✔ **Beaches:** All the Atlantic beaches here are good places to surf, body surf, or just let the waves comb your hair. **Daytona Beach,** Seabreeze Boulevard to Volusia Avenue east of A1A, is the center of the nerve-jarring action, with numerous concessionaires renting rafts, beach bikes, and such (☎ 386-239-7873; www.volusia.org). The **Daytona Beach Boardwalk,** just east of where U.S. 92 crosses A1A and dives into the ocean, is arguably one of the top five people-watching places in Florida, and it offers a cheesy, midway-style arcade to sweeten (or sour) the pot. **Ormond Beach,** Highway 40 at A1A, is a quieter version (sans boardwalk and odd characters) of its Daytona counterpart (☎ 386-239-7873; www.ormondchamber.com). **Ponce Inlet,** south of Port Orange off A1A, is almost as peaceful (☎ 386-239-7873; www.volusia.org).

✔ **Fishing:** More than 25 vessels offer half- and full-day charters into the Atlantic Ocean, where you may hook a tuna, wahoo, or grouper. **Charters by Cindy/Rainbow Charters** (☎ 866-356-1334; www.daytonabeachfishing.com) charges $450 half-day and $700 to $900 full-day rates for up to six people. **Cookie Cutter Sport Fishing** (☎ 386-304-0006; www.charternet.com/fishers/cookiecutter) offers the same charter options for $550 to $2,000.

✔ **Golf:** In addition to the following options, you can find more local golf information on the Web at www.golf.com and www.floridagolfing.com. If you like surfing the old-fashioned way, request course information from the **Florida Sports Foundation** (☎ 850-488-8347) or **Florida Golfing** (☎ 877-222-4653). Here are a couple of the better local courses:

  • **Deltona Hills Golf and Country Club,** 1120 Elkcam Blvd., Daytona (☎ 386-789-4911), has rolling hills and fairways. Greens fees are $25 to $40 in the winter and under $25 in the summer.

  • **Daytona Beach Golf Club,** 600 Wilder Blvd. (☎ 386-258-3119), has twin courses — the south course has fairways adorned with palm trees and lakes, and the north course offers rolling fairways with lush vegetation. Greens fees are $25 to $40 in the winter and under $25 in the summer.

✔ **Parks: Washington Oaks State Park,** 6400 Oceanshore Blvd./A1A, Palm Coast (☎ 386-446-6780; www.floridastateparks.org/washingtonoaks), is a 19th-century plantation turned 400-acre park that stretches from the Atlantic to the Matanzas River. You can take guided tours, but exploring the ornamental gardens, tidal pools, and dunes on your own is much more fun. The park is 14 miles north of Flagler Beach (about 35 miles north of Daytona Beach) on A1A. Admission is $3.75 per car.

Shopping

There are some shopping "districts" in and around Daytona, but remember that this is a tourist zone and has all the related trappings — overpriced antiques shops on one side and trinket shacks on the other. Look for the tackiest souvenirs along Atlantic Avenue/A1A, especially near the boardwalk (where U.S. 92 connects with A1A). Most shops sell barely-there bathing suits, seashells, and T-shirts decorated with some of the world's most forgettable expressions.

If you're into yard sales and produce stands on a moderately large scale, the **Daytona Beach Flea and Farmers Market,** U.S. 92 at I-95, (☎ **386-253-3330;** www.daytonafleamarket.net) is a funky place to shop for produce, "junque," and white-elephant gifts Friday through Sunday, from 8 a.m. to 5 p.m.

Main St. Inc., 512 Canal St. (☎ **386-423-3131;** http://volusia.com/nsbmainstreetinc), in the New Smyrna Beach Downtown Historic District, has a scattering of antiques dealers, jewelers, and home-furnishing shops. There's also a farmer's market on Saturdays from 7 a.m. to 1 p.m.

Riverfront Marketplace, 300 S. to 300 N. Beach St., Daytona Beach (☎ **386-872-3272;** www.riverfrontmarketplace.com), offers dozens of restaurants, shops, boutiques, salons, a day spa, bars, a live theater, and the Halifax History Museum.

Volusia Mall, 1700 International Speedway Blvd. (☎ **386-253-6783;** www.volusiamall.net), has more than 100 stores anchored by Macy's, Dillard's, and Sears. Some smaller nearby strip centers feature stores such as T.J. Maxx.

Living It Up After Dark

In addition to the following, you can find a lot of action along the main beach strip, A1A/Atlantic Avenue. You should also check the Daytona Beach *News-Journal* for its Friday entertainment section.

Bars

600 North, 600 N. Atlantic (☎ **904-255-4471**), is *Baywatch* revisited, with buxom bikini babe staffers who have actually been extras on the show, and a year-round spring-break vibe with assorted drinking and thong-sporting contests.

The **Boot Hill Saloon,** 310 Main St. (☎ **904-258-9506**), is a bluesy, brew-sy honky-tonk especially popular during race and bike weeks. If line dancing is your thang, then scoot your boots over to the **Rockin' Ranch,** 801 S. Nova Rd. (☎ **904-947-0785**), an uber fun country-western bar with live music and even line-dancing lessons.

Main Street and **Seabreeze Boulevard** on the beach are happening areas where dozens of bars (and a few topless shows) cater to leather-clad bikers.

A popular beachfront bar for more than 40 years, the **Ocean Deck Restaurant & Beach Club,** 127 S. Ocean Ave. (☎ **386-253-5224;** see listing under "Dining Out" earlier in this chapter), is packed with a mix of locals and tourists, young and old, who come for live music and cheap drinks. Reggae or ska bands play after 9:30 p.m. There's valet parking after dark, or leave your vehicle at Ocean Deck's Reggae Republic surf shop on Atlantic Avenue.

The **River Deck Night Club & Restaurant,** 2739 S. Ridgewood, Ormond Beach (☎ 386-761-0022), features live dance tunes, Wednesday, Friday, and Saturday. **Frank's Front Row,** 308 Seabreeze, Daytona Beach (☎ 386-255-9221), has live contemporary music nightly. Neither has a cover charge.

Performing arts

The **Peabody Auditorium,** 600 Auditorium Blvd., Daytona Beach (☎ 386-671-3460; www.peabodyauditorium.org), is home to the Daytona Beach Symphony Society, the Civic Ballet of Volusia County, and the Concert Showcase of Florida. It also hosts touring companies.

The modern **Ormond Beach Performing Arts Center,** 399 N. U.S. Hwy. 1 (☎ 386-676-3375; www.ormondbeach.org/pac), is home to professional, community, and children's theater productions, and it offers classes in the performing arts. Volusia County's largest venue, **Ocean Center,** 101 N. Atlantic Ave. (☎ 386-254-4500; www.oceancenter.com), offers sporting events such as rodeos and occasional concerts.

Day-tripping to Ocala

Before it became a major breeding center for thoroughbred race horses, Ocala's main claim to fame was serving as an occasional movie and television set. Johnny Weissmuller (arguably the best Tarzan ever), and Lloyd Bridges (from the old *Sea Hunt* television show), got into the swim and filmed at **Silver Springs.**

Today, this full-fledged attraction 60 miles west of Daytona has dual faces. **Silver Springs** is a throwback-but-modernized Florida attraction that lures guests with glass-bottom boat rides above crystal-clear springs, a jungle cruise (remember, this is north central Florida, where *jungle* translates into "swamps" or "scrub land"), a safari ride, and encounters with panthers, alligators, crocodiles, bears, and other critters. (Admission: $32.99 adults, $23.99 kids 3–12; add $2 to get into Wild Waters on the same day.) **Wild Waters,** a neighboring water park, costs $23.99 adults, $20.99 kids 3 to 12 by itself. It has a wave pool, water slides, and plenty more. Silver Springs also has a country-music concert series (☎ 352-236-2121; www.silversprings.com and www.wildwaterspark.com).

Ocala Carriage and Tours is a delightful way to see some of the area's horse farms or the city's downtown historic district while being lullabyed by the clippity-clop of a draft horse's hoofs. The 70-minute tours cost

$95 for up to four adults and two kids (☎ **877-996-2252;** www.ocala carriage.com).

Ocala Stud Farm (☎ **352-237-2171**) and **Double Diamond** (☎ **352-237-3834**) also offer walking or driving farm tours, and **Young's Paso Finos** (☎ **352-867-5273**) and **Ocala Foxtrotter Ranch** (☎ **352-347-5551**) offer horseback rides.

 You can get more information on these and other activities as well as hotels and restaurants from the **Ocala/Marion County Chamber of Commerce** (☎ **352-629-8051;** www.ocalacc.com).

Fast Facts

Area Code
The local area code is **386.**

Hospitals
The region's major hospital is Halifax Medical Center, 303 N. Clyde Morris Blvd., Daytona Beach (☎ 386-254-4000).

Information Sources
You can contact the Daytona Beach Convention and Visitors Bureau, 126 E. Orange Ave. (☎ 800-554-0415; www.daytonabeach.com), from 9 a.m. to 5 p.m. on weekdays.

Maps
The visitors bureau (see "Information Sources," earlier in this section) is a great place to get maps, before or after you arrive. You can also find good maps at your rental-car agency and inside convenience stores, which sell them for $3 to $5.

Newspapers
The *News Journal* (☎ 386-252-1511) is the local paper and publishes an informative Friday entertainment section.

Post Offices
There are post offices at 220 N. Beach St., Daytona Beach, and 260 Williamson Blvd., Ormond Beach. For other local branches, call ☎ 800-275-8777.

Taxes
The sales tax is 6 percent; hotels tack on an additional 5.5 percent.

Taxis
The main taxi company is Yellow Cab (☎ 386-255-5555). Its rates are $2.60 to start the meter and $1.60 per additional mile.

Transit Information
Volusia County's public system, VOLTRAN (☎ 386-756-7496), runs buses and trolleys throughout the area. Fares are $1 for adults, 50¢ for seniors, kids, or riders with disabilities. There's also a free tram to the beach if you park in the $5-per-day lot at Earl Street and Atlantic Avenue, near Adventure Landing (☎ 386-756-7496). Trams run every 15 minutes, 9 a.m. to 11 p.m. daily.

Weather
To check weather forecasts online, go to www.weathercenter.com or surf over to the National Weather Service's site at www.nws.noaa.gov. You also can get information by watching the Weather Channel on TV or visiting its Web site (www.weather.com).

Chapter 21

Northeast Florida

● ●

In This Chapter

▶ Getting to know Northeast Florida
▶ Drinking from the fountain of youth in the oldest U.S. city
▶ Catching the critters at Jacksonville Zoo
▶ Go-karting around: Adventure Landing
▶ Seeing a 19th-century sugar plantation

● ●

*R*emember Ponce de León from your high school history class? Well, it turns out he was a better dreamer than an astronomer. He was supposed to land at Bimini and find the "fountain of youth" that would keep Jolly Ol' King Ferdinand and his daughter, Juana the Mad (we're not making that up), on their thrones forever. But Ponce bounced his azimuth off the wrong star and wound up near present-day Cape Canaveral. Instead of eternal life and the hand of Juana, he got hissing snakes, angry natives, and alligators that were delighted to sample a little Spanish take-out.

As for the fabled fountain, well, St. Augustine has one, complete with a gift shop selling glow-in-the-dark key chains. The fountain itself is indoors. It even has a dome. And if you sip the water, you're making a *big* mistake. It contains sulfur, which, as anyone who's ever been held captive in chemistry class knows, smells like rotten eggs.

More on that domed scandal later in this chapter, but for now, here's my three-minute thumbnail on this region.

After you drive away from the coast, the Great Northeast is about as rural as Florida gets. The St. Johns River is the interior's biggest attraction. Although the river is a magnet for anglers, boaters, and other river rats, for most tourists it's little more than a reference point or a backdrop for some other activity, closer to the coast.

Due to the lack of action away from the coast, this chapter's tour bus stays near the Atlantic. I divide this region into two general areas, south to north. The oldest city in the United States, St. Augustine offers a lot to do, especially if you like to live history. Although Jacksonville is the largest city in Northeast Florida, it's mainly an insurance and banking center but does have a few interesting attractions for visitors. Its neighbors,

Fernandina Beach and Amelia Island, have colorful histories but, again, not much in the way of attractions.

Now, queue up Willie Nelson's gem "On the Road Again," and I can you get started down the road to Northeast Florida.

Getting a Feel for Northeast Florida

It's kind of ironic that the alleged Fountain of Youth is located in America's oldest European settlement. Alas, St. Augustine is like a fine wine — it has aged beautifully in all its 17th-century glory. Families love it here not just because it's steeped in history, hence educational for the kids, but because the old-world vibe is conducive to romance.

Jacksonville, on the other hand, isn't exactly romantic. The once industrial city has gotten hipper in a cosmopolitan way thanks, in part, to the 2005 SuperBowl and all the celebrities who came with it. Jax, as it's fondly known, has a riverfront that is akin to NYC's South Street Seaport and a downtown that's trying to come into its own with new restaurants, bars, and attractions. Not so far from Jax is Amelia Island — now that's romantic

Located on the northernmost barrier island of Florida, Amelia Island features 13 miles of gorgeous beach with a quaint Victorian-style town. Just 45-minutes northeast of downtown Jax, Amelia Island is the ideal getaway for couples looking to escape "city" life.

St. Augustine

Established in 1565, **St. Augustine** is the oldest continuously settled city in the United States. The city, which blissfully refuses to indulge in Botox treatments, offers visitors a bounty of history in its architecture, attractions, and accommodations. At least a half-dozen places in town claim to be the oldest something or other. A few of them actually are. In addition to the history, St. Aug has a delightfully European, old-world feel to it with bona fide cobblestone streets, winding roads, excellent restaurants, and even a bit of nightlife. (Skip ahead to see a map of St. Augustine.)

Getting there

The farther north you travel, the easier it is to drive from other parts of the country, but air travel is the arrival-and-departure method of choice.

By plane

Jacksonville International Airport (☎ **904-741-4902;** www.jaxports. com), which is 43 miles north of St. Augustine, serves this area. A dozen major lines, including **American, Continental, Delta, Northwest,** and **US Airways,** fly in and out of here. **Avis, Budget, Dollar, Enterprise, Hertz,**

St. Augustine

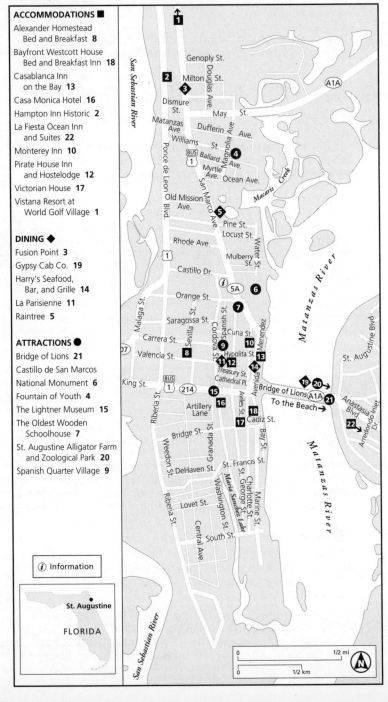

ACCOMMODATIONS ■

Alexander Homestead
  Bed and Breakfast **8**

Bayfront Westcott House
  Bed and Breakfast Inn **18**

Casablanca Inn
  on the Bay **13**

Casa Monica Hotel **16**

Hampton Inn Historic **2**

La Fiesta Ocean Inn
  and Suites **22**

Monterey Inn **10**

Pirate House Inn
  and Hostelodge **12**

Victorian House **17**

Vistana Resort at
  World Golf Village **1**

DINING ◆

Fusion Point **3**

Gypsy Cab Co. **19**

Harry's Seafood,
  Bar, and Grille **14**

La Parisienne **11**

Raintree **5**

ATTRACTIONS ●

Bridge of Lions **21**

Castillo de San Marcos
  National Monument **6**

Fountain of Youth **4**

The Lightner Museum **15**

The Oldest Wooden
  Schoolhouse **7**

St. Augustine Alligator Farm
  and Zoological Park **20**

Spanish Quarter Village **9**

ⓘ Information

St. Augustine

FLORIDA

0   1/2 mi

0   1/2 km

National, and **Thrifty** have rental-car desks on the airport's lower level. Taxi and shuttle services from Jacksonville to St. Augustine are cost-prohibitive.

By car

From the north, take I-95 south to Highway 16, then go east into the city, and go south on U.S. 1/Ponce de Leon Boulevard. From the west, take I-10 to I-95 and follow the preceding directions. From the Midwest, follow I-75 to I-10, then I-95.

Getting around

The city's historic downtown is small and user-friendly enough that I recommend you park your car and hoof it along the cobbled, winding streets of St. Augustine's historic district. For parking information, see "By car," later in this chapter.

Here are some other options for getting around town:

By car

In addition to U.S. 1 (which becomes Ponce de Leon Boulevard in the city), A1A is the main north–south route, and it stays pretty close to the water. In town, you may also use Cordova and St. George streets to travel north and south. East–west routes include Highways 16 and 312, King Street, and May Street.

On-street parking is nonexistent in St. Augustine's historic district, and metered parking lots are difficult to find and are often full. Your best bet is to park in the large municipal lots behind the visitor center on Castillo Drive. The $3 fee is good for two consecutive days, so you may leave and return at will. Plus, most of the top historic attractions are within walking distance of the center, as it is virtually across the street from the Old City Gates.

By taxi

For a taxi, call **Yellow Cab** (☎ 904-824-6888) or **Ancient City Cab** (☎ 904-824-8161). St. Augustine taxis use a complicated zone system, but figure on spending $2 to $8 for one person and $1.50 for each extra body. Those rates will get you to most parts of the city.

By guided tour

St. Augustine Historical Sightseeing Tours (☎ 904-826-4218; www.infoperson.com/no1tours.htm) offers a one-hour sightseeing jaunt plus you can use its trolleys to get to 20 stops around town for up to three days ($16 adults, $7 kids 6–11, free for children under 6). This is an inexpensive way to travel the downtown historic district.

I tell you about two others guided tours later in this chapter under "Going on a guided tour."

Staying in style

St. Augustine has plenty of moderate and inexpensive hotels. If you want a unique experience, however, stay in one of the city's bed-and-breakfasts, many of which occupy restored historic homes. Note, however, that kids usually aren't welcome; ditto for smokers. The **Historic Inns of St. Augustine,** P.O. Box 5268, St. Augustine, FL 33085-5268 (www.staugustine inns.com), provides visitors with a list describing its member properties.

Hotel rates increase significantly on weekends, when the city is usually inundated with visitors, so try coming during the week to lower your costs. Also, don't forget to add the hotel tax of 9 percent to your budget.

All the accommodations listed here offer free parking, air-conditioning, and pools, unless otherwise noted.

The top hotels

Alexander Homestead Bed and Breakfast
$$ St. Augustine

Victor, Victorian! This restored 1888 home is a Kodak moment, to say the least. One room has a Jacuzzi, two have fireplaces, and each have lavender sachets tucked away in drawers, their own private porches, and antiques. Gourmet breakfasts include homemade French toast with almond syrup, and at night, you can have a glass of complimentary brandy to go along with your complimentary chocolate. Even better, coffee is delivered directly to your door in the morning so there's no need to really have to stir yourself too much. The only drawback is the lack of a pool.

See map p. 398. 14 Sevilla St. ☎ *888-292-4147 or 904-826-4147.* www.alexander homestead.com. *To get there: Located east of U.S. 1, just south of Orange Street. Rack rates: Mon–Thurs $159–$179, Fri–Sun $169–$199. AE, DISC, MC, V.*

Casa Monica Hotel
$$–$$$ St. Augustine

You've really arrived in St. Augustine if you stay at the Casa Monica Hotel. Most of the guest quarters are spacious and fully modern hotel rooms, with Iberian-style armoires, wrought-iron headboards, and tapestry drapes. "Premium" rooms have sitting areas with sofas and easy chairs. Much more interesting are the "signature suites" installed in the building's two tile-topped towers and fortresslike central turret. Each of these one- to four-bedroom units is unique. One in the turret has a half-round living room with gun-port windows overlooking the historic district, while a three-story town-house model in one of the towers has a huge whirlpool bathroom on its top floor. The hotel's restaurant, 95 Cordova, is one of the city's best. For $15 a day, guests can use the pools, restaurants, and other facilities at The Serenata Beach Club, an exclusive oceanfront club located ten minutes from the hotel.

See map p. 398. 95 Cordova St. (at King Street). ☎ **800-648-1888** or 904-827-1888. Fax: 904-827-0426. www.casamonica.com. To get there: Take U.S. 1/Ponce de Leon Boulevard south to King Street, and then left to Cordova. Parking: $12.75 valet. Rack rates: $149–$239. AE, DC, DISC, MC, V.

Hampton Inn Historic
$–$$ St. Augustine

This 52-room chain motel is 6 blocks (1 mile) north of the historic district. It isn't luxurious, but it's near the heart of the action and the privately run sightseeing trolleys (see "Getting around," earlier in this chapter) stop here. It presents a clean option for those on tighter budgets. Rates include continental breakfast, and all local phone calls are free.

See map p. 398. 2050 N. Ponce de Leon Blvd./U.S. 1. ☎ **800-426-7866** or 904-829-1996. Fax: 904-829-1988. www.hamptoninn.com. To get there: On U.S. 1, just north of downtown. Rack rates: Feb–Apr $105–$185, May–Sept $95–$175, Oct–Nov $85–$165, Dec–Jan $110–$200. AE, CB, DC, DISC, MC, V.

Monterey Inn
$–$$ St. Augustine

A family-owned motel, this 59-unit property overlooks Matanzas Bay and, like the Hampton earlier, it comes with an affordable price. The guest rooms are tight on space but clean and comfortable. Efficiencies are available.

See map p. 398. 16 Avenida Menendez (between Cuna Street and Hypolita Street). ☎ **904-824-4482**. Fax: 904-829-8854. www.themontereyinn.com. To get there: Located at U.S. 1 Business Route and A1A. Rack rates: $59–$159, though weekday rates are as low as $39. AE, DC, DISC, MC, V.

Victorian House
$$ St. Augustine

This 1897 Victorian find comes complete with wraparound porch and converted carriage house divided into four units, all of which have TVs and private entrances. Kids are more than welcome at the carriage house, but they aren't allowed to stay in the main house, not that they'd want to anyway — there are no TVs. The main house features four units, all of which are decked out in antiques. Continental breakfast is included in the rates.

See map p. 398. 11 Cadiz St. (between Aviles and Charlotte streets). ☎ **877-703-0432** or 904-824-5214. Fax: 904-824-7990. www.victorianhouse-inn.com. To get there: From A1A, take the Vilano Beach Bridge to Orange Street. Make slight right. Turn left on Cordova Street, left onto King Street, right onto Aviles Street and then left onto Cadiz Street. Rack rates: $95–$165. AE, DC, DISC, MC, V.

Runner-up hotels

If you can't find something already listed that suits you, consider this five-pack of choices.

Bayfront Westcott House Bed and Breakfast Inn

$$ St. Augustine Overlooking Matanzas Bay, this two-story, Key West–style, wood-frame house offers rare opportunities for an uncluttered view from the porch, the second-story veranda, and a shady courtyard. The rooms — some with bay windows, two-person whirlpool tubs, and working fireplaces — are exquisitely furnished and immaculate. *See map p. 398. 138 Avenida Menendez, just south of A1A and the Bridge of Lions.* ☎ **800-558-3455** *or 904-824-1681.* www.bayfrontinn.com.

Casablanca Inn on the Bay

$$ St. Augustine Here's a 1914 Mediterranean-style house that faces the bay and offers beautifully decorated rooms plus free beer, wine, soft drinks, and cookies. No pool, however. *See map p. 398. 24 Avenida Menendez, between Hypolita Street and Treasury Street.* ☎ **800-826-2626** *or 904-829-0928.* www.casablancainn.com.

Coquina Gables Oceanfront Bed & Breakfast

$ St. Augustine Beach Set oceanfront, the inn has a great room with a fireplace, luxurious suites named for famous authors, a gourmet breakfast, and a nice beach. *1 F St.* ☎ **904-461-8727.** www.coquinagables.com.

La Fiesta Ocean Inn and Suites

$$ St. Augustine Beach This modest property offers comfortable motel-style rooms, large suites, and a nice beach. *See map p. 398. 810 A1A/Beach Blvd.* ☎ **800-852-6390** *or 904-471-2220.* www.lafiestainn.com.

Pirate Haus Inn & Hostelodge

$ St. Augustine Located in the heart of the historic district, this Hosteling International member offers bargain rates if you don't mind the spartan quarters, the lack of a pool, and, in the case of some rooms, sharing a bath. It's best known for its all-you-can-eat pancake breakfast, which is included in the rock-bottom rates. *See map p. 398. 32 Treasury St.* ☎ **904-808-1999.** www.piratehaus.com.

Dining out

When you consider St. Augustine's popularity with the tourist crowd, it isn't surprising that the city is loaded with tourist-trap restaurants and fast-food joints. That said, the dining in town is, on the whole, pretty good and fairly priced. The local cuisine is (no surprise!) seafood mixed with a variety of other cuisines. **Note:** All Florida restaurants and food-serving bars are smoke-free.

Don't forget to add the 6 percent sales tax to your meal budget.

Fusion Point
$ St. Augustine ORIENTAL/SUSHI

This eatery offers a mix of cuisines from the Far East. On the sushi side, a big appetite can turn this $ eatery into a $$ or $$$ one. Specialties include spicy Thai chicken, steak tempura, and *yum-yum rolls* (a deep-fried sushi roll).

See map p. 398. 237 San Marco Ave. ☎ *904-823-1444. To get there: Located on San Marco/U.S. 41 Business Route, just north of the heart of town. Reservations not accepted. Sushi: $1.25–$3 per item; $2.50–$8 per roll. Main courses: $8–$18. MC, V. Open: Daily 5–10 p.m.*

Gypsy Cab Co.
$$ St. Augustine NEW AMERICAN

The menu changes frequently in this restaurant that looks like a gaudy house built in the '40s or '50s (which it is). The "urban cuisine" here is among the city's most interesting and is expertly prepared by the chef-owner, Ned Pollack. Try the black-bean soup and veal with bacon-horseradish cream, if available. As a capper, I recommend Amaretto cheesecake or Key lime pie. The Gypsy Bar & Grill (next door) serves lunch from 11 a.m. to 4 p.m. weekdays.

See map p. 398. 830 Anastasia Blvd./A1A. ☎ *904-824-8244. To get there: Located on A1A, 1 mile south of the Bridge of Lions. Reservations accepted. Main courses: $10–$19, with many in the $16–$18 range. AE, DC, DISC, MC, V. Open: Daily 5:30–10 p.m.*

Harry's Seafood, Bar, and Grille
$–$$ St. Augustine NEW ORLEANS/SEAFOOD

Come to this Cajun restaurant hankering for crawdad étouffée, spicy gumbo, chicken-and-andouille-sausage jambalaya, and other treats straight out of N'awlins. You can't go wrong with the shrimp en brochette (jumbos stuffed with Monterey Jack cheese, wrapped in bacon, and grilled). There are almost enough under-$15 entrees to make it a $ restaurant.

See map p. 398. 46 Avenida Menendez. ☎ *904-824-7765. To get there: On Avenida Menendez near Hypolita. Reservations accepted. Main courses: $10–$24. AE, MC, V. Open: Daily 11 a.m.–10 p.m.*

La Parisienne
$$–$$$ St. Augustine FRENCH

An accidental tourist in these parts, La Parisienne is a welcome respite from all the nearby Americana. Despite its name, this lovely dining room evokes the French countryside, with a rough-hewn beamed-pine ceiling, lace-curtained windows, and ladder-back chairs. Changing seasonally, the menu always features fresh seafood, and in fall you'll see venison and quail.

See map p. 398. 60 Hypolita St. ☎ *904-829-0055. To get there: Between Spanish and Cordova streets. Reservations accepted. Main courses: $19–$28. AE, DISC, MC, V. Open: Tues–Fri 5–9 p.m., Sat–Sun 11 a.m.–3 p.m. and 5–9 p.m.*

Raintree
$$ St. Augustine CONTINENTAL

I highly doubt that the Victorians who originally lived in this 1877 house ate as well as you will at Raintree, best known for its cashew-encrusted pork tenderloin mignonettes with a champagne and ruby raspberry sauce, beef Wellington, and rack of New Zealand lamb. A list of over 300 wines ain't too shabby, either.

See map p. 398. 102 San Marco Ave. ☎ 904-824-7211. To get there: Located on San Marco Avenue at Bernard Street. Reservations accepted. Main courses: $15–$24. AE, DC, MC, V. Open: Sun–Thurs 6–9:30 p.m., Fri–Sat 6–10 p.m.

Exploring St. Augustine

History is the highlight in St. Augustine, with 144 blocks of houses and buildings that are on the National Register of Historic Places. The historic district centers on St. George Street, a few blocks east of U.S. 1. Much of the action takes place on St. George, the Avenida Menendez, King Street, San Marco Avenue, Castillo Drive, or across the Bridge of Lions, which leads to Anastasia Island.

The top attractions

Bridge of Lions
St. Augustine

An Italian sculptor carved the two king of beasts on the historic Bridge of Lions, which goes from the mainland to Anastasia Island. Alas, the artist left a few physical attributes off his lions, and legend has it that he was subjected to such ridicule by townies that he stabbed himself with a blunt sculpting knife. The Bridge, located where U.S. 1/San Marco turns into Anastasia Boulevard and crosses the Intracoastal Waterway, is one of the most photographed (and congested, thanks to a drawbridge and barge traffic) sights in town.

See map p. 398.

Castillo de San Marcos National Monument
St. Augustine

Built in the 18th century, this stoic Spanish fortress includes plenty of bastions, dungeons, and artillery positions to explore. Additionally, the National Park Service puts on a number of events here, including torchlight tours and reenactments. Most folks can see it all in one to two hours.

See map p. 398. 1 E. Castillo Dr. (at San Marco Avenue). ☎ 904-829-6506, ext. 234. www.nps.gov/casa. *Admission: $5 adults, $2 kids 6–16, free for children 5 and under. Open: Daily 8:45 a.m.–4:45 p.m.*

Fountain of Youth
St. Augustine

Earlier in this chapter, I promised to get back to (drumroll, please) Ponce de León's quest. So, here you are. This fountain's for you, if you're the kind who flushes, er, spends money on anything. If you go, I hope you remember my warning about this foul-tasting liquid. There is also a planetarium where you can stargaze at the dome, a 45-minute tour that gets downright silly, and the inevitable Ponce de Leon Gift Shop. Allow 90 minutes to see everything.

See map p. 398. 11 Magnolia Ave. ☎ 800-356-8222 or 904-829-3168. www.fountain ofyouthflorida.com. *Admission: $5.75 adults, $4.75 seniors, $2.75 kids 6–12. Open: Daily 9 a.m.–5 p.m.*

The Lightner Museum
St. Augustine

Dating to 1888, this cutie began life as Henry Flagler's elaborate, Spanish Renaissance–style resort spa. These days it makes a gorgeous museum that has substantial collections of cut glass, vases, and wood-jointed dolls. The first floor has a row of shops. You can also meet a mummy, equally dead birds, samples of Victorian glassblowing, and a collection of rocks, minerals, and Native-American artifacts in period cases. Allow two hours to see the highlights.

See map p. 398. 75 King St. ☎ 904-824-2874. www.lightnermuseum.org. *To get there: Located at King and Cordova. Admission: $6 adults, $2 kids 12–18, free for children 11 and under. Open: Daily 9 a.m.–5 p.m.*

The Oldest Wooden Schoolhouse
St. Augustine

This is one of many "oldests" in this city (others include a house, store, jail, and so on). Built in 1763, the red-cedar schoolhouse is held together by wooden pegs and nails that were made by hand. Today, the last class — held in 1864 — is re-created for visitors. You'll be ready to bolt when the bell rings 45 minutes later (if not before).

See map p. 398. 14 George St. ☎ 904-829-9729. www.oldestschoolhouse.com. *Admission: $3 adults, $2.50 seniors, $2 kids 6–12, free for children 5 and under. Open: Daily 9 a.m.–5 p.m.*

St. Augustine Alligator Farm and Zoological Park
St. Augustine

It's not as historic as some landmarks, but it is the oldest continuously running reptile retreat in Florida, having opened in 1893. The main attraction is **Land of Crocodiles,** home to all 23 species of these critters. Until 1999, its star resident was Gomek, an 18-foot, 1,800-pound Porosus crocodile that, in his native New Guinea, munched on water buffaloes and slow-moving humans. Alas, Gomek has gone to that big swamp in the sky, but his skin has been stuffed so you can sit on him and get your picture taken. The park also has alligator, snake, and bird shows. Figure on staying four to five hours.

See map p. 398. 999 Anastasia Blvd. ☎ *904-824-3337.* www.alligatorfarm.com. *To get there: Located across the Bridge of Lions on A1A. Admission: $14.95 adults, $8.95 kids 5–11, free for children 4 and under. Open: Daily 10 a.m.–6 p.m. (until 5 p.m. in winter).*

Spanish Quarter Village
St. Augustine

If the kids complain about how hard they've got it these days, take them here and they'll never complain again. Okay, well, they will at least appreciate what they've got! A living-history village, it dates to 1740 and features blacksmiths, weavers, and woodworkers, among other tradespeople. The nearby **City Gate,** on San Marco near Orange, was erected in 1808 by the Spanish as a defensive wall. **Mission of Nombre de Dios,** west of San Marco Avenue on Old Mission Road at the Intracoastal, goes way back to 1565 and has a 208-foot cross that's visible from 25 miles at sea. It's where the first Catholic Mass in the United States was said, but Mass is no longer offered there. Allow two to four hours to see it all.

See map p. 398. 29 St. George St. ☎ *904-823-4569.* www.oldcity.com/spanish quarter. *To get there: Located between Cuna Street and Orange Street. Admission: $6.50 adults, $5.50 seniors, $4.00 kids 6 and older, free for children 5 and under. Open: Sun–Thurs 9 a.m.–5:30 p.m., Fri–Sat 9 a.m.–9 p.m.*

Finding more cool things to see and do

If you need a break from sightseeing and want to catch a ray on the beach or snag a grouper that could feed an army, you can choose from several other outdoor recreational activities. And when you're ready to hit the touring trail again, you may want to try one of the tour companies that offer specialized programs for visitors, later in this chapter.

✔ **Beaches: Vilano Beach,** on the north side of St. Augustine Inlet on A1A, is a public beach with restrooms, volleyball courts, and picnic areas. After you cross the Bridge of Lions, **Yankee Beach** is the first stop on Anastasia Island. It earned its name because many northern tourists never venture beyond it. Those who do, find **Anastasia Island State Recreation Area** (☎ 904-461-2033; www.abfla.com/ parks/Anastasia/anastasia.html). This 1,700-acre bird sanctuary has 5 miles of beaches, lagoons, sabal palms, and sea oats, growing wild from 20-foot dunes. Admission costs $5 per car.

✔ **Fishing:** Snapper, grouper, amberjack, and other species are common catches in the Atlantic Ocean. You can catch a large charter boat from **Sea Love Marina,** 250 Vilano Rd./A1A N. (☎ 904-824-3328; www.sealovefishing.com). Day-trips are $50; $40 kids 14 and under.

✔ **Golf:** You can obtain local course information online at www.golf.com and www.floridagolfing.com, or you can call the **Florida Sports Foundation** (☎ 850-488-8347) or **Florida Golfing** (☎ 877-222-4653). The popular-but-pricey **World Golf Village** (☎ 904-940-6088; www.wgv.com) offers 54 holes, including The Slammer and The Squire, a fairly open course with kind greens. Greens fees are $110 and up in winter, $86 to $110 in summer. **St. Johns County Golf Course,** 4900 Cypress Links Blvd., St. Augustine (☎ 904-825-4900; www.sjcgc.com), is forgiving of the average player and his or her wallet — fees here are $25 to $40 year-round.

Going on a guided tour

St. Augustine Historical Sightseeing Tours (☎ 904-826-4218; www.infoperson.com/no1tours.htm) offers a one-hour sightseeing tour that also entitles you to transportation on its trolleys for three days ($15 adults, $5 kids 6–11, free for children under 6).

St. Augustine Transfer Company (☎ 904-829-2391) offers 45-minute to 1-hour horse-drawn carriage tours through the historic district. Tours cost $20 for adults, $10 for kids 6 to 11; free for children under 6; minimum $80 for a private carriage. You can flag a carriage down at the bayfront area.

Ancient City Tours (☎ 800-597-7177 or 904-797-0807; www.ancientcitytours.net) offers several guided tours, including a theater tour and an evening ghost walk. Prices begin at $7.

Shopping

St. Augustine doesn't have any special shopping areas, but you can find an assortment of shops, scattered throughout the historic district, that sell everything from antiques to local hot sauces. The heart of the district is a pedestrians-only area on **St. George Street** between Cuna Street and Cathedral Place. The trolleys make frequent stops here.

There are two outlet malls on Highway 16, near I-95. **Belz Factory Outlet World** (☎ 904-826-1311; www.belz.com) has 65 shops, including Tommy Hilfiger, Liz Claiborne, Timberland, and Royal Doulton. The **St. Augustine Outlet Center** (☎ 904-825-1555; www.staugustineoutlets.com) houses 95 stores, including Coach, Donna Karan, Company Store, and Brooks Brothers.

Living it up after dark

St. Augustine has dozens of small bars scattered along the beach and inside the historic district. **Ann O'Malley's,** 23 Orange St. (☎ 904-825-4040), is a friendly Irish pub that pours a good selection of ales, stouts, and drafts. **A1A Ale Works,** 1 King St. (☎ 904-829-2977), is a microbrewery that attracts a young-to-middle-age crowd. The **Oasis Deck & Restaurant,** 4000 U.S. A1A (☎ 904-471-3424), has live music or a DJ most nights.

Jacksonville, Amelia Island, and Fernandina Beach

Jacksonville is part Navy town and part business destination, though it has a few fun attractions and nice beaches. Along the St. Johns River, downtown Jax is rather vibrant, a center of activity during weekdays and on weekend afternoons and evenings when locals hang out at restaurants and bars at Jacksonville Landing and the Southbank Riverwalk — two dining and entertainment complexes that have helped revitalize the downtown area. (See maps for Jacksonville, Amelia Island, and Fernandina Beach later in this chapter.) To its north, you'll find Amelia Island, a natural, upscale resort area, and Fernandina Beach, which has much of the area's history (but is nothing, in scope, like St. Augustine).

Getting there

Here, we go back to the usual three transportation modes: planes, trains, and automobiles.

By plane

Jacksonville International Airport (☎ 904-741-4902; www.jaxports. org) has a dozen major carriers, including **American, Continental, Delta, Northwest, TWA,** and **US Airways. Avis, Budget, Dollar, Enterprise, Hertz, National,** and **Thrifty** have rental-car desks on the airport's lower level. **Gator City Taxi and Shuttle** (☎ 904-355-8294) charges $24 to $96 for up to four passengers, depending on where you want to go in the county. The airport is 45 minutes from Amelia Island, 25 minutes from Fernandina Beach, and 15 minutes from downtown Jacksonville.

By car

From the north, take I-95 south. From the west, take I-10 to I-95. From the Midwest, follow I-75 to I-10, then I-95.

By train

Amtrak (☎ 800-872-7245; www.amtrak.com) has a terminal in downtown Jacksonville at 3570 Clifford Lane, off U.S. 1 and just north of 45th Street.

Getting around

Jacksonville is a large city, and Fernandina Beach and Amelia Island are about 30 miles north of town. Unless you're going to stick close to a base camp, you're going to need wheels of one sort or another. I recommend a rental car as your best mode of transportation.

Jacksonville

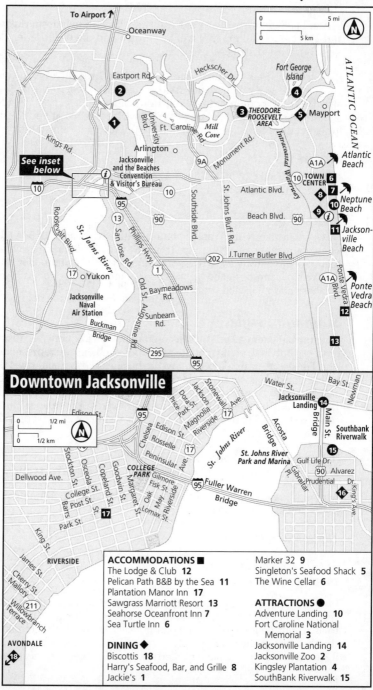

To Airport ↑

Oceanway

Eastport Rd

Heckscher Dr.

Fort George
Island

2

University Blvd.

Ft. Caroline Rd.

3 THEODORE
ROOSEVELT
AREA

Mill
Cove

4

5 Mayport

ATLANTIC OCEAN

1

Kings Rd.

Arlington

Jacksonville
and the Beaches
Convention
& Visitor's Bureau

Monument Rd.

Intracoastal Waterway

A1A

Atlantic
Beach

**See inset
below**

9A

10

10 TOWN
CENTER

6
7
8

See inset below

10

95

Southside Blvd.

St. Johns Bluff Rd.

Atlantic Blvd.

10 Neptune
Beach

9

St. Johns River

13

Phillips Hwy.

San Jose Rd.

90

Beach Blvd.

90

11 Jackson-
ville
Beach

Roosevelt Blvd.

17

Yukon

Old St. Augustine Rd.

Baymeadows
Rd.

1

202

J.Turner Butler Blvd.

A1A

Ponte Vedra Blvd.

Ponte
Vedra
Beach

Jacksonville
Naval
Air Station

Sunbeam
Rd.

Buckman
Bridge

12

295

95

13

Downtown Jacksonville

Water St.

Bay St.

Newnan

Edison St.

95

Dora St.

Jackson

Price

Stonewall

Ave.

Magnolia

Riverside

17

Jacksonville
Landing

14

Main St.

Acosta
Bridge

Main St. Bridge

Southbank
Riverwalk

Chelsea

Edison St.

Rosselle

17

Peninsular Ave.

St. Johns River

St. Johns River
Park and Marina

Gulf Life Dr.

15

Dellwood Ave.

Stockton St.

Osceola

College St.

Copeland St.

Goodwin St.

COLLEGE
PARK

Gilmore St.

Margaret St.

Fisk St.

Oak

May

Lomax St.

Riverside

95

Fuller Warren
Bridge

Gibraltar
Pl.

90 Alvarez

Prudential

Dr.

King's Ave.

16

Post St.

Barrs

Park St.

17

King St.

RIVERSIDE

James St.

Cherry St.

Mallory

Willowbranch
Terrace

211

AVONDALE

18

ACCOMMODATIONS ■
The Lodge & Club **12**
Pelican Path B&B by the Sea **11**
Plantation Manor Inn **17**
Sawgrass Marriott Resort **13**
Seahorse Oceanfront Inn **7**
Sea Turtle Inn **6**

DINING ◆
Biscottis **18**
Harry's Seafood, Bar, and Grille **8**
Jackie's **1**

Marker 32 **9**
Singleton's Seafood Shack **5**
The Wine Cellar **6**

ATTRACTIONS ●
Adventure Landing **10**
Fort Caroline National
 Memorial **3**
Jacksonville Landing **14**
Jacksonville Zoo **2**
Kingsley Plantation **4**
SouthBank Riverwalk **15**

By car

I-10 and I-95 enter the heart of the city. I-295, with help from Highways 9A and 115, creates a loop that will help you avoid the traffic-laden downtown business district.

Bay Street divides the north and south. Main Street divides the east and west. But be wary of any address that has *East, West, North,* or *South* attached to it; compass directions don't always correspond to addresses and street signs. The best thing to do is ask someone at your destination for exact directions from your starting point to your finish line.

By taxi

Gator City Taxi (☎ 904-355-8294) charges $1.25 to get in and $1.25 for each mile thereafter.

By bus

Fares on **Jacksonville Transportation Authority** buses (☎ 904-630-3125; www.jtaonthemove.com) range from 75¢ to $1.50. Remember, though, that public bus routes are the worst mode of transportation for tourists — they're slow and designed primarily for commuters and locals heading to business and shopping venues.

Staying in style

Jacksonville offers a variety of accommodations, from upscale resorts to business hotels to chain motels. A number of chains are represented along I-95. The downtown hotels cater to the business crowd, and rates there are higher during the week but can drop quite a bit on weekends. The beach hotels tend to be less expensive from December through March. The Jacksonville Convention and Visitors Bureau (see "Information" in "Fast Facts" at the end of this chapter) provides visitors with a list of accommodations in the area.

Hotel taxes add a whopping 9½ to 14 percent to your bill, depending on where you stay in this region, so ask when making a reservation.

Accommodations listed here offer free parking, air-conditioning, and pools unless otherwise noted.

The top hotels

Amelia Island Plantation
$$–$$$$ **Amelia Island**

Magnificent landscaping complements this self-contained, 1,350-acre resort, which offers accommodations ranging from standard motel rooms to luxurious condos, villas, and penthouses. Although motel rooms are distinctly no-frills, the condos, villas, and penthouses show price has its privileges in the form of designer toiletries, wood (rather than near-cardboard)

Amelia Island and Fernandina Beach

ACCOMMODATIONS ■
Amelia Island Plantation **8**
Elizabeth Pointe Lodge **6**
Fairbanks House **4**
Florida House Inn **2**
Ritz Carlton **7**

DINING ◆
Beech Street Grill **5**

ATTRACTIONS ●
BEAKS **9**
Centre Street **3**
Fort Clinch State Park **1**
Little & Big Talbot Island
   State Parks **9**

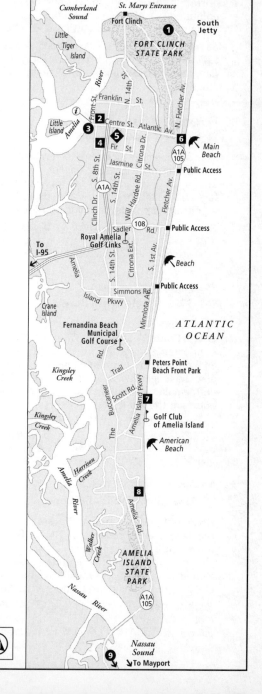

furniture, and other niceties. A free tram every 15 minutes provides transportation throughout the property. The resort's all-inclusive rates allow unlimited use of three championship golf courses, 23 clay tennis courts, and a health club. The Plantation also has a 13,200-square-foot spa.

See map p. 411. 3000 First Coast Hwy. ☎ *888-261-6161 or 904-261-6161. Fax: 904-277-5945.* www.aipfl.com. *To get there: Located on A1A, on the south end of the island. Rack rates: $135–$945; $236–$1,185 all-inclusive recreation package. AE, DC, DISC, MC, V.*

Fairbanks House
$$–$$$ Fernandina Beach

This smoke-free (including the grounds) bed-and-breakfast delivers turn-of-the-century Victorian charm with heart-of-pine floors, a wonderful mahogany staircase, and 12-foot ceilings. Its dozen rooms, suites, and cottages have king- or queen-size beds and a Jacuzzi, claw-foot tub, or shower. A gourmet breakfast is included. Kids over 12 are welcome.

See map p. 411. 227 S. Seventh St. ☎ *888-891-9882 or 904-277-0500. Fax: 904-277-3103.* www.fairbankshouse.com. *To get there: Located south of Centre Street, just west of A1A. Rack rates: $160–$275. AE, DISC, MC, V.*

The Lodge & Club
$$$–$$$$ Ponte Vedra Beach

This is one of two upscale resorts under the same umbrella. The second is **The Ponte Vedra Inn & Club** (☎ 800-234-7842). All 66 of the large and comfortable units at The Lodge & Club were renovated to the tune of $4.5 million and offer an ocean view from their balconies or patios. They also have garden tubs or Jacuzzis, refrigerators, window seats, and coffeemakers. Privileges include use of the 2 golf courses and 15 tennis courts at the Inn & Club.

See map p. 409. 607 Ponte Vedra Blvd. (at Corona Road). ☎ *800-243-4304. Fax: 904-273-0210.* www.pvresorts.com. *To get there: Located off A1A, 20 miles south of Jacksonville. Rack rates: Rooms $209–$380, suites $300–$439. AE, DC, DISC, MC, V.*

Sawgrass Marriott Resort
$$–$$$$ Ponte Vedra Beach

Home of the PGA's annual Players Championship in March, this is one of the largest golf resorts in the United States, with 99 holes of golf. Accommodations range from standard hotel rooms to comfortable villas, suites, and condos. Some suites have full kitchens, minibars, and coffeemakers. Other perks include a steak-and-seafood restaurant, two health clubs, eight tennis courts, and several kids' programs.

See map p. 409. 1000 PGA Tour Blvd. ☎ *800-457-4653 or 904-285-7777. Fax: 904-285-0906.* www.marriotthotels.com/jaxsw. *To get there: Located south of Jacksonville, off A1A between Highway 210 and Butler Boulevard. Parking: $9 valet,* *free self-parking. Rack rates: Rooms $129–$395, suites and condos $225–$695. AE, DC, DISC, MC, V.*

Seahorse Oceanfront Inn
$–$$ Neptune Beach

The Seahorse is a 1950s-style, few-frills motel with clean rooms, some of which offer a view of the Atlantic Ocean from balconies or patios. Some accommodations have kitchenettes, and several restaurants are nearby. The pool bar, The Lemon Bar, is quite the happening watering hole.

See map p. 409. 120 Atlantic Blvd. ☎ **800-881-2330** *or 904-246-2175. Fax: 904-246-4256.* www.seahorseresort.com. *To get there: Go to Atlantic Boulevard and First Street. Rack rates: Motel rooms Sun–Thurs $99, Fri–Sat $119; suite (sleeps six) Sun–Thurs $200, Fri–Sat $225. AE, DC, DISC, MC, V.*

Sea Turtle Inn
$$–$$$$ Atlantic Beach

This eight-story hotel is a touch nicer than the Seahorse (see previous listing) and offers 193 spacious rooms with partial or full ocean views, data-ports, refrigerators, and coffeemakers. Some rooms have balconies. Free coffee and weekday newspapers are available. A lounge and restaurant are on the premises.

See map p. 409. 1 Ocean Blvd. ☎ **800-874-6000** *or 904-249-7402. Fax: 904-249-1119.* www.seaturtle.com. *To get there: Located at the ocean and Atlantic Boulevard. Rack rates: $99–$349. AE, DC, DISC, MC, V.*

Runner-up hotels

Here are four other lodging choices, in case those listed above haven't lit a spark yet.

Elizabeth Pointe Lodge

$$ Fernandina Beach   Built in 1991 by B&B gurus David and Susan Caples, this Nantucket-style beach house has big-paned windows that look out from the comfy library (with stone fireplace) and dining room to an expansive front porch and the surf beyond. All 20 rooms have amazing, oversized bathrooms. *See map p. 411. 98 S. Fletcher Ave.* ☎ **800-772-3359** *or 904-277-4851.* www.elizabethpointelodge.com.

Florida House Inn

$$ Fernandina Beach   Open since 1857, this bed-and-breakfast's 15 rooms boast antique armoires, heart-of-pine floors, and private baths. Breakfast is included, but a pool isn't. No smoking; not recommended for children. *See map p. 411. 20 S. Third St.* ☎ **800-258-3301** *or 904-261-3300.* www.floridahouseinn.com.

Pelican Path B&B by the Sea

$$ **Jacksonville Beach** Rooms in this modern, oceanfront bed-and-breakfast have refrigerators and coffeemakers. Oceanfront rooms have king-size beds and spa tubs. *See map p. 409. 11 N. 19th Ave.* ☎ *888-749-1177 or 904-241-2407.* www.pelicanpath.com.

Plantation Manor Inn

$$ **Jacksonville** Located in the downtown historic district near the St. Johns River, this nine-unit bed-and-breakfast has a lap pool. No smoking; not recommended for children. *See map p. 409. 1600 Copeland St.* ☎ *904-384-4630.* www.plantationmanorinn.com.

Ritz-Carlton

$$$–$$$$ **Amelia Island** This posh golf-and-tennis resort has 450 ocean-view and oceanfront rooms. *See map p. 411. 4750 Amelia Island Pkwy.* ☎ *800-241-3333 or 904-277-1100.* www.ritzcarlton.com.

Dining out

As in the rest of Florida, seafood rules in Jacksonville and its surrounding towns, although you can find a variety of cuisines available in a decent range of prices. ***Remember:*** All Florida restaurants and food-serving bars are smoke-free.

Sales tax ranges from 6 to 7 percent in this region.

Beech Street Grill
$$–$$$ **Fernandina Beach** NEW AMERICAN

Housed in a historic two-story home, this perennial award-winner is a North Florida favorite. Skillful service and a grand atmosphere enhance the fantastic cuisine. Joys on the menu include scamp grouper in a macadamia-nut crust with mango chili salsa, and seared veal loin with chive-whipped potatoes. Beech Street also has an extensive wine list.

See map p. 411. 801 Beech St. ☎ *904-277-3662. To get there: On A1A at Eighth Street. Reservations recommended. Main courses: $22–$35. AE, DC, DISC, MC, V. Open: Nightly 6–10 p.m.*

Biscottis
$–$$ **Jacksonville** ECLECTIC

Located in the trendy Avondale neighborhood, Biscottis exudes a very East Villagey vibe. Grab a table out on the sidewalk and people watch over a cup of coffee as you choose from daily specials such as pan-seared tuna or pork loin. Sandwiches, salads, and pizzas are also top-notch. Biscottis also owns B.B.'s, a hot restaurant south of the Southbank Riverwalk.

See map p. 409. 3556 St. John's Ave. ☎ *904-387-2060. To get there: Between Talbot and Ingleside avenues. Reservations not accepted. Main courses: $5–$20. AE, DC,*

DISC, MC, V. Open: Mon 11 a.m.–10 p.m., Tues–Thurs 7 a.m.–10 p.m., Fri 7 a.m.–midnight, Sat 8 a.m.–midnight, Sun 8 a.m. –3 p.m.

Harry's Seafood, Bar, and Grille
$$ Jacksonville   NEW ORLEANS/SEAFOOD

Déjà vu. This is a branch of the same six-restaurant chain that I list under St. Augustine, and it's worth repeating. The cuisine is Cajun-inspired and the atmosphere is friendly. Try the shrimp en brochette (jumbos stuffed with Monterey Jack cheese, wrapped in bacon, and grilled) or Cajun popcorn (crawdad tails lightly breaded, fried, and served with a remoulade).

See map p. 409. 1018 N. Third St. ☎ 904-247-8855. To get there: Go south from Atlantic Beach on Third Street, the main beach road. Reservations accepted. Main courses: $10–$24. AE, MC, V. Open: Daily 11 a.m.–10 p.m.

Jackie's
$ Jacksonville   SEAFOOD

Almost all the entrees at this nautically themed restaurant cost under $15, including fried or broiled shrimp, oysters, catfish, grouper, and scallops. The menu also features a number of combination seafood platters, including a couple of dishes that serve two people. You can dine inside or eat on the outdoor deck, which has a view of the Trout River.

See map p. 409. 8132 Trout River Dr. ☎ 904-764-0120. To get there: Just south of St. Johns River off Main Street/U.S. 1. Reservations accepted. Main courses: $9–$29. AE, MC, V. Open: Daily 11 a.m.–10 p.m.

Marker 32
$$–$$$ Jacksonville   AMERICAN

Enjoy the view of the Intracoastal Waterway and its sail- and motorboats while you dig into an inventive menu that features chipotle-rubbed beef tenderloin with roasted-tomato demi-glace; grilled salmon with cucumber-mango salad; or marinated scallops with wilted spinach, slaw, and horseradish potatoes.

See map p. 409. 14549 Beach Blvd. ☎ 904-223-1534. To get there: Take Beach Boulevard ½ mile west of the Intracoastal Waterway Bridge. Reservations suggested. Main courses: $16–$28.50. AE, DISC, MC, V. Open: Daily 5–10 p.m.

Singleton's Seafood Shack
$–$$ Mayport   SEAFOOD

This old–school, rustic fish camp has been serving every kind of fresh-off-the-boat seafood since 1969. Unlike most fish camps that love the deep fryer, this one manages to use the fryer without destroying the fresh seafood taste. Blackened mahimahi rocks, as does the Cajun shrimp. No need to go to N'awlins for po'boys either — they've got delicious ones here of the oyster and shrimp variety.

See map p. 409. 4728 Ocean St. ☎ *904-246-4442. To get there: Located at A1A at the St. Johns River Ferry Landing. Main courses: $10–$18; sandwiches $2–$7. AE, DISC, MC, V. Open: Sun–Thurs 10 a.m.–9 p.m., Fri–Sat 10 a.m.–10 p.m.*

The Wine Cellar
$$–$$$ Jacksonville   CONTINENTAL

This exclusive restaurant offers fine dining in an intimate, old-world setting, with dining inside or on the outdoor brick terrace. The pecan-crusted rack of lamb and sesame-seared ahi tuna over enoki mushrooms and Asian greens help lift the menu two cuts above the norm. There's a long wine list, and some servers have been here since the restaurant rang its opening bell in 1974.

See map p. 409. 1314 Prudential Dr. ☎ **904-398-8989.** www.winecellarjax.com. *To get there: Located on the east side of the St. Johns River, near the Riverwalk. Reservations recommended. Main courses: $14–$27. AE, MC, V. Open: Mon–Fri 11 a.m.–2 p.m., Mon–Sat 5:30–10 p.m.*

Exploring the Jacksonville area

Jacksonville may cater more to business travelers than tourists, but there are still some dandy attractions, ranging from charming historic districts to animals that love to get into the act.

The top attractions

Adventure Landing
Jacksonville Beach

Kids and kids at heart have a ball in this amusement park, where you can challenge an 18-hole miniature golf course, do battle laser-tag style, tear it up in a go-kart, or try your hand at video games. Shipwreck Island, Adventure Landing's water park, will keep you cool with pools, hydro slides, and tube runs, including one that has a 40-foot vertical drop. Allow two to four hours. *Note:* The water park is only open from May until September.

See map p. 409. 1944 Beach Blvd. (at 20th Street). ☎ **904-246-4388.** www.adventure landing.com. *To get there: Take Atlantic Boulevard east to St. Johns Bluff Road, make a right, and go left on Beach Boulevard. Admission: Prices vary by attraction, from $5.99–$19.99 for adults, $3.99–$16.99 for kids. Open: Sun–Thurs noon–9 p.m., Fri noon–midnight, Sat 11 a.m.–midnight.*

BEAKS
Big Talbot Island

It's an acronym for Bird Emergency Aid and Kare Sanctuary, and it's a neat eco stop, where staffers raise and care for thousands of injured or deformed birds, including bald eagles, ospreys, pelicans, and owls. BEAKS also cares for deer, but birds come first. In addition to the one-hour round-trip from Jacksonville, plan to spend one to two hours visiting.

See map p. 411. 12084 Houston Ave. ☎ *904-251-2473 (expect a message about how to care for an injured bird but leave a message of your own, and they'll call back).* ww4.choice.net/~matschca/beaks.html. *To get there: It's complicated; ask for directions when you call. Admission: You'll feel guilty without leaving a donation. Open: Tues–Sun noon–4 p.m.*

Centre Street
Fernandina Beach

Centre Street and Historic Fernandina Beach offer a self-charted walking tour that costs nothing but calories. The 50-block downtown historic district is loaded with Victorian and Queen Anne homes that date to the town's birth as a port in the mid-19th century. Grab a tour map from the Chamber of Commerce, located in the old depot, 102 Centre St. (☎ **800-226-3542** or 904-261-3248). It's open between 9 a.m. and 5 p.m. Monday through Friday. If you have strong legs, good shoes, and a desire to shop, this is worth three to four hours of your time.

See map p. 411.

Fort Caroline National Memorial
Jacksonville

This is a shrine to the short-lived French Huguenot settlement founded here in 1564. The park has a replica of the fort, a museum of French and Native-American artifacts, and a trail.

See map p. 409. 12713 Fort Caroline Rd. ☎ *904-641-7155.* www.nps.gov/foca. *To get there: Take Atlantic Boulevard east, head past Southside Expressway, turn on Monument Boulevard, and follow the signs. Admission: Free. Open: Daily 9 a.m.–5 p.m.*

Fort Clinch State Park
Fernandina Beach

The sign is small, and most passersby don't have a clue that this treasure is just over the dunes. After you slap through the mosquitoes, there's a small museum and store and then a crushed-shell trail through coastal scrub to the fort. A small museum-style interpretive center is on the grounds, but the rangers are what really make this site unique. Dressed in wool uniforms (even in summer), they give a stark but frequently humorous look at a soldier's life in the 1860s. In addition to living-history lessons, the fort offers candlelight tours many Friday and Saturday evenings. On the first weekend of the month, some 40 volunteers demonstrate the daily routines of a surgeon's office, carpentry shop, forge, and kitchen. An hour or two should be all you need to see the park.

See map p. 411. 2601 Atlantic Ave. ☎ *904-277-7274.* www. dep.state.fl.us/ parks/district2/fortclinch/index.asp. *To get there: Located 1 mile from the ocean on A1A. Admission: $5 per car. Open: Daily 8 a.m. to sundown.*

Jacksonville Landing
Downtown Jacksonville

Resembling New York City's South Street Seaport, Boston's Faneuil Hall, Miami's Bayside, and Baltimore's Inner Harbor, this glass-and-steel complex on the north bank of the river serves as the focus of downtown activity. Yeah, you may see a mime or two occasionally, and there's a Hooter's, a Ruby Tuesday, and a Starbuck's, but there's also amazing local live music, good nonchain sushi, Thai, and Mexican, too. Unlike in the other cities, this complex is not just for tourists and is command central for many locals looking for a lively day/night out. There are more than 65 stores here, but shopping is secondary to dining and entertainment. You can choose from a half-dozen full-service restaurants plus an inexpensive food court with indoor and outdoor seating overlooking the river. The Landing is the scene of numerous special events, ranging from arts festivals to baseball-card shows, and outdoor rock, blues, country, and jazz concerts on weekends. Call or check the Web site to find out what's going on during your stay.

See map p. 409. 2 Independent Dr. (between Main and Pearl streets), on the St. Johns River. ☎ *904-353-1188.* www.jacksonvillelanding.com. *To get there: From I-95, take exit 107 downtown to Main Street, go over the Blue Bridge, and turn left at Bay Street. Then go 2 blocks and make a left on Laura Street, which dead-ends at the Landing. Admission: Free. Open: Mon–Thurs 10 a.m.–8 p.m., Fri–Sat 10 a.m.–9 p.m., Sun noon–5:30 p.m.; bars and restaurants open later.*

Jacksonville Zoo
Jacksonville

Lions, tigers, white rhinos, cheetahs, jaguars, warthogs, anteaters, and lowland gorillas. Wow! This city zoo has grown up in recent years and is one of the top five in Florida. Pay attention to the thatched roof when you enter — Zulu craftsmen built it. The newest attraction, *Range of the Jaguar,* opened in the spring of 2004 to the tune of $15.4 million. Although this spotlight features the jaguar, you will see other animals here as well, such as golden lion tamarins, tapirs, capybaras, giant river otters, anteaters, and a variety of bird, reptile, amphibian, and fish species including the anaconda. Allow two to four hours to see it all.

See map p. 409. 8605 Zoo Rd. ☎ *904-757-4463.* www.jaxzoo.org. *To get there: Take I-95 exit 124A and go east on Heckscher Drive. Admission: $9.50 adults, $8 seniors, $5 kids 3–12. Open: Daily 9 a.m.–5 p.m.*

Kingsley Plantation
Jacksonville

Here's a lesson on 19th-century Florida plantation life and slavery. Built in 1817 by Zephaniah Kingsley, this plantation grew sugar cane and sea-island cotton. The site has a well-preserved plantation house as well as the ruins of 23 slave quarters that were built from oyster shell and sand. There are ranger-guided tours, but scheduling is a bit inconsistent, so call to check on times. Allow one to two hours to catch the highlights.

See map p. 409. On the Avenue of Palms. ☎ *904-251-3537. To get there: Located north of Mayport U.S. Naval Station on A1A; follow the signs west on Palmetto Avenue (a gravel road). Admission: Free. Open: Daily 9 a.m.–5 p.m.*

Little and Big Talbot Island State Parks
Mayport

Little Talbot is a 2,500-acre preserve with salt marshes, hammocks, and Atlantic dunes, along with 4 miles of gorgeous beaches carved by erosion and decorated by rocks and driftwood. You may also spot some of the park's river otters. Located on the same stretch of coastline, Big Talbot Island State Park has some spectacular bluffs, the ruins of two plantations, and five marked trails that wind through dunes, salt marshes, tidal creeks, and prairie. If you're a park or beach buff, allow three to four hours.

See map p. 411. 20 miles northeast of downtown Jacksonville. ☎ *904-251-2320. To get there: Little and Big Talbot islands are off A1A, north of the Mayport Naval Station. Admission: $4 per car at Little Talbot, $2 per car at Big Talbot. Open: Daily 8 a.m to dusk.*

SouthBank Riverwalk
Jacksonville

Walkers, joggers, tourists, and people-watchers frequent this 1.2-mile boardwalk on the south side of the St. Johns River. At night, it's colorfully illuminated. By day, the biggest attraction is the **Museum of Science and History,** located at Museum Circle and San Marco Boulevard (☎ **904-396-7062;** www.themosh.org), which has some interactive exhibits for kids. The Riverwalk also has occasional seafood and arts festivals.

See map p. 409. On the riverbank, beside Main Street Bridge (between San Marco and Ferry Street). ☎ *904-396-4900. To get there: Take I-95 to Prudential Drive, exit right, and follow the signs. Museum admission: $6 adults, $4.50 seniors, $4 kids 3–12. Museum hours: Mon–Fri 10 a.m.–5 p.m., Sat 10 a.m.–6 p.m., Sun 1–6 p.m.*

Finding more cool things to see and do
This section offers a few additional things to do, including some for folks with special tastes:

- ✔ **Baseball:** The **Jacksonville Suns,** a Class AA Minor-League affiliate of the Los Angeles Dodgers, play 70 home games from early April to early September at **Wolfson Park,** 1201 E. Duval St. (☎ **904-358-2846;** www.jaxsuns.com). Tickets run from $3 to $15.50.

✔ **Beaches:** The four most popular bathing spots are **Atlantic Beach (also a popular surfing beach)** (east end of Highway 10), **Neptune Beach** (on A1A, 1 mile south of Highway 10), **Jacksonville Beach** (east end of U.S. 90), and **Ponte Vedra Beach** (Highway 203, 2 miles south of Butler Boulevard). There is no admission charge for any of these beaches.

✔ **Fishing: Captain Dave Sipler's Sportfishing** (☎ 904-642-9546; www.captdaves.com) is one of several guide services offering charters for small groups. The rate for three people is $325 for a six-hour fishing trip that goes after tarpon, kingfish, drum, redfish, flounder, and other species.

✔ **Football:** The National Football League's **Jacksonville Jaguars** play their preseason and regular-season home games at **Alltel Stadium,** One Alltel Stadium Place (☎ 904-633-2000; www.jaguars.com). Prices start at about $35, but single-game tickets can be hard to come by, depending on the team's opponent.

✔ **Golf:** The **Golf Club of Jacksonville,** 10440 Tournament Lane (☎ 904-779-2100), has rolling, tree-lined fairways and, with fees under $25 year-round, is an affordable course. **Baymeadows Golf Club,** 7981 Baymeadows Circle W., Jacksonville (☎ 904-731-5701; www.baymeadowsgolf.com), offers water hazards on ten holes and plenty of doglegs. Greens fees run between $41 and $65 year-round.

You can obtain local course information online at www.golf.com and www.floridagolfing.com, or you can call the **Florida Sports Foundation** (☎ 850-488-8347) or **Florida Golfing** (☎ 877-222-4653).

✔ **Kayaking: Kayak Amelia** (☎ 904-321-0697; www.kayakamelia.com) offers an assortment of guided excursions off the Intracoastal Waterway. Prices range from $55 to $95.

Shopping

San Marco Square, at San Marco and Atlantic boulevards, south of the river, is a quaint shopping district in the middle of a stunning residential area. Shops in meticulously refashioned Mediterranean-revival buildings sell antiques and home furnishings, in addition to wares such as clothing, books, and records.

Another worthwhile neighborhood to explore is the **Avondale/Riverside** historic district southwest of downtown on St. Johns Avenue between Talbot Avenue and Boone Park, on the north bank of the river. More than 60 boutiques, antiques stores, art galleries, and cafes line the wide, tree-lined avenue.

Nearby, the younger set hangs out at **Five Points,** on Park Street at Avondale Avenue, where used-record stores, vintage clothiers, coffee shops, and funky art galleries stay open late.

The **Avenues Mall,** 10300 Southside Blvd., Jacksonville (☎ 904-363-3060), has 150 stores, including such anchors as Dillard's and Sears. **Jacksonville Landing** (see listing in "The Top Attractions" earlier in this chapter) has about 65 shops, plus a number of restaurants.

Living it up after dark

Check the "Weekend" section in the *Florida Times-Union* (www.jacksonville.com) on Fridays for up-to-the-minute entertainment news.

Bars

Jacksonville Landing, 2 Independent Dr., on the St. Johns River (☎ 904-353-1188; www.jacksonvillelanding.com), stages periodic festivals and outdoor rock, jazz, blues, and country concerts.

Fernandina Beach's **Palace Saloon,** at Centre and Second streets (☎ 904-261-6320), was Florida's oldest continuously run watering hole (dating to the Rockefellers' and Carnegies' days), until a fire turned the lights out in February 1999. It reopened a month later. The bar offers rock or blues on Friday and Saturday nights. As an added bonus, you'll hear haunting stories about a lovable former bartender called "Uncle Charlie."

Out at Town Center, at the ocean end of Atlantic Boulevard, one of several popular spots is **Ragtime Tavern & Taproom,** 207 Atlantic Blvd. (☎ 904-241-7877), where local groups play live jazz and blues Wednesday through Sunday nights. Weekends, especially, the place is really jumping and the crowd is young, but it's lively rather than rowdy. Across the street is the **Sun Dog Diner,** at 207 Atlantic Blvd. (☎ 904-241-8221), with nightly acoustic music and decent diner food. If these don't fit your mood, walk around Town Center until you find something you like. The **Freebird Café,** 200 N. 1st St. (☎ 904-246-2473), is a two-story homage to native Jacksonville band Lynyrd Skynyrd, run by late lead singer Ronnie Van Zant's widow and daughter and featuring live music six nights a week as well as pretty good nouveau Southern cuisine. Music fans of a different genre shouldn't miss **Stella's Piano Café,** 1521 Margaret St. (☎ 904-353-2900), a restaurant housed in an old Victorian home with a second-floor piano bar.

Performing arts

The **Florida Times Union Center for the Performing Arts,** 300 Water St., Jacksonville (☎ 904-630-3900; www.jacksonville.com/community/tu-center), hosts Broadway shows, big-name concerts, and dance companies. Its Robert E. Jacoby Hall is home to the **Jacksonville Symphony Orchestra** (☎ 904-354-5547), which performs from early fall through spring.

Fast Facts

Area Code

The local area code is **904**.

Hospitals

The following hospitals are in the immediate area: Baptist Medical Center, 800 Prudential Dr., Jacksonville (☎ 904-202-2000); Baptist Medical Center/Nassau, 1250 S. 18th St., Fernandina Beach (☎ 904-321-3500); Flagler Hospital, 400 Heath Park Blvd., St. Augustine (☎ 904-819-5155); Memorial Hospital Jacksonville, 3525 University Blvd. S. (☎ 904-399-6111).

Information

Good sources of information include the St. Johns County Visitors and Convention Bureau, 88 Riberia St. (☎ 800-653-2489; www.visitoldcity.com); the Jacksonville & the Beaches Convention and Visitors Bureau, 201 E. Adams St. (☎ 800-733-2668; www.jaxcvb.com); and the Amelia Island Tourist Development Council, 102 Centre St. (☎ 800-226-3542; www.ameliaisland.org).

Mail

U.S. post offices are located at 3000 Spring Park Rd., in downtown Jacksonville, and at 99 King St., in St. Augustine. To find a branch near your hotel, call ☎ 800-275-8777.

Maps

Ask for maps at the information sources listed earlier in this section. Rental-car agencies (including those at the airport) are another good source of maps, as are convenience stores, which sell them for $3 to $5.

Newspapers

The *Florida Times-Union* (☎ 904-359-4111; www.jacksonville.com) in Jacksonville covers this region.

Safety

Because Jacksonville is a large city, it has the crime that you would normally associate with a major metropolis. Always stick to well-lit, populated tourist areas, and even then be aware of your surroundings.

Taxes

Florida assesses a 6 percent sales tax on everything except groceries and medicine. Hotels raise the total to anywhere from 9½ percent to 14 percent, depending on the region.

Taxis

For a taxi, call Yellow Cab (☎ 904-824-6888) or Ancient City Cab (☎ 904-824-8161). St. Augustine taxis use a complicated zone system, but figure on spending $2 to $8 for one person and $1.50 for each extra body. Those rates will get you to most parts of the city. Gator City Taxi (☎ 904-355-8294) in Jacksonville charges $1.25 to get in and $1.25 for each mile thereafter.

Weather Updates

To check weather forecasts online, go to www.weathercenter.com or surf over to the National Weather Service's site at www.nws.noaa.gov. You also can get information by watching the Weather Channel (www.weather.com).

Part VII
The Part of Tens

The 5th Wave   By Rich Tennant

First of all, these limes were originally harvested in horse drawn buggys. That's where their name comes from. Secondly, they're less expensive than Key limes, tastier than Key limes, and more plentiful than Key limes. So how about it? Can I get you a nice piece of Buggy Lime pie?

In this part . . .

*A*h, tradition. In *For Dummies* guides, "The Part of Tens" is where I serve up plenty of useful and fun information that I couldn't fit anywhere else in the book. I point you to more of Florida's finest beaches — the state has over 1,100 miles of coastline, and I highlight the best spots for swimming, snorkeling and shelling. In addition, I dish out information about Florida's unique eats, from crab claws to Key lime pie. Getting hungry? Read on.

Chapter 22

The Top Ten Florida Beaches

*T*here are two kinds of beaches in Florida: those that the TV ads trumpet and those that are less-discovered gems. The former includes some of the places I visit in earlier chapters, such as Miami Beach, Fort Lauderdale Beach, Daytona Beach, Clearwater Beach, and so on. The latter are off the beaten path. In many cases they're in state parks or preserves.

These off-the-path beaches are less crowded, and vacationers who walk the extra mile are rewarded with features that are often extraordinary — towering sand dunes, wind-bent sea oats, powder-fine sand, crystal-clear water, solitude, good shelling, or a combination of these features.

One of the founders of the Real Florida Beach Club is Dr. Stephen Leatherman, a professor and geologist at Florida International University. Several years ago he earned the nickname "Dr. Beach" for his annual ranking of the best stretches of sand in the world, released around Memorial Day each year. He uses more than 50 criteria (like width, sand softness, safety, water temperature, wave size, bugs, trash, and amenities) to come up with his top-ten list of beaches. My method, based on plain-old creature comforts, is much less scientific. But in many cases, I agree with Dr. B. Here are my favorites, listed from south to north.

Bahia Honda State Park (Big Pine Key)

Bahia Honda (that's *deep bay* in Spanish) is the only state park in the lower Keys and one of the rare beaches in this area. Fact is, this is the only natural beach in the Keys. Can it get any better than brilliant white sand, turquoise water, and a brisk breeze? The park's 524 acres include dunes, coastal mangroves, and hammocks. In addition, the white-sand beach has deep water close to the shore, making it good for snorkeling. (You may find lobster and starfish in 3 feet of water.) While you're here, climb aboard what's left of the old Henry Flagler rail line and enjoy the panorama of the surrounding Keys.

Although the swimming is good here, be careful of the deep water and the currents off the park.

36850 Overseas Hwy., Big Pine Key. ☎ *305-872-2353. To get there: Located 12 miles south of Marathon on Overseas Highway (Mile Marker 37.5). Admission: $4 per vehicle and 50¢ per person.*

Bill Baggs Cape Florida State Recreation Area (Miami/Key Biscayne)

This park is where the neon don't shine and certainly the most secluded beach in Miami. With its historic lighthouse (originally built in 1825) and native flora, the park provides a welcome respite from the hustle and bustle of this international city. But watch out for the raccoons and other critters that are more than happy to walk off with your picnic basket, among other things.

1200 Crandon Blvd., Key Biscayne. ☎ *305-361-5811. To get there: From the mainland, take U.S. 1 south to Rickenbacker Causeway and cross to Key Biscayne, and then follow the signs. Admission: $5 per car (up to eight people).*

Matheson Hammock Park Beach (South Miami)

This tranquil beach beckons with an enclosed, man-made lagoon that's flushed naturally by the tidal action of adjacent Biscayne Bay. The bay's warm waters and a backdrop of a tropical hardwood forest surround the park and are a favorite of many a fashion photographer. It has a full-service marina, snack bar, and restaurant built into a coral-rock building.

9610 Old Cutler Rd., South Miami. ☎ *305-665-5475. To get there: Take Highway 826 to North Kendall Drive, continue 3¾ miles to Red Road/SW 57th Avenue, turn left on Red Road, then turn right back onto Kendall and go ¾ mile to Old Cutler Road, turn right and follow signs. Admission: $4 per car.*

Naples Beach (Naples)

Many Florida cities and towns have beaches, but few are as lovely as the gorgeous 10-mile strip that runs in front of Naples's famous Millionaires' Row. You don't have to be rich to wander its length, peer at the mansions, and stroll on historic Naples Pier to catch a sunset over the Gulf.

25 12th Ave South, Naples. ☎ 239-213-3062. To get there: Go west on 5th Avenue South and turn left at 2nd Street South, which becomes Gordon Drive. Turn right onto 12th Avenue South. Admission: Free.

Cayo Costa State Park (Captiva Island)

These days, deserted tropical islands with great beaches are scarce in Florida, but this 2,132-acre barrier strip of sand, pine forests, mangrove swamps, oak hammocks, and grasslands provides a genuine get-away-from-it-all experience. Access is only by boat from nearby Gasparilla, Pine, and Captiva islands.

P.O. Box 1150, Boca Grande. ☎ 941-964-0375. To get there: Located directly south of Boca Grande. Accessible only by passenger ferry or private boat. Reservations are required on the ferry service. Call Tropic Star of Pine Island at ☎ 239-283-0015. Admission: $1 per person.

Siesta Beach (Sarasota)

This beach is short, just a quarter of a mile long, but it's also 500 feet wide. The tide has pounded the sand granules for so long that they feel like fine flour beneath your toes. (This is the kind of sand that squeaks like snow when you walk on it.) By Gulf of Mexico standards, it has good swimming (the water is a little on the warm side and very tame by Atlantic standards, but there's virtually no undertow). You're going to have a hard time finding a better place to chill out. Just sit at the water's edge and let the small waves lap at your legs. Lifeguards add to the safety level. Siesta Beach gets a little crowded with families at times (it's Sarasota's most popular beach), but there's a 700-car parking lot, and the price is right.

948 Beach Rd., Siesta Key (near Sarasota). ☎ 941-861-2150. To get there: Heading west on State Road 72, cross U.S. 41 and the Intracoastal Waterway. At the road's end, turn right at Midnight Pass and follow the signs. Admission: Free.

Fort DeSoto Park (St. Petersburg)

Here, you'll get a good tan *and* a history lesson that goes well beyond the latest, trashy summer page turner. At Fort DeSoto Park, you not only have 1,136 acres of five interconnected islands and 3 miles of unfettered beaches, but a fort, for which the park was named, that's listed on the National Register of Historic Places, nature trails, fishing piers, a 2.25-mile canoe trail, and spectacular views of Tampa Bay and the Gulf.

3500 Pinellas Bayway South, St. Petersburg. ☎ 727-582-2267. To get there: From the north, take I-275 south to exit 17 (Pinellas Bayway). Go west to the second stoplight. Turn left (south). This will lead you directly into the park. Admission: Free.

Caladesi Island State Park (Dunedin)

This 3-mile-long island is among the best shelling locations in Florida. The no-vehicles policy means that you don't need to worry about noise or air pollution. It's secluded with soft sand, sea grass, small dunes, and a variety of birds, including blue herons. You may have the opportunity to see the resident dolphins performing off the beach, and in summer, you'll probably see the crawl marks left by nesting loggerhead turtles. To get there, use the ferry at Honeymoon Island State Recreation Area (see Chapter 15).

3 Causeway Blvd., Dunedin. ☎ 727-469-5918. To get there: From Clearwater, go north on U.S. 19, and then west on Curlew Road, which leads to Honeymoon Island and the ferry. Admission: $4 per vehicle, plus $7 adults, $3.50 kids 4–12 for the ferry to the island.

Washington Oaks State Park (Palm Coast)

This park gets lost in the tourist shuffle between Daytona Beach to the south and St. Augustine to the north, which is all the better for those who visit. Originally part of an early-19th-century plantation, the 400-acre park reaches from the Atlantic Ocean to the Matanzas River. A hammock and marsh are on one side, but a beautifully rocky beach across the way presents my favorite picture. The waves' constant pounding on the coquina rocks gives the beach a ghostly, other-world-like orange hue.

 The depressions in the rock and tide pools are neat places to search for mussels, limpets, and barnacles. Although the rocks make swimming a little hazardous, a short walk to either side gets you clear of them.

6400 Oceanshore Blvd., Palm Coast (about 20 miles south of St. Augustine). ☎ 386-446-6780. To get there: From Daytona Beach, take A1A north 48 miles to the park entrance. Admission: $3.25 per car.

Little Talbot Island State Park (Jacksonville)

Actually, this 2,500-acre park is on Little *and* Big Talbot Islands. Salt marshes, hammocks, and Atlantic dunes (these are tall puppies) complement more than 4 miles of gorgeous beaches, marshes, and centuries-old live oaks. Fiddler crabs scurry about the beach, and lucky visitors get a glimpse of the park's river otters.

This is another place to see a rocky beach carved by erosion, as well as plenty of driftwood formations. On the trails and observation platform, you'll see some of the nearly 200 species of land, wading, and sea birds that come to the island. Despite the major city just south of the park and a large Navy base, this is one of Florida's least-spoiled beaches.

12157 Heckscher Dr., Jacksonville. ☎ *904-251-2320. To get there: From Jacksonville, follow Highway A1A 20 miles northeast. Admission: $3.25 per car.*

Chapter 23

Ten or More of Florida's Favorite Foods

*I*n this chapter, I cheat — twice.

First, I list more than ten items here.

Second, while some of these dishes are true Florida specialties, I remind you that this state is a melting pot. So much of the food that you find on restaurant menus or in the supermarket is someone else's recipe. Most of what's presented as Cracker cuisine (think grits, and such) has roots in Alabama, Georgia, or some other Southern state that ends in a vowel. Our food also shows a substantial (and delicious) Cuban and Latin influence, as well as a Caribbean flair.

The local cuisine is sometimes called *Floribbean*. I don't think any self-respecting Cracker, Cuban, or Caribbean islander would ever concoct a name like that. The culprit was a trio of froufrou chefs who were tired of answering questions like "Is the Early Bird Special Florida's version of, say, Pan Asian cuisine?" The result: a fusion of Floridian, Caribbean and Latin ingredients that, while extremely tasty, doesn't come cheap.

I steer clear of *Floribbean* in this part and instead deal with some older and more conventional staples because they give you a far better feel for the foods you'll see on menus or in grocers' aisles throughout the state.

Ambrosia

There's something whimsical about the name and this salad. It blends mandarin oranges, pineapple, coconut, marshmallows, and sour cream into a mouth-watering explosion of taste.

Citrus Fruits

Winter is the big season for Florida oranges, grapefruit, and tangerines. Nevertheless, you can find them, or their imported cousins, sold year-round at roadside stands or grocery stores and supermarkets. Although they aren't citrus, strawberries are another sweet and very popular wintertime treat.

Conch

These critters live in those shells that you find in souvenir shops, take back home, and (after a carafe of wine) put to your ear and swear that you can hear the ocean.

 Conch (pronounced *konk*) can be tough, so cooks whack the heck out of it with a tenderizing mallet before serving it. That's if you want it in chowder or fried, two of the most common ways conch is prepared. Conch fritters are another favorite. Although conch is also served in salads, it tends to be grainy and not real sweet, unless you have the courage to try it raw. Those brave enough find a faint almond flavor.

Cuban Cuisine

Florida had a sizable Hispanic population even before Fidel Castro, but since 1959 the population has increased dramatically. The Tampa and Miami areas have large Latin bases — the reason for such a strong Cuban/Spanish influence in our food.

To sample a day's worth of Cuban delights, begin at breakfast with a wedge of hot, buttered Cuban bread dunked in a cup of *café con leche* — strong coffee cut with milk. Things get downright funky after that. Specialties include *frijoles negros* (black beans), *arroz con pollo* (chicken and yellow rice), *boliche* (tender, sausage-stuffed beef), Cuban mojo-roast pork, *salteado* (chorizo, onion, and pepper stew), and deviled crab with hot sauce. Arguably, though, it doesn't get any better than *paella* — rice buried under a blanket of treats that may include mussels, clams, shrimp, scallops, lobster, oysters, crab claws, chicken, and/or pork. If you have room, try your luck with *flan,* egg custard dripping in caramel sauce.

Divinity

Divinity should be called dentists' delight. It's instant tooth decay (but, oh, what fun you're going to have getting there). This chewy candy is composed of a ton of sugar, corn syrup, egg whites, vanilla, and pecans.

Florida Lobster

Like conch, Florida lobster tends to be grainy and not very sweet, especially in inland restaurants. It's also commonly served broiled with butter. Many places cheat and give you margarine.

My advice: Leave the lobsters to the Mainers or Caribbean islanders.

Grits

Like other Southerners, real backwoods Floridians know "gree-its" is a two-syllable word. Grits are corn, coarsely ground to a slurry. The trick is to eat them before they congeal into something that resembles a hockey puck. Salt, pepper, and butter are allowed. Some folks like to add cheese, but in a real Cracker diner adding cheese will get you almost as many disapproving stares as using sugar — a common mistake made by Northerners who mistake grits for Cream O' Wheat.

Key Lime Pie

If it's green, send it back to the kitchen. The real stuff is yellow, thanks to the backyard fruit grown throughout much of South Florida. Pretenders use the wrong limes or — and this is true sacrilege — green food coloring. Key lime pie usually comes with a graham-cracker or regular crust and is usually made with condensed milk (not low-fat). This dessert is tangy and tart and sometimes has a dollop of whipped cream and a slice of lime on top. One variation uses meringue.

Mullet

No, I don't mean the much lambasted hair style, if you could call it that, made popular by the likes of Billy Ray Cyrus and described by many as "business in the front, party in the back," although you may spot many of those around certain parts of Florida. This local *fish* has dark, fatty meat and a pretty strong flavor when compared to white-meat fish. Mullet is more common in down-home, shorts-are-welcome restaurants than in the fancier establishments. It's usually served smoked or fried with a light cornmeal wrapping. The roe (fish eggs) is often sent to the Orient, where it's considered a delicacy.

Seafood

Florida's Gulf and Atlantic coasts and its inland waters cast forth a delightful menu of marine cuisine. Depending on the time of year and your location, you can feast on Apalachicola oysters, Fernandina Beach shrimp,

St. Johns River blue crabs, Florida Bay lobsters and conch, Gulf shrimp, and Cedar Key clams. Grouper, mahimahi, largemouth bass, speckled perch, and trout are also menu regulars.

Stone Crab Claws

In season from mid-October until May, this catch is the crab world's answer to Maine lobster, a sweet treat that results in a heck of a lot more meat and a lot less work than if you choose blue crabs. Steamed or boiled, these claws are close to heaven when dipped in butter. They're also at the top of the price chart.

Appendix

Quick Concierge

• •

*T*his handy section is where I condense all the practical and pertinent information — from airline phone numbers to mailbox locations — you need to make sure that you have a successful and stress-free vacation. And if you believe there is no such thing as too much preparation, I give you some additional resources to check out.

Florida A to Z: Facts at Your Fingertips

AAA

If you belong to the American Automobile Association, you can contact your local office for maps and optimum driving directions or call ☎ 800-222-1134 and ask to be transferred to the office nearest your location. Some other auto clubs also have service agreements with AAA, so ask your club whether this is the case before you leave. You can get information online at www.aaa.com.

American Express

You can reach the card company's Travel Service offices nationally by calling ☎ 800-297-3429.

Banks

Banks are generally open Monday through Friday from 9 a.m. to 3 or 4 p.m. (Drive-in windows usually are open until 6 p.m. on Friday.) ATMs honoring Cirrus, Honor, Plus, and other systems are commonly found in most malls, banks, and convenience stores, such as 7-Eleven and Circle K, as well as at larger tourist attractions, resorts, and shopping venues. To locate an ATM near your hotel in Florida, contact either of the two most popular networks: Cirrus (☎ 800-424-7787; www.mastercard.com/cardholder services/atm) and Plus (☎ 800-843-7587; www.visa.com/atms).

Credit Cards

American Express, MasterCard, and Visa are universally accepted in all but a few places. Carte Blanche, Diner's Club, and Discover are also accepted in many locations. We list the accepted credit cards under hotel and restaurant entries.

Most credit card companies have an emergency toll-free number to call if your card is lost or stolen; they may be able to wire you a cash advance immediately or deliver an emergency credit card in a day or two. Call the following emergency numbers in the United States: American Express ☎ 800-221-7282 (for cardholders and traveler's check holders); MasterCard ☎ 800-307-7309 or 636-722-7111; Visa ☎ 800-847-2911 or 410-581-9994. For other credit cards, call the toll-free number directory at ☎ 800-555-1212.

Emergencies

All of Florida uses **911** as the emergency number for police, fire departments, ambulances, and other critical needs. There's also a 24-hour, toll-free number for the **Poison Control Center** (☎ 800-282-3171).

For less urgent requests, call ☎ 800-647-9284, a number sponsored by the Florida Tourism Industry Marketing Corporation, the state's tourism promotion board. Its operators speak more than 100 languages and can provide general directions, as well as help with lost travel papers and credit cards, medical problems, accidents, money transfers, airline confirmations, and much more.

Information

Visit Florida, 661 E. Jefferson St., Suite 300, Tallahassee, FL 32301 (☎ 888-735-2872; www.flausa.com), is the state's official tourism office. You can order a copy of *Great Florida Getaways* and the *Florida Vacation Guide* plus brochures on golf, fishing, camping, and biking.

See "Fast Facts" in the destination chapters for local tourist information sources. Also, see "Where to Get More Information," later in this appendix.

To get local telephone information, dial ☎ 411.

Liquor Laws

Florida law requires you to be 21 years old or older before you can buy or consume alcohol. And the state is very strict about enforcing the law. You can get into parimutuels and bars where food is served at an earlier age. *Note:* Liquor stores in Florida are open Monday through Saturday, except Election Day. Depending on the region, they're closed all or part of Sunday.

Mail

If you want to receive mail on your vacation and you aren't sure of your address, your mail can be sent to you, in your name, care of General Delivery at the main post office of the city or region where you expect to be (see "Fast Facts" in the destination chapters). You can get the address and phone number of any post office in the area that you visit by calling ☎ 800-275-8777.

Maps

AAA and other auto clubs offer good Florida maps to members. You can also find maps in bookstores and libraries in your hometown. Most Florida convenience stores sell local maps for $3 to $5. If you rent a car, ask the rental agent for a local map — many of the agencies carry thorough ones. You can also request maps from many of the tourist information bureaus listed in the "Fast Facts" sections of some destination chapters. Web sites such as MapQuest (www.mapquest.com) or computer software such as Microsoft Streets & Trips are other good sources for maps.

Police

In any emergency, call **911.** If you have a cellular phone and need highway help, dial ***FHP** for the Florida Highway Patrol.

Restrooms

Foreign visitors often complain that public toilets are hard to find, but Florida is no worse than most U.S. destinations. True, there are no restrooms on the streets, but you can usually find one in a bar, restaurant, hotel, museum, department store, convenience store, attraction, fast-food barn, or service station — and it will probably be clean. In particular, Mobil service stations have made a public pledge to provide exceptionally clean bathrooms, most decorated with homey touches. Note, however, that restaurants and bars in resorts or heavily visited areas may reserve their restrooms for the use of their patrons. Some establishments display a notice that toilets are for the use of patrons only. You can ignore this sign or, better yet, avoid arguments by paying for a cup of coffee or a soft drink, which will qualify you as a patron. Within the theme parks, restrooms will be clearly marked on the handout park maps.

Safety

Stay alert and remain aware of your immediate surroundings. Putting your valuables in a safe-deposit box (inquire at your hotel's front desk) is a good idea, although nowadays many hotels are equipped with in-room safes. Keep a close eye on your valuables when you're in a public place — restaurant, theater, and even an airport terminal. Renting a locker is always preferable to leaving your valuables in the trunk of your car, even in the theme-park lots. Be cautious, even in the parks, and avoid carrying large amounts of cash in a backpack or fanny pack. If you rent a car, carefully read the safety instructions that the rental company provides. Never stop in a dark area, and remember that children should never ride in the front seat of a car equipped with air bags.

Smoking

On July 1, 2003, a constitutional amendment banned smoking in Florida's public workplaces, including restaurants and bars that serve food. Stand-alone bars that serve virtually no food are exempt, as are designated smoking rooms in hotels and motels. Even so, hotel accommodations for smokers are evaporating; the same goes for smoking areas in many public places, such as stadiums. Some of the major attractions do provide areas for smokers (although they're usually outdoors).

Taxes

Florida's state sales tax is 6 percent, and many municipalities add an additional 1 percent or more to that. In general, you can expect to add 11 to 14 percent to your hotel bill and 6 to 7 percent to most everything else — except groceries and health supplies or medical services. If you rent a car, be prepared to fork over an additional 20 percent or more in taxes.

Time Zone

Florida, for the most part, is on Eastern standard time from late fall until mid-spring and then on Eastern daylight saving time (one hour later) for the rest of the year. That means, when it's noon here, it's 7 a.m. in Honolulu, 8 a.m. in Anchorage, 9 a.m. in Vancouver and Los Angeles, 11 a.m. in Winnipeg and New Orleans, and 5 p.m. in London. The Panhandle (not reviewed in this book), however, operates on central time, which is one hour behind the rest of the state. So when it's noon in Miami, it's 11 a.m. in Pensacola.

Weather

To check weather forecasts online, go to www.weathercenter.com, or surf over to the National Weather Service's site at www.nws.noaa.gov. You also can get information by watching the Weather Channel (www.weather.com). Local forecast contacts are listed under "Fast Facts" in the destination chapters.

Toll-Free Numbers and Web Sites

Airlines

Aer Lingus
☎ 800-474-7424 in the U.S.
☎ 01-886-8888 in Ireland
www.aerlingus.com

Air Canada
☎ 888-247-2262
www.aircanada.ca

America West Airlines
☎ 800-235-9292
www.americawest.com

American Airlines
☎ 800-433-7300
www.aa.com

BMI
No US number
www.flybmi.com

British Airways
☎ 800-247-9297
☎ 0345-222-111 or 0845-77-333-77
  in Britain
www.british-airways.com

Continental Airlines
☎ 800-525-0280
www.continental.com

Delta Air Lines
☎ 800-221-1212
www.delta.com

Northwest Airlines
☎ 800-225-2525
www.nwa.com

Pan American Airways
☎ 800-359-7262
www.flypanam.com

Song
☎ 800-359-7664
www.flysong.com

Southwest Airlines
☎ 800-435-9792
www.southwest.com

United Airlines
☎ 800-241-6522
www.united.com

US Airways
☎ 800-428-4322
www.usairways.com

Virgin Atlantic Airways
☎ 800-862-8621 in the continental
United States
☎ 0293-747-747 in Britain
www.virgin-atlantic.com

Major hotel and motel chains

Baymont Inns & Suites
☎ 800-301-0200
www.baymontinns.com

Best Western International
☎ 800-528-1234
www.bestwestern.com

Clarion Hotels
☎ 800-CLARION
www.clarionhotel.com or
www.hotelchoice.com

Comfort Inns
☎ 800-228-5150
www.hotelchoice.com

Courtyard by Marriott
☎ 800-321-2211
www.courtyard.com or www.
marriott.com

Days Inn
☎ 800-325-2525
www.daysinn.com

Doubletree Hotels
☎ 800-222-TREE
www.doubletree.com

Econo Lodges
☎ 800-55-ECONO
www.hotelchoice.com

Fairfield Inn by Marriott
☎ 800-228-2800
www.marriott.com

Four Seasons
☎ 800-819-5053
www.fourseasons.com

Hampton Inn
☎ 800-HAMPTON
www.hampton-inn.com

Hilton Hotels
☎ 800-HILTONS
www.hilton.com

Holiday Inn
☎ 800-HOLIDAY
www.basshotels.com

Howard Johnson
☎ 800-654-2000
www.hojo.com

Hyatt Hotels & Resorts
☎ 800-228-9000
www.hyatt.com

Inter-Continental Hotels & Resorts
☎ 888-567-8725
www.interconti.com

ITT Sheraton
☎ 800-325-3535
www.starwood.com

Knights Inn
☎ 800-843-5644
www.knightsinn.com

La Quinta Motor Inns
☎ 800-531-5900
www.laquinta.com

Marriott Hotels
☎ 800-228-9290
www.marriott.com

Motel 6
☎ 800-4-MOTEL6 (800-466-8356)
www.motel6.com

Omni
☎ 800-THEOMNI
www.omnihotels.com

Quality Inns
☎ 800-228-5151
www.hotelchoice.com

Radisson Hotels International
☎ 800-333-3333
www.radisson.com

Ramada Inns
☎ 800-2-RAMADA
www.ramada.com

Red Carpet Inns
☎ 800-251-1962
www.reservahost.com

Red Roof Inns
☎ 800-843-7663
www.redroof.com

Renaissance
☎ 800-228-9290
www.renaissancehotels.com

Residence Inn by Marriott
☎ 800-331-3131
www.marriott.com

Ritz-Carlton
☎ 800-241-3333
www.ritzcarlton.com

Rodeway Inns
☎ 800-228-2000
www.hotelchoice.com

Sheraton Hotels & Resorts
☎ 800-325-3535
www.sheraton.com

Sleep Inn
☎ 800-753-3746
www.sleepinn.com

Super 8 Motels
☎ 800-800-8000
www.super8.com

Travelodge
☎ 800-255-3050
www.travelodge.com

Westin Hotels & Resorts
☎ 800-937-8461
www.westin.com

Wyndham Hotels and Resorts
☎ 800-822-4200 in Continental U.S.
   and Canada
www.wyndham.com

Car-rental agencies

Advantage
☎ 800-777-5500
www.advantagerentacar.com

Alamo
☎ 800-327-9633
www.goalamo.com

Avis
☎ 800-331-1212 in Continental U.S.
☎ 800-TRY-AVIS in Canada
www.avis.com

Budget
☎ 800-527-0700
www.budget.com

Dollar
☎ 800-800-4000
www.dollar.com

Enterprise
☎ 800-325-8007
www.enterprise.com

Hertz
☎ 800-654-3131
www.hertz.com

National
☎ 800-CAR-RENT
www.nationalcar.com

Payless
☎ 800-PAYLESS
www.paylesscarrental.com

Rent-A-Wreck
☎ 800-535-1391
www.rentawreck.com

Thrifty
☎ 800-367-2277
www.thrifty.com

Where to Get More Information

If you want some more information on accommodations, dining, attractions, or just about anything else involving Florida, you won't find it difficult to come by. In the upcoming sections, I list a host of places that offer tourist information, maps, and brochures.

Online sources

✔ **Absolutely Florida** (www.funandsun.com): It's an unofficial line, but this excellent Web site is overflowing with Florida information on topics ranging from lodging and restaurants to nightspots and nude beaches.

✔ **Beach Directory** (www.beachdirectory.com): This virtual guide to the beaches around Florida includes tours, maps, beach recommendations, and information on lodging and dining near the coast. It also includes information on Orlando.

✔ **OfficialTravelInfo.com** (www.officialtravelinfo.com): This Internet-only source provides links to many Florida destinations. Use the world map to click on "North America," and then from the menu beneath it click on "United States," "Florida," and the city you want.

Official state welcome centers

You can get information on the go by stopping in at the official state welcome center at these locations:

✔ **I-10:** To find this welcome center, travel 16 miles west of Pensacola, Florida.

✔ **I-75:** This location is about 1½ miles south of the Florida-Georgia border and 4 miles north of Jennings, Florida.

✔ **I-95:** This center is located 7 miles north of Yulee, Florida.

✔ **State Road 231:** You can visit this branch right after you cross into Florida from Georgia. It's 3 miles north of Campbellton, Florida.

Other sources of information

Here are a few other contacts on the statewide side:

✔ **Accommodations:** Information on accommodations throughout the state is available from the **Florida Hotel and Motel Association,** P.O. Box 1529, Tallahassee, FL 32302 (☎ **850-224-2888;** www.flahotel.com).

✔ **Attractions:** Contact the **Florida Attractions Association,** P.O. Box 10295, Tallahassee, FL 32302 (☎ **850-222-2885;** www.floridaattractions.com), for information about discount tickets and a guide map on special things to see and do in Florida.

✔ **Campgrounds:** If you're interested in camping while you're in the Sunshine State, get in touch with the **Florida Association of RV Parks and Campgrounds,** 1340 Vickers Dr., Tallahassee, FL 32303-3041 (☎ **850-562-7151;** www.florida-camping.com).

✔ **Historical sites and resources:** History buffs can get a line on cool places to visit from the **Division of Historic Resources,** Department of State, R.A. Gray Building, 500 S. Bronough St., Tallahassee, FL 32399-0250 (☎ **850-245-6300;** www.dos.state.fl.us).

✔ **Inns:** Learn a lot about the state's B&Bs from Florida Bed & Breakfast Inns, P.O. Box 6187, Palm Harbor, FL 34684 (☎ **800-524-1880;** www.bbonline.com/fl/fbbi/index.html).

✔ **Sports:** Active travelers and sports nuts can contact the **Florida Sports Foundation,** 2964 Wellington Circle N., Tallahassee, FL 32308 (☎ **850-488-8347;** www.flasports.com), for a variety of information about pro, amateur, and recreational sports. You also can get free guides about fishing, boating, golf, and spring training.

✔ **State forests:** Nature lovers should contact the **Florida Division of Forestry,** 3125 Conner Blvd., Tallahassee, FL 32399-1650 (☎ **850-488-4274;** www.fl-dof.com/state_forests/index.html).

✔ **State parks:** If a trip to a state park is on your agenda, contact the **Department of Environmental Protection,** Office of Recreation and Parks, Mail Station 535, 3900 Commonwealth Blvd., Tallahassee, FL 32399-3000 (☎ **850-488-9872;** www.dep.state.fl.us/parks).

✔ **Tourist assistance:** For 24-hour assistance regarding things such as lost credit cards, wallets, traveler's checks, and passports, or to get travel directions, call ☎ **800-656-8777.**

Index

• J •

• *P* •

• *Q* •

• *R* •

Notes

Notes

BUSINESS, CAREERS & PERSONAL FINANCE

0-7645-5307-0   0-7645-5331-3 *†

Also available:
- Accounting For Dummies †
  0-7645-5314-3
- Business Plans Kit For Dummies †
  0-7645-5365-8
- Cover Letters For Dummies
  0-7645-5224-4
- Frugal Living For Dummies
  0-7645-5403-4
- Leadership For Dummies
  0-7645-5176-0
- Managing For Dummies
  0-7645-1771-6

- Marketing For Dummies
  0-7645-5600-2
- Personal Finance For Dummies *
  0-7645-2590-5
- Project Management For Dummies
  0-7645-5283-X
- Resumes For Dummies †
  0-7645-5471-9
- Selling For Dummies
  0-7645-5363-1
- Small Business Kit For Dummies *†
  0-7645-5093-4

HOME & BUSINESS COMPUTER BASICS

0-7645-4074-2   0-7645-3758-X

Also available:
- ACT! 6 For Dummies
  0-7645-2645-6
- iLife '04 All-in-One Desk Reference For Dummies
  0-7645-7347-0
- iPAQ For Dummies
  0-7645-6769-1
- Mac OS X Panther Timesaving Techniques For Dummies
  0-7645-5812-9
- Macs For Dummies
  0-7645-5656-8
- Microsoft Money 2004 For Dummies
  0-7645-4195-1

- Office 2003 All-in-One Desk Reference For Dummies
  0-7645-3883-7
- Outlook 2003 For Dummies
  0-7645-3759-8
- PCs For Dummies
  0-7645-4074-2
- TiVo For Dummies
  0-7645-6923-6
- Upgrading and Fixing PCs For Dummies
  0-7645-1665-5
- Windows XP Timesaving Techniques For Dummies
  0-7645-3748-2

FOOD, HOME, GARDEN, HOBBIES, MUSIC & PETS

0-7645-5295-3   0-7645-5232-5

Also available:
- Bass Guitar For Dummies
  0-7645-2487-9
- Diabetes Cookbook For Dummies
  0-7645-5230-9
- Gardening For Dummies *
  0-7645-5130-2
- Guitar For Dummies
  0-7645-5106-X
- Holiday Decorating For Dummies
  0-7645-2570-0
- Home Improvement All-in-One For Dummies
  0-7645-5680-0

- Knitting For Dummies
  0-7645-5395-X
- Piano For Dummies
  0-7645-5105-1
- Puppies For Dummies
  0-7645-5255-4
- Scrapbooking For Dummies
  0-7645-7208-3
- Senior Dogs For Dummies
  0-7645-5818-8
- Singing For Dummies
  0-7645-2475-5
- 30-Minute Meals For Dummies
  0-7645-2589-1

INTERNET & DIGITAL MEDIA

0-7645-1664-7   0-7645-6924-4

Also available:
- 2005 Online Shopping Directory For Dummies
  0-7645-7495-7
- CD & DVD Recording For Dummies
  0-7645-5956-7
- eBay For Dummies
  0-7645-5654-1
- Fighting Spam For Dummies
  0-7645-5965-6
- Genealogy Online For Dummies
  0-7645-5964-8
- Google For Dummies
  0-7645-4420-9

- Home Recording For Musicians For Dummies
  0-7645-1634-5
- The Internet For Dummies
  0-7645-4173-0
- iPod & iTunes For Dummies
  0-7645-7772-7
- Preventing Identity Theft For Dummies
  0-7645-7336-5
- Pro Tools All-in-One Desk Reference For Dummies
  0-7645-5714-9
- Roxio Easy Media Creator For Dummies
  0-7645-7131-1

* Separate Canadian edition also available

† Separate U.K. edition also available

Available wherever books are sold. For more information or to order direct: U.S. customers visit www.dummies.com or call 1-877-762-2974.
U.K. customers visit www.wileyeurope.com or call 0800 243407. Canadian customers visit www.wiley.ca or call 1-800-567-4797.

SPORTS, FITNESS, PARENTING, RELIGION & SPIRITUALITY

0-7645-5146-9

0-7645-5418-2

Also available:

- Adoption For Dummies
  0-7645-5488-3
- Basketball For Dummies
  0-7645-5248-1
- The Bible For Dummies
  0-7645-5296-1
- Buddhism For Dummies
  0-7645-5359-3
- Catholicism For Dummies
  0-7645-5391-7
- Hockey For Dummies
  0-7645-5228-7

- Judaism For Dummies
  0-7645-5299-6
- Martial Arts For Dummies
  0-7645-5358-5
- Pilates For Dummies
  0-7645-5397-6
- Religion For Dummies
  0-7645-5264-3
- Teaching Kids to Read
  For Dummies
  0-7645-4043-2
- Weight Training For Dummies
  0-7645-5168-X
- Yoga For Dummies
  0-7645-5117-5

TRAVEL

0-7645-5438-7

0-7645-5453-0

Also available:

- Alaska For Dummies
  0-7645-1761-9
- Arizona For Dummies
  0-7645-6938-4
- Cancún and the Yucatán
  For Dummies
  0-7645-2437-2
- Cruise Vacations For Dummies
  0-7645-6941-4
- Europe For Dummies
  0-7645-5456-5
- Ireland For Dummies
  0-7645-5455-7

- Las Vegas For Dummies
  0-7645-5448-4
- London For Dummies
  0-7645-4277-X
- New York City For Dummies
  0-7645-6945-7
- Paris For Dummies
  0-7645-5494-8
- RV Vacations For Dummies
  0-7645-5443-3
- Walt Disney World & Orlando
  For Dummies
  0-7645-6943-0

GRAPHICS, DESIGN & WEB DEVELOPMENT

0-7645-4345-8

0-7645-5589-8

Also available:

- Adobe Acrobat 6 PDF
  For Dummies
  0-7645-3760-1
- Building a Web Site For Dummies
  0-7645-7144-3
- Dreamweaver MX 2004
  For Dummies
  0-7645-4342-3
- FrontPage 2003 For Dummies
  0-7645-3882-9
- HTML 4 For Dummies
  0-7645-1995-6
- Illustrator CS For Dummies
  0-7645-4084-X

- Macromedia Flash MX 2004
  For Dummies
  0-7645-4358-X
- Photoshop 7 All-in-One Desk
  Reference For Dummies
  0-7645-1667-1
- Photoshop CS Timesaving
  Techniques For Dummies
  0-7645-6782-9
- PHP 5 For Dummies
  0-7645-4166-8
- PowerPoint 2003 For Dummies
  0-7645-3908-6
- QuarkXPress 6 For Dummies
  0-7645-2593-X

NETWORKING, SECURITY, PROGRAMMING & DATABASES

0-7645-6852-3

0-7645-5784-X

Also available:

- A+ Certification For Dummies
  0-7645-4187-0
- Access 2003 All-in-One Desk
  Reference For Dummies
  0-7645-3988-4
- Beginning Programming
  For Dummies
  0-7645-4997-9
- C For Dummies
  0-7645-7068-4
- Firewalls For Dummies
  0-7645-4048-3
- Home Networking For Dummies
  0-7645-42796

- Network Security For Dummies
  0-7645-1679-5
- Networking For Dummies
  0-7645-1677-9
- TCP/IP For Dummies
  0-7645-1760-0
- VBA For Dummies
  0-7645-3989-2
- Wireless All In-One Desk Reference
  For Dummies
  0-7645-7496-5
- Wireless Home Networking
  For Dummies
  0-7645-3910-8

HEALTH & SELF-HELP

0-7645-6820-5 *†   0-7645-2566-2

Also available:
- Alzheimer's For Dummies
  0-7645-3899-3
- Asthma For Dummies
  0-7645-4233-8
- Controlling Cholesterol For Dummies
  0-7645-5440-9
- Depression For Dummies
  0-7645-3900-0
- Dieting For Dummies
  0-7645-4149-8
- Fertility For Dummies
  0-7645-2549-2

- Fibromyalgia For Dummies
  0-7645-5441-7
- Improving Your Memory For Dummies
  0-7645-5435-2
- Pregnancy For Dummies †
  0-7645-4483-7
- Quitting Smoking For Dummies
  0-7645-2629-4
- Relationships For Dummies
  0-7645-5384-4
- Thyroid For Dummies
  0-7645-5385-2

EDUCATION, HISTORY, REFERENCE & TEST PREPARATION

0-7645-5194-9   0-7645-4186-2

Also available:
- Algebra For Dummies
  0-7645-5325-9
- British History For Dummies
  0-7645-7021-8
- Calculus For Dummies
  0-7645-2498-4
- English Grammar For Dummies
  0-7645-5322-4
- Forensics For Dummies
  0-7645-5580-4
- The GMAT For Dummies
  0-7645-5251-1
- Inglés Para Dummies
  0-7645-5427-1

- Italian For Dummies
  0-7645-5196-5
- Latin For Dummies
  0-7645-5431-X
- Lewis & Clark For Dummies
  0-7645-2545-X
- Research Papers For Dummies
  0-7645-5426-3
- The SAT I For Dummies
  0-7645-7193-1
- Science Fair Projects For Dummies
  0-7645-5460-3
- U.S. History For Dummies
  0-7645-5249-X

Get smart @ dummies.com®

- **Find a full list of Dummies titles**
- **Look into loads of FREE on-site articles**
- **Sign up for FREE eTips e-mailed to you weekly**
- **See what other products carry the Dummies name**
- **Shop directly from the Dummies bookstore**
- **Enter to win new prizes every month!**

* Separate Canadian edition also available
† Separate U.K. edition also available

Available wherever books are sold. For more information or to order direct: U.S. customers visit www.dummies.com or call 1-877-762-2974.
U.K. customers visit www.wileyeurope.com or call 0800 243407. Canadian customers visit www.wiley.ca or call 1-800-567-4797.